JESUS AND
HIS CONTEMPORARIES

JESUS AND
HIS CONTEMPORARIES

Comparative Studies

CRAIG A. EVANS

BRILL ACADEMIC PUBLISHERS, INC.
BOSTON • LEIDEN
2001

Library of Congress Cataloging-in-Publication Data

Evans, Craig A.
    Jesus and his contemporaries: comparative studies/by Craig A. Evans.
        p. cm.—
    Originally published: 1995.
    Includes bibliographical references and indexes.
    ISBN 0-391-04118-5 (alk. paper)
        1. Jesus Christ—Biography—Public life. 2. Jesus Christ—Friends and
    associates. 3. Messiah. 4. Jesus Christ—Historicity. I. Title.

BT340 .E93 2001
232.9'01—dc21
[B]   2001035753

ISBN 0-391-04118-5

PRINTED IN THE UNITED STATES OF AMERICA

CONTENTS

SYNTHESIS

PREFACE

Jesus and His Contemporaries: Comparative Studies constitutes a collection of studies that approach the study of Jesus of Nazareth from a historical and contextual perspective. In my judgment much of the current discussion pays insufficient attention to history, parallel traditions, and relevant figures and events. Instead, discussion often focuses on a cluster of sayings, sometimes devoid of a realistic and adequately documented context, from which various images of the "historical Jesus" emerge. We are introduced to Jesuses who are Cynics, sages, iconoclasts, and subversives. We are told that traditional images of Jesus are uncritical and unfounded—the products of Christian dogmatism.

In North America this discussion has taken its most self-conscious and purposeful shape in the context of the Jesus Seminar, whose members meet twice a year to discuss and assess the sayings of Jesus. One of the goals of the Seminar has been to produce a red-letter edition of the Gospels, highlighting what Jesus did and did not say. This particular goal has been realized with the publication of *The Five Gospels*, edited by Robert W. Funk, the Seminar's founder, and Roy W. Hoover.[1] But the conclusions presented by this work are dubious at many points, revealing many of the weaknesses alluded to above. In an insightful and stinging review Richard B. Hays remarks: "The depiction of Jesus as a Cynic philosopher with no concern about Israel's destiny, no connection with the concerns and hopes that animated his Jewish contemporaries, no interest in the interpretation of Scripture, and no message of God's coming eschatological judgment is—quite simply—an ahistorical fiction, achieved by the surgical removal of Jesus from his Jewish context."[2] I heartily concur with Hays.

The present collection of studies, though not assembled or written

---

[1]   R. W. Funk and R. W. Hoover (eds.), *The Five Gospels* (New York: Macmillan, 1993). The Seminar is now preparing studies devoted to the question of Jesus' actions.

[2]   R. B. Hays, "The Corrected Jesus," *First Things* 43 (May, 1994) 43-48, here p. 47.

specifically with the Jesus Seminar in mind, makes a serious attempt to interpret important elements of Jesus' life, death, and teaching in a historical, Jewish context. There is no attempt here to present a comprehensive life of Jesus. Indeed, the approach is not systematic, but topical. Although certain important topics have not been treated (such as Jesus and the Pharisees and the interpretation of the Law), the topics that have been chosen hopefully will highlight several important features of Jesus' life, activities, and death. They treat issues that in my judgment must be taken into account if a "historical Jesus," realistically situated in his time and place, has any chance of emerging. The Jesus that emerges may or may not be politically correct, as defined by academics and social critics at the moment, but he makes sense in context of first-century Israel's interpretation of its past and its hopes for the future.

I wish to thank the respective editors and directors of *Biblische Zeitschrift, Bulletin for Biblical Research*, and *Theological Studies* for permission to reprint copyrighted materials. A word of thanks is also due Professor Martin Hengel who accepted this work for the Arbeiten zur Geschichten des antiken Judentums und des Urchristentums. I would also like to salute my colleagues here at the University for providing a stimulating context in which research and critical thinking are both encouraged and rewarded.

Craig A. Evans   October, 1994
Trinity Western University
Langley, British Columbia

ABBREVIATIONS

AB	Anchor Bible
ABD	D. N. Freedman (ed.), *The Anchor Bible Dictionary* (6 vols., New York: Doubleday, 1992)
ABRL	Anchor Bible Reference Library
AGJU	Arbeiten zur Geschichte des antiken Judentums und des Urchristentums
AGSU	Arbeiten zur Geschichte des Spätjudentums und Urchristentums
AnBib	Analecta biblica
ANRW	*Aufstieg und Niedergang der römischen Welt*
ANTJ	Arbeiten zum Neuen Testament und Judentum
APOT	R. H. Charles (ed.), *Apocrypha and Pseudepigrapha of the Old Testament* (2 vols., Oxford: Clarendon, 1913)
ArBib	The Aramaic Bible
ASOR	American Schools of Oriental Research
ATR	*Anglican Theological Review*
BA	*Biblical Archaeologist*
BAR	*Biblical Archaeologist Reader*
BARev	*Biblical Archaeology Review*
BASOR	*Bulletin of the American Schools of Oriental Research*
BASORSup	Bulletin of the American Schools of Oriental Research, Supplements
BBR	*Bulletin for Biblical Research*
BETL	Bibliotheca ephemeridum theologicarum lovaniensium
BEvT	Beiträge zur evangelischen Theologie
Bib	*Biblica*
BJRL	*Bulletin of the John Rylands University Library of Manchester*
BJS	Brown Judaic Studies
BibOr	Biblica et orientalia
BJRL	*Bulletin of the John Rylands University Library of Manchester*
BK	*Bibel und Kirche*
BNTC	Black's New Testament Commentary
BR	*Biblical Research*
BTB	*Biblical Theology Bulletin*
BZ	*Biblische Zeitschrift*
BZNW	Beihefte zur *Zeitschrift für die neutestamentliche Wissenschaft*
CBQ	*Catholic Biblical Quarterly*
CBQMS	Catholical Biblical Quarterly Monograph Series
CG	Coptic Gnostic Codex
CH	Calwer Hefte
CIJ	J. B. Frey, *Corpus Inscriptionum Judaicarum* (2 vols., Rome: Pontificio Istituto di Archeologia Cristiana, 1936-52)
CJT	*Canadian Journal of Theology*

ConBNT	Coniectanea biblica, New Testament
CPJ	V. A. Tcherikover and A. Fuks (eds.), *Corpus Papyrorum Judaicarum* (2 vols., Cambridge: Harvard University Press, 1957-60)
CRINT	Compendia rerum iudaicarum ad novum testamentum
CSR	*Christian Scholars Review*
CTMis	*Currents in Theology and Mission*
DJD	Discoveries in the Judaean Desert
DownRev	*Downside Review*
DSD	*Dead Sea Discoveries*
EKKNT	Evangelisch-katholischer Kommentar zum Neuen Testament
EncJud	*Encyclopaedia Judaica* (1971)
ER	R. H. Eisenman and J. M. Robinson, *A Fascimile Edition of the Dead Sea Scrolls* (2 vols., Washington: Biblical Archaeology Society, 1991)
ErFor	Erträge der Forschung
ETL	*Ephemerides theologicae lovanienses*
EvQ	*Evangelical Quarterly*
EvT	*Evangelische Theologie*
ExpTim	*Expository Times*
FB	Forschung zur Bibel
FZPT	*Freiburger Zeitschrift für Philosophie und Theologie*
GNS	Good News Studies
Greg	*Gregorianum*
HNT	Handbuch zum Neuen Testament
HSCP	*Harvard Studies in Classical Philology*
HSS	Harvard Semitic Studies
HTKNT	Herders theologischer Kommentar zum Neuen Testament
HTKNTSup	Herders theologischer Kommentar zum Neuen Testament, Supplements
HTR	*Harvard Theological Review*
HUCA	*Hebrew Union College Annual*
IBR	Institute for Biblical Research
IBS	*Irish Biblical Studies*
ICC	International Critical Commentary
IEJ	*Israel Exploration Journal*
IJPR	*International Journal for Philosophy of Religion*
IKZ	*Internationale katholische Zeitschrift*
Int	*Interpretation*
JANESCU	*Journal of the Ancient Near Eastern Society of Columbia University*
JBL	*Journal of Biblical Literature*
JBR	*Journal of Bible and Religion*
JES	*Journal of Ecumenical Studies*
JETS	*Journal of the Evangelical Theological Society*
JJS	*Journal of Jewish Studies*
JNES	*Journal of Near Eastern Studies*
JQR	*Jewish Quarterly Review*
JQRMS	Jewish Quarterly Review Monograph Series

JR	*Journal of Religion*
JRH	*Journal of Religious History*
JRS	*Journal of Roman Studies*
JSJ	*Journal for the Study of Judaism in the Persian, Hellenistic and Roman Period*
JSNT	*Journal for the Study of the New Testament*
JSNTSup	Journal for the Study of the New Testament Supplement Series
JSOTSup	Journal for the Study of the Old Testament Supplement Series
JSP	*Journal for the Study of the Pseudepigrapha*
JSPSup	Journal for the Study of the Pseudepigrapha Supplement Series
JSS	*Journal of Semitic Studies*
JTS	*Journal of Theological Studies*
KEK	Kritisch-exegetischer Kommentar über das Neue Testament
LCL	Loeb Classical Library
LTK	*Lexicon für Theologie und Kirche*
MeyerK	H. A. W. Meyer (ed.), Kritisch-exegetischer Kommentar über das Neue Testament
MHUC	Monographs of the Hebrew Union College
MTS	Marburger Theologische Studien
NCB	New Century Bible
NIC	New International Commentary
NIGTC	New International Greek Testament Commentary
NovT	*Novum Testamentum*
NovTSup	Novum Tetamentum, Supplements
NTD	Das Neue Testament Deutsch
NTS	*New Testament Studies*
NTTS	New Testament Tools and Studies
OTS	*Oudtestamentische Studiën*
PAM	Palestine Archaeological Museum (in reference to numbered photographs of the Dead Sea Scrolls)
PEQ	*Palestine Exploration Quarterly*
PG	J. Migne (ed.), *Patrologia graeca*
PL	J. Migne (ed.), *Patrologia latina*
PSBSup	*Princeton Seminary Bulletin Supplement*
QD	Quaestiones disputatae
RB	*Revue biblique*
Ref	*Reformatio*
REJ	*Revue des études juives*
RelS	*Religious Studies*
RelSRev	*Religious Studies Review*
RevQ	*Revue de Qumran*
RHPR	*Revue d'histoire et de philosophie religieuses*
RHR	*Revue de l'histoire des religions*
RL	*Religion in Life*
RNT	Regensburger Neues Testament
RSB	*Religious Studies Bulletin*
RSR	*Recherches de science religieuse*
RTL	*Revue théologique de Louvain*

RVV   Religionsgeschichtliche Versuche und Vorarbeiten
SAC   Studies in Antiquity & Christianity
SANT   Studien zum Alten und Neuen Testament
SBEC   Studies in the Bible and Early Christianity
SBL   Society of Biblical Literature
SBLDS   Society of Biblical Literature Dissertation Series
SBLMS   Society of Biblical Literature Monograph Series
SBLRBS   Society of Biblical Literature Resources for Biblical Study
SBLSP   Society of Biblical Literature Seminar Papers
SBS   Stuttgarter Bibelstudien
SBT   Studies in Biblical Theology
SCHNT   Studia ad corpus hellenisticum novi testamenti
Scr   *Scripture*
SEÅ   *Svensk exegetisk årsbok*
SFSHJ   South Florida Studies in the History of Judaism
SHT   Studies in Historical Theology
SJ   Studia Judaica
SJLA   Studies in Judaism in Late Antiquity
SJT   *Scottish Journal of Theology*
SKKNT   Stuttgarter Kleiner Kommentar: Neues Testament
SNTS   Society for New Testament Studies
SNTSMS   Society for New Testament Studies Monograph Series
SNTU   Studien zum Neuen Testament und seiner Umwelt
SPB   Studia postbiblica
SSEJC   Studies in Scripture in Early Judaism and Christianity
SSN   Studia semitica neerlandica
SSS   Semitic Study Series
SL   *Studia liturgica*
ST   *Studia theologica*
STDJ   Studies on the Texts of the Desert of Judah
Str-B   [H. Strack and] P. Billerbeck, *Kommentar zum Neuen Testament*
             aus Talmud und Midrasch (5 vols., Munich: Beck, 1922-61)
SubBib   Subsidia biblica
SVTP   Studia in veteris testamenti pseudepigrapha
TBl   *Theologische Blätter*
TDNT   *Theological Dictionary of the New Testament*
Th   *Theology*
TQ   *Theologische Quartalschrift*
TrinJ   *Trinity Journal*
TRu   *Theologische Rundschau*
TS   *Theological Studies*
TSAJ   Texte und Studien zum antiken Judentum
TToday   *Theology Today*
TU   Texte und Untersuchungen
TynBul   *Tyndale Bulletin*
TZ   *Theologische Zeitschrift*
USQR   *Union Seminary Quarterly Review*
VC   *Vigiliae christianae*

VT	*Vetus Testamentum*
VTSup	Vetus Testamentum, Supplements
WBC	Word Biblical Commentary
WUNT	Wissenschaftliche Untersuchungen zum Neuen Testament
YJS	Yale Judaica Series
ZAW	*Zeitschrift für die alttestamentliche Wissenschaft*
ZKT	*Zeitschrift für katholische Theologie*
ZNW	*Zeitschrift für die neutestamentliche Wissenschaft*
ZTK	*Zeitschrift für Theologie und Kirche*

CHAPTER ONE

RECENT DEVELOPMENTS IN JESUS RESEARCH: PRESUPPOSITIONS, CRITERIA, AND SOURCES

The present work presupposes the gains of and attempts to make a modest contribution to the so-called Third Quest of the historical Jesus.[1] In this opening chapter it will be useful to clarify what I regard as the real gains of the discussion of the last twenty years or so. These are treated under the headings of (1) presuppositions, (2) authenticity criteria, and (3) sources.

---

[1]   The Old Quest and the New Quest, if not always adequately understood, have been surveyed, summarized, and analyzed often enough that it is not necessary to expose the readers of the present book to yet another presentation of this fascinating history of research. For the classic assessment of the Old Quest, see A. Schweitzer, *Von Reimarus zu Wrede: Eine Geschichte des Leben-Jesu-Forschung* (Tübingen: Mohr [Siebeck], 1906); ET: *The Quest of the Historical Jesus: A Critical Study of its Progress from Reimarus to Wrede* (London: Black, 1910; with Introduction by J. M. Robinson, New York: Macmillan, 1968); rev. *Die Geschichte der Leben-Jesu-Forschung* (Tübingen: Mohr [Siebeck], 1913; 6th ed., 1951). Schweitzer's treatment should be augmented by C. Brown, *Jesus in European Protestant Thought, 1778–1860* (SHT 1; Durham: Labyrinth, 1985), and E. G. Lawler, *David Friedrich Strauss and His Critics: The Life of Jesus Debate in Early Nineteenth-Century German Journals* (New York: Lang, 1986). For the classic statement on the New Quest, see J. M. Robinson, *A New Quest of the Historical Jesus* (SBT 25; London: SCM, 1959); German ed., *Kerygma und historischer Jesus* (Zürich and Stuttgart: Zwingli, 1960; 2nd ed., 1967), as well as the helpful summary by H. Zahrnt, "Die Wiederentdeckung des historischen Jesus," in Zahrnt, *Die Sache mit Gott: Die protestantische Theologie im 20. Jahrhundert* (Munich: Piper, 1966) 326-81; ET: "The Rediscovery of the Historical Jesus," in Zahrnt, *The Question of God: Protestant Theology in the Twentieth Century* (New York: Harcourt, Brace & World, 1969) 253-94. For an assessment of the current discussion, see E. P. Sanders, *Jesus and Judaism* (London: SCM; Philadelphia: Fortress, 1985) 1-3; J. P. Meier, "The Historical Jesus: Rethinking Some Concepts," *TS* 51 (1990) 3-24; W. R. Telford, "Major Trends and Interpretive Issues in the Study of Jesus," in B. D. Chilton and C. A. Evans (eds.), *Studying the Historical Jesus: Evaluations of the State of Current Research* (NTTS 19; Leiden: Brill, 1994) 33-74.

PRESUPPOSITIONS

The presuppositions of the Third Quest differ from those of the Old and New Quests in several important areas. I shall treat these under three broad subheadings: (1) myth and miracle, (2) historical value of the Gospels, and (3) theological apologetics. Not all will agree with my assessment of these topics, but I think most will agree that the Third Quest represents a major break from the assumptions and methods that characterize the first two centuries of historical Jesus research (ca. 1770s to 1970s).[2]

1. Myth and Miracle. The secondary literature of the last two decades or so suggests that mythology's role in scholarship concerned with the historical Jesus has been eclipsed. Superficially this is seen in the noticeable decline in the number of books and articles that even speak of myth in relation to the question of the historical Jesus.[3] In the 1980s only a handful of studies have appeared that are concerned with myth, and in these doubt is expressed as to the future of the demythologizing hermeneutic itself.[4] What is more significant is the fact that most of the recent significant books published on the historical Jesus make little or no reference to the problem of myth or demythologization. In contrast to the systemic skepticism that characterized much of German and North American scholarship, often a concomitant of assumptions about myth in the Gospels, Jesus research in recent years has reflected a greater optimism that the Gospels can yield the data necessary for an intelligible reconstruction of the ministry of Jesus. This is seen in the fact that virtually all of these works make historically plausible suggestions as to how Jesus

---

[2]   Parts of the discussion that follows summarize my essay, "Life-of-Jesus Research and the Eclipse of Mythology," *TS* 54 (1993) 3-36.

[3]   See my *Life of Jesus Research* (NTTS 13; Leiden: Brill, 1989) 99-100.

[4]   For recent reviews, see J. Macquarrie, "A Generation of Demythologizing," in J. P. van Noppen (ed.), *Theolinguistics* (Brussels: Vrije Universiteit, 1981) 143-58, and K. H. Schelkle, "Entmythologisierung in existentialer Interpretation," *TQ* 165 (1985) 257-66. For an essay that ponders the future of demythologization, see U. Luz, "Rückkehr des mythologischen Weltbildes: Überlegungen bei einer neuen Lektüre von Bultmann's Programm der Entmythologisierung," *Ref* 33 (1984) 448-53. For an essay that offers a positive assessment of demythologization, see M. J. de Nys, "Myth and Interpretation: Bultmann Revisted," *IJPR* 11 (1980) 27-41. For a negative assessment, see D. Cairns, "A Reappraisal of Bultmann's Theology," *RelS* 17 (1981) 469-85.

understood himself and his mission, things that Bultmann and others a generation ago thought beyond reach. What accounts for this change in thinking? And more to the point of the present discussion, why has mythology dropped out of the mainstream of the discussion?

I believe that the perception of myth as a problem for historical Jesus research has abated for two reasons: (1) a historical, as opposed to metaphysical, approach to the miracle stories is now pursued and (2) theologically-driven apologetics have subsided. The latter point will be taken up in the next section, but the former point will be treated here.

Concerning the question of miracles in the traditions about Jesus Bruce Chilton has advised: ". . . historical enquiry must . . . rest content with a reasoned, exegetical account of how what is written came to be, and how that influences our appreciation of the received form of the text. *The historical question centers fundamentally on what people perceived, and how they acted on their perception.*"[5] Scholars interested in the historical Jesus will do well to heed Chilton's advice. The scientific or metaphysical problem of how to define a miracle is just that—a scientific and metaphysical problem. It is not an item that should bring historical inquiry to a standstill. The historian need not know just exactly how Jesus healed someone or just exactly what happened when a person was exorcized of a "demon." The question that the historian needs to answer is did Jesus do those sorts of things and, if he did, what did they mean to his contemporaries?[6]

---

[5]   B. D. Chilton, "Exorcism and History: Mark 1:21-28," in D. Wenham and C. Blomberg (eds.), *The Miracles of Jesus* (Gospel Perspectives 6; Sheffield: JSOT Press, 1986) 253-71, quotation from p. 265 (my emphasis). Twenty years ago the same point was made by P. J. Achtemeier, "Miracles and the Historical Jesus: A Study of Mark 9:14-29," *CBQ* 37 (1975) 471-91, esp. p. 488: "human beings react to reality as they perceive and understand it."

[6]   A major problem that attends any attempt to distinguish a mythological world view from a "scientific" world view is that in a certain sense all human observation and description is to some extent "mythological." Herein I believe lies a major flaw in Bultmann's "scientific" understanding of miracles and the demythologising hermeneutic that attempts to deal with them. For studies that address this problem, see I. Henderson, *Myth in the New Testament* (SBT 7; London: SCM, 1952); idem, "Karl Jaspers and Demythologizing," *ExpTim* 65 (1953-54) 291-93; R. F. Aldwinckle, "Myth and Symbol in Contemporary Philosophy and Theology: The Limits of Demythologizing," *JR* 34 (1954) 267-79; A. D. Galloway, "Religious Symbols and Demythologising," *SJT* 10 (1957) 361-69.

Neither must the historian ascertain the historicity of each and every miracle story or even the historicity of any one in particular. It is enough to observe that Jesus was widely held as a miracle worker by his contemporaries.

The miracles of Jesus are interpreted more carefully and more realistically in context, with the result that they are now viewed primarily as part of charismatic Judaism, either in terms of piety or in terms of restoration theology (or both).[7] The older notion that the miracle tradition is relatively late and of Hellenistic origin,[8] perhaps

---

7   Years ago P. Fiebig (*Jüdische Wundergeschichten des neutestamentlichen Zeitalters* [Tübingen: Mohr (Siebeck), 1911]) gathered together the Jewish miracle stories of the New Testament period. The potential relevance of these stories has been recently and very helpfully explored by G. Vermes, *Jesus the Jew: A Historian's Reading of the Gospels* (London: Collins, 1973) 58-82. Vermes has concluded that Jesus' miracles place him within the context of charismatic Judaism (see esp. pp. 69, 79). Although some have criticized Vermes' inference that Jesus was essentially a Jewish hasid, or holy man, most agree that Jesus' ministry of miracles parallels more closely the lives of Jewish personalities such as Honi, Hanina ben Dosa, or Theudas, than it does the lives of various hellenistic magicians and wonder-workers, who have been put forward. For his part, Sanders (*Jesus and Judaism*, 170-73) thinks that Theudas offers the closest parallel. See also O. Betz, "Jesu Heiliger Krieg," *NovT* 2 [1957] 116-37. Betz discusses passages in Josephus that describe promised wonders (*J.W.* 2.13.4 §259 vs. *Ant.* 20.5.1 §97; *J.W.* 2.13.5 §262 vs. *Ant.* 20.8.7 §176) and then compares them to Jesus' wonders. Also see B. Lindars, "Elijah, Elisha and the Gospel Miracles," in C. F. D. Moule (ed.), *Miracles: Cambridge Studies in their Philosophy and History* (London: Mowbray, 1965) 61-79; C. Brown, "Synoptic Miracle Stories: A Jewish Religious and Social Setting," *Forum* 2.4 (1986) 55-76.

8   R. Bultmann, *Die Geschichte der synoptischen Tradition* (2nd ed., Göttingen: Vandenhoeck & Ruprecht, 1931); ET: *History of the Synoptic Tradition* (Oxford: Blackwell, 1968). Bultmann asserts that the "Hellenistic origin of [most of] the miracle stories is overwhelmingly the more probable" (ET, p. 240). His assumption of the non-Palestinian origin of the miracle tradition is made clear by this statement: ". . . in Q [which contains almost no miracle stories] the picture of Jesus is made essentially from the material of the Palestinian tradition, while in Mark and most of all in his miracle stories Hellenism has made a vital contrib-tion" (p. 241). A similar position is adopted by M. Dibelius, *Die Formgeschichte des Evangeliums* (Tübingen: Mohr [Siebeck], 1919); ET: *From Tradition to Gospel* (London: James Clarke, 1971). According to Dibelius, the miracle tradition is remote and unhistorical: "[The presence of miracle stories] often, but not always, means a degeneration of the tradition, removing it further from the historical reality . . ." (ET, p. 99). Indeed, the miracle tradition is basically non-Christian (cf. p.

the product of *theios aner* ideas,[9] has been largely abandoned. Ongoing research has provided us with more precise knowledge of the historical, social, and religious context of first-century Palestine.[10] Studies in the miracles themselves have taken important steps forward, resulting in more nuanced assessments of miracle, medicine, and magic.[11]

---

102). This conclusion, which is patently false, will be taken up below in chap. 5.

[9] The "Divine Man [θεῖος ἀνήρ]" concept is a synthetic creation of the History of Religions School. Some have thought that the divine man idea aids interpretation of the Gospel miracle tradition, e.g. H. D. Betz, *Lukian von Samosata und das Neue Testament: Religionsgeschichtliche und Paränetische Parallelen* (Berlin: Akadamie, 1961); G. Petzke, *Die Traditionen über Apollonius von Tyana und das Neue Testament* (SCHNT 1; Leiden: Brill, 1970); P. J. Achtemeier, "Gospel Miracle tradition and the Divine Man," *Int* 26 (1972) 174-97. Betz (pp. 100-101) presupposes that a *Gesamtkonzeption* of the divine man was handed down from ancient Greek literature to the time of the early church. Such a "complete concept," however, does not exist. For a convenient summary of the criticisms leveled against this theory, see H. C. Kee, *Miracle in the Early Christian World: A Study in Sociohistorical Method* (New Haven and London: Yale University, 1983) 297-99. For further criticisms, see D. L. Tiede, *The Charismatic Figure as Miracle Worker* (SBLDS 1; Missoula: Scholars Press, 1972); M. Hengel, *Der Sohn Gottes: Die Entstehung der Christologie und die jüdisch-hellenistische Religionsgeschichte* (Tübingen: Mohr [Siebeck], 1975) 50-53; ET: *The Son of God* (Philadelphia: Fortress, 1976) 31-32; C. H. Holladay, *Theios Aner in Hellenistic Judaism: A Critique of the Use of This Category in New Testament Christology* (SBLDS 40; Missoula: Scholars Press, 1977); B. L. Blackburn, "'Miracle Working ΘΕΙΟΙ ΑΝΔΡΕΣ' in Hellenism (and Hellenistic Judaism)," in Wenham and Blomberg (eds.), *Miracles of Jesus*, 185-218; idem, *'Theios Aner' and the Markan Miracle Traditions: A Critique of the Theios Aner Concept as an Interpretative Background of the Miracle Traditions Used by Mark* (WUNT 2.40; Tübingen: Mohr [Siebeck], 1991); E. Koskenniemi, *Apollonius von Tyana in der neutestamentlichen Exegese* (WUNT 2.61; Tübingen: Mohr [Siebeck], 1994).

[10] S. Freyne, *Galilee from Alexander the Great to Hadrian: A Study of Second Temple Judaism* (Wilmington: Glazier; Notre Dame: Notre Dame University, 1980); idem, *Galilee, Jesus and the Gospels: Literary Approaches and Historical Investigations* (Philadelphia: Fortress, 1988); R. A. Horsley, *Jesus and the Spiral of Violence: Popular Jewish Resistance in Roman Palestine* (San Francisco: Harper & Row, 1987); idem and J. S. Hanson, *Bandits, Prophets, and Messiahs: Popular Movements at the Time of Jesus* (San Francisco: Harper & Row, 1985). For a survey of the relevant historical and archaeological data, see J. H. Charlesworth, *Jesus within Judaism* (ABRL; New York: Doubleday, 1988).

[11] H. C. Kee, *Miracle in the Early Christian World*; idem, *Medicine, Miracle*

As a consequence of the change in assumptions, the miracle stories are now treated seriously and are widely accepted by Jesus scholars as deriving from Jesus' ministry. Major studies on the historical Jesus discuss the miracles, whether in general terms or in reference to specific miracles, with little or no discussion of myth or the philosophical issues at one time thought to be necessary for any assessment of the miracle traditions in the Gospels.[12] Several specialized studies have appeared in recent years, which conclude that Jesus did perform miracles.[13] There have been also a few attempts at

---

and *Magic in New Testament Times* (SNTSMS 55; Cambridge: Cambridge University, 1986); E. Yamauchi, "Magic or Miracle? Disease, Demons and Exorcisms," in Wenham and Blomberg (eds.), *The Miracles of Jesus*, 89-183.

[12]   Many of the most significant studies in Jesus in recent years take the miracles seriously into account, e.g. Vermes, *Jesus the Jew*, 58-82; M. Smith, *Jesus the Magician* (San Francisco: Harper & Row, 1978) 8-20; B. F. Meyer, *The Aims of Jesus* (London: SCM, 1979) 154-58; A. E. Harvey, *Jesus and the Constraints of History* (London: Duckworth, 1982) 105-18; Sanders, *Jesus and Judaism*, 157-73; M. J. Borg, *Jesus: A New Vision* (San Francisco: Harper & Row, 1987) 57-75; B. Witherington, *The Christology of Jesus* (Minneapolis: Fortress, 1990) 145-77.

[13]   R. H. Fuller, *Interpreting the Miracles* (Philadelphia: Westminster, 1963); German ed., *Die Wunder Jesu in Exegese und Verkündigung* (Düsseldorf: Patmos, 1967). Fuller concludes that "the tradition that Jesus did perform exorcisms and healings (which may also have been exorcisms originally) is very strong" (p. 39). Fuller's positive assessment anticipated the critical affirmations that have been heard in more recent years. G. Theissen, *Urchristliche Wundergeschichten: Ein Beitrag zur formgeschichtlichen Erforschung der synoptischen Evangelien* (Gütersloh: Mohn, 1974); ET: *The Miracle Stories of the Early Christian Tradition* (Philadelphia: Fortress, 1983) 277: "There is no doubt that Jesus worked miracles, healed the sick and cast out demons"; Achtemeier, "Miracles and the Historical Jesus," 471-91; O. Betz and W. Grimm, *Wesen und Wirklichkeit der Wunder Jesu* (ANTJ 2; Frankfurt am Main and Bern: Lang, 1977); Smith, *Jesus the Magician*, 101: "In most miracle stories no explanation at all is given; Jesus simply speaks or acts and the miracle is done by his personal power. This trait probably reflects historical fact"; D. Zeller, "Wunder und Bekenntnis: zum Sitz im Leben urchristlicher Wundergeschichten," *BZ* 25 (1981) 204-22; G. Maier, "Zur neutestamentlichen Wunderexegese im 19. und 20. Jahrhundert," in Wenham and Blomberg (eds.), *The Miracles of Jesus*, 49-87, 79: "Historische Forschung kann heute mit guten Gründen sagen, dass Jesus damals Wunder getan hat"; Sanders, *Jesus and Judaism*, 157: "There is agreement on the basic facts: Jesus performed miracles, drew crowds and promised the kingdom to sinners"; H. Hendrickx, *The Miracle Stories of the Synoptic Gospels* (London: Chapman; San Francisco: Harper &

delineating criteria for ascertaining the historicity or non-historicity of individual miracle stories. For example, Engelbert Gutwenger has argued that the miracles can be assessed against criteria similar to those used for ascertaining the authenticity of the sayings tradition.[14] Franz Mussner has gone much further in arguing that the miracles of Jesus in the Gospels portray the *ipsissima facta Jesu*.[15] Mussner has scored some important points, but his conclusion may go beyond the evidence. Rudolf Pesch reasons, *pace* Mussner, that if the *ipsissima verba Jesu* cannot normally be recovered, it is not likely that *ipsissima facta* can either.[16] Nevertheless, he too concludes that Jesus performed miracles. Alfred Suhl has reached a similar conclusion, arguing that the miracle tradition is ultimately rooted in the historical Jesus (and not the early church, as many of the form critics had supposed).[17] René Latourelle has offered one of the most detailed and systematic treatments of criteria for evaluating the historicity of the miracles of Jesus.[18] Although his work contains many useful insights, it is flawed by a pronounced, and at times overriding, theological apologetic.[19] Criteria

---

Row, 1987) 22: "Yes, we can be sure that *Jesus performed real signs which were interpreted by his contemporaries as experiences of an extraordinary power*" (his emphasis); Witherington, *Christology*, 155: "That Jesus performed deeds that were perceived as miracles by both him and his audience is difficult to doubt."

[14]   E. Gutwenger, "Die Machtweise Jesu in formgeschichtlicher Sicht," *ZKT* 89 (1967) 176-90.

[15]   F. Mussner, *Die Wunder Jesu: Eine Hinführung* (Schriften zur Katechetik 10; Munich: Kösel, 1967); ET: *The Miracles of Jesus: An Introduction* (Notre Dame: University of Notre Dame, 1968).

[16]   R. Pesch, *Jesu ureigene Taten? Ein Beitrag zur Wunderfrage* (QD 52; Freiburg: Herder, 1970); idem, "Zur theologischen Bedeutung der 'Machttaten' Jesu. Reflexionen eines Exegeten," *TQ* 152 (1972) 203-13.

[17]   A. Suhl, *Die Wunder Jesu: Ereignis und Überlieferung* (Gütersloh: Mohn, 1968). Although some still argue that the miracle tradition reflects the history of the early church and its faith, more than it does the history of Jesus (e.g. G. Schille, *Die urchristliche Wundertradition: Ein Beitrag zur Frage nach dem irdischen Jesus* [Arbeiten zur Theologie 29; Stuttgart: Calwer, 1967]), this view appears to be waning.

[18]   R. Latourelle, "Authenticité historique des miracles de Jésus: Essai de critériologie," *Greg* 54 (1973) 225-62. Most of this essay (pp. 229-61) has appeared in Latourelle, *Miracles de Jésus et théologie du miracle* (Paris: Cerf; Montreal: Bellarmin, 1986); ET: *The Miracles of Jesus and the Theology of Miracles* (New York: Paulist, 1988) 54-69.

[19]   The massive study by H. van der Loos (*The Miracles of Jesus* [NovTSup 9;

have been worked out here and there in other studies that, together with the better points argued by Mussner and Latourelle, form the basis for a critical, historical evaluation of the miracles of Jesus. These criteria are articulated in chap. 5 below.

Third Quest scholars recognize that an accurate and reasonably complete picture of the historical Jesus cannot emerge if the miracle tradition is ignored or discarded. It is simply impossible to speak meaningfully about the "historical Jesus" if it is a Jesus stripped of what was probably the most distinctive feature of his public ministry— his miracles.[20] If Jesus was not known by his contemporaries to have performed miracles, and if miracles of such quality and quantity were not actually expected of an agent of redemption (whatever one's messianic views), then how can we account for the sheer preponderance of miracles in the Jesus tradition?[21] In my judgment the miracle stories belong to the same "bedrock" of tradition to which scholars have in the past so confidently assigned the parables.[22]

2. Historical Value of the Gospels. The New Testament Gospels are

---

Leiden: Brill, 1965]) suffers from the same weaknesses. Although van der Loos makes some good points in support of this miracle or that, his theological apologetic often leads him beyond what can be reasonably claimed on historical grounds. Moreover, some of his assertions are simply gratuitous (see pp. 235-36). No rigorous criteria are developed and employed.

[20]   Meyer (*Aims of Jesus*, 158) senses this when he says that it is "a mistake in historical interpretation to adopt a minimizing attitude toward the miracles of Jesus."

[21]   Kee (*Medicine, Miracle and Magic*, 128) concludes that "the phenomenon of healing in the gospels and elsewhere in the New Testament is a central factor in primitive Christianity, and was so from the beginning of the movement. It is not a later addendum to the tradition, introduced in order to make Jesus more appealing to the Hellenistic world, but was a major feature of the Jesus tradition from the outse[t]. Indeed, it is almost certainly a part of the historical core of that tradition, even though it is likely to have been embellished in the process of transmission."

[22]   It is for this reason, among others, that I cannot view as promising the results of the recent studies by B. L. Mack, *A Myth of Innocence: Mark and Christian Origins* (Philadelphia: Fortress, 1988) and J. D. Crossan, *The Historical Jesus: The Life of a Mediterranean Jewish Peasant* (San Francisco: HarperCollins, 1991). For both the miracle tradition plays a negligible role. Mack finds the Marcan portrait not only unreliable, but even misleading. Because he imports quantities of material of dubious worth Crossan conjures up a Jewish cynic and leaves the reader wondering what Jesus said and did to get himself crucified and to generate a following that survived his death. More will be said about Crossan shortly.

now viewed as useful, if not essentially reliable, historical sources. Gone is the extreme skepticism that for so many years dominated Gospel research.[23] Representative of many is the position of E. P. Sanders and Marcus Borg, who have concluded that it is possible to recover a fairly reliable picture of the historical Jesus. For example, Borg notes that more and more scholars are coming to the conclusion that "we can sketch a fairly full and historically defensible portrait of Jesus."[24] Similarly, Sanders comments: "The dominant view today seems to be that we can know pretty well what Jesus was out to accomplish, that we can know a lot about what he said, and that those two things make sense within the world of first-century Judaism."[25] With regard to Mark, some critical interpreters, although still recognizing his theological motives and redactional activities, believe that the Marcan evangelist has treated his tradition in a conservative manner.[26]

---

[23] To be fair, one must remember that much of the skepticism in the first half of the twentieth century was in reaction to the positivistic historiography of the Old Quest that sought to extract from the Gospels the mental, psychological, and spiritual development of Jesus. The "lives" generated by this thinking deserved to be regarded with skepticism.

[24] Borg, *Jesus: A New Vision*, 15.

[25] Sanders, *Jesus and Judaism*, 2. For evidence of this "dominant view" he cites (p. 355 n. 14) H. Schürmann, "Zur aktuellen Situation der Leben-Jesu-Forschung," *Geist und Leben* 46 (1973) 300-310, and G. Aulén, *Jesus in Contemporary Historical Research* (Philadelphia: Fortress, 1976) viii, 3. See also W. R. Farmer, *Jesus and the Gospel: Tradition, Scripture, and Canon* (Philadelphia: Fortress, 1982), who says with regard to the Gospels: "We have access to a large body of first-rate historical evidence that is decisive in answering important questions about Jesus" (p. 21). Other studies that view the Gospels in a similar light include those by Meyer, *The Aims of Jesus*; Harvey, *Jesus and the Constraints of History*; R. Riesner, *Jesus als Lehrer: Eine Untersuchung zum Ursprung der Evangelien-Überlieferung* (WUNT 2.7; Tübingen: Mohr [Siebeck], 1981; 4th ed., 1994); idem, "Der Ursprung der Jesus-Überlieferung," *TZ* 38 (1982) 493-513; A. F. Zimmermann, *Die urchristlichen Lehrer: Studien zum Tradentenkreis der διδάσκαλοι im frühen Urchristentum* (WUNT 2.12; Tübingen: Mohr [Siebeck], 1984); G. N. Stanton, *The Gospels and Jesus* (Oxford: Oxford University, 1989) 150-64; Witherington, *Christology*, 1-31; E. E. Ellis, "Gospels Criticism: A Perspective on the State of the Art," in P. Stuhlmacher (ed.), *The Gospel and the Gospels* (Grand Rapids: Eerdmans, 1991) 26-52; Stuhlmacher, "The Theme: The Gospel and the Gospels," in Stuhlmacher (ed.), *The Gospel and the Gospels*, 1-25, esp. 2-12.

[26] See R. Pesch, *Das Markusevangelium* (HTKNT 2.1-2; Freiburg: Herder,

This more positive assessment of the Gospels does not, however, herald a return to the naive positivism which characterized much of the Old Quest. No one is arguing for another round of psycho-analysing Jesus. Bultmann believed that we could know nothing of Jesus' "personality." In this he was certainly correct. It is impossible to reconstruct a psychological profile or trace the development of Jesus' consciousness. Third Quest scholarship is not interested in attempting this. Third Quest scholarship may not be as skeptical as New Quest scholars or their predecessors, but it is critical, perhaps even more critical, in that it has rejected certain questionable assumptions and conclusions held and promoted by form critics. Among these is the assumption that the early Church freely invented sayings of Jesus,[27] or that certain laws govern the development and transmission of oral traditions.[28]

3. Theological Apologetics. Unlike the earlier quests, the Third

---

1976-77) 1.63-67; 2.1-25; M. Hengel, *Studies in the Gospel of Mark* (Philadelphia: Fortress, 1985) 32-41; R. A. Guelich, *Mark 1–8:26* (WBC 34A; Dallas: Word, 1989) xxxiii-xxxiv. By "conservative" I mean that the evangelist has *conserved* the dominical tradition, as opposed to having freely and extensively edited it or having created it altogether.

27   In my judgment the thesis of M. E. Boring (*Sayings of the Risen Jesus: Christian Prophecy in the Synoptic Tradition* [SNTSMS 46; Cambridge: Cambridge University Press, 1982]; *The Continuing Voice of Jesus* [Louisville: Westminster/ John Knox, 1991]), to the effect that much of dominical tradition arose through early Christian prophecy, is no longer persuasive or widely held. Boring is certainly right in finding that much of the dominical tradition has been reinterpreted, largely through recontextualization, but there is little objective evidence of wholesale creation. For criticisms of Boring's conclusions, see D. E. Aune, *Prophecy in Early Christianity and the Ancient Mediterranean World* (Grand Rapids: Eerdmans, 1983) 240-42 (on Jesus tradition, see pp. 153-88); D. Hill, *New Testament Prophecy* (Atlanta: John Knox, 1979) 5-9 (on Jesus tradition, pp. 48-69). Aune and Hill are responding to Boring's dissertation and to earlier studies presented in the SBLSP (1973, 1974, 1976, 1977) and *JBL* (1972). For an earlier statement that is compatible with Boring's conclusions, see F. W. Beare, "Sayings of the Risen Jesus in the Synoptic Tradition," in W. R. Farmer et al. (eds.), *Christian History and Interpretation* (J. Knox Festschrift; London: Cambridge University Press, 1967) 161-81.

28   For an excellent critique of this assumption, see E. P. Sanders, *The Tendencies of the Synoptic Tradition* (SNTSMS 9; Cambridge: Cambridge University Press, 1969).

Quest is not driven by theological-philosophical concerns.[29] There has been a shift away from a philosophical orientation to a historical orientation. Gone is the lively and often convoluted discussion of *Geschichte* and *Historie* as meaningfully distinct categories. The matter is simply no longer debated.[30] Likewise, the related concern to

---

[29]   See, e.g. R. Bultmann, "New Testament and Mythology," in *Kerygma and Myth: A Theological Debate* (London: SPCK, 1957) 1-44: "[The universe is a] "self-subsistent unity immune from the interference of supernatural powers" (p. 7). For similar thinking addressed specifically to the question of miracles, see also Bultmann, "Zur Frage des Wunder," in Bultmann, *Glauben und Verstehen* (2 vols., Tübingen: Mohr [Siebeck], 1954) 1.214-28; ET: "The Problem of Miracle," *RL* 27 (1958) 63-75; idem, *Faith and Understanding*, 249: "*The idea of miracle has, therefore, become untenable and it must be abandoned*" (Bultmann's emphasis). For Bultmann the facticity of Jesus' miracles is irrelevant. The deistic heritage is obvious. For a philsophical analysis of miracles in the thinking of Spinoza, Reimarus, Hume, Strauss, Feuerbach, and Bultmann, see E. Keller and M.-L. Keller, *Der Streit um die Wunder* (Gütersloh: Mohn, 1968); ET: *Miracles in Dispute: A Continuing Debate* (London: SCM, 1969; repr. 1984).

[30]   As part of their rationale for the New Quest, in which a stronger historical link between the historical Jesus and the Christ of faith is established, Bultmann's pupils advocated a new understanding of history (which involved, of course, a new understanding of *Geschichte* and *Historie*) in which subjective appropriation of theological, or existential, truths was believed to be the essence of historiography, not the recording of (objective) facts; cf. J. M. Robinson, *The Problem of History in Mark* (SBT 21; London: SCM, 1957) 16-20. But this understanding has not escaped significant criticism. P. Merkley ("New Quests for Old: One Historian's Observations on a Bad Bargain," *CJT* 16 [1970] 203-18) has criticized the leading advocates of the New Quest for misinterpreting and misappropriating the views of the late historian R. G. Collingwood, concluding that these scholars simply do not understand history and historiography. Moreover, the distinction between "authentic" and "authoritative," a distinction often made, or at least assumed, by the leading advocates of the New Quest, is also problematic. With regard to this problem, see R. H. Stein, "'Authentic' or 'Authoritative'? What is the Difference?" *JETS* 24 (1981) 127-30. Stein and Merkley have in mind the sort of thinking so aptly expressed by Robinson, *New Quest of the Historical Jesus*, 99-100 n. 3: "One may however observe that material regarded as wholly 'unauthentic' in terms of positivistic historiography may not seem nearly as 'unauthentic' in terms of modern historiography. For a saying which Jesus never spoke may well reflect accurately his historical significance, and in this sense be more 'historical' than many irrelevant things Jesus actually said." Clearly, what Robinson means here by "historical" is not what too many historians today (or at any time, for that matter) would recognize as the proper sense of the word. If words are allowed to have their

find a Jesus relevant for the Christian kerygma seems also to have
receded. In responding to his pupils thirty years ago Bultmann
summed up their principal disagreement: "In the time of the [Old
Quest] . . . the emphasis lay upon establishing the difference between
Jesus and the kerygma. Today [i.e. the New Quest] it is the reverse: the
emphasis lies on the working out of the unity of the historical Jesus and
the Christ of the kerygma."[31] Bultmann's succinct statement of the
essential point of difference between the Old and New Quests is
certainly accurate and it also reveals how different the current mode of
Jesus research is. The question of the role of the kerygma is hardly
raised today. Life of Jesus research is characterized today more by an
interest *in history rather than in faith.* In the case of Sanders, this is
explicitly stated.[32] For this reason, scholars tend to talk of "life of Jesus
research," as opposed to a "quest."[33] Consequently the debate over the
legitimacy or illegitimacy of research into the historical Jesus, an item
to which great importance was attached throughout most of this
century, has simply ceased. To raise it now would strike most as odd,
even atavistic.

Other items that often have provoked controversy have subsided.
For example, scholars, both Jewish and Christian, are in essential
agreement that the Jewish religious-political leadership of Jerusalem,

conventional meaning, then one should realize that "authentic" ought to imply that
the saying in question goes back to Jesus, while "inauthentic" ought to imply that it
does not. Whether a saying (that goes back to Jesus or not) has existential relevance
for a person is quite another matter. For further criticism, see J. P. Mackey, *Jesus
the Man and the Myth* (New York: Paulist, 1979) 10-51; Meyer, *Aims of Jesus,*
51-54; J. Gnilka, *Jesus von Nazaret: Botschaft und Geschichte* (HTKNTSup 3;
Freiburg: Herder, 1990) 11-34; Meier, "The Historical Jesus," 3-24; idem, *A
Marginal Jew: Rethinking the Historical Jesus. Volume One: The Roots of the
Problem and the Person* (ABRL; New York: Doubleday, 1991) 26-31. Meier ("The
Historical Jesus," 3-24) offers a helpful discussion of what it properly means to
speak of the "historical" Jesus. He wisely recommends dropping the confusing and
dubious distinction between the *historische* Jesus and the *geschichtliche* Jesus.

31   Bultmann, *Das Verhältnis,* 5-6; ET, p. 15.

32   With regard to the theological significance of Jesus, Sanders (*Jesus and
Judaism,* 2) states: "The present work is written without that question in mind."

33   See J. H. Charlesworth, "Research on the Historical Jesus," *Proceedings of
the Irish Biblical Association* 9 (1985) 19-37; idem, "From Barren Mazes to Gentle
Rappings: The Emergence of Jesus Research," *Princeton Seminary Bulletin* 7
(1986) 221-30. For convenience I shall continue to speak of the "Third Quest."

in collaboration with the Roman governor, played an important role in Jesus' death. Few today would argue either that the Romans played little or no role or that the Jewish leadership was uninvolved. What happened to Jesus of Nazareth was probably not too much different from happened a generation later to Jesus ben Ananias, where we find the Jewish leadership working in concert with the Roman governor to silence a prophet of doom.

AUTHENTICITY CRITERIA

From the New Quest to the present the criteria for assessing the probability of the authenticity of given pericopes or isolated sayings have received much attention. In my judgment, in recent years the various criteria have been carefully sorted out, with dubious criteria culled out from among those that are more useful. Probably the best presentation of the criteria has come from John Meier.[34] There are six criteria that should be considered valid. I shall treat them in what I regard as more or less their order of importance.

1. Historical Coherence. Material that coheres with what we know of Jesus' historical circumstances and the principal features of his life should be given priority. This is a point that Sanders has made, and I think it has merit. We may expect authentic material to help explain "why [Jesus] attracted attention, why he was executed, and why he was subsequently deified."[35] Material that does not clarify these questions is not automatically excluded, of course, but priority must be given to

---

34   Meier, *A Marginal Jew*, 167-95. For further discussion, with more detail and more examples, see R. H. Stein, "The 'Criteria' for Authenticity," in R. T. France and D. Wenham (eds.), *Studies of History and Tradition in the Four Gospels* (Gospel Perspectives 2; Sheffield: JSOT Press, 1980) 225-63; C. A. Evans, "Authenticity Criteria in Life of Jesus Research," *CSR* 19 (1989) 6-31. For a finely nuanced—at times "hair-splitting"—review of the criteria, see D. Polkow, "Method and Criteria for Historical Jesus Research," in K. H. Richards (ed.), *Society of Biblical Literature 1987 Seminar Papers* (SBLSP 26; Atlanta: Scholars, 1987) 336-56. For French and German assessments of the criteria, see R. Latourelle, "Critères d'authenticité des Évangiles," *Greg* 55 (1974) 609-38; F. Lentzen-Deis, "Kriterien für die historische Beurteilung der Jesusüberlieferung in den Evangelien," in K. Kertelge (ed.), *Rückfrage nach Jesus: Zur Methodik und Bedeutung der Frage nach dem historischen Jesus* (QD 63; Freiburg: Herder, 1974) 78-117.
35   Sanders, *Jesus and Judaism*, 7.

material that does clarify them.

We must ask how it was that an itinerant teacher from Galilee was put to death on a Roman cross. For this reason Meier calls it the "Criterion of Rejection and Execution."[36] I think that this is the single most important feature that must be taken into account in any work that wishes to be taken seriously. The problem with many of the interpretations of Jesus that have been presented in the last two decades is that they do not realistically explain this problem. They come up with interesting Jesuses who reflect, usually along politically-correct lines, the values of twentieth-century academia. Some of this may constitute good sociology, even avant-garde theology, but it is not good historiography.

In my judgment this criterion should be given first place. In saying this I am in essential agreement with Sanders, who, I realize, has been criticized for giving priority to fairly well establishment *facts*, as opposed to the *sayings* of Jesus, which is where most studies traditionally have begun.[37] I side with Sanders here for two reasons: (1) The original context of the sayings of Jesus, with rare exceptions, is lost. Consequently, even if we are relatively certain of the authenticity of a significant core of sayings, we are seldom certain of the original setting in which they were uttered and, therefore, of what precisely they originally meant. As I see it, interpretation of the sayings is more vulnerable to the whims of modern subjectivity than are events and "facts." Obviously the "facts" have to be interpreted also, and subjectivity remains a problem, but their context is more certain. (2) Non-Christian sources support certain important facts and so provide significant information for comparative study. As will be argued below, we have no reliable sources of Jesus' sayings outside of the New Testament. Even if some of these sources were to be accepted as containing historically trustworthy tradition, they give us no useful information as to the setting and context of the sayings. From this I conclude that the historical framework, made up of several fairly certain facts, must first be clarified and then used as a primary criterion for determining what sayings and episodes ought be considered the stronger candidates of authentic tradition and how they

---

36   Meier, *A Marginal Jew*, 177.

37   See Sanders, *Jesus and Judaism*, 10-22. The Jesus Seminar, which focuses almost exclusively on the sayings of Jesus, will be treated below.

should be interpreted. Sanders has identified the "almost indisputable facts" as follows:

1. Jesus was baptized by John the Baptist.
2. Jesus was a Galilean who preached and healed.
3. Jesus called disciples and spoke of there being twelve.
4. Jesus confined his activity to Israel.
5. Jesus engaged in a controversy about the Temple.
6. Jesus was crucified outside Jerusalem by the Roman authorities.
7. After his death Jesus' followers continued as an identifiable movement.
8. At least some Jews persecuted at least parts of the new movement (Gal 1:13, 22; Phil 3:6), and it appears that this persecution endured at least to a time near the end of Paul's career (2 Cor 11:24; Gal 5:11; 6:12; cf. Matt 23:34; 10:17).[38]

To these facts one can add a few more complementary details. I think that it is highly probable that Jesus was viewed by the public as a prophet, that he spoke often of the kingdom of God, that his Temple controversy involved criticism of the ruling priests, and that the Romans crucified him as "king of the Jews." We shall find that many of the sayings of Jesus cohere with these historical elements, often times either explaining them or being explained by them.

2. Multiple Attestation. Multiple attestation refers to material that appears in two or more independent sources. This material may be regarded as primitive, though not necessarily authentic. Multiple attestation confirms that material was not generated by one evangelist or another (or their respective communities), but must have been in circulation some years before the Gospels and their sources were composed.[39] Thus, multiple attestation does not guarantee authenticity; it only guarantees antiquity.[40]

Nevertheless, given the nature of the task—that of discovering the

---

[38] Sanders, *Jesus and Judaism*, 11.

[39] The criterion of multiple forms demonstrates the same thing; cf. C. H. Dodd, *History and the Gospel* (New York: Scribner's, 1937) 91-101. Ideas that appear in two or more forms of tradition (e.g. sayings, parables, stories) may be regarded as ancient and widespread. Examples would include the kingdom of God, association with sinners, and certain halakic disputes.

[40] It has also been argued, and I think rightly in most cases, that the burden of proof shifts in favor of authenticity when material is multiply attested; cf. H. K. McArthur, "The Burden of Proof in Historical Jesus Research," *ExpTim* 82 (1970-71) 116-19.

essential facts of the life and death of Jesus of Nazareth, a man who lived some two thousand years ago and did not himself record any of his teachings—multiply attested material should be given careful consideration. As it so happens, much of what is multiply attested has often been regarded as authentic, not only because it is multiply attested, but because it often enjoys the support of other criteria.[41]

The degree of importance attached to the criterion of multiple attestation has reached new levels in John Dominic Crossan's recently published work on the historical Jesus.[42] In his reconstruction of the historical Jesus he disallows all material that is not multiply attested.[43] Crossan, of course, knows that not everything multiply attested is authentic, nor is everything singly attested inauthentic. He believes that since multiple attestation is the only truly objective criterion, it should be the foundational criterion. There is, to be sure, an element of truth to this line of reasoning.

But is the criterion of multiple attestation genuinely objective, at least as it employed by Crossan and some of his sympathizers? I have my doubts. Many of the sayings that Crossan has identified as multiply attested are multiply attested only if it is granted that various apocryphal and extra-canonical sources be regarded as independent of the canonical Gospels. A few years before the publication of *The Historical Jesus*, Crossan offered us his inventory of the "primary stratum." For example, he asserts that the best attested saying ("ask,

---

[41] F. C. Burkitt (*The Gospel History and Its Transmission* [3rd ed., Edinburgh: T. & T. Clark, 1911] 148-66) identified thirty-one multiply attested sayings. (Burkitt presupposed the Two Document Hypothesis and did not make use of any of the agrapha or apocryphal gospels.) Whereas R. Bultmann (*The History of the Synoptic Tradition* [Oxford: Blackwell, 1972]) regarded only a quarter of these sayings as authentic, the Jesus Seminar, which is scarcely less skeptical, judged eleven of these sayings "pink" (i.e. probably from Jesus), thirteen "gray" (i.e. possibly from Jesus), and only seven "black" (i.e. definitely not from Jesus); cf. R. W. Funk (ed.), *The Gospel of Mark: Red Letter Edition* (Sonoma: Polebridge, 1991). In perusing their publications, one observes that sayings attested not only in the canonical Gospels, but also in extra-canonical sources (which are understood by many in the Jesus Seminar to be independent sources), are frequently the sayings that win "red" and "pink" votes. More will be said about this below.

[42] Crossan, *The Historical Jesus*.

[43] "My methodological discipline in this book forbids the use of single attestations for reconstructing the historical Jesus"; Crossan, *The Historical Jesus*, 257; cf. similar expressions on pp. xxxi-xxxiii and 410.

seek, knock") is attested in "six independent sources": (1) *Gospel of Thomas* (§2, §92, §94, POxy654 §2), (2) Q (Luke 11:9-10 = Matt 7:7-8), (3) Mark 11:24, (4) John (14:13-14; 15:7, 16; 16:23-24, 26), (5) *Dialogue of the Savior* (§9-12, §20, §79-80), and (6) *Gospel of the Hebrews* (§4).[44] But do we really have *six* independent sources? I think that here it is more appropriate to speak of two (Mark and Q), possibly three (Mark, Q, and John). I have little confidence that the sayings in *Thomas* are independent, and no confidence whatsoever that they are independent in *Dialogue* or *Hebrews*.

Other examples are much more problematic. Of the 107 complexes that Crossan has identified, 55 are multiply attested only because of their appearance in the *Gospel of Thomas* and/or in other extra-canonical sources. Five more complexes are attested *only* in these sources.[45] If these sources are secondary (being directly or indirectly dependent on the canonical Gospels), as many scholars believe, then more than one half of Crossan's inventory loses its claim to multiple attestation.

What I find particularly interesting is that there are so few complexes made up solely of extra-canonical materials. In other words, almost all "multiply attested" material, as Crossan defines it, is material that occurs in at least one of the canonical Gospels. I think that this is one more indication that all of the credible material ultimately derives from the canonical Gospels themselves. If *Thomas* and some of the other apocryphal gospels are truly independent, or at least contain independent traditions, and in some cases even antedate the canonical Gospels, why is there not a larger number of sayings attested only by the extra-canonical sources? I suspect that there are not more such sayings in these sources because they (the sources) are not in fact primitive and independent. More will be said about this controversial issue below in the section concerned with sources.

Multiple attestation, then, remains an important and useful criterion. But it should not be used to exclude singly attested material, nor should excessive reliance on this criterion lead us to draw upon questionable sources whose traditions may not in all probability be independent of

---

[44]   J. D. Crossan, "Materials and Methods in Historical Jesus Research," *Forum* 4.4 (1988) 3-24, esp. 15-16, 23. See also Crossan, *The Historical Jesus*, 435 (§4).

[45]   Crossan, "Materials and Methods," 13-22.

the canonical Gospels.

3. Embarrassment. By "embarrassing," I mean material that is perceived by the evangelists as awkward, as in need of qualification, and perhaps even deletion. It may also be material that is contrary to the editorial tendency of the evangelist himself. Nevertheless, despite the awkwardness and the potential embarrassment, the material is preserved. It is reasoned, and I think cogently, that this material is preserved because it is ancient and widespread.[46] As Meier has put it: "It is highly unlikely that the Church went out of its way to create the cause of its own embarrassment."[47]

Several examples immediately come to mind. The baptism of Jesus, which is related by Mark, evidently with little discomfort for the evangelist (Mark 1:9-11), becomes increasingly qualified in its retelling in the later Gospels. Matthew tells us that John the Baptist was initially unwilling to baptize Jesus (Matt 3:13-15). The Lucan account leaves us with the impression that Jesus was baptized after John had been imprisoned (Luke 3:18-22). The Fourth Gospel omits reference to Jesus' baptism altogether (John 1:29-34). The apocryphal gospels add embellishments of their own. The words spoken from heaven in the version presented by *GHeb* §2 are expanded and significantly christologized. All of this leaves the impression that the baptism of Jesus created a measure of embarrassment for the early Church (cf. Acts 19:1-7). Jesus' relationship to John the Baptist could not be denied, but it could be explained and qualified. Another good example is seen in the tradition of Jesus' allusion to Ps 22:1. Mark's presentation of Jesus' cry from the cross, "My God, my God, why have You forsaken me?" (Mark 15:34), is replaced by much more reassuring

---

[46]   See D. G. A. Calvert, "An Examination of the Criteria for Distinguishing the Authentic Words of Jesus," *NTS* 18 (1972) 209-19. Calvert comments: "The inclusion of material which does not especially serve his purpose may well be taken as a testimony to the authenticity of that material, or at least to the inclusion of it in the tradition of the Church in such a clear and consistent way that the evangelist was loath to omit it" (p. 219). This criterion is not precisely the same as that of the criterion of embarrassment, but it is cognate. In the case of the latter, authenticity is supported when the tradition cannot easily be explained as the creation of the Church in general; in the case of the former, authenticity is supported when the tradition cannot easily be explained as the creation of a given evangelist or his community.

[47]   Meier, *A Marginal Jew*, 169.

utterances in Luke (23:46) and in John (19:30). Again we are left with
the impression that the early Church, at least a significant part of it,
was uncomfortable with this tradition. Numerous other details in the
Marcan Gospel are either touched up (e.g. 3:33-34; 4:38, 40; 7:24-30)
or omitted (e.g. 7:31-37; 8:22-26). All of these "embarrassing"
Marcan materials have good claim to authenticity.

Other important examples of embarrassment are seen in the question
that the imprisoned John the Baptist puts to Jesus: "Are you the one
who comes, or do we look for another?" (Matt 11:2-6 = Luke 7:18-
23). It is extremely improbable that the early Church would invent
such an exchange between John and Jesus. Surely a tradition which
expresses doubt about Jesus cannot have been the creation of the early
Church. Jesus' discussion of Ps 110:1, in which he appears to distance
himself from Davidic messianology (Mark 12:35-37), is yet another
example in which the criterion of embarrassment supports the
authenticity of the pericope, even if the original setting and meaning
remain obscure. Again, we must ask why the early Church would
create a saying in which Jesus appears to question Davidic descent,
which elsewhere in the New Testament is affirmed (cf. Rom 1:3), and
a saying in which he appears to question the appropriateness of Ps
110:1, a passage which was very important for the early Church's
articulation of christology. Jesus' action in the Temple (Mark 11:15-
18), complete with a saying about the Temple's destruction (Mark
14:58; Acts 6:13-14), and his admission that he does not know the
eschatological hour (Mark 13:32) are also good candidates for this
criterion.

4. Dissimilarity. Defined and put into practice as it was during the
heyday of redaction criticism, the criterion of dissimilarity (or
discontinuity, as it was sometimes called) is problematic. Norman
Perrin gave this criterion its classic definition: "the earliest form of a
saying we can reach may be regarded as authentic if it can be shown to
be dissimilar to characteristic emphases both of ancient Judaism and of
the early Church."[48] In recent years it has been soundly criticized.[49]

---

[48]   N. Perrin, *Rediscovering the Teaching of Jesus* (London: SCM; New York:
Harper & Row, 1967) 39. For a similar statement of the principle, see E.
Käsemann, *Essays on New Testament Themes* (SBT 41; London: SCM, 1964) 37.
[49]   See the studies by M. D. Hooker, "On Using the Wrong Tool," *Th* 75
(1972) 570-81, esp. 574-75; D. L. Mealand, "The Dissimilarity Test," *SJT* 31

There are at least two problems with this understanding of the criterion: (1) Jesus was a Jew; we should expect his teachings and actions to reflect Jewish ideas and customs. Why must authentic materials be dissimilar to "characteristic emphases . . . of ancient Judaism"? This thinking, which is clearly rooted in Rudolf Bultmann's *History of the Synoptic Tradition* and presupposed in his *Jesus*,[50] in my opinion grows out of a theology that places great emphasis on how Jesus was different from (i.e. "superior to") Judaism. In essence what we have in Bultmann and his pupils is apologetics, not history. So far as the requirements of logic are concerned, there are no legitimate grounds for skepticism simply because dominical tradition sometimes reflects characteristic emphases of first-century Judaism.[51] Jesus was, moreover, the founder of a movement that was devoted to him and to his teaching. Should we not then expect many of Jesus' emphases to carry over into the movement? It is reasoned that since much of the Church's teaching is indebted to the teaching of Jesus, it is probable

(1978) 41-50; Stein, "The 'Criteria' for Authenticity," 240-45; Chilton, *A Galilean Rabbi and His Bible Jesus' Own Interpretation of Isaiah* (London: SPCK, 1984) 86-87; Sanders, *Jesus and Judaism*, 16-17, 252-55; Evans, "Authenticity Criteria," 15-16; E. P. Sanders and M. Davies, *Studying the Synoptic Gospels* (London: SCM; Philadelphia: Trinity Press International, 1989) 301-33.

50   For example, see Bultmann, *The History of the Synoptic Tradition*, 102-108; esp. idem, *Jesus* (Berlin: Deutsche Bibliothek, 1926) esp. 15-18; ET: *Jesus and the Word* (New York: Scribner's, 1934) esp. 12-15. I refer to these pages in *Synoptic Tradition* because they illustrate Bultmann's skepticism with regard to various proverbial sayings attributed to Jesus *because of their similarities with rabbinic proverbial sayings*. There is simply no good reason for doubting the authenticity of dominical tradition simply because it parallels genres and styles of first-century Palestine. Skepticism must be justified on other grounds.

51   In sharp contrast to Bultmann and his pupils, Geza Vermes has emphasized the Jewish parallels, not only as authentic in most cases, but as essential for understanding Jesus; cf. Vermes, *Jesus the Jew*; idem, *Jesus and the World of Judaism* (London: SCM; Philadelphia: Fortress, 1983); idem, *The Religion of Jesus the Jew* (London: SCM; Minneapolis: Fortress, 1993). Other Jewish scholars have emphasized the importance of Jesus' Jewishness; cf. D. Flusser, *Jesus in Selbstzeugnissen und Bilddokumenten* (Rowohlts Monographien 140; Hamburg: Rowohlt, 1968); ET: *Jesus* (New York: Herder & Herder, 1969); P. Lapide, *Der Rabbi von Nazaret: Wandlungen des jüdischen Jesus-bildes* (Trier: Spee, 1974). The Jewish interest in Jesus has been recently discussed by D. A. Hagner, *The Jewish Reclamation of Jesus: An Analysis and Critique of Modern Jewish Study of Jesus* (Grand Rapids: Zondervan, 1984).

that some of the early Church's emphases grew out of those of Jesus' teaching. Sayings that cohere with early Christian emphases but are in various ways inconsistent with other sayings are appropriate candidates for exclusion. (2) Employment of the criterion of dissimilarity has also been criticized for its tendency too readily to exclude material. Instead, the criterion should be used to ascertain a core of reasonably certain material. In other words, the criterion is valid in a *positive* not *negative* application.

Although the criterion of dissimilarity has been criticized, it has in a certain sense also been rehabilitated. Dissimilarity to early Judaism has been dropped, as it should be, while dissimilarity to emphases in the early Church is applied with greater nuance. Material cannot be disqualified simply because it is in continuity with the teaching of the early Church, it should be disqualified if it appears to reflect ideas that are inconsistent with the *Sitz im Leben Jesu*.[52] Indeed, often authentic material is given new applications that serve well the Church's interests and needs, but these new applications are not the same as those in their orignal setting. This point has been illustrated in studies by James Sanders, who speaks of the hermeneutics of "prophetic criticism."[53] Sanders has made the point that what for Jesus was meant as a prophetic challenge and criticism of conventional wisdom (such as a warning not to presume who is elect and who is not, or who will be judged and who will be blessed) could in a later context be used in terms of the hermeneutics of "insiders vs. outsiders." Therefore, an unnuanced and uncritical reading of the Nazareth sermon in Luke 4 and many of the parables could lead to the erroneous conclusion that these materials were produced by the early Church, as expressions of debate and controversy with the synagogue. "Jesus could not have meant that," some reason. Therefore, "Jesus could not have said it." But these two statements must be distinguished. The former is often true, but the latter does not necessarily follow.[54]

---

[52] Evans, "Authenticity Criteria," 26-27.

[53] J. A. Sanders, "From Isaiah 61 to Luke 4," in J. Neusner (ed.), *Christianity, Judaism and Other Greco-Roman Cults* (M. Smith Festschrift; Part One: New Testament; SJLA 12; Leiden: Brill, 1975) 75-106; revised and repr. in C. A. Evans and J. A. Sanders, *Luke and Scripture: The Function of Sacred Tradition in Luke-Acts* (Minneapolis: Fortress, 1993) 46-69.

[54] For more discussion of Jesus' use of Scripture, especially as it reflects the hermeneutics of prophetic criticism, see B. D. Chilton and C. A. Evans, "Jesus and

5. Semitisms and Palestinian Background. Meier subdivides this criterion into two related criteria: "Traces of Aramaic" and "Palestinian Environment." He admits that they have some value in making negative assessments (i.e. linguistic and environmental elements foreign to first-century Palestine probably do not derive from Jesus, but from later, non-Palestinian segments of the early Church). But he doubts that these criteria have much value for making positive judgments.[55] All that Semitisms and Palestinian features prove is that a given saying originated in an Aramaic-speaking Palestinian community, not that it necessarily originated with Jesus. To an extent, Meier is right. There is no question that Joachim Jeremias and others sometimes claimed too much on the basis of Aramaic and Palestinian elements.[56] Nevertheless, I think these criteria do make an important contribution, perhaps mostly in a general way.

The Gospels are written in Greek and yet they purport to record the sayings of Jesus who in all probability spoke primarily in Aramaic. If these Greek sayings in reality represent the utterances of the Aramaic-speaking Jesus,[57] we should expect to find traces of the Aramaic language. And indeed we do. We find Aramaic words and idioms that are foreign to Greek but at home in Aramaic.[58] Aramaic language and

---

Israel's Scriptures," in Chilton and Evans (eds.), *Studying the Historical Jesus*, 281-335, esp. 309-33.

55   Meier, *A Marginal Jew*, 178-80. A similar negative evaluation is offered by Sanders and Davies, *Studying the Synoptic Gospels*, 333-34.

56   For illustrations, see J. Jeremias, *Neutestamentliche Theologie. Erster Teil: Die Verkündigung Jesu* (Gütersloh: Mohn, 1971) 14-45; ET: *New Testament Theology: The Proclamation of Jesus* (London: SCM; New York: Scribner's, 1971) 3-37. See also the older work by G. Dalman, *Die Worte Jesu mit Berücksichtung des nach kanonischen jüdischen Schrifttums und der aramäistischen Sprache erörtert* (Leipzig: Hinrichs, 1898) 13-34; ET: *The Words of Jesus* (Edinburgh: T. & T. Clark, 1902) 17-42.

57   On the question of the language(s) spoken by Jesus, see J. A. Fitzmyer, "The Languages of Palestine in the First Century A.D.," *CBQ* 32 (1970) 501-31; idem, "Methodology in the Study of the Aramaic Substratum of Jesus' Sayings in the New Testament," in J. Dupont (ed.), *Jésus aux origines de la christologie* (BETL 40; Gembloux: Duculot, 1975) 73-102; both rev. and repr. in Fitzmyer, *A Wandering Aramean: Collected Aramaic Essays* (SBLMS 25; Missoula: Scholars Press, 1979) 1-56; and S. E. Porter, "Jesus and the Use of Greek in Galilee," in Chilton and Evans (eds.), *Studying the Historical Jesus*, 123-54.

58   For a recent study reassessing the criteria used in identifying the presence of

Palestinian elements do not of course prove the authenticity of any given saying, though they add a measure of support and, in general, they instill in the historian the confidence that the tradition is ancient and bears the characteristics one should expect of authentic dominical tradition. I believe that it is therefore appropriate to regard the criteria of Semitisms and Palestinian background as playing an important supporting role with respect to the other criteria.[59]

6. Coherence. Finally, the criterion of coherence (or consistency) should also be considered as a valid canon of authenticity. It justifies the broadening of the core of material established as authentic through appeal to the criteria described above. Accordingly, material that coheres or is consistent with material judged authentic may also be regarded as authentic.[60] However, Meier rightly warns that this criterion should not be applied too rigorously, especially negatively, to exclude material as inauthentic.[61]

The potential danger in this criterion lies in too quickly assuming what the essence of Jesus' message was and in insisting that material cohere quite closely to this essence. One may observe an interesting division among Jesus scholars in appeals to this criterion. During the New Quest and its aftermath scholars were confident that Jesus' message was eschatological.[62] This led Charles Carlston to argue that

---

Semitisms, see E. C. Maloney, *Semitic Interference in Marcan Syntax* (SBLDS 51; Chico: Scholars Press, 1981).

[59]   For a lucid and compelling demonstration of the value of targumic tradition for the identification and clarification of potentially authentic dominical tradition, see Chilton, *Galilean Rabbi*; idem, "Targumic Transmission and Dominical Tradition," in France and Wenham (eds.), *Studies of History and Tradition*, 21-45.

[60]   See Perrin, *Rediscovering the Teaching of Jesus*, 43.

[61]   Meier, *A Marginal Jew*, 176-77.

[62]   The eschatological criterion, sometimes called the criterion of "proleptic eschatology," arose from J. Weiss, *Die Predigt Jesu vom Reiche Gottes* (Göttingen: Vandenhoeck & Ruprecht, 1892; 2nd ed., 1900); ET: *Jesus' Proclamation of the Kingdom of God* (Chico: Scholars Press, 1985). Weiss's position won a ringing endorsement from A. Schweitzer, *Von Reimarus zu Wrede: Eine Geschichte des Leben-Jesu-Forschung* (Tübingen: Mohr [Siebeck], 1906); ET: *The Quest of the Historical Jesus: A Critical Study of its Progress from Reimarus to Wrede* (London: A. & C. Black, 1910; with Introduction by J. M. Robinson, New York: Macmillan, 1968). The criterion was refined by R. Bultmann, *Theologie des Neuen Testaments* (2 vols., Tübingen: Mohr [Siebeck], 1948-53; 5th ed., 1965) 1.2-10; ET: *Theology of the New Testament* (2 vols., New York: Scribner's, 1951-

authentic material "fit reasonably well into the eschatologically based demand for repentance that was characteristic of Jesus' message."[63] But not all Jesus scholars agree that an "eschatologically based demand for repentance" was "characteristic of Jesus." On the one hand, Sanders agrees that Jesus' message was eschatological, but he doubts that Jesus demanded repentance.[64] On the other hand, Marcus Borg and many of the members of the Jesus Seminar doubt that Jesus preached an eschatological message.[65]

Dubious Criteria. In my opinion there are at least two dubious criteria. On their own merits they really prove nothing so far as the question of the historical Jesus is concerned, although they may tell us things about the editing of the tradition. The first has been called the criterion of "least distinctive features." Bultmann argued for this criterion. According to him: "Whenever narratives pass from mouth to mouth the central point of the narrative and general structure are well preserved; but in the incidental details changes take place, for imagination paints such details with increasing distinctiveness."[66]

---

55) 1.3-11; and employed by non-Bultmannians as well; cf. W. G. Kümmel, *Verheissung und Erfüllung: Untersuchung zur eschatologischen Verkündigung Jesu* (Basel: Majer, 1945; 2nd ed., Zürich: Zwingli, 1953) 47-57; ET: *Promise and Fulfillment: The Eschatological Preaching of Jesus* (SBT 23; London: SCM, 1957) 54-64; R. Schnackenburg, *Gottes Herrschaft und Reich: Eine biblisch-theologische Studie* (Freiburg: Herder, 1959) 135-48; ET: *God's Rule and Kingdom* (New York: Herder & Herder, 1963) 160-77; Jeremias, *Neutestamentliche Theologie*, 101-105; ET: *New Testament Theology*, 97-102.

63   C. E. Carlston, "A *Positive* Criterion of Authenticity?" *BR* 7 (1962) 33-44, esp. 34.

64   Sanders, *Jesus and Judaism*, 123-56 (on eschatology), 200-211 and 277-80 (on repentance). For criticism of Sanders's views of Jesus and repentance, see B. D. Chilton, "Jesus and the Repentance of E. P. Sanders," *TynBul* 39 (1988) 1-18.

65   M. J. Borg, "A Temperate Case for a Non-Eschatological Jesus," *Forum* 2 (1986) 81-102; R. W. Funk and R. W. Hoover (eds.), *The Five Gospels* (New York: Macmillan, 1993) 40.

66   R. Bultmann, "The New Approach to the Synoptic Problem," *JR* 6 (1926) 337-62, quotation from p. 345. This essay has been reprinted in Bultmann, *Existence and Faith* (New York: Harper & Row, 1960) 35-54. See also Bultmann's essay, *Die Erforschung der Synoptischen Evangelien* (2nd ed., Giessen: Töpelmann, 1930), in which he speaks of the "laws governing popular narrative and tradition"; ET: "The Study of the Synoptic Gospels," in Bultmann and K. Kundsin, *Form Criticism* (New York: Harper & Row, 1934) 11-76. The criterion of greater/lesser distinctiveness underlies many of his form-critical judgments, as seen

Consequently, he and others believe that the least distinctive tradition has the best claim to authenticity. But the data do not offer much support for this belief. Sanders and others have shown that there "are no hard and fast laws of the development of the Synoptic tradition," with the tradition becoming more and sometimes less distinctive in its transmission.[67] A related version of this criterion, which runs in virtually the opposite direction from Bultmann's proposal, has to do with "vividness in narration." It is argued that "vivid" details smack of authenticity; perhaps, in the case of Mark, indicating genuine Petrine tradition.[68] But, as Meier points out, vivid details may be due to effective Christian story-tellers, not necessarily to eye-witness testimony.[69]

The second dubious criterion is the aforemention criterion of "proleptic eschatology." This criterion lacks validity because it assumes what needs to be proven. Whether or not Jesus held to an eschatological interpretation of the kingdom of God, and if so in what sense, cannot be decided upon in advance and then be used as a criterion for determining the authenticity of other materials. Such an approach is circular. Jesus' view of eschatology and/or the kingdom can be appealed to (i.e. as suggested with respect to the criterion of coherence) only when it has been established on other grounds.

The reconstructions and interpretations found in the present book presuppose the valid criteria described above. With regard to the sayings of Jesus, no particular criterion is given priority, nor is any particular passage or cluster of passages. Rather, I rely on clusters of material that are in various ways mutually supportive and are always meaningfully contextualized in the relatively well established historical parameters of Jesus' public life. The approach that I take has been succinctly stated by Sanders: "The method which is being

---

in his *History of the Synoptic Tradition.*

[67]   Sanders, *Tendencies of the Synoptic Tradition*, 272-75, quotation from p. 272. For additional criticisms, see L. R. Keylock, "Bultmann's Law of Increasing Distinctiveness," in G. F. Hawthorne (ed.), *Current Issues in Biblical and Patristic Interpretation* (M. C. Tenney Festschrift; Grand Rapids: Eerdmans, 1975) 193-210; Sanders and Davies, *Studying the Synoptic Gospels*, 127-28; Meier, *A Marginal Jew*, 182.

[68]   V. Taylor, *The Gospel According to St. Mark* (2nd ed., London: Macmillan; New York: St. Martin's, 1966) 135-49.

[69]   Meier, *A Marginal Jew*, 180-82.

followed more and more, and the one which it seems necessary to follow in writing about Jesus, is to construct hypotheses which, on the one hand, do rest on material generally considered reliable without, on the other hand, being totally dependent on the authenticity of any given pericope."[70]

SOURCES

Another important issue that confronts scholars concerned with Jesus research has to do with the evaluation of extra-canonical sources. These sources fall into two principal categories: (1) agrapha and apocryphal gospels which purport to contain the sayings of Jesus; and (2) early non-Christian writers who happen to refer to Jesus. Whereas the second category has occasioned some controversy—more in the past than in the present—in recent years it has been the first category that has sparked most of the controversy and is, in my opinion, largely responsible for the widely divergent views of Jesus held today in respectable scholarly circles. We shall review this category first.

1. Agrapha and Apocryphal Gospels. The Jesus materials found in these sources (1) either parallel material preserved in the canonical Gospels, (2) or supplement this material. There is little of the latter that has commanded serious attention. As has already been noted, Crossan has identified only five complexes of "multiply attested" material extant exclusively in extra-canonical sources. Thus the debate chiefly centers on the former, that is, on the material that parallels what we find in the canonical Gospels. At the heart of this debate is the question whether or not some or much of these parallels in extra-canonical sources is independent of and more primitive than the canonical Gospels themselves. Scholarly opinion on this question is sharply divided.

The division can be readily perceived by simply reviewing some of the major works on Jesus that have appeared in recent years. B. F. Meyer, A. E. Harvey, and E. P. Sanders attach no importance to the agrapha and the apocryphal gospels.[71] Indeed, most major Jesus

---

70   Sanders, *Jesus and Judaism*, 3.
71   Meyer, *The Aims of Jesus*; Harvey, *Jesus and the Constraints of History*; Sanders, *Jesus and Judaism*. It is worth noting that Bultmann (*History of the Synoptic Tradition*, 374) regarded the apocryphal gospels as nothing more than "legendary adaptations and expansions." Two recent German publications maintain

scholars, in fact, do not. In his first volume of an anticipated three volume-work Meier also has concluded that these extra-canonical sources do not offer the serious exegete anything of real value.[72] Although French and German scholarship has shown some interest in the agrapha and apocryphal gospels for purposes of Jesus research, extensive use of these materials appears to be primarily an American phenomenon.[73]

Several faculty and graduates from Claremont and Harvard, along with Dominic Crossan and several members of the Jesus Seminar, are convinced that the agrapha and apocryphal (or extra-canonical, as they prefer to call them) gospels contain independent, ancient, and sometimes superior readings.[74]

---

this view; cf. Gnilka, *Jesus von Nazaret*, 22-34; R. Schnackenburg, *Die Person Jesu Christi im Spiegel der vier Evangelien* (HTKNTSup 4; Freiburg: Herder, 1993) 355.

[72] Meier, *A Marginal Jew*, 112-66.

[73] The classic German work was that of J. Jeremias, *Unbekannte Jesusworte* (Zürich: Zwingli, 1947; 2nd ed., Gütersloh: Bertelsmann, 1951; 3rd ed., 1961); ET: *The Unknown Sayings of Jesus* (London: SPCK, 1957; 2nd ed., 1964). Most German scholars have been less sanguine with respect to the value of the extra-canonical sources; cf. O. Hofius, "Unbekannte Jesusworte," in Stuhlmacher (ed.), *Das Evangelium und die Evangelien* (WUNT 28; Tübingen: Mohr [Siebeck], 1983) 355-82; ET: "Unknown Sayings of Jesus," in Stuhlmacher (ed.), *The Gospel and the Gospels*, 336-60. Helmut Koester is a notable exception. From the appearance of his German dissertation (*Synoptische Überlieferung bei den apostolischen Vätern* [TU 65; Berlin: Akademie, 1957]) to his subsequent numerous publications in German and in English, he has advocated the antiquity and independence of some of the extra-canonical sources. See his "Apocryphal and Canonical Gospels," *HTR* 73 (1980) 105-30, as well as his more recent *Ancient Christian Gospels: Their History and Development* (London: SCM; Philadelphia: Trinity Press International, 1990). His work and that of some of his students have lent important support to Crossan and other members of the Jesus Seminar.

[74] Besides Koester's *Ancient Christian Gospels*, see R. Cameron, *The Other Gospels: Non-Canonical Gospel Texts* (Philadelphia: Westminster, 1982); J. D. Crossan, *The Cross that Spoke: The Origins of the Passion Narrative* (San Francisco: Harper & Row, 1988); idem, *Four Other Gospels: Shadows on the Contours of Canon* (rev. ed., Sonoma: Polebridge, 1992); R. J. Miller (ed.), *The Complete Gospels* (Sonoma: Polebridge, 1992); S. J. Patterson, *The Gospel of Thomas and Jesus* (Sonoma: Polebridge, 1993); and Funk and Hoover, *The Five Gospels*. Several works that concern Q reflect these assumptions; cf. J. S. Kloppenborg, *The Formation of Q: Trajectories in Ancient Wisdom Collections*

Crossan's work, which consists not only of a comprehensive study of the historical Jesus, but of several studies concerned with various extra-canonical gospels, illustrates quite well the views of this small, but influential coterie of American scholars who attach great importance to these sources. Crossan's study of the extra-canonical gospels has led him to the following dates, as well as identifications of various putative early editions:[75] *Gospel of Thomas* (earliest edition: 50s C.E.), *Egerton Gospel* (i.e., Papyrus Egerton 2: 50s C.E.), Fayyum Fragment (50s C.E.), Papyrus Oxyrhynchus 1224 (50s C.E.), *Gospel of the Hebrews* (50s C.E.), *Cross Gospel* (= a pruned version of the *Gospel of Peter*: 50s C.E.), *Gospel of the Egyptians* (earliest version: 60s C.E.),[76] *Secret Gospel of Mark* (early 70s C.E.), Papyrus Oxyrhynchus 840 (80s C.E.), *Gospel of Thomas* (later draft: 60s or 70s C.E.), *Dialogue Collection* (= a pruned version of the Coptic Gnostic tractate *Dialogue of the Savior*: late [?] 70s C.E.), *Apocryphon of James* (dating from first half of second century C.E., but containing tradition reaching back to the 50s C.E.), *Gospel of the Nazoreans* (150s C.E.), *Gospel of the Ebionites* (150s C.E.), and *Gospel of Peter* (150s C.E.). Crossan claims that the *Gospel of Thomas*, the *Egerton Gospel*, Papyrus Vindobonensis Greek 2325, Papyrus Oxyrhynchus 1224, the *Gospel of the Hebrews*, and the *Gospel of the Egyptians*, are independent of the New Testament Gospels, with the *Dialogue of the Savior* and the *Apocryphon of James* containing independent traditions. He further concludes that the *Cross Gospel*, which is now imbedded in the *Gospel of Peter*, is the passion narrative on which all four of the New Testament Gospels are based.[77] Given this chrono-

---

(Studies in Antiquity & Christianity; Philadelphia: Fortress, 1987); A. D. Jacobson, *The First Gospel: An Introduction to Q* (Sonoma: Polebridge, 1992); B. L. Mack, *The Lost Gospel: The Book of Q & Christian Origins* (San Francisco: Harper-Collins, 1993). These scholars primarily emphasize the extra-canonical gospels, as opposed to the agrapha. For readers who may not know, Polebridge is the publishing arm of the Jesus Seminar.

[75] Crossan, *The Historical Jesus*, 427-34. The dates noted in the parentheses refer not to the dates of the extant MSS, but to the conjectured dates of the autographs.

[76] This *Gospel of the Egyptians*, of which only six fragments are preserved in various patristic writings, is not to be confused with the gnostic *Gospel of the Egyptians* (CG III, 2).

[77] See Crossan, *The Cross that Spoke*, 404.

logical scheme, it is not surprising that Crossan often concludes that traditions contained in the apocryphal gospels that parallel those of the New Testament Gospels are more primitive and historically superior. Often he finds the earliest, most original form of Jesus' teaching in the extra-canonical gospels. Crossan's source analysis contributes to his picture of the historical Jesus in significant ways.

But are these extra-canonical gospels ancient and independent of the canonical Gospels? Although some of the evidence is open to opposing interpretations, there is significant evidence that suggests that the extra-canonical gospels are dependent on the canonical Gospels, either directly or—as is often the case—indirectly. This is true in the cases of the *Gospel of Thomas*, the *Gospel of Peter*, Papyrus Egerton 2, and the *Secret Gospel of Mark*, four apocryphal gospels to which appeal these days is often made. Comparative study of these sources suggests that they are secondary and probably not earlier than the second century. We may review them briefly.[78]

Gospel of Thomas. The *Gospel of Thomas* survives in Coptic as the second tractate in Codex II of the Nag Hammadi library and partially in Greek in Oxyrhynchus Papyri 1, 654, and 655. POxy654 contains *GThom* Prologue, §1–7, and a portion of §30. POxy1 contains *GThom* §26–33. POxy655 contains *GThom* §24, §36–39, §77. Although the point has been disputed, it appears that most scholars contend that *Thomas* was originally composed in Greek and that the Oxyrhynchus Papyri stand closer to the original form of the tradition.

There are several factors that should give us pause before accepting the Jesus Seminar's high estimation of *Thomas* as an ancient and independent source. First, this writing alludes to more than half of the writings of the New Testament (i.e. Matthew, Mark, Luke, John, Acts, Romans, 1–2 Corinthians, Galatians, Ephesians, Colossians, 1 Thessalonians, 1 Timothy, Hebrews, 1 John, Revelation),[79] which suggests that *Thomas* could very well be little more than a collage of New Testament and apocryphal materials which have been interpreted, often allegorically, in such a way as to advance second and third-

---

[78] For a much fuller critique of the uncritical use of extra-canonical sources, see J. H. Charlesworth and C. A. Evans, "Jesus in the Agrapha and Apocryphal Gospels," in Chilton and Evans (eds.), *Studying the Historical Jesus*, 479-533.

[79] Cf. C. A. Evans, R. L. Webb, and R. A. Wiebe, *Nag Hammadi Texts and the Bible: A Synopsis and Index* (NTTS 18; Leiden: Brill, 1993) 88-144.

century gnostic ideas. Second, the traditions contained in *Thomas* hardly reflect a setting that pre-dates the writings of the New Testament, which is why Dominic Crossan and others attempt to extract an early version of *Thomas* from the Coptic and Greek texts that are now extant. Third, there is present in *Thomas* a significant amount of material that is distinctive to Matthew ("M"), Luke ("L"), and John.[80] If *Thomas* really does represent an early, independent collection of material, then how is one to explain the presence of so much M, L, and Johannine material? Perhaps sensing this problem, Koester assigns all of the L parallels, and a few of the M parallels to Q.[81] But such a move appears gratuitous. It is much more likely that the presence of M, L, and Johannine elements in *Thomas* indicates that the latter, at least in its extant Coptic form, has been influenced by the canonical Gospels. Fourth, features characteristic of Matthean and Lucan *redaction* are also found in *Thomas*,[82] even in the Greek sayings preserved at Oxyrhynchus (compare Mark 4:22; Luke 8:17; POxy655 §5).

For these reasons many scholars doubt the historical value of the *Gospel of Thomas*.[83] It remains possible, of course, that a few forms of sayings in *Thomas* might be early and independent,[84] but the priority assigned to it by the Jesus Seminar and a few others seems to me to be wholly unwarranted.

Gospel of Peter. Since the discovery of a portion of the *Gospel of Peter* about one century ago scholars have disagreed over the question of its relationship to the canonical Gospels. In recent years Dominic Crossan, Helmut Koester, and a few of the latter's Harvard students

---

[80]   For a listing of the M, L, and Johannine elements in *Thomas*, see Charlesworth and Evans, "Jesus in the Agrapha and Apocryphal Gospels," 498. M appears fifteen times, L six times, and Johannine material five times.

[81]   Koester, *Ancient Christian Gospels*, 86-107.

[82]   For several examples of Matthean and Lucan redaction in *Thomas*, see Charlesworth and Evans, "Jesus in the Agrapha and Apocryphal Gospels," 499-500.

[83]   See Meier, *A Marginal Jew*, 123-41.

[84]   See the careful approach taken by B. D. Chilton, "The Gospel According to Thomas as a Source of Jesus' Teaching," in D. Wenham (ed.), *The Jesus Tradition Outside the Gospels* (Gospel Perspectives 5; Sheffield: JSOT Press, 1984) 155-75; idem, *The Temple of Jesus: His Sacrificial Program Within a Cultural History of Sacrifice* (University Park: Penn State Press, 1992) 116-19.

have argued that underlying *Peter* is a primitive passion source that is
not only independent of the canonical Gospels but is possibly their
source.[85] But this position is very dubious. Even that part of *Peter*,
which Crossan has extracted (in an attempt to prune away the obvious
secondary elements) and labeled the *Cross Gospel*, is replete with
redactional elements from the Synoptic Gospels, especially those found
in Matthew.[86] The evidence leads Meier to conclude that *Peter* is a
second-century "pastiche of traditions from the canonical Gospels,
recycled through the memory and lively imagination of Christians
who have heard the Gospels read and preached upon many a time."[87]
Moody Smith's rhetorical question only underscores the problematical
dimension of Crossan's hypothesis: "[I]s it thinkable that the tradition
began with the legendary, the mythological, the anti-Jewish, and
indeed the fantastic, and moved in the direction of the historically
restrained and sober?"[88] The only plausible answer to this question is
"No."

Papyrus Egerton 2. Papyrus Egerton 2 consists of four fragments.
The fourth fragment yields nothing more than one illegible letter. The
third fragment yields little more than a few scattered words. The first
and second fragments offer four (or perhaps five) stories that parallel
Johannine and Synoptic materials. Papyrus Köln 255 constitutes a
related fragment of the text.

The first vignette describes controversy between Jesus and his
opponents, who are referred to as lawyers and rulers. Jesus tells them
to "search the scriptures, in which [they] think [they] have life." They
reply that they know full well that "God spoke to Moses," but they do
not know where Jesus has come from. They then take up stones "to

---

[85] Koester, *Ancient Christian Gospels*, 240; idem, "Überlieferung und
Geschichte der frühchristlichen Evangelienliteratur," *ANRW* 2.25.2 (1984) 1463-
1542, esp. 1487-88, 1525-27; Cameron, *The Other Gospels*, 77-78; Crossan, *The
Cross that Spoke*, 404; idem, *Four Other Gospels*, 89-90.

[86] See Charlesworth and Evans, "Jesus in the Agrapha and Apocryphal
Gospels," 505-14; J. B. Green, "The Gospel of Peter: Source for a Pre-Canonical
Passion Narrative?" *ZNW* 78 (1987) 293-301. Green concludes that the *Gospel of
Peter* is nothing more than an embellishment based on the Gospel of Matthew.

[87] Meier, *A Marginal Jew*, 117-18.

[88] D. M. Smith, "The Problem of John and the Synoptics in Light of the
Relation between Apocryphal and Canonical Gospels," in A. Denaux (ed.), *John
and the Synoptics* (BETL 101; Leuven: Peeters, 1992) 147-62, here p. 150.

32   JESUS AND HIS CONTEMPORARIES

stone" Jesus, "laid hands on him," and attempted to arrest him. But
they were unable, "because his hour . . . had not yet come." The
allusions to various Johannine stories are obvious.[89] The second
vignette is an elaboration on the story of the healing of the leper (Mark
1:40-44), complete with the telltale presence of Matthean redaction
(cf. Matt 8:2a, in contrast to Mark 1:40a). The third episode constitutes
a combination of Johannine and Synoptic elements (John 3:2 + Mark
12:14 + Luke 6:46 + Mark 7:6-7). Crossan and Koester think that
rather than a secondary admixture of Johannine and Synoptic
elements, the third episode is evidence of "a stage before the distinction
of Johannine and Synoptic traditions was operative."[90] But such an
explanation is problematic. This episode appears to be more of a
pastiche of loosely related statements[91] than a primitive, coherent,
unified tradition whose components would later be separated and
placed into new contexts in at least three of the canonical Gospels. The
fourth vignette is so fragmentary that it is not certain what is being
described. Apparently Jesus responds to a question with an object
lesson. He stands at the bank of the Jordan River, extends his hand,
sows seed over the water, which then apparently bears fruit, causing
the people to rejoice. This curious tale is reminiscent of an apocryphal
story in the *Infancy Gospel of Thomas* in which the boy Jesus sowed a
handful of seed that yielded a remarkable harvest (*InfanThom* 10:1-2
[Latin]; *InfanThom* 12:1-2 [Greek MS A]).

Although the hypothesis of Crossan and Koester remains a
possibility, the evidence available at this time suggests that in all
probability Papyrus Egerton 2 represents nothing more than a second-
century conflation of Synoptic and Johannine elements, rather than
primitive first-century material on which the canonical Gospels
depended. The presence of at least one apocryphal tale akin to those of
the least historically viable traditions only strengthens this conviction.

Secret Gospel of Mark. The history of the controversy surrounding
the discovery and publication of the purported letter of Clement of

[89]   See Charlesworth and Evans, "Jesus in the Agrapha and Apocryphal
Gospels," 515-16.
[90]   Crossan, *Four Other Gospels*, 183; cf. Koester, *Ancient Christian Gospels*,
207; idem, "Überlieferung und Geschichte," 1488-90, 1522.
[91]   See Charlesworth and Evans, "Jesus in the Agrapha and Apocryphal
Gospels," 521-24. Here it is pointed out that Justin Martyr often patched together
loosely related sayings.

Alexandria to one Theodorus, in which is embedded what Clement calls the *Secret Gospel of Mark*, need not be rehearsed here.[92] The lack of scholarly verification of the find is as well known as Clement's credulity. Thus, in my view it is extremely precarious to build complicated theories of Gospel development, as Crossan and Koester have done, on the basis of *Secret Mark*'s alleged relationship to canonical Mark.[93] Even if the Clementine letter is genuine (and many qualified scholars are prepared to accept it), I have little confidence in Clement's story about the origins of *Secret Mark*. In all probability *Secret Mark*, if such really existed, is a second century revision of canonical Mark. As such it has nothing to offer serious Jesus research.[94]

The significance of this brief review of the four extra-canonical sources, to which the Jesus Seminar and its sympathisers attach much importance, lies in showing how flimsy the foundation is on which so much hypothesis and literary reconstruction are made to rest.[95] Their

[92] See Charlesworth and Evans, "Jesus in the Agrapha and Apocryphal Gospels," 526-28.

[93] Crossan, *Four Other Gospels*, 108; Cameron, *The Other Gospels*, 68-69; H. Koester, "History and Development of Mark's Gospel: From Mark to Secret Mark and 'Canonical' Mark," in B. C. Corley (ed.), *Colloquy on New Testament Studies: A Time for Reappraisal and Fresh Approaches* (Macon: Mercer University, 1983) 35-58, here p. 56. Koester's proposals are pursued further by P. Sellew, "*Secret Mark* and the History of Canonical Mark," in B. A. Pearson (ed.), *The Future of Early Christianity* (H. Koester Festschrift; Minneapolis: Fortress, 1991) 242-57.

[94] H. Merkel, "Appendix: the 'Secret Gospel' of Mark," in W. Schneemelcher (ed.), *New Testament Apocrypha. Volume One: Gospels and Related Writings* (rev. ed., Cambridge: Clarke; Louisville: Westminster/John Knox, 1991) 106-109; idem, "Auf den Spuren des Urmarkus? Ein neuer Fund und seine Beurteilung," *ZTK* 71 (1974) 123-44. In the latter item Merkel rightly remarks: "Damit wird es unmöglich, aus dem neuen Text zusätliche Informationen über den historischen Jesus zu erhalten."

[95] In his 1993 SNTS presidential address, Martin Hengel expressed his doubts about the antiquity of three of the four apocryphal gospels that I have just reviewed: ". . . der heute beliebte Versuch, spätere sogenannte apokryphe Evangelientexte, allen voran das Thomasevangelium oder den rätselhaften Papyrus Egerton und das Petrusevangelium vorzudatieren bzw. in ihnen ältere vorevangelische Quellen zu entdecken, haben mich in keiner Weise überzeugt"; M. Hengel, "Aufgaben der neutestamentlichen Wissenschaft," *NTS* 40 (1994) 321-57, quotation from p. 332. F. Neirynck ("The Historical Jesus: Reflections on an Inventory," *ETL* 70 [1994]

work has a learned, critical appearance in which comparison among "all the sources" is made. But special pleading, a tendency to opt for implausible explanations, and the frequent failure to take into account second through fourth-century practices of loose quotation and conflation (as plainly observed in patristic sources) call into question the efficacy of the Seminar's results.

What influence the Jesus Seminar's high regard for extra-canonical sources has in its efforts to reconstruct the historical Jesus is clearly illustrated in Crossan's publications. Many of the readings that Crossan judges to be the most original form of the tradition will strike most as farfetched. For example, *GHeb* §2 is said to contain the most original account of Jesus' baptism: "And it came to pass when the Lord was come up out of the water, the whole fount of the Holy Spirit descended upon him and rested on him and said to him: My son, in all the prophets was I waiting for thee that thou shouldest come and I might rest in thee. For thou art my rest; thou art my first-begotten Son that reignest for ever."[96] Is it probable that this is the "earliest text"?[97] On the contrary, is not Mark's simpler description (cf. Mark 1:10-11) more primitive? In my view, the *Gospel of the Hebrews* offers an embellished version of the New Testament Gospels. Again, when the Egerton Papyrus tells us that the leper who approached Jesus explained how he got leprosy (PEger2 §2: "[I was] wandering with lepers and eating with them"), is it not more probable that what we have here is an embellishment of the version found in the Synoptics? This is the same sort of apocryphal embellishment that one can find elsewhere (cf. the embellishment of Mark 3:1 in *GNaz* §10). As another example, Crossan thinks that *Sib. Or.* 8:273-278 ("With a word he shall make the winds to cease, and calm the sea while it rages walking on it . . . And from five loaves and a fish of the sea . . . He shall feed five thousand . . . and then taking all the fragments left over He will fill twelve baskets . . .") is "independent of the canonical Gospels."[98] He is inclined to this view because the Oracle follows a sequence of sea and meal, which Crossan thinks is more original, rather than the Synoptic

---

221-34) has also reviewed these apocryphal materials and has reached the same conclusion.

[96]   Crossan, *The Historical Jesus*, 232-33.
[97]   Crossan, *The Historical Jesus*, 232.
[98]   Crossan, *The Historical Jesus*, 406.

sequence of meal and sea. This conclusion, however, is highly problematic. There is no good reason to think that lines 273-278 of the eighth *Sibylline Oracle* constitute a distinct and primitive unit. There is nothing that indicates that these lines ever existed outside of their present context. Lines 251-336 make up an elaborate poem devoted to Christ. This poem draws on several New Testament writings and on a few later writings, such as *Barnabas* and *Shepherd of Hermas*, and probably should not be dated earlier than the end of the second century. The chance that any part of this poem, which alludes to events in the life and passion of Jesus, actually contains material independent of the New Testament Gospels is very slight indeed.

The real problem in all of this is that Crossan's uncritical use of these apocryphal gospels leads to a distortion of the portrait of the historical Jesus. For example, preference for the purged versions of Jesus' teaching found in the *Gospel of Thomas*, a document that shows little interest in Jewish salvation history or commercial and business matters, lends support to Crossan's portrait of Jesus as Cynic. In most cases the parables of *Thomas* make better sense viewed as abridged and gnosticized versions of the Synoptic parables, rather than the latter as embellished expansions of the former. If this is true, and there are many scholars who think it is, then *Thomas'* material is not particularly helpful and could even be misleading.

Perhaps the most convoluted and least convincing example is Crossan's treatment of the history of the passion narrative. He would have us believe that the *Cross Gospel*, which must be extracted from the second-century *Gospel of Peter*, contains the foundation narrative on which Mark and the other New Testament Gospels are based.[99] Crossan wonders why Mark was willing to follow the *Cross Gospel* for the Passion, but not for the resurrection. This question is not difficult to answer, if we approach the problem the other way around: *Cross Gospel* and Mark parallel one another in the Passion narrative, because Mark provided one; they do not parallel one another in the Easter

---

[99]   Crossan relies on the earlier work of J. Denker (*Die theologiegeschichtliche Stellung des Petrusevangeliums: Ein Beitrag zur Frühgeschichte des Doketismus* [Bern and Frankfurt: Lang, 1975) who argued that Peter's scriptural apologetic, in that it was implicit rather than explicit, antedated the Synoptic Gospels. Although he disagrees with Crossan's conclusion that a putative "Cross Gospel" underlies the four canonical Gospels, Koester (*Ancient Christian Gospels*, 240) believes that the *Gospel of Peter* is essentially independent of the canonicals.

narrative, because Mark did not provide one. In other words, what we are employing here is the same logic that argues for Markan priority over Matthew and Luke: Where there is no Mark (such as an Easter narrative, complete with resurrection appearances), Matthew and Luke diverge. We may now expand this rule of thumb: Where there is no Mark, Matthew and Luke diverge, leaving the *Cross Gospel* and other apocryphal gospels no other choice but to draw upon Matthew and Luke and occasionally upon Mark's later and spurious ending.

Crossan marshalls another argument against the priority of the Markan Passion narrative by suggesting that the most original expression is found in *Barn.* 7:6-12. He believes that the earliest form that the tradition took was a "prophetic passion," which was only later developed by the *Cross Gospel* into a "narrative passion." I wonder if Crossan has not again got it backwards. Surely *Barnabas* 7 is a forerunner of the kind of theological rumination seen, for example, in Melito's *Paschal Homily*, and the already mentioned poem in *Sibylline Oracles* 8, both of which offer theologically rich interpretations of Jesus' life and death. *Barnabas*, Melito, and others in the second, third, and fourth centuries sifted the Old Testament for types and parallels that added greater significance to the Passion. Jesus was compared to the Passover Lamb, to Temple sacrifice, to the binding of Isaac, and, as in the case of *Barnabas*, to the scapegoat. So far as trajectories are concerned, I think it much more likely that the question of "what happened?" preceded the question of "what did it mean?" In other words, narrative forms of the Passion preceded prophetic and theological forms of the Passion.

One reason that Crossan thinks that a narrative Passion is secondary is that the disciples had no idea what happened: "Jesus' followers had fled upon his arrest and knew nothing whatsoever about his fate beyond the fact of crucifixion itself."[100] What argues against this assumption—never mind the utter implausibility in the assertion itself that Jesus' followers never found out from anyone what transpired—is the tradition of Peter's denial of Jesus. I think that it is highly unlikely that Mark or the early Church would invent a story about Peter cursing and denying that he knew Jesus. It is true that Mark apparently intended to portray the disciples as weak, confused, and lacking faith. But one should not infer from this theological tendency, which in my

---

[100] Crossan, *The Historical Jesus*, 392.

estimation redaction critics in the past have exaggerated, wholesale creation of such elements as Judas' betrayal and Peter's denial. Even Kim Dewey, who attributes a very active editorial role to the evangelist, thinks that Mark inherited and developed, rather than created, the tradition that Peter denied Jesus.[101] Paul certainly knew of the betrayal and arrest (1 Cor 11:23). After all, Mark's claim that "all [the disciples] forsook him and fled" (14:50), which Crossan evidently accepts, is as likely part of the evangelist's negative portrayal of the disciples as anything else. If the denial tradition is historical, which seems quite likely, then we have Peter at least in close enough proximity to know something of what happened following Jesus' arrest. And even if he was not, is it really likely that Jesus' followers never learned of some of the things that happened to Jesus? Crossan's refusal to interact with major scholars who hold to a higher assessment of the reliability of Mark's tradition, especially his Passion narrative,[102] is a frustrating weakness of his book.

I have discussed at length Crossan's book on the historical Jesus because it offers a full and recent treatment of the subject produced by a prominent member of the Jesus Seminar.[103] It reflects the kind of results one might expect working from the conclusion (sometimes little more than assumption) that the extra-canonical gospels are of similar, even greater value for reconstructing the historical Jesus. It might also be worthwhile to say a few things about *The Five Gospels*, the Seminar's recently published colorized version of the canonical Gospels (plus *Thomas*), which clearly identifies what is judged to be authentic, inauthentic, and what lies somewhere in between.[104] Richard

---

[101] K. Dewey, "Peter's Curse and Cursed Peter," in W. Kelber (ed.), *The Passion in Mark* (Philadelphia: Fortress, 1976) 96-114.

[102] See M. Hengel, *Studies in the Gospel of Mark* (Philadelphia: Fortress, 1985); Pesch, *Das Markusevangelium*.

[103] The reader should not infer from this comment any slight of Marcus Borg or Bruce Chilton, whose books on Jesus (see esp. Borg, *Conflict, Holiness and Politics in the Teachings of Jesus* [SBEC 5; New York and Toronto: Mellen, 1984]; idem, *Jesus: A New Vision*; Chilton, *A Galilean Rabbi*; idem, *The Temple of Jesus*) are among the very best produced by members of the Jesus Seminar. Borg's and Chilton's books, in that they reflect few of the idiosyncrasies of the Seminar, do not serve as exemplars nearly as well as do Crossan's.

[104] On the Jesus Seminar's color ratings, see Funk and Hoover, *The Five Gospels*, 36, as well as n. 41 above.

Hays has written an incisive review of this book.[105] He criticises the methods of the Seminar in four important areas. The first area concerns the dating and evaluation of sources. This is a point that has been addressed above. Hays shares my skepticism concerning the early dating and independence of the *Gospel of Thomas*, as well as some of the other extra-canonical sources. The results are indeed curious. Whereas *Thomas* is credited with three "red" sayings (i.e. §20, §54, §100), Mark is credited with only one (Mark 12:17). Regrettably, the editors neglect to inform their readers that the Seminar's high assessment of *Thomas* is not shared by too many outside of their circle.

The second aspect of the Seminar's methods that concerns Hays is their use of the criterion of dissimilarity. A high percentage of Synoptic material is regarded as suspect because it is too Jewish or too Christian. As argued above, such a negative use of this criterion is unnecessary and unrealistic and leads to questionable results. Hays rightly observes that "the 'Jesus' who emerges from this procedure is necessarily a free-floating iconoclast, artificially isolated from his people and their Scripture, and artificially isolated from the movement that he founded."[106]

Thirdly, Hays objects to the Seminar's preference for a non-eschatological Jesus. We end up with a Jesus who frequently speaks of the kingdom of God, but never with an eschatological nuance, and we end up with disciples who fail to grasp this basic, distinguishing point in their master's teaching. It seems that the disciples completely misunderstood Jesus: He was not Israel's Messiah and there was no eschatological kingdom on which Israel could pin its hopes. The Seminar believes that it is impossible to reconcile the ideas of the presence of the kingdom and the coming of the kingdom.

Finally, Hays rightly criticises the Seminar for failing to place Jesus' sayings in historical context. The Jesus of the Jesus Seminar is essentially innocuous, at best a pest, and hardly a serious threat. Why would Jewish authorities take seriously a Jewish cynic? Why would anybody? Why would the Romans crucify as "king of the Jews" an itinerant teller of parables? Hays comments: "The Jesus constructed by the Jesus Seminar is a talking head, whose teachings bear no intelligible

---

[105] R. B. Hays, "The Corrected Jesus," *First Things* (May, 1994) 43-48. See also the review by F. Neirynck, *ETL* 70 (1994) 160-62.

[106] Hays, "The Corrected Jesus," 45.

relation to his death on a cross."[107] This is an important point, and it is the point where the Seminar and its sympathisers begin to flounder. For example, Burton Mack, who rejects Mark's passion account as pure fiction, is at a loss to explain Jesus' death. He lamely concludes that Jesus got caught up in a riot and ended up sentenced to death.[108] David Seeley, Mack's student, sensing this problem, proposes that Jesus' death "was probably just a mistake," that is, Pilate failed to realize that Jesus' talk of a kingdom did not really pose any threat to Rome.[109] Seeley's solution has borrowed a page right out of the Fourth Evangelist's apologetic, in which the Johannine Jesus assures the readers of the late first-century Roman Empire: "My kingdom is not of this world" (John 18:36). Seeley's proposal should be warmly received by fundamentalists, but most critical historians will find it dubious. Crossan does better than Mack and Seeley, but not by much. He allows that Jesus probably did act and speak in some manner that was critical of or threatening toward the Temple establishment and that this could account for Jesus' death.[110] The hostility of Israel's religious authorities becomes intelligible, but we are still in the dark with respect to the Roman execution, at least with respect to the *titulus* which indicated Jesus' crime: his claim to be "king of the Jews."[111]

Hays sums up the heart of the problem: "The depiction of Jesus as a Cynic philosopher with no concern about Israel's destiny, no connection with the concerns and hopes that animated his Jewish contemporaries, no interest in the interpretation of Scripture, and no message of God's coming eschatological judgment is—quite simply— an ahistorical fiction, achieved by the surgical removal of Jesus from his Jewish context."[112] I quoted this statement in the Preface of this book and I quote it again here because the point that Hays has made cannot be overemphasized. The Seminar's tendency to isolate Jesus

---

[107] Hays, "The Corrected Jesus," 46.

[108] Mack, *A Myth of Innocence*, 88-89.

[109] D. Seeley, "Was Jesus like a Philosopher? The Evidence of Martyrological and Wisdom Motifs in Q, Pre-Pauline Traditions, and Mark," in D. J. Lull (ed.), *Society of Biblical Literature 1989 Seminar Papers* (SBLSP 28; Atlanta: Scholars Press, 1989) 540-49.

[110] Crossan, *The Historical Jesus*, 359-60.

[111] The authenticity of the inscription upon the *titulus*, which is widely accepted, is taken up elsewhere.

[112] Hays, "The Corrected Jesus," 47.

from so many parallel forms of thought and expression, as well as from parallel individuals of action, leaves us with a Jesus that I very much doubt would have been relevant or intelligible to his contemporaries.

2. *Non-Christian Sources.* Much less contentious is the discussion concerning the relative importance of the various non-Christian sources. But the significance of these sources is not adequately appreciated by many members of the Jesus Seminar. In a recent publication I have reviewed these materials; I offer here a summary of my conclusions.[113]

There are several sources which over the years have been viewed as having some value for historical Jesus research, but which today are regarded as dubious. Rabbinic sources belong to this category. It seems highly improbable that any of the several references to Jesus (usually as Yeshu or Yeshu ha-Noṣri) is based on anything more than second-hand acquaintance with Christian teachings and the canonical Gospels.[114] In my opinion, had Christianity not survived the early second century, there would be no references to Jesus in the Talmud or the midrashim. The same holds true for the "additions" in the Slavonic (or Old Russian) version of Josephus' *Jewish War*,[115] as well as for the Yosippon (or Josippon), a Hebrew version which dates from the ninth or tenth centuries.[116] These writings tell us nothing of Jesus that stems from ancient sources that are independent of the New Testament Gospels.

113 C. A. Evans, "Jesus in Non-Canonical Sources," in Chilton and Evans (eds.), *Studying the Historical Jesus*, 443-78.

114 See J. Maier, *Jesus von Nazareth in der talmudischen Überlieferung* (ErFor 82; Darmstadt: Wissenschaftliche Buchgesellschaft, 1978) 263-75; Meier, *A Marginal Jew*, 94-98. The teaching attributed to Jesus in *b. 'Abod. Zar.* 16b–17a, through Jacob of Kefar Sekania (James?), may be one instance of potentially genuine material that the Talmud has preserved independently of Christian sources.

115 L. H. Feldman, "Flavius Josephus Revisited: The Man, His Writings, and His Significance," *ANRW* 2.21.2 (1984) 763-862, esp. 771-74.

116 E. Bammel, "Jesus as a Political Agent in a Version of the Josippon," in E. Bammel and C. F. D. Moule (eds.), *Jesus and the Politics of His Day* (Cambridge: Cambridge University Press, 1984) 197-209; repr. in Bammel, *Judaica: Kleine Schriften I* (WUNT 37; Tübingen: Mohr [Siebeck], 1986) 289-301; S. Bowman, "Sefer Yosippon: History and Midrash," in M. Fishbane (ed.), *The Midrashic Imagination: Jewish Exegesis, Thought, and History* (Albany: State University of New York, 1993) 280-94.

There are other sources which may be of minimal value, though various uncertainties usually accompany them. The reference to the darkness at the time of Jesus' death, attributed to one Thallus, may indicate the existence in first-century non-Christian circles of some knowledge of Jesus' passion.[117] However, even if this is true, we learn nothing new. One Mara bar Serapion, in a letter to his son, refers to Jesus as the Jews' "wise king."[118] But the date of this missive cannot be established with certainty. Proposed dates range from the first to the third centuries. Suetonius' confusing reference to the explusion from Rome of Jews who during the reign of Claudius had been "instigated by Chrestus" (*Divus Claudius* 25.4) at best tells us that in the early second century a Roman historian possessed an imperfect knowledge of the new movement. Pliny the Younger's letter to Emperor Trajan leaves us with a record of early Christians' suffering at the hands of the Roman government (*Epistles* 10.96). From interrogations Pliny has learned that Christians gather regularly, sing hymns "to Christus as to a god," and partake of an innocent meal (by which is probably meant the eucharist). The calumnies of Celsus, to the effect that Jesus was little more than a magician (cf. Origen, *Contra Celsum* 1.6, 38, 46, 68, 71; 2.9, 14, 16; 3.1; 5.51; 6.42), reflect Jewish criticism of Jesus, which evidently had its roots in the time of Jesus itself (cf. Matt 12:24 = Luke 11:15; Mark 3:22). This very criticism will resurface in later rabbinic traditions (cf. *b. Sanh.* 107b; *b. Soṭa* 47a). Lucian of Samosata refers to Christians who worship "the man who was crucified in Palestine" for introducing a new cult (*Peregrinus* §11, §13). Lucian's comments show that by the middle of the second century literate Romans knew that Christians worshipped the crucified Jesus of Palestine. But again, this fact adds nothing new to our inventory.

There are, however, two important non-Christian sources for the historical Jesus. Although we learn nothing new from these sources, we do obtain important corroboration of significant factors. The first is provided by the Jewish historian Josephus; the second is provided by the Roman official and historian Tacitus. The latter will be treated first

---

[117] Julius Africanus, *Chronography* §18.

[118] For Syriac text and translation, see W. Cureton, *Spicilegium Syriacum: Containing Remans of Bardesan, Meliton, Ambrose and Mara bar Serapion* (London: Rivingtons, 1855) 43-48 [text—Syriac pagination], 73 [translation—Arabic pagination].

and briefly; much more attention will be accorded the former.

Tacitus. Cornelius Tacitus (c. 56–c. 118) was proconsul of Asia (112–113), friend of Pliny the Younger, and author of *Annals* and the *Histories*. Only portions of these works are extant. In *Annals* 15.44 he provides a passing reference to Jesus that is of some limited importance:

> Therefore, to squelch the rumor [that the burning of Rome had taken place by order], Nero supplied (as culprits) and punished in the most extraordinary fashion those hated for their vice, whom the crowd called "Christians." Christus, the author of their name, had suffered the death penalty during the reign of Tiberius, by sentence of the procurator Pontius Pilate. The pernicious superstition was checked for a time, only to break out once more, not merely in Judea, the origin of the evil, but in the capital itself, where all things horrible and shameful collect and are practiced.

Meier rightly remarks that the "passage is obviously genuine. Not only is it witnessed in all the manuscripts of the *Annals*, the very anti-Christian tone of the text makes Christian origin almost impossible."[119] The hostility toward Christians in general and the failure to mention the resurrection of Jesus are strong arguments for the authenticity of the passage, as well as for its independence.[120] The importance of the text lies in its corroboration of the Gospels' claim that Jesus died under the authority of Pontius Pilate and was the founder of the movement that had come to be called after his name.

Josephus. The most important non-Christian source for the historical Jesus is found in Josephus' *Jewish Antiquities*, penned sometime in the final decade of the first century. Jesus is mentioned in two passages. The first is the so-called Testimonium Flavianum. According to this controversial and disputed text Josephus describes Jesus in the following terms (*Ant.* 18.3.3 §63-64):

> At this time there appeared Jesus, a wise man, *if indeed one ought to call him a man.* For he was a doer of amazing deeds, a teacher of persons who receive truth with pleasure. He won over many Jews and many of the Greeks. *He was the Messiah.* And when Pilate condemned him to the cross,

---

119 Meier, *A Marginal Jew*, 90.

120 See H. Fuchs, "Tacitus über die Christen," *VC* 4 (1950) 65-93; A. Kurfess, "Tacitus über die Christen," *VC* 5 (1951) 148-49; T. D. Barnes, "Legislation against the Christians," *JRS* 58 (1968) 32-50; E. M. Smallwood, *The Jews under Roman Rule* (SJLA 20; Leiden: Brill, 1976) 217-19

the leading men among us having accused him, those who loved him from the first did not cease to do so. *For he appeared to them the third day alive again, the divine prophets having spoken these things and a myriad of other marvels concerning him.* And to the present the tribe of Christians, named after this person, has not disappeared.

This passage has aroused a great deal of interest among scholars. Some have maintained that the passage is wholly authentic; others think that it is wholly spurious. Most today regard the passage as authentic but edited.[121] Meier has argued, and I think plausibly, that the three italicized portions represent Christian interpolations. They are the only parts of the Testimonium that affirm Jesus from a Christian point of view. Their deletion, moreover, does not interrupt the flow of the passage.

Further support for the authenticity of the Testimonium is found in an analysis of its vocabulary and style. Years ago H. St. J. Thackeray observed: "The evidence of language, which, on the one hand, bears marks of the author's style, and on the other is not such as a Christian would have used, appears to me decisive."[122] Meier's recent study leads to the same conclusion.[123] Finally, Meier makes a very good point when he notes that the Testimonium does not exaggerate the part that the Jewish leaders played in Jesus' death. On the basis of the Gospels alone an early Christian interpolator would have in all probability portrayed the Jewish leaders as villains. If the passage were a later interpolation, say from the fourth century, then it would be hard to understand why it does not reflect the antipathy that many Christians felt toward the Jewish people. The Testimonium reads the way we should expect it to, if it were authored by a Jew before the emergence of Jewish-Christian animosities.[124]

The principal support for the authenticity of the Testimonium lies in the second passage which refers to Jesus, albeit only incidently. The

---

[121] J. P. Meier, "Jesus in Josephus: A Modest Proposal," *CBQ* 52 (1990) 76-103; idem, *A Marginal Jew*, 56-69. For fuller bibliography representing the diversity of opinion concerning the question of the authenticity of the Testimonium Flavianum, see Evans, "Jesus in Non-Christian Sources," 466-67 nn. 57-59.

[122] H. St. J. Thackeray, *Josephus, the Man and the Historian* (New York: Jewish Institute of Religion, 1929) 137. See the detailed analysis of vocabulary and style on pp. 140-48.

[123] Meier, "Jesus in Josephus," 90-92.

[124] Meier, *A Marginal Jew*, 65-66.

reference is found in *Ant.* 20.9.1 §200-201:

> He (Ananus) convened the council of judges and brought before it the
> brother of Jesus—the one called "Christ"—whose name was James, and
> certain others. Accusing them of transgressing the law he delivered them up
> for stoning. But those of the city considered to be the most fair-minded and
> strict concerning the laws were offended at this and sent to the king secretly
> urging him to order Ananus to take such actions no longer.

There are no compelling reasons for rejecting this passage as inauthentic. There is nothing Christian, or positive, in the reference to
James and Jesus. The whole point seems to be to explain why Ananus
was deposed as High Priest. Furthermore, the designation, "brother of
Jesus," contrasts with Christian practice of referring to James as the
"brother of the Lord" (cf. Gal 1:19; Eusebius, *Hist. Eccl.* 2.23.4). It is
not surprising, therefore, that, in the words of Louis Feldman, "few
have doubted the genuineness of this passages on James."[125]

The authenticity of the second, shorter passage lends support to the
authenticity of the earlier passage.[126] The reference to "Jesus the one
called 'Christ'" ('Ιησοῦ τοῦ λεγομένου Χριστοῦ) clearly implies a prior
reference. In all probability the Testimonium Flavianum is that prior
reference.[127]

Several important inferences may be drawn from the two Josephan
passages. The first has to with Jesus' fate in Jerusalem. The sequence of
events in Josephus roughly corresponds to what we find in the Gospels
and Acts: Jesus is a wonderworker and teacher who attracted a large
following. The Jewish "first men" (i.e. ruling priests and members of
the Sanhedrin)[128] bring to Pilate charges against Jesus. The Roman
governor condemns Jesus to the cross. But despite his death, the "tribe
of Christians," named after Jesus (thus implying awareness that Jesus
was called "Christ"), remains loyal to Jesus, while his brother James,

---

[125] L. H. Feldman, *Josephus X* (LCL 456; London: Heinemann; Cambridge:
Harvard University, 1965) 108 n. a, as cited, with approval, by Meier, *A Marginal
Jew*, 59. The story of James being thrown from the pinnacle of the Temple (from
Hegesippus, as reported by Eusebius, *Hist. Eccl.* 2.23.11-18), although obviously
legendary, appears to be based on tradition parallel to, but independent of, the story
preserved in Josephus.

[126] It is also quoted by Eusebius, *Hist. Eccl.* 2.23.22.

[127] See the discussion in Meier, *A Marginal Jew*, 57-59.

[128] On this identification of "first men," see Evans, "Jesus in Non-Christian
Sources," 472-73.

apparently a leader of the Palestinian Church, is martyred some years later.

The bare outline that Josephus provides takes on added significance when we recall that a few scholars recently have called into question the Gospels' presentation of Jesus' death as a result of his public teaching. As already mentioned, Mack has questioned the Gospels' presentation of Jesus' death as a direct consequence of his prior activities and teachings. He has to assert this, of course, for he recognizes that his Cynic Jesus would have been a threat to no one. Unable to account for Jesus' death, he gratuitously asserts that the causes cannot be known and that Mark's account is narrative fiction.[129]

One wonders from what source Josephus gathered his information concerning Jesus and James. Since Josephus says nothing about Jesus' resurrection, Meier has concluded, rightly in my judgment, that Josephus probably did not learn of Jesus and James from Christian sources.[130] Because what he relates has to do with the execution of both, it is possible that his sources were official records. Feldman entertains this possibility, but it can be no more than a conjecture.[131] In any case, the source of the Testimonium was in all probability not a Christian one.

Summary and Assessment

The major gains of the Third Quest are seen principally in the critical reassessment of the presuppositions and criteria. As to presuppositions, there is a more positive evaluation of the historicity of the canonical Gospels. These writings are seen as essentially reliable and capable of providing the data necessary for productive Jesus research. The Synoptic Gospels, and even the Fourth Gospel to a limited extent, are being fully exploited by scholars, which has enabled the Third Quest to move ahead with a degree of confidence that form and redaction critics earlier this century would have thought impossible.

---

[129] Mack, *A Myth of Innocence*, 282; cf. Seeley, "Was Jesus like a Philosopher?" 548.

[130] Meier, *A Marginal Jew*, 67-68.

[131] L. H. Feldman, "The *Testimonium Flavium*: The State of the Question," in R. F. Berkey and S. A. Edwards (eds.), *Christological Perspectives* (H. K. McArthur Festschrift; New York: Pilgrim, 1982) 179-99, 288-93, esp. 194-95.

What in large measure has brought on this recent and more positive assessment of the Gospels has been the critical reevaluation of the criteria of authenticity, as well as careful rethinking of what the goal of Jesus research really is. The Third Quest is not a quest for a Jesus that is relevant for Christian faith, which is what drove the Old and New Quests. The Third Quest is a historically-driven interest in understanding Jesus and the emergence of what would become Christianity. Many of the participants may have theological interests in the discussion and in its results, but the discussion itself is not governed by some sort of "correct" understanding of self or the kerygma. What relevance the results of Jesus research may have for the Church or for the individual is a question that theologians and individuals can decide for themselves. But theological agenda do not in current mainstream scholarship dictate the goals, presuppositions, or methods of Jesus research.

Today the trend has been the greater appreciation of the historical context and environment in which the life and teaching of Jesus must be interpreted. The discovery and (eventual) publication of the Dead Sea Scrolls, as well as a host of material lumped together as the Old Testament Pseudepigrapha, have greatly enhanced the opportunities to engage in comparative and contextual study. Ongoing archaeology and cognate studies have supplemented significantly the grist which the mills of the Third Quest may now grind.

Martin Hengel and his colleagues at Tübingen have played a very important role in generating this return to history, not simply by calling scholars back to the primary sources, but by calling scholars back to the *relevant* sources.[132] A major concern in the present book is to study several important facets of Jesus' life and teaching against

---

[132] One immediately thinks of M. Hengel, *Die Zeloten: Untersuchungen zur jüdischen Freiheitsbewegung in der Zeit von Herodes I. bis 70 n. Chr.* (AGJU 1; Leiden: Brill, 1961; 2nd ed., 1976); ET: *The Zealots: Investigations into the Jewish Freedom Movement in the Period from Herod I until 70 A.D.* (Edinburgh: T. & T. Clark, 1989); as well as studies by Otto Betz, *Jesus: Der Messias Israels* (WUNT 42; Tübingen: Mohr [Siebeck], 1987), Otfried Hofius, *Jesu Tischgemeinschaft mit den Sündern* (CH 86; Stuttgart: Calwer, 1967), and Peter Stuhlmacher (ed.), *Das Evangelium und die Evangelien: Vorträge vom Tübinger Symposium 1982* (WUNT 28; Tübingen: Mohr [Siebeck], 1983). This bibliography represents but a sampling. In his 1993 SNTS presidential address Hengel ("Aufgaben," 339) warns of the decline in historical and philological exegesis.

what are judged to be the relevant background sources. It is my belief that an accurate and compelling portrait of the historical Jesus cannot emerge apart from such comparative study. A "close reading" of the Gospels that does not take into account Jesus' contemporaries and the events and traditions which conditioned their thinking and actions can never provide us with such a portrait.

But not all agree as to what these relevant background sources are. Should we give priority to the Dead Sea Scrolls, Josephus, the Old Testament Pseudepigrapha, and early rabbinica? Or should we give priority to gnostic sources, magical papyri, and Greco-Roman literature? One's position here will have a profound impact on the results of investigation. If one assigns priority to the second cluster of sources, which admittedly cannot always be neatly isolated from the first, one may very well conclude that Jesus was a Cynic, in which case it is best to compare his sayings and activities, as Gerald Downing and Dominic Crossan have done,[133] to those of Cynics and Cynic-Stoics of the Greco-Roman world. Or one may conclude that he was a philosopher, or even a wit. But do these portraits realistically explain Jesus' death and the movement that arose in its aftermath?

In my judgment some of the scholarship that is part of the Third Quest is faulty through its questionable use of potentially irrelevant sources. The appeal to certain Greco-Roman materials, as the most relevant backdrop against which we may understand Jesus' activities and teachings, and the priority assigned to certain apocryphal gospels, from which Jesus' teachings are reconstructed and his activities understood, have led to eccentric and misleading portraits of the historical Jesus. In some ways this tendency, which may strike some as curious, is in reality nothing new, but is rooted in the assumptions and methods of the History of Religions School from the beginning of the twentieth century.[134]

---

[133] Crossan, *The Historical Jesus*; F. G. Downing, *Christ and the Cynics: Jesus and Other Radical Preachers in First-Century Tradition* (JSOT Manuals 4; Sheffield: JSOT Press, 1988). The latter is the Greco-Roman "Strack-Billerbeck" for Jesus research; and like it, Downing's parallels are beset with contextual and chronological problems.

[134] One thinks of Bultmann's efforts to explain the origin of Pauline and Johannine christology by appeal to fifth-century Mandaean sources, which were themselves full of allusions to New Testament passages and Christian ideas. Never able to appreciate the methodological error in this procedure James Robinson and

This book will present numerous parallels between various deeds and sayings of Jesus. I am well aware that mere parallels do not and cannot resolve all of the problems. And I am also well aware of Samuel Sandmel's warning concerning what he called "parallelomania,"[135] a warning of which we were reminded by E. P. Sanders in the Historical Jesus seminar during the 1993 SNTS meeting in Chicago. (He told us that every New Testament scholar, as a sort of antidote, should read Sandmel's essay weekly.) Sandmel's warning and Sanders's reminder are salutary, to be sure, but New Testament interpretation, unless it is content to be subjective, cannot avoid comparative study of parallels (and Sanders did not suggest that it could). The observation and analysis of parallels give us the perspective that we need in order to understand sufficiently the literature that we study. Little in the New Testament can be adequately understood apart from the study of parallels, from the analysis of individual words themselves to attempts to reconstruct chains of events.[136]

The chapters that follow are grouped under two sub-headings. The first looks at Jesus and his rivals. The point of these chapters is to explore the diversity of beliefs and actions taken by various individuals, beliefs and actions which appear related to the teachings and activities of Jesus. From these chapters it becomes possible to compare Jesus better to his approximately contemporary rivals. The early Church regarded Jesus as Israel's Messiah and "savior." In what ways was Jesus like or unlike other Jewish deliverers? The chapters in Part One address this question. The goal is to understand better the *Sitz im Leben Jesu*.

The second cluster of chapters falls under the sub-heading of Jesus and his opponents. These chapters narrow the focus of discussion by raising questions that specifically concern the principal elements of Jesus' teachings and actions and the question why the Jewish and

---

Helmut Koester, the last of Bultmann's students, have in more recent times appealed to third and fourth-century Coptic sources, which, like the Mandaean sources, were also full of allusions to the New Testament. What were minimized or ignored in this effort to isolate and understand the ingredients that went into the articulation of New Testament christology were the older and more relevant materials of Palestinian and Diaspora Judaism.

[135]   S. Sandmel, "Parallelomania," *JBL* 81 (1962) 2-13.

[136]   Though in different words, these were among the very points members of the Historical Jesus seminar raised in response to Sanders's comments.

Roman authorities executed him in the manner they did.

The Epilogue will draw together some of the main conclusions of the book. These will be synthesized in an effort to present a coherent picture of the ministry and christology of Jesus. The Epilogue will also offer a few suggestions for understanding the emergence of Christian theology and its indebtedness to Jesus' teaching.

PART ONE

JESUS AND HIS RIVALS

CHAPTER TWO

MESSIANIC CLAIMANTS
OF THE FIRST AND SECOND CENTURIES

WERE THERE MESSIANIC CLAIMANTS IN THE TIME OF JESUS?

In a recent and substantial study of New Testament christology
Marinus de Jonge refers to studies by Richard Horsley and John
Hanson, in which they "do not hesitate to speak of popular *messianic*
movements, assuming that Judas, Simon, and Athronges and their
followers were inspired by popular memories and expectations
concerning David, who, after all, had in his younger days been a
successful leader of a sizable band of brigands (1 Sam[uel] 21–30),
before being installed as king in Jerusalem and becoming the founder
of the Davidic dynasty. This is an attractive theory, but unfortunately
difficult to substantiate from literary sources: we have only Josephus'
very one-sided presentation of the facts."[1] De Jonge does not reject out
of hand Horsley's and Hanson's conclusion—he admits that Simon bar
Gioras and Menaḥem could very well have had "messianic preten-
sions"[2]—but he is reluctant to affirm it with as much confidence as
they.

Part of the problem, quite apart from the incomplete and biased
information that Josephus has provided us, is the definition of
"Messiah." This is a highly complex and difficult question which de
Jonge himself has addressed in several important essays.[3] The

---

[1]   M. de Jonge, *Christology in Context: The Earliest Christian Response to
Jesus* (Philadelphia: Westminster, 1988) 164. De Jonge refers to R. A. Horsley,
"Popular Messianic Movements Around the Time of Jesus," *CBQ* 46 (1984) 471-
95; and to Horsley and J. S. Hanson, *Bandits, Prophets, and Messiahs: Popular
Movements at the Time of Jesus* (San Francisco: Harper & Row, 1988) 88-134.
    This is merely another round in an old debate. For a defense of understanding
the Jewish resistance in messianic terms, see M. Hengel, *The Zealots: Investigations into the Jewish Freedom Movement in the Period from Herod I until 70 A.D.*
Edinburgh: T. & T. Clark, 1989) 290-302.
[2]   De Jonge, *Christology in Context*, 165.
[3]   M. de Jonge, "The Use of the Word 'Anointed' in the Time of Jesus,"

principal problem, as I see it, is the diversity of messianic views and the even greater diversity of eschatologies. Recent collections of studies edited by Jacob Neusner and James Charlesworth underscore and document this diversity.[4]

I wonder if de Jonge's hesitation to view Simon bar Gioras and Menaḥem, as well as others, as messianic claimants has to do with an assumption regarding what *the* Messiah was supposed to do. Because the reports of Josephus lack detail and tell us nothing of any theological rationale or eschatological expectation that may have been entertained by Simon bar Gioras and Menaḥem, it might be argued that there is insufficient evidence to view them as messianic claimants. But what was the theology of King David, the messianic archetype? Beyond a henotheistic loyalty to Yahweh, a belief that God was to be worshipped in Jerusalem, and the conviction that he, David, was the "Lord's anointed," there is little "Davidic" theology—and no eschatology—to be found in the Old Testament narratives. Judas and Athronges, and later Simon bar Gioras and Menaḥem, even as described by Josephus, parallel the model of David. Would these men and others who dared to place a diadem upon their heads and call themselves "king" think of themselves in any other sense than as Israel's rightful "anointed" rulers? Is it not probable that the traditions of David would serve as the model? And, if they did, the interpretations that had grown up around them would surely come into play.

We must always bear in mind that in the Mediterranean world of late antiquity accession to the throne was as religious and theological, as it was political. Roman emperors, and the Greek despots before them, were hailed in deified terms.[5] But more importantly, in Israel's sacred

NovT 18 (1966) 132-48; idem, "Messianic Ideas in Later Judaism," *TDNT* 9 (1974) 509-17; idem, "The Use of ὁ χριστός in the Passion Narratives," in J. Dupont (ed.), *Jésus aux origines de la christologie* (BETL 40; Gembloux: Duculot; Leuven: Leuven University Press, 1975) 169-92; repr. in de Jonge, *Jewish Eschatology, Early Christian Christology and the Testaments of the Twelve Patriarchs: Collected Essays* (NovTSup 63; Leiden: Brill, 1991) 63-86; idem, "The Earliest Christian Use of *Christos*: Some Suggestions," *NTS* 32 (1986) 321-43.

4   J. Neusner et al. (eds.), *Judaisms and Their Messiahs at the Turn of the Christian Era* (Cambridge: Cambridge University Press, 1987); J. H. Charlesworth (ed.), *The Messiah: Developments in Earliest Judaism and Christianity* (Minneapolis: Fortress, 1992).

5   POxy 1453.11 reads: Καίσαρ[α] θεὸν ἐκ θεοῦ. A third-century B.C.E.

traditions themselves, the anointed king is regarded as in some sense God's son: "You are My son, today I have begotten you" (Ps 2:7); "I will be his Father, and he shall be My son" (2 Sam 7:14; cf. 1 Chr 17:13; Ps 89:26).

In view of these scriptural traditions in which David the Lord's anointed, Israel's king par excellence and messianic template, as well as in view of the pagan custom in late antiquity to view the king as Lord, Savior, God, or son of God, I think that it is highly dubious to distinguish merely political royal claimants from messianic royal claimants. That is, the presumption should be that any Jewish claim to Israel's throne is in all probability a messianic claimant in some sense. The claimant's understanding of eschatology, that is, in what sense his accession to the throne answered Israel's prophetic hope, will tell us much more precisely in what sense he understood his "anointing," and therefore in what sense he was a messiah.

The sticking point, as I see it, is whether or not any of these men

---

inscription from Halicarnassus (British Museum, no. 906) is in honor of Πτολεμαίου τοῦ σωτῆρος καὶ θεοῦ ("Ptolemy, Savior and God"). A first-century B.C.E. inscription from Ephesus describes Julius Caesar as τὸν ἀπὸ Ἄρεως καὶ Ἀφροδε[ί]της θεὸν ἐπιφανῆ καὶ κοινὸν τοῦ ἀνθρωπίνου βίου σωτῆρα ("the manifest God from Mars and Aphrodite, and common Savior of human life"). Compare Titus 2:13: ἐπιφάνειαν τῆς δόξης τοῦ μεγάλου θεοῦ καὶ σωτῆρος ἡμῶν Ἰησοῦ Χριστοῦ. The following inscriptions refer to Ptolemy XIII (62 B.C.E.) and to Ptolemy XIV and Cleopatra (52 B.C.E.), respectively. The first was found over a door of a Temple of Isis on the island of Philae. The second comes from Alexandria: τοῦ κυρίου βασιλ[έ]ος θεοῦ ("of the lord king god"); τοῖς κυρίοις θεοῖς μεγίστοις ("to the lords, the greatest gods"). An inscription from Priene refers to the birthday of Augustus as [ἡ γενέθλιος] τοῦ θεοῦ ("the offspring of god"). Another birthday inscription refers to Augustus as τοῦ θηοτάτου Καίσαρο[ς] ("of the most divine Caesar"). An inscription from Pergamum reads: [Αὐτοκράτ]ορ[α Κ]αίσαρα [θ]εοῦ υἱὸν θεὸν Σεβαστὸ[ν] [πάσης] γῆ[ς κ]αὶ θ[α]λάσσης [ἐ]π[όπ]τ[ην] ("The Emperor, Caesar, son of god, the god Augustus, the overseer of every land and sea"). A marble inscription from Magnesia reads in reference to Nero: Γερμανικὸν τὸν υἱὸν τοῦ μεγίστου θεῶν Τιβερίου Κλαυδίου Καίσαρος Σεβάστου Γερμανικὸς σου Αὐτοκράτορ ("Germanicus the son the greatest of the gods, Tiberius Claudius; Caesar Augustus Germanicus your Emperor"). See A. Deissmann, *Light from the Ancient East* (New York: Harper & Row, 1927) 344-54. Finally, another inscription from Halicarnassus refers to Augustus as: Δία δὲ πατρῷον καὶ σωτῆρα τοῦ κοινοῦ τῶν ἀνθρώπων γένους ("Hereditary God and Savior of the common race of humanity" [Δία is the acc. of Ζεύς]). See *TDNT* 7 (1971) 1012.

interpreted their bids for royal power in eschatological terms. Did Athronges or Simon expect the arrival of a Davidic kingdom, with their coronation and subsequent (hoped for) victory over Rome? Had Josephus related this kind of information, de Jonge of course would not dispute Horsley and Hanson. But Josephus does not tell us this directly. However, he does admit that a prophecy was a major factor in stirring up the people: "But what more than all else incited them to the war was an ambiguous oracle, likewise found in their sacred scriptures, to the effect that at that time one from their country would become ruler of the world. This they understood to mean someone of their own race, and many of their wise men went astray in their interpretation of it. The oracle, however, in reality signified the sovereignty of Vespasian, who was proclaimed Emperor on Jewish soil" (*J.W.* 6.5.4 §312-314).[6] This Jewish prophecy seems to have been known, independently of Josephus, by Tacitus (*Hist.* 5.13),[7] and Suetonius (*Div. Vesp.* 4.5).[8] It probably had something to do with Josephus' prophecy of Vespasian's accession to the throne (*J.W.* 3.8.9 §399-402), a prophecy which Cassius Dio (*Hist. Rom.* 66.1.2-4)[9] and

---

[6]   Trans. H. St. J. Thackeray, *Josephus III* (LCL 210; London: Heinemann; Cambridge: Harvard University, 1928) 467.

[7]   "The majority firmly believed that their ancient priestly writings contained the prophecy that this was the very time when the East should grow strong and that men starting from Judaea should possess the world. This mysterious prophecy had in reality pointed to Vespasian and Titus, but the common people, as is the way of human ambition, interpreted these great destinies in their own favour, and could not be turned to the truth even by adversity"; trans. C. H. Moore, *Tacitus III* (LCL 249; London: Heinemann; Cambridge: Harvard University, 1931) 199.

[8]   "There had spread over all the Orient an old and established belief, that it was fated at that time for men coming from Judaea to rule the world. This prediction, referring to the emperor of Rome, as afterwards appeared from the event, the people of Judaea took to themselves; accordingly they revolted . . ."; trans. J. C. Rolfe, *Suetonius II* (LCL 38; London: Heinemann; Cambridge: Harvard University, 1914) 289.

[9]   "Now portents and dreams had come to Vespasian pointing to the sovereignty long beforehand . . . and Nero himself in his dreams once thought that he had brought the car of Jupiter to Vespasian's house. These portents needed interpretation; but not so the saying of a Jew named Josephus; he, having earlier been captured by Vespasian and imprisoned, laughed and said: 'You may imprison me now, but a year from now, when you have become emperor, you will release me'"; trans. E. Cary, *Dio's Roman History VIII* (LCL 176; London: Heinemann; Cam-

Appian (*Hist. Rom.* 22, according to Zonaras, *Epitome Hist.* 11.16)[10] also relate.

To which scriptural oracle did Josephus, Tacitus, and Suetonius refer? The two most likely candidates are Gen 49:10 ("the scepter shall not depart from Judah") and Num 24:17 ("a star [LXX: ἄστρον] shall come forth out of Jacob, and a scepter shall rise out of Israel"). Of the two, the latter is the most likely. The fact that Josephus tells us in this context that one of the omens that incited the Jewish people to revolt was a star (ἄστρον) in the sky (*J.W.* 6.5.3 §289) suggests that this is so. Moreover, there are several texts from antiquity that either quote or allude to Num 24:17 (e.g. *T. Judah* 24:1-6; 1QM 11:4-9; possibly Philo, *Vit. Mos.* 1.52 §290; *De praem. et poen.* 16 §95). According to rabbinic tradition Num 24:17 is applied to Simon ben Kosiba, who is dubbed "bar Kokhba," or "son of the star": "A star [כוכב] goes forth from Jacob; a Koziba [כוזבא] goes forth from Jacob" (*y. Ta'an.* 4.5).

Josephus' reference to the "ambiguous oracle" should make it clear that what inspired the people to revolt and induced the people to follow certain royal claimants or prophetic figures was the strong belief that prophecy was in the process of fulfillment. As many of the Pseudepigrapha and Dead Sea Scrolls make clear (not to mention the New Testament itself), eschatological expectations were in the air in first-century Palestine. It is probable, therefore, that the various figures who summoned followings did so out of the belief that they were playing a part in the anticipated eschatological drama, a drama which would culminate in the defeat of Rome and the restoration of Israel.[11]

From these considerations I conclude that Horsley's and Hanson's depiction of several of the leaders of Israel's freedom movement as messianic figures, that is, charismatic figures "anointed" for the task of liberating and restoring Israel, can with qualification be accepted. The respective visions of these men no doubt differed; so also did their methods. And it cannot be doubted that some of these individuals may

---

bridge: Harvard University, 1925) 259-61. Cf. Josephus, *J.W.* 3.8.9 §399-408.

[10] "For Josephus, as he himself related it, found in the sacred writings a certain oracle signifying when some one from their country would rule the inhabited world . . . This oracle Appian also also mentions in his twenty-second book of his Roman history"; my translation.

[11] See A. Schalit, "Die Erhebung Vespasians nach Josephus, Talmud und Midrasch: Zur Geschichte einer messianischen Prophetie," *ANRW* 2.2 (1975) 208-327, esp. 235-55.

very well have been little more than the opportunists and brigands that Josephus portrayed them to be. But it is also very probable that several understood themselves and their actions in terms of Israel's sacred prophecies, particularly the star prophecy of Num 24:17, and hoped, with Heaven's assistance, to liberate Israel and restore the kingdom.

MESSIAHS, PROPHETS, AND DELIVERERS

In the first and second centuries of the Common Era several persons evidently claimed some form of messianic status. The forms that these claims took were not uniform. Some were royal, with David as the model. Others prophetic, usually with Moses as the model. Others were priestly, usually with Melchizedek as the model. Review of the claims and activities of these figures helps clarify the "messianic context" of the time and place in which Jesus lived, and the later interpretive backgrounds against which the New Testament authors wrote.

1. Biblical and Historical Precedents. Although "messiah" (i.e. "anointed one," from משׁח/χρίειν) is often understood in terms of the royal "son of David," in reality messianic concepts in late antiquity were quite diverse. If we understand "messiah" to mean one who believes himself to be anointed by God in order to play a leading role in the restoration of Israel, a restoration which may or may not involve the Davidic monarchy, then it is correct to speak of anointed kings, anointed prophets, and anointed priests. There is evidence that there were several individuals in the period of time under considera- tion who qualify for inclusion in one or more of these three categories. All of these cateogries are rooted in biblical and historical precedents.

Kings. The concept of the "anointed" king derives from early biblical history. Saul was anointed king (1 Sam 15:1); later David was anointed (1 Sam 16:13). David, of course, became the archetype of the anointed king, whose heir was likened to God's son (2 Sam 7:11-16; Pss 18:50; 89:20; 132:17), and the basis for future hope (Isa 9:2-7; 11:1-10; cf. v. 2 in the Targum: "And a king shall come forth from the sons of Jesse, and a Messiah"). Kings were sometimes prophets as well. The spirit of prophecy came upon King Saul (1 Sam 10:6-13; 19:23-24). King David also was able to prophesy (1 Sam 16:13; 2 Sam 23:1-7; cf. Josephus, *Ant.* 6.8.2 §166 [where he also casts out demons]; Acts 2:29-30). At the end of 11QPsalms[a] we are told that "All these [psalms and songs] he [David] spoke through prophecy which was given him from before the Most High" (27:11). Kings apparently also functioned as priests (1 Sam 14:35 [Saul]; 2 Sam 6:12-19 [David]; 2 Sam 8:18 [David's sons]; 1 Kgs 3:15 [Solomon]; cf. Ps 110:1-4).

The hopes pinned on Zerubbabel may very well have been the earliest instance of post-Davidic messianism (Neh 7:7; 12:1, 47; Hag 1:14; 2:20-23; Zech 3:8; 4:6-10; 6:12-14; Sir 49:11-12). Probably of great influence was the portrait of the expected Messiah in *Psalms of Solomon* 17–18, where he is described as a warrior, a wise ruler, and one who will purge Jerusalem. Herod the Great, who had been appointed "King of the Jews" by the Roman Senate in 40 B.C.E., and whose marriage three years later to Mariamme I, of the Hasmonean family, which was probably intended to strengthen his claim to the throne, may very well have thought of himself as some sort of messiah (Josephus, *J.W.* 1.17.4 §331: "[considered] a man of divine favor"; see also *b. B. Bat.* 3b–4a). The account of Herod's attempt to destroy Jesus may imply that the Matthean evangelist regarded the former as some sort of messianic rival of the latter (Matt 2:1-18).

Prophets. Prophets, as well as kings, were "anointed." This is seen in a variety of texts, biblical and post-biblical: God told Elijah to anoint Hazael, king of Syria, Jehu, king of Israel, and Elisha "to be prophet" in Elijah's place (1 Kgs 19:15-16). It is significant that the anointing of Elisha is parallel to the anointing of the two kings. With reference to the wandering patriarchs God warned gentile kings: "Touch not my anointed ones, do my prophets no harm!" (1 Chr 16:22 = Ps 105:15; cf. Gen 20:7). A particularly instructive example comes from Isa 61:1-2: "The Spirit of the Lord God is upon me, because the Lord has anointed me to bring good tidings to the afflicted." According to the Targum the anointed one is none other than the prophet himself: "The prophet said: 'The spirit of prophecy is upon me . . . .'" In *Mek.* on Exod 20:21 (*Baḥodeš* §9) the passage is applied to Moses. At Qumran (11QMelch 2:4-20; 1QH 17:14) and in the New Testament (Luke 4:18-19; 7:22 = Matt 11:5) Isa 61:1-2 seems to have been understood in prophetic/messianic terms.

Another important idea was the "prophet-like-Moses" theme, for this idea was as kingly as it was prophetic.[12] At many points in rabbinic

---

[12] See H. M. Teeple, *The Mosaic Eschatological Prophet* (SBLMS 10; Philadelphia: SBL, 1957); W. A. Meeks, *The Prophet-King: Moses Traditions and*

tradition Moses was compared with the Messiah. Like the Messiah (*Pesiq. R.* 33.6; *Frag. Tg.* Exod 12:42), so Moses was thought to have come into existence prior to the creation of the universe (*T. Mos.* 1:14; cf. *Pesiq. R.* 15.10; and the comparison between the Exodus and Israel's eschatological restoration in *Pesiq. R. Kah.* 5.8; *Sipre Deut.* §130 [on Deut 16:3]; *Tg.* Lam 2:22). Comparisons between Moses and David may also imply comparison between Moses and Messiah: "You find that whatever Moses did, David did . . . As Moses became king in Israel and in Judah . . . so David became king in Israel and in Judah" (*Midr. Ps.* 1.2 [on Ps 1:1]). Both Moses and David "gave their lives for Israel" (*Sipre Deut.* §344 [on Deut 33:3]). Although these traditions are late, they probably represent embellishments of earlier comparisons between Moses and Messiah. Christians, of course, made their own comparisons (John 1:14-18; Acts 3:22-23; 7:37; Heb 3:1-6; 8:5-6; *Sib. Or.* 8:250: "Moses prefigured [Christ]").

Undoubtedly the most influential prophetic figure in Jesus' lifetime was his contemporary John the Baptist. His baptizing activity around the Jordan, his disciples, the crowds, his eventual arrest and execution, all suggest that he should be included among the other charismatic prophets of this period (Mark 1:2-9; 6:14-29; Matt 3:7b-12; Luke 3:7b-9, 16-17; John 1:19-28; Acts 19:1-7; Josephus *Ant.* 18.5.2 §116-119).

Priests. In very old tradition priests appear as kings. Melchizedek, priest-king of Salem, is an obvious example (Gen 14:18; cf. Ps 110:1-4). As were kings, priests also were anointed. Aaron, the brother of Moses was anointed *and crowned* (cf. Exod 29:6-7; cf. Pseudo-Philo, *Bib. Ant.* 13:1). All priests were to be anointed (Lev 16:32). Zadok, the founder of a high-priestly line, was anointed (1 Chr 29:22; cf. 2 Chr 31:10). After the collapse of the Davidic dynasty, the High Priest was often the highest Jewish authority. High Priest Onias III ruled Jerusalem (2 Maccabees 3–4). Jason the priest attempted to gain control of Jerusalem when he thought Antiochus IV had died (2 Macc 5:5-7). After the successful Maccabean revolt, the Hasmonean family not only served as high priests, thus usurping the Zadokite succession,

the Johannine Christology (NovTSup 14; Leiden: Brill, 1967); J.-A. Bühner, *Der Gesandte und sein Weg im 4. Evangelium: Die kultur- und religionsgeschichtlichen Grundlagen der johanneischen Sendungschristologie sowie ihre traditionsgeschichtliche Entwicklung* (WUNT 2.2; Tübingen: Mohr [Siebeck], 1977).

but even regarded themselves as kings (Aristobulus I [104-103 B.C.E.], cf. Josephus, *J.W.* 1.3.1 §70; Ant. 13.11.1 §301; and Jannaeus [103-76 B.C.E.], cf. Josephus, *Ant.* 13.12.1 §320; *b. Sanh.* 107b). Reflecting the Hasmonean period, the *Testaments of the Twelve Patriarchs* anticipated a priestly ruler, as well as kingly ruler (*T. Sim.* 7:2; *T. Judah* 21:2; *T. Joseph* 19:6). Qumran looked for an "anointed [priest] of Aaron," who would serve alongside the "anointed of Israel" (CD 12:23–13:1, 21; 14:19; 1QS 9:11). Christians believed that Jesus was not only prophet and king, but was also the heavenly High Priest (Heb 5:1-6), whose death ended the need for a priesthood or for further sacrifice (Heb 7:27-28; 9:23-26).

Even in later rabbinic tradition the anointed priest plays a part in the messianic era. Commenting on Zech 4:14 ("There are the two anointed ones who stand by the Lord"): "This is in reference to Aaron and the Messiah" (*'Abot R. Nat.* A 34.4). In *Tg. Ps.-J.* Num 25:12, enriched with phrases from Isa 61:1 and Mal 3:1, Eleazar, Aaron's son, is told that he will be made "the messenger of the covenant . . . to announce redemption at the end of days."

2. Messianic Kings. Our best historical source for the Herodian-Roman period is Josephus. Unfortunately, because of his bias, it is not always easy to distinguish bona fide messianic claimants from those who were truly no more than criminals. Josephus tended to denigrate these claimants as deceivers, impostors, and brigands. For example, he says: "Judea was filled with brigandage. Anyone might make himself a king [βασιλεύς] . . . causing trouble to few Romans . . . but bringing the greatest slaughter upon their own people" (*Ant.* 17.10.8 §285). This comment certainly betrays Josephus' cynical attitude toward the liberation movements of the first century. But despite this pejorative assessment, several of these aspirants in all probability were messianic claimants whose goal was the liberation of Israel.[13] The following figures sought to rule Israel and bring about political, if not religious, restoration.[14]

---

[13]   B. Witherington (*The Christology of Jesus* [Minneapolis: Fortress, 1990] 84-85) has also lent his support to Horsley's and Hanson's line of interpretation.

[14]   For a review of the period following the death of Herod, see S. Safrai and M. Stern (eds.), *The Jewish People in the First Century* (CRINT 1.1; Assen: Van Gorcum; Philadelphia: Fortress, 1974) 277-82; E. M. Smallwood, *The Jews under Roman Rule from Pompey to Diocletian: A Study in Political Relations* (SJLA 20; Leiden: Brill, 1981) 105-19.

Judas (of Sepphoris, Galilee) son of Hezekiah the "brigand chief." In the wake of Herod's death (4 B.C.E.) Judas plundered the royal arsenals and attacked other kingly aspirants (*Ant.* 17.10.5 §271-272; *J.W.* 2.4.1 §56). According to Josephus this man "became a terror to all men by plundering those he came across in his desire for great possessions and in his ambition for royal honor [ζηλώσει βασιλείου τιμῆς]." Although Josephus does not say explicitly, presumably Judas, as well as many of the other insurrectionists of this period of time, was subdued by Varus, the Roman governor of Syria, who quelled rebellion in Galilee, Samaria, Judea, Jerusalem, and Idumea (cf. *Ant.* 17.10.9-10 §286-298; *J.W.* 2.5.1–3 §66-79).[15]

Simon of Perea, a former royal servant. Evidently this Simon was another opportunist who arose after Herod's death. According to Josephus he was a handsome man of great size and strength, who "was bold enough to place the diadem on his head [διάδημά τε ἐτόλμησε περιθέσθαι], and having got together a body of men, he was himself also proclaimed king [αὐτὸς βασιλεὺς ἀναγγελθείς] by them in their madness, and he rated himself worthy of this beyond anyone else. After burning the royal palace in Jericho, he plundered and carried off the things seized there. He also set fire to many other royal residences . . ." (*Ant.* 17.10.6 §273-276; *J.W.* 2.4.2 §57-59: "he placed the diadem on himself [περιτίθησιν μὲν ἑαυτῷ διάδημα]"). His claim to kingship was even noted by Tacitus (*Hist.* 5.9: "After the death of Herod . . . a certain Simon seized the title king [*regium nomen*]"). Simon was eventually slain by Gratus (4 B.C.E.).[16]

Athronges the shepherd of Judea. According to Josephus one Athronges, "remarkable for his great stature and feats of strength," though a mere shepherd of no special ancestry or character, "dared to (gain) a kingdom [ἐτόλμησεν ἐπὶ βασιλείᾳ]." "Having put on the diadem [ὁ δὲ διάδημα περιθέμενος]," he began giving orders, exercising and retaining "power for a long while [4-2 B.C.E.], for he was called king [βασιλεῖ τε κεκλημένῳ]" (*Ant.* 17.10.7 §278-284; *J.W.* 2.4.3 §60-65: "He himself, like a king [αὐτὸς δὲ καθάπερ βασιλεύς], handled matters of graver importance. It was then that he placed the diadem on himself [ἑαυτῷ περιτίθησιν διάδημα]"). He and his brothers

---

[15] For a summary of this man's activities and a study of his "dynasty," see Hengel, *The Zealots*, 330-37.

[16] See Hengel, *The Zealots*, 327-28.

eventually surrendered to Archelaus.[17]

Judas (of Gamala) the Galilean.[18] I regard Judas the Galilean as one
of the anointed kings, and not simply as a bandit, because of his "bid
for independence" (*Ant.* 18.1.1 §4) and because of his mention in Acts
5:37, thus putting him in the company of Jesus and Theudas, both
prophets and probably both messianic claimants. Furthermore, the fact
that Judas' son Menaḥem claimed to be a messiah could suggest that he
had inherited his kingly aspirations from his father (which may be
hinted at by Josephus himself in *J.W.* 2.17.8 §433-434). Probably not
the same person as Judas son of Hezekiah, this Judas called on his
countrymen not to submit to the census administered by Quirinius, the
Roman governor who had replaced the deposed Archelaus (*Ant.*
18.1.1 §4-10; *J.W.* 2.8.1 §118). According to Acts, the Pharisee
Gamaliel said that "Judas the Galilean arose in the days of the census
and drew away some of the people after him; he also perished, and all
who followed him were scattered" (5:37). (This passage is
problematic, especially if the "Theudas" of Acts 5:36 is the Theudas of
45 C.E.) It is significant that a parallel is drawn between Judas and
Theudas (who will be considered below), at least in that both
movements ended in the deaths of their leaders. (Josephus does not tell
us what became of Judas.) Josephus describes Judas' movement as a
"rebellion" and as a "a bid for (national) independence," as well as a
"fourth philosophy." It is perhaps significant that at the mention of
Judas' call for civil disobedience Josephus goes on to summarize the
disturbances of the first century and to suggest that it was this sort of
thinking that led to violence and bloodshed that ultimately culminated
in the catastrophe of 66-70 C.E. (*Ant.* 18.1.1 §10: "My reason for
giving this brief account of [the events that led up to the war] is chiefly
that the zeal which Judas and Saddok inspired in the younger element
meant the ruin of our cause"). Therefore, although Judas' personal
role seems to have been principally that of a teacher, the effect of his
teaching warrants regarding him as yet another founder of a
movement that opposed foreign domination and, by implication,
advocated the establishment of an independent kingdom of Israel. The
crucifixion of his sons Jacob and Simon under Governor Tiberius

---

17   See Hengel, *The Zealots*, 328.
18   Judas of Gamala may be Judas of Sepphoris; see Hengel, *The Zealots*, 331-
32.

Alexander (46-48 C.E.) may also have had something to do with rebellion (*Ant.* 20.5.2 §102).

It is worth remarking that the context in which Judas and Saddok are described strongly suggests that the latter, a Pharisee, was a teacher. Following the description of Judas and Saddok, the principal figures who sowed the seeds of ruin, as Josephus viewed it, we are treated to the principal religious factions, or "philosophies," of the Jewish people. Josephus tells his Roman readers of the Pharisees (*Ant.* 18.1.3 §12-15), the Sadducees (*Ant.* 18.1.4 §16-17), and the Essenes (*Ant.* 18.1.5 §18-22). He then returns to Judas the Galilean, calling his faction the "fourth philosophy," which he admits was Pharisaic (*Ant.* 18.1.6 §23-25). What I think this "philosophy" really was was an eschatological movement that was made up of Pharisees and non-Pharisees. They looked to the Deity (τὸ θεῖον) for assistance, they were filled with devotion (*Ant.* 18.1.1 §5) and a passion for liberty, convinced that God alone was their sovereign (*Ant.* 18.1.6 §23).[19] According to Josephus this teaching infected the thinking of Jews and helped set the stage for the rebellion. Allowing for the obvious bias, I think Josephus is describing more than just a militant philosophy, but a worldview very much influenced by prophetic and apocalyptic scriptural traditions, such as the "ambiguous oracle" discussed above. These traditions, in diverse forms, lay behind most, perhaps even all, of the freedom movements in the first century. The presence of an underlying theological-apocalyptic premise adds further justification for speaking of these would-be liberators as messianic figures.[20]

Menaḥem (grand)son of Judas the Galilean. Josephus tells us that Menaḥem (*ca.* 66 C.E.), either the son or the grandson of Judas the Galilean, plundered Herod's armory at Masada, arming his followers as well as other "brigands," and then "returned like a king [βασιλεύς] to Jerusalem, became the leader of the revolution, and directed the siege of the palace." His followers occupied the Roman barracks and

---

[19] For further discussion, see M. Black, "Judas of Galilee and Josephus' 'Fourth Philosophy'," in O. Betz, L. Haacker, and M. Hengel (eds.), *Josephus Studien* (Göttingen: Vandenhoeck & Ruprecht, 1974) 45-54. In my view, Hengel (*The Zealots*, 123) rightly perceives the teaching of Judas and Saddok as having an "eschatological perspective."

[20] For discussion concerning the Pharisees' attitude toward and role in the first Jewish revolt, see C. Roth, "The Pharisees of the Jewish Revolution of 66–73," *JSS* 7 (1962) 63-80.

eventually caught and killed Ananias the high priest. As a result of his accomplishments, Josephus tells us, Menaḥem, believing himself unrivalled, became an "insufferable tyrant [τύραννος]." Finally, insurgents loyal to Eleazar son of Ananias the high priest rose up against him. Menaḥem, "arrayed in royal [βασιλικῇ] apparel," was attacked while in the Temple. Although he initially managed to escape and hide, he was eventually caught, dragged out into the open, tortured, and put to death (*J.W.* 2.17.8-9 §433-448). It is possible, but I think improbable, that he is the Menaḥem referred to in a tradition that tells of the birth of King Messiah, whose name is Menaḥem son of Hezekiah, born on the day that the Temple was destroyed (*y. Ber.* 2.4; cf. *b. Sanh.* 98b; *Num. Rab.* 13.5 [on Num 7:12]).[21]

John of Gischala son of Levi. Initially John of Gischala was commander of the rebel forces in Gischala (*J.W.* 2.20.6 §575). He later became part of the zealot coalition (*J.W.* 4.1.1-5 §121-146; 5.3.1 §104-105; 5.6.1 §250-251) which, having been forced to retreat into Jerusalem, gained control of most of the city and installed a high priest of its own choosing (*J.W.* 4.3.6 §147-150; 4.3.8 §155-161). Although Josephus describes him as little more than a power-hungry brigand (*J.W.* 2.21.1 §585-589), apparently John did have kingly aspirations. Josephus tells us that he aspired to "tyrannical power [τυραννιῶντι]," "issued despotic [δεσποτικώτερον] orders," and began "laying claim to absolute sovereignty [μοναρχίας]" (*J.W.* 4.7.1 §389-393). Fearing the possibility that John might achieve "monarchical rule [μοναρχίας]," many of the zealots opposed him (*J.W.* 4.7.1 §393-394; see also 4.9.11 §566, where the Idumeans turn against the "tyrant"). When the city was finally overrun, John surrendered and was imprisoned for life (*J.W.* 6.9.4 §433). Later in his account of the Jewish war Josephus evaluates John much in the same terms as he does Simon bar Giora (*J.W.* 7.8.1 §263-266; in 4.9.10 §564-565 they are compared as the tyrants "within" and "without" Jerusalem; in 6.9.4 §433-434 Josephus also compares their respective surrenders). One of John's worst crimes was his "impiety towards God. For he had unlawful food

---

21 Hengel, *The Zealots*, 293-97, 331-32, 358-59, 362-66. The idea that the Menaḥem of the talmudic tradition is the Menaḥem of the first revolt was argued by R. Meyer, *Der Prophet aus Galiläa: Studie zum Jesusbild der drei ersten Evangelien* (repr. Darmstadt: Wissenschaftliche Buchgesellschaft, 1970 [orig. 1940]) 76-77. Hengel (*The Zealots*, 296-97) accepts the identification.

served at his table and abandoned the established rules of purity of our forefathers" (*J.W.* 7.8.1 §264). What apparently was so reprehensible to Josephus the Pharisee, of priestly descent, was probably no more than different halakot, ones which were evidently more lenient and more popular. The disgust that Josephus shows is reminiscent of reactions that Jesus' table manners sometimes evoked (cf. Mark 2:15-17; 7:2; Luke 15:1-2).[22]

Simon bar Giora of Gerasa. The most important leader of the rebellion was Simon bar Giora (from Aramaic בר גיורא = "son of the proselyte"), a man from Gerasa (or Jerash).[23] Simon distinguished himself with military prowess and cunning (*J.W.* 2.19.2 §521; 4.6.1 §353; 4.9.4 §510; 4.9.5 §514-520). He drew a large following by "proclaiming liberty for slaves and rewards for the free" (*J.W.* 4.9.3 §508; 4.9.7 §534 ["forty thousand followers"]). His army was "subservient to his command as to a king [βασιλέα]" (*J.W.* 4.9.4 §510). Josephus avers that early on in his career Simon had shown signs of being tyrannical (*J.W.* 2.22.2 §652 [τυραννεῖν]; 4.9.3 §508 [ὁ δὲ τυραννιῶν]; 5.1.3 §11; 7.2.2 §32 [ἐτυράννησεν]; 7.8.1 §265 [τύραννον]). Simon subjugated the whole of Idumea (*J.W.* 4.9.6 §521-528). The ruling priests, in consultation with the Idumeans and many of the inhabitants of the city, decided to invite Simon into Jerusalem to protect the city from John of Gischala (*J.W.* 4.9.11 §570-576). Simon entered the city and took command in the spring of 69 C.E. (*J.W.* 4.9.12 §577). Among the leaders of the rebellion "Simon in particular was regarded with reverence and awe . . . each was quite prepared to take his very own life had he given the order" (*J.W.* 5.7.3 §309). By his authority, coins were minted declaring the "redemption of Zion."[24]

---

22   U. Rappaport, "John of Gischala: From Galilee to Jerusalem," *JJS* 33 (1982) 479-93; Hengel, *The Zealots*, 371-76.

23   O. Michel, "Studien zu Josephus: Simon bar Giora," *NTS* 14 (1968) 402-408; Hengel, *The Zealots*, 297-98, 372-76.

24   B. Kanael, "The Historical Background of the Coins 'Year Four . . . of the Redemption of Zion'," *BASOR* 129 (1953) 18-20. Kanael argues that Simon bar Giora minted the copper coins whose legend reads: "Year Four of the Redemption of Zion," in contrast to John of Gischala's silver coins, minted earlier, whose legend reads: "Year Three of the Freedom of Zion." He claims further that this difference "throws light on the differences between Simon and John: John strove only for political freedom, while Bar Giora stood at the head of a Messianic movement; hence his coins bear the inscription 'redemption of Zion'" (p. 20). I doubt

Finally defeated and for a time in hiding, Simon, dressed in white tunics and a purple mantle, made a dramatic appearance before the Romans on the very spot where the Temple had stood (*J. W.* 7.2.2 §29). He was placed in chains (*J. W.* 7.2.2 §36), sent to Italy (*J. W.* 7.5.3 §118), put on display as part of the victory celebration in Rome (*J. W.* 7.5.6 §154), and was finally executed (*J. W.* 7.5.6 §155).[25]

Lukuas of Cyrene. During the reign of Trajan (98–117 C.E.)[26] the Jewish inhabitants of Judea, Egypt, and Cyrene revolted. According to Eusebius, our most reliable source for this affair:

> In the course of the eighteenth year [115 C.E.] of the reign of the Emperor a rebellion of the Jews again broke out and destroyed a great multitude of them. For both in Alexandria and in the rest of Egypt and especially in Cyrene, as though they had been seized by some terrible spirit of rebellion, they rushed into sedition against their Greek fellow citizens, and increasing the scope of the rebellion in the following year started a great war while Lupus was governor of all Egypt. In the first engagement they happened to overcome the Greeks, who fled to Alexandria and captured and killed the Jews in the city, but though thus losing the help of the townsmen, the Jews of Cyrene continued to plunder the country of Egypt and to ravage the districts in it under their leader Lucuas. The Emperor sent against them Marcius Turbo with land and sea forces including cavalry. He waged war vigorously against them in many battles for a considerable time and killed many thousands of Jews, not only those of Cyrene but also those of Egypt who had rallied to Lucuas, their king [Λουκούᾳ τῷ βασιλεῖ αὐτῶν]. The Emperor suspected that the Jews in Mesopotamia would also attack the inhabitants and ordered Lusius Quietus to clean them out of the province. He organized a force and murdered a great multitude of the Jews there, and for this reform was appointed governor of Judaea by the Emperor. The Greek authors who chronicle the same period have related this narrative in these very words [*Hist. Eccl.* 4.2.1-5].[27]

---

that this difference in wording can support the weight of such an inference.

[25]   Still standing in Rome today, not far from the Forum, is the Arch of Titus in which this victory parade is depicted. On one side of the inside of the arch Titus and his chariot and horses are depicted, on the other side of the inside of the arch the Jewish captives are depicted, along with the menorah, golden trumpets, and other utensils from the Temple.

[26]   See K. H. Walters, "The Reign of Trajan, and its Place in Contemporary Scholarship (1960–72)," *ANRW* 2.2 (1975) 381-431.

[27]   Trans. by K. Lake and J. E. L. Oulton, *Eusebius: Ecclesiastical History* (2 vols., LCL 153, 265; London: Heinemann; Cambridge: Harvard University Press, 1926-32) 1.305, 307.

Cassius Dio mentions this revolt, but calls the Jewish leader Andreas (*Hist. Rom.* 68.32; 69.12–13).[28] Although Dio's claim that hundreds of thousands perished is probably an exaggeration, the papyri and archaeological evidence confirm that the revolt was widespread and very destructive.[29] Appian himself barely escaped Egypt, having witnessed the destruction of the temple of Nemesis by Jewish rebels (*Bell. Civ.* 2.90). Among other buildings destroyed were temples dedicated to Apollo and Hecate. In Cyrene the rebels destroyed temples dedicated to Apollo, Artemis, Hecate, Demeter, and possible temples dedicated to Pluto, Isis, and others. Our scanty sources indicate that much of North Africa had to be rebuilt and repopulated following the end of the war.[30]

---

28   It is conjectured that Lukuas and Andreas were one and the same person and that his full name may have been Λουκούας ὁ καὶ ʼΑνδρέας; cf. P. M. Fraser, "Hadrian and Cyrene," *JRS* 40 (1950) 77-90, esp. 83-84.

29   See E. Schürer, *The History of the Jewish People in the Age of Jesus Christ* (3 vols., rev. and ed. by G. Vermes, F. Millar, and M. Black; Edinburgh: T. & T. Clark, 1973-87) 1.530-33; A. Fuks, "The Jewish Revolt in Egypt (A.D. 115–117) in the Light of the Papyri," *Aegyptus* 33 (1953) 131-58; V. A. Tcherikover and A. Fuks (eds.), *Corpus Papyrorum Judaicarum* (2 vols., Cambridge: Harvard University Press, 1957-60) 1.85-93; A. Fuks, "Aspects of the Jewish Revolt in A.D. 115-117," *JRS* 15 (1961) 98-104; Walters, "The Reign of Trajan," 426-27; Smallwood, *The Jews under Roman Rule*, 389-427; M. Hengel, "Messianische Hoffnung und politischer 'Radikalismus' in der 'jüdisch-hellenistischen Diaspora': Zur Frage der Voraussetzungen des jüdischen Aufstandes unter Trajan A.D. 115-117," in D. Hellholm (ed.), *Apocalypticism in the Mediterranean World and the Near East: Proceedings of the International Colloquium on Apocalypticism, Uppsala, August 12–17, 1979* (Tübingen: Mohr [Siebeck], 1983), 655-86; L. L. Grabbe, *Judaism from Cyrus to Hadrian* (2 vols., Minneapolis: Fortress, 1992) 2.565-69.

30   Tcherikover and Fuks (eds.), *Corpus Papyrorum Judaicarum*, 1.87 nn. 77-79, 1.90 n. 81; Fraser, "Hadrian and Cyrene," 77-90; S. Applebaum, "The Jewish Revolt in Cyrene in 115–117, and the Subsequent Recolonisation," *JJS* 2 (1951) 177-86. An inscription found at Cyrene records Hadrian's order to rebuild the public baths and other buildings: Imp(erator) Caesar divi Trajani | Parthici fil(ii) divi Nervae Neros | Trajanus-Hadrianus Aug(ustus) pontif(ex) max(imus) trib(unicius) potest(as) III co(n)s(ul) III balineum | cum porticibus et sphaeristeris ceteris | veadjacentibus ovae tumulto Judaico | dirvta et exusta erant civitati | Cyrenensium restititui jussit ("The Emperor Caesar, of deified Trajan the Parthian son of deified Nerva Nero, Trajan-Hadrian Augustus chief pontiff thrice (proclaimed, holder of) tribunician power, thrice consul, ordered the bath, with the porticos and the ball-

Several papyri provide us with disjointed but vivid details relating to the war and to its aftermath.[31] *CPJ* no. 435 (115 C.E.), an edict from Rutilius Lupus, Roman Prefect of Egypt, refers to a "battle [μάχη] between the Romans and the Jews." In *CPJ* no. 436 (115 C.E.?) an anxious sister urges her brother not to go out without a guard (φυλακή). *CPJ* no. 438 (probably 116 C.E.) tells of a defeat at the hands of the Jewish insurgents: "The one hope and expectation that was left was the push of the massed villagers from our district against the impious Jews; but now the opposite has happened. For on the 20th our forces fought and were beaten and many of them were killed [. . .] now, however, we have received news from men coming from [. . .] that another legion of Rutilius arrived at Memphis on the 22nd and is expected." *CPJ* no. 439 (117 C.E.?) reports that a "slave was coming from Memphis to bring the good news of his (i.e. Apollonius') victory and success." In *CPJ* no. 443 (117 C.E.) Apollonius requests a leave to tend to his damaged estates. *CPJ* no. 444 (late 117 C.E. or early 118 C.E.) refers to the recent "Jewish disturbances," while *CPJ* no. 445 (perhaps early 118 C.E.) refers to the confiscation of Jewish property. Finally, *CPJ* no. 450 (late 199 C.E. or early 200 C.E.) expresses gratitude to the people of Oxyrhynchus for their "friendship to the Romans which they exhibited in the war against the Jews [κατὰ τὸν πρὸς Ἐιουδαίους πόλεμον συμμαχήσαντες], giving aid then and even now keeping the day of victory as a festival every year."

Although we cannot be certain, given the fragmentary, biased, and often unreliable sources, it is probable that Lukuas the Jewish "king" was regarded in messianic terms. This is probable not only because "Messiah" was understood to be a king, but the destruction of pagan temples and the resulting references to the Jews as "impious" make it clear that a religious factor played an important role in the war, whatever the specific cause or causes of it. Moreover, the intensity of the fighting, which led to exaggerated charges of savagery, testifies to the dedication and zeal of the Jewish insurgents. All of these factors suggest that Lukuas was regarded as the Messiah and that the war was a

---

courts and other adjacent enclosures, (which) were destroyed and burned in the Jewish rebellion [*tumultus Judaicus*], of the city of the Cyrenians to be restored"); cf. S. Perowne, *Hadrian* (London: Hodder and Stoughton, 1960) pl. 2.

[31]   All of these papyri can be found in Tcherikover and Fuks (eds.), *Corpus Papyrorum Judaicarum*, 2.228-60.

battle for the restoration of Israel.[32]

Simon ben Kosiba. Apparently Simon, either the son of a man named Kosiba or from a village (or valley) by that name, was the principal leader of the second Jewish rebellion against Rome (132-35 C.E.). (The rabbis often spell his name with the letter "z" to make a word play with "lie.") According to rabbinic tradition, Rabbi Aqiba, contrary to other rabbis, regarded Simon as the Messiah (*y. Ta'an.* 4.5). Another tradition adds: "Bar Koziba reigned two and a half years, and then said to the rabbis, 'I am the Messiah.' They answered, 'Of Messiah it is written that he smells [instead of sees] and judges: let us see if he [Bar Koziba] can do so" (*b. Sanh.* 93b). Administering justice by smelling, instead of seeing, is an allusion to Isa 11:3-5 ("He shall not judge by what his eyes see, or decide by what his ears hear; but with righteousness he shall judge the poor, and decide with equity for the meek of the earth . . ."). The talmudic passage goes on to say that Simon failed and so was slain. According to *y. Ta'an.* 4.5 (cf. *m. Ta'an.* 4:6; *b. Giṭ.* 57a-b; *Lam. Rab.* 2:2 §4) Simon was defeated at Bether because of arrogance against heaven ("Lord of the Universe, neither help us nor hinder us!") and violence against Rabbi Eleazar, one of Israel's revered teachers.

No doubt because of his ultimate defeat and the disastrous consequences for Israel, the rabbis were very critical of Simon. The evidence suggests, however, that initially he was quite successful. Legends such as his catching and throwing back Roman siege stones may be remnants of popular stories in which Simon had been depicted in a much more favorable light. (According to Jerome [*Against Rufinus* 3.31] Simon deceived the people with fraudulent miracles.) Apparently Aqiba found something appealing about him. In fact, it was Simon's military success, the tradition tells us, that led the famous rabbi to recognize Simon as the Messiah (*Lam. Rab.* 2:2 §4). According to Moses Maimonides, "Rabbi Aqiba, the greatest of the sages of the Mishna, was a supporter of King Ben Kozeba, saying of him that he was King Messiah. He *and all the contemporary sages* regarded him as the King Messiah, until he was killed for sins which he had committed" (*Mishneh Torah, Melakhim* 11:3, my emphasis). For these reasons, as well as the fact that the Romans subdued Judea only

---

32   So Tcherikover and Fuks (eds.), *Corpus Papyrorum Judaicarum,* 1.90: "the only reason [for the revolt] was the Messianic character of the whole movement."

with great difficulty, it is probable that Simon enjoyed widespread popularity and support. It is quite possible that the persecution against Christians described by Justin Martyr had to do with their refusal to acknowledge the messiahship of Simon: "During the Jewish war Bar Kochebas, the leader of the Jewish rebellion, commanded Christians to be led away to terrible punishment, unless they denied Jesus as the Messiah and blasphemed" (*1 Apol.* 31.6). According to Eusebius, "Bar Kochebas . . . claimed to be a luminary who had come down to them from heaven" (*Hist. Eccl.* 4.6.2).

Simon became known as "Bar Kokhba" because of a word-play between his name and the star of Num 24:17-19, a passage widely regarded as messianic: "A star [כוכב] shall come out of Jacob, and a scepter shall rise out of Israel; it shall crush the forehead of Moab, and break down all the sons of Sheth. Edom [= Rome] shall be dispossessed . . . ." The earliest messianic interpretation of this verse is apparently found in the *Testament of Judah*: "And after this there shall arise for you a Star from Jacob . . . This is the Shoot of God . . . Then he will illumine the scepter of my kingdom, and from your root will arise the Shoot, and through it will arise the rod of righteousness for the nations, to judge and to save all that call on the Lord" (24:1-6). Not only are there allusions to Numbers 24, there are important allusions to Isa 11:1-5 as well. At Qumran Num 24:17-19 seems to have been understood in a messianic sense: "Yours is the battle! From [you] comes the power . . . as you declared to us in former times, 'A star has journeyed from Jacob, a scepter has arisen from Israel . . .' And by the hand of your Anointed Ones . . . you have announced to us the times of the battles . . . " (1QM 11:4-9); "And the Star [alluding to Amos 9:11 in line 15] is the Seeker of the Law who came to Damascus; as it is written, 'A star has journeyed out of Jacob and a scepter is risen out of Israel.' The scepter is the Prince of the all the congregation, and at his coming 'he will break down all the sons of Seth'" (CD 7:18-21; cf. 1QSb 5:27-28; 4QTest 9-13). In the Targums the messianic interpretation of Num 24:17 is explicit: ". . . a king shall arise out of Jacob and be anointed the Messiah out of Israel" (*Onqelos*); ". . . a mighty king of the house of Jacob shall reign, and shall be anointed Messiah, wielding the mighty scepter of Israel" (*Ps.-Jonathan*); "A king is destined to arise from the house of Jacob, a redeemer and ruler from the house of Israel, who shall slay the mighty ones . . . who shall destroy all that remains of the guilty city, which is Rome" (*Frag. Tg.*

Num 24:17-19). This messianic interpretation of Numbers 24 is likely what lies behind Matt 2:1-12: the magi have seen the Messiah's "star" and have concluded that the "king of the Jews" has been born. Philo alluded to the passage: "For 'there shall come a man,' says the oracle, and leading his host to war he will subdue great and populous nations, because God has sent to his aid the reinforcement which befits the godly" (*De praem. et poen.* 16 §95). It may also be the passage which Josephus called the "ambiguous oracle" (*J.W.* 6.5.4 §312-313; cf. 3.8.9 §400-402), which, as noted above, was known to several Greco-Roman writers.

But the messianic kingdom that Simon hoped to establish was crushed by the Romans. In the wake of this defeat Aqiba may have reassessed his view of Simon, as could be seen in J. Neusner's translation of *y. Ta'an.* 4.5: "A disappointment shall come forth out of Jacob."[33] Aqiba's retraction of his earlier messianic interpretation of Dan 7:9, and possibly the length of the messianic reign, may also have had something to do with Simon's defeat. For Aqiba and many other rabbis, if the scattered and anecdotal sources can be trusted, the defeat proved costly. The edict of Hadrian forbade Jews to enter Jerusalem and from possessing or teaching Torah. The period is referred to as the "age of the edict" (*b. Šabb.* 60a; *m. Ta'an.* 4:6; *Mek.* on Exod 20:6 [*Baḥodeš* §6]; see also Cassius Dio, *Hist. Rom.* 69.12.2; Eusebius, *Hist. Eccl.* 4.6.4: "Hadrian then commanded that by a legal decree and ordinances the whole nation should be absolutely prevented from entering from thenceforth even the district around Jerusalem"; *Dem. Ev.* 6.18.10). Jerusalem's name was changed to Aeilia Capitolina (cf. Cassius Dio, *Hist. Rom.* 69.12.1). Aqiba violated the edict, was imprisoned (*t. Sanh.* 2.8; cf. *t. Ber.* 2.13; *b. 'Erub.* 21b; *b. Yebam.* 105b, 108b; *y. Yebam.* 12.5), and was cruelly tortured and put to death (*b. Yebam.* 62b; *Lev. Rab.* 13.5 [on Lev 11:4-7]; *Song Rab.* 2:7 §1; *b. Ber.* 61b; *b. Menaḥ.* 29b).[34]

---

33   J. Neusner, *Messiah in Context: Israel's History and Destiny in Formative Judaism* (Philadelphia: Fortress, 1984) 95. I do not in fact think that Neusner's interpretation of this passage is correct; see chap. 4 below.

34   Smallwood, *The Jews under Roman Rule*, 428-66; Grabbe, *Judaism from Cyrus to Hadrian*, 2.569-81. The most important study on the Bar Kokhba revolt has been produced by P. Schäfer, *Der Bar Kokhba-Aufstand: Studien zum zweiten jüdischen Krieg gegen Rom* (TSAJ 1; Tübingen: Mohr [Siebeck], 1981). The value of Schäfer's work lies in its critical assessment of the primary literature.

The Bar Kokhba rebellion will be given much fuller treatment in chap. 4. The sources are especially problematic. The paragraphs above offer no more than a summary of the principal texts and traditions. A critical assessment of their historical value will be undertaken in chap. 4.

3. Messianic Prophets. Even those who claimed to be prophets had intentions not too different from the kingly aspirants. They too wished to liberate Israel, and consequently provoked violent response from the Romans. Although their respective understandings of leadership, or messiahship, may have differed from those who attempted to wear the diadem (in that they may have expected a little more of Heaven's aid), their attempts at modeling their leadership after Moses strongly suggest that they too were part of the struggle to restore Israel. Part of Moses typology was the "wilderness summons," an idea probably related to Isa 40:3 ("In the wilderness prepare the way of the Lord"), a passage cited in Christian (Mark 1:2-3), Qumran (1QS 8:12-14; 9:19-20), and other (Bar 5:7; *T. Mos.* 10:1-5) sources. In the case of Christians (at least with regard to John the Baptist) and Essenes, the passage was acted upon quite literally: they went out into the wilderness to prepare the way of the Lord. Synoptic warnings about not heeding a summons to the wilderness (cf. Matt 24:26) and various claims of false Christs (cf. Mark 13:21-22 par) surely have in mind the people of whom Josephus wrote. At many points there are suggestive parallels (Mark 13:21-22; Matt 24:26; Luke 17:20-23; 21:8; cf. Josephus, *Ant.* 17.10.7 §278-284; 20.8.6 §168; 20.8.10 §188; *J.W.* 2.13.5 §261-263; *J.W.* 6.5.4 §315). One of the characteristics of these prophets is the promise of a "sign [σημεῖον]." For this reason it may be appropriate to call these prophets "sign prophets," in contrast to the oracular prophets.[35]

The Anonymous Samaritan. Josephus tells us that during the administration of Pontius Pilate (26–36 C.E.) a certain Samaritan (36 C.E.), whom he calls a liar and demagogue, convinced many of his people to follow him to Mount Gerizim where he would show them the place where their sacred Temple vessels were buried. (The Samaritan

---

[35] P. W. Barnett, "The Jewish Sign Prophets A.D. 40–70—Their Intentions and Origin," *NTS* 27 (1981) 679-97; Hengel, *The Zealots*, 229-45; R. A. Horsley, "Popular Prophetic Movements at the Time of Jesus: Their Principal Features and Social Origins," *JSNT* 26 (1986) 3-27.

temple on Mount Gerizim had been destroyed by John Hyrcanus in 128
B.C.E. [Josephus, *Ant.* 13.9.1 §256].) Pilate sent a detachment of
troops, which routed the pilgrims before they could ascend the
mountain (*Ant.* 18.4.1 §85-87). This episode, although not a Jewish
affair, parallels the type of thinking found in Jewish regions (i.e.
Galilee and Judea). This Samaritan "uprising" probably had to do with
the Samaritan hope for the appearance of the *Taheb*, the "restorer,"
whose coming was expected in keeping with the promise of Deut
18:15-18 (cf. *Memar Marqah* 4:12; John 4:20, 25: "Our [Samaritan]
fathers worshipped on this mountain [i.e. Mount Gerizim] . . . I know
that Messiah is coming . . . when he comes, he will show us all things").
As such, it is another example of the messianic fervor and unrest of the
region in this period of time.

   Theudas. During the administration of Fadus (44–46 C.E.) Josephus
tells us that "a certain impostor named Theudas persuaded the majority
of the populace to take up their possessions and follow him to the
Jordan River. He stated that he was a prophet and that at his command
the river would be parted and would provide easy passage. With this
talk he deceived many" (*Ant.* 20.5.1 §97-98). The Roman governor
dispatched the cavalry, which scattered Theudas' following. The
would-be prophet was himself decapitated and his head put on display
in Jerusalem. Acts 5:36 tells us that he had a following of about four
hundred men. Although he regarded himself as a "prophet [προ-
φήτης]," Josephus calls Theudas an "impostor [γόης]" who "deceived
many." (Note the similar description in 2 Tim 3:13: "evil men and
impostors will go from bad to worse, deceiving and being deceived."
Judging by Philo's usage [*Spec. Leg.* 1.58 §315], a γόης was the precise
opposite of the genuine προφήτης.) Theudas' claim to be able to part
the Jordan River is an unmistakable allusion either to the crossing of
the Red Sea (Exod 14:21-22) or to the crossing of the Jordan River
(Josh 3:14-17), part of the imagery associated with Israel's redemption
(cf. Isa 11:15; 43:16; 51:10; 63:11).[36] In either case, it is probable that
Theudas was claiming to be the prophet "like Moses" (Deut 18:15-19;
cf. 1 Macc 4:45-46; 14:41; 9:27). As such, he was claiming to be more

---

   [36] Hengel (*The Zealots*, 229-30) also draws our attention to *LivProph*
[*Ezekiel*] 3:5-9, which describes the prophet Ezekiel dividing the river Chebar. This
tradition, which parallels the story about Theudas, is yet another reflection of the
crossing of the Red Sea.

than a mere prophet; he was claiming to be a messianic figure.

The Anonymous Egyptian (Jew).[37] At the outset of the section in which he speaks of the Egyptian, Josephus tells us that "impostors and deceitful men persuaded the crowd to follow them into the wilderness. For they said that they would show them unmistakable wonders and signs according to God's foreknowledge." They and many of their following "were brought before (Governor) Felix" and "were punished" (*Ant.* 20.8.6 §168). Felix's response suggests that the proclamations and activities of these men were not viewed as politically innocent. Indeed, Josephus tells us that these "madmen" promised their followers "signs of freedom" (*J.W.* 2.13.4 §259). Felix himself regarded these actions as "preliminary to insurrection" (*J.W.* 2.13.4 §260). In this the governor was probably correct. As to the Egyptian, Josephus reports: "At this time [ca. 56 C.E.] there came to Jerusalem from Egypt a man who said that he was a prophet [προφήτης] and advised the masses of the common people to go out with him to the mountain called the Mount of Olives, which lies opposite the city . . . For he asserted that he wished to demonstrate from there that at his command Jerusalem's walls would fall down, through which he promised to provide them an entrance into the city" (*Ant.* 20.8.6 §169-170). Felix promptly dispatched the cavalry, which routed and dispersed the following. However, the Egyptian himself escaped. In the parallel account in *Jewish War* Josephus calls the Egyptian a "false prophet" and "impostor" who, with a following of thirty thousand, "proposed to force an entrance into Jerusalem and, after overpowering the Roman garrison, to set himself up as tyrant [τυραννεῖν] over the people" (*J.W.* 2.13.5 §261-163). The hoped-for sign of the walls falling down was probably inspired by the story of Israel's conquest of Jericho, led by Joshua the successor of Moses (Josh 6:20). This Egyptian is mentioned in other sources as well. According to Acts 21:38 a Roman tribune asked Paul: "Are you not the Egyptian, then, who recently stirred up a revolt and led the four thousand men of the Assassins out into the wilderness?" It is possible that the rabbis may have confused Jesus, also thought to have spent time in Egypt where he acquired knowledge of magic (*b. Sanh.* 107b; cf. Origen, *Contra Celsum* 1.38), with the Egyptian. It is interesting to note that according

---

[37] That this man was meant to be understood as Jewish seems most probable, cf. Hengel, *The Zealots*, 231.

to the accounts in Acts and in *Jewish War* the Egyptian summoned people "out into the wilderness." This wilderness summons, as well as the Joshua-like sign of the walls falling down, is very likely part of the prophet-like-Moses theme, or some variation of it, that evidently lay behind much of the messianic speculation of the first century. Moreover, the fact that this Jewish man was known as the man from Egypt might also have had to do with some sort of association with Moses.

Anonymous "Impostor." In a context in which he described the troubles brought on by the *sicarii* Josephus reports that "Festus [ca. 61 C.E.] also sent a force of cavalry and infantry against those deceived by a certain impostor who had promised them salvation [σωτηρία] and rest [παῦλα] from troubles, if they chose to follow him into the wilderness [ἐρημία]. Those whom Festus sent destroyed that deceiver and those who had followed him" (*Ant.* 20.8.10 §188). It is likely that this "impostor" was another messianic prophet, probably in keeping with the prophet-like-Moses theme (as the wilderness summons would seem to indicate). The impostor's promise of rest, moreover, may have had something to do with Ps 95:7b-11, a passage warning Israelites not to put God to the test, as they did at Meribah and Massah "in the wilderness [ἔρημος]," and consequently fail to enter God's "rest [κατάπαυσις]" (cf. Exod 17:1-7; Num 20:1-13). Although the parallel is not precise, it is worth noting that this passage is cited and commented upon in Hebrews (3:7–4:13), a writing in which Jewish Christians are exhorted not to neglect their "salvation [σωτηρία]" (2:3) but to "strive to enter that rest [κατάπαυσις]" (4:11).

Jonathan the refugee. Following the Roman victory over Israel, one Jonathan fled to Cyrene. According to Josephus this man, by trade a weaver, was one of the sicarii. He persuaded many of the poorer Jews to follow him out into the desert, "promising to show them signs and apparitions" (*J.W.* 7.11.1 §437-438; *Life* 76 §424-425). Catullus the Roman governor dispatched troops who routed Jonathan's following and eventually captured the leader himself (*J.W.* 7.11.1 §439-442). Although Josephus does not describe Jonathan as a (false)prophet, it is likely that this is how the man viewed himself, as the desert summons would imply.

4. Messianic Priests. Although there were eschatological ideas that envisioned the appearance of messianic priests, some based on the Hasmonean model (*T. Reub.* 6:10-12; *T. Judah* 21:2-3), others based on Melchizedek (Hebrews 5, 7–8; perhaps 11QMelch), there are no clear examples of messianic priestly claimants in the period under consideration. It is possible that the Samaritan (see §3 above), who hoped to find the sacred vessels of the Samaritan temple, had some priestly ideas. And possibly the zealots thought that they were installing an anointed high priest (one "Phanni," possibly of Zadokite lineage) on the threshhold of the restoration of the kingdom (Josephus, *J.W.* 4.3.8 §155-157). But this is doubtful, since Phanni, described by Josephus as clownish, incompent, and reluctant, was probably no more than a pawn in the hands of the rebels. Thus, it would appear that although there were many who made kingly and prophetic claims, evidently none attempted to fulfill the restorative ideas associated with the anointed high priest.

5. Later Messianic Claimants. Following the defeat of Simon in 135 C.E. it would be three centuries before the reappearance of messianic fervor. Based on various calculations it was believed that Messiah would come either in 440 C.E. (cf. *b. Sanh.* 97b) or in 471 C.E. (cf. *b. 'Abod. Zar.* 9b). Other dates were suggested. Answering this expectation, one "Moses of Crete" (ca. 448 C.E.) promised to lead the Jewish people through the sea, dry-shod, from Crete to Palestine. At his command many of his followers threw themselves into the Mediterranean. Some drowned; others were rescued. Moses himself disappeared (cf. Socrates Scholasticus, *Hist. Eccl.* 7.38; 12.33). Evidently Moses typology had continued to play an important role in shaping restoration hopes.

A variety of other pseudo-messiahs appeared in the Islamic period (especially in the eighth century), during the later crusades (especially in the twelfth and thirteenth centuries), and even as late as the six-teenth, seventeenth, and eighteenth centuries.[38]

Summary and Assessment

Whether and how Jesus related to these messianic figures have been matters of ongoing debate. S. G. F. Brandon compared Jesus to the would-be kings who attempted to liberate Israel through violent overthrow of her Roman masters. Taking seriously his Roman crucifixion as "king of the Jews," between two "zealots," Brandon argued that Jesus attempted to overthrow the Jewish-Roman rule in

---

[38] Cf. *Jewish Encyclopedia* 10.252-55.

Jerusalem: "Jesus met at the hands of the Romans the same fate suffered by Judas of Galilee and his two sons, and on either side of the cross that bore his title 'The King of the Jews' was crucified a λῃστής, as the Romans contemptuously called Israel's resistance fighters, the Zealots."[39] Although Brandon's thesis had the effect of raising the political question of Jesus' activities,[40] his conclusion has not been followed.

Martin Hengel, whose dissertation on the zealots was a major stimulus for Brandon, quickly offered a devastating critique of Brandon's thesis.[41] Hengel shows how at many points Jesus' teaching was incompatible with the methods and objectives of the Jewish resistance.[42] Jesus' "zeal" was for a piety that included love for one's enemies (Matt 5:21-26, 38-48) and an openness toward non-Torah observant Jews, that is, the "sinners" (Mark 2:15-17; Matt 11:19 = Luke 7:34). In a saying that has strong claim to authenticity, Jesus explicitly rejects the philosophy of the resistance: "All those grasping a sword will die by a sword" (Matt 26:52).[43] Hengel concludes, rightly in my estimation, that Jesus sought to bring about Israel's renewal through the transformation of the individual.

In numerous studies Richard Horsley has advanced the discussion by suggesting that Jesus challenged society itself, especially Israel's religious leaders.[44] Probably acting in a manner reminiscent of the classical prophets, Jesus criticized the Temple establishment. Fully

---

39   S. G. F. Brandon, *Jesus and the Zealots: A Study of the Political Factor in Primitive Christianity* (Manchester: Manchester University Press; New York: Scribner's, 1967) 358; cf. idem, *The Trial of Jesus of Nazareth* (New York: Stein and Day, 1968) 140-50.

40   For an important and recent collection of pertinent studies, see E. Bammel and C. F. D. Moule (eds.), *Jesus and the Politics of His Day* (Cambridge: Cambridge University, 1984).

41   M. Hengel, *War Jesus Revolutionär?* (CH 110; Stuttgart: Calwer, 1970); ET: *Was Jesus a Revolutionist?* (Philadelphia: Fortress, 1971); review of Brandon, *Jesus and the Zealots*, in *JSS* 14 (1969) 231-40. See also Hengel's related work, *Victory over Violence* (Philadelphia: Fortress, 1973).

42   Hengel, *The Zealots*, 181, 301-302, 339-41.

43   The logion presupposes the Aramaic paraphrase of Isa 50:11. For discussion, see B. D. Chilton, *A Galilean Rabbi and His Bible: Jesus' Use of the Interpreted Scripture of His Time* (GNS 8; Wilmington: Glazier, 1984) 98-101.

44   R. A. Horsley, *Jesus and the Spiral of Violence: Popular Jewish Resistance in Roman Palestine* (San Francisco: Harper & Row, 1987).

confident that the kingdom of God had begun to dawn, Jesus called for a profound change in his society. It was this criticism of the Temple establishment, combined with the call for change, that made Jesus dangerous in the eyes of his contemporaries. The studies of Horsley and Hengel, though disagreeing at points, have helped clarify the social and political dimension within which Jesus' teaching and activities should be interpreted.[45]

Of the two types of would-be messianic deliverers active in the time of Jesus, most scholars appear to agree that Jesus resembles the "sign" prophets more than he does the popular royal claimants.[46] But I think three qualifications are necessary: (1) Although it is true that Jesus did offer his healing activity as evidence to the imprisoned John the Baptist that he really was the "one who is coming" (Matt 11:2-6 = Luke 7:18-23), Jesus did not offer a "sign," at least not of the magnitude of those promised by Theudas, the Egyptian Jew, and others. Indeed, we are told that when asked, Jesus flatly refused to give a "sign [$\sigma\eta\mu\epsilon\hat{\iota}o\nu$]" (Mark 8:11-12; Luke 11:16).[47] I would add also that although Josephus tells us of the various signs offered by the sign prophets, he describes Jesus as a teacher and "doer of amazing deeds" (*Ant.* 18.3.3. §63-64). Josephus says nothing about Jesus promising a sign. So it seems that not even Josephus lumps Jesus into exactly the same category as Theudas and the Egyptian Jew.

(2) Vestiges of royal, Davidic elements still linger in the Gospel traditions, which the evangelists may have wished to tone down or to expurgate altogether. The tradition of the heavenly voice that echoes

---

[45]   Horsley is critical of Hengel and others for speaking of the "zealots," as if they were a disinct movement or party. The zealots emerged as a coalition of rebel groups during the first war with Rome; cf. R. A. Horsley, "Ancient Jewish Banditry and the Revolt against Rome, A.D. 66–70," *CBQ* 43 (1981) 409-32; idem, "Menahem in Jerusalem: A Brief Messianic Episode among the Sicarii—Not 'Zealot Messianism'," *NovT* 27 (1985) 334-48; idem, "The Zealots: Their Origin, Relationship and Importance in the Jewish Revolt," *NovT* 28 (1986) 159-92.

[46]   Horsley and Hanson, *Bandits, Prophets, and Messiahs*, 257-58; E. P. Sanders, *Jesus and Judaism* (London: SCM; Philadelphia: Fortress, 1985) 172.

[47]   In the Fourth Gospel Jesus' miracles are explicitly and programmatically termed "signs [$\sigma\eta\mu\epsilon\hat{\iota}\alpha$]" (cf. 2:11, 23; 3:2; 4:48, 54; passim). Note how the parallel to the Synoptic refusal to give a sign becomes reinterpreted in John 2:18-22. The sign that Jesus will give will be the raising up of his body. This relates in some way to the "sign of Jonah" material found in Matt 12:38-39.

Ps 2:7 (Mark 1:11; 9:7), the "son of David" utterances (Mark 10:47-48; 11:10), the Davidic genealogies and birth narratives (Matthew 1–2; Luke 1–3), the non-controversial way that Paul speaks of Jesus as the son of David (Rom 1:3-4), and the regular and persistent habit of referring to Jesus as the Messiah[48] are all indications that royal ideas were part of the Jesus movement from the very beginning. The proclamation of the kingdom in itself, moreover, may suggest a royal dimension to Jesus' teaching and sense of purpose. And, of course, and perhaps most important of all, remains the fact of Jesus' Roman crucifixion as "king of the Jews" (Mark 15:26).

(3) Bruce Chilton has reminded us that the title most frequently applied to Jesus is "rabbi" (cf. Matt 26:25, 49; Mark 9:5; 10:51; 11:21; 14:45; John 1:38, 49; 3:2; 4:31; 6:25; 9:2; 11:8).[49] Even the miracles, primarily on the basis of which Geza Vermes concludes that Jesus is best compared to Ḥoni and Ḥanina ben Dosa,[50] are consistent with the identification of rabbi. These famous holy men are called rabbis, while to other rabbis well known for their halakot miracles are attributed.[51] Bruce Chilton wonders if the comparison to Saddok and to other activist rabbis might be more appropriate.[52]

---

[48] As is argued in chap. 12, I think that it is probable that the idea of Jesus as being in some sense "anointed" derives from Jesus himself, probably as part of his interpretation of Isa 52:7 and 61:1-2. That Jesus understood this anointing in a prophetic sense seems clear, but what is less clear is if he understood it in a royal, Davidic sense. I think that he probably did, but I say this with much hesitation. The royal implication of "anointed" is quite ancient, deriving from Scripture itself, often in reference to King David (2 Sam 2:4; 12:7; 22:51; 23:1; Pss 2:2; 89:21; 132:17), and is given an idealistic, somewhat eschatological usage in the *Psalms of Solomon* 17–18. In rabbinic literature the epithet "King Messiah" becomes a commonplace.

[49] Chilton, *A Galilean Rabbi*, 34.

[50] G. Vermes, *Jesus the Jew: A Historian's Reading of the Gospels* (London: Collins; Philadelphia: Fortress, 1973) 72-82.

[51] The point is made by B. D. Chilton, *The Temple of Jesus: His Sacrificial Program Within a Cultural History of Sacrifice* (University Park: Penn State Press, 1992) 92 n. 5.

[52] See the book cited in the preceding note. Chilton offers important points of comparison between Jesus and individuals such as the teachers who incited the crowd to pelt Jannaeus with lemons (Josephus, *Ant.* 13.13.5 §372-373), the teachers who persuaded several young men to cut down the golden eagle (*J.W.* 1.33.2–4 §648-655; *Ant.* 17.6.2–4 §149-167), Hillel who taught that sacrificial animals had to be "owned" by the offerer before being offered (*t. Ḥag.* 2.11; *y.*

(4) Chilton has also highlighted certain aspects of Jesus' teachings and actions in which it appears that he has assumed priestly perogatives (Mark 1:40-44, cleansing of the leper; Matt 17:24-26, pronouncement on Temple tax; Mark 7:1-8, 14-23, on what defiles; Mark 12:41-44, on gifts to the Temple). Chilton believes that Jesus' understanding of the Temple lies behind his statements on forgiveness (Matt 5:23-24; Luke 7:47) and on acceptance of outcasts (Luke 10:29-37; 18:9-14).[53] Jesus' views of the Temple and his concerns for purity will be pursued further in subsequent chapters.

Some scholars have argued that Jesus is better compared against other figures. As just mentioned, Vermes prefers to compare Jesus to Jewish "holy men," while Morton Smith thinks that magician is the most suitable category. This aspect of comparison involves other aspects of the Jesus tradition; they will be taken up in chap. 5.

Ḥag. 2.3), and Simeon ben Gamaliel who protested the overpricing of doves (*m. Ker.* 1:7).

[53] Chilton, *The Temple of Jesus*, 121-36.

CHAPTER THREE

JESUS AND THE MESSIANIC TEXTS FROM QUMRAN:
A PRELIMINARY ASSESSMENT OF THE RECENTLY
PUBLISHED MATERIALS

With the publication of the remainder of the Dead Sea Scrolls in 1991 scholars are now at last in a position to begin work, so far as it touches on Qumran and related matters, that is truly comprehensive. Robert Eisenman, who had already played a key role in publishing the photographs of these materials,[1] has published, along with co-author Michael Wise, a selection of fifty documents from Cave 4.[2] Several of these documents had not been published previously; many had not been discussed. The Biblical Archaeology Society has also begun to publish the texts of the documents from Cave 4. Thus far Ben Zion Wacholder and Martin Abegg, Jr., have produced three fascicles of a series of volumes that will present all of the unpublished Hebrew and Aramaic texts of Cave 4.[3] Their reconstructions have set before the academic

---

[1]   R. H. Eisenman and J. M. Robinson, *A Facsimile Edition of the Dead Sea Scrolls* (2 vols., Washington: Biblical Archaeological Society, 1991). Coinciding with the publication of this facsimile edition was the announcement of Huntington Library (San Marino, California) that scholars would be permitted to examine its colleection of photographs of the Dead Sea Scrolls.

[2]   R. H. Eisenman and M. O. Wise, *The Dead Sea Scrolls Uncovered: The First Complete Translation and Interpretation of 50 Key Documents Withheld for Over 35 Years* (Shaftesbury: Element, 1992). Not all will agree with some of the reconstructions and translations proposed by the authors of this volume. For criticisms of several aspects of this work, see A. S. van der Woude's review in *JSJ* 24 (1993) 298-99, and the review article by D. J. Harrington and J. Strugnell, "Qumran Cave 4 Texts: A New Publication," *JBL* 112 (1993) 491-99. Harrington and Strugnell comment that this book "must be used with great caution" (p. 499).

[3]   B. Z. Wacholder and M. G. Abegg, Jr., *A Preliminary Edition of the Unpublished Dead Sea Scrolls: The Hebrew and Aramaic Texts from Cave Four* (Washington: Biblical Archaeology Society, 1991-94). The Princeton Theological Seminary Dead Sea Scrolls Project should also be mentioned. Under the director-ship of J. H. Charlesworth, a team of some twenty-five scholars is working toward the production of new critical editions and translations of the Qumran sectarian documents. So far this team has produced a valuable tool in the form of J. H.

community the badly needed raw data with which a fresh assessment of the Dead Sea Scrolls and their significance for early Judaism and Christianity can get under way. Detailed analyses of these documents are needed and will no doubt be forthcoming in the years to come. For now it will be useful to consider in a preliminary fashion what impact, if any, these newly published texts might have for life of Jesus research. The essay will begin with a summary of the messianic and related texts that have been available for some time. Scholarly interpretation of these texts will be briefly reviewed. The second part of the essay will then present the newly published texts that appear to have relevance for investigating Qumran's messianology. The third part of the essay will look at a few of the newly published texts that although not messianic they may have relevance for Jesus research.

Older Bibliography: M. Burrows, "The Messiahs of Aaron and the New Testament (DSD IX, 11)," *ATR* 34 (1952) 202-206; K. G. Kuhn, "Die beiden Messias Aarons und Israels," *NTS* 1 (1954-55) 168-79; tr. and repr. "The Two Messiahs of Aaron and Israel," in K. Stendahl (ed.), *The Scrolls and the New Testament* (New York: Harper & Row, 1957) 54-64; idem, "Die beiden Messias in den Qumrantexten und die Messiasvorstellung in der rabbinischen Literatur," *ZAW* 70 (1958) 200-208; K. Schubert, "Zwei Messiasse aus dem Regelbuch von Chirbet Qumran," *Judaica* 11 (1955) 216-35; idem, "Der alttestamentliche Hintergrund der Vorstellung von den beiden Messiassen im Schriftum von Chirbet Qumran," *Judaica* 12 (1956) 24-28; idem, "Die Messiaslehre in den Texten von Chirbet Qumran," *BZ* 1 (1957) 177-97; L. H. Silberman, "The Two 'Messiahs' of the Manual of Discipline," *VT* 5 (1955) 77-82; W. H. Brownlee, "Messianic Motifs of Qumran and the New Testament," *NTS* 3 (1956-57) 12-30, 195-210; E. L. Ehrlich, "Ein Beitrag zur Messiaslehre der Qumransekte," *ZAW* 68 (1956) 234-43; W. S. LaSor; "The Messiahs of Aaron and Israel," *VT* 6 (1956) 425-29; idem, "The Messianic Idea in Qumran," in M. Ben-Horin et al. (eds.), *Studies and Essays in Honor of Abraham A. Neuman* (Leiden: Brill, 1962) 343-64; M. Black, "Messianic Doctrine in the Qumran Scrolls," in K. Aland and F. L. Cross (eds.), *Studia Patristica 1* (TU 63; 2 vols., Berlin: Akademie, 1957) 1.441-59; R. E. Brown, "The Messianism of Qumrân," *CBQ* 19 (1957) 53-82; idem, "J. Starcky's Theory of Qumran Messianic Development," *CBQ* 28 (1966) 51-57; idem, "The Teacher of Righteousness and the Messiah(s)," in M. Black (ed.), *The Scrolls and Christianity* (SPCK Theological Collections 11; London: SPCK, 1969) 37-44, 109-12; R. Gordis, "The 'Begotten' Messiah in the Qumran Scrolls," *VT* 7 (1957)

Charlesworth (ed.), *Graphic Concordance to the Dead Sea Scrolls* (Tübingen: Mohr [Siebeck]; Louisville: Westminster/John Knox, 1991). A second concordance is planned, following the publication of the critical editions, which will present the data in their conventional analytical format (see the end of n. 137 below).

191-94; A. S. van der Woude, *Die messianische Vorstellungen der Gemeinde von Qumran* (SSN 3; Assen: van Gorcum; Neukirchen: Neukirchen-Vluyn, 1957); idem, "Le Maître de Justice et les deux messies de la communauté de Qumrân," in *La secte de Qumrân et les origines chrétiennes* (RechBib 4; Bruges: Desclée de Brouwer, 1959) 121-34; J. Gnilka, "Die Erwartung des messianische Hohenpriesters in den Schriften von Qumran und im Neuen Testament," *RevQ* 2 (1959-60) 395-426; J. Liver, "The Doctrine of the Two Messiahs in the Sectarian Literature in the Time of the Second Commonwealth," *HTR* 52 (1959) 149-85; M. Smith, "What is Implied by the Variety of Messianic Figures?" *JBL* 78 (1959) 66-72; J. Héring, "Encore le messianisme dans les écrits de Qoumran," *RHPR* 41 (1961) 160-62; J. F. Priest, "Mebaqqer, Paqid, and the Messiah," *JBL* 81 (1962) 55-61; idem, "The Messiah and the Meal in 1QSa," *JBL* 82 (1963) 95-100; R. B. Laurin, "The Problem of Two Messiahs in the Qumran Scrolls," *RevQ* 4 (1963-64) 39-52; J. Starcky, "Les quatre étapes du messianisme à Qumran," *RB* 70 (1963) 481-505; E. Lohse, "Der König aus Davids Geschlecht: Bemerkungen zur messianischen Erwartung der Synagoge," in O. Betz et al. (eds.), *Abraham unser Vater: Juden und Christen im Gespräch über die Bibel* (O. Michel Festschrift; AGJU 5; Leiden: Brill, 1963) 337-45; L. Stefaniak, "Messianische oder eschatologische Erwartungen in der Qumransekte?" in J. Blinzler et al. (eds.), *Neutestamentliche Aufsätze* (J. Schmid Festschrift; Regensburg: Pustet, 1963) 294-302; K. Weiss, "Messianismus in Qumran und im Neuen Testament," in H. Bardtke (ed.), *Qumran-Probleme* (Berlin: Akademie, 1963) 353-68; E. A. Wcela, "The Messiah(s) of Qumran," *CBQ* 26 (1964) 340-49; H. Braun, *Qumran und das Neue Testament* (2 vols., Tübingen: Mohr [Siebeck], 1966) 2.75-84; R. Deichgräber, "Zur Messiaserwartung der Damaskusschrift," *ZAW* 78 (1966) 333-43; A. J. B. Higgins, "The Priestly Messiah," *NTS* 13 (1966-67) 211-39; M. de Jonge, "The Use of the Word 'Anointed' in the Time of Jesus," *NovT* 8 (1966) 132-48; W. Grundmann, "Die Frage nach der Gottessohnschaft des Messias im Lichte von Qumran," in S. Wagner (ed.), *Bibel und Qumran: Beiträge zur Erforschung der Beziehungen zwischen Bibel- und Qumranwissenschaft* (H. Bardtke Festschrift; Berlin: Evangelische Haupt-Bibelgesellschaft, 1968) 86-111; G. Vermes, *The Dead Sea Scrolls: Qumran in Perspective* (Philadelphia: Fortress, 1977) 182-88, 194-97; A. Caquot, "Le messianisme qumrânien," in M. Delcor (ed.), *Qumrân: Sa piété, sa théologie et son milieu* (BETL 46; Gembloux: Duculot; Louvain: Leuven Univeristy Press, 1978) 231-47; E. Schürer, *The History of the Jewish People in the Age of Jesus Christ: Vol. II* (rev. and ed. by G. Vermes, F. Millar, and M. Black; Edinburgh: T. & T. Clark, 1979) 550-54.

Recent Bibliography: O. Betz, "Die Bedeutung der Qumranschriften für die Evangelien des Neuen Testaments," *BK* 40 (1985) 54-64; repr. in Betz, *Jesus: Der Messias Israels. Aufsätze zur biblischen Theologie* (WUNT 42; Tübingen: Mohr [Siebeck], 1987) 318-32; S. Talmon, "Waiting for the Messiah: The Spiritual Universe of the Qumran Covenanters," in J. Neusner et al. (eds.), *Judaisms and their Messiahs at the Turn of the Christian Era* (Cambridge and New York: Cambridge University Press, 1987) 111-37; idem, "The Concepts of Māšîaḥ and

Messianism in Early Judaism," in J. H. Charlesworth (ed.), *The Messiah: Developments in Earliest Judaism and Christianity* (Minneapolis: Fortress, 1992) 79-115; L. H. Schiffman, "Messianic Figures and Ideas in the Qumran Scrolls," in Charlesworth (ed.), *The Messiah*, 116-29; idem, *The Eschatological Community of the Dead Sea Scrolls* (SBLMS 38; Atlanta: Scholars, 1989); J. J. Collins, "The *Son of God* Text from Qumran," in M. C. De Boer (ed.), *From John to Jesus: Essays on Jesus and New Testament Christology in Honour of Marinus de Jonge* (JSNTSup 84; Sheffield: JSOT Press, 1993) 65-82; idem, "The Works of the Messiah," *DSD* 1 (1994) 98-112.

I. THE TEXTS

In the following pages all of the messianic texts will be presented, translated, and briefly commented upon (including those that are disputed). Page numbers and plate numbers will also be given. The principal works that offer these plates and transcriptions are abbreviated as follows:

Allegro	J. M. Allegro, "Further Messianic References," *JBL* 75 (1956) 174-87
Beyer	K. Beyer, *Die aramäischen Texte vom Toten Meer* (Göttingen: Vandenhoeck & Ruprecht, 1984)
Broshi	M. Broshi (ed.), *The Damascus Document Reconsidered* (Jerusalem: Israel Exploration Society and the Shrine of the Book, 1992)
Burrows I	M. Burrows (ed.), *The Dead Sea Scrolls of St. Mark's Monastery.* Vol. 1: *The Isaiah Manuscript and the Habakkuk Commentary* (with J. C. Trever and W. H. Brownlee; New Haven: ASOR, 1950)
Burrows II	M. Burrows (ed.), *The Dead Sea Scrolls of St. Mark's Monastery.* Vol. 2, fasc. 2: *The Manual of Discipline* (with J. C. Trever and W. H. Brownlee; New Haven: ASOR, 1951)
DJD 1	D. Barthélemy and J. T. Milik, *Qumran Cave I* (DJD 1; Oxford: Clarendon, 1955)
DJD 5	J. M. Allegro, *Qumrân Cave 4 I (4Q158–4Q186)* (DJD 5; with A. A. Anderson; Oxford: Clarendon, 1968)
DJD 7	M. Baillet, *Qumrân Grotte 4 III (4Q482–4Q520)* (DJD 7; Oxford: Clarendon, 1982)
ER	R. H. Eisenman and J. M. Robinson, *A Facsimile Edition of the Dead Sea Scrolls* (2 vols., Washington: Biblical Archaeology Society, 1991) [refs. are to plate numbers]
EW	R. H. Eisenman and M. O. Wise, *The Dead Sea Scrolls Uncovered* (Shaftesbury: Element, 1992)
Fitzmyer	J. A. Fitzmyer, *Essays on the Semitic Background of the New Testament* (London: Chapman, 1971; repr. as SBLSBS 5; Missoula: Scholars, 1974)

Horgan   M. P. Horgan, *Pesharim: Qumran Interpretations of Biblical Books* (CBQMS 8; Washington: Catholic Biblical Association, 1979)

Lohse   E. Lohse, *Die Texte aus Qumran: Hebräisch und Deutsch* (3rd ed., Munich: Kösel, 1981)

PAM   Palestine Archaeological Museum [refs. are to accession numbers of photographs]

Rabin   C. Rabin, *The Zadokite Documents* (Oxford: Clarendon, 1958)

Schechter   S. Schechter, *Fragments of a Zadokite Work* (Cambridge: Cambridge University Press, 1910; repr. with Prolegomenon by J. A. Fitzmyer; New York: Ktav, 1970)

Sukenik   E. L. Sukenik, *The Dead Sea Scrolls of the Hebrew University* (ed. N. Avigad; Jerusalem: Magnes, 1955)

Trever   J. C. Trever, *Scrolls from Qumrân Cave I* (Jerusalem: Shrine of the Book, 1974)

Vermes   G. Vermes, *The Dead Sea Scrolls in English* (3rd ed., Sheffield: JSOT Press, 1987)

WA   B. Z. Wacholder and M. G. Abegg, *A Preliminary Edition of the Unpublished Dead Sea Scrolls: The Hebrew and Aramaic Texts from Cave Four* (3 fascicles, Washington: Biblical Archaeology Society, 1991-94)

Yadin   Y. Yadin, *The Scroll of the War of the Sons of Light against the Sons of Darkness* (Oxford: Oxford University Press, 1962)

Zeitlin   S. Zeitlin, *The Zadokite Fragments* (JQRMS 1; Philadelphia: Dropsie College, 1952)

1. CD 7:18-21 (= 4QD^b [4Q266] 3 iv 7-10 = 4QD^f [4Q268] 5:2-4)

והכוכב הוא דורש התורה	18
הבא דמשק כאשר כתוב דרך כוכב מיעקב וקם שבט	19
מישראל השבט הוא נשיא כל העדה ובעמדו וקרקר	20
את כל בני שת	21

"[18]. . . And the star is the Seeker of the Law [19]who came to Damascus; as it is written, 'A star has journeyed out of Jacob and a sceptre is risen [20]out of Israel' [Num 24:17]. The sceptre is the Prince [נשיא] of the whole congregation, and at his coming 'he will break down [21]all the sons of Seth' [Num 24:17]."

Text: Broshi 22-23; Zeitlin pl. VII; Schecter 112; Rabin 31; Lohse 80. For 4QD^b, see WA 1.8. For 4QD^f, of which only two words and a few letters are visible, see WA 1.50.

Although unusual in applying part of the passage to the "Seeker of the Law" (= the Teacher of Righteousness), the interpretation of Num

24:17 otherwise coheres with the messianic interpretation that we find in the Targums and elsewhere.[4] The "Prince" probably refers to the expected Messiah.[5] The expectation that the Prince "will break down all the sons of Seth" is at variance with Eisenman's "slain Messiah" interpretation of 4Q285 (see below). The relationship between CD 6:2–8:3 and CD 19 presents problems of its own.[6]

2. CD 12:23–13:1

בקץ הרשעה עד עמוד משוח[7] אהרן   23
וישראל   1

"[23]. . . during the time of ungodliness until the appearance of the Messiah [משוח] of Aaron [1]and Israel . . ."

Text: Broshi 32-35; Zeitlin pls. XII-XIII; Schecter 106-107; Rabin 63-65; Lohse 92.

The anticipation of the "appearance of the 'Anointed One' (or 'Messiah') of Aaron and Israel" is expressed several times in CD. A. S. van der Woude takes the passage in a messianic sense.[8] Whether one Messiah is envisioned here, or two (the point is debated), only comparison with other passages will make clear. The paraphrase in *Tg.* Isa 16:1 (משיחא דישראל) supports the view that the "Messiah of

---

4   See Rabin 30 n. 3 (on CD 7:19). *Tg. Onq.* Num 24:17b reads: "A king will emanate from Jacob, and the Messiah will be consecrated from Israel; and he will kill the princes from Moab and rule over all of humankind." The other Pentateuch targums paraphrase the verse similarly. The phrase, "a star comes forth from Jacob" (דרך כוכב מיעקוב), probably in reference to the teacher of righteousness, is also attested in 4Q269 (D^d) 5:3.

5   So A. S. van der Woude, *Die messianischen Vorstellungen der Gemeinde von Qumrân* (SSN 3; Assen: Van Gorcum, 1957) 58, 74; J. Maier, *Die Texte vom Toten Meer* (2 vols., Munich and Basel: Reinhardt, 1960) 2.53. For more recent studies, see G. J. Brooke, "The Amos-Numbers Midrash (CD 7,13b–8,1a) and Messianic Expectation," *ZAW* 92 (1980) 397-404; M. A. Knibb, *The Qumran Community* (Cambridge: Cambridge University Press, 1987) 63; F. M. Strickert, "Damascus Document VII 10–20 and Qumran Messianic Expectation," *RevQ* 12 (1985-87) 327-49. The epithet, "Prince of the whole congregation," occurs elsewhere (cf. 1QM 5:1; 4Q376 1 iii 1).

6   See Rabin 26-42; J. Murphy-O'Connor, "A Literary Analysis of Damascus Document VI, 2–VIII, 3," *RB* 78 (1971) 210-32; idem, "The Original Text of CD 7:9–8:2 = 19:5-14," *HTR* 64 (1971) 379-86.

7   Broshi (33 n. 5) reads משיח.

8   Van der Woude, *Die messianischen Vorstellungen*, 29.

Israel" is a royal, Davidic figure.

3. CD 14:18-19 (= 4QD^b [4Q266] 18 iii 11-13 = 4QD^f [4Q268] 13:1-3)

18 [   ] וזה פרוש המשפטים אשר [יתהלכו⁹ בהם בקץ]

19 [הרשעה עד עמוד משי]ח אהרן וישראל ויכפר עונם]   [

"^{18}[. . .] And this is the exact statement of the ordinances in which [they shall walk ^{19}until the Messi]ah [משיח] of Aaron and Israel appears and expiates their iniquity."

Text: Broshi 36-37; Zeitlin pl. XIV; Schechter 105; Rabin 71; Lohse 96. For text of 4QD^b, see WA 1.20; for 4QD^f, see WA 1.53.

The reading in 4QD^b confirms the partially extant "Messiah." Only "Aaron and Israel" is extant in 4QD^f. In this instance the text may have in view only one anointed person. Expiating sin is, after all, a priestly function. (Eisenman translates "will atone for their sins," probably to draw Qumran language closer to that of the New Testament and to further his idiosyncratic interpretations.[10]) K. G. Kuhn's supposition that CD's singular references to the "Messiah of Aaron and Israel" are the result of a Medieval copyist's confusion is undermined by the discovery of the singular "Messiah" in the fragments of CD found in Cave 4.[11] But van der Woude nevertheless thinks "Messiah of Aaron and Israel" is eliptical for "Messiah of Aaron *and Messiah of* Israel."[12] In this case, it is the "Messiah of Aaron" who "expiates" the iniquity of the people. This one must be an anointed priest. The "Messiah of Israel" is the expected Davidic Messiah.

4. CD 19:9-11

9   והשומרים אותו הם עניי הצאן

---

[9]   Broshi (37) restores ישפטו ("they shall judge").

[10]   EW 162.

[11]   K. G. Kuhn, "The Two Messiahs of Aaron and Israel," in K. Stendahl (ed.), *The Scrolls and the New Testament* (New York: Crossroad, 1992) 54-64, 256-59. See esp. 59-60. Rabin (31 n. 1 on 7:21a [= 19:11]) wonders if the plural is the mistake. Knibb (*The Qumran Community*, 60) admits that the singular may be shorthand for the "Messiah of Aaron and (Messiah of) Israel," but he is of the opinion that CD, unlike other writings of Qumran, expected only one Messiah, the "Messiah of Aaron and Israel."

[12]   Van der Woude, *Die messianischen Vorstellungen*, 32-33, 60-61, 74.

אלה ימלטו בקץ הפקדה והנשארים ימסרו לחרב בבוא משיח   10

אהרן וישראל   11

"9. . . Those who heed Him are the poor of the flock; [10]they will be saved at the time of visitation. But others will be delivered up to the sword at the coming of the Messiah [משיח] of [11]Aaron and Israel."

Text: Broshi 42-43; Zeitlin pl. XIX-XX; Schechter 101; Rabin 31, 79; Lohse 100.

In lines 7-9 Zech 13:7 is quoted. The following comment makes it clear that the members of Qumran understood themselves as the "sheep" of Zechariah's prophecy. The shepherd who is struck down may have been understood as the community's founder (Teacher of Righteousness?), but the text does not say. It is interesting that early Christians applied this text to Jesus (cf. Mark 14:27).

The anticipation that the "others will be delivered up to the sword when the Messiah of Aaron and Israel comes" is consistent with CD 7:18-21. Although there is no requirement that the messianic expectations of CD and 4Q285 be identical (since, after all, diversity of views is common enough in early Judaism in general and in the Dead Sea Scrolls themselves), the portrait of the "Messiah of Aaron and Israel" breaking down the sons of Seth and putting Israel's enemies to the sword does tell against Eisenman's understanding of 4Q285, that the Messiah will be slain by the Prince of the Kittim (see below). If Eisenman's interpretation is correct, then we have sharply divergent views concerning the fate of the Messiah. Either he slays Israel's enemies, as is taught in CD and elsewhere, or he is himself slain.

5. CD 19:33–20:1

כן כל האנשים אשר באו בברית   33

החדשה בארץ דמשק ושבו ויבגדו ויסורו מבאר מים החיים: 34

לא יחשבו בסוד עם ובכתבם לא יכתבו מיום האסף   35

מורה היחיד עד עמוד משיח מאהרן ומישראל   1

"33. . . Likewise, none of the men who enter the new [34]covenant in the land of Damascus, and who have turned back and betrayed it and departed from the fountain of living waters, [35]shall be numbered among the assembly of the people or inscribed in its book from the day of the gathering in of [1]the Teacher of the assembly until the appearance of the Messiah [משיח] from Aaron and from Israel."

Text: Broshi 44-47; Zeitlin pl. XIX-XX; Schecter 100-101; Rabin 37; Lohse 104.

This text offers a warning to would-be apostates to the effect that there can be no readmission into the community.[13] This ban on readmission was to remain in effect "from the day of the gathering in (i.e. death) of the Teacher of the assembly until the appearance of the Messiah."[14]

6. 1Q30 1 i 2-6

[	מ[שיח הקודש]	]	2
[	ב[שלישית את כול]	]	3
[	ס[פרים חומשם]	]	4
[	[ויותר על ארבעת]	]	5
[	[ופשיהם לפי]	]	6

"2[. . .] the holy [Me]ssiah [. . .]
3[. . . in the] third (place) all the [. . .]
4[. . . b]ooks of the five [. . .]
5[. . .] and the rest on the four [. . .]
6[. . .] and their interpretations [. . .]"

Text: PAM 40.438, 40.500; DJD 1.132-33 (+ pl. XXX).

1Q30 is a Hebrew liturgical text, in which appears a reference to "a/the holy [Me]ssiah" (מ[שיח הקודש]); cf. משיחו הקודש ("his holy anointed ones") in CD 6:1. It is impossible to determine with any certainty which "anointed one" is in mind, either the anointed priest ("Messiah of Aaron") or the anointed layman ("Messiah of Israel").

In the Gospels (esp. Mark 1:24 = Luke 4:34; cf. John 6:69; Acts 4:27: τὸν ἅγιον παῖδά σου Ἰησοῦν), Jesus is called the "holy one" (ὁ ἅγιος τοῦ θεοῦ). It is not clear in these contexts if "Holy One" has a Messianic connotation. In the Old Testament the epithet is applied to Aaron (Ps 106:16), Elisha (2 Kgs 4:9), and Samson (Judg 16:17). It has been suggested that the latter lies behind the reference to Jesus, as part of a wordplay involving Nazareth (נצר) and "holy one" (נזיר). This could be, but it does not account for the expression in 1Q30, which uses קודש, not נזיר.

---

[13] See P. R. Davies, *The Damascus Covenant: An Interpretation of the "Damascus Document"* (JSOTSup 25; Sheffield: JSOT Press, 1982) 181-86.

[14] So van der Woude, *Die messianischen Vorstellungen*, 38. See also Knibb, *The Qumran Community*, 72.

Because the Dead Sea Scrolls do speak of a "Messiah of Aaron" and because Scripture calls Aaron "holy" (קֹדֶשׁ/ἅγιος), it is prudent to assume that 1Q30 is referring to the expected anointed priest, not to the "anointed one of Israel."

Van der Woude, however, rejects the restoration [מ]שיח הקודש, proposing instead רוח הקודש ("the Holy Spirit").[15] The photographical plate is so poor, that it is not possible to decide the question. If van der Woude is correct, then the fragment has no bearing on the concerns of this study.

7. 1QS 4:19b-21a

ואז תצא לנצח אמת תבל כיא התגוללה בדרכי רשע	19
בממשלת עולה עד	
מועד משפט נחרץ הואז יברר אל באמתו כול מעשי גבר	20
וזקק לו מבני איש להתם כול רוח עולה מתכמי	
בשרו ולטהרו ברוח קודש מכול עלילות רשעה	21

"[19]Then truth, which has been defiled in the ways of wickedness during the dominion of falsehood until [20]the time of judgment, shall arise in the world for ever. God will then purify by His truth all the deeds of man and will put in the refining furnace a certain one from among the sons of men. He will banish all spirit of falsehood from [21]his flesh, and purify him of all wicked deeds with the Spirit of holiness."

Text: Shrine Photograph 7104; Trever 67 (= pl. IV); Burrows II col. IV; Lohse 14.

Bo Reicke and William Brownlee have argued that the reference to "a certain one from among the sons of men" is a messianic figure.[16] Appealing to *Tg.* Isa 53:10 and to Qumran's treatment of the Servant passages, Brownlee translates line 20 as follows: "At that time God will purify by His truth all the deeds of a man; and He will refine him more

---

15 Van der Woude, *Die messianischen Vorstellungen*, 165.

16 B. Reicke, *Handskrifterna från Qumrân* [Symbolae Biblicae Upsalienses 14; Uppsala: Wretmans, 1952] 70; W. H. Brownlee, "The Servant of the Lord in the Qumran Scrolls II," *BASOR* 135 (1954) 33-38; idem, "John the Baptist in the New Light of Ancient Scrolls," *Int* 9 (1955) 71-90, esp. 88; idem, *The Meaning of the Qumrân Scrolls for the Bible: With Special Attention to the Book of Isaiah* (Oxford and New York: Oxford University Press, 1964) 206-207.

than the sons of men."[17] By suffering, the Servant Messiah would become refined and able to bring about God's kingdom. Brownlee also appeals to 1QH 3 (see below). He contends that "the challenges to the individual interpretation of [1QS 4:20] are not well founded," concluding that "this passage refers to an anointed prophet, rather than to a royal Messiah."[18] Indeed, Brownlee believes that 1QS 4:20 has conclusively established a messianic interpretation for Isa 52:13-15. Nevertheless, van der Woude strongly disagrees: "Nowhere in this passage is a messianic figure spoken of."[19] But Brownlee and Reicke may be correct. Brownlee's interpretation may receive support from an interesting variant in 1QIsaiah[a], which will be considered below.

8. 1QS 9:9b-11

וכול עצת התורה לוא יצאו ללכת   9

בכול שרירות לבם ונשפטו במשפטים   10

הרשונים אשר החלו אנשי היחד לתיסר בם

עד בוא נביא ומשיחי אהרון וישראל   11

"[9]And they shall not depart from any counsel of the Law to walk [10]in all the stubbornness of their heart, but they shall be governed by the first ordinances in which the members of the community began their instruction, [11]until the coming of the Prophet and the Anointed Ones [משיחי] of Aaron and Israel."

Text: Shrine Photograph 7109; Trever 72 (= pl. IX); Burrows II col. IX; Lohse 32.

Unlike the earlier references in CD, this time we have the plural "anointed ones" of Aaron and Israel. The plural supports the view that CD's singular "messiah of Aaron and of Israel" really does refer to two anointed ones.[20] It is also likely that the two messianic figures found in the *Testaments of the Twelve Patriarchs*, one expected from

---

17   Brownlee, *The Meaning of the Qumrân Scrolls*, 207.

18   Brownlee, *The Meaning of the Qumrân Scrolls*, 209; cf. 145-46.

19   Van der Woude, *Die messianischen Vorstellungen*, 89-96, with quotation from p. 96. See also the notes in Maier, *Die Texte vom Toten Meer*, 2.21. Knibb (*The Qumran Community*, 102-103) believes that the author is using "man" collectively and is speaking of a purified remnant (i.e. the Qumran community).

20   M. Burrows ("The Messiahs of Aaron and Israel (DSD IX,11)," *ATR* 34 [1952] 202-206) rightly interprets CD 12:23–13:1, 19:9-11, and 20:1 in view of the plural "anointed ones" in 1QS 9:9-11. So also van der Woude, *Die messianischen Vorstellungen*, 76-78.

the tribe of Levi and the other expected from the tribe of Judah, correspond to Qumran's "messiahs of Aaron and Israel." More will be said on this below.

In one of the first detailed discussions of 1QS, Brownlee identified the "Prophet" as the Messiah, and the "anointed ones of Aaron" as Qumran's priests and the "anointed ones of Israel" as Qumran's lay members.[21] This interpretation, however, is unlikely.

The most natural interpretation of the passage is that the "anointed of Aaron" is the anticipated rightful High Priest and the "anointed of Israel" is the royal Messiah, probably Davidic, while the "prophet" is in all probability the promised prophet of Deut 18:15-18 (see below for further discussion of this point).[22]

9. 1QSa (= 1Q28a) 2:11-21

[ה]וא [זה מו]שב אנשי השם [קריאי] מועד לעצת היחד אם יו[לי]ד	11
[אל] א[ת] המשיח אתם יבוא [הכוהן] ראש כול עדת ישראל וכול	12
א[חיו בני] אהרון הכוהנים [קריאי] מועד אנושי השם וישבו	13
ל[פניו איש] לפי כבודו ואחר [ישב מש]יח ישראל וישבו לפניו ראש[י]	14
א[לפי ישראל אי]ש לפי כבודו כמ[עמדו] במחניהם וכמסעיהם וכול	15
רשי א[בות הע]דה עם חכמ[י] עדת הקודש] ישבו לפניהם איש לפי	16
כבודו ו[אם לשול]חן יחד יוע[דו] או לשתות הת[י]רוש וערוך השולחן	17
היחד [ומסך ה]תירוש לשתות [אל ישלח] איש את ידו ברשת	18
הלחם ו[התירוש] לפני הכוהן כיא [הוא מ]ברך את רשית הלחם	19
והתירו[ש ושלח] ידו בלחם לפנים ואח[ר יש]לח משיח ישראל ידיו	20
בלחם [ואחר יבר]כו כול עדת היחד א[יש לפי] כבודו	21

"... [11][h]e. [This is the sit]ting of the men of renown [called] to assembly for the council of the community when [God] will have be[got]ten [יוליד] [12]the Messiah [המשיח] among them. [The Priest] shall enter [at] the head of all the congregation of Israel, then all [13][the chiefs of the sons] of Aaron the priests [called] to the assembly, men

---

21   W. H. Brownlee, *The Dead Sea Manual of Discipline: Translation and Notes* (BASORSup 10–12; New Haven: American Schools of Oriental Research, 1951) 35-36 n. 19.

22   Van der Woude, *Die messianischen Vorstellungen*, 75-89; Maier, *Die Texte vom Toten Meer*, 2.32-33; Knibb, *The Qumran Community*, 139-40. For comparisons with other double Messiah traditions (such as Samaritan and Jewish sectarian), see E. Bammel, "Zu 1QS 9, 10f," in Bammel, *Judaica* (WUNT 37; Tübingen: Mohr [Siebeck], 1986) 112-14.

of renown; and they shall sit [14][before him], each according to his rank. And afterwards, [the Mess]iah [משיח] of Israel [shall enter]; and the chiefs of [15][the tribes of Israel] shall sit before him, each according to his rank, according to their [position] in their camps and during their marches; then all [16]the heads of fa[mily of the con-gre]gation, together with the wise me[n of the holy congregation], shall sit before them, each according to [17]his rank. And [when] they gather for the community tab[le], [or to drink w]ine, and arrange the [18]community table [and mix] the wine to drink, let no man [stretch out] his hand over the first-fruits [19]of bread and [wine] before the Priest; for [it is he who] shall bless the first fruits of bread and [20]w[ine, and shall] first [stretch out] his hand over the bread. And after[wards], the Messiah [משיח] of Israel shall [str]etch out his hands [21]over the bread. [And afterwards,] all the congregation of the community shall [bl]ess, ea[ch according to] his rank."

Text: PAM 40.060, 40.062, 40.549, 42.926; DJD 1.110-11, 117-18 (+ pl. XXIV); Lohse 50.

Dominique Barthélemy entitled 1QSa "Règle de la Congrégation" (after the opening words: וזה הסרך לכול עדת ישראל), but Geza Vermes is probably correct to call it "The Messianic Rule," since the text pertains to "the last days" (2:1) and describes the Messiah presiding over the community banquet.[23] 1QSa is apparently related to 1QM and may be describing the community banquet that follows the final victory over the sons of darkness.[24]

Besides lacunae in lines 11 and 12, the left-hand part of the document is badly discolored, making restoration of the text very difficult. As presented in the text above, Barthélemy restores the last word of line 11 to read: "When God will have begotten [יוליד] the Messiah." However, J. T. Milik thinks that the text should read "when God will have brought [יוליך] the Messiah."[25] Shemaryahu Talmon agrees; he translates: "when (God) shall lead to them the (Davidic?)

---

23 DJD 1.108; Vermes 100.
24 See A. Dupont-Sommer, *The Essene Writings from Qumran* (Gloucester: Peter Smith, 1973) 71; DJD 1.108; Vermes 100; J. F. Priest, "The Messiah and the Meal in 1QSa," *JBL* 82 (1963) 95-100. For a recent study of 1QSa, see L. H. Schiffman, *The Eschatological Community of the Dead Sea Scrolls* (SBLMS 38; Atlanta: Scholars Press, 1989).
25 DJD 1.117.

Anointed."[26] Rejecting both of these restorations Geza Vermes has suggested the reading: "when the (Priest) Messiah shall summon [יוֹעִיד] them."[27] Restoring the text differently at several points, H. Neil Richardson proposes the reading: " . . . when [the prophet] will be born [יִוָּלֵד]." The Messiah will go in with them [because he is] the head of all the congregation of Israel."[28]

In my judgment three factors support Barthélemy's original restoration: (1) in the photograph the last letter seems to be a daleth (in any event, it is too short to be a final kaph);[29] (2) most of the scholars who studied the scroll in the early 1950s (when the leather text was in better condition than it is today) were convinced that יוליד was the correct reading;[30] and (3) the controversial restoration is completely in step with Ps 2:2, 7: "The kings of the earth set themselves, and the rulers take counsel together, against the Lord and his Messiah [מְשִׁיחוֹ] . . . He said to me: "You are My son, today I have begotten [יְלִדְתִּיךָ] you." Given the language of Ps 2:2, 7 there is nothing unusual or unexpected

---

26   S. Talmon, "The Concepts of *Māšîaḥ* and Messianism in Early Judaism," in J. H. Charlesworth (ed.), *The Messiah: Developments in Earliest Judaism and Christianity* (Minneapolis: Fortress, 1992) 79-115, esp. 110 n. 73. This reading was eventually accepted by F. M. Cross, *The Ancient Library of Qumran* (Garden City: Doubleday, 1961) 87.

27   Vermes 102; cf. idem, *The Dead Sea Scrolls: Qumran in Perspective* (Philadelphia: Fortress, 1977) 196. Knibb (*The Qumran Community*, 153-54) accepts Vermes's restoration. Schiffman (*The Eschatological Community*, 53-54) reads: אם י[חוע]ד [בעת קץ] המשיח אתם ("when [at the end] (of days) the messiah [shall assemble] with them"). For other proposals, see Maier, *Die Texte vom Toten Meer*, 2.158-59. Van der Woude (*Die messianischen Vorstellungen*, 99) finds the restoration of lines 11-12 so doubtful that he proposes no reading.

28   H. N. Richardson, "Some Notes on 1QSa," *JBL* 76 (1957) 108-22, esp. 116-17.

29   Infrared has confirmed the dalith; cf. Richardson, "Some Notes," 116 n. 53.

30   See J. A. Fitzmyer, "The Aramaic 'Elect of God' Text from Qumran Cave 4," *CBQ* 27 (1965) 348-72; repr. in Fitzmyer, *Essays on the Semitic Background of the New Testament* (London: Chapman, 1971) 127-60, esp. 153 n. 27; J. J. Collins, "The Son of God Text," in M. C. De Boer (ed.), *From Jesus to John: Essays on Jesus and New Testament Christology* (M. de Jonge Festschrift; JSNTSup 84; Sheffield: JSOT Press, 1993) 65-82, esp. 78-79. Barthélemy's restoration has also been accepted by M. Hengel, *The Son of God* (Philadelphia: Fortress, 1976) 44: "when (God) brings it about that the Messiah is born among them."

in restoring 1QSa 2:11-12 to read: "when God will have begotten the Messiah."[31] Accepting and defending Barthélemy's restoration as the original and correct reading, Robert Gordis thinks that the reading in 1QSa was based on Ezek 36:12 אָדָם עֲלֵיכֶם וְהוֹלַדְתִּי (as suggested by the reading presupposed by the LXX: καὶ γεννήσω ἐφ᾽ ὑμᾶς ἀνθρώπους).[32] This is possible, but Ps 2:2, 7 remains the most probable background text.[33]

Various New Testament writings apply this verse to Jesus in a messianic sense (Acts 13:33; Heb 1:5; with possible allusions in Mark 1:11; 9:7; John 1:49; Rom 1:3-4). Outside of Christianity this Psalm was understood in a messianic sense (b. Sukk. 52a; Midr. Ps 2.9 [on Ps 2:7]), possibly as early as the first century (4 Ezra 7:28-29, if the reference to "My son the Messiah" is indeed to Psalm 2). The exegesis in the fragmentary opening lines of 4QFlor may presuppose Ps 2:7, as well as the related 2 Sam 7:11-16 (note their linkage in Heb 1:5).[34] A fourth factor in support of Barthélemy's restoration may be found in the related passages below. Accepting the reading יוליד does not, however, require a literal interpretation. For example, Philip Sigal assumes too much, when he concludes that 1QSa 2:11-15 attests "the idea of a divine conception of the Messiah."[35] What 1QSa attests is not a divine conception, but the confidence that someday God will raise up

---

[31] For a discussion of the problem in general, as well as the specific question of Psalm 2 and 1QSa 2:11-12, see R. Gordis, "The 'Begotten' Messiah in the Qumran Scrolls," VT 7 (1957) 191-94; O. Michel and O. Betz, "Von Gott gezeugt," in W. Eltester (ed.), Judentum Urchristentum Kirche (J. Jeremias Festschrift; BZNW 26; Berlin: Töpelmann, 1960) 2-23; W. Grundmann, "Die Frage nach der Gottessohnschaft des Messias im Lichte von Qumran," in S. Wagner (ed.), Bibel und Qumran: Beiträge zur Erforschung der Beziehungen zwischen Bibel- und Qumranwissenschaft (H. Bardtke Festschrift; Berlin: Evangelische Haupt-Bibelgesellschaft, 1968) 86-111, esp. 100-105.

[32] Gordis, "The 'Begotten' Messiah," 193. The verb in MT Ezek 36:12 is וְהוֹלַכְתִּי.

[33] M. Smith ("'God's Begetting the Messiah' in 1QSa," NTS 5 [1958-59] 218-24) accepts יוליד, but thinks that it refers to an anointed priest or to some other consecrated individual, not to the Messiah.

[34] See D. Goldsmith, "Acts 13:33-37: A Pesher on 2 Samuel 7," JBL 87 (1968) 321-24; G. J. Brooke, Exegesis at Qumran: 4QFlorilegium in Its Jewish Context (JSOTSup 29; Sheffield: JSOT Press, 1985) 209.

[35] P. Sigal, "Further Reflections on the 'Begotten' Messiah," Hebrew Annual Review 7 (1983) 221-33.

a messianic figure.

10. 1QSb (= 1Q28b) 5:20-29

[	למשכיל לברך את נשיא העדה אשר]	20

[ ]תו וברית ה[י] חד יחדש לו להקים מלכות עמו 21
לעול[ם ולשפוט בצדק אביונים]

[ו]להוכיח במי[שר לע]נוי ארץ ולהתהלך לפניו תמים 22
בכול דרכי] [

ולהקים ברי[ת קדשו ב]צר לדורשי[ו י]ש[אכ]ה אדוני לרום 23
עולם וכמגדל ע[ו]ז בחומה

נשגבה ה[כיתה עמים] בעז [פי]כה בשבטכה תחרים ארץ וברוח שפתיכה 24
תמית רשע[ע]ים עם רוח עצ]ה וגבורת עולם רוח דעת ויראת אל והיה 25
צדק אזור [מותניכה ואמונ]ה אזור חלציכה [ו]ישם קרניכה ברזל 26
ופרסותיכה נחושה

תנגח כפ[ר ותרמוס עמ]ים כטיט חוצות כיא אל הקימכה לשבט 27
למושלים לפ[ניכה יקדמו וישתחוו וכול לא]ומים יעובדוכה ובשם 28
קודש[יונברכה

והייתה כא[רי]ה   [כה טרף ואין משי[ב] ופרשו [ק]ליכה על [הארץ] 29

"20. . . for the maskil to bless the Prince [נשיא] of the congregation who [. . .] 21and for whom He will renew the covenant of the community, that he may restore the kingdom of His people for ev[er and judge the poor with justice, 22and] that he may rule with e[quity the hum]ble of the land and walk before Him perfectly in all the ways [of truth . . .] 23and that he may restore [His holy] coven[ant at the time] of the [distress of those who seek (Him)]. May Adonai [rai]se [you] to everlasting heights, and as a forti[fied] tower upon a 24steep wall. And [you shall strike the peoples] by the might of your [mouth]; you shall devastate the earth by your scepter, and by the breath of your lips 25you shall slay the ungodly. [The Spirit of couns]el and eternal might [shall be upon you], the Spirit of knowledge and of the fear of God. 26And righteousness shall be the girdle [of your loins, and faith] the girdle of your haunches. May He make your horns of iron and your hooves of bronze. 27May you toss like a you[ng bull and trample the peo]ples like the mud of the streets. For has established you as a scepter over 28the rulers. [Before you they will stand up and bow down. And all the] nations shall serve you. He shall strengthen you by His holy Name, 29and you shall be as a [lion . . . the] prey which none can bring back; and may your swift ones ride over [the earth]."

Text: PAM 40.069, 40.075, 40.076; DJD 1.127-29 (+ pl. XXIX, frag. 25); Lohse 58.

Set in a context of eschatological blessings,[36] the text alludes to parts of Isa 11:1-5 (cf. lines 21-26), possibly with an allusion to Gen 49:10 (cf. line 24). This passage describes the political Messiah (although only called "Prince" [נשיא]), who will be a great warrior, a guardian of the poor, a man of piety and righteousness. He is expected to anihilate Israel's enemies, usher in the long awaited era of salvation, foretold by the prophets, and compel the nations to serve Israel.[37] On the last line, see 1QM 12:9: "And our horsemen are like the clouds and like the mists of dew which cover the earth."

11. 1QH 3:9-10

9 והרית גבר הצרהבחבליה כיא במשברי מות תמליט זכר
ובחבלי שאול יגיח
10 מכור הריה פלא יועץ עם גבורתו

"9And she who is great with the male child was distressed by her pains, for in the throes of death will she be delivered of a man-child. And with hellish pains 10from the womb (lit. "furnace") of the pregnant woman will break forth a wonderful Counselor with his might."

Text: Shrine Photograph 4239; Sukenik pl. XXXVII; Lohse 122.

The words, פלא יועץ עם גבורתו ("wonderful counselor with his might"), echo the language of Isa 9:5 [E6]: פלא יועץ אל גבור ("wonderful Counselor, mighty God"). But is the passage messianic? The question has been hotly debated. Dupont-Sommer says that the passage "obviously refers to the Messiah," to whom the Community will give birth.[38] Krister Stendahl appears to understand the passage similarly.[39]

---

36 R. Leivestad, "Enthalten die Segenssprüche 1QSb eine Segnung des Hohenpriesters der messianischen Zeit?" *ST* 31 (1977) 137-45; Schiffman, *The Eschatological Community*, 72-76. For parallels, see Maier, *Die Texte vom Toten Meer*, 2.161.

37 Van der Woude, *Die messianischen Vorstellungen*, 116.

38 Dupont-Sommer, *Essene Writings*, 208; idem, "La Mère du Messie et la mère de l'Aspic dans un hymne de Qoumran," *RHR* 147 (1955) 174-88.

39 K. Stendahl, "The Scrolls and the New Testament: An Introduction and a

J. V. Chamberlain also argues for a messianic interpretation.[40] But this interpretation is contested by Lou Silberman.[41] As alluded to above, Brownlee thinks the passage is messianic.[42] Menahem Mansoor doubts the messianic interpretation[43] and van der Woude rejects it outright.[44] Van der Woude concludes that the passage is not messianic, but is descriptive of the time of "messianic woes."[45] He could be correct, but the specific description of the pregnant woman who will give birth to the "Wonderful Counselor" could very well be, all the metaphor notwithstanding, a poetic-prophetic reference to the birth of an expected messianic figure, much as in the reference in 1QSa 2:11-12. On also thinks of Revelation 12, which describes a woman giving birth to a messianic figure.[46]

12. 1QM (= 1Q33) 5:1-2

1   ועל מ[גן] נשיא כול העדה יכתבו שמ[ו ו]שם ישראל ולוי ואהרון ושמות
שנים עשר שבטי ישראל כתול[ד]ותם

2   ושמות שנים עשר שרי שבטידם

"[1]And on the s[taf]f of the Prince [נשיא] of the whole Community they shall write [his] name [and] the names of Israel, Levi, and Aaron, together with the names of the twelve tribes according to their genealogy [2]and the names of the twelve chiefs of their tribes."

Perspective," in Stendahl (ed.), *The Scrolls and the New Testament* (New York: Harper, 1957; repr. New York: Crossroad, 1992) 1-17, esp. 12. See also more recently E. M. Laperrousaz, "Le mère du Messie et la mère de l'Aspic dans les Hymnes de Qumrân: Quelques remarques sur la structure de 1QH III, 1–18," in P. Lévy and E. Wolff (eds.), *Mélanges d'histoire des religions offerts à H. C. Puech* (Paris: Presses universitaires de France, 1974) 173-85.

40   J. V. Chamberlain, "Another Thanksgiving Psalm," *JNES* 14 (1955) 32-41; idem, "Further Elucidation of a Messianic Thanksgiving Psalm from Qumran," *JNES* 14 (1955) 181-82.

41   L. H. Silberman, "Language and Structure in the Hodayot (1QH3)," *JBL* 75 (1956) 96-106.

42   W. H. Brownlee, "Messianic Motifs of Qumran," *NTS* 3 (1956-57) 12-30, 195-210; idem, *Meaning*, 274-81. Brownlee believes that the "man-child" is drawn from Isa 66:7, while the "pregnant woman" is drawn from Isa 7:14.

43   M. Mansoor, *The Thanksgiving Hymns* (Leiden: Brill, 1961) 90-92, 112-13.

44   Van der Woude, *Die messianischen Vorstellungen*, 144-56.

45   Van der Woude, *Die messianischen Vorstellungen*, 156. For additional notes, see Maier, *Die Texte vom Toten Meer*, 2.75-76.

46   See Knibb, *The Qumran Community*, 174-76.

Text: Shrine Photograph 3369; Sukenik pl. XX; Yadin 278-79; Lohse 190.

The passage assumes that the "Prince of the whole Community" is superior to the "twelve chiefs" (cf. 4QpIsa[d] 1:6-7), which only lends support to viewing this Prince [נשיא] as the expected Messiah,[47] and probably the Davidic Messiah at that. Moreover, this Prince is probably to be understood as the Prince described in 1QSb 5:20-29.[48] Writing the names of the twelve tribes also coheres with the expectation expressed in *Pss. Sol.* 17:28 that the Davidic Messiah will "distribute them upon the land according to their tribes." This tradition reflects hopes earlier expressed in Ezekiel, which in 37:15-28 anticipates the reunion of the tribes of Israel, over which "David . . . will be . . . prince [נשיא] forever" (37:25; cf. 34:24).[49]

13. 1QM (= 1Q33) 11:4-9

לכה המלחמה ומאת[כה] הגבורה	4
ולוא לנו ולוא כוחנו ועצום ידינו עשה חיל כיא בכוחכה	5
ובעוז חילכה הגדול כא[שר] הגדתה	
לנו מאז לאמור דרך כוכב מיעקוב קם שבט מישראל	6
ומחץ פאתי מואב וקרקר כול בני שית	
וירד מיעקוב והאביד שריד [מ]עיר והיה אויב ירשה	7
וישראל עשה חיל וביד משיחיכה	
חוי תעודות הגדתה לנו ק[ץ] מלחמות ידיכה להכבד	8
באויבינו להפיל גדודי בליעל שבעת	
גוי הבל ביד אביוני פדותכה [בכו]ח ובשלום לגבורר פלא	9

"4. . . Yours is the battle! From [You] comes the power; [5](the battle) is not ours. Not our might nor the strength of our hands display valor; as You declared [6]to us in former times, 'A star has journeyed from Jacob, a scepter has arisen from Israel; and he shall crush the temples of Moab and overturn all the sons of Seth. [7]And he shall rule from Jacob and shall cause the survivors of the city to perish. And the enemy shall become a conquered land and Israel shall display its valor' [Num 24:17-19]. And by the hand of Your anointed ones [משיחיכה], [8]the seers of things ordained, You have announced to us the

---

47   Van der Woude, *Die messianischen Vorstellungen*, 133-35; Maier, *Die Texte vom Toten Meer*, 2.119.

48   Van der Woude, *Die messianischen Vorstellungen*, 134-35.

49   On the significance of "Prince," as opposed to "King," see van der Woude, *Die messianischen Vorstellungen*, 135.

times of the battles of Your hands, in which You will be glorified in our enemies; in which You will bring down the hordes of Belial, the seven [9]nations of vanity into the hand of the poor whom you have redeemed [by the migh]t and fullness of wonderful power."

Text: Shrine Photograph 3375; Sukenik pl. XXVI; Yadin 310-11; Lohse 204.

In CD 7:20 we are told that the "Scepter" is the prince of the congregation, while the "star from Jacob" is the "seeker of the Law" (i.e. teacher of righteousness). There is no reason to interpret the present passage differently from the others that quote the passage from Numbers 24. That the "scepter" should be understood in terms of a Davidic prince is supported by the reference to David's defeat of Goliath in lines 1-2.[50] Again we have coherence with the targumic tradition (all four principal pentateuch targumim). Regarding line 7, the reference is probably to the Old Testament prophets, e.g. "touch not My anointed ones" (1 Chr 16:22; Ps 105:15; cf. CD 2:12; 6:1; 6Q15 [= 6QD] 3:4).[51]

14. 4QPatrBles (= 4Q252) 5:1-7

[לוא] יסור שליט משבט יהודה בהיות לישראל ממשל	1
[לוא י]כרת יושב בוא לדויד כי המחקק היא ברית המלכות	2
[אל]פי ישראל המה הרגלים עד בוא משיח הצדק צמח	3
דויד כי לו ולזרעו נתנה ברית מלכות עמו עד דורות עולם אשר	4
שמרה [ ] התורה עם אנשי היחד כי	5
[ ] היא כנסת אנשי	6
[הקודש] נתן [	7

"[1]'A monarch will [not] be wanting to the tribe of Judah' [Gen 49:10] when Israel rules, [2][and] a (descendant) seated on it (the throne) will [not] be wanting to David. For 'the (commander's) staff' [Gen 49:10] is the covenant of kingship, [3][and] the 'feet' [cf. Gen 49:11] are [the thou]sands of Israel, 'until' the coming of the Messiah [משיח] of righteousness, the branch of [4]David [צמח דויד]; for to him and to his seed has been given the covenant of kingship over his people for everlasting generations, because [5]he has kept [. . .] the Law together with the men of the community. For [6][. . .] it is the assembly of the

---

50   Pace Maier, *Die Texte vom Toten Meer*, 2.127. Maier thinks that in this instance the interpretation of Numbers 24 is not messianic.

51   So van der Woude, *Die messianischen Vorstellungen*, 123-24.

men of [7][holiness . . .] he gave."

Text: PAM 41.319, 41.584, 41.816, 42.585, 42.609, 43.253, 43.381; Allegro 174-76 (+ pl. I); ER 1289, 1375; EW 87, 89 (+ pl. V); Lohse 246; WA 2.215.

4QPatrBles is in reality the fifth column of a much larger text that may be described as either a pesher on Genesis (WA 2.212: "Pesher Genesis[a]"), a Genesis apocryphon, or a florilegium (EW 77: "A Genesis Florilegium"). It gives evidence of the characteristics of all three. Pesher-like exegesis is plainly evident (4:1-2, 5, 6), yet it appears to be a retelling of certain episodes of Genesis (1:1–2:7 concerns Noah; 2:8–3:8 concerns Abraham; 3:12-13 concerns Jacob; 4:1–6:3 concerns Jacob's blessings upon his sons) and so is an apocryphon of sorts. As does 4QFlor, 4Q252 strings together various Old Testament passages from different contexts (Gen 6:3 in 1:2; Gen 9:25-27 in 2:5-7; Gen 36:12 + Exod 17:14 in 4:1-3; Gen 49:3-4 in 4:3-5), to show how they relate to the story or to the fulfillment of a given verse within the story.

The introduction of a messianic interpretation of Gen 49:10 is little more than a digression and apparently does not represent a major concern of the document as a whole. There is not a hint of messianism anywhere else in this document. The epithets צמח דויד ("branch of David") and משיח הצדק ("Messiah of righteousness") are derived from the Old Testament (cf. Jer 23:5; 33:15; Zech 3:8; 6:12).[52] The promise לו ולזרעו ("to him and to his seed") probably alludes to 2 Sam 7:12 (which is quoted and interpreted in 4QFlor 1:10-13) and is understood to be fulfilled in the appearance of the "branch of David."[53]

15. 4QFlorilegium (= 4Q174 or 4QMidrEsch) 1:7-13, 18-19

7   לפניו מעשי תורה ואשר אמר לדויד ו[הניחו]תי לכה מכול
    אויביכה אשר יניח להמה מכ[ול]
8   בני בליעל המכשילים אותמה לכלותמ[ה ולבלע]מה כאשר באו

---

52   Allegro 175; van der Woude, *Die messianischen Vorstellungen*, 172; Maier, *Die Texte vom Toten Meer*, 2.164.

53   Van der Woude, *Die messianischen Vorstellungen*, 172; Maier, *Die Texte vom Toten Meer*, 2.164; H. Stegemann, "Weitere Stücke von 4QpPsalm 37, von 4Q Patriarchal Blessings und Hinweis auf eine unedierte Handschrift aus Höhle 4Q mit Exerpten aus dem Deuteronomium," *RevQ* 6 (1967-69) 211-17. On כנסת used in positive sense in line 6, see 4QpNah 3 iii 7. On the restoration of אנשי הקודש, see 1QS 5:13; 8:17; 9:8; CD 20:2, 5, 7.

במחשבת [ב]ל[ל"]י[על להכשיל ב]ני

9 א[ן ר] ולחשוב עליהמה מחשבות און למ[סר נ]פש

לבליעל במשגת א[ן ת]מה

10 [ה]גיד לכה יהוה כיא בית יבנה לכה והקימותי את זרעכה אחריכה

והכינותי את כסא ממלכתו

11 [לעול]ם אני [א]ה[ן] יה[ן] לוא לאב והוא יהיה לי לבן הואה צמח דויד

העומד עם דורש התורה אשר

12 [ישב על כסא] בצי[ן בא]חרית הימים כאשר כתוב והקימותי

את סוכת דויד הנופלת היאה סוכת

13 דויד הנופל[ת א]שר יעמוד להושיע את ישראל

18 [למה רגש]ו גויים ולאומים יהג[ו ריק ית]יצבו

[מלכי ארץ ור]ונים נוסדו יחד על יהוה ועל

19 [משיחו פ]שר הדבר [מלכי הגו]יים וה[רגשו על] בחירי

ישראל באחרית הימים

"7. . . . And concerning that which He said to David, 'I [will give] you [rest] from all your enemies' [2 Sam 7:11b]. (This means) that He will give them rest from al[l] 8the sons of Belial who will seek to cause them to stumble that they may destroy them and [swallow] them [up], just as they came with a plot of [Be]l[ia]l to cause the s[ons] of 9ligh[t] to stumble and to devise wicked plots against them, deli[vering] his [s]oul to Belial in their wi[cked] straying. 10'[And] Yahweh [de]clares to you that He will build you a house; and I will raise up your seed after you, and I will establish his royal throne 11[forev]er. I wi[ll be] a father to him and he shall be My son' [2 Sam 7:11c, 12b-c, 13, 14a]. This is the 'branch of David' [צמח דויד] who will stand with the Interpreter of the Law, who 12will sit on the throne in Zion at the end of days; as it is written, 'I will raise up the tent of David which is fallen' [Amos 9:11]. This is the 'fallen tent of 13David' who will stand to save Israel."

"18['Why do] the nations [rag]e and the peoples imag[ine a vain thing? The kings of the earth set] themselves, [and the ru]lers take counsel together against the LORD and against 19[His Messiah' [Ps 2:1-2]. The in]terpretation of the passage (concerns) [the kings of the na]tions who will [rage against] the elect (pl.) of Israel at the end of days . . ."

Text: PAM 42.605, 42.608, 42.623, 43.423, 43.440; Allegro 176-77; DJD 5.53-57 (+ pls. XIX-XX); Lohse 256-58.

In this text we encounter explicit messianic exegesis of 2 Sam 7:11-
14. Nathan's oracle is eschatologized and directly applied to the
"branch of David [צֶמַח דָּוִיד] who will stand with the interpreter of
Torah, who will sit on the throne in Zion at the end of days." Although
alluding to Jer 33:15-17 ("In those days and at that time I cause a
righteous branch [צֶמַח] to spring forth for David [דָּוִד] . . . David shall
never lack a man to sit on the throne"), we are told that all of this will
be in fulfillment of Amos 9:11, a text which Christians understood as
fulfilled in the inclusion of Gentiles into the Church (cf. Acts 15:14-
18).[54] The expectation of this Davidide is quite clear: he is to rule and
save Israel.[55] Column one ends with a quotation of Ps 2:1-2 and its
interpretation. Although little of the interpretation has survived, it is
clear that it concerns the eschatological battle. It is important to note
that in this presentation of the final battle the Messiah evidently plays a
role (which is not clear in 1QM).[56]

16. 4QpIsa[a] (= 4Q161) 7-10 iii 22-29 [= 8-10:17-24 in DJD 5]

[פשר הפתגם על צמח] דויד העומד באח[רית הימים להושיע את]	22
[ישראל ולכלות את או] יבו ואל יסומכנו ב[רוח ג]בורה [[	23
ואל יתן לו כ[סא כבוד נזר ק[ודש] ובגדי ריקמו[ת]]	24
ואל ישים שבט] בידו ובכול הג[וא]י[ם ימשול ומגוג]	25
כו[ל העמים תשפוט חרבו ואשר אמר לוא]	26
[למראה עיניו ישפוט] ולוא למשמע אוזניו יוכיח פשרו אשר	27
[וכאשר יורדהו כן ישפוט ועל פיהם]	28
[עמו יצא אחד מכוהני השם ובידו בגדי]	29

---

54   Amos 9:11 is also treated in a messianic sense in later rabbinic (b. Sanh.
96b-97a) and targumic exegesis.

55   See J. M. Allegro, "Fragments of a Qumran Scroll of Eschatological
Midrashim," JBL 77 (1958) 350-54; Y. Yadin, "A Midrash on 2 Sam VII and Ps I-II
(4 Q Florilegium)," IEJ 9 (1959) 95-98; van der Woude, Die messianischen
Vorstellungen, 172-75; Knibb, The Qumran Community, 260-61.

56   A. Steudel ("4QMidrEschat: 'A Midrash on Eschatology' (4Q174 +
4Q177)," in J. Trebolle Barrera and L. Vegas Montaner [eds.], The Madrid
Qumran Congress: Proceedings of the International Congress on the Dead Sea
Scrolls Madrid 18-21 March, 1991 [STDJ 11; 2 vols., Leiden: Brill, 1992] 2.531-
41) has argued that 4Q174 and 4Q177 are fragments of the two copies of the same
document. She believes that 4Q174 is from the beginning part, while 4Q177 is
from the middle of the document. If she is correct, then the anticipated Davidide of
4Q174 may play a part in the victory over Belial, described in 4Q177 12-13 i 1-11.

"22[The interpretation of the matter concerns the branch of] David, who will appear at the en[d of days to save 23Israel and to exterminate] his [ene]mies. And God will sustain him with [a 'mi]ghty [spirit' (Isa 11:2) . . 24 . . And God will give him a th]rone of glory, a h[oly] crown, and garments of variegated stu[ff . . 25 . . And God will place a scepter] in his hand, and over all the n[ation]s he will rule, and Magog 26[. . . al]l the peoples will his sword judge, and when it says, 'neither 27[will he judge by appearances] nor will he decide on hearsay' [Isa 11:3b], the interpretation of it is that 28[. . .] and as they teach him, so will he judge, and according to their command 29[. . .] with him. One of the priests of repute will go out, and in his hand the garments of . . ."

Text: PAM 41.805, 42.620, 43.431; Allegro 177-81 (+ pls. II-III); DJD 5.11-15 (+ pls. IV-V); Horgan 75-76, 85-86.

Allegro and Horgan restore צמח in line 22, though it could be נצר, as in Isa 11:1. In favor of צמח is its appearance in 4QPatrBles 5:3-4 and 4QFlor 1:11. On the restoration of lines 22-23, see 4QFlor 1:7-13; 1QpHab 13:3; 1QM 11:11; 13:16. The reference in line 25 to placing a "[scepter] in his hand," if restored correctly, is probably an allusion to Gen 49:10. Qumranic exegesis of Gen 49:10 is consistent with what we find in the present text. In the same line "Magog" probably derives from Ezekiel (38:2; 39:6; cf. Gen 10:2). "Gog" is mentioned in 1QM 11:16, where it will be punished by God in the last days (cf. Rev 20:8). Line 28 makes it clear that the expected Davidide will obey the priests. This is in step with what is observed elsewhere: the lay Messiah submits to the priestly Messiah. There is one other allusion that is worth noting briefly: 4QpIsaa 2-6 ii 14 reads "[his] rod" (Isa 10:26), which is probably what is referred to in 2-6 ii 19: "[. . . the rod is] the prince [נשיא] of the community." This interpretation of Isa 10:22–11:5 is completely in step with what is said elsewhere of the Davidic Branch or Prince. The exegesis of 4QpIsaa is thoroughly messianic.[57]

---

[57]   Allegro 181-82; van der Woude, *Die messianischen Vorstellungen*, 180-82; J. Carmignac, "Notes sur les Pesharîm," *RevQ* 3 (1961-62) 505-38, esp. 511-15; J. M. Rosenthal, "Biblical Exegesis of 4QpIs," *JQR* 60 (1969-70) 27-36; J. D. Amousine, "A propos de l'interprétation de 4 Q 161 (fragments 5–6 et 8)," *RevQ* 8 (1974) 381-92.

17. 4QpsDan ar^a (= 4Q246; *olim* 4QpsDan A or 4QpsDan^d) 1:1–2:9

[וכדי דחלה רבהה על]והי שרת נפל קדם כרסיא	1
[אדין אמר למלכא חיי מ]לכא לעלמא אתה רגז ושניך	2
[זיו אנפיך ועלי]בא חזוך וכלא אתה עד עלמא	3
[תמלך ויהוון עבדיך ר]ברבין עקה תתא על ארעא	4
[ולהוה קרב בעממיא] ונחשירין רב במדינתא	5
[די יעבדון גדודי] מלך אתור ומצרין	6
[להוה עמהון ברם אף ברך] רב להוה על ארעא	7
[וכל עממיא שלם עמה י]עבדון וכלא ישמשן	8
[לה והוא בר אל ר]בא יתקרא ובשמה יתכנה	9

ברה די אל יתאמר ובר עליון יקרונה כזיקיא	1
די חזיתא כן מלכותהן תהוה שנ[ין] ימלכון על	2
ארעא וכלא ידשון עם לעם ומדינה למד[ינ]ה	3
vacat עד יקום עם אל וכלא יניח מן חרב	4
מלכותה מלכות עלם וכל ארחתה בקשט ידי[ן]	5
ארעא בקשט וכלא יעבד שלם חרב מן ארעא יסף	6
וכל מדינתא לה יסגדון אל רבא באילה	7
הוא ועבד לה קרב עממין ינתן בידה וכלהן	8
ירמה קדמוהי שלטנה שלטן עלם וכל תחומי	9

". . . [1]\[when great fear\] settled \[u\]pon him, he fell down before the throne. [2]\[Then he said to the king, 'Live,\] O King, forever! You are vexed, and changed [3]\[is the complexion of your face; de\]pressed is your gaze. (But) you shall rule over everything forever! [4]\[And your deeds will be g\]reat. (Yet) distress shall come upon the earth; [5]\[there will be war among the peoples\] and great carnage in the provinces, [6]\[which the bands of\] the king of Assyria \[will cause. And E\]gypt [7]\[will be with them. But your son\] shall be great upon the earth, [8]\[and all peoples sh\]all make \[peace with him\], and they all shall serve [9]him.\] (For) he shall be called \[son of\] the \[gr\]eat \[God\], and by his name shall he be named. [1]He shall be hailed 'Son of God' [ברה די אל], and they shall call him 'Son of (the) Most High' [בר עליון]. Like comets [2]that one sees, so shall be their kingdom. (For some) year\[s\] they shall rule upon [3]the earth and shall trample everything (under foot); people shall trample upon people, province upon \[pro\]vince, [4](*vacat*) until there arises the people of God, and everyone rests from the sword. [5](Then) his kingdom (shall be) an everlasting kingdom, and all his ways (shall be) in truth. He shall jud\[ge\] [6]the land with truth, and everyone shall make peace. The sword will cease from the land,

[7]and all the provinces shall pay him homage. The great God, by his might, [8]shall make war for him. Peoples He shall put in his hand; and all of them [9]He shall cast before him. His dominion (shall be) an everlasting dominion, and all of the territories of [the earth shall be his]!'"[58]

Text: PAM 42.601, 43.236; EW 68-71 (+ pl. IV); J. A. Fitzmyer, "4Q246: The 'Son of God' Document from Qumran," *Bib* 74 (1993) 153-74 (+ pl.).

This fragmentary text describes a prophecy given to a distressed king. He is assured that he will have a son who will be hailed as "Son of God" and that this son will enjoy victory, peace, and an eternal kingdom. But is this royal heir a messianic figure? Many have thought so, but Joseph Fitzmyer, among others, has expressed reservations.

A few points seem to favor a messianic identification of the royal heir. The first is what appear to be parallels with Isa 10:20–11:16, a passage which is interpreted in a messianic sense in at least three other Qumran texts (1QSb 5, 4QpIsa[a], 4Q285) and possibly in others (4QMess ar, 4Q286/287). There are five important parallels between 4Q246 and Isa 10:20–11:16, especially as we find it in the Aramaic: (1) In both passages Assyria and Egypt are viewed as Israel's principal enemies (Isa 10:24; 11:15-16; 4Q246 1:6; cf. 1QM 1:2, 4, where Assyrian and Egyptian enemies are juxtaposed). The targum also interprets Isa 10:20–11:16 eschatologically. (2) Both passages speak of a royal heir who "will judge [ידין] in truth [בקשט]" (*Tg.* Isa 11:4; 4Q246 2:5-6; cf. *Pss. Sol.* 17:26-29, where the anticipated actions of the Davidic Messiah are described in similar terms). (3) Both passages expect the royal heir to bring peace (שלם) to the land (ארעא) (*Tg.* Isa 11:6; 4Q246 2:6; 1:8). (4) Both passages anticipate the submission of the nations to the royal heir (*Tg.* Isa 11:10, 14; 4Q246 2:7; 1:8-9; cf. *Pss. Sol.* 17:21-25, 30, where the Davidic Messiah subjugates Israel's enemies). (5) God, "the mighty God" (Isa 10:21; 4Q246 2:7), is the royal heir's true "might," who will defeat his enemies (*Tg.* Isa 10:33-34; 11:11, 15; 4Q246 2:7-9).

---

58   Translation and reconstruction are based on J. A. Fitzmyer, "The Contribution of Qumran Aramaic to the Study of the New Testament," *NTS* 20 (1973-74) 382-407; repr., in Fitzmyer, *A Wandering Aramean: Collected Aramaic Essays* (SBLMS 25; Missoula: Scholars Press, 1979) 85-113, esp. 92-93 [references are to the reprint]; and idem, "4Q246," 155-57. In a few places I depart from Fitzmyer. I wish to acknowledge the helpful suggestions made by James M. Lindenberger.

A second point that supports the messianic interpretation of 4Q246 is the possible parallel with Ps 89:27-28(E26-27): "He shall cry to Me, 'You are my Father, my God, and the Rock of my salvation.' And I will make him the first-born, the highest of the kings of the earth." These verses hark back to the Davidic Covenant of 2 Samuel 7.

A third indication that 4Q246 may in fact be messianic are the parallels with Luke 1:32-35, which are applied to Jesus as Israel's Messiah. Several phrases in the Lucan angelic announcement parallel the statements in 4QpsDan arᵃ.[59]

Luke	4Q246
οὗτος ἔσται μέγας (1:32)	(1:7) ברך רב להוה
υἱὸς ὑψίστου κληθήσεται (1:32)	(2:1) ובר עליון יקרונה
κληθήσεται υἱὸς θεοῦ (1:35)	(2:1) ברה די אל יתאמר
βασιλεύσει . . . εἰς τοὺς αἰῶνας (1:33)	(2:5) מלכותהה מלכות עלם

A fourth point that supports the messianic interpretation of 4Q246 lies in the fact that in the Synoptic tradition Jesus is called "Son of God" (Matt 4:3, 6; 16:1; Mark 3:11; 15:39) and is addressed as the "Son of the Most High," by the Gerasene demoniac: υἱὲ τοῦ θεοῦ τοῦ ὑψίστου (Mark 5:7; Luke 8:28). In all probability these epithets were understood in a messianic sense and so were applied to Jesus.

Such parallels as these notwithstanding, Fitzmyer resists the inference that the person to whom the Aramaic scroll refers is a messianic figure.[60] In his earlier study he remarked that the "text represents a Jewish composition and that the titles are predicated of some person of Jewish background, possibly historical, but more likely expected. He is not, however, called משיח, an anointed agent of Yahweh."[61] In his more recent treatment of this passage Fitzmyer again concludes that the messianic interpretation is problematic. "The text should be understood as a sectarian affirmation of God's provision and guarantee of the Davidic dynasty. But just as not every king of old who sat on David's throne was given the title 'Messiah,' so too it is not clear that the successor to the enthroned king will necessarily be a Messiah, even though the text grants that he will be 'Son of God' and 'Son of the Most High.' I continue to think that that successor may be a

---

59   Fitzmyer, "Qumran Aramaic," 91-94; idem, *The Gospel According to Luke I-IX* (AB 28; Garden City: Doubleday, 1981) 347-48; idem, "4Q246," 174.

60   Fitzmyer, "Qumran Aramaic," 93, 102-107; idem, *Luke I-IX*, 206.

61   Fitzmyer, "Qumran Aramaic," 93, 102-107; idem, *Luke I-IX*, 206.

son of the enthroned king."[62]

Fitzmyer raises six points that he regards as problematic for the messianic interpretation of 4Q246.[63] Of these only one is pertinent: the fact that the word משיח itself does not appear. The other points raise legitimate questions about assumptions that scholars often bring to this text, but they do not in themselves weaken the case for a messianic interpretation. Although the word "Messiah" does not appear, it seems very probable that talk of an *expected* Jewish person who will be hailed as "Son of God" and "Son of the Most High" is messianic talk of some sort, perhaps along the lines observed in 4QFlor. It is true, as Fitzmyer says, that "not every king of old who sat on David's throne was given the title 'Messiah'," but what is more to the point is that none of the *historical* descendants of David was ever called "Son of God." Not even David himself is explicitly called "Son of God." The two Old Testament passages from which such an idea could be inferred (i.e. 2 Sam 7:11b-16; Ps 2:7) came to be interpreted messianically (at Qumran and elsewhere) and in all probability gave rise to the idea of calling Messiah "Son of God."[64]

4Q246 contains a prophecy of the coming of a royal heir who will be called "Son of God" and "Son of the Most High," who will subdue the Gentiles, who "will judge in truth," and whose kingdom will be eternal. These titles and qualities are ascribed to Jesus, whom first-century Christians regarded as Israel's Messiah. This fact in itself suggests "Son of God" and "Son of the most High" could very well have been messianic titles. Therefore, the messianic interpretation, though admittedly not certain, seems to make the best sense. Recently John Collins has commented that "the messianic interpretation should be preferred."[65] I agree with Collins. If the text does not refer to a

---

62   Fitzmyer, "4Q246," 174.

63   Fitzmyer, "4Q246," 170-74.

64   Other (derivative) passages include Isa 9:5; Ps 89:4-5[E3-4]; 1 Chr 17:13; 22:10; 28:6.

65   Collins, "The *Son of God* Text," 80. Otto Betz has come to the same conclusion; O. Betz, "Spricht ein Qumran-Text vom gekreuzigten Messias?" in O. Betz and R. Riesner, *Jesus, Qumran und der Vatikan: Klarstellungen* (Giessen: Brunnen; Freiburg: Herder, 1993) 103-20, esp. 115-18; ET: "Does a Qumran Text speak of the Crucified Messiah?" in Betz and Riesner, *Jesus, Qumran and the Vatican: Clarifications* (New York: Crossroad, 1994) 83-98, esp. 93-97. See also É. Puech, "Fragment d'une Apocalypse en Araméen (4Q 246 = pseudo-Dan) et le 'Royaume de Dieu'," *RB* 99 (1992) 98-131.

messianic figure, to whom does it refer?

18. 4QMess ar (= 4Q536) 3 i 4-11

בעלימותה להוה כלהון [כאנ]וש די לא ידע מדע[ם עד] עדן די   4
[י]נדע תלתת ספריא   vacat   [   ]   vacat   5
[בא]דין יערם וידע שו[ן]כלא [שן חזון למאתה לה על ארכובת[ה]   6
ובאבוהי ובא[ב]ד]התוהי [ ] חין וקינה עמה לה[ ]ו]ן מלכה וערמומ[ן]ה   7
[ו]ידע רזי אנשא וחוכמתה לכול עממיא תהך וידע רזי כול חייא   8
[וכ]ול חשבוניהון עלוהי יסופו ומסרת כול חייא שגיא תהוא   9
[וימטון כול ח]שבונוהי בדי בחיר אלהא הוא מולדה ורוח נשמוהי   10
[ח]שבונוהי להוון לעלמין [   ]   vacat   11

"[4]In his youth he will become like all of them [. . . like a ma]n who does not know anyth[ing, until] the time when [5]he will have come to know the three books. [6][Th]en he will become wise and will be disc[rete . . .] visions will come to him upon [his] knees (in prayer). [7]And with his father and his forefa[th]ers [. . .] life and old age; he will acquire counsel and prudence, [8][and] he will know the secrets of humankind. His wisdom will spread to all peoples, and he will know the secrets of all living things. [9][Al]l their plans against him will cease, and the opposition of all the living will be great. [10][But all of] his [p]lans [will succeed], because he is the Elect of God [בחיר אלהא]. His birth [מולדה] and the spirit of his breath [. . .] [11]his [p]lans will endure forever . . ."

Text: PAM 43.591; ER 1538; EW 33-37.

In an early publication, Jean Starcky argued that 4Q536 is messianic; and he named it accordingly.[66] But this interpretation has been disputed.[67] Is the בְּחִיר אֱלָהָא a messianic figure? The exact expression

[66]   J. Starcky, "Un texte messianique araméen de la grotte 4 de Qumran," *Ecole des langues orientales anciennes de l'Institut Catholique de Paris: Mémorial du cinquantenaire 1914-1964* (Travaux de l'Institut Catholique de Paris 10; Paris: Bloud et Gay, 1964) 51-66.

[67]   For example, Fitzmyer (*The Dead Sea Scrolls: Major Publications and Tools for Study* [SBLRBS 20; Atlanta: Scholars, 1990] 55) says that the text is "misnamed; it is not messianic." Vermes 305: "It is just as likely, however, that the text alludes to the miraculous birth of Noah." L. H. Schiffman ("Messianic Figures and Ideas in the Qumran Scrolls," in J. H. Charlesworth [ed.], *The Messiah: Developments in Earliest Judaism and Christianity* [Minneapolis: Fortress, 1992] 116-29, esp. 127) has also questioned the messianic interpretation.

does not occur in the Old Testament. But we do find references to
"Moses, his chosen one" (מֹשֶׁה בְחִירוֹ, Ps 106:23), to "my chosen one . . .
David my servant" (דָוִד עַבְדִּי . . . בְחִירִי, Ps 89:4[E3]), and to "my Servant
. . . my chosen one" (עַבְדִּי . . . בְחִירִי, Isa 42:1). Interestingly enough, all
three of these personages—Moses, David, and the Servant of the
Lord—become messianic models in one context or another in subsequent writings and traditions.[68] Nowhere else in the Dead Sea Scrolls
thus far published do we encounter an "elect one." (The plural occurs
twice in reference to the Community itself; cf. 1QpHab 10:13; 4QFlor
1:19.) The singular form, which appears to have a titular function,
occurs several times in the Similitudes of Enoch (i.e. *1 Enoch* 37–71).
But how early is this part of the Enochic tradition? Although I have
little confidence in Milik's suggestion that the work derives from a
second century Jewish Christian, who has intentionally colored *1
Enoch*'s presentation of the Elect One/Son of Man after the traditions
of the New Testament Gospels,[69] the antiquity of the Similitudes
remains an open question. (None of the fragments of this work found
at Qumran belong to this part of the book.) I have to agree with
Fitzmyer in this instance, that in itself the designation "Elect One" is
not a clear indication that 4QMess ar is messianic.[70] Of course, the
references to Jesus as God's "chosen one" (cf. Luke 9:35: ὁ υἱός μου ὁ
ἐκλελεγμένος; John 1:34 [𝔓5vid א* Ambrose]: οὗτός ἐστιν ὁ ἐκλεκτός)
could very well be evidence that a designation such as בְחִיר אֱלָהָא would
have been understood in messianic terms in the first century.[71]
Moreover, the statement in line 8, "His understanding will spread to all
peoples, and he will know the secrets of all living things" (cf. 1 Kgs
4:29-34; Sir 47:12-17), has a Solomonic ring to it that could imply that
the "Elect One" is a son of David.

Perhaps of equal interest is the reference to the "birth" of the figure.

---

68 Elsewhere in the Dead Sea Scrolls we find מושה משיחו, "Moses His
anointed" (4Q377 2 ii 5).

69 J. T. Milik, *Ten Years of Discovery in the Wilderness of Judaea* (SBT 26;
London: SCM, 1959) 33. The problem with Milik's proposal is that there really is
nothing in the *Similitudes* that can be identified as distinctly Christian.

70 Fitzmyer, "The Aramaic 'Elect of God' Text," 152-53.

71 This point remains valid, even if the wording of Luke 9:35 reflects redaction
and the wording of John 1:34 is nothing more than a second-century textual variant.
The point is that these readings indicate that some thought it appropriate to refer to
Jesus, a messianic figure, as God's "elect."

Unfortunately the first two or three words of line 11 are missing, so we do not know what is said about "his birth and the spirit of his breath." Fitzmyer suggests supplying either "are blessed" or "are of God."[72] He finds no difficulty with the latter alternative, in view of 1QSa 2:11-12. I agree. The expression, "spirit of his breath," may be an allusion to Isa 11:4: בְּרוּחַ שְׂפָתָיו. There are other possible points of contact with Isaiah 11. In line 6 this person will gain "knowledge," in lines 7 and 8 he will be endowed with "counsel" and "wisdom." All of these qualities describe the branch of David in Isa 11:2, especially as rendered in the Targum, which is not surprising given its language. The messianic interpretation that the Targum gives to Isaiah 11 (cf. vv. 1, 6), that 4QpIsa[a] 7-10 iii 1-29 apparently gives to Isa 10:33–11:3, and that 1QSb 5:20-29 appears to give Isa 11:1-5 may be significant and may suggest that 4QMess ar is messianic after all.[73]

19. 4QTestimonia (= 4Q175) 1-20

וידבר . . . . אל מושה לאמור שמעת את קול דברי	1
העם הזה אשר דברו אליכה היטיבו כול אשר דברו	2
מי נתן ויהיה לבבם זה לדם לירא אותי ולשמור את כול	3
מצותי כול היומים למעאן יטב לדם ולבניהם לעולם	4
נבי אקים לאהמה מקרב אחידמה כמוכה ונתתי דברי	5
בפיהו וידבר אליהמה את כול אשר אצונו והיה האיש	6
אשר לוא ישמע אל דברי אשר ידבר הנבי בשמי אנוכי	7
אדרוש מעמו	8
וישא משלו ויאמר נאום בלעם בנבעור ונאם הגבר	9
שהתם העין נואם שומע אמרי אל וידע דעת עליון אשר	10
מחזה שדי יחזה נופל וגלו עין אראנו ולוא עתהא	11
אשורנו ולוא קרוב דרך כוכב מיעקוב ויקום שבט מישראל ומחץ	12
פאתי מואב וקרקר את כול בני שית	13

---

[72] Fitzmyer, "The Aramaic 'Elect of God' Text," 153.

[73] It is puzzling why Fitzmyer ("The Aramaic 'Elect of God' Text," 149-50) so quickly dismisses the possibility of allusion to Isa 11:2. It is accepted by J. Carmignac, "Les horoscopes de Qumran," RevQ 18 (1965) 199-217, esp. 214. Fitzmyer suspects that the text may refer to the birth of Noah (as in 1QapGen 2:1-5 and in frag. 1 of 4Q534/536; for additional references, see Fitzmyer, "The Aramaic 'Elect of God' Text," 158-59). However, Fitzmyer has to concede that nowhere is Noah called the "elect of God." Even if the fragment under consideration is concerned with Noah, the ancient worthy may very well have been understood as a messianic type.

וללוי אמר הבו ללוי תמיך ואורך לאיש חסידך אשר   14
נסיתו במסה ותרבהו על מי מריבה האמר לאביו   15
ולאמו לידעתיכהו ואת אחיו לוא הכיר ואת בנו לוא   16
ידע כי שמר אמרתכה ובריתך ינצר ויאירו משפטיך ליעקוב   17
תורת כה לישראל ישימו קטורה באפך לכליל על מזבהך   18
ברך . . . . חילו ופעל ידו תרצה מחץ מתנים קמו ומשנאו   19
בל יקומו   20

"[1]And the LORD spoke to Moses, saying, 'You have heard the words of this people [2]which they have spoken to you. All they have said is good. [3]Oh, if only they could have this same heart to fear me and to keep all [4]my commandments all the days, that it be good for them and for their children, forever!' [Deut 5:28-29]. [5]'I will raise up from among their brethren a prophet like you. I will put my words [6]into his mouth and he shall say all that I will command him. Whoever [7]will not listen to my words which this prophet shall utter in my name, I Myself will [8]call him to account' [Deut 18:18-19]. [9]And he uttered his message and said, 'Oracle of Balaam, son of Beor, and oracle of the man [10]whose eye is clear; oracle of the one who hears the sayings of El, and knows the knowledge of Elyon; who [11]observes the vision of Shaddai, who falls down and his eye is uncovered. I see him, but not now; [12]I watch him, but not near. A star shall march forth from Jacob, and a scepter shall rise from Israel; and it shall crush the [13]temples of Moab and destroy all the sons of Seth' [Num 24:15-17]. [14]And of Levi (Jacob) said, 'Give to Levi your Thummim, and your Urim to your loyal bondsman, whom [15]you tested at Massah, and with whom you strove at the waters of Meribah; who said to his father [16]and to his mother, "I do (not) know you"; and whose brother(s) he did not acknowledge and whose sons he did not recognize. [17]For he kept your words and guarded your covenant; he shall make your judgments clear to Jacob, [18]your Torah to Israel. He shall set incense before you, and a whole burnt offering on your altar. [19]Bless his might, O LORD, and accept the work of his hands. Smite the loins of his adversaries and those who hate him, [20]that they may never rise again' [Deut 33:8-11]."

Text: PAM 40.603, 41.796, 43.757; Allegro 182-87; DJD 5.57-60 (+ pl. XXI); Lohse 250.

Most interpreters have viewed 4QTestimonia as a collection of texts which for the most part were understood messianically.[74] Some have proposed that the quotations correspond to the three eschatological figures of 1QS 9:11 ("the Prophet and the Anointed Ones of Aaron and Israel"): Deut 5:28-29 and Deut 18:18-19 in lines 1-8 apply to the awaited Prophet like Moses (note the paragraph break between lines 8 and 9); Num 24:15-17 in lines 9-13 (again note the paragraphing) apply to the Messiah of Israel; while Deut 33:8-11 in lines 14-20 apply to the priestly Messiah.[75] This is probably correct, but Fitzmyer cautions that things may be a bit more complicated than this.[76]

The opening quotation of Deut 5:28-29 in lines 1-4 is interesting. There is some evidence that suggests that this passage was at times interpreted eschatologically. Although found in a very late source, the following midrash may have some relevance: "[The Lord] said: 'Oh, if only they could have this same heart to fear me and to keep all my commandments all the days' [Deut 5:26(E29)]; and . . . the disciple Moses . . . said: 'Would that all the Lord's people were prophets!' [Num 11:29]. Neither the words of the [Lord] nor the words of the disciple [Moses] are to be fulfilled in this world, but the words of both will be fulfilled in the world to come: The words of the [Lord], 'A new heart also will I give you and you shall keep My ordinances' [Ezek 36:26], will be fulfilled; and the words of the disciple, 'I will pour out My Spirit upon all flesh; and your sons and your daughters shall prophesy' [Joel 2:28], will also be fulfilled" (*Midr. Ps* 14.6 [on 14:7]).[77] In other words, Ezek 36:26 is understood as the specific

---

[74] Vermes 295; van der Woude, *Die messianischen Vorstellungen*, 182; Knibb, *The Qumran Community*, 263-66.The messianic interpretation of this passage has been contested recently by J. Lübbe, "A Reinterpretation of 4QTestimonia," *RevQ* 12 (1985-87) 187-97. But van der Woude ("Fünfzehn Jahre Qumranforschung (1974–1988)," *TRu* 57 [1992] 1-57, esp. 32-33) does not find his objections persuasive. Neither do I.

[75] Vermes 295; van der Woude, *Die messianischen Vorstellungen*, 184; Dupont-Sommer, *Essene Writings*, 317. See also Knibb, *The Qumran Community*, 265-66.

[76] Fitzmyer, "'4QTestimonia'," 84. Fitzmyer notes that in CD 7:18-20 Num 24:17 is applied to two figures, the "Seeker of the Law" and the "Prince of the Congregation." Whereas the latter is probably to be identified as the "Messiah of Israel," the former is probably the Teacher of Righteousness. In my judgment this point does not weaken the three-fold correlation that has been proposed.

[77] Translation based on W. G. Braude, *The Midrash on Psalms* (2 vols., YJS 13; New Haven: Yale University, 1959) 1.186. A similar and much earlier midrash

fulfillment of the wish that God expressed in Deut 5:26 (even as Joel
2:28 is understood as the specific fulfillment of Moses' wish expressed
in Num 11:29). The wishes of God and of Moses "will be fulfilled in
the world to come."

Another indication that Deut 5:28-29 may have been interpreted
eschatologically is its placement, together with Deut 18:18-19, in the
Samaritan Pentateuch between vv. 18(E21) and 19(E22) of Exodus
20.[78] The appearance of Deut 5:28-29 and Deut 18:18-19 (in that
order), precisely as we find these passages in 4QTest is probably more
than coincidence. Indeed, the opening words of line 1, which introduce
the quotation of Deut 5:28-29, agree exactly with the wording found in
Exod 20:18b(E21b) of the Samaritan Pentateuch (but not the
Masoretic Text): וידבר .... אל משה לאמור.[79] Apparently Deut 18:15-19
was a foundational text for the Samaritan doctrine of the *Taheb*
("restorer"), who was expected "to come into the world" and
"announce all things" (John 6:14; 4:25). Besides the explicit quotations
in 4QTest 5-8 and in Acts (3:22-23; 7:37), we may have allusions to
Deut 18:15-19, all from an eschatological perspective, in intertestamental texts (1 Macc 4:46; 14:41; *T. Levi* 8:15; *T. Benj.* 9:2; 1QS
9:11) and in first-century texts (John 1:21, 25; 4:25; 6:14; 7:40;
Josephus, *Ant.* 18.4.1 §85-86). Thus, the linkage with Deut 18:18-19
could suggest that Deut 5:28-29 was also understood eschatologically
and, if we follow the lead of rabbinic interpretation, may have
expressed the hope that in the last days God's people will finally obey
Torah faithfully.

---

is found in *Mek.* on Exod 22:20-23 (*Neziqin* §18) in which Deut 5:26, Isa 66:22,
and Isa 59:20-21 are cited back-to-back, with the concluding comment: "All the
more is it to be expected that in this world your days will be prolonged and you will
live to see children and grandchildren and that you will also merit life in the age to
come."

78   Shortly after Allegro published a portion of 4QTest this was observed by P.
W. Skehan, "The Period of the Biblical Texts from Khirbet Qumrân," *CBQ* 19
(1957) 435-40, esp. 440; cf. R. E. Brown, "Messianism of Qumrân," *CBQ* 19
(1957) 53-82, esp. 82; J. A. Fitzmyer, "'4QTestimonia' and the New Testament,"
TS 18 (1957) 513-37; repr. in Fitzmyer, *Essays on the Semitic Background of the
New Testament*, 59-89. References are to the reprint. For Fitzmyer's comments on
the Samaritan Pentateuch, see p. 83.

79   Skehan, "The Period of the Biblical Texts from Khirbet Qumrân," 435.

20. 4QTanḥumim (= 4Q176) 1-2 i 1-11

[	ועשה פלאכה והצדק בעמכה והי[ו]	1
[	מקדשכה וריבה עם ממלכות על דמ[	2
	ירושלים וראה נבלת כהניכ[ה]	3
ואין קובר ומן סגר ישעיה תנחומים[נחמו נחמו עמי]	4
יומר אלוהיכם דברו על לב ירושלים וק[ראו אליה כיא	5
מלאה צבא[ה] כיא	
נרצה עוונה כיא לקחה מיד • • • • כפלים בכול חטותיהא	6
קול קורה	
במדבר פנו דרך • • • • ישר ב[ערבה] מסלה לאלוהינ[ו]	7
כול גיא ינשא	
[וכול הר וגב]עה ישפלו והיה העקוב למי[שור]	8
והרכסים לב[ק]עה	
[ונגלה כ]בוד • • • • ואתה ישראל עב[די י]עק[ו]ב [אשר	9
ב[חרת]י[כה]	
זרע אבר[הם אהבי אשר חזקתיכה [מקצות] ה[א]רץ ומאצילהא	10
[קראתיכה ואמר] לכה עבדי אתה [בחרתיכה ולוא מאסת]י[ך]	11

"¹And he will accomplish Your miracles and Your righteousness among Your people. And they will [. . .] ²Your sanctuary, and will dispute with kingdoms over the blood of [. . .] ³Jerusalem and will see the bodies of Your priests [. . .] ⁴'and none to bury them' [Ps 79:3]. From the Book of Isaiah: Consolations—'[Comfort, comfort My people], ⁵says your God. Speak to the heart of Jerusalem and c[ry to her that] her [bondage is completed], that ⁶her punishment is accepted, that she has received from the hand of the LORD double for all her sins. A voice cries ⁷in the wilderness: Prepare the way of the LORD; make straight in the desert a highway for our God. Every valley shall be lifted up, ⁸and every mountain and hill be made low; and the uneven ground shall become level, and the rough places a plain. ⁹And the [gl]ory of the LORD [shall be revealed]' [Isa 40:1-3]. 'And you, Israel, [My ser]vant, Jacob [whom I ha]ve chosen, ¹⁰[the seed of Abra]ham, My beloved; you whom I took [from the ends] of the [ea]rth and from its farthest corners ¹¹[I called you, saying] to you, "You are My servant; [I have chosen you and not cas]t [you off]"' [Isa 41:8-9]."

Text: PAM 40.609, 41.309, 41.316, 41.812, 41.813, 42.606, 43.427; DJD 5.60-63 (+ pls. XXII-XXIII); Vermes 302.

Drawing heavily on Isaiah 40–55 4QTanḥumim offers consolation to Jerusalem. It may be implied that the prophetic consolations will be realized following the eschatological battle, to which the opening lines probably make reference. Although no messianic figure is mentioned (unless he is the subject of line 1), the struggle that is anticipated, as well as the implied victory, is consistent with texts in which a messianic figure does play a part. Important to note are such verses as Isa 40:1-3 (1-2 i 4-9), Isa 49:7, 13-17 (1-2 ii 1-6); Isa 43:1-2 (3:1-3); Isa 43:4-6 (4-5 i 1-5); Isa 51:22-23 (6-7 i 1-3); Isa 52:1-3; 54:4-10 (8-11 i 1-17); Zech 13:9 (15:2-5).

21. 11QMelchizedek (= 11Q13) 2:13-20

מיד ב]ליעל	ומלכי צדק יקום נק]מ[ת מש]פ[טי א]ל	13
	ומיד כול] רוחי גורל[ו	
כ]ול	ובעזרו כול אלי [מרומים ה]ואה א[	14
	בני ח]י[ל והפ] [	
	הזואת הואה יום ה]ישועה א[שר אמר [אל עליו ביד	15
	ישע]יה הנביא אשר אמר [מה] נאוו	
	על הרים רגל]י[מבש]ר] משמיע שלום מב]שר טוב	16
	משמיע ישוע]ה אומר לציון [מלך] אלוהיך	
	פשרו ההר]י[ם [דברי] הנביא]ם[המה א]שר [	17
	נב]א[לכול [אבילי ציון]	
מבשר]	המבשר הו]אה מ]שיח הרו]ח[אשר אמר דנ]יאל	18
[	טוב משמי]ע ישועה] הואה הכ]תו[ב עליו אשר [אמר	19
	לנח]ם[א]בילי ציון] ל]ה]שכילמה בכול קצי הע]ו[לם	20

"13And Melchizedek will avenge with the vengeance of the judgments of Go[d . . . from the hand of Be]lial and from the hand of all [the spirits of] his [lot.] 14And to this help are all the heavenly ones [on high.] He [. . .] all sons of might and [. . .] 15this. This is the day [of salvation about w]hich [God] spoke [through the mouth of Isa]iah the prophet who said: '[How] beautiful 16upon the mountains are the feet of him who brings good news, who announces peace, who brings glad tid[ings of good, who proclaims salva]tion, who says to Zion: Your Heavenly One is [King]' [Isa 52:7]. 17Its interpretation (is this): The mount[ai]ns are [the words] of the prophet[s], those w[ho . . .] proph[esied] to all [those who mourn in Zion.] 18'And he who brings good news'—th[is is the Me]ssiah [(מ)שיח)] of the Spir[it], of whom Dan[iel] speaks [. . . 'He who brings glad tidings] 19of good, who

proclaim[s salvation]'—that is what is written concerning him, when
He speaks [. . .] ²⁰to 'com[fort those who] m[ourn in Zion] to
[in]struct them in all the ages of the wo[rld]."

Text: PAM 43.979; A. S. van der Woude, "Melchisedek als himmlische Erlöser-
gestalt in den neugefundenen eschatologischen Midraschim aus Qumran Höhle XI,"
OTS 14 (1965) 354-73 (+ pls. I-II); M. de Jonge and A. S. van der Woude, "11Q
Melchizedek and the New Testament," *NTS* 12 (1966) 301-26.

11QMelchizedek is made up of fourteen fragments, from which
most of one column can be restored along with a few words from two
other columns.[80] In important ways it resembles 4QFlorilegium. In the
opening lines parts of Lev 25:9-13 and Isa 61:1-3 are quoted or alluded
to and presented from an eschatological perspective (line 4: "Its
meaning for the end of days concerns the captives"; line 7: "In the year
of the last jubilee"; line 9: "Melchizedek's year of favor"; line 13: "will
avenge with the vengeance of the judgments of God"; line 17: "all those
who moun in Zion"; line 20: "to comfort those who mourn in Zion").
The principal passage seems to be Lev 25:9-13, parts of which are
quoted at the beginning (lines 2 and 6) and end (line 26), with Isa 61:1-
2 running like a thread throughout most of the column (see lines 4, 6,
9, 13, 18). Another important passage is Isa 52:7, which along with Isa
61:1-2, is alluded to in 1QH 15:15, 18:14-15, and 4Q521 (see below
for discussion of this text).

Leaving aside the interesting question of the precise identity and
function of the figure called "Melchizedek,"[81] the identification of the

---

80 The difficulties involved in the restoration of this fragmentary text (the relationship of the fragments, what belongs to which column, etc.) are notorious. See
J. A. Fitzmyer, "Further Light on Melchizedek from Qumran Cave 11," *JBL* 86
(1967) 25-41; J. Carmignac, "Le document de Qumran sùr Melkisedeq," *RevQ* 7
(1970) 343-78; J. T. Milik, "Milkî-ṣedeq et Milkî-reša' dans les anciens écrits juifs
et chrétiens," *JJS* 23 (1972) 95-144, esp. 96-109, 124-26; J. A. Sanders, "The Old
Testament in 11Q Melchizedek," *JANESCU* 5 (1973) 373-82; F. L. Horton, *The
Melchizedek Tradition* (SNTSMS 30; Cambridge: Cambridge University Press,
1976) 64-82; P. J. Kobelski, *Melchizedek and Melchireša'* (CBQMS 10;
Washington: Catholic Biblical Association, 1981) 3-23; E. Puech, "Notes sur le
manuscrit de XIQMelkîsédeq," *RevQ* 12 (1985-87) 483-513; G. J. Brooke,
"Melchizedek (11QMelch)," *ABD* 4 (1992) 687-88. N.B. What Kobelski and
others identify as column 2, Fitzmyer and others at one time identified as column 1.

81 Van der Woude ("Melchisedek als himmlische Erlösergestalt," 366-73)
identifies Melchizedek as Michael, an identification which may receive support from

"herald" of Isa 52:7 as the "Messiah," possibly of Dan 9:25, calls for attention. In his initial publication of the text, van der Woude restored line 18 to read: המבשר הו[אה המ[שיח הוא[ה] אשר אמר ד[נ ("the 'herald' is that Messiah of whom (?) speaks"),[82] which is followed by Fitzmyer.[83] In a subsequent publication co-authored with Marinus de Jonge, van der Woude restored the fourth word to read הרו[ח].[84] With the last word restored to דניאל, the line now reads: המבשר הו[אה מ[שיח הרו[ח] אשר אמר דנ[י]אל ("the 'herald' is the Messiah of the Spirit, of whom Daniel speaks"). If the second restoration is correct, then the text may have intended to identify the herald as the one anointed by the Spirit of Isa 61:1,[85] as well as the messianic figure of Daniel 9.

There is evidence that Jesus may have thought of himself as the one "anointed" of the Spirit of Isaiah 61. The text is alluded to in his reply to John the Baptist (Matt 11:2-6 = Luke 7:18-23) and is formally quoted in the Nazareth Sermon (Luke 4:18-19). Whereas the latter passage is problematic, given Luke's reworking of the tradition (cf. Mark 6:1-6), the former passage rests on reasonably firm ground.[86] The early Church's failure to exploit Isa 61:1-2 for its christology (with the possible exception of the Lucan evangelist—whose interest at this point is concerned more with election theology than it is with christology) adds to the probability that the utterance of Matt 11:5-6 =

---

similar identification in late rabbinic tradition (cf. *b. Ḥag.* 12b; *b. Šeb.* 62a); but for some misgivings, see Fitzmyer, "Further Light on Melchizedek," 32.

82   Van der Woude, "Melchisedek als himmlische Erlösergestalt," 358.

83   Fitzmyer, "Further Light on Melchizedek," 27.

84   M. de Jonge and A. S. van der Woude, "11Q Melchizedek and the New Testament," *NTS* 12 (1965-66) 301-26, esp. 302. For the restoration of דניאל, see Fitzmyer, "Further Light on Melchizedek," 27, 40.

85   Proposed by Y. Yadin, "A Note on Melchizedek and Qumran," *IEJ* 15 (1965) 152-54, and accepted by de Jonge and van der Woude, "Melchizedek and the New Testament," 306-307; M. P. Miller, "The Function of Isa 61:1-2 in 11Q Melchizedek," *JBL* 88 (1969) 467-69; Kobelski, *Melchizedek*, 6, 21. Miller's essay is helpful for appreciating the interpretive role that Isa 61:1-2 plays in 11QMelchizedek. The linkage of Isa 52:7 with 61:1-2 would have been facilitated by the common key word מבשר.

86   R. Bultmann, *The History of the Synoptic Tradition* (Oxford: Blackwell, 1972) 110; B. F. Meyer, *The Aims of Jesus* (London: SCM, 1979) 157; A. E. Harvey, *Jesus and the Constraints of History* (London: Duckworth, 1982) 140-53; D. C. Allison and W. D. Davies, *The Gospel According to Saint Matthew* (3 vols., Edinburgh: T. & T. Clark, 1988-) 2.244-46.

Luke 7:22-23 does indeed derive from Jesus.

Nor does the New Testament explicitly identify Jesus as the herald of Isa 52:7. Indeed, Paul applies the passage (in the plural) to the apostles of Christ (Rom 10:15). At best we have allusions to this passage in later traditions that possibly make this identification (cf. Acts 10:36; Eph 2:17; 6:15). If Isa 52:7 played a role in Jesus' self-understanding—and the saying about not bringing peace (Matt 10:34) may in some way allude to it[87]—it probably was linked to Isa 61:1-2, perhaps in some sense as we see these texts linked in 11QMelchizedek.[88]

Daniel Miner's proposed restoration of line 17 (which was not followed above) could also have significance for Jesus research. He detects in this line an allusion to Isa 56:7 and so restores as follows:[89]

פשרו ההר [אשר אמר] הביאו[תי]המה א[ל הר קדשי כיא בית]
תפ[ ]לה] לכול [העמים יקרא]

Its interpretation: "the mountains," of which He says, "I will bring them to

---

[87]   If this saying does indeed derive from Jesus, the original point may have been to question popular assumptions concerning the implications of the peace announced by Isa 52:7.

[88]   Rabbi Yohanan is said to have identified the "herald" of Isa 52:7 as the Messiah (*Pesiq. R.* 15.14/15 = *Pesiq. R. Kah.* 5.9). In *Pesiq. R.* 35.4 the herald is Elijah who appears three days before the appearance of the Messiah; in *Lev. Rab.* 9.9 (on 7:11-12) Messiah will bring peace, as seen in Isa 52:7. In *Pesiq. R. Kah.* Supplement 5.4 the herald is identified variously as Moses, Isaiah, or David.

The targumic rendering of Isa 52:7 ("the kingdom of your God is revealed"), as well as the targumic interpretation of and way of speaking about the kingdom of God in all probability have relevance for understanding Jesus' proclamation of the kingdom; cf. B. D. Chilton, "Regnum Dei Deus Est," *SJT* 31 (1978) 261-70; idem, *God in Strength: Jesus' Announcement of the Kingdom* (SNTU 1; Freistadt: Plöchl, 1979; repr. BibSem 8; Sheffield: JSOT Press, 1987) 89; idem, *The Glory of Israel: The Theology and Provenience of the Isaiah Targum* (JSOTSup 23; Sheffield: JSOT, 1982) 77-81. On the relevance of 11QMelchizedek for Jesus research, see also D. E. Aune, "A Note on Jesus' Messianic Consciousness and 11Q Melchizedek," *EvQ* 45 (1973) 161-65; O. Betz, "Jesus' Gospel of the Kingdom," in P. Stuhlmacher (ed.), *The Gospel and the Gospels* (Grand Rapids: Eerdmans, 1991) 53-74, esp. 58-60. According to Betz: "But did *Jesus himself* understand himself to be a מבשר in the sense of the [Isa 52:7 and 61:1-2]? I believe one can confidently answer Yes" (p. 59). Betz also notes the importance of the Targum's rendering of Isa 52:7.

[89]   D. F. Miner, "A Suggested Reading for 11Q Melchizedek 17," *JSJ* 2 (1971) 144-48, esp. 145.

My holy mountain, for my house will be called a house of prayer for all peoples."

If Miner's restoration is correct,[90] then we have another important point of agreement with dominical tradition. According to Mark 11:17, Jesus quoted part of Isa 56:7 and alluded to Jer 7:11, when he took action in the Temple: "My house will be called a house of prayer for all the nations, but you have made it a 'cave of robbers'."

The appearance together of Isa 61:1-2 and Isa 56:7 in 11QMelchizedek may clarify an important feature of Jesus' ministry and suggest in what sense he acted within the Temple precincts. It is possible that as the herald of Isaiah 61 Jesus challenged the Temple establishment to prepare itself for the fulfillment of Isa 56:7, when all nations come to Jerusalem to worship.

22. 1QIsaiah[a]

1QIsa[a] 42:18-19 (= Isa 51:4-5)

4   [18]Listen to Me, My people,
         and give ear to Me, My nation;
      For Law proceeds from Me,
         and My just rule for a light to the peoples.
5   [19]I speed My vindication ever nearer,
         My Salvation has gone forth,
         and *his* arms will rule the peoples;
      Far shores wait for *him*,
         and for *his* arm they hope.

1QIsa[a] 44:1-4 (= Isa 52:14-15)

14   [1]As many were astonished [2]at you—
         I so anointed his appearance beyond anyone (else),
         and his form beyond that of (other) sons of men—
15   [3]So shall he *sprinkle* many nations *because of himself*,
         and kings shall shut their mouths;
      For that which [4]had not been told them they have seen,
         and that which they had not heard they have understood.

---

90   Kobelski (*Melchizedek*, 6, 20-21) restores the line as presented in the text above. With some hesitation, Sanders ("The Old Testament in IIQ Melchizedek," 374-75) follows Miner.

1QIsaᵃ 50:23-26 (= Isa 62:10-12)
10   ²³Pass out through the gates,
          clear the way for the people.
       Build up, build up the highway;
          free it from stones *of stubbing.*
       Say ²⁴*among* the peoples:
11   "Behold, the Lord!"
       Summon him to the end of the earth;
          say to Maiden Zion:
       ²⁵"Look! your Salvation has come.
          See, his reward is with him.
12   They shall be called the Holy People,
          the Redeemed of the Lord;
       and you ²⁶shall be called Sought Out,
          a city not deserted."

Text: Shrine Photographs 7042, 7044, 7050; Trever 49, 51, 57 (= pls. XLII, XLIV, L); Burrows I cols. XLII, XLIV, L.

W. H. Brownlee and J. V. Chamberlain have argued that in a few instances the text of 1QIsaiahᵃ has been messianized.[91] In the first passage Brownlee believes that the shift from the first person to the third person in 1QIsaᵃ 42:18-19 (= Isa 51:4-5) is intended to introduce the Servant of the Lord. "My Salvation" is to be understood as the Servant, whose "arms will rule the peoples." In the second passage, Brownlee argues that the reading משחתי in 44:2 (= Isa 52:14) represents a deliberate substitution of "anointed" (מְשַׁחְתִּי) for "marred" (MT: מִשְׁחַת). The idea of being "anointed more than anyone else" may be paralleled in Ps 45:8[E7]: "Therefore God, your God has anointed you with the oil of gladness more than your fellows." Brownlee concludes that this variant "would seem to indicate the sect's belief that the highest embodiment of the Servant of the Lord would be the Messiah."[92] The fact that both Isa 52:13–53:12 and Psalm 45 are interpreted messianically in the Targum[93] lends a measure of support

---

91   W. H. Brownlee, "The Servant of the Lord in the Qumran Scrolls I," *BASOR* 132 [1953] 8-15, esp. 9; idem, *Meaning*, 193-215, 292-96; J. V. Chamberlain, "Functions of God as Messianic Titles in the Complete Qumran Isaiah Scroll," *VT* 5 (1955) 366-72, esp. 369 n. 1.
92   Brownlee, "The Servant of the Lord," 10.
93   *Tg.* Isa 52:13: "Behold, my Servant, the Messiah, shall prosper, he shall be

to Brownlee's interpretation. In the third passage, Brownlee suspects that השמיעו (MT: הִשְׁמִיעַ) should be vocalized as הִשְׁמִיעוֹ, so that it would read: "Behold, the Lord has summoned him," that is, the messianic Servant, who, as in the first passage, is called "My Salvation" (50:25 = Isa 62:11).

Not too many have followed Brownlee and Chamberlain. The textual variants are open to other interpretations. Van der Woude, for example, believes that 1QIsaª 44:1-4 should be understood in a collective sense.[94]

Summary

On the basis of these texts[95] scholars have summarized Qumran's

---

exalted and increase, and shall be very strong"; *Tg.* Ps 45:3: "Your beauty, O King Messiah, surpasses that of ordinary men. The spirit of prophecy has been bestowed upon your lips; therefore, the Lord has blessed you forever."

94   Van der Woude, *Die messianischen Vorstellungen*, 165-69.

95   In his survey van der Woude discusses numerous passages under the heading, "the messianic texts of Qumran." He cites the following, which I have not included in my listing: (1) Concerning CD 2:2-13 it is the reference to anointed prophets in line 12 that makes this passage "messianic": "And He made known to them His holy Spirit by the hand of His anointed ones [משיחו, which should probably read משיחי] and He showed the truth" (2:12-13). The reading is admittedly difficult, but the context makes it clear that the reference is to the prophets, not to a messianic figure. After a detailed discussion of the debate surrounding this passage, van der Woude (*Die messianischen Vorstellungen*, 20) rightly concludes that CD 2:12-13 makes no contribution to Qumran's messianology. (2) In CD 5:15-6:3 we find a reference to the "anointed ones": "the land was ravaged because they preached rebellion against the commandments of God given by the hand of Moses and of His holy anointed ones [משיחו, which again should probably read משיחי]" (5:21-6:1). Again van der Woude (*Die messianischen Vorstellungen*, 27) rightly concludes that the reference is to the pre-exilic prophets and so has nothing to offer to our understanding of Qumran's messianic ideas. On the plural as the right reading, see van der Woude, *Die messianischen Vorstellungen*, 165. (3) Van der Woude (*Die messianischen Vorstellungen*, 126-33) also discusses various passages concerned with the "chief priest" who conducts the war (e.g. 1QM 13:1-2; 15:4-8; 16:11-14; 18:3-6; 19:9-13). He points out (p. 129) that the mere fact that in 1QM no mention is made of the Davidic Messiah at the time of the final battle, but rather extensive mention is made of the "High Priest" (as in the forementioned passage), is evidence of the high regard the Community had for the priestly Messiah: "The Aaronide is vastly superior to the Davidide." It also shows to what extent the Community interpreted the final battle as a sacral act. Nevertheless, according to 4Q285 5:4-5 the "Prince of the Community" will take part in the final battle against

messianic expectation in terms of diarchy, that is, a joint rule shared by a priestly Messiah, the "anointed of Aaron," and a Davidic Messiah, the "Anointed of Israel."

There is nothing novel about Qumran's messianic diarchy; it has its roots in the Old Testament (esp. MT and *Tg.* Zech 3:6-10; 6:9-15; cf. juxtaposition of Aaron/Israel, e.g. Ps 115:9-10, 12; 118:3; 135:19)[96] and probably is the presupposition of the *Testaments of the Twelve Patriarchs.* It is not necessary to conclude, as did R. H. Charles, that the *Testaments* exhibit two competing messianologies—one priestly (of Levi), the other Davidic (of Judah).[97] Rather, the *Testaments* reflect the diarchic understanding as it arose in the intertestamental period.[98]

---

the Kittim. 4Q376 1 iii 1-3 prescribes the actions of the "Prince of all the Community" during a time of war. But the text may not be eschatological. (4) Another passage speaks of the "valiant man of battle [גבור המלחמה]" and "man of glory [איש כבוד]" (1QM 12:9-10). The reference is not to a human messianic figure, but to God himself (cf. Exod 15:3, where we are told that "Yahweh is a man of war [איש מלחמה יהוה]"). Van der Woude (*Die messianischen Vorstellungen,* 139) rightly rejects the passage as having messianic meaning. (5) Brownlee ("The Incarnation in the Light of Ancient Scrolls," *The United Presbyterian* 113.5 [1955] 12-13, 15) understands 1QM 17:5b-9 in a messianic sense: "He will send final assistance by the power of the great angel to the lot whom He has redeemed, and to the servant of Michael in the midst of the gods, and the dominion of Israel shall be over all flesh" (p. 12). Brownlee's translation and interpretation are questionable. I have to agree with van der Woude (*Die messianischen Vorstellungen,* 144) that the passage is not messianic, but only describes Michael's role in the final eschatological battle. (6) Van der Woude (pp. 157-65) also discusses passages in 1QpHab (e.g. 5:1-6, which speaks of God's "elect," but the noun should probably be understood as a singular; 8:1-3; 8:13–9:2; 9:9-12, where if "elect" be singular in these cases, it probably refers to the Teacher of Righteousness; 11:2-6). They either refer to the Teacher of Righteousness or to the community as a whole.

96   See the essay by P. D. Hanson, "Messiahs and Messianic Figures in Proto-Apocalypticism," in Charlesworth (ed.), *The Messiah,* 67-75, esp. 69-71; cf. J. J. M. Roberts, "The Old Testament's Contribution to Messianic Expectation," in Charlesworth (ed.), *The Messiah,* 39-51, esp. 50.

97   R. H. Charles, "The Testaments of the Twelve Patriarchs," in Charles (ed.), *The Apocrypha and Pseudepigrapha of the Old Testament* (2 vols., Oxford: Clarendon, 1913) 2.294. Charles believed that the Levitical Messiah was advocated by the original author of the *Testaments* (cf. *T. Reub.* 6:7-12; *T. Levi* 8:14; 18:1-14; *T. Dan* 5:10-11). After the ḥasidim (early Pharisees, as Charles understood them) broke with the Hasmoneans, a later editor championed a Judahite Messiah (cf. *T. Judah* 24:5-6; *T. Naph.* 4:5).

98   See esp. Kuhn's essay, "The Two Messiahs," 57-58; Vermes, *The Dead*

Side by side a royal descendant of David and a Zadokite high priest would rule over restored Israel. It is has been suggested that the emphasis of the two messiahs, one of Aaron and one of Israel, may have originated as a corrective of the merger of the high priestly and royal offices during the Hasmonean period.[99]

Qumran's diarchic perspective may entail more than its messianic views; it may have to do with the community's interpretation of its origin, as reflected in CD 1:5-7: "And in the age of (his) wrath . . . he remembered them and caused the root [שורש] he had planted to sprout [ויצמח] (again) from Israel and Aaron." This probably alludes to Ezek 17:6: "And (the twig) sprouted [ויצמח] and became a low spreading vine, and its branches turned toward him, and its roots [ושרשיו] remained where it stood. So it became a vine, and brought forth branches and put forth foliage." As the context seems to suggest, the passage is referring to the founding of the community. This restored plant, "from Israel and Aaron," will provide the environment out of which the "anointed ones of Aaron and Israel" will spring forth. Talmon rightly comments that the messianic dualism developed later in the document is mirrored here.[100] "Roots" and "sprout" recall passages which became part of the messianic stock, e.g. Isa 11:1: "There shall come forth a shoot from the stump of Jesus, and a branch shall grow out of his roots [ומשרשיו]"; and probably also Isa 53:2: "For he grew up before him like a young plant [וכשרש], and like a root out of dry ground . . ." (see also Jer 33:15; Zech 3:8; 6:12).

But difficulties attend any attempt to summarize or synthesize the messianology of Qumran. Lawrence Schiffman has reminded us of an important caveat concerning the "definition of the corpus to be studied."[101] Not everything found in the Judean desert necessarily reflects Qumran's view. Some ideas may reflect "minority opinions."

Sea Scrolls: Qumran in Perspective, 184-86, 194-97; Fitzmyer, "The Aramaic 'Elect of God' Text," 129-40; S. Talmon, "Waiting for the Messiah: The Spiritual Universe of the Qumran Covenanters," in J. Neusner et al. (eds.), *Judaisms and their Messiahs at the Turn of the Christian Era* (Cambridge and New York: Cambridge University Press, 1987) 111-37, esp. 122-31; idem, "The Concepts of Māšîaḥ," 101-103; Schiffman, "Messianic Figures," 118-29.

99   For this view, see A. Hultgård, *L'Eschatologie des Testaments des Douze Patriarches* (2 vols., Stockholm: Almquist & Wiksell, 1977) 1.60-69.

100   Talmon, "The Concepts of Māšîaḥ," 105.

101   Schiffman, "Messianic Figures," 116-17.

Some ideas may have been widely held at different periods in the history of the community. For example, in the case of 1QS 9:9-11, which speaks of "Messiahs," the passage is not found in what is regarded as the oldest copy of the Scroll of Rules. Schiffman well illustrates the diversity (and relative paucity) of messianic views at Qumran. We cannot therefore expect a coherent, unified doctrine. But the corpus of materials should play a restraining role. Whereas there may very well be a diversity of opinions, options that are widely out of step with the corpus as a whole should be viewed with suspicion, especially if poorly attested (i.e. based on restored text or on speculations of historical background). We must be prepared to accept the fact that we cannot tie together all the loose ends.[102] What contribution the recently published messianic texts may make will now be considered.

II. RECENTLY PUBLISHED MESSIANIC TEXTS FROM QUMRAN

23. 4Q521 1 ii 1-14

‏השׁ[מים והארץ ישמעו למשיחו‎ [	1
‏וכל א[שר בם לוא יסוג ממצות קדושים‎ [	2
‏התאמצו מבקשי אדני בעבדתו‎ *vacat*	3
‏הלוא כזאת תמצאו את אדני כל המיחלים בלבם‎	4
‏כי אדני חסידים יבקר וצדיקים בשם יקרא‎	5
‏ועל ענוים רוחו תרחף ואמונים יחליף בכחו‎	6
‏יכבד את חסידים על כסא מלכות עד‎	7
‏מתיר אסורים פוקח עורים זוקף כ[פופים]‎	8
‏ל[עו]לם אדבק [בו]שלים ובחסדו [אבטח‎ [	9

---

[102] One of the loose ends in Qumran research concerns the myterious Teacher of Righteousness. Who this person was and what, if anything, he had to do with the founding of the Community, continues to be debated. In 1982 Philip Davies proposed that the "teacher of righteousness" was a messianic title (*The Damascus Covenant*, 119-25). Although the suggestion has its attractions, it does not carry conviction; cf. M. A. Knibb, "The Teacher of Righteousness—A Messianic Title?" in P. R. Davies and R. T. White (eds.), *A Tribute to Geza Vermes: Essays on Jewish and Christian Literature and History* (JSOTSup 100; Sheffield: JSOT Press, 1990) 51-65. Earlier van der Woude (*Die messianischen Vorstellungen*, 165) had concluded that the historical Teacher of Righteousness is not "a messianic figure ... rather he is the priest-prophet 'to whom God made known all the mysteries of the words of His servants the prophets' (1QpHab 7:4-5), the second Moses, the preparer of the way of the two Messiahs, but he is not himself a Messiah."

[   ] חקדש לוא יתאחר [וט]ובו   10
[   ] ונכבדות שלוא היו מעשה אדני כאשר י[11
                      אז ירפא חללים ומתים יחיה ענוים יבשר   12
קד]ושים ינהל ירעה [ב]ם יעשה   [ש]   [   ]   13
[   ]וכלו כ[   ]   14

"¹[. . . the hea]vens and the earth will obey His Messiah, ²[. . . and all
th]at is in them. He will not turn aside from the commandments of the
holy ones. ³Take strength in His service, (you) who seek the Lord.
⁴Will you not find the Lord in this, all you who wait patiently in your
hearts? ⁵For the Lord will visit the pious ones, and the righteous ones
He will call by name. ⁶Over the meek His Spirit will hover, and the
faithful He will restore by His power. ⁷He will glorify the pious ones
on the throne of the eternal kingdom. ⁸He will release the captives,
make the blind see, raise up the do[wntrodden.] ⁹For[ev]er I shall
cling to Him . . .], and [I shall trust] in His lovingkindness, ¹⁰and [His]
goo[dness . . .] of holiness will not delay [. . .] ¹¹And as for the
wonders that are not the work of the Lord, when He [. . .] ¹²then he
will heal the slain, resurrect the dead, and announce glad tidings to
the poor. ¹³[. . .] He will lead the [hol]y ones; he will shepherd
[th]em; he will do [. . .] ¹⁴and all of it . . ."

Text: PAM 43.604; ER 1551; EW 19-23 (+ pl. I).

4Q521 has aroused considerable interest.[103] The opening statement
that the "heavens and earth will obey [or hear] His Messiah" (1 ii 1) and
the allusions to Isa 61:1, which parallel dominical tradition, are the
principal features. According to this text, "He will release the captives,
make the blind see, raise up the downtrodden . . . then he will heal the
slain [or sick], resurrect the dead, and announce glad tidings to the
poor" (1 ii 8, 12). The references to healing the slain (or sick) and
raising the dead cohere with a saying found in Q, as the following
columns illustrate:

---

[103] See R. H. Eisenman, "A Messianic Vision," *BARev* 17.6 (1991) 65; E.
Puech, "Une Apocalypse messianique (4Q521)," *RevQ* 15 (1992) 475-519; M. O.
Wise and J. D. Tabor, "The Messiah at Qumran," *BARev* 18.6 (1992) 60-65; Betz,
"Spricht ein Qumran-Text vom gekreuzigten Messias?" 111-15; ET: "Does a
Qumran Text speak of the Crucified Messiah?" 90-93; J. J. Collins, "The Works of
the Messiah," *DSD* 1 (1994) 98-112.

Q (Matt 11:5 = Luke 7:22)	Isaiah 35 + 61	4Q521
he cured many of diseases		he will heal the slain
blind receive sight	blind receive sight	make blind see
lame walk	lame walk	
lepers are cleansed		
deaf hear	deaf hear	
dead are raised up		resurrect the dead
poor have good	poor have good	poor have good
news preached	news preached	news preached

Jesus' words clearly allude to Isa 35:5-6 and 61:1-2, but the reference to the dead being raised up is not found in these passages from Isaiah. However, this element appears in 4Q521. Even Luke's introductory summary, "he cured many of diseases" (cf. Luke 7:21), approximates 4Q521's "he will heal the slain." Given the evident importance of this Isaianic tradition for Jesus' self-understanding,[104] the parallels with this scroll could be very significant. One cannot help but wonder if it is more than coincidence that in replying to an imprisoned and questioning John the Baptist (Matt 11:2-6 = Luke 7:18-23), who may very well have had some contact with members of the Qumran sect, Jesus not only alludes to Scripture that was important to this community (cf. 11QMelch 2:4, 6, 9, 13, 18; 1QH 15:15; 18:14-15), he paraphrases it as they did.

There could be one important discrepancy, however. Whereas Jesus applies to himself the salvific activities of Isaiah 35 and 61, in 4Q521 it is God who appears to be the agent of healing and resurrection. It is Adonai, mentioned in line 5, who is the antecedent of the verbs of line 8. Adonai appears again in line 11, so he may be the antecedent of the verbs in line 12 as well, though the lacuna at the end of line 11 and the beginning of line 13 leave open the possibility of another actor. So whereas the heavens and the earth may obey the Lord's Messiah, it seems that it will be the Lord himself who will release the captive, heal the slain, raise the dead, and announce glad tidings. It is this last item—the act of announcing the glad tidings to the poor, which is an allusion to Isa 61:1 and possibly Isa 52:7—that supports the possibility that the subject of the verbs in line 12 is the previously mentioned Messiah.

24. 4QSerekh Milḥamah (= 4Q285) 5:1-6

כאשר כתוב בספר] ישעיהו הנביא וניקפ[ו]   ]   1

---

[104] On the authenticity of the tradition, see n. 86 above.

[סבכי היער בברזל ולבנון באדיר י]פול ויצא חוטר מגזע ישי   2

[ונצר משרשיו יפרה פשרו   [צמח דויד ונשפטו את   3

[[והמיתו נשיא העדה צמ]ח דויד [4

[[בתופי]ם ובמחוללות וצוה כוהן [5

[הרואש   ח]ללי[י] כתיים [ ] לל[ ] [6

"¹[. . . as it is written in the book of] Isaiah the prophet, 'And felled will be ²[thickets of the forest with an axe, and Lebanon by a mighty one will f]all. A shoot will arise from the roots of Jesse, ³[and a branch from his roots will bear fruit.' Its interpretation is . . .] the Branch of David. And they will judge the ⁴[. . .] And the Prince of the community, the Bran[ch of David], will put him to death ⁵[. . . with tambouri]ne and with dancing. And the Priest will command [. . . ⁶the sl]ai[n of the] Kitti[m] . . ."

Text: PAM 41.282, 41.468, 41.708, 42.260, 42.370, 43.325; ER 224, 321, 409, 739, 1352; EW 27-29 (+ pl. II [= frag. 7 in EW 29]); WA 2.225.

Fragment 5 (or 7), lines 1-6, of this text quickly became controversial when Robert Eisenman claimed that it spoke of a slain Messiah.[105] According to him, line 4 should read: "and they will put to death the Leader of the Community, the Branch of David." But Eisenman's interpretation and translation are problematic. The text is clearly a midrash on parts of Isaiah 10-11,[106] which elsewhere is understood to describe the Messiah's victory over Israel's enemies (cf. 4QpIsaᵃ 7-10 iii 1-29; and 1QM 19:9-13, which speaks of victory and the slain Kittim, i.e. Romans). Is it conceivable that the covenanters of Qumran believed that the eschatological "Branch of David" would appear only to be slain by the Romans?

Markus Bockmuehl has argued convincingly that the most natural vocalization of the radicals of the key word in line 4 is וְהֵמִיתוֹ ("and he will kill him"), rather than Eisenman's problematic וְהֵמִיתוּ ("and they

---

105 Eisenman made public statements to this effect. His position appears in EW 24-29 and is defended by J. D. Tabor, "A Pierced or Piercing Messiah?—The Verdict is Still Out," BARev 18.6 (1992) 58-59, with a reply by G. Vermes on p. 59.

106 In line 2 WA reads מגזע ("from the roots"), EW reads מטע ("from the planting"). The reading of the former is probably correct, given the allusion to Isa 11:1, which reads מִגֵּזַע. On the antiquity of the tradition that understands "Lebanon" as a reference to the Gentile nations that oppose Israel, see G. Vermes, "Lebanon," in Vermes, Scripture and Tradition in Judaism (SPB 4; Leiden: Brill, 1973) 26-39.

will kill"), with נשיא העדה ("the Prince of the Community") understood as the object, not the subject, of the verb.[107] Both syntax and context support Bockmuehl's interpretation.

Eisenman may have been misled by a questionable translation in line 5. According to him, the fragmentary line reads: "with woundings, and the high priest will command . . ." But ם ובמחוללות[is better understood as "with tambourine and with dancing" (restoring the first word as בתופים on analogy with Exod 15:20; cf. Judg 11:34; 4QpIsaᶜ 25 iii 2). In other words, this fragmentary line is describing the celebration that follows the military victory. While noncombatants sing and dance,[108] the high priest gives orders pertaining to the disposal of the corpses of the enemy. Against such a setting the death of the Branch of David seems completely out of place. It is better to translate the fragment as "the Branch of David will put him to death."[109]

It appears then that 4Q285 does not offer an interpretation of the Davidic Messiah that is appreciably different from what had been previously observed in the other scrolls. Once again we encounter the expectation of the appearance of a mighty figure who will rout the Romans (i.e. the Kittim) and, according to this text, possibly slay the Roman emperor himself.

25. 4Q554 11[?]:15-22

[באתרה ומלכות מ]   15

---

[107] M. Bockmuehl, "A 'Slain Messiah' in 4Q Serekh Milḥamah (4Q285)?" *TynBul* 43 (1992) 155-69, esp. 165-66. For further discussion, see G. Vermes, T. H. Lim, and R. P. Gordon, "The Oxford Forum for Qumran Research Seminar on the Rule of War from Cave 4 (4Q285)," *JJS* 43 (1992) 85-94 (see enlarged, computer-enhanced photograph on p. 87); Betz, "Spricht ein Qumran-Text vom gekreuzigten Messias?" 103-10. Bockmuehl and Vermes identify the text as the fifth fragment (so do Wacholder and Abegg); Eisenman identifies it as the seventh. Bockmuehl and the Oxford Forum have recently received solid support from M. G. Abegg, Jr., "Messianic Hope and 4Q285: A Reassessment," *JBL* 113 (1994) 81-91. Abegg presents an impressive array of lexical support for this position.

[108] I proposed this restoration in C. A. Evans, "The Recently Published Dead Sea Scrolls and the Historical Jesus," in B. D. Chilton and C. A. Evans (eds.), *Studying the Historical Jesus: Evaluations of the Current State of Research* (NTTS 19; Leiden: Brill, 1994) 547-65, here 553-54. It was gratifying to see the same conclusion reached independently by Abegg, Jr., "Messianic Hope," 90-91.

[109] So also Abegg, Jr., "Messianic Hope," 88-89. In my view, Abegg's study should put the "slain Messiah" interpretation to rest.

16   [כתיא באתרה כלהון בסוף כלהון]   [
17   [אחרין שגיאן ורשין עמהון מ]   [
18   [עמהון אדום ומואב ובני עמון]   [
19   [די בבל ארעא כלה לא יש.]   [
20   [ויבאשון לזרעך עד עדן די.]   [
21   [בכל עממ]ין[מלכות[א] ב.ל]   [
22   [ויעב]דון [ ] בהון עממין]   [

". . . [15]after him and the kingdom of [. . .] [16]the Kittim after him, all of them one after another [. . .] [17]others great and poor with them [. . .] [18]with them Edom and Moab and the Ammonites [. . .] [19]of Babylon. In all the earth no [. . .] [20]and they will oppress your descendants until such time that [. . .] [21]among all natio[ns, the] kingdom [. . .] and the nations shall ser[ve] them [. . .]"

Text: PAM 41.940, 43.564, 43.589; ER 521, 1512, 1536; EW 41-46 (+ pl. III); Beyer 222.

4Q554 is another Aramaic edition of a text that has been called the "New Jerusalem" (cf. 1QJN ar [= 1Q32], 2QJN ar [= 2Q24], 4QJN hebr [= 4Q232], 5QJN ar [= 5Q15], 11QJN ar).[110] In lines 15-22, of what may have orignally been the eleventh column, we find mention of "the kingdom" (line 15), the "Kittim after him" (line 16), a prediction that "they shall oppress your descendants until such time   . . . " (line 20), and what may be a prophecy of eventual triumph: "among all the nations, the kingdom . . . and the nations shall serve them . . ." (lines 21-22). Although certainty is not possible, given the fragmentary condition of this part of the scroll, it is probable that once again we have expressed the anticipation of a military triumph and the establishment of a kingdom that will dominate the nations. It will be at this time that the "New Jerusalem" (described earlier) will become a reality.

26. 4Q522 1 ii 1-8

1   [   ]   ]ן להשכין שם את אה.. ב[[

---

110 For discussion, see M. Baillet, J. T. Milik, and R. de Vaux, Les 'Petites Grottes' de Qumrân: Exploration de la falaise, Les grottes 2Q, 3Q, 5Q, 6Q, 7Q à 10Q, Le rouleau de cuivre (DJD 3; Oxford: Clarendon, 1962) 184-93; J. Starcky, "Jérusalem et les manuscrits de la mer Morte," Le Monde de la Bible 1 (1977) 38-40; J. Licht, "An Ideal Town Plan from Qumran—The Description of the New Jerusalem," IEJ 29 (1979) 45-59; Beyer 214-22.

2 העתים כי הנה בן נולד לישי בן פרץ בן יה[ודה   וילכד]
3 את סלע ציון ויורש משם את כל האמורי ב[   ]
4 לבנות את הבית ליהוה אלוהי ישראל זהב וכסף [   ]
5 ארזים וברושים יב[י]א מ[ן]לבנון לבנותו ובני הסטן [   ]
6 יכהן שם ואיש .. מ[   ]..[   ] ואה.[ ] [כה]   [ ]
7 ו[   ].ן מן השמ.[   ] ודוד יהו[ה]ן ישכין לבטח]   [ ]
8 [ש]מים עמו ישכון [ל]עד ועתה האמורי ם והכנענ[י   ]

"[1] [. . .] to establish there the [. . .] [2]the times, for a son is about to be born to Jesse, son of Perez, son of Ju[dah. . . . and he shall capture] [3]the rock of Zion, and he will dispossess from there all the Amorites [. . .] [4]to build the House for the Lord, the God of Israel. Gold and silver [. . .] [5]cedars and cypress will he bring from Lebanon to build it, and the sons of Satan [. . .] [6]he will serve there as priest and a man [. . .] your [. . .] [7][. . .] from the [. . .] And the Lord will establish David securely [. . .] [8][He]aven will dwell with him forever . . . ."

Text: PAM 43.606; ER 1553; EW 89-92.

At first glance, the text seems to be little more than a paraphrase of the biblical story of David and the building of the Temple. Although a paraphrase of the promise in 2 Samuel 7 that God will establish David's throne forever, lines 7-8 ("And the Lord will establish David securely [. . . He]aven will dwell with him forever") may have been intended to add an eschatological dimension to the passage.[111]

27. 4QTestament of Naphtali (= 4Q215) 4(?):2-10

2 וצרת מצוק ונסוי שחת ויצרפו בם לבחירי צדק מח.ל .ש.
3 בעבור חס[יד]ו כיא שלם קץ הרשע וכול עולה ת[עבו]ר
4 באה עת ה[צ]דק ומלאההארץ דעה ותהלח אל בו כ[יא]
5 בא קץ השלום וחוקי אמת ותעודת הצדק להשכיל [כול אנש]
6 בדרכי אל ובנכורות מעשיו [יתוסרו ע]ד עולמי עד כול ב[ריאה]
7 תברכנו וכול אנש ישתחוה לו [ויהיה לב]בם אח[ד] כיא הואה [הכין]
8 פעולתם בטרם הבראם ועבודת הצדק פלג גבולותם [הגביל]
9 בדורותם כיא בא ממשל הצדק הטוב וירם כסא ה[משיח]
10 ומודה גבה השכל ערמה ותושיה נבחנו במעש[י] קו[ו]דש[ו]

[111] Baillet, Milik, and de Vaux, Les 'Petites Grottes' de Qumrân, 179; E. Puech, "Fragments du Psaume 122 dans un manuscript hébreu de la grotte iv," RevQ 9 (1977-78) 547-54.

". . . ²and great distress and trials of destruction. And some among them shall be purified to become the elect of righteousness [. . .]. ³for the sake of his pious [on]es. For the era of evil has been completed, and all sinfulness will pas[s away]; ⁴the time of righteousness has come, and the earth will be full of knowledge and praise of God. F[or] ⁵the era of peace has come, and the laws of truth and the testimony of righteousness, to teach [all men] ⁶the ways of God and the mightiness of His works; [they shall be instructed un]til all eternity. All cr[eation] ⁷will bless Him, and every man will bow down before Him in worship, and their he[arts will be] as one. For He [prepared] ⁸their actions before they were created, and [measured out] the service of righteousness as their portion ⁹in their generations. For the rule of righteousness (and) goodness has come, and He has raised up the throne of the [Messiah.] ¹⁰And Wisdom will increase greatly. Insight and understanding will be confirmed by the works of [His] Holiness . . ."

Text: PAM 41.915, 43.237; ER 512, 1273; EW 157-60.

Evidently part of the Hebrew version of *Testament of Naphtali*,¹¹² 4Q215 4:2-10 foretells the time when "righteousness has come, and the earth will be full of knowledge and praise of God" (line 4). It will be an "era of peace," when the "laws of truth and the testimony of righteousness" will be taught to all of humanity (line 5). It will be the time when God will have "raised up the throne of the [Messiah]" (line 9). Eisenman proposes the restoration of Messiah in line 9. The proposal fits the context and could be correct.

28. 4Q287 10:13

[נח]ה על משיחו רוח קוד]ש   ]   13

"¹³. . . the Holy Spirit [rest]ed upon His Messiah . . ."

or:

---

112 For the Medieval Hebrew fragments of the *Testament of Naphtali*, see M. Gaster, "The Hebrew Text of one of the Testaments of the XII Patriarchs," *Proceedings of the Society of Biblical Archaeology* 16 (1894) 33-49, 109-17; R. H. Charles, *The Greek Versions of the Testaments of the Twelve Patriarchs* (Oxford: Clarendon, 1908; repr. Hildesheim: Georg Olms, 1960) 239-44; M. de Jonge, *The Testaments of the Twelve Patriarchs: A Study of Their Text, Composition, and Origin* (Leiden: Brill, 1953) 52-60.

[‏[ולוא ידבר סר]ה על משיחי רוח קוד‏[שו   13

"¹³. . . and the Holy Spirit [will not speak rebell]ion against My
anointed . . ."

Text: PAM 41.588, 42.418, 43.314; ER 1349; EW 222-30 (+ pl. XXI); WA
3.111.

The first reconstruction is that proposed by Eisenman and Wise; the
second is by Wacholder and Abegg. The line is restored from the
bottom (i.e. 13th) line of fragment 10 (or 3 in Eisenman and Wise) of
4Q287, a text which is probably the same as 4Q286, as one extensive
verbal overlap seems to suggest (4Q286 7 ii 1-12 = 4Q287 6:1-11).

The first reconstruction is inspired by Isa 11:2 (‏וְנָחָה עָלָיו רוּחַ יהוה‏),
where נוּחַ is used. Indeed, the fragment could be alluding to this
prophetic passage, which is interpreted in a messianic sense elsewhere
in the Dead Sea Scrolls (cf. 4QpIsaᵃ 7-10 iii 15, 23; 1QSb 5:25). The
Targum may also be relevant, which reads: "And a king shall come
forth from the sons of Jesse, and the Messiah [‏משיחא‏] shall be exalted
from the sons of his sons. And a spirit before the Lord shall rest [‏ותשרי‏]
upon him" (*Tg.* Isa 11:1-2a). In the Aramaic tradition ‏שרה/שרי‏ is found
in the context of the Shekinah resting upon someone or dwelling
among persons (cf. *b. Sanh.* 39a).[113] These traditions have relevance
for the interpretation of the story of Jesus' baptism (cf. Matt 3:16 =
Mark 1:10 = Luke 3:22; John 1:32: "I saw the Spirit descend as a dove
from heaven, and it remained on him") and possibly his use of Isa 61:1
("The Spirit of the Lord is upon me"; cf. Luke 4:18; Matt 11:4-5 =
Luke 7:22).

The second restoration is analogous to Jer 29:32: "he has spoken
rebellion against the Lord" (‏סרה דבר על־יהוה‏) and Deut 13:5: "he has
spoken rebellion against the Lord your God" (‏דבר־סרה על־יהוה אלהיכם‏).
This restoration is also supported by 4Q270 9 ii 14 (‏סרה על משיחי‏). If
the restoration is guided by passages such as these, then 4Q287 may
have been a warning concerning false prophets who will speak against
God's "anointed." Whether this anointed person is an anointed
prophet, an anointed priest, an anointed temporal king, or an anointed
eschatological king (i.e. Messiah) is impossible to determine given the
fragmentary condition of the text.

---

[113] Milik, "Milkî-ṣedeq et Milkî-reša'," 130-35; Kobelski, *Melchizedek*, 42-48.

29. 4Q369 1 ii 4-12

[	לזרעו לדורותם אחזת עולמים וכו̇ל	4
[	ומשפטיכה הטובים בררתה לו ל]	5
[	באור עולמים ותשימהו לכה בן בכו̇ר]	6
[	כמהו̇ לשר ומושל בכול תבל ארצ̇ה [	7
[	ע] חרת [שמים וכבוד שחקים סמכת]ה עליו	8
[	[ ]. ומלאך שלומכה בעדתו והו]א	9
[	[נתן]לו חוקים צדיקים כאב לב]ן̇	10
[	[ ]. אהבתו תדבק נפשכה לע] ולם	11
[	[ ]. ה כי בם כבו̇דכ]ה שמת]ה̇].	12

". . . ⁴to his seed for all time an eternal possession. And al[l . . .] ⁵and You have made clear to him Your good judgments [. . .] ⁶in eternal light. And You made him a first-bo[rn] son to You [. . .] ⁷like him for a prince and ruler in all Your earthly land [. . ⁸ . . the] cr[own of the] heavens and the glory of the clouds [You] have set [on him . . ⁹ . .] and the angel of Your peace among his assembly. And H[e . . . ¹⁰gave] to him righteous statutes, as a father to [his s]on [. . ¹¹ . .] his love your soul cleaves to for[ever. ¹². . .] because by them [you established] your glory [. . .]"

Text: PAM 41.518, 42.834, 43.357; ER 342, 1041; WA 2.233; DJD 13 (to appear).

The promise in line 4, "to his seed for all time an eternal possession," probably has to do with the land itself. It has been promised to someone's offspring as an eternal possession. But who is this someone? Is he the one in line 5 to whom God made clear his "good judgments"? 4QPatrBles 5:4 may offer a pertinent parallel: "For to him (i.e. David) and to his seed was granted the Covenant of kingship over his people for everlasting generations . . ." If the parallel in 4QPatrBles is relevant, then the person referred to in line 5 may be a messianic figure who is promised rulership. The phrase in line 10, "as a father to his son," reminds us of 2 Samuel 7 and its Davidic messianic inter- pretation in 4QFlor. In any case, he is probably the same person in lines 5-6, whom instructed "in eternal light" God "made a first-born son." In 4Q458 15:1 we find בכורי ("My first-born"), but the fragment is tiny and the context is uncertain.¹¹⁴ In the Old Testament בֵּן בְּכוֹר occurs a few times (almost always with suffixes; cf. Exod 4:22 in

---

114 The context may be messianic. We read of what could be a messianic figure earlier in 4Q458. See 2 ii 3-6 in the text below.

reference to Israel; and 4Q504 1-2 iii 6: לישראל בני בכורי ["Israel My first-born son"]). It is much more common for בְּכוֹר to appear alone.

Of the three biblical figures who are referred to in the Old Testament as God's "elect one" (see discussion of 4QMess ar above), only David is referred to as God's "first-born." Psalm 89:21, 27-28 (E20, 26-27) provides an instructive parallel: "I have found David, My servant; with holy oil I have anointed him [מְשַׁחְתִּיו] . . . he shall cry to me, 'You are My Father . . .' and I will make him the first-born [בְּכוֹר], the highest of the kings of the earth." This Psalm offers three important parallels with 4Q369 1 ii 6-10: (1) David calls God his Father, which parallels line 10, "as a father to his son"; (2) the Psalmist says that God "will make him the first-born," which parallels line 6, "You made him a first-born son to you"; and (3) the Psalmist says that God's first-born will be "the highest of the kings of the earth," which finds a partial parallel in line 7, "like him for a prince and ruler in all Your earthly land."[115]

30. 4Q458 2 ii 3-6

[	ויאבדהו ואת חילו]	3
[	ותבלע את כל הערלים ותק . .]	4
[	ויצדקו והלך על הרום ה]	5
[	משיח בשמן מלכות ה]	6

"³And he will destroy him and his army [. . .] ⁴And you will swallow up all the uncircumcised, and you will [. . .] ⁵And they will be righteous, and he will ascend to the height [. . .] ⁶one anointed [משיח] with the oil of the kingdom of the . . ."

Text: PAM 40.618, 41.854, 43.544; ER 1493; WA 2.288; EW 48-49.

In the second fragment of 4Q458 we read of the destruction of someone's army and of the anointing of someone else with the "oil of the kingdom." In all probability we have another text that foretells the coming of the Messiah, the defeat of Israel's enemies, and the establishment of the eschatological kingdom.

This person "anointed [משיח] with the oil of the kingdom" could be the "first-born" referred to later in a small fragment (cf. 15:1).[116] The phrase itself approximates language used in reference to David: "I

---

115 See Collins, "The Son of God Text," 79.
116 For text, see WA 2.290.

have found David my servant, with my holy oil [בשמן קדשי] I have anointed him" (Ps 89:21[E20]; cf. 11QPsᵃ 28:11: וימשחני בשמן הקודש ["he will anoint me with holy oil"]).[117] The Psalm goes on to call David God's "first-born" (v. 28[E27]). But being "anointed with the oil of the kingdom" is unique.

The prediction in line 5 that this expected figure "will ascend to the height [הרום]" may be related to 1QSb 5:23: "May Adonai raise him (i.e. the Prince of the Community) to everlasting heights [לרום]." See also the discussion of 4Q491 below. One is also reminded of Ps 68:19(E18): "You ascended to the heights [למרום], leading captives in Your train, and receiving gifts among men." This text is quoted in the New Testament and is applied to the risen Christ (Eph 4:8).

31. 4Q434/436 "Hymns of the Poor" 3:1-7

1	[ ] כה.[ ] [ ].ח להנחם על אבלה ענוה ה:]		
2	גוים [ש]חת ולאומים יכרית ורשעים]	חרש [
3	מעשי שמים וארץ ויגיעו וכבודו מלוא[	א]מדם
4	יכפר ירב טוב ונחמם טוב הש]	לאכול [
5	פריה וטובה *vacat*	
6	כאיש אשר אמו תנחמנו כן ינחמם בירושל]ם כחהן] על כלה עליה	
7	[ ] [ ]לם ושם] א[ ] כסאו לעולם ועד וכבודו]	וכל גוים]

"¹[. . .] your [. . .] to be comforted on account of her mourning; her affliction He [. . .] ²nations [He will de]stroy, and peoples cut off, and the wicked [. . .] He fashioned ³the works of heaven and earth, and they met, and His glory filled [. . .] their [tr]uth ⁴will make atonement. Goodness will multiply, and the goodness of the [. . .] comfort them [. . .] to eat ⁵its fruit and its goodness. ⁶Like a man whose mother comforts him, so will He comfort them in Jerusal[em . . . and like a bridegroom] over the bride, over her ⁷[. . .] and He will put [. . . and He will lift u]p his throne forever and ever. And His glory [. . .] and all the Gentiles . . ."

Text: PAM 43.528; ER 1478; EW 239.

This text appears to comprise a series of hymns in which the covenanters give thanks to God for comforting them and for revealing to them His truth. God will "comfort the poor" (1:1), which may

---

117 This Psalm, or at least the latter part of it, is paraphrased messianically in the Targum; cf. vv. 51-52.

allude to Isa 11:4 ("with righteousness he will judge the poor") and Isa 61:2 ("to comfort those who mourn"). See also 2 i 2-3. God has "made the crooked places straight" (2 i 9), which is an allusion to Isa 40:4. The third fragment is of particular interest.

Given the fragmentary state of the text it is difficult to tell whose throne will be lifted up. Is it God's throne, or is it Messiah's? The expression, "so will He comfort them in Jerusalem [כן ינחמם בירושלם]," in all probability is an allusion to Isa 40:1-2: "Comfort, comfort My people . . . speak tenderly to Jerusalem." The text is eschatologically interpreted in the Dead Sea Scrolls, as seen in 4QTanḥ 1-2 i 4, and quite possibly messianically interpreted, as seen in 11QMelch 2:20. The same could be the case here. The day will come when God will comfort Jerusalem, exalt the Messiah, and crush Israel's enemies.

The statement, "their [t]ruth 4will make atonement" (lines 3-4), is reminiscent of 1QS 9:3-5: "They shall expiate guilty rebellion and sinful infidelity . . . without the flesh of burnt offering and the fat of sacrifices, but the offering of the lips in accordance with the Torah will be as an agreeable odor of righteousness, and perfection of way shall be as the voluntary gift of a delectable oblation." Elsewhere the community describes itself as an "expiation for the earth" (1QS 8:10). Perhaps also related is 4QFlor 1:6-7: "He has commanded a sanctuary of men to be built for Himself, that there they may send up, like the smoke of incense 7before Him, the works of the Torah." Elements of both of these texts are found in 4Q251 3:7-9: "[When] there are in the Council of the Community fif[teen men, perfect in everything which has been revealed in all the Law 8and the Pr]ophets, the Council of the Communi[ty] shall be founded [on truth . . .] 9of (God's) favor, and a pleasing fragrance to make atonement for the land, from a[ll evil . . .]."

32. 4Q381 15:7-9

כי אתה] תפאתה הדו ואני משיחך אתבננתי	]	7
אודי]עך כי הודעתי והשכיל כי השכלתני	]	8
כי בשמך אלהי בקרא ואל ישועתך[	]	9

"7[. . . For You] are the glory of its splendor. And I Your Messiah have gained understanding. 8[. . . I will make] You known, because You instructed me, and I will teach, because You taught me. 9[. . .] For on Your name, my God, we shall call for Your salvation . . ."

Text: PAM 43.226; E. M. Schuller, *Non-Canonical Psalms from Qumran: A*

Pseudepigraphic Collection (HSS 28; Atlanta: Scholars Press, 1986) 94 + pl. II.

Eileen Schuller has noted several parallels with Psalm 89. Lines 4-7 contain allusions to Ps 89:10-12, 14, 7, and possibly 18. The statement in line 7, "I Your Messiah," may presuppose Ps 89:21 (cf. vv. 39, 52), while line 8 may allude to Ps 32:8 ("I will instruct you [אשכילך] and teach you the way should go"), a Psalm which in the Masoretic Text is attributed to David. One is also reminded of Ps 51:13 ("I will teach transgressors Your ways"). Line 9 may also echo phrases from various Davidic Psalms (e.g., 54:1: אלהים בשמך הושיעני; 116:4: ובשם־יהוה אקרא). The Masoretic Text attributes Psalm 54 to David, while rabbinic tradition attributes Psalm 116 to David (cf. *Midr. Ps.* 116.1 [on 116:1]).

Although Schuller acknowledges that ואני משיחך אתבננתי could be translated, "and I Your Messiah have gained understanding," she believes that the context suggests that the translation be "As for me, I have gained understanding from Your discourse." Here she takes the noun as מִ(ן) + שִׂיחַ + ךָ.[118] This is possible, of course, but the allusions to Psalm 89, which are quite clear, and the possible allusions to Psalms 32, 54, and 116 strongly suggest that David or one of his descendants, the Lord's Anointed, is in view. If this is true, the noun makes perfect sense as מְשִׁיחֶךָ, the very form which appears in Ps 89:39, 52. If taken this way, then the text is saying that the Lord's Messiah, having gained understanding, will be able to make God known and to teach. The idea of David teaching God's ways is, as noted in the preceding paragraph, expressed in the Psalter.

What is not clear, however, is the perspective of this psalm. There is nothing in it that would suggest that it was understood in an eschatological sense. Originally it may have been understood as referring to the historical David or possibly to his descendants. But this does not necessarily preclude an eschatological interpretation (such as is given Psalm 37).[119] It is possible that from this psalm the Messiah of the Eschaton was expected to be a teacher.

---

[118] Schuller, *Non-Canonical Psalms from Qumran*, 28, 97, 101-102.

[119] In 4QpPs 37 the wisdom sayings and promises of Ps 37:7-24 are understood in an eschatological sense. 4Q381 17 may be eschatological.

III. OTHER POTENTIALLY RELEVANT TEXTS FOR JESUS RESEARCH

33. 4QBeatitudes (= 4Q525) 2:1-8

1 בלב טהור ולוא רגל על לשונו אשרי תוקיה ולוא יתמוכו

2 בדרכי עולה אש[רי] הגלים בה ולוא יביעו בדרכי אולת אשרי דורשיה

3 בבור כפים ולוא ישחרנה ב[לב] מרמה אשרי אדם השיג חוכמה ויתהלך

4 בתורת עליון ויכן לדרכיה לבו ויתאפק ביסוריה ובנגיעיה ירצה ימ[י]ד

5 לוא יטושנה בעוני מצר[יו] ובעת צוקה לוא יעחבנה ולוא

ישכחנה [בימי פ]חד

6 ובענות נפשו לוא יג[ע]ל[נה] כי בה יהגה תמיד ובצרתו

ישח[ח בתורת אל ובכו]ל

7 היותו בה [יהגה וישיחנה תמיד] לנגד עיניו לבלתי לכת בדרכי [עולה   ]

8 [   ]ה יחד ויתם לבו אלוה[   ]ם

"[Blessed is he who walks] ¹with a pure heart and who does not slander with his tongue. Blessed are they who hold fast to her (i.e. Wisdom's) laws and do not hold ²to the ways of evil. Bless[ed] are they who rejoice in her and do not overflow with the ways of folly. Blessed are they who ask for her ³with clean hands and do not seek her with a deceitful [heart]. Blessed is the man who grasps hold of Wisdom and walks ⁴in the Torah of the Most High and directs his heart to her ways and restrains himself with her disciplines and always accepts her chastisements ⁵and does not cast her off in the misery of [his] affliction[s] nor forsake her in a time of trouble, nor forget her in [days of ter]ror, ⁶and in the meekness of his soul, does not despis[e her], but rather always meditates on her, and when in affliction, occupies himself [with Torah; who al]l ⁷his life [meditates] on her [and places her continually] before his eyes so he will not walk in the ways of [evil .. ⁸..] in unity and his heart if perfect. God . . ."

Text: PAM 43.595, 43.596, and 43.608; ER 1542, 1543, and 1554; EW 172-77 (+ pl. XII).

As soon as 4Q525 became available the significance of the beatitudes was appreciated. Émile Puech has produced the first critical study.[120] He concludes that there originally were eight beatitudes followed by a ninth longer one. His argument is supported by the observation of the

---

[120] É. Puech, "4Q525 et les péricopes des béatitudes en Ben Sira et Matthieu," *RB* 98 (1991) 80-106. For a popular assessment, see B. T. Viviano, "Beatitudes Found Among the Dead Sea Scrolls," *BARev* 18.6 (1992) 53-55, 66.

presence of eight short beatitudes in Sir 14:20-27 (cf. 25:7-11) and
Matthew's eight short beatitudes (Matt 5:3-10) followed by a ninth
longer one (Matt 5:11-12). Because the fragmentary text of 4Q525
2:1-8 preserves only four short beatitudes and the final longer one,
Puech infers that that lower part of the first column contained three,
and probably four, beatitudes. He also reconstructs the opening lines of
col. 1 to read: "[Words (or proverbs) of David (or of Solomon son of
David), which he spok]e (or [wrot]e) by the wisdom God gave to him
[to . . . acquir]e wisdom and disci[pline,] to understand [. . .] to
increase kn[owledge of wisdom . . .]" (4Q525 1:1-2).

There are several intriguing parallels with teaching attributed to
Jesus, especially that found in Matthew's version of the Sermon on the
Mount. Consider the following sampling:

> [Blessed is he who walks] with a pure heart (4Q525 2:1).
> Blessed are the pure in heart (Matt 5:8).
>
> Blessed are those who rejoice in her (4Q525 2:2).
> Blessed are you when men revile you . . . rejoice and be glad (Matt 5:11-
> 12).
>
> Blessed is the man who . . . in the meekness of his soul, does not despise
> her (4Q525 2:3-6).
> In the meekness of righteousness bring forth [your] words . . . (4Q525
> 4:20).
> Blessed are the meek (Matt 5:5).
>
> As you hear, answer accordingly . . . And with patience utter (your words)
> and answer truthfully before officers . . . (4Q525 4:22, 25).
> Let what you say be simply "Yes" or "No"; anything more than this comes
> from evil (Matt 5:37).
>
> . . . his heart is perfect (4Q525 2:8)
> The perfect will thrust aside evil (4Q525 4 ii 6)
> . . . perfection because of your word, and perfection . . . (4Q525 4:4)
> You, therefore, must be perfect, as your heavenly Father is perfect (Matt
> 5:48; cf. 4Q525 4:11: "God [your] Father").
>
> Blessed are they who ask for her (4Q525 2:2)
> Ask, and it will be given to you . . . For every one who asks receives
> (Matt 7:7-8; cf. Jas 4:2).
>
> . . . or what grows of its own they shall gat[her . . .] burned, and every
> weed [He uprooted . . . (4Q525 10 vi 7-8).
> Every tree that does not bear good fruit is cut down and thrown into the

fire (Matt 7:19; cf. Matt 13:24-30: "Gather the weeds first and bind them in bundles to be burned").

The differences between the beatitudes of 4Q525 and those of Jesus are also very important. Jesus' beatitudes are eschatological; each blessing concludes with a promise: "for theirs is the kingdom of heaven," or "for they shall inherit the earth" (Matt 5:3, 5). In 4Q525 the beatitudes are not eschatological; they reflect concern with life in the present world.[121]

It is also of interest to note that there are parallels with the Jacobean tradition (itself recognized to have many affinities with the dominical tradition, especially that of the Sermon on the Mount). The admonition to "guard against the stumbling block of the tongue" and the danger of being "ensnared by a tongue [of evil?]" (4Q525 4:26-27) parallel similar warnings in James (1:26; 3:2-8).

34. 4Q416/418 9 ii + 10 i 5-8

מהר תן אשר	5
לו יקח כיסכה ובדבריכה אל תמעט רוהכה בכל הון אל ימר	6
רוח קודשכה	
כיא אין מחיר שוה [בנפשכה מן]של אוטכה ברצון שחר	7
פניו וכלשונו	
[דבר בו] ואז תמצא חפצכה]	8

"⁵. . . (Therefore), quickly return whatever ⁶belongs to him; otherwise he will take your purse. In your affairs, do not compromise your spirit. Do not exchange your Holy Spirit for any riches, ⁷because no price is worth [your soul.] Willingly seek the face of him who has authority over your storehouse, and in his own tongue ⁸[speak with him.] In that way you will find satisfaction . . ."

Text: PAM 43.589, 43.511; ER 1536, 1461; EW 248, 253 (+ pl. XXII).

The restoration of the text is based on combining components of the overlapping fragments 9 (col. ii) and 10 (col. i). Another parallel from the Sermon on the Mount suggests itself. "Make friends quickly with your accuser, while you are going with him to court, lest your accuser hand you over to the judge, and the judge to the guard, and you be put in prison; truly, I say to you, you will never get out till you have paid

---

121 The point is made by Viviano, "Beatitudes," 66.

the last penny" (Matt 5:25-26). Consider also Mark 8:36-37: "What does it profit one, to gain the whole world and forfeit his soul? For what would a person give in exchange for his soul?" The theme of the Holy Spirit as gift may also be relevant: "If you then, who are evil, know how to give good gifts to your children, how much more will the heavenly Father give the Holy Spirit to those who ask him" (Luke 11:13; cf. Matt 7:11, which reads differently).

35. 4Q542 1 i 4-7

וכען בני אזדהרו בירותתא די משא למא לכון   4

די יהבו לכון אבהתכון ואל תתנו ירותתכון לנכראין ואחסנותכון   5

לכיליאין ותהון לשפלו ולנבלו בעיניהון ויבסרון עליכון די   6

להון תותבין לכון ולהון עליכון ראשין   7

"⁴. . . And now, my sons, look after your inheritance that was bequeathed to you, ⁵which your fathers gave to you. Do not give your inheritance to foreigners, nor your heritage ⁶to violent men, lest you be regarded as humiliated in their eyes, and foolish, and they trample upon you, for ⁷they will come to dwell among you and become the ranking men over you."

Text: PAM 42.600, 43.565; ER 923, 1513; EW 149 (+ pl. IX).

The verb בסר means either to "tread upon" or to "contemn." The warning not to give away Israel's heritage to foreigners, lest they "trample (or tread) upon" the Israelites could very well parallel Jesus' similar warning to his disciples in Matt 7:6: "Do not give what is holy to dogs, nor cast your pearls before swine, lest they trample them with their feet and, turning, should tear you to pieces." Jesus is not speaking of literal trampling or tearing, but of suffering expressions of contempt and abuse.

The passage may also have some relevance for first century Jewish views of foreign taxation. If 4Q542 is speaking of foreign taxation, then it is an emphatic call to the Jewish people not to pay. Such a stance coheres with an element commonly found in the various liberation movements that arose in Israel in the first century. The question of whether or not Jews should pay Roman tax was put to Jesus (cf. Mark 12:13-17). Jesus' ambiguous answer would probably not have satisfied the author of 4Q542; it may not have satisfied his opponents either (cf. Luke 23:2: "We found this man . . . forbidding the payment of taxes to

Caesar").[122]

36. 4QHalakah A (= 4Q251) 2:5-7

אל יעל איש בהמה אשר תפול   5

א[ל] המים ביום השבת ואם נפש אדם היא אשר תפול אל המי[ם]   6

[ביום] השבת ישלח לו את בגדו להעלותו בו   7

"5. . . A man should not lift cattle which has fallen [6]in[to] the water on the Sabbath day. But if it is a human who has fallen into the wat[er [7]on the day of] the Sabbath, he will throw him his garment to lift him out with it. But he will not lift an implement . . ."

Text: PAM 43.307 and 43.308; ER 1342 and 1343; EW 204.

4Q251 is made up of several fragments concerned with legal interpretation. There are several parallels to 1QS, especially in fragment 3. The second fragment sets forth a halakah concerned with what is permissible on the Sabbath. In it we have here a halakic interpretation that is sharply at variance with that attributed to Jesus: "Which one of you, having a son (or donkey) or an ox that has fallen into a well, will not immediately pull him out on a sabbath day?" (Luke 14:5; cf. Matt 12:11; Luke 13:15).[123] Elsewhere the covenanters expressed similar strict rulings. According to CD 11:13-17 (= 4QD[e] 10 v 18-21) it is wrong to "assist a beast in giving birth on the Sabbath day." Jesus evidently presupposed the more lenient ruling of the Pharisees, who permitted one to lift an animal out of the water (for rabbinic views, see *m. Yoma* 8:6; *Mek.* on Exod 22:2 [*Neziqin* §13]; *b. Šabb.* 128b; *Eccl. Rab.* 9:7 §1).

37. 4Q390 2 i 9-10

[ ] [אשר לר]ה[ע] הו יגזלו ויעשוקו איש את רעהו את מקדשי יטמאו   9

[ ] ו]את [מ]עדי .. [.]ם ובבני[הם] יחללו[ן] את זר[ע]ם   10

כוהניהם יחמסו

"9. . . They will rob their neigh[b]ors and oppress one another and defile My Temple [10][. . . and] My festivals [. . .] through [their]

[122] For further discussion of 4Q542, see E. Puech, "Le Testament de Qahat en araméen de la Grotte 4 (4QTQah)," *RevQ* 15 (1991) 23-54; R. H. Eisenman, "The Testament of Kohath," *BARev* 17.6 (1991) 64.

[123] See Milik, *Ten Years of Discovery*, 111.

children they will pollu[te] their seed. Their priests will commit
violence . . ."

Text: PAM 43.506; EW 55-56. See Dimant for improvement in restoration of text
and translation.

Part of a survey of Israel's history, 4Q390 2 i 9-10 gives expression
to complaints of priestly corruption.[124] The description here of
oppression and corruption is reminiscent of other complaints of high
priestly corruption and violence. Devorah Dimant has detected
parallels between 2 i 8-10 and certain pseudepigraphal writings (cf. *T.
Levi* 17:11; 16:1-2; *T. Mos.* 5:4; *Pss. Sol.* 2:3; 8:12), as well as
parallels with other writings of Qumran (cf. CD 4:18; 6:6, 11; 8:4, 7;
20:23; 1QpHab 8:10; 12:8-9). From this she concludes that 4Q390 was
not authored by the Qumran community, but was inherited, along with
certain pseudepigraphal writings (such as the *Testaments of the
Twelve Patriarchs* and *Jubilees*) that voiced criticisms of the Temple
establishment, with which the Qumran community agreed.[125]

Dimant is probably correct, but this does not mean that the members
of Qumran would have viewed these criticisms as inapplicable to their
own time. The criticisms of the "Wicked Priest" and his supporters
(1QpHab 8:11; 9:5, 12; 12:6-9, 10) may very well have been applied to
many of the High Priests during the Herodian and Roman period.
Indeed, the criticisms found in *T. Mos.* 7:3-10, which apply to the
ruling priests during the reign of Herod's sons, are quite similar to the
criticisms that originally referred to the Hasmonean priests. Many of
the complaints against the ruling priests of the first century parallel
those from the earlier period (cf. Josephus, *Ant.* 20.8.8 §179-181;
20.9.2 §205-207; 20.9.4 §213; and in the rabbinic literature, see *m.
Ker.* 1:7; *t. Menah.* 13.18-21; *t. Zebah.* 11.16-17; *b. Pesah.* 57a).

Criticism of the ruling priestly establishment forms an important
part of the backdrop against which the actions of Jesus in Jerusalem

---

[124] For discussion, see D. Dimant, "New Light from Qumran on the Jewish
Pseudepigrapha — 4Q390," in Trebolle Barrera and Vegas Montaner (eds.),
Proceedings of the International Congress on the Dead Sea Scrolls, 2.405-47 (+
pl. 25); EW 53-54. Dimant calls the text 4QpsMos[e]. J. Strugnell had thought that
4Q390 was part of the 4QpsEzek collection (= 4Q385-391). Dimant disagrees,
concluding that "most of the fragment assigned to 4Q385-390 are, in fact, copies of
the *PsMos* work rather than that of *PsEz*" ("New Light from Qumran," 411).

[125] Dimant, "New Light from Qumran," 445-47.

should be understood (cf. Mark 11–14).[126] 4Q390 provides an important link between Qumranic criticisms found in some of the older pseudepigraphal writings.

38. 4Q525 5:2-5a

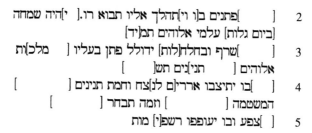

2	י]היה שמחה	פתנים בו וי]תהלך אליו תבוא רו.[
		ביום גלות] עלמי אלוהים תמ]יד[
3	מלכ]ות	שרף ובחלחלות] ידולל פתן בעליו [
		אלוהים] תני]נים תש] [
4	[	בו יתיצבו אררי]ם לנ]צח וחמת תנינים]
		המשטמה] וזמה תבחר] [
5		צפע ובו יעופפו רשפ]י] מות]

"2 . . . serpents in [it, and you will] go to him, you will enter [. . .] there will be joy [on that day] the mysteries of God [are revealed] for[ever. . . .] ³burn. By poi[sons] will a serpent weaken his lords [. . . the Kingd]om of God [. . . vip]ers [. . .] ⁴In him they will take their stand. They are accursed for[ever] and the venom of vipers [. . .] the Mastema [. . .] you choose depravity [. . .] ⁵and in him the demons of death take flight . . ."

Text: PAM 43.595, 43.596, and 43.608; ER 1542, 1543, and 1554; EW 173-77 (+ pl. XII).

4Q525 5:2-5a is in such poor condition that it is not possible to trace a line of thought throughout the text. But the appearance of certain words and phrases could be quite important nonetheless.

The possible association of "kingdom of God" and authority over "demons" is suggestive.[127] One thinks of the well-known dominical

[126] See C. A. Evans, "Jesus' Action in the Temple and Evidence of Corruption in the First-Century Temple," in D. J. Lull (ed.), *Society of Biblical Literature 1989 Seminar Papers* (SBLSP 28; Atlanta: Scholars, 1989) 522-39 (see now chap. 8 below); idem, "Opposition to the Temple: Jesus and the Dead Sea Scrolls," in J. H. Charlesworth (ed.), *Jesus and the Dead Sea Scrolls* (ABRL; New York: Doubleday, 1992) 235-53.

[127] The restoration of [ממלכ]ות אלוהים] is admittedly risky. If the restoration is valid, it would be one of the few instances of the precise phrase, "kingdom of God," outside of Jesus and early Christian literature. In Greek (βασιλεία τοῦ θεοῦ) the phrase occurs in *Pss. Sol.* 17:3; Wis 10:10; Philo, *Spec. Leg.* 4.32 §164 (cf. *Mut. Nom.* 23 §135; *Som.* 2.43 §285). In Aramaic (מלכותא דיהוה/דאל) the phrase occurs in *Tg.* Isa 24:23; 31:4; 40:9; 52:7; *Tg.* Obad 21; *Tg.* Mic 4:7-8; *Tg.* Zech

saying: "If I by the finger of God cast out demons, then the kingdom of God has come upon you" (Luke 11:20; cf. 10:17). The apparent promise to have power over serpents and vipers is also reminiscent of another dominical saying: "Behold, I have given you authority to tread upon serpents and scorpions, and over all the power of the enemy; and nothing shall hurt you" (Luke 10:19). Compare also 4Q525 4:11: ". . . and on the [backs] of your [enemies] you will tread [תדרוך] . . ." The dominical tradition and the expressions in 4Q525 4 and 5 cohere with the idea found in *T. Levi* 18:12: "And Beliar shall be bound by him (i.e. the coming priest), and he shall give power to his children to tread upon the evil spirit." One is also reminded of the story of Ḥanina ben Dosa's encounter with the poisonous lizard. The lizard (or snake) bites Ḥanina's foot and dies (*t. Ber.* 3.20; *b. Ber.* 33a).

39. 4QMᵃ (= 4Q491) 11 i 11-18

11	[הושיביני אל עליון בתוך] תמימי
12	עו]למים כסא עוז בעדת אלים בל ישבו בו כול מלכי קדם ונדיביהמה
	לוא] יקרבו לו[אדומי
13	ל]כבודי לוא ידמה ולוא ירומם זולתי ולוא יבוא ביא כיא אני ישבתי
	ב[עיד]ה בשמים ואין
14	מחי]יבים אני עם אלים אתחשב ומכוני בעדת קודש לוא כבשר תאו]תי
	בלבד] כול יקר לי בכבוד
15	אלי מעו]ן הקודש [א]יא לבוז נחשב ביא ומיא בכבודי ידמה ליא מיא
	הו]א] כבאי ים ישוב וספר
16	על תמור]תי מיא יש]חק ל]צערים כמוני ומיא [לסבו]ל רע הדמה ביא
	ואין [נ]שניתי בהוריה לוא תדמה
17	תורתי לדברי איש] ומיא יגודוניא בפת]חי פיא] ומזל שפתי מיא יכיל
	ומיא יועדני וידמה במשפטי
18	לוא יעמוד נגד]יא אניא עם אלים אחש]ב ו]כבודיא עם בני המלך
	לוא [פ]ז ולוא כתם אופירים [ידמה לכמתי]

"¹¹[El 'Elyon gave me a seat among] those perfect ¹²forever, a mighty throne in the congregation of the gods. None of the kings of the East shall sit in it and their nobles shall not [come near it]. No Edomite ¹³shall be like me in glory. And none shall be exalted save me, nor shall come against me. For I have taken my seat in the [congregation] in the heavens, and none ¹⁴[find fault with me]. I shall

---

14:9 (cf. *Tg. Neof.* Exod 15:18; *Tg. Ezek* 7:7, 10).

be reckoned with gods and established in the holy congregation. I do not desire [gold], as would a man of flesh; everything precious to me is the glory [15]of [my God. The status] of a holy Temple, not to be violated, has been attributed to me, and who can compare with me in glory? What voyager will return and tell [16][of my equivalent]? Who [laughs] at griefs as I do? And who is like me [in bearing] evil? Moreover, if I lay down the law in a lecture [my instruction] is beyond comparison [17][with any man's]. And who will attack me for [my utterances]? And who will contain the flow of my speech? And who will call me into court and be my equal? In my legal judgments [18][none will stand against] me. I shall be reckoned with gods, and my glory, with [that of] the king's sons. Neither refined gold, nor gold of Ophir [can match my wisdom]."

Text: PAM 42.045, 42.473, 42.474; DJD 7.26-27 (+ pl. VI); M. Smith, "Ascent to the Heavens and Deification in 4QMª," in L. H. Schiffman (ed.), *Archaeology and History in the Dead Sea Scrolls: The New York University Conference in Memory of Yigael Yadin* (JSPSup 2; Sheffield: JSOT Press, 1990) 181-88.

Maurice Baillet entitled 4Q491 11 i 8-24, "cantique de Michel."[128] But in view of the fact that the angel Michael does not occur in the hymn, nor in any of the proximate material, there is reason to doubt this identification. In recent studies, Morton Smith argues that column 1 of fragment 11 contains the remains of three hymns, with the middle one (lines 12-19) describing the ascent of a person (not Michael or any other angel) into heaven. Smith's restoration and translation are give above.[129]

Related materials have been observed in 4Q427 and 4Q471.[130] The following lines in 4Q427 are of special interest:

[7] . . . Great is God who ac[ts wonderfully],
[8]for he casts down the haughty spirit so that there is no remnant,
and lifts up the poor from the dust to [the eternal height].

---

[128] DJD 7.26.

[129] M. Smith, "Two Ascended to Heaven—Jesus and the Author of 4Q491," in Charlesworth (ed.), *Jesus and the Dead Sea Scrolls*, 290-301. His translation is on p. 296. At several points Smith proposes restorations different from those proposed by Baillet. See also Smith, "Ascent to the Heavens and Deification in 4QMª," 181-88.

[130] See E. Schuller, "A Hymn from a Cave Four Hodayot Manuscript: 4Q427 7 i + ii," *JBL* 112 (1993) 605-28.

[9]and to the clouds he magnifies him in stature,
and (he is) with the heavenly beings in the congregation
of the community (7 ii 7-9).

[16] . . . What is flesh in relation to these things?
How are [dust and clay] to be reckoned [17]to recount these things continually
and to take a stand in place [before you
and come into community with] [18]the sons of heaven? (7 ii 16-18)[131]

Smith concludes that in this hymn we have evidence of the belief that certain pious persons could attain to a sort of quasi deification through ascent into heaven. That deification at Qumran was the goal or was actually believed to be attainable is doubtful,[132] but Smith's suggestion that what we have here is a human gaining entry into the heavenly realm and actually taking a seat among celestial beings deserves careful consideration.

The idea of heavenly exaltation, which may also be reflected in 1QSb 5:23, 4Q458 2 ii 5, and in some of the hymns of 1QH, could have relevance for Jesus research. Smith has suggested that the concept could clarify the christology of the Fourth Gospel,[133] but I wonder if it might also have relevance for understanding Jesus' reply to Caiaphas: "You will see the Son of Man seated at the right hand of Power, coming with the clouds of heaven" (Mark 14:62). This saying is often dismissed as a Christian confession that presupposes Jesus' resurrection and heavenly exaltation. But 4Q491 may offer evidence that ideas of heavenly exaltation could be entertained apart from death and resurrection. Furthermore, if Smith's restoration of line 15 is correct ("[The status] of a holy Temple, not to be violated, has been attributed to me"), then we may have here a pertinent parallel with sayings attributed to Jesus in which he was likened to the Temple (cf. Mark 14:58; cf. John 2:19-22).

40. 4QŠirŠabb[a-f] (= 4Q400-405) + MasŠŠ (excerpts)

רום מלכות[כ]כה	1
רום מלכותו	2
תפארת מלכותכה	3
תשבוחות מלכותכה בקדושי ק[ד]ושים	4

---

[131] Schuller, "4Q427 7 i + ii," 611.

[132] See the criticism offered by Schuller, "4Q427 7 i + ii," 627 n. 42.

[133] Smith, "Two Ascended to Heaven," 298-99.

וספרו הוד מלכותו 5

שמי מלכות כב[וד]כה 6

[בכול] שמי מלכות 7

מה[ל]לי מלכותו כבודו 8

בהדר תשבחות כבוד מלכותו 9

תשבחות כול אלוהים עם הדר כול מלכ[ותו] 10

ומשכן רוש רום כבוד מלכותו 11

מושב ככסא מלכותו 12

ממלכות מושבי כבוד למרכבו[ת] 13

כסאי.. כבוד מלכותו 14

ראשי ממלכות ממלכות קדושים למלך הקודש 15

בכול מרומי מקדשי מלכות כבודו

מלכות כבוד מלך כול א[לוהים] 16

1. "[Your] lofty kingdom" (4Q400 1 ii 1)
2. "His lofty kingdom" (4Q403 1 i 8; 1 i 14; 4Q405 3 ii 4; MasŠŠ 2:20)
3. "the beauty of Your kingdom" (4Q400 1 ii 3)
4. "the praiseworthiness of Your kingdom among the holiest of the h[oly ones]"(4Q400 2:1; 4Q401 14 i 7)
5. "and they declare His kingdom"(4Q400 2:3)
6. "the heavens of Your glor[ious] kingdom" (4Q401 14 i 6)
7. "[in all] the heavens of His kingdom" (4Q400 2:3-4)
8. "[who pr]aise His glorious kingdom" (4Q403 1 i 25)
9. "in the splendor of praise is the glory of His kingdom" (4Q403 1 i 32)
10. "the praises of all the gods together with the splendor of all His kingdom" (4Q403 1 i 32-33)
11. "And the tabernacle of highest loftiness, the glory of His kingdom" (4Q403 1 ii 10)
12. "a seat like the throne of His kingdom" (4Q405 20 ii-21-22 2)
13. "the kingdom . . . glorious seats of the chariot thrones" (4Q405 20 ii-21-22 4)
14. "the throne of His glorious kingdom" (4Q405 23 i 3)
15. "the chiefs of the realm of the holy ones of the King of holiness in all the heights of the sanctuaries of His glorious kingdom" (4Q405 23 ii 11-12)
16. "the glorious kingdom of the King of all the g[ods]" (4Q405 24:3)

Text: PAM 43.473 (4Q400), 43.510 (4Q401), 42.807 (4Q403), 42.967 + 43.498

+ 43.500 (4Q405), 7039-200 (MasŠŠ); C. Newsom, *Songs of the Sabbath Sacrifice: A Critical Edition* (HSS 27; Atlanta: Scholars Press, 1985) 90, 110, 136, 172, 188, 209, 226, 267, 303, 322, 332, 341 + pls. I, II, IV, VI, X, XI.

The significance of the frequent references to kingdom in MasŠŠ and 4QŠirŠabb[a-f] lies in the fact that it is a heavenly kingdom; it is not an earthly kingdom over which the scion of David will some day rule. Although the precise epithet "kingdom of God" is never used, it is God's kingdom nonetheless. We find "Your kingdom," "His kingdom," and "kingdom of the King of all the gods." The close association of kingdom with God may lend a measure of support to Bruce Chilton's contention that for Jesus the kingdom of God was nothing other than God's disclosure of himself.[134] These descriptive phrases must be taken into consideration in the study of Jesus' understanding of the kingdom.

Of interest also is excerpt 13: "the kingdom . . . glorious seats of the chariot thrones" (4Q405 20 ii-21-22 4).[135] Such language may bear some relationship to Jesus' promise to his disciples that some day, "when the Son of man shall sit on his glorious throne" (or when the Father assigns Jesus a kingdom, according to the Lucan version), they too would "sit on twelve thrones, judging the twelve tribes of Israel" (Matt 19:28 = Luke 22:29-30). Commentators have rightly recognized that this logion alludes to Daniel 7 and Ps 122:4-5. In the former passage we are offered a vision of heaven in which thrones are set up, one like a son of man appears, and a kingdom is assigned to God's saints. In the latter passage Jerusalem is greeted as the place where the tribes of Israel go up to be judged before thrones of the house of David. That both of these passages are juxtaposed in a later midrash (*Midr. Tanḥ. B Qedošin* §1) which, in trying to account for the plurality of thrones in Dan 7:9, concludes that the thrones are for the "great ones" of Israel may have relevance for understanding Jesus' concept of the kingdom.[136]

---

[134] Chilton has presented his thesis in several publications (see n. 88 above). For a recent statement, see B. D. Chilton, "The Kingdom of God in Recent Discussion," in Chilton and Evans (eds.), *Studying the Historical Jesus*, 255-80.

[135] For text and translation, see Newsom, *Songs of the Sabbath Sacrifice*, 303, 306.

[136] For further discussion of this midrash, see chap. 11 below.

Summary and Assessment

The recently published materials from Cave 4 offer much new and useful data for ongoing Jesus research. There are specific highlights from the "messianic texts": (1) Perhaps the most remarkable feature is the striking parallel between 4Q521 and the dominical tradition (Q: Matt 11:5 = Luke 7:22). (2) The exciting but misguided "slain Messiah" interpretation notwithstanding, 4Q285's explicit association of the scion of David with the final triumph over Rome in itself is of importance. The fragment adds important bits of information to the sect's interpretation of Isaiah 10–11. (3) 4Q369's reference to a prince whom God will make a "first-born son" may add yet another tantalizing datum to Qumranian messianology. (4) Ideas of ascent to heaven may be found in 4Q427, 4Q458, and 4Q491. The reference in 4Q458 could be of special significance, since it may refer to an anointed individual.

Other texts of potential significance for Jesus research should include (5) the beatitudes of 4Q525, in which purity and meekness are emphasized, (6) 4Q525, in which a possible reference to the kingdom of God and power of the "demons of death" are juxtaposed, and (7) the Songs of the Sabbath Sacrifice, in which there is frequent reference to God's kingdom.

Perhaps the most important aspect of the Dead Sea Scrolls is the general observation of their relevance for the *Sitz im Leben Jesu*. This of course was observed from the moment of the publication of the first finds. Many found the parallels so striking that theories were soon forthcoming in which it was asserted that Jesus had been a member of the Dead Sea community or that he and the Teacher of Righteousness were one and the same. Although few today maintain such theories, the importance of the Dead Sea Scrolls for New Testament interpretation in general and for Jesus research in particular is widely recognized.[137]

---

[137] For older studies, see O. Cullmann, "The Significance of the Qumran Texts for Research into the Beginnings of Christianity," *JBL* 74 (1955) 213-26; H. Braun, "The Significance of Qumran for the Problem of the Historical Jesus," in C. E. Braaten and R. A. Harrisville (eds.), *The Historical Jesus and the Kerygmatic Christ: Essays on the New Quest of the Historical Jesus* (Nashville: Abingdon, 1964) 69-78; idem, *Qumran und das Neue Testament* (2 vols., Tübingen: Mohr [Siebeck], 1966) 2.54-102; W. H. Brownlee, "Jesus and Qumran," in F. T. Trotter (ed.), *Jesus and the Historian* (E. C. Colwell Festschrift; Philadelphia: Westminster, 1968) 52-81. For more recent studies, see H. C. Kee, "The Bearing of the

It is amazing how this feature is so under-appreciated by the Jesus Seminar in its penchant for situating Jesus largely outside of the thoughtworld of first century Palestine. As we shall see in the other chapters of this book, time and time again the principal themes and modes of Jesus' teaching, as well as his activities, are closely paralleled by his Jewish contemporaries, contemporaries who are rooted in the ancient sacred traditions and customs that make up the Jewish faith.

Dead Sea Scrolls on Understanding Jesus," in R. J. Hoffmann and G. A. Larue (eds.), *Jesus in History and Myth* (Buffalo: Prometheus, 1986) 54-75; J. H. Charlesworth, *Jesus Within Judaism* (ABRL 1; New York: Doubleday, 1988) 54-76; idem (ed.), *Jesus and the Dead Sea Scrolls*.

The bibliography for particular aspects of Jesus and the Dead Sea Scrolls is immense. In his 1993 SNTS Presidential Address Martin Hengel ("Aufgaben der neutestamentlichen Wissenschaft," *NTS* 40 [1994] 321-57, esp. 342-43) speaks of the "Zeichen eines neuen Qumranfrühlings," which will continue to shed light on "die Frage der Messianität Jesu." The present chapter has attempted to make a contribution to this "Qumran spring" and its relevance for Jesus research.

Three more recent publications should be mentioned: E. Tov (ed.), *The Dead Sea Scrolls on Microfiche* (Leiden: Brill, 1993); F. García Martínez, *The Dead Sea Scrolls Translated* (Leiden: Brill, 1994); and—the first volume in the Princeton series mentioned above in n. 3—J. H. Charlesworth (ed.), *The Dead Sea Scrolls: Hebrew, Aramaic, and Greek Texts with English Translations. Volume 1: Rule of the Community and Related Documents* (Tübingen: Mohr [Siebeck]; Louisville: Westminster/John Knox, 1994).

EXCURSUS ONE

EARLY MESSIANIC TRADITIONS IN THE TARGUMS

Compared to the targums to the Prophets and the Writings, the Pentateuch Targums are relatively conservative in finding messianic implications in the text. Onqelos interprets only two passages in a messianic sense: Gen 49:10-12; Num 24:17-24. Neofiti has a few more: Gen 3:15; 49:10-12; Exod 12:42; Num 11:26; 24:7, 17-24. The list grows longer in the Fragment Targums: Gen 3:15; 49:1, 10-12; Exod 12:42; Num 11:26; 24:7, 17-24. The largest number of passages interpreted messianically are found in Pseudo-Jonathan: Gen 3:15; 35:21; 49:1, 10-12; Exod 17:16; 40:9-11; Num 23:21; 24:17-24; 25:19; Deut 30:4-9.

Numerous passages in the Targums to the Prophets are understood in a messianic sense: 1 Sam 2:7-10; 2:35; 2 Sam 22:28-32; 23:1-5; 1 Kgs 5:13; Isa 4:1-6; 9:5-6; 10:24-27; 11:1-16; 14:29-30; 16:1-5; 28:5-6; 42:1-9; 43:10; 52:13–53:12; Jer 23:1-8; 30:8-11, 21; 33:12-26; Ezek 17:22-24; 34:20-31; 37:21-28; Hos 2:2; 3:3-5; 14:5-8; Mic 4:8; 5:1-3(E2-4); Hab 3:17-18; Zech 3:8; 4:7; 6:12-13; 10:4; and 12:10 (according to Codex Reuchlinianus).

A host of messianic passages can also be found in the Targums to the Writings: Pss 18:28-32(E27-31); 21:1-8; 45:7-18; 61:7-9(E6-8); 72:1-20; 80:15-18(E14-17); 89:51-52(E50-51); 132:10-18; Song 1:8, 17; 4:5; 7:4, 12-14; 8:1-4; Ruth 1:1; 3:15; Lam 2:22; 4:22; Qoh 1:11; 7:24; Esth (II) 1:1; 1 Chr 3:24.

Several of these texts in all probability reflect traditions dating to the first century C.E. or earlier. A few others may also derive from the first century, but the evidence is too meager to be certain. The following paragraphs will review these early texts and the evidence for their antiquity.[1]

---

[1] For text of Pseudo-Jonathan, see E. G. Clarke, *Targum Pseudo-Jonathan of the Pentateuch: Text and Concordance* (Hoboken: Ktav, 1984); for text of Neofiti, see A. Díez Macho, *Neophyti 1: Targum Palestinense MS de la Biblioteca Vaticana* (6 vols., Madrid and Barcelona: Consejo Superior de Investigaciones

1. Gen 3:15. In the middle of the oracle of judgment pronounced
upon the serpent for tempting Eve, the reptile is told: "I will put
enmity between you and the woman, and between your seed and her
seed; he shall bruise your head, and you shall bruise his heel" (RSV).
The Neofiti, Fragment, and Pseudo-Jonathan Targums see in this
passage hope that in the future, in the day of King Messiah, humanity
will cease its quarrels and make peace. The paraphrases of the
respective Targums are quite similar. Neofiti's reading is as follows:

ובעל דבבו אשוי ביניך ובין איתתה ובין בניך ובין בנה ויהוי

כד יהוון בניה נטרין אורייתא ועבדין פקודייה יהוון מתכוונין

לך ומחיין יתך לראשך וקטלין יתך וכד יהוון שבקין פקודי

דאוריתא תהוי מתכוין ונכת יתיה בעקבה וממרע יתיה ברם

לבריה יהוי אסו ולך חויה לא יהוי אסו דעתידין אינון מעבד

שפיותיה בעוקבה ביומא דמלכא משיחא:

"And enmities will I put between you and the woman and between your
sons and her sons. And it shall be when her sons observe the Law and put
into practice the commandments they will aim at you and smite you on the
head and kill you; but when they forsake the commandments of the Law
you will aim at and wound him on his heel and make him ill. For her son,
however, there will be a remedy, but for you, serpent, there will be no
remedy, for they will make peace in the future, in the day of King
Messiah."[2]

In Irenaeus Gen 3:15 is explicitly understood in a messianic sense

---

Científicas, 1968-77); for text of the Fragment targums, see M. L. Klein, *The
Fragment Targums of the Pentateuch According to their Extant Sources* (AnBib 76;
2 vols., Rome: Biblical Institute Press, 1980); for texts of Onqelos, the Prophets,
and the Writings (less the Psalms), see A. Sperber, *The Bible in Aramaic Based on
Old Manuscripts and Printed Texts* (5 vols., Leiden: Brill, 1959-73); for text of
Psalms, see P. de Lagarde, *Hagiographa Chaldaice* (Leipzig: Teubner, 1873). In
addition to these volumes, I have consulted P. de Lagarde, *Prophetai Chaldaice*
(Leipzig: Teubner, 1872), M. Aberbach and B. Grossfeld, *Targum Onkelos to
Genesis* (New York: Ktav, 1982), and J. F. Stenning, *The Targum of Isaiah*
(Oxford: Clarendon, 1949).

For a convenient survey and commentary, see S. H. Levey, *The Messiah: An
Aramaic Interpretation* (MHUC 2; Cincinnati: Hebrew Union College–Jewish
Institute of Religion, 1974). Levey does not take into account Neofiti. For a
summary and assessment, see J. Neusner, *Messiah in Context: Israel's History and
Destiny in Formative Judaism* (Philadelphia: Fortress, 1984) 239-47.

2   Trans. by M. McNamara and M. Maher, in Díez Macho, *Neophyti 1*,
1.503-504.

(cf. *Adv. Haer.* 21.1). The Church father understood the passage as fulfilled in the birth of Jesus and in his final victory over Satan. But was Gen 3:15 understood in a messianic sense by any of the New Testament writers? There is some evidence that it was.

Paul may be alluding to this tradition, when he tells the Roman Christians that "the God of peace will soon crush Satan under your feet" (Rom 16:20). Not only do we find the reference to crushing Satan under foot, which seems to be an allusion to Gen 3:15, but his reference to "the God of peace" coheres with the interpretation of Gen 3:15 that we have preserved in the Aramaic tradition.

Jesus may also have alluded to it in Luke 10:18-19: "I saw Satan fall like lightning from heaven. Behold, I have given [διδόναι] you authority [ἐξουσία] to tread [πατεῖν] upon serpents and scorpions, and over all the power of the enemy; and nothing shall hurt you." Treading upon serpents and scorpions (understood as Satan's forces),[3] in association with the fall of Satan, could very well be an allusion to the crushing of Satan's head in Gen 3:15.[4] The assurance that "nothing shall hurt" his disciples coheres with the Targum's assurance that the children of the woman will find a remedy in the messianic age. The later saying attributed to Rabbi Levi may be relevant: "In the messianic age all will be healed, except the serpent" (*Gen. Rab.* 20.5 [on 3:15]).[5]

The idea of trampling upon Satan and his agents predates the New Testament. According to *T. Levi* 18:10-12 the awaited deliverer[6]

> shall open the gates of Paradise and shall remove the threatening sword against Adam and shall give [διδόναι] to the saints to eat from the Tree of Life and the spirit of holiness shall be upon them and Beliar shall be bound

---

[3]   In the targums Satan is often associated with serpents and scorpions; cf. P. Grelot, "Étude critique de Luc 10,19," *RSR* 69 (1981) 87-100, esp. 92-96. For an example of "Satan" (שטן) in first century Aramaic, see 4QTLevi ar[a] 1:17.

[4]   Cf. also Ps 91:13.

[5]   This tradition may underlie Rev 12:17 καὶ ὠργίσθη ὁ δράκων ἐπὶ τῇ γυναικί, καὶ ἀπῆλθεν ποιῆσαι πόλεμον μετὰ τῶν λοιπῶν τοῦ σπέρματος αὐτῆς, τῶν τηρούντων τὰς ἐντολὰς τοῦ θεοῦ καὶ ἐχόντων τὴν μαρτυρίαν Ἰησοῦ. On the relationship between Luke 10:18-19 and Revelation 12, see M.-E. Boismard, "Rapprochements littéraires entre l'évangile de Luc et l'Apocalypse," in J. Schmid and A. Vögtle (eds.), *Synoptische Studien* (A. Wikenhauser Festschrift; Munich: Zink, 1953) 53-63, esp. 55-58; Grelot, "Luc 10,19," 97.

[6]   Although a priestly figure, the deliverer of *T. Levi* 18 should probably be understood as a messianic figure, whose "star shall rise in heaven like a king" (v. 3, alluding to Num 24:17).

by him and he shall give authority [ἐξουσία] to his children to tread [πατεῖν] on evil spirits [πνεύματα].

I suspect that Gen 3:15 is part of the scriptural tradition that lies behind *T. Levi* 18. The references to Paradise and to the removal of the sword that drove Adam from it strongly suggest that treading upon the evil spirits is an interpretation of the promise that the seed of Eve would someday crush Satan's head. As the common words indicate, Jesus' utterance in Luke 10:18-19 is surely related to *T. Levi* 18:10-12.

Finally, the anticipated struggle "between [Satan's] sons and [the woman's] sons" may form part of the backdrop of the vitriolic exchange in John 8. The Aramaic interpretation of Gen 3:15 may very well be the presupposition behind the accusation that the Johannine Jesus levels against his opponents: "you are of your father the devil" (John 8:44).[7]

Although the extant targumic tradition in all probability represents a later embellished form of the tradition, complete with emphasis on keeping Torah faithfully, the messianic nuance itself probably derives from the first century or earlier, as attested by New Testament and pseudepigraphal writings.[8]

2. Gen 49:10-12. All four Pentateuch Targums understand Jacob's blessing of his son Judah in a messianic sense. The royal dimension of the blessing readily lent itself to messianic interpretation: "The scepter shall not depart from Judah, nor the ruler's staff from between his feet, until Shiloh comes; and to him shall be the obedience of the peoples" (RSV, slightly modified). The Aramaic reads, according to Neofiti:

10 לא פסקין מלכין מין דבית יהודה ואף לא ספרין מלפי אוריה
מבני בנוי עד זמן דייתי מלכא משיחא דדידיה היא מלכותא וליה
ישתעבדון כל מלכוותא:
11 מה יאי הוא מלכא משיחא דעתיד למיקם מן מדבית יהודה אסר
חרציה ונפק לקרבא על שנאוי ומקטל מלכין עם שלטונין מסמק

---

7   See G. Reim, "Joh. 8.44—Gotteskinder/Teufelskinder: Wie antijudaistisch ist 'Die wohl antijudaistischste Äusserung des NT'?" *NTS* 30 (1984) 619-24. Reim relates John 8:39-47, particularly v. 44, especially to Gen 4:1-16 in the targums.

8   For further discussion in support of an early date of the targumic paraphrase of Gen 3:15, see McNamara, *The New Testament and the Palestinian Targum to the Pentateuch* (AnBib 27A; 2nd ed., Rome: Biblical Institute, 1978) 217-22; J. Michl, "Der Weibessame (Gen 3,15) in Spätjudentum und frühchristlicher Auffassung," *Bib* 33 (1952) 371-401.

טורייא מדם קטיליהון ומחוור גלמתא מתרבי גובריהון לבושי
מעגעגין בדמא מדמי לרפוס ענבים:
מה ייאיין עיני דמלכא משיחא מן חמרא זכוא דלא למיחמי בהון   12
גילוי עריין מלמשפך בהון דם זכיי שנוי נקיין מחלבא מלמיכל
בהון חמיסיין וגזילין יסמקון טורייא מן גפני ומעצרתא מן חמרא
ויתחוורון גלמתא מן סגי עבור ועדרין דען:

"[10]Kings shall not cease from among those of the house of Judah, and
neither (shall) scribes teaching the Law from his sons' sons until the time
King Messiah shall come whose is the kingship; to him shall all the
kingdoms be subject. [11]How beautiful is King Messiah who is to arise from
among those of the house of Judah. He girds his loins and goes forth to
battle against those that hate him; and he kills kings with rulers, and makes
the mountains red from the blood of their slain and makes the valleys white
from the fat of their warriors. His garments arc rolled in blood; he is like a
presser of grapes. [12]How beautiful are the eyes of King Messiah; more than
pure wine lest he see with them the revealing of nakedness or the shedding
of innocent blood. His teeth are purer than milk, lest he eat with them things
that are stolen or robbed. The mountains will become red from his vines and
the vats from wine; and the hills will become white from the abundance of
grain and flocks of sheep."[9]

The most significant variant among the Targums is found in
Onqelos' paraphrase of v. 11: עמא יבנון היכליה ("the people shall build
his Temple"). Although Onqelos' reading overall is simpler, this
reference to building the Temple probably reflects the post-70 C.E.
hope, rather than a prophecy of the building of the first Temple.[10] But
the messianic interpretation is itself is much earlier.

Qumran provides evidence of early messianic interpretation of Gen
49:10-12: "[1]'A monarch will [not] be wanting to the tribe of Judah'
[Gen 49:10] when Israel rules, [2][and] a (descendant) seated on it (the
throne) will [not] be wanting to David. For 'the (commander's) staff'
[Gen 49:10] is the covenant of kingship, [3][and] the 'feet' [cf. Gen 49:11]
are [the thou]sands of Israel, 'until' the coming of the Messiah [משיח] of
righteousness, the branch of [4]David [צמח דויד]; for to him and to his
seed has been given the covenant of kingship over his people for
everlasting generations, because [5]he has kept [. . .] the Law together
with the men of the community" (4QPatrBles [= 4Q252] 5:1-7). The
passage is probably alluded to in 4QpIsa[a] (= 4Q161) 7-10 iii 25 as

---

9   Trans. by McNamara and Maher, in Díez Macho, Neophyti 1, 1.635.
10   On the development of the tradition, see Aberbach and Grossfeld, Genesis,
287-88 n. 25.

well: "And God will place a scepter] in his hand, and over all the n[ation]s he will rule" (see the discussions of these texts in chap. 3 above).

The LXX may also witness the presence of an implied messianic interpretation, especially as seen in v. 10:

οὐκ ἐκλείψει ἄρχων ἐξ Ιουδα καὶ ἡγούμενος ἐκ τῶν μηρῶν αὐτοῦ, ἕως ἂν ἔλθῃ τὰ ἀποκείμενα αὐτῷ, καὶ αὐτὸς προσδοκία ἐθνῶν.

"A prince will not fail from Judah, nor a leader from his loins, until the things reserved for him should come—even he, the expectation of nations."

McNamara points out that the Targums to Gen 49:11-12 parallel at important points Rev 19:11-16, an apocalyptic passage that describes the faithful warrior Messiah.[11] The beauty of his "eyes" (Rev 19:12; *Tgs.* Gen 49:12), his blood-soaked garments (Rev 19:13; *Tgs.* Gen 49:11), and the picture of the Messiah as a presser of grapes (Rev 19:15; *Tgs.* Gen 49:11) strongly suggest that the dramatic picture of Revelation 19 reflects interpretive traditions associated with Jacob's blessing of his son Judah in Genesis 49, traditions which are now preserved in all of the Pentateuch Targums.[12]

3. Num 24:17-24. This is the second and only other passage which is taken in a messianic sense by all four Pentateuch Targums. Balaam's oracle, intended as a curse upon Israel but transformed into a blessing, sees one who is not yet present: "a star shall come forth out of Jacob, and a scepter shall rise out of Israel; it shall crush the forehead of Moab, and break down all the sons of Sheth" (RSV). Of the readings of the four Targums, which parallel one another fairly closely, that of Onqelos is probably the earliest. Discussion will be limited to v. 17:

חזיתיה ולא כען סכיתיה וליתוהי קריב כד יקום מלכא מיעקב
ויתרבא משיחא מישראל ויקטיל רברבי מואב וישלוט בכל בני אנשא:

"I see him, but not now; I behold him, but he is not near; when a king shall arise out of Jacob and be anointed the Messiah out of Israel. He shall slay the princes of Moab and reign over all mankind."[13]

Although Onqelos' reading overall is simplest and probably the earliest, the variant reading "king," without the explicit mention of

---

11   McNamara, *The New Testament and the Palestinian Targum*, 230-33.

12   For other possible traces of early messianic exegesis of Gen 49:10-12, see Heb 7:14; Rev 5:5.

13   Trans. by Levey, *The Messiah*, 21.

"Messiah," which is found in Neofiti and the Fragment Targum, could be a more primitive reading. (Pseudo-Jonathan agrees with Onqelos in reading "anointed Messiah.")

Messianic interpretation of Num 24:17 is amply attested in the first century or earlier (cf. *T. Judah* 24:1-6; CD 7:20; 1QM 11:4-9; possibly Philo, *Vit. Mos.* 1.52 §290; *De praem. et poen.* 16 §95). As argued above in chap. 2, Num 24:17 is probably the "ambiguous oracle" which Josephus understood as fulfilled in Vespasian's accession to the throne (*J.W.* 6.5.4 §312-314). The LXX itself seems to reflect to some degree messianic interpretation:

Δείξω αὐτῷ, καὶ οὐχὶ νῦν· μακαρίζω, καὶ οὐκ ἐγγίζει· ἀνατελεῖ ἄστρον ἐξ Ἰακὼβ, καὶ ἀναστήσεται ἄνθρωπος ἐξ Ἰσραήλ· καὶ θραύσει τοὺς ἀρχηγοὺς Μωὰβ καὶ προνομεύσει πάντας υἱοὺς Σήθ.

"I shall point him out, though not now; I bless (him), though he is not near. A star will arise out of Jacob; even a man will arise from Israel. And he will strike the princes of Moab and he will plunder all the sons of Seth."

See Matt 2:3; 2 Pet 1:19; Rev 22:16. This oracle is likely what lies behind Simon ben Kosiba's title, "Bar Kokhba." See chap. 4 for further discussion of the Bar Kokhba tradition.

4. 1 Sam 2:1-10. The final verse of Hannah's song of thanksgiving invited messianic interpretation: "The Lord will judge the ends of the earth; he will give strength to his king, and exalt the power of his anointed" (RSV). In the Targum her song becomes an apocalyptic prophecy: "And Hannah prayed in a spirit of prophecy" (v. 1), which goes on to speak of the Philistines, Assyrians, Babylonians, Greeks, the Hasmoneans, and Esther and Mordecai. In true apocalyptic style, Hannah's reworked song foresees judgment of Israel's enemies, who will be cast into Gehenna. The concluding verse probably understands the "anointed" in terms of the expected Messiah. The Aramaic reads:

יוי יתבר בעלי דבבא דקימין לאבאשא לעמיה עליהון
מן שמיא בקל רם ישקיף יוי יעביד פורענות דין מגוג
ומשרית עממין חטופין דאתן עמיה מסיפי ארעא ויתין
תוקפא למלכיה וירבי מלכות משיחיה:

"The Lord shall shatter the adversaries who arise to do evil to His people; He shall blast them with a loud noise issuing from heaven. The Lord shall exact punishment from Gog and from the marauding armies of the nations who come with him from the ends of the earth. He shall give strength to His king, and shall make great the kingdom of His Messiah."[14]

Daniel Harrington believes that the Aramaic form of Hannah's song probably took shape in the aftermath of the destruction of Jerusalem in 70 C.E.[15] He is probably correct. Harrington and Anthony Saldarini further conclude that in the Aramaic tradition the text is understood as messianic.[16] The Magnificat (Luke 1:46-55), which is clearly modeled after Hannah's song, suggests that 1 Sam 2:1-10 may have been understood, at least in part, in a messianic sense and possibly before 70 C.E.

That Luke intended the infancies of Samuel and Jesus to parallel one another seems clear enough.[17] The summary of the young Samuel's growth (1 Sam 2:26: "Now the boy Samuel continued to grow both in stature and in favor with the Lord and with men") is clearly echoed in Luke's summary of Jesus: "And Jesus increased in wisdom and in stature, and in favor with God and man" (Luke 2:52). Luke provides this summary following Jesus' visit to the Temple (Luke 2:41-51), in which the lad tells his perplexed parents that it was necessary for him to be in his "Father's house" (2:49). Samuel's summary likewise appears in the context of the boy growing up in the Temple (1 Sam 1:28; 2:11, 18-20). But it is in the comparison of the two canticles themselves that we find the most important parallels:

Luke 1	*1 Samuel 2*
My soul magnifies the Lord (v. 47). . . . for He has regarded the humble estate of His servant (v. 48).	My heart exults in the Lord (v. 1). . . . if You will look on the affliction of of Your servant, and remember me . . . (1:11)
He has put down the mighty from their thrones, and exalted those of low degree (v. 52).	The bows of the mighty are broken, but the feeble gird on strength (v. 4).

---

14   Trans. by Levey, *The Messiah*, 34. Compare also the translation in D. J. Harrington and A. J. Saldarini, *Targum Jonathan of the Former Prophets* (ArBib 10; Wilmington: Glazier, 1987) 105-106.

15   D. J. Harrington, "The Apocalypse of Hannah: Targum Jonathan of 1 Samuel 2:1-10," in D. M. Golomb (ed.), *"Working With No Data": Semitic and Egyptian Studies Presented to Thomas O. Lambdin* (Winona Lake: Eisenbrauns, 1987) 147-52.

16   Harrington and Saldarini, *Targum Jonathan of the Former Prophets*, 106 n.10.

17   See J. A. Sanders, "Ναζωραῖος in Matthew 2.23," in C. A. Evans and W. R. Stegner (eds.), *The Gospels and the Scriptures of Israel* (JSNTSup 104; SSEJC 3; Sheffield: JSOT Press, 1994) 116-28, esp. 123-25.

He has filled the hungry with good things, and the rich he has sent empty away (v. 53).	Those who were full have hired themselves out for bread, but those who were hungry have ceased to hunger (v. 5).

It is difficult to resist the conclusion that the Magnificat in some way is related to the Aramaic paraphrase of Hannah's song, which has become a prophecy of Israel's turbulent future, concluding with the appearance of the Messiah. 1 Samuel 2:10 is understood in a Davidic sense in *Mek.* on Exod 15:12-16 (*Širata* §9); in a few other places it is taken in an eschatological sense (cf. *Lam. Rab.* 2:3 §6; *Midr. Sam.* §5; *Midr. Ps.* 75.5 [on 75:11]).

5. *Isa 11:1-16.* In the Hebrew, Isaiah's oracle anticipates the coming forth of "a shoot from the stump of Jesse, even a branch (that) shall grow out of his roots" (v. 1). This Davidic descendant will be endowed with God's Spirit and will be able to judge Israel faithfully and usher in a time of lasting peace. The roots of Old Testament messianic expectation are to be found in this passage and in 2 Samuel 7. The passage readily invited explicit messianic paraphrasing, as seen in the Targum, especially in vv. 1 and 6:

1   ויפוק מלכא מבנוהי דישי ומשיחא מבני בנוהי יתרבי:

6   ביומוהי דמשיחא דישראל יסגי שלמא בארעא וידור דיבא עם אימרא
ונמרא עם גדיא ישרי ועגל ואריה ופטים כחדא ויניק זעיר מדבר להון:

"And a king shall come forth from the sons of Jesse, and the Messiah shall be exalted from the sons of his sons."

"In the days of the Messiah of Israel shall peace increase in the land, and the wolf shall dwell with the lamb, and the leopard shall lie down with the kid, and the calf and the lion and the fatling together, and a little suckling child will lead them."[18]

With respect to v. 6, Bruce Chilton has made the pertinent observation that the meturgeman's eschatology appears to predate that of the authors of 4 Ezra 12:34 and 2 Bar 40:4, who imagined that the appearance of Messiah was but a prelude to the final divine drama.[19] In contrast to these late first-century views, the Targum appears to

---

[18]   Trans. by B. D. Chilton, *The Isaiah Targum* (ArBib 11; Wilmington: Glazier, 1987) 28.

[19]   B. D. Chilton, *The Glory of Israel: The Theology and Provenience of the Isaiah Targum* (JSOTSup 23; Sheffield: JSOT Press, 1982) 88.

envision the messianic era as itself the final age.

The LXX enhances the messianic potential of the text, especially in v. 10:

Καὶ ἔσται ἐν τῇ ἡμέρᾳ ἐκείνῃ ἡ ῥίζα τοῦ Ἰεσαι καὶ ὁ ἀνιστάμενος ἄρχειν ἐθνῶν, ἐπ' αὐτῷ ἔθνη ἐλπιοῦσιν, καὶ ἔσται ἡ ἀνάπαυσις αὐτοῦ τιμή.

"And there shall be in that day the root of Jesse, even he who arises to rule over the nations; in him the nations will hope, and his place of rest will be an honor."

The paraphrase, "he who arises to rule over the nations," makes explicit the triumphalistic aspect of the anticipated branch of David.

Qumran understood Isaiah 11 messianically. 1QSb 5:21-26 alludes to parts of Isa 11:1-5: "the Prince [נשיא] of the congregation who . . . and for whom He will renew the covenant of the community, that he may restore the kingdom of His people for ev[er and judge the poor with justice, and] that he may rule with e[quity the hum]ble of the land" (lines 20-22). Isaiah 11 is understood messianically in 4QpIsa^a (= 4Q161) 7-10 iii 22-29: "[The interpretation of the matter concerns the branch of] David, who will appear at the en[d of days to save ²³Israel and to exterminate] his [ene]mies. And God will sustain him with [a 'mi]ghty [spirit' (Isa 11:2) . . . And God will give him a th]rone of glory, a h[oly] crown" (lines 22-24). 4QMess ar (= 4Q536) 3 i 10 may allude to Isa 11:4, though whether or not 4QMess ar is itself messianic is disputed. 4Q287 10:13 ("the Holy Spirit [rest]ed upon His Messiah") may allude to Isa 11:2. (For further discussion of these texts, see chap. 3 above.)

Several parts of Isa 11:1-16 are alluded to in the New Testament, though most of these allusions are found in books written in the late first century or in the second. Only one allusion is found on the lips of Jesus: "Do not judge according to appearance [κατ' ὄψιν], but judge the just judgment" (John 7:24; cf. Isa 11:3). In all probability, of course, we have here an utterance of the Johannine community in conflict with a synagogue that has rejected the Christian message. The Matthean fulfillment, "He shall be called a Nazarene" (Matt 2:23), probably has something to do with the נצר of Isa 11:1.[20] These are allusions at best; in Rom 15:12 Paul quotes LXX Isa 11:10 and explicitly applies the passage to Jesus. From this we may infer that the messianic interpretation of Isaiah 11 was known to Christians no later than the middle

---

[20]   Again see Sanders, "Ναζωραῖος in Matthew 2.23," 127-28.

of the first century.

6. Isa 42:1-9. Two of Second Isaiah's Servant Songs are understood in a messianic sense in the Isaiah Targum. The first is Isa 42:1-9, but only in some MSS.[21] The question of the Targum's "original" reading is not important; what is important is that there is some evidence that Isa 42:1-9 was understood in some circles as having to do with the Messiah. Not only does "Messiah" appear in some of the Aramaic texts of Isa 42:1-9, the passage is given a messianic interpretation elsewhere. The Aramaic of v. 1, with the disputed variant in brackets, reads as follows:

הא עבדי [משיחא] אקרבניה בחירי דאתרעי ביה מימרי אתין רוח קודשי
עלוהי דיני לעממין יגלי:

"Behold my servant [the Messiah], I will bring him near, my chosen in whom my Memra is pleased; I will put my Holy Spirit upon him, he will reveal my judgment to the peoples."[22]

There are several important allusions to this passage in the New Testament. The heavenly voice that speaks at the baptism and transfiguration of Jesus ("You are my son in whom I am pleased") has probably alluded to Isa 42:1.[23] The Matthean evangelist explicitly cites Isa 42:1-4, as fulfilled in Jesus' public ministry (cf. Matt 12:18-21). Matthew's quotation is based on the Hebrew, with some influence from the LXX and the Targum.[24] Given Matthew's emphasis in portraying Jesus as Israel's Messiah (cf. 1:1, 16-18; 2:4; 16:20), it does seem likely that the evangelist's interest in applying Isa 42:1-4 to Jesus lay, at least in part, to a messianic understanding of the passage.

4QMess ar (= 4Q536) 3 i 10 ("he is the Elect of God [בחיר אלהא]") may contain an allusion to Isa 42:1, but as noted above, there is some doubt about whether or not this text is speaking of a messianic figure.

---

21 Levey (*The Messiah*, 59) accepts the reading, following Lagarde and the Warsaw edition. Stenning, Sperber, and Chilton omit it. For the MSS and texts that include משיחא, see Sperber, *The Bible in Aramaic*, 3.84.

22 Trans. by Chilton, *The Isaiah Targum*, 81.

23 See the discussion in D. C. Allison and W. D. Davies, *The Gospel according to Saint Matthew* (2 vols., ICC; Edinburgh: T. & T. Clark, 1988-91) 1.336-39; B. D. Chilton, *A Galilean Rabbi and His Bible: Jesus' Use of the Interpreted Scripture of His Time* (GNS 8; Wilmington: Glazier, 1984) 129-31.

24 K. Stendahl, *The School of St. Matthew and Its Use of the Old Testament* (rev. ed., Philadelphia: Fortress, 1968) 115; R. H. Gundry, *The Use of the Old Testament in St. Matthew's Gospel* (NovTSup 18; Leiden: Brill, 1967) 110-16.

7. Isa 52:13–53:12. The mysterious and much discussed Suffering
Servant Song in the Targum is taken not only in a messianic sense, but
in a triumphalistic sense. The Servant Messiah does not suffer; his
enemies suffer. He is not crushed by the iniquities of his people; the
Temple is, which he will rebuild. He is not led like a lamb to the
slaughter; he will lead the wicked to their slaughter. His grave is not
assigned with the wicked; he will deliver the wicked to Gehenna. The
transformation of the text is remarkable. Below are 52:13, 53:4, 53:5,
and 53:10, which may have relevance for the New Testament:

13 הא יצלח עבדי משיחא יראם ויסגי ויתקף לחדא:

4   בכין על חובנא הוא יבעי ועויתנא בדיליה ישתבקן ואנחנא
    חשיבין כתישין מחן מן קדם יוי ומענן:

5   והוא יבני בית מקדשא דאיתחל בחובנא אתמסר בעויתנא ובאלפניה
    שלמיה יסגי עלנא ובדנתנהי לפתגמוהי חובנא ישתבקן לנא:

10 ומן קדם יוי הות רעוא למצרף ולדכאה ית שארא דעמיה בדיל
    לנקאה מחובין נפשהון יחזון במלכות משיחהון יסגון בנין
    ובנן יירכון יומין ועבדי אוריתא דיוי ברעותיה יצלחון:

"Behold, my servant the Messiah, shall prosper, he shall be exalted and
increase, and shall be very strong."

"Then he will beseech concerning our sins and our iniquities for his sake
will be forgiven; yet we were esteemed wounded, smitten before the Lord
and afflicted."

"And he will build the sanctuary which was profaned for our sins, handed
over for our iniquities; and by his teaching his peace will increase upon us,
and in that we attach ourselves to his words our sins will be forgiven us."

"Yet before the Lord it was a pleasure to refine and to cleanse the remnant of
his people, in order to purify their soul from sins; they shall see the
kingdom of their Messiah, they shall increase sons and daughters, they shall
prolong days; those who perform the law of the Lord shall prosper in his
pleasure."[25]

Bo Reicke and William Brownlee have argued that the reference in
1QS 4:20 to "a certain one from among the sons of men" is the
messianic figure of Isaiah's Suffering Servant Song.[26] Appealing to

---

25   Trans. by Chilton, *The Isaiah Targum*, 103-105.
26   B. Reicke, *Handskrifterna från Qumrân* [Symbolae Biblicae Upsalienses
14; Uppsala: Wretmans, 1952] 70; W. H. Brownlee, "The Servant of the Lord in

Tg. Isa 53:10 and to Qumran's treatment of the Servant passages, Brownlee translates line 20 as follows: "At that time God will purify by His truth all the deeds of a man; and He will refine him more than the sons of men."[27] By suffering, the Servant Messiah would become refined and able to bring about God's kingdom. Brownlee finds further support for his interpretation in 1QIsa[a] 44:1-4 (= Isa 52:14-15), where in 52:14 a variant could suggest that the Servant's face is "anointed." But Brownlee's proposals have not won general acceptance (see the discussion above in chap. 3). The Dead Sea Scrolls do not, therefore, provide clear evidence of a pre-Christian messianic interpretation of the Suffering Servant Song.

However, the Suffering Servant Song is quoted or alluded to in several New Testament passages, which could suggest that it was understood in a messianic sense in the first century.[28] It may be, as Morna Hooker has argued, that scholars have in the past over estimated the influence that the Servant concept had in the formation of early christology,[29] but the fact remains that several New Testament writers seem interested to relate Jesus in various ways to certain aspects of the Servant. Indeed, in a few places verbatim quotations are applied to him (cf. Matt 8:17 = Isa 53:4; John 12:38 = Isa 53:1; Acts 8:32-33 = Isa 53:7-8; Rom 10:16 = Isa 53:1; Rom 15:21 = Isa 52:15; 1 Pet 2:24-25 = Isa 53:5-6).

An important point of thematic coherence between the Aramaic version of the Song and the New Testament Gospels concerns sin and the Servant's intercession in behalf of his people. Whereas the Hebrew text in 53:4-5, 10 speaks of infirmities and disease, the Aramaic speaks of sins and iniquities. The association of these ideas is present in Jesus' ministry: Matt 9:1-8 = Mark 2:1-12 = Luke 5:17-26 (the healing/forgiving of the paralytic). The clearest example of the targumic interpretation of *heal* in terms of *forgiveness* is seen in Isa 6:10, to

---

the Qumran Scrolls II," *BASOR* 135 (1954) 33-38; idem, "John the Baptist in the New Light of Ancient Scrolls," *Int* 9 (1955) 71-90, esp. 88; idem, *The Meaning of the Qumrân Scrolls for the Bible: With Special Attention to the Book of Isaiah* (Oxford and New York: Oxford University Press, 1964) 206-207.

27 Brownlee, *The Meaning of the Qumrân Scrolls*, 207.

28 For a convenient summary, see C. H. Dodd, *According to the Scriptures* (London: Nisbet, 1952) 92-94.

29 M. D. Hooker, *Jesus and the Servant: The Influence of the Servant Concept of Deutero-Isaiah in the New Testament* (London: SPCK, 1959).

which Jesus alludes in Mark 4:12.[30] Although the Matthean evangelist quotes Isa 53:4 as fulfilled in Jesus' healing ministry (Matt 8:14-17), he expects his readers and hearers to understand his ministry of healing in the light of the angelic announcement made at the outset of his Gospel, viz. that Jesus' purpose is to "save his people from their sins" (Matt 1:21).

The opening verse of Isaiah's Suffering Servant Song appears to play a very important role in the fourth evangelist's christology. Drawing upon the principal verbs in the Greek version, the evangelist has Jesus speak of the impending hour in which he is to be "lifted up" (ὑψωθῆναι) and "glorified" (δοξασθῆναι). Both of these verbs are drawn from LXX Isa 52:13, especially as they come into play in John 12.[31]

Given the influence of this Isaianic Song in the New Testament and given the fact of its explicit messianic presentation in the Targum, it is probable that the messianic interpretation of Isa 52:13–53:12 did not originate in early Christianity, but predated it. It is to be admitted that the Targum's triumphalistic picture of the Messiah in all probability took its shape between 70 and 135 C.E., as Chilton has argued,[32] but this does not mean that the passage was not viewed in a messianic sense prior to this time. Although over-arguing the point, Robert Aytoun's claim that Jewish interpreters would have been reluctant to messianize the Suffering Servant Song after the rise of Christianity does have some merit.[33] I believe that the messianic interpretation of this passage

---

[30]   On this passage, see Chilton, *A Galilean Rabbi and His Bible*, 90-98; C. A. Evans, *To See and Not Perceive: Isaiah 6.9-10 in Early Jewish and Christian Interpretation* (JSOTSup 64; Sheffield: JSOT Press, 1989) 69-76 (on the targum) and 91-106 (on Mark).

[31]   See C. A. Evans, "Obduracy and the Lord's Servant: Some Observations on the Use of the Old Testament in the Fourth Gospel," in C. A. Evans and W. F. Stinespring (eds.), *Early Jewish and Christian Exegesis: Studies in Memory of William Hugh Brownlee* (Homage 10; Atlanta: Scholars Press, 1987) 221-36.

[32]   Chilton, *The Glory of Israel*, 91-96. The prediction that the Messiah "will rebuild the Temple" clearly points to a date after 70. That rebuilding the Temple was a messianic task to begin with is based on the original building of the Temple, which was Solomon's task, and Zechariah's promise that the "Branch" would build a new Temple (Zech 6:12). What links this task to the Servant of the Aramaic Isaiah is the fact that in Zechariah the Branch is also called the Lord's "Servant" (Zech 3:8).

[33]   R. A. Aytoun, "The Servant of the Lord in the Targum," *JTS* 23 (1921-22) 172-80. See Chilton's criticisms of Aytoun's conclusions in *The Glory of Israel*,

in the Targum survives, despite its exploitation in Christian theology, because it was ancient and widely held. The triumphalistic interpretation, perhaps prompted to some extent by the rise of Simon ben Kosiba as "Bar Kokhba," would have countered Christians' emphasis on suffering, while the defeat of Bar Kokhba would not have had the effect of eliminating the messianic interpretation altogether but of further eschatologizing it.

8. *Jer 23:5.* In a scathing oracle the prophet Jeremiah condemns Judah's leaders as corrupt shepherds who have plundered and scattered God's flock. In sharp contrast to these faithless rulers, the prophet reassures the people, God will some day "raise up for David a righteous branch and he shall reign as king." Elsewhere in the prophets (Jer 33:15; Zech 3:8; 6:12) "Branch" becomes a name for an awaited righteous king and so easily lent itself to messianic interpretation. The Targum understands this "righteous branch" as the Messiah:

הא יומיא אתן אמר יוי ואקים לדויד משיח דצדקא
וימלוך מלכא ויצלח ויעביד דין דקשוט וזכו בארעא:

"Behold, the days are coming, says the Lord, when I shall raise up for David a righteous Messiah, and he shall reign as king, and prosper, and shall enact a righteous and meritorious law in the land."[34]

There is a modicum of evidence that suggests that Jer 23:5 was understood in a messianic sense prior to the emergence of the Targum. The LXX speaks of God raising up to David ἀνατολὴν δικαίαν ("a righteous rising"), which is probably intended as an enhancement of the passage. More impressive is what appears to be an allusion to Jer 23:5 in *Pss. Sol.* 17:32, in which the context is clearly messianic:

καὶ αὐτὸς βασιλεὺς δίκαιος διδακτὸς ὑπὸ θεοῦ ἐπ' αὐτούς, καὶ οὐκ ἔστιν ἀδικία ἐν ταῖς ἡμέραις αὐτοῦ ἐν μέσῳ αὐτῶν, ὅτι πάντες ἅγιοι, καὶ βασιλεὺς αὐτῶν χριστὸς κυρίος.

"And he will be a righteous king over them, taught by God. There will be no unrighteousness in their midst in his days, for all shall be holy, and their king shall be the Lord Messiah."

This "righteous" king could well be an allusion to the righteous branch of Jer 23:5. There may be allusions to the passage in the New Testament. Paul's description of Christ Jesus as the believers'

_____

92-93, 156-57 nn. 11 and 14.

[34] Trans. based on Levey, *The Messiah*, 68-69.

"wisdom" and "righteousness" may echo the prophetic text (1 Cor 1:30). In the very next verse Paul quotes from Jer 9:24 (1 Cor 1:31), so it is possible that the apostle was thinking of Jeremiah. The Good Shepherd discourse in John 10, in which previous shepherds are referred to as thieves and robbers, may also presuppose the targumic interpretation of Jeremiah's shepherd oracle.

9. *Mic 5:1.* Micah consoled Judah with the prophecy that "a ruler" (מוֹשֵׁל) would some day come forth, "whose goings forth are from of old, from ancient days" (E5:2). The passage readily lent itself to a messianic interpretation, though the Aramaic paraphrase is careful to explain in what sense this figure is from ancient times:

ואת בית לחם אפרת כזעיר הויתא לאתמנאה באלפיא דבית יהודה
מנך קדמי יפוק משיחא למהוי עביד שולטן על ישראל ודי שמיה
אמיר מלקדמין מיומי עלמא:

"And you, O Bethlehem Ephrath, you who were too small to be numbered among the thousands of the house of Judah, from you shall come forth before Me the Messiah, to exercise dominion over Israel, he whose name was mentioned from before, from the days of creation."[35]

The Micah paraphrase is echoed in *Ps.-J.* Gen 35:19-21, parts of which read:

19   ומיתת רחל ואתקברת באורח אפרת היא בית לחם:
21   ... אתרא דהתמן עתיד דיתגלי מלכא משיחא בסוף יומייא:

"And Rachel died and was buried on the way to Ephrath, that is Bethlehem. . . . the place from which the King Messiah will reveal himself at the end of days."

The passage is quoted in Matt 2:6 and alluded to with a bit of irony in John 7:42. It is clear from these passages that Mic 5:1(E2) was understood in a messianic sense in the first century. In the context of the first one, we are told that Herod "gathered together the chief priests and scribes of the people and inquired of them where the Messiah [ὁ χριστός] should be born. They told him, 'In Bethlehem of Judea; for so it is written . . .'" (Matt 2:4-5). In John's Gospel the crowd muses: "Does not Scripture say that 'from the seed of David,' and 'from Bethlehem' the village from which David hailed the Messiah [ὁ χριστός] 'comes'?" (John 7:42). The first allusion is to 2 Sam 7:12, while the second and third allusions are to Micah.

---

35   Trans. by Levey, *The Messiah*, 93.

A few more targumic texts may reflect messianic tradition dating to the first century. They include the following:

10. Exod 12:42. The Targum's expansion of Exod 12:42, which speaks of the first Passover observance, is one of the most remarkable pieces of interpretation found in the Targums. Both the Fragment Targum and Neofiti take the passage in a messianic sense. The "fourth night" paragraph reads, following the Fragment Targum:

לילא רביעאה כד ישלים עלמא קציה למתפרקה עבדי רישעה ישתיצון
ונירי דפרזלא יתברון ומשה יפוק מן גו מדברא ומלכא משיחא מן גו רומא
דין ידבר בריש ענה ודין בריש ענה ומימרא דיי יהוי ביני תרויהון ואנא
והינון מהלכין כחדא הוא ליל פיסחא קודם יי נטיר ומזומן לכל בני
ישראל לדרייהון:

"The fourth night: when the world will read its fixed time to be redeemed; the evil-doers will be destroyed, and the iron yokes will be broken; and Moses will go forth from the midst of the wilderness and the King Messiah from on high: this one will lead at the head of the cloud (*or* flock), and that one will lead at the head of the cloud (*or* flock); and the Word of the Lord will be between both of them; and I and they will proceed together. This is the Passover night before the Lord; it is preserved and prepared for all the Israelites, through their generations."[36]

The depiction of King Messiah going forth "on high" and at the head of the "cloud" may be an allusion to Dan 7:13, which in the New Testament (cf. Mark 14:61-62) and in rabbinic literature is taken in a messianic sense (cf. *b. Sanh.* 98a). The association of Messiah with Passover is seen in the New Testament, in both Paul (1 Cor 5:7: "Christ our Passover") and in the fourth Gospel, which likens Jesus' execution to the sacrifice of the Passover lamb (cf. 1:29, 36; and chaps. 18–19).[37]

---

36   Trans. based on Klein, *The Fragment-Targums of the Pentateuch*, 2.126. I disagree with Klein's reading "from Rome." It should be "from on high," which makes better sense of the context. The word רומא can be read either רוּמָא ("height") or רוֹמָא ("Rome"). The former makes the best sense, given the subsequent reference to "flock" (ענה or ענא), which is probably meant as an allusion to "cloud" (עננא); cf. the translation and comments of McNamara and Maher in Díez Macho, *Neophyti 1*, 2.442 nn. 1-2. Levey (*The Messiah*, 12-13) reads "cloud."

37   See C. A. Evans, *Word and Glory: On the Exegetical and Theological Background of John's Prologue* (JSNTSup 89; Sheffield: JSOT Press, 1993) 181-84; and esp. S. E. Porter, "Can Traditional Exegesis Enlighten Literary Analysis of the Fourth Gospel? An Examination of the Old Testament Fulfillment Motif and the Passover Theme," in Evans and Stegner (eds.), *The Gospels and the Scriptures of Israel*, 396-428.

The linking of Moses and Messiah, often in terms of typology, is also found in rabbinic literature (cf. *Sipre Deut.* §130 [on 16:3]; *Pesiq. R.* 15.10; *Pesiq. R. Kah.* 5.8) and in the New Testament.[38]

11. Num 11:26. In response to a grumbling and faithless people, the Spirit of the Lord descended upon seventy elders gathered about the Tabernacle, who then began to prophesy for a short time. But two men who had not gone out to the Tabernacle, Eldad and Medad (or Modad), "prophesied in the camp." The Fragment Targum and Neofiti supply us with the content of their prophecy:

ואשתיירו תרין גברין במשריתה שמה דחד אלדד ושמה דתניינה
מידד ושרת עליהון רוח קודשה אלדד הוה מתנבא ואמר הא סלוי
סלק מן ימא ויהוי לישראל לתקלה ומידד הוה מתנבא ואמר הא
משה נביא מסתלק מן גו משריתה ויהושע בר נון משמש נשיותיה
בתריה ותרוייהון מתנבביין כחדא ואמרין בסוף עקב יומיא גוג ומגוג
סלקין לירושלם ובידוי דמלכא משיחה אינון נפלין ושבע שנין
ידלקון בני ישראל מן מני זייניהון וחרש לא יפקון ואינון הוון מן
שבעתי חכימיה דמתפרשין ולא נפקו שבעתי חכימיה מן משריתה
עד אלדד ומדד מתנבאין במשריתה:

> "And two men remained in the camp, the name of one was Eldad and the name of the second was Medad, and the Holy Spirit rested upon them. Eldad prophesied and said: 'Behold, quail come up from the sea and shall become a stumbling-block for Israel.' And Medad prophesied and said: 'Behold, Moses the prophet is taken up from the midst of the camp and Joshua bar Nun exercises his leadership in his stead.' And both of them prophesied together, saying: 'At the very end of days Gog and Magog ascend on Jerusalem and they fall at the hand of King Messiah, and for seven years the children of Israel shall kindle fires from their implements of war; and the carpenters wil not have to go out.' And these were from the seventy wise men who were set apart. And the seventy wise men did not leave the cample while Eldad and Medad were prophesying in the camp."[39]

Pseudo-Jonathan is vividly eschatological, but not messianic. The paraphrase offers a prophecy that predicts the appearance of a king from the land of Magog who gathers the nations against Israel. But they all will be destroyed by a blast of fire issuing forth from beneath God's throne. While beasts and birds of carrion feast on their corpses, the dead of Israel will be resurrected and will receive rewards. The prophecy of Eldad and Medad is also understood in a predictive sense

---

38   See Levey, *The Messiah*, 13.
39   Trans. based on McNamara in Díez Macho, *Neophyti 1*, 4.540.

in *Sipre Num.* §95 (on 11:26), but not nearly in such detail.

The association of the Spirit with the Messiah (cf. 1 Cor 14:5 and Num 11:29) seen in the New Testament may have something to do with this association in Num 11:26. Moses' comment about all of God's people having the Spirit may have had something to do with Pentecost. In at least one rabbinic midrash the prophecy of Joel 2:28 is understood to be the fulfillment of Moses' wish in Num 11:29 that all Israel receive God's Spirit and prophesy (*Midr. Ps.* 14.6 [on 14:7]). The relationship is admittedly tenuous. Nevertheless, the fact that the prophecy of Eldad and Medad appears also to be related in some ways to Revelation[40] and apparently was the central feature of a pseudepigraphon known to the author of the *Shepherd of Hermas*[41] increases the probability that the prophecy of Num 11:26 was in early times understood eschatologically and even messianically. Therefore, the Aramaic paraphrase of Num 11:26 may very well preserve first century (or earlier) tradition.

12. Isa 9:5-6. The Hebrew form of the oracle ascribes remarkable virtues to the child who has been born, the son who has been given, who will sit on the throne of David and whose kingdom will last forever. The Targum not only identifies the Davidide as the Messiah, but it is careful to assign the epithets "Mighty God" and "Eternal Father" to the Lord, and not to the Messiah:

5   אמר נביא לבית דויד ארי רבי אתיליד לנא בר אתיהיב לנא
 וקביל אוריתא עלוהי למיטרה ואתקרי שמיה מן קדם מפלי עיצא
אלהא גיברא קיים עלמא משיחא דשלמא יסגי עלנא ביומוהי:

6   סגי רבו לעבדי אוריתא ולנטרי שלמא לית סוף על כורסי דויד
ועל מלכותיה לאתקנא יתה ולמבנה בדינא ובזכותא מכען ועד
עלמא במימרא דיוי צבאות תתעביד דא:

"The prophet said to the house of David, 'For to us a child is born, to us a

---

40   See McNamara, *The New Testament and the Palestinian Targum*, 235-37.

41   The only extant fragment of the work is found in Hermas, *Vision* 2.3.4: ἐγγὺς κύριος τοῖς ἐπιστρεφομένοις, ὡς γέγραπται ἐν τῷ Ἐλδὰδ καὶ Μωδάτ, τοῖς προφητεύσασιν ἐν τῇ ἐρήμῳ τῷ λαῷ ("'The Lord is near those who turn to him,' as it is written in the (Book of) Eldad and Modat, who prophesied to the people in the wilderness"). There is a quotation of "the prophetic word" (ὁ προφητικὸς λόγος) in 2 *Clem.* 11:2-4 that may also be a fragment of this lost work. E. G. Martin ("Eldad and Modad," in J. H. Charlesworth [ed.], *The Old Testament Pseudepigrapha* [2 vols., Garden City: Doubleday, 1983-85] 2.463-65) dates the *Book of Eldad and Modat* to sometime before the second century C.E.

son is given; and he will accept the law upon himself to keep it, and his name will be called before the Wonderful Counselor, the Mighty God, existing forever, "The Messiah in whose days peace will increase upon us." Great pride will belong to those who perform the law, and for those who keep peace there will be no end, upon the throne of David and upon his kingdom, to establish it and to build it with judgment and with virtue from this time forth and forever. By the Word of the Lord of hosts this will be done.'"[42]

Isaiah 9:5-6(E6-7) may function in a messianic sense at Qumran.[43] Parts of Isa 9:1-6 are quoted or alluded to in various places in the New Testament in reference to Jesus (see esp. Matt 4:15-16 [cf. Isa 8:23–9:1(E9:1-2)], John 1:45; Eph 2:14 [cf. Isa 9:5] and Luke 1:32-33; John 12:34 [cf. Isa 9:6]), suggesting that the passage was understood in a messianic sense in the first century. The LXX seems to understand the passage in a messianic sense. We find in the Greek version a similar effort to avoid applying to the Davidide divine epithets ("and his name is called 'The Messenger of Great Counsel'").

13. Jer 33:15 = Zech 3:8; 6:12. "Branch" (צֶמַח) becomes a virtual technical term in Jer 33:15, Zech 3:8, and 6:12: "Behold, the man whose name is the Branch: for he shall grow up in his place, and he shall build the Temple of the Lord." Parts of these three texts read as follows:

אקים לדויד משיח דצדקא׃

האנא מיתי ית עבדי משיחא ויתגלי׃

הא גברא משיחא שמיה עתיד דיתגלי ויתרבי ויבני ית היכלא דייי׃

"I will raise up for David a righteous Messiah" (Jer 33:15).
"Behold, I bring My Servant, the Messiah, who is to be revealed" (Zech 3:8).
"Behold, the man, 'The Messiah' is his name. He is destined to be revealed

---

42   Trans. based on Chilton, *The Isaiah Targum*, 21.

43   A. Dupont-Sommer (*The Essene Writings from Qumran* [Gloucester: Peter Smith, 1973] 208; idem, "La Mère du Messie et la mère de l'Aspic dans un hymne de Qoumran," *RHR* 147 [1955] 174-88) thinks that the reference in 1QH 3:9-10 to the "Wonderful Counselor with his might" is clearly a messianic reference. This is argued also by J. V. Chamberlain, "Another Thanksgiving Psalm," *JNES* 14 (1955) 32-41; idem, "Further Elucidation of a Messianic Thanksgiving Psalm from Qumran," *JNES* 14 (1955) 181-82, and W. H. Brownlee, "Messianic Motifs of Qumran," *NTS* 3 (1956-57) 12-30, 195-210. But others disagree. See the fuller discussion above in chap. 3.

and to be anointed, and he shall build the Temple of the Lord" (Zech 6:12).

There are no quotations or allusions in the New Testament to any of these texts. The messianic interpretation of "Branch" in Jer 23:5, which may be first century, could suggest that these other Branch passages may also have been understood in a messianic sense in the first century. The LXX's rendering of Zech 6:12 ('Ανατολή) may have had messianic overtones. Messianic interpretation of Zech 6:12 is found in rabbinic literature (cf. *Num. Rab.* 18.21 [on 16:4]). But this tradition is late; so is the hope of rebuilding the Temple (cf. *Gen. Rab.* 97sup [on 49:8]). However, the idea of the Messiah being revealed may be a primitive element, for it is attested in 4 Ezra 7:28 (Syriac): "My son the Messiah shall be revealed with those who are with him" (cf. 2 Bar 29:3; 39:7). It may even be attested in John 1:31: ". . . in order that he might be revealed [ἵνα φανερωθῇ] to Israel I came baptizing in water."

14. Ps 45:3. The dedication to the king in v. 2(E1) and the reference to anointing in v. 8(E7) invited messianic paraphrasing of this Psalm. Verse 3(E2) in the Targum is particular interest, because it may derive from the first century. The Hebrew reads: "You are the fairest of the sons of men; grace is poured upon your lips; therefore God has blessed you forever." The text reads according to the Targum:

שופרך מלכא משיחא עדיף מבני נשא אתיהיב:
רוח נבואה בספוותך מטול כן ברכינך יהוה לעלמא:

"Your beauty, O King Messiah, is greater than that of the sons of men. The spirit of prophecy has been placed upon your lips; therefore, the Lord has blessed you forever."

There are a few indications that some of the messianic ideas of *Tg.* Psalm 45 may have been known in the first century. First, Ps 45:6-7 is quoted and applied to Jesus (as the "Son") in Heb 1:8-9. It is plausible that an Aramaic messianic interpretation of this Psalm was partly what drew the author's attention to it. Secondly, as has been argued by Günter Reim, *Tg.* Psalm 45 may have contributed to Johannine christology.[44] Thirdly, *Tg. Ps.-J.* and *Tg. Neof.* Gen 49:11, which as argued above contain early messianic ideas, appear to have been influenced by *Tg.* Ps 45:3. The former read: "How beautiful is King Messiah who is to arise from among those of the house of Judah."

---

[44] G. Reim, "Jesus as God in the Fourth Gospel: The Old Testament Background," *NTS* 30 (1984) 158-60.

15. Ps 72:1. The opening verse of the Psalm, "Give the king Your judgments, O God, and Your righteousness to the king's son," is probably what prompted the messianization of Psalm 72. In the Aramaic it reads:

על ידוי דשלמה אתאמר בנבואה אלהא הילכות דינך
משיחא הב וצדקתך לבריה דדוד מלכא:

"By the hand of Solomon, spoken through prophecy. O God, give the halakot of Your justice to the King Messiah , and Your righteousness to the son of King David."

The messianic interpretation of this Psalm may account for Matthew's interest in showing how gifts were given to the newborn Messiah (cf. Matt 2:11; Ps 72:10-11, 15). This tradition may also be reflected in Rev 22:26, which describes the nations bringing gifts to the new Jerusalem, over which the messianic Lamb will rule.

16. Ps 89:51-52. Two of the final three verses of Psalm 89 (E50-51) are taken in a messianic sense in the Targum. This is not surprising, given the reference to God's "anointed." What makes the Aramaic messianic is the shift in temporal aspect. The Hebrew Psalm envisions current taunting of God's anointed, whereas in the Aramaic Israel's enemies scoff at the Messiah's delay, thus implying a future anointed one. The Targum reads:

51   אידכר יהוה חיסודא דעבדך סוברית בעטפי כל
גידופידהון דסגיעין עממין:

52   די חסידו בעלי דבבך יהוה די חסידו איחור רושמת
ריגלי משיחך יהוה:

"Remember, O Lord, the revilement of Your servant; I bore in my bosom all the blasphemies of many nations, with which Your enemies have scoffed, O Lord, with they have scoffed at the delay of the footsteps of Your Messiah, O Lord."[45]

These verses may be alluded to in 1 Pet 4:14. There is some significant verbal similarity between the LXX and the Petrine text. LXX Ps 88:51 reads: οὗ ὠνείδισαν οἱ ἐχθροί σου, κύριε, οὗ ὠνείδισαν τὸ ἀντάλλαγμα τοῦ χριστοῦ σου ("whereby Your enemies have reviled You, Lord, whereby they reviled the recompense of Your Christ"). 1 Peter reads: εἰ ὀνειδίζεσθε ἐν ὀνόματι Χριστοῦ, μακάριοι, ὅτι τὸ τῆς δόξης καὶ τὸ τοῦ θεοῦ πνεῦμα ἐφ' ὑμᾶς ἀναπαύεται ("If you are reviled

---

45   Trans. based on Levey, *The Messiah*, 121.

for the name of Christ, you are blessed, because the spirit of glory and of God rests upon you"). The passage appears in *m. Soṭa* 9:15 in a description of the woes that accompany the coming of the Messiah (the tradition also appears in *Song Rab.* 2:13 §4). What could suggest that this messianic interpretation is early is the fact that many of the messianic details in *m. Soṭa* 9:15 that surround the quotation of Ps 89:52(E51) have early antecedents.[46]

In making use of the Targums for Jesus research and for the interpretation of the Gospels I recommend the comparative method that Bruce Chilton has developed. His work, as well as that of others, has been fruitful in identifying points of dictional and thematic or exegetical coherence between targumic and dominical traditions. The following examples should serve to clarify and justify the method.[47]

There are three clear examples of dictional coherence between sayings of Jesus and readings found in the Isaiah Targum. A fourth example from Pseudo-Jonathan will also be considered. (1) The paraphrase of Isa 6:9-10 in Mark 4:12 concludes with ". . . and *it be forgiven* them." Only the Isaiah Targum reads this way.[48] The Hebrew and the LXX read "heal." Perceiving this dictional coherence, Chilton rightly suspects that the Isaiah Targum has preserved an interpretation that in an earlier form was known to Jesus and his contemporaries.[49] The well known criterion of dissimilarity argues for the authenticity

---

[46] See C. A. Evans, "Mishna and Messiah 'in Context': Some Comments on Jacob Neusner's Proposals," *JBL* 112 (1993) 267-89, esp. 285-88.

[47] Fuller discussions of many of these examples will be found in B. Chilton, *God in Strength: Jesus' Announcement of the Kingdom* (SNTU 1; Freistadt: Plöchl, 1979; repr. BibSem 8; Sheffield: JSOT Press, 1987); idem, *A Galilean Rabbi and His Bible*, 57-147; idem and C. A. Evans, "Jesus and Israel's Scriptures," in Chilton and Evans (eds.), *Studying the Historical Jesus: Evaluations of the State of Current Research* (NTTS 19; Leiden: Brill, 1994) 281-335, esp. 299-309.

[48] The Peshitta also reads this way, but it is dependent upon the Targum (and the LXX in other places); cf. Evans, *To See and Not Perceive*, 77-80, 195 (for the notes).

[49] Chilton, *A Galilean Rabbi and His Bible*, 90-98. Despite the verbatim agreement between the Targum and Mark 4:12, M. D. Goulder ("Those Outside (Mk. 4:10-12)," *NovT* 33 [1991] 289-302) has recently claimed that the former has nothing to do with the latter. Goulder's explanation of the parallel is not convincing and has been answered in Chilton and Evans, "Jesus and Israel's Scriptures," 302-304.

of this strange saying, for the tendencies in both Jewish[50] and
Christian[51] circles were to understand this Isaianic passage in a way
significantly different from the way it appears to be understood in the
Marcan tradition. (2) The saying, "All those grasping a sword by a
sword will perish" (Matt 26:52), coheres dictionally with *Tg.* Isa
50:11: "Behold, all you who kindle a fire, who grasp a sword! Go, fall
in the fire which you kindled and on the sword which you grasped!"
Chilton observes that the items that the Targum has added to the
Hebrew text are the very items that lie behind Jesus' statement.[52] (3)
Jesus' saying on Gehenna (Mark 9:47-48), where he quotes part of Isa
66:24, again reflects targumic diction. This verse in the Hebrew and
the LXX says nothing about Gehenna, but it does in the Targum: ". . .
will not die and their fire shall not be quenched, and the wicked shall
be judged in Gehenna . . . ."[53] The verse is alluded to twice in the
Apocrypha (Jdt 16:17; Sir 7:17), where it seems to be moving beyond
temporal punishment (which appears to be the primary thrust of
Hebrew Isaiah) toward eschatological judgment. But the implicit
association of Gehenna with Isa 66:24 is distinctly targumic. And, of
course, the targumic paraphrase is explicitly eschatological, as is Jesus'
saying. (4) Chilton and others think that the distinctive reading found
in *Tg. Ps.-J.* Lev 22:28 ("My people, children of Israel, as our Father
is merciful in heaven, so shall you be merciful on earth") lies behind
Jesus' statement in Luke 6:36: "Become merciful just as your Father is
merciful."[54] Matthew (5:48) reads: "Father in heaven." Although it is
unnecessary to claim that Jesus has actually quoted the Targum, as has
been suggested,[55] or even less plausibly that the Targum has quoted

---

[50]   See *Mek.* on Exod 19:2 (*Baḥodeš* §1); b. *Roš Haš.* 17b; b. *Meg.* 17b; y.
Ber. 2.3; *Sed. Elij. Rab.* §16 (82-83); *Gen. Rab.* 81.6 (on Gen 42:1).

[51]   See Matt 13:11b-17; Luke 8:10; Acts 28:26-27; John 12:40. The latter is an
exception, serving the Fourth Evangelist's distinctive scriptural apologetic.

[52]   Chilton, *A Galilean Rabbi and His Bible*, 98-101.

[53]   Chilton, *Isaiah Targum*, 128; idem, *A Galilean Rabbi and His Bible*, 101-7.

[54]   Chilton, *A Galilean Rabbi and His Bible*, 44; cf. McNamara, *The New
Testament and the Palestinian Targum*, 133-38; idem, *Targum and Testament*
(Grand Rapids: Eerdmans, 1972) 118-19; R. Le Déaut, *The Message of the New
Testament and the Aramaic Bible* (SubBib 5; Rome: Biblical Institute, 1982) 31;
idem, "Targumic Literature and New Testament Interpretation," *BTB* 4 (1974) 243-
89, esp. 246.

[55]   A. T. Olmstead, "Could an Aramaic Gospel be Written?" *JNES* 1 (1942)
41-75, esp. 64.

him,[56] the parallel demands explanation. The most probable one is that
the Targum has preserved a saying that circulated in first-century
Palestine (cf. *y. Ber.* 5.3; *y. Meg.* 4.9), a saying which Jesus was
remembered to have uttered himself.

There are two good examples of thematic or exegetical coherence
between targumic and dominical traditions. The Parable of the
Vineyard Tenants (Mark 12:1-12 par) is based on Isaiah's Song of the
Vineyard (Isa 5:1-7), as the dozen or so words in the opening lines of
the Marcan parable clearly indicate. But Isaiah's parable was directed
against the "house of Israel" and the "men of Judah" (cf. Isa 5:7). In
contrast, Jesus' parable is directed against the "ruling priests, scribes,
and elders" (cf. Mark 11:27), who evidently readily perceived that the
parable had been told "against them" and not against the general
populace (cf. Mark 12:12). Why was this parable so understood, when
it is obviously based on a prophetic parable that spoke to the nation as a
whole? Chilton and others have rightly pointed to the Isaiah Targum,
which in place of "tower" and "wine vat" reads "sanctuary" and "altar"
(cf. Isa 5:2 and *Tg.* Isa 5:2),[57] institutions which will be destroyed (cf.
Isa 5:5 and *Tg.* Isa 5:5). The Isaiah Targum has significantly shifted
the thrust of the prophetic indictment against the priestly
establishment. Jesus' parable seems to reflect this orientation: the
problem does not lie with the vineyard; it lies with the caretakers of the
vineyard.[58] A few of these components appear outside of the New
Testament and the Isaiah Targum. In *1 Enoch* 89:66-67 the Temple is
referred to as a "tower." Its (first) destruction is referred to, but
without any apparent allusion to Isaiah 5. This Enochic tradition
appears in *Barn.* 16:1-5, where it is applied to the second destruction,
but without reference to either Isaiah 5 or Mark 12. Thus the
coherence between *Tg.* Isaiah 5 and Mark 12 is distinctive and
probably cannot be explained away as coincidence.

Even the much-disputed quotation of Ps 118:22-23 may receive
some clarification from the Targum. Although Chilton suspects that
the citation of Ps 118:22-23 derives from the church and not from
Jesus, Klyne Snodgrass has argued plausibly that its presence is due to a

---

[56]   See M. Black, *An Aramaic Approach to the Gospels and Acts* (3rd ed.,
Oxford: Clarendon Press, 1967) 181.

[57]   This allegorizing interpretation appears also in the Tosefta (cf. *t. Me'il.*
1.16; *t. Sukk.* 3.15).

[58]   Chilton, *A Galilean Rabbi and His Bible*, 111-14.

play on words between "the stone" (הָאֶבֶן) and "the son" (הַבֵּן), which probably explains the reading in *Tg.* Ps 118:22: "The young man which the builders abandoned . . . ."[59] This kind of word play is old and is witnessed in the New Testament (cf. Matt 3:9 par: "from these stones God is able to raise up children [which in Aramaic originally could have been "sons"] to Abraham"; cf. Luke 19:40). The quotation was assimilated to the better known Greek version, since it was used by Christians for apologetic and christological purposes (cf. Acts 4:11; 1 Pet 2:4, 7) and possibly because second generation Christians were unaware of the original Aramaic word play.[60]

A second example of exegetical coherence between targumic and dominical tradition is found in Jesus' exchange with the scribe who asks what is necessary to inherit eternal life (Luke 10:25-28). The assurance given to the scribe, "Do this and you will live" (Luke 10:28), after his recitation of the double commandment (cf. Deut 6:5; Lev 19:18), contains an allusion to Lev 18:5: "You shall keep My statutes and My ordinances, which if a person *do*, he *shall live* by them" (with the pertinent elements emphasized).[61] But Lev 18:5 in the Greek and Hebrew versions has to do only with life in the present age; in these versions the text says nothing about *eternal life*, the point of the scribe's question. In the Targum, however, Lev 18:5 is understood in an eschatological sense: "You should observe My ordinances and My laws, which, if a person practices them, he shall live by them *in eternal life*" (*Tg. Onq.* Lev 18:5; cf. *Tg. Ps.-J.* Lev 18:5: " . . . he shall live by *them in eternal life and shall be assigned a portion with the righteous*"). This eschatological understanding of Lev 18:5 may also be witnessed in *Pss. Sol.* 14:1-5 and CD 3:12-20. What we seem to have here is yet one more instance of exegetical coherence between targumic and dominical tradition.[62]

---

59   K. R. Snodgrass, *The Parable of the Wicked Tenants: An Inquiry into Parable Interpretation* (WUNT 27; Tübingen: Mohr [Siebeck], 1983) 111; C. A. Evans, "On the Vineyard Parables of Isaiah 5 and Mark 12," *BZ* 28 (1984) 82-86, esp. 85.

60   See the fuller discussion of this parable in chap. 10 below.

61   Luke's τοῦτο ποίει καὶ ζήσῃ closely approximates the LXX's ἃ ποιήσας ἄνθρωπος ζήσεται ἐν αὐτοῖς.

62   For futher discussion of this example, see C. A. Evans, "'Do This and You Will Live': Targumic Coherence in Luke 10:25-28," in P. V. M. Flesher (ed.), *Targumim and New Testament Interpretation* (Targum Studies; Atlanta: Scholars Press, forthcoming).

Other examples of thematic or exegetical coherence may include charges of disrespect for the prophets (compare *Tg.* Isa 28:11 with Matt 5:12 = Luke 6:23; Matt 23:37 = Luke 13:34) and what appears to be a dominical emphasis on private revelation (compare *Tg.* Isa 48:6 with Matt 13:17 = Luke 10:24).[63]

Concluding Comments

What this survey shows is that whereas much, even most, of the messianic tradition in the Targums derives from times after the New Testament, a fair portion of it reflects interpretive traditions and ways of speaking from the first century and even earlier. Bruce Chilton's work on the Isaiah Targum has shown how at many points Jesus' utterances, as well as his general concept of the kingdom of God, cohere with targumic language and themes. Jesus research cannot, therefore, neglect the Targums.

---

[63] Chilton, *A Galilean Rabbi and His Bible*, 133-36. Although approaching the subject of private revelation differently, W. Grimm (*Jesus und das Danielbuch. Band I: Jesu Einspruch gegen das Offenbarungssystem Daniels* [ANTJ 6.1; Frankfurt am Main: Peter Lang, 1984]) arrives at a similar conclusion. Grimm primarily treats Matt 11:25-27 = Luke 10:21-22 and Luke 17:20-21. His thesis is that Jesus believed that God disclosed the secrets of the Kingdom to the pure and innocent, not to the professional religious authorities. Elsewhere Grimm (*Die Verkündigung Jesu und Deuterojesaja* [ANTJ 1; 2nd ed., Frankfurt am Main: Peter Lang, 1981] 112) discusses the relevance of Isaiah for Matt 13:17 = Luke 10:24.

CHAPTER FOUR

WAS SIMON BEN KOSIBA RECOGNIZED AS MESSIAH?

In a well known passage Rabbi Aqiba is said to have recognized Simon ben Kosiba as "the Messiah" (*y. Ta'an.* 4.5 = *Lam. Rab.* 2:2 §4). The tradition is cited often and usually without raising either the question of its authenticity or the more general question of whether or not Simon was recognized by anyone as Israel's Messiah.[1] However, given the more critical orientation of scholars of rabbinica in recent years—and here I think especially of Jacob Neusner—, as well as the fact that the surviving relics of that struggle (especially the Bar Kokhba coins and letters) never refer to Simon as Messiah, this tradition should not be accepted without careful review.

The many problems that attend investigation of the Bar Kokhba revolt have been treated at length by scholars with much greater expertise in this subject than I possess. In most of these particulars I defer to them and accept their conclusions without debate. Of the recent studies that I judge to be the most helpful are those by Leo Mildenberg and Peter Schäfer. The former, whose specialty is numismatics, has concluded that Hadrian (117–138 C.E.), as part of his policy of Romanization, visited Judea in 130 C.E.; that at the time of his visit he announced his plans to rebuild and rename Jerusalem as Aelia Capitolina and erect a temple in honor of Jupiter; that although this announcement was resented by some Jews, it was Hadrian's ban on circumcision that was the primary cause of the revolt; that the Jewish people were united but overpowered by Rome only after a long and costly war; and that his successor Antoninus Pius (138–161 C.E.) repealed the ban, in the case of Jews only, in order to remove the offense that had provoked the rebellion.[2]

---

[1]   Among the most competent works, see E. Schürer, *The History of the Jewish People in the Age of Jesus Christ (175 B.C.–A.D. 135)* (3 vols., rev. G. Vermes and F. Millar; Edinburgh: T. & T. Clark, 1973-87) 1.543-44; E. M. Smallwood, *The Jews under Roman Rule* (SJLA 20; Leiden: Brill, 1976) 439-40.

[2]   L. Mildenberg, "Bar Kokhba Coins and Documents," *HSCP* 84 (1980)

Schäfer agrees with Mildenberg at certain points. He too doubts that Hadrian's decision to found a Roman colony at the site of the ruins of Jerusalem instigated the rebellion, though he believes that the Jewish people would have been more accepting of this plan than Mildenberg is prepared to allow. Schäfer agrees with Mildenberg's generally negative assessment of the worth of rabbinic sources. But he disagrees with Mildenberg's argument that the Jewish people were united behind the rebels and their leader Simon ben Kosiba. He likens Judea at the time of the revolt to the Maccabean period. Some Jews were accepting of Hadrian's Romanization policy, others were not. Those calling for revolt, Schäfer believes, were priests hoping to restore Israel's political and religious autonomy.[3] Mildenberg, however, believes that it was the ban on circumcision that provoked the rebellion and that this rebellion was widely supported in Judea.

I find most of the conclusions of Schäfer and Mildenberg convincing. Schäfer's suggestion of division among the Jewish people is plausible. There was, after all, division among the Jews in all of their wars. The fact that the rebellion was limited to Judea and that Simon had difficulty, as his correspondence indicates, in maintaining loyalty and order among his own followers point to dissension and divisions. But the magnitude and duration of the war strongly suggest that the division was not on the order of what the Jewish people experienced in the first war with Rome. If we accept the Maccabean analogy, we should imagine that certain priests took an active role in promoting the cause and that most Jews answered.[4] Some did so reluctantly, perhaps fearful of retaliation if they did not. The disputed passage in *t. Šabb.* 15.9 may very well relate to these people, who either had not been circumcised at all or had had epispasm and then during the revolt felt it necessary to be (re)circumcised.

311-35; idem, *The Coinage of the Bar Kokhba War* (Typos: Monographien zur antiken Numismatik 6; Frankfurt am Main: Sauerländer, 1984).

3   P. Schäfer, *Der Bar Kokhba-Aufstand: Studien zum zweiten jüdischen Krieg gegen Rom* (TSAJ 1; Tübingen: Mohr [Siebeck], 1981); idem, "Hadrian's Policy in Judaea and the Bar Kokhba Revolt: A Reassessment," in P. R. Davies and R. T. White (eds.), *A Tribute to Geza Vermes: Essays on Jewish and Christian Literature and History* (JSOTSup 100; Sheffield: JSOT Press, 1990) 281-303. The first item provides an invaluable catalogue of the primary data.

4   See M. Hengel, "Hadrians Politik gegenüber Juden und Christen," *JANESCU* 16-17 (1984-85) 153-82, esp. 180-81.

I am persuaded that the major factor in instigating the rebellion, in driving the religious establishment to promote it, and in the widespread support for the rebellion, was the ban on circumcision, as Mildenberg has argued. The statement found in *Scriptores Historiae Augustae* may be decisive: *Moverunt ea tempestate et Iudaei bellum, quod vetabantur mutilare genitalia* ("At this time also the Jews began a war, because they were forbidden to mutilate the genitals [i.e. practise circumcision]"; *Vita Hadriani* 14.2). The repeal of this ban early in the administration of Antoninus Pius (*Digesta* 48, 8.11.1) lends further support to this interpretation.[5]

I disagree with Mildenberg, however, concerning the question of Simon ben Kosiba's possible messianic recognition. He states: "Shim'on ben Kosiba was not the longed for Messiah of the Jews and never pretended to be so. This we know for a fact from the rebel coins, letters and documents."[6] I disagree. We certainly do not know any such thing for a fact. In some of the coins and letters Simon is called "Prince" (נשיא),[7] which at Qumran and possibly in Ezek 37:24-25 was understood in messianic terms. It is not at all clear that *Nasi* cannot have the same meaning in the coins and letters. Our literary sources, though scanty and biased, agree on one thing: Simon ben Kosiba was regarded as a messianic claimant of one sort or another.

I have to agree with Schäfer, who very cautiously suggests that Aqiba may very well have recognized Simon as Messiah.[8] I believe the

---

5   Mildenberg, *Coinage of the Bar Kokhba War*, 105: "This [i.e. the ban on circumcision] and only this was the catalyst, the decisive cause of the Bar Kokhba War."

6   Mildenberg, *Coinage of the Bar Kokhba War*, 102; idem, "Bar Kokhba Coins and Documents," 313-15. A similar conclusion has also been reached by G. S. Aleksandrov, "The Role of 'Aqiba in the Bar-Kokhba Rebellion," *REJ* 132 (1973) 65-77, esp. 73-74.

7   In his correspondence Simon refers to himself as "Prince of Israel" (נסיא ישראל) or "Prince over Israel" (נסיא על ישראל). "Prince" is spelled variously נסיא or נשיא. Most of these letters have not been published in full. For a report, which contains excerpts of the letters (= 5/6ḤevEp 1–15), see Y. Yadin, "Expedition D," *IEJ* 11 (1961) 36-52; 12 (1962) 227-57. Only in one of the Murabba'at letters (= Mur 24) does Simon does refer to himself as "Prince of Israel."

8   P. Schäfer, "R. Aqiva und Bar Kokhba," in Schäfer, *Studien zur Geschichte und Theologie des rabbinischen Judentums* (AGJU 15; Leiden: Brill, 1978) 65-121; idem, "Rabbi Aqiva and Bar Kokhba," in W. S. Green (ed.), *Approaches to Ancient Judaism: Volume II* (BJS 9; Chico: Scholars Press, 1980)

principal reason that Mildenberg rejects a messianic identification for
Simon is due to his assumed, but unexamined, definition of Messiah.
For example, he states: "Even though this messianic pun [viz. bar
Kosiba/bar Kokhba] may have been current during the war, the Jewish
fighters and partisans should not be pictured as having actually
believed that Shim'on ben Kosiba was the Messiah; the Judaean Desert
documents make clear that the Jews knew their leader was a man like
themselves. The creative pun on the leader's name in Aramaic would
simply have given the Jews a popular rallying cry for their cause."[9]

This statement immediately raises two questions: (1) What kind of
"Messiah" does Mildenberg have in mind? Does he assume that there
was a single, widely accepted concept of the Messiah and that this
Messiah was not a man like other men?[10] I find this thinking very
problematic. If Josephus in 68 C.E. could apply Num 24:17 (the
"ambiguous oracle") to General Vespasian—a foreign conqueror of
Israel, why could not Aqiba in 133 or 134 C.E. apply this oracle to
Simon ben Kosiba—a Torah-observant Jew who hoped to liberate
Israel? Simon's messiahship seems to have been a very earth-bound,
David-like rule intended to liberate Israel from Gentile oppressors.[11]
(2) Would an identification of Simon with the star of Num 24:17 be no
more than a "popular rallying cry"? On the contrary, would it not
imply much more, at least to many of Simon's followers? Given the

---

113-30. Less cautious is Adele Reinhartz ("Rabbinic Perceptions of Simeon bar
Kosiba," *JSJ* 20 [1989] 171-94) who speaks of "irrefutable evidence for the
messianic identification of Bar Kosiba" (p. 192). I believe that the evidence is
compelling, but hardly irrefutable.

    9   Mildenberg, *Coinage of the Bar Kokhba War*, 76.

    10   This is often the kind of thinking entertained by Christians, who uncritically
define Jewish messianism in terms of New Testament christology. New Testament
christology represents expressions of Jewish messianism to be sure, but it is not
comprehensive. Features of New Testament christology were wholly unacceptable
to many Jews, while many Jewish messianic ideas never found their way into the
matrix of New Testament christology. For major works sensitive to the pluralism of
messianic ideas, see J. Neusner et al. (eds.), *Judaisms and Their Messiahs at the
Turn of the Christian Era* (Cambridge: Cambridge University Press, 1987); J. H.
Charlesworth (ed.), *The Messiah: Developments in Earliest Judaism and
Christianity* (Minneapolis: Fortress, 1992).

    11   This is the view of Schäfer, "Rabbi Aqiva and Bar Kokhba," 120; and
Reinhartz, "Rabbinic Perceptions of Simeon bar Kosiba," 190.

messianic interpretation of Num 24:17 at Qumran[12] and in the Targums it seems that calling Simon the "son of the star" would imply that he was indeed regarded as the Messiah (however that is to be defined).[13]

The balance of this paper (1) will survey the most important primary sources that touch on the question of the messianic recognition of Simon. It (2) will also explore the messianic ideas that are associated with Rabbi Aqiba and then it (3) will compare these ideas with certain dominical traditions

MESSIANIC TRADITIONS ABOUT SIMON BEN KOSIBA

Although we have no detailed history of the Bar Kokhba revolt (132–135 C.E.), as we have of the first revolt (66–70 C.E.) described in Josephus' *Jewish War*, some Roman and Christian writers do refer to it and in a few cases discuss it, while some of the rabbinic writings refer to it and relate various anecdotes. In addition to the useful data that this literature provides,[14] much helpful information may be gleaned from the coins, official correspondence of Simon ben Kosiba, and archaeology.

Roman Writers

Four Roman writers provide us with significant information concerning the Bar Kokhba revolt. Three of them are historians (Appian, Dio, and an unknown biographer); the fourth was a personal friend and confidant of Emperor Marcus Aurelius (Fronto). Appian (c. 95–165 C.E.) and Fronto (c. 100–176 C.E.) were contemporaries of the revolt, while Dio wrote in the third century. The fourth writer, the anonymous author of the *Scriptores Historiae Augustae*, a late fourth-century collection of imperial biographies that is not always reliable, also refers to the revolt (quoted above).

Appian refers to three Roman destructions of Jerusalem: "The Jewish nation alone resisted, and Pompey conquered them [63 B.C.E.],

---

[12]   Whereas it is true that the *bar kokhba* pun coheres with Qumran's interpretation of Num 24:17, there is not enough evidence to conclude that Simon was an Essene, as has been argued by L. E. Toombs, "Barcosiba and Qumrân," *NTS* 4 (1957) 65-71.

[13]   On the messianic interpretation of Num 24:17 at Qumran and in the Targums, see chap. 3 and excursus 1.

[14]   The Bar Kokhba revolt is alluded to in the Samaritan Chronicles (Chronicle IV [*Sepher Yehoshua*] chap. 47). But the account is quite legendary and unreliable.

sent their king, Aristobulus, to Rome, and destroyed [κατέσκαψεν] their greatest and to them holiest city Jerusalem, as Ptolemy, the first king of Egypt, had formerly done. It was afterward rebuilt and Vespasian destroyed [κατέσκαψεν] it again, and Hadrian did the same [αὖθις] in my time" (*Hist. Rom.* 11: *The Syrian Wars* 8 §50).[15]

Appian's examples are not really parallel. Other than a collapsed tower and a breach in the wall, Jerusalem suffered little at the hands of Pompey and his men (cf. Josephus, *J.W.* 1.7.4 §149; *Ant.* 14.4.4 §69). The city was hardly "destroyed" (κατασκάπτειν can also mean to "demolish," "level," or "raze"). The second taking of Jerusalem, of course, resulted in the complete destruction of the city and temple. In this case κατασκάπτειν is quite appropriate and is in fact the very word that Josephus uses (*J.W.* 7.1.1 §1). The extent of destruction in the third taking of Jerusalem is unclear, principally because we do not know to what extent the city had been rebuilt following the end of the first revolt. (See Dio below who also uses κατασκάπτειν to describe the capture of Jerusalem.) There is also some doubt as to whether or not Simon ben Kosiba actually occupied Jerusalem.

On the occasion of the defeat and destruction by the Parthians of the legate Severianus and his legion in Armenia (162 C.E.) Cornelius Fronto offered the following words of consolation to Emperor Marcus Aurelius Antoninus: "The God who begat the great Roman race has no compunction in suffering us to faint at times and be defeated and wounded . . . But always and everywhere he turned our sorrows into successes and our terrors into triumphs. But not to hark back too far into ancient times, I will take instances from your own family . . . under the rule of your grandfather Hadrian what a number of soldiers were killed by the Jews . . . ."[16] It is significant that Fronto would refer to the Bar Kokhba war as an illustration of past Roman defeats and wounds. He probably regarded the Bar Kokhba revolt as an example not of defeat, for Rome won the war, but as an example of a grievous wound, in view of the numerous casualties. Fronto's comparison of the Jewish war with the Parthian war offers important corroboration to aspects of Dio's history.

---

15   Adaptation of H. White, *Appian's Roman History II* (LCL 3; Cambridge: Harvard University, 1912-13) 199.
16   Trans. C. R. Haines, *The Correspondence of Marcus Cornelius Fronto II* (LCL; Cambridge: Harvard University, 1919-20) 21-23.

Cassius Dio provides us with the longest and most detailed account of the Bar Kokhba revolt. The relevant portions are as follows:

> At Jerusalem [Hadrian] founded a city in place of the one which had been razed to the ground, naming it Aelia Capitolina, and on the site of the temple of the god he raised a new temple to Jupiter. This brought on a war of no slight importance nor of brief duration, for the Jews deemed it intolerable that foreign races should be settled in their city and foreign religious rites planted there. So long, indeed, as Hadrian was close by in Egypt and again in Syria, they remained quiet . . . but when he went farther way, they openly revolted . . . Hadrian sent against them his best generals. First [or the best] of these was Julius Severus, who was dispatched from Britain, where he was governor, against the Jews. Severus did not venture to attack his opponents in the open at any one point, in view of their numbers and their desperation, but by intercepting small groups, thanks to the number of his soldiers and his under-officers, and by depriving them of food and shutting them up, he was able, rather slowly, to be sure, but with comparative little danger, to crush, exhaust and exterminate them. Very few of them in fact survived. Fifty of their most important outposts and nine hundred and eighty-five of their most famous villages were razed to the ground. Five hundred and eighty thousand men were slain in the various raids and battles, and the number of those that perished by famine, disease and fire was past finding out. Thus nearly the whole of Judaea was made desolate . . . . Many Romans, moreover, perished in this war. Therefore Hadrian in writing to the senate did not employ the opening phrase commonly affected by the emperors, "If you and your children are in health, it is well; I and the legions are in health." (*Hist. Rom.* 69.12.1–14.3)[17]

Dio provides us with several important details: (1) The Jewish war effort was extensive, widely supported ("in view of their numbers"), and initially successful. This is the most likely inference to be drawn from the necessity to dispatch Julius Severus the "best" (which is probably what πρῶτος means here) of Rome's generals, all the way from one end of the empire to the other. From Dio's reference to "their desperation" we probably should infer extreme commitment, even fanaticism, on the part of the Jewish people, and not despair, as Dio's word (ἀπόγνωσις) could imply. (2) The destruction of Judea and the Jewish people was catastrophic. The Jews were hunted and "exterminated." "Very few of them survived." The city of Jerusalem, as well as numerous fortresses and villages were destroyed [κατα-

---

17   Trans. E. Cary, *Dio's Roman History VIII* (LCL 176; Cambridge: Harvard University, 1914-27) 449-51.

σκάπτειν]. Jewish military casualties, Dio would have us believe, exceeded half a million, while the number of deaths from the side effects of the war "was past finding out." Dio's numbers may be exaggerated (and probably are), but their preciseness does suggest that they are based on some sort of official counts. If these numbers are no more than literary hyperbole, then why not say one thousand villages, instead of "nine hundred and eighty-five," or five hundred thousand, instead of "five hundred and eighty thousand"? (3) Rome suffered heavy losses also. Dio is either unwilling or unable to report the number of Roman casualties. He says "many," which in the context of the comparison with the Jewish losses suggests that the Roman losses may have been enormous. Hadrian's personal presence in Judea, as well as his omission of the customary opening phrase ("I and the legions are in health") from his reports support this suggestion. Fronto's consoling words to Marcus Aurelius, in which he compares Hadrian's losses to those suffered in Armenia ("what a number of soldiers were killed by the Jews"), add further support.

Christian Writers

Three early Christian writers (Justin Martyr, Eusebius, and Jerome) refer to the Bar Kokhba revolt. A fourth, the anonymous author of the *Epistle of Barnabas*, probably refers to the situation immediately preceding the revolt.[18] Justin Martyr (110–165 C.E.) and the author of *Barnabas* (c. 130? C.E.) were contemporaries of the revolt. Eusebius (c. 260–339/340 C.E.) and Jerome (c. 347–419 C.E.) lived much later.

In his *Dialogue with Trypho the Jew* Justin Martyr says: "Christ said among you that he would give the sign of Jonah, exhorting you to repent . . . in order that your nation and city might not be taken and destroyed, as they have been destroyed . . . yet even when your city is captured, and your land ravaged, you do not repent" (108.1, 3).[19] The destruction to which Justin refers here is probably that resulting from both wars with Rome. But in his first *Apology* he makes explicit reference to Bar Kokhba: "[The prophetic books] are also in the possession of all Jews throughout the world; but they, though they read, do not understand what is said, but count us foes and enemies;

---

[18]   Epiphanius (ca. 315–403 C.E.) refers to the rebuilding of Jerusalem with the new name of Aelia (*On Weights and Measures* 14-15 [*PG* 43.260-61]).

[19]   *PG* 6.725-26.

and, like yourselves, they kill and punish us whenever they have the power, as you can well believe. For in the Jewish war which lately raged, Barchochebas [βαρχωχέβας],[20] the leader of the revolt of the Jews, gave orders that Christians alone should be led away to cruel punishments, unless they should deny Jesus the Christ and blaspheme" (*1 Apol.* 31.5-6).[21]

Eusebius provides the fullest Christian description of the Bar Kokhba revolt, though only as an aside. His primary concern is tracing the history of the church and the succession of the bishops in Judea. He reports that "until the siege of the Jews . . . their whole church at that time consisted of Hebrews who had continued Christian from the Apostles down to the siege at the time when the Jews again rebelled from the Romans and were beaten in a great war [οὐ μικροῖς πολέμοις]" (*Hist. Eccl.* 4.5.2).[22] When he finishes his tracing of the succession, he gives an account of the war and its effects upon Christianity in Judea:

> The rebellion of the Jews once more progressed in character and extent, and [Tineius] Rufus, the governor of Judaea, when military aid had been sent him by the Emperor, moved out against them, treating their madness without mercy. He destroyed in heaps thousands of men, women, and children, and under the law of war, enslaved their land. The Jews were at that time led by a certain Bar Chochebas, which means "star," [βαρχωχέβας ὄνομα, ὃ δὴ ἀστέρα δηλοῖ] a man who was murderous and a bandit, but relied on his name, as if dealing with slaves, and claimed to be a luminary who had come down to them from heaven [ἐξ οὐρανοῦ φωστὴρ αὐτοῖς κατεληλυθώς] and was magically enlightening [ἐπιλάμψαι τερατευόμενος, lit. "(supposedly) performing wonders to enlighten"] those who were in misery. The war reached its height in the eighteenth year of the reign of Hadrian in Beththera [Βήθθηρα],[23] which was a strong citadel not very far

---

In Justin and Eusebius Bar Kokhba's name appears as Βὰρ Χωχέβας (with or without a space), or simply as Χωχέβας or Χοχεβᾶς. Jerome spells it *Barchochebas* and *Bar-chochabas*.

21 *PG* 6.376-77.

22 *PG* 20.309.

23 That is, Bethar, the city in which Simon made his final stand. In Eusebius the city is spelled variously as Βήθθηρα, Βέθθερ, or Βίθθηρ (Βιθήρ and Βιθθηρά in other sources), while in Hebrew sources it appears as בֵּיתָּר‎, בֵּיתֵּר‎, ביתר‎, or בֵּתֵּר‎. The modern Arab village of Bittir is situated adjacent the ancient site, about seven miles southwest of Jerusalem. The villagers call the ancient site Khirbet el Yahud ("the Jewish ruins"). Some scholars dispute the tradition that this was the site of Simon's final battle.

from Jerusalem; the siege lasted a long time before the rebels were driven to their final destruction by famine and thirst and the instigator of their madness paid the penalty he deserved. Hadrian then commanded that by a legal decree and ordinances the whole nation should be absolutely prevented from entering from thenceforth even the district round Jerusalem, so that not even from a distance could it see its ancestral home. Ariston of Pella tells the story. Thus when the city came to be bereft of the nation of the Jews, and its ancient inhabitants had completely perished, it was colonized by foreigners, and the Roman city which afterwards arose changed its name, and in honour of the reigning emperor Aelius Hadrian was called Aelia. The church, too, in it was composed of Gentiles, and after the Jewish bishops the first who was appointed to minister to those there was Marcus. (*Hist. Eccl.* 4.6.1-4)[24]

Eusebius' account coheres with the Roman writers in its description of the human catastrophe. Thousands of men, women, and childern were destroyed "in heaps" (ἀθρόως) with the result that Jerusalem's "ancient inhabitants . . . completely perished." The depopulation of the region was so extensive that the ethnic character of the Christian church in Judea was completely transformed. The destruction of Judea is alluded to in Eusebius' *Chronicle*, where he says that the "Jews took up arms and devastated Palestine during the period in which the governor of the province was Tineius Rufus, to whom Hadrian sent an army in order to crush the rebels" (*Hadrian Year 16*).[25] In *Demonstratio Evangelica* Eusebius adds: "we have seen in our own time Sion once so famous ploughed with yokes of oxen by the Romans and utterly devastated, and Jerusalem, as the oracle says [Isa 1:8], deserted like a lodge" (6.13).[26] Also of importance is Eusebius' description of Bar Kokhba as a "luminary who had come down to them from heaven, performing miracles to enlighten the miserable." The tradition that Simon performed wonders of some sort agrees with the traditions found in Jewish sources. The church historian is aware that Simon was called the "star." Although he says nothing of Christian persecution in *Historia Ecclesia*, he does mention it briefly in the *Chronicle*: "Cochebas, prince of the Jewish sect, killed the Christians

---

[24] Trans. K. Lake, *Eusebius: The Ecclesiastical History II* (LCL 153; Cambridge: Harvard University, 1926-32) 311-13 (*PG* 20.309-16).

[25] *PG* 19.558.

[26] Trans. W. J. Ferrar, *Demonstratio Evangelica* (2 vols., London: SPCK; New York: Macmillan, 1920) 2.15 (*PG* 22.436).

with all kinds of persecutions, (when) they refused to help him against the Roman troops" (*Hadrian Year 17*).[27]

Jerome adds a little to what has already been seen. He says that the "citizens of Judea came to such distress that they, together with their wives, their children, their gold and their silver, in which they trusted, remained in underground tunnels and deepest caves" (*Comm. in Isa.* on 2:15).[28] The relatively recent discoveries in several caves in Naḥal Ḥever of relics and remains from the Bar Kokhba revolt confirm Jerome's statement. He also contributes to the tradition of Bar Kokhba as wonder worker, when he says that "that famed Bar Chochebas, the instigator of the Jewish uprising, fanned a lighted blade of straw in his mouth with puffs of breath so as to give the impression that he was spewing out flames" (*Rufinus* 3.31).[29]

The Christian writers call Bar Kokhba "leader" and "instigator," but never "Messiah." Nevertheless, references to persecution may imply that Bar Kokhba had made messianic claims. According to Justin Martyr, Christians "alone" were tortured and executed if they did not renounce Jesus as Messiah (ὁ χριστός). Presumably, this renunciation was required because Bar Kokhba *alone* was recognized as Israel's Messiah, not the Jesus of Christian beliefs. So far as we know, Christians were the only sect among second-century Jews to hold fiercely to a particular person as Israel's "Messiah." Eusebius' claim that Christians were persecuted if they refused to aid Bar Kokhba coheres with Justin's statement. (It also is in agreement with one of the Bar Kokhba letters that threatens punishment for failing to fight for the cause; see below.) Christians' refusal to support the revolt was probably due not to pacifism, but to their refusal to recognize neither Bar Kokhba's messianic identification nor the goals of the revolt itself.

Rabbinic Writings

In the rabbinic writings the earliest and most explicit tradition that Simon ben Kosiba was recognized as Messiah is found in the gemara of the Palestinian Talmud.[30] According to *y. Ta'an.* 4.5 (commenting on

---

27 *PG* 19.558.

28 *PL* 24.51.

29 *PL* 23.480.

30 The earliest date for the completion of Talmud Yerushalmi is 400 C.E. See A. Goldberg, with M. Krupp, "The Palestinian Talmud," in S. Safrai (ed.), *The Literature of the Sages. First Part: Oral Tora, Halakha, Mishna, Tosefta, Talmud,*

m. Ta'an. 4:6, "and Beter was captured and the city [of Jerusalem] was ploughed up"):

1. תני רבי שמעון בן יוחי עקיבה רבי היה דורש
2. דרך כוכב מיעקב דרך כוזבא מיעקב
3. רבי עקיבה כד הוה חמי בר כוזבה הוה אמר דין הוא מלכא משיחא
4. אמר לו רבי יוחנן בן תורתא
5. עקיבה יעלו עשבים בלחייך ועדיין בן דוד לא יבא

"[1]Rabbi Simeon ben Yoḥai taught: 'Aqiba, my master, used to interpret [2]"a star [כוכב] goes forth from Jacob" [Num 24:17]—Kozeba [כוזבא] goes forth from Jacob.'" [3]Rabbi Aqiba, when he saw Bar Kozeba, said: 'This is the King Messiah.' [4]Rabbi Yoḥanan ben Torta said to him: [5]'Aqiba! Grass will grow on your cheeks and still the son of David does not come!'"[31]

As framed, this tradition leaves one with the impression that Aqiba's positive assessment of "Bar Kozeba"[32] was not shared by other rabbis. Yoḥanan ben Torta, a minor authority, has told the great master that he would be long dead before Messiah appears. Jacob Neusner understands this tradition as made up of two contradictory components: the first part denying the messiahship of Simon (*i.e.* lines 1-2), with the second part identifying Simon as messiah (line 3). "What we have is simply two separate opinions of Aqiba."[33] I disagree. Although it is possible that the first part betrays Aqiba's later disillusionment with Simon (in which case it should read, "A disappointment/lie [כּוֹזְבָא] shall come forth out of Jacob," which is the way Neusner has taken it), I think that it is more likely that the first part of this tradition (lines 1-2) is a unified whole. Aqiba meets Simon ben Kosiba and concludes that he has met the Messiah, the "star" of which Num 24:17 spoke. Aqiba's original wording did not involve two puns, but only one: "a

External Tractates (CRINT 2.3; Assen: Van Gorcum; Philadelphia: Fortress, 1984) 303-22.

31   My translation.

32   The Rabbis spelled the name variously כּוֹזְבָה ,כּוֹזְבָה, or כּוֹזִיבָא, never referring to Simon as "bar Kokhba" (though in one MS of *Seder 'Olam* the name בר כככא does appear). In the letters found at Naḥal Ḥever and Murabba'at Simon's name is spelled with either ס or שׂ. More will be said on this below.

33   J. Neusner, *Messiah in Context: Israel's History and Destiny in Formative Judaism* (Philadelphia: Fortress, 1984) 95.

star [כוכב] goes forth from Jacob" [Num 24:17]—Kosiba [כוסבא] goes
forth from Jacob."[34] Elsewhere in rabbinic writings Simon's name is
understood as "disappointment" or "lie," but I do not think that this
was the original understanding of Aqiba's utterance. The Palestinian
Talmud has spelled Simon's name with a ז, as is the practice in rabbinic
literature. Consequently, Aqiba's original affirmation of Simon has
been transformed: The "star" has not come forth from Jacob, a "liar"
has. This is in fact the point of the further reinterpreting of the parallel
tradition that we find in *Lam. Rab.* 2:2 §4.

However, all five lines of material quoted and translated above may
not have been originally a unit. Unlike the Hebrew statements in lines
1-2 and 5, Aqiba's statement in line 3 ("This is the King Messiah") is in
Aramaic, and is probably a later insertion. But this does not mean that
it is itself late or inauthentic, as will be argued below.

The Aqiba tradition appears in the later midrash on Lamentations.
According to this version, Aqiba's interpretation is corrected by Rabbi
Judah ha-Nasi: "Rabbi Yoḥanan said: 'Rabbi (i.e. Judah ha-Nasi) used
to expound "A star [*kokab*] shall come forth out of Jacob" [Num 24:17]
thus: "Do not read כוֹכָב [star] but כּוֹזָב [lie]"'" (*Lam. Rab.* 2:2 §4).[35] Not
only does this interpretation differ from Aqiba's, but the framers of
the Lamentations midrash have substituted it for Aqiba's interpretation, placing it alongside of Aqiba's recognition of Simon as Messiah.
What we have here is a later reworking of the older tradition
perserved in the Palestinian gemara. The later compilers and editors of
the talmudic and midrashic tradition apparently have taken care to
portray Aqiba's views as shared by no one else.

Nevertheless, the Palestinian Talmud attributes messianic interpretation of Num 24:17 to at least one another rabbi. According to *y. Ned.*
3.8 (commenting on *m. Ned.* 3:10-11a):

1. רבי גרשום בשם רבי אחא
2. דרך כוכב מיעקב:
3. ממי דרך כוכב ועתיד לעמוד מיעקב:

"[1]Rabbi Gershom in the name of Rabbi Aḥa: [2]"'A star goes forth

---

[34]   So also Schäfer, "Rabbi Aqiva and Bar Kokhba," 119; cf. idem, *Der Bar
Kokhba-Aufstand*, 55-57.

[35]   Trans. A. Cohen, "Lamentations," in H. Freedman and M. Simon (eds.),
Midrash Rabbah (10 vols., London and New York: Soncino, 1983) 8.157.

from Jacob" [Num 24:17]. ³From whom will the star go forth? (From) him who is destined to arise from Jacob.'"

Aqiba's messianic interpretation of Num 24:17 was not unusual; it was common. Besides Rabbis Gershom and Aḥa, all four of the Pentateuch Targums paraphrase the passage in a messianic manner (see excursus 1) and, as seen in chaps. 2 and 3, Qumran and other early sources understand the passage messianically. What is remarkable about *y. Ta'an.* 4.5 is its attempt to portray Aqiba as the lone, even opposed, voice recognizing Simon. It is quite possible that this fictive portrait does not represent the general attitude of the rabbis toward Simon ben Kosiba. Not only is there evidence of an editorial bias within the sources themselves, but there is explicit evidence, albeit quite late and uncorroborated, that Aqiba was not alone in his positive assessment of Simon. It is intriguing to find that Moses Maimonides, over against the Talmud itself, believed that Simon enjoyed wide-spread support among the rabbis: "Rabbi Aqiba, the greatest of the sages of the Mishna, was a supporter of King Ben Kozeba, saying of him that he was King Messiah. He *and all the contemporary sages* regarded him as the King Messiah, until he was killed for sins which he had committed" (*Mishneh Torah, Melakhim* 11:3, emphasis added).³⁶ Obviously, the opinion of a Jewish scholar writing half a millenium after the completion of the Talmud cannot be accepted as historical fact without further ado. But it will be argued below, when other considerations are taken into account, that Maimonides' statement is in all probability closer to the truth than what we find in the Talmud and the midrash on Lamentations.

There is no doubt, of course, that the disillusionment that followed Bar Kokhba's defeat gave rise to repudiation, criticism, and sarcasm. Simon ben Kosiba went from *bar kokhba* ("son of the star") to *bar kozeba* ("son of the lie/disappointment"). The tradition also tried to show that the rabbis recognized early on that Simon was not the Messiah: "Bar Koziba was king for two and a half years, and then said to the Rabbis: 'I am Messiah [משיח אנא].' They said to him: 'Of Messiah it is written that he smells and judges [cf. Isa 11:2-3]. Let us see if he smells and judges.' When they saw that he could not smell and judge,

---

36   My translation. Note that "Koziba" here in Maimonides carries no pejorative connotation.

they killed him" (b. Sanh. 93b).[37] This tradition is of no historical value but provides further evidence of the effort to debunk the defeated Simon.[38]

Nevertheless, the tradition does admit that Simon showed military prowess: "And what used Bar Koziba to do? He would catch the missiles from the enemie's catapults on one of his knees and hurl them back, killing many of the foe. On that account Rabbi Aqiba [proclaimed him Messiah]" (Lam. Rab. 2:2 §4).[39] Simon, of course, did not literally catch siege stones and throw them back at the Romans. Nevertheless, this fanciful tradition does suggest that Simon enjoyed some success against the Romans.[40] It has also been suggested that he may have made use of captured Roman catapults.[41] When Hadrian saw that Simon was dead, he said: "If his God had not slain him who could have overcome him?" (Lam. Rab. 2:2 §4; Pesiq. R. 30.3).[42] Although criticizing ben Kosiba for arrogance, he is viewed as a hero of sorts.

Jewish sources agree that the resulting slaughter was great: "Emperor Hadrian slew eighty thousand myriads of human beings at Bethar" (Lam. Rab. 2:2 §4; Gen. Rab. 65.21 [on 27:22]; "eight hundred thousand," according to y. Ta'an. 4.5; "not a soul escaped," according to 'Abot R. Nat. A 38.3).[43] Hadrian said to Aquila: "See how I have degraded (the people of Israel), and how many of them I have slain" (Exod. Rab. 30.12 [on 21:1]).[44] Elsewhere we are told that Hadrian "killed in the city of Bethar four hundred thousand myriads, or as some say, four thousand myriads" (b. Giṭ. 57b).[45] God will judge

---

[37]   My translation.

[38]   For a critical assessment of this text and other related ones, see Schäfer, Der Bar Kokhba-Aufstand, 57-58. Schäfer remarks that we have here "a purely literary composition without any historical value" (p. 58). The claim that "the rabbis" killed Simon is quite remarkable.

[39]   Cohen, "Lamentations," 158.

[40]   The resident Roman legions, X Fretensis and VI Ferrata, probably suffered heavy losses. It has also been suggested that XXII Deiotariana may have been annihilated; cf. Smallwood, The Jews under Roman Rule, 446-47.

[41]   Smallwood, The Jews under Roman Rule, 446 n. 71.

[42]   Cohen, "Lamentations," 159.

[43]   Cohen, "Lamentations," 157.

[44]   S. M. Lehrman, "Exodus," in Freedman and Simon (eds.), Midrash Rabbah, 3.360.

[45]   Trans. M. Simon, "Gittin," in I. Epstein (ed.), The Babylonian Talmud (18 vols., London: Soncino, 1978) 9.266 (and n. 5).

Rome, according to Rabbi Berekiah, because "Hadrian slew in Bethar four hundred myriads of thousands of human beings" (*Song Rab.* 2:17 §1).[46] "How many battles did Hadrian fight? Two teachers give an answer. One said it was fifty-two and the other fifty-four" (*Lam. Rab.* 2:2 §4).[47]

The rabbis spared no hyperbole in describing the extent and gruesomeness of the Jewish slaughter: Rivers of blood flowed to the sea; Hadrian built a fence out of corpses from Tiberius to Sepphoris; only his successor (Antoninus Pius) permitted burial; the gentiles fertilized their vineyards with the blood of the slain; great numbers of phylacteries were found at Bethar; children were wrapped in Torah scrolls and burned (*b. Giṭ.* 57a, 57b–58a; *Lam. Rab.* 2:2 §4; *Seder Elijah* §151 [28]); Jews hid in caves (literally so, in light of the Bar Kokhba letters found in the cave at Naḥal Ḥever, along with cooking utensils and various personal belongings); and Jews starved (*Lam. Rab.* 1:16 §45; *Midr. Ps* 17.13 [on 17:14]). The memory of the disaster was such that ben Kosiba's generation became known as the "generation of destruction" (*Esth. Rab.* 3.7 [on 1:9]; *Song Rab.* 1:3 §3; 8:6 §4; *Midr. Ps* 16.4 [on 16:4], where it is identified as one of the three generations of suffering). These traditions have no historical value beyond corroborating in colorful ways the magnitude of the disaster in Judea and its enduring painful memory.[48]

Bar Kokhba Letters and Coins

The Bar Kokhba coins and letters provide valuable insight and in some instances confirmation of the histories and traditions in the writings surveyed above. Three letters from Simon ben Kosiba were found at Wadi Murabba'at in the early 1950s.[49] Fifteen more, one of which was written on wood, were discovered at Naḥal Ḥever in 1960

---

46   M. Simon, "Song of Songs," in Freedman and Simon (eds.), *Midrash Rabbah*, 9.142.

47   Cohen, "Lamentations," 166.

48   For a critical assessment of these texts and other related ones, see Schäfer, *Der Bar Kokhba-Aufstand*, 136-93.

49   That is, Mur 24, Mur 43MurEpBarCᵃ, and Mur 44MurEpCᵇ, all from cave 2. The Murabba'at finds have been published in P. Benoit, J. T. Milik, and R. de Vaux, *Les grottes de Murabba'at* (2 vols., DJD 2; Oxford: Clarendon, 1961) 1.122-34, 159-63; 2.pls. 35-37 and 46.

and 1961 by Yigael Yadin.[50] The "wooden letter" begins "Simon bar Kosiba, Prince [נְשִׂיא] over Israel."[51] Other letters refer to Simon as "Prince of Israel";[52] so do some of the coins.[53] Although nowhere is Simon called "Messiah," the letters and coins suggest that this is very likely how "Prince of Israel" was understood.

Some coins read on the obverse, "Simon[54] Prince [נשיא] of Israel," and on the reverse, "Year One of the Redemption [גאלת] of Israel." Others read on the obverse, "Year Two of the Freedom [חרות] of Israel," and on the reverse, "Simon Prince of Israel." Several coins refer to "Simon the Prince" and to the "freedom of Jerusalem."[55] A few depict the Temple, some with what could be a star above it, others depict palm branches, citron, grape bunches, trumpets, and oil-libation jugs.[56] All of these symbols indicate, as Yadin rightly comments, "the Messianic nature of the war."[57] The image of the Temple probably indicates the hope of rebuilding the Temple, a task that the Isaiah meturgeman thought fell to the Messiah.[58] Given that Simon was called

---

[50] I.e., 5/6ḤevEp 1-15; cf. Yadin, "Expedition D" (see n. 7 above); idem, *Bar-Kokhba* (London: Weidenfeld and Nicolson, 1971) 113-39; B. Lifshitz, "Papyrus grecs du désert de Juda," *Aegyptus* 42 (1962) 240-56 (+ pls.); J. A. Fitzmyer, "The Bar Cochba Period," in Fitzmyer, *Essays on the Semitic Background of the New Testament* (London: Chapman, 1971) 305-54. For text and translation of the Aramaic letters, see J. A. Fitzmyer and D. J. Harrington, *A Manual of Palestinian Aramaic Texts* (BibOr 34; Rome: Biblical Institute Press, 1978) 158-63.

Several of Simon's letters found at Naḥal Ḥever read: "From Simon ben [*or* bar] Kosiba . . ." (משמעון בן [בר] כוסבה). Two letters spell Kosiba with שׁ; and among the letters and documents of Murabba'at it is sometimes spelled כוסבא. One letter is written in Greek, and spells the leader's name, Σιμων Χωσιβα, thus possibly settling the question of which vowel (e or i) or consonant (z or s) was used; cf. Yadin, "Expedition D," 11 (1961) 44; idem, *Bar-Kokhba*, 132; Lifshitz, "Papyrus grecs," 248.

[51] Yadin, "Expedition D," 11 (1961) 41; idem, *Bar-Kokhba*, 122, 124.

[52] Yadin, "Expedition D," (1962) 255.

[53] Yadin, *Bar-Kokhba*, 20-21; Schürer, *History of the Jewish People*, 1.606.

[54] Lit. "Šime'on."

[55] L. Y. Rahmani, "The Coins from the Cave of Horror," *IEJ* 12 (1962) 200; Mildenberg, *The Coinage of the Bar Kokhba War*, 29-31; Yadin, *Bar-Kokhba*, 24-25; Schürer, *History of the Jewish People*, 1.606.

[56] Yadin, *Bar-Kokhba*, 24-25.

[57] Yadin, *Bar-Kokhba*, 27.

[58] Cf. *Tg.* Isa 53:5: "and [the Messiah] will build the sanctuary"; cf. *Tg.* Zech

bar kokhba and given that his name also appears on coins that bear the image of the Temple, the star emblem is probably meant to allude to his title, "Son of the Star," and may also imply that Simon hoped to rebuild the Temple.[59]

The coins' proclamations of Israel's "redemption" and Jerusalem's "freedom" cohere with several of the petitions of the *Amidah*: "Redeem [גאל] us for the sake of Thy Name. Blessed art Thou, O Lord, the Redeemer [גואל] of Israel" (§7); "Blow the great horn of our freedom [חרות]" (§10); and "Be merciful, O Lord our God, towards Jerusalem, Thy city, and towards Zion, the abiding place of Thy glory, and towards the kingdom of the house of David, Thy righteous Messiah. Blessed art Thou, O Lord, God of David, the builder of Jerusalem" (§14).[60]

One of the Bar Kokhba documents, a lease deed, begins "On the twenty-eighth of Marhsehvan, the third year of Simon bar Kosiba, Prince of Israel, at En-gedi."[61] Dating the document "the third year of Simon bar Kosiba" follows the dating conventions of the time, that is, noting the given year of a monarch's rule (cf. Luke 3:1: "In the fifteenth year of the reign of Tiberius Caesar"). Compare the dating in 5/6HevBA 14, one of the letters belonging to Babatha, a young woman who may have been related to Simon ben Kosiba: "In the ninth year of Emperor Trajan Hadrian Caesar Augustus..."[62] Simon's letter implies the recognition of Simon, in pointed contrast to Hadrian the Roman emperor, as Israel's king.

6:12-13; *Tg.* Song 1:17. B. D. Chilton (*The Glory of Israel: The Theology and Provenience of the Isaiah Targum* [JSOTSup 23; Sheffield: JSOT Press, 1983] 93-96) thinks that this Aramaic tradition took form in the period between the wars with Rome.

59   So P. Volz, *Die Eschatologie der jüdischen Gemeinde im neutestamentlichen Zeitalter* (Hildesheim: Olm, 1966) 210; Chilton, *Glory of Israel*, 96. The "star" identification is disputed by Mildenberg, "Bar Kokhba Coins and Documents," 315; and Reinhartz, "Rabbinic Perceptions," 174. Mildenberg and other numismatists contend that the "star" is nothing more than a rosette and so has no messianic significance whatsoever.

60   For text see G. Dalman, *Die Worte Jesu* (Leipzig: Hinrichs, 1898) 299-301 (Palestinian rescension), and chap. 6 below.

61   Yadin, "Expedition D," 12 (1962) 250, cf. p. 255; idem, *Bar-Kokhba*, 176-78.

62   For text, see N. Lewis, *The Documents from the Bar Kokhba Period in the Cave of Letters: Greek Papyri* (Jerusalem: Israel Exploration Society, 1989) 55.

In a few cases the content of the Bar Kokhba letters also reflects Simon's regal authority. In one, Simon orders the confiscation of a quantity of wheat. In another he threatens Jonathan bar Be'ayan and Masabal bar Simon, recipients of several of the letters, with punishment if they do not bring him the men of Tekoa (to fight). In a related letter Simon threatens to burn the homes of those who shelter deserters. In another, Simon requests more men. Failure to comply with his orders will result in punishment. Simon will himself "deal with the Romans." One letter, signed by Samuel bar 'Ami, orders the arrest and disarming of a certain Yeshua.[63]

The use of the title "prince" (נָשִׂיא) does not in itself militate against a messianic interpretation. This is so for two reasons. First, נָשִׂיא is sometimes used to refer to the king. We see this when Ahijah the prophet tells Jeroboam of the impending division of the kingdom: "I will not take the whole kingdom out of [Solomon's] hand; but I will make him prince [נָשִׂיא] all the days of his life, for the sake of David my servant" (1 Kgs 11:34). Similar usage is found centuries later at Qumran. In what is probably a reference to the anticipated Messiah, the War Scroll speaks of "the name of the prince [הַנָּשִׂיא] of the myriad" (1QM 3:16; cf. 1QSa 2:12, 14, 20; CD 14:19; 19:10; 20:1). One passage appears to equate "prince" with the "Branch of David" (4Q285, see below). Another passage apparently refers either to one of the Hasmonean priest-kings or to the oft-married Herod the Great: "And concerning the prince [הַנָּשִׂיא] it is written, 'He shall not multiply wives for himself' [Deut 17:17]. As for David, he did not" do the evil deeds that have been done by Israel's recent rulers (CD 5:1-2). It should be noted that Deut 17:14-20, from which the quotation was taken, contains legislation concerning Israel's king (מֶלֶךְ, v. 15). Second, and more importantly, "prince" appears to be Ezekiel's preferred title for the awaited messianic deliverer. "Prince" and "king" are placed in a parallel relationship in one eschatological passage with messianic implications: "My servant David shall be king [מֶלֶךְ] over them; and they shall all have one shepherd . . . and David my servant shall be their prince [נָשִׂיא] for ever" (Ezek 37:24-25). In this context "prince" and "king" are synonymous. Elsewhere in Ezekiel the awaited Davidic king is called נָשִׂיא (44:3; 45:16; 46:2, 4, 8, 12, 16, 17, 18; 48:21, 22); while Israel's king in Ezekiel's time is called נָשִׂיא

63 Yadin, "Expedition D," 11 (1961) 41-49; idem, Bar-Kokhba, 125-26.

(12:10, 12; 21:25).

The coins and letters also provide evidence of Simon's commitment to Jewish faith and practice. In one letter Simon directs Jonathan and Masabala to send to him one Eleazar bar Hitta "before the Sabbath." The implication is that there can be no travel on the Sabbath. In another letter directions are given regarding a supply of wheat. But again, despite the urgency, the Sabbath is to be honored.[64] Yet another letter requests the provisions necessary for the celebration of the Feast of Tabernacles. Among the items that Simon requires are palm branches and citrons, items also found depicted on the Bar Kokhba coins.[65]

Simon ben Kosiba's devotion to Jewish faith is consistent with messianic expectation, for the Messiah was expected to keep the Law faithfully.[66] The messianic picture in the Isaiah Targum, which reflects interpretive traditions that probably antedate the Bar Kokhba revolt, emphasizes this point.[67] Messiah's ministry, moreover, is to be "conducted with a priestly colleague,"[68] which is what we find in "Eleazar the priest," whose name appears on some of the Bar Kokhba coins and who may be the Eleazar of Modiin associated with Simon in the rabbinic tradition,[69] thus adding to the impression that religious/

---

64   Yadin, *Bar-Kokhba*, 128, 139. Mur 44: "[observe] the Sabbath"; cf. Fitzmyer, "The Bar Cochba Period," 340.

65   Yadin, *Bar-Kokhba*, 24-25, 128-33. See also Smallwood, *The Jews under Roman Rule*, 453.

66   In the generations following the defeat of Simon, the Messiah was sometimes portrayed as a learned student of Torah; cf. Neusner, *Messiah in Context*, 189-91. In the targums the Messiah obeys and protects the Law, including Halakah (*Frag. Tg.* Gen 49:10, 12; *Tg.* Isa 9:5-6; *Tg.* Song 8:1), expounds the Law (*Tg.* Isa 42:1, 4, 7), and even enforces the Law (*Tg.* Isa 53:11, 12).

67   Chilton, *The Glory of Israel*, 87-88.

68   Chilton, *The Glory of Israel*, 23-24, 96. The association of High Priest and Messiah is probably implied in *Tg.* Isa 22:15-25, while the pairing of these figures is made explicit in *Tg.* 1 Sam 2:35: "I will raise up before me a trustworthy priest . . . and I will establish for him an enduring reign and he will serve my Messiah all the days"; and *Tg.* Zech 6:13: "He [Messiah] will build the Temple of the Lord . . . and there will be a High Priest on his throne, and there will be a counsel of peace between them."

69   Yadin, *Bar-Kokhba*, 24-25; Smallwood, *The Jews under Roman Rule*, 440. It is interesting to note that this Eleazar is said to have taught that if the Sabbath was kept, God would give Israel Messiah and the kingdom of David (*Mek.*

messianic convictions were a major driving force behind the rebellion.

All of these considerations lead me to conclude that at some point in the war Simon ben Kosiba was recognized as Israel's Messiah, the Lord's Anointed who was destined to liberate Jerusalem and restore Israel. If Mildenberg is correct in his contention that the catalyst of the war was Hadrian's ban on circumcision, which if complied with meant the end of Judaism and the Jewish people, then the appearance of a messianic savior is understandable. But the most compelling evidence lies in the Aqiba confession and the hostile testimony to this confession that we find in Justin Martyr and repeated in other fathers such as Eusebius. Aqiba's interpretation of Num 24:17 clearly has caused embarrassment for the rabbinic tradition. Shortly we shall see the same kind of embarrassment with respect to Aqiba's messianic views which are not explicitly linked to Simon ben Kosiba. Invoking the "criterion of embarrassment" (see chap. 1 above) I contend that the rabbinic tradition would not embarrass itself by inventing a tradition in which Rabbi Aqiba, the revered master of halakah, is portrayed as applying Num 24:17 to Simon ben Kosiba, a tradition which the rabbis then have to find ways of debunking. I think that it is much more reasonable to assume that the tradition is authentic and that the Aramaic statement, "This is the King Messiah," approximates the actual words of Aqiba. Confirmation is found in the hostile statement of Justin Martyr, that the leader of the Jewish revolt was called "Bar Chochebas." If Simon was not called *bar kokhba*, the "son of the star," then what motivation could Justin Martyr have had for calling him this? Why would anyone, Jewish or Christian, call Simon the "son of the star" following his defeat? Christians had no motivation for doing so; they preferred to liken him to a criminal or fraud. The rabbis had no motivation to do so; they preferred to liken him to a liar and impostor. Even the negative pun on his name, *bar kozeba* ("son of the lie"), is best explained as an attempt to erase the original pun of *bar kokhba*.

If we conclude that Simon ben Kosiba was in fact called the "son of the star," as a deliberate allusion to Num 24:17, then I think that it is very probable that he was thought of as a messianic deliverer. But this does not mean that he was thought of in supernatural terms, as in some of the highly speculative messianology found in some circles, or that

---

on Exod 16:25 [*Vayassa'* §5]).

his kingdom would usher in the eschatological age (though some of his
followers may have thought that it would).

AQIBA'S MESSIANOLOGY

Outside of Num 24:17 there is no other Old Testament passage that
can with certainty be related to Simon. The tradition that relates Simon
to Isaiah 11 has no serious claim to historicity (*b. Sanh.* 93b). Other
passages may have been applied to Simon, but his defeat and the
catastrophe that it brought upon Israel did not encourage the
preservation of positive traditions.

Aqiba's messianic interpretation of the plural "thrones" of Dan 7:9
is one tradition, however, that warrants careful consideration for two
reasons: (1) it comes from Aqiba, the author of the tradition that
applied Num 24:17 to Simon ben Kosiba, and (2) his interpretation
elicited a similar negative reaction from his colleagues and from the
editors of the rabbinic tradition. Because Aqiba's interpretation of Dan
7:9 formed a part of his messianology, there exists then the possibility
that his interpretation was intended to relate in some way to Simon.
The pertinent texts are are found in *b. Sanh.* 38b = *b. Ḥag.* 14a and
Midr. Tanḥ. B on Lev 19:1-2 (*Qedošin* §1).

The passage in *b. Sanh.* 38b (commenting on *m. Sanh.* 4:5, "that the
heretics should not say, 'There are many ruling powers in heaven'—
again to proclaim the greatness of the Holy One") finds itself in an
interesting context. The tradition is repeated almost verbatim in *b.
Ḥag.* 14a, with Isa 66:1 appended as scriptural support for the interpretation offered by Rabbi Eleazar ben Azariah. We shall examine the
shorter and more original version in *b. Sanh.* 38b:

1. עד די כרסוון רמיו כאי איכא למימר:
2. אחד לו ואחד לדוד דתניא אהד לו ואחד לדוד:
3. דברי רבי עקיבא: אמר לו רבי יוסי עקיבא:
4. עד מתי אתה עושה שכינה חול אלא אחד לדין ואחד לצדקה:
5. קבלה מיניה או לא קבלה מיניה תא שמע דתניא:
6. אחד לדין ואחד לצדקה :דברי רבי עקיבא: אמר לו רבי אלעזר בן עזריא
7. עקיבא מה לך אצל הגדה: כלך אצל נגעים ואהלות:
8. אלא אחד לכסא ואחד לשרפרף כסא לישב עליו שרפרף להדום רגליו:

"¹'Till thrones were placed' [Dan 7:9]—what is there to say? ²One
(throne) for Him and one for David, even as has been taught: 'One

was for Him and one was for David'—[3]the words of Rabbi Aqiba. Rabbi Yose said to him, [4]'Aqiba, how long will you profane the Shekinah? Rather, one (throne) is for justice and one for mercy.' [5]Did he accept (this answer) from him or not accept it from him? Come (and) hear what has been taught: [6]'One (throne) is for justice and the other for mercy'—the words (now) of Rabbi Aqiba. Rabbi Eleazar ben Azariah said to him, [7]'Aqiba, what do you have to do with Aggada? Occupy yourself with Nega'im and Ohaloth—[8]but one as a throne and one as a footstool: a throne for a seat and a footstool for support of His feet.'"[70]

Midr. Tanḥ. B on Lev. 19:1-2 (*Qedošin* §1):

1. וידבר יהוה אל־משה לאמר: דבר אל בני־ישראל ואמרת אליהם
2. קדשים תהיו [כי קדוש אני יהוה אלהיכם]:
3. זה שאמר הכתוב: ויגבה יהוה צבאות במשפט [והאל הקדוש נקדש בצדקה]:
4. אימתי נעשה הקדוש ברוך הוא גבוה בעולמו: כשיעשה דין
5. ומשפט באומות העולם שנאמר נצב לריב יהוה ועומד לדין עמים:
6. וכן הוא ואומר [חזה] הוית עד [די כרסון] רמיו:
7. מהו כרסוון: וכי כסאות הרבה הן: והכתיב
8. ואראה את יהוה יושב על כסא [רם ונשא וכתיב מלך יושב על כסא על כסא דין]:
9. מהו כרסוון: רבי יוסי הגלילי ורבי עקיבא:
10. חד אמר כורסוון זה הכסא ואפופרין שלו: וחד אמר אלו כסאות של
11. אומות העולם שעתיד הקדוש ברוך הוא להפכן שנאמר
12. והפכתי את כסא ממלכות והשמדתי חוזק ממלכות הגוים:
13. תדע שכן הוא כורסוון יתיב אין כתיב כאן אלא רמיו
14. וכתיב סוס ורוכבו רמה בים: ורבנן אמרין:
15. מהו כורסוון לעתיד לבא: הקודש ברוך הוא יושב והמלאכים נותנים
16. כסאות לגדולי ישראל והם יושכים: הקדש ברוך הוא יושב
17. כאב בית דין עמהם ודנין לאומות העולם שנאמר
18. יהוה במשפט יבא עם זקני עמו ושריו:
19. על זקני עמו אין כתיב כאן אלא עם זקני [שריו]
20. מלמד שהקודש ברוך הוא יושב עם הזקנים ושרי ישראל ודן לאומות העולם:
21. ומי הן אלו כסאות: בית דוד וזקני ישראל שנאמר
22. כי שם ישבו כסאות למשפט כסאות לבית דוד:
23. אמר רבי פנחס בשם רבי חלקיה [הדרומי] בשם רבי ראובן: אם אתה אומר
24. כי שם ישבו כסאות למשפט כסאות בית דוד
25. ומה ועתיק יומין יתיב שהוא יושב ביניהם כאב בית דין

---

[70]   My translation.

26. ודן עמהם את האומות לפיכך: כתיב עד די כורסוון רמיו:

"[1]And the Lord spoke to Moses, saying: 'Speak to the sons of Israel and say to them: [2]"Be holy [because I the Lord your God am holy]"' [Lev 19:1]. [3]This is what the passage says: 'The Lord of hosts will be exalted in judgment [and the holy God will make himself holy in righteousness]' [Isa 5:16]. [4]When will the Holy One, blessed be He, be exalted in this world? When he passes sentence [5]and makes judgment on the peoples of the world, as it says: 'The Lord has stationed himself for the litigation; He stands to judge peoples' [Isa 3:13]. [6]And thus it says: 'I kept looking until thrones were set up' [Dan 7:9]. [7]How is it 'thrones'? Are there really many thrones? But it is written: [8]'I saw the Lord sitting upon a throne [high and lifted up' [Isa 6:1]; and it is written: 'A king sits on a throne of judgment' [Prov 20:8].] [9]How is it 'thrones'? Rabbi Yose the Galilean and Rabbi Aqiba (discussed this question). [10]One said: '"Thrones"—this refers to the throne and to its footstool.' The other said: 'These are the thrones that belong to [11]the people of the world, which the Holy One, blessed be He, is about to overthrow, as it says: [12]"I will overthrow the throne of the kingdoms and I shall destroy the strength of the kingdoms of the nations" [Hag 2:22]. [13]You should know that "thrones were placed" is not written here, but "were cast down"; [14]as it is written: "Horse and rider he cast into the sea" [Exod 15:1].' Our rabbis say: [15]'What does "thrones" mean in the world to come? The Holy One, blessed be He, will sit and the angels will give [16]thrones to the great ones of Israel, and they will sit. And the Holy One, blessed be He, will sit [17]as presiding Judge with them. They will judge the peoples of the world, as it says: [18]"The Lord comes in judgment with the elders of His people and His princes" [Isa 3:14]. [19]"Against" the elders of His people it is not written here, but "with" the elders [and His princes], [20]teaching that the Holy One, blessed be He, sits with the elders and princes of Israel to judge the peoples of the world. [21]And whose are these thrones? (They belong to) the house of David and to the elders of Israel, as it says: [22]"For there sit thrones for judgment, thrones for the house of David" [Ps 122:5].' [23]Rabbi Phineas said in the name of Rabbi Ḥilqiah [the southern] in the name of Rabbi Reuben: 'When you say, [24]"For there sit thrones for judgment, thrones for the house of David," [25]what can "the Ancient of Days sat down" [Dan

7:9] mean, if not that He sits between them as presiding Judge [26]and with them judges the peoples? Therefore, it is written: "until thrones were set up" [Dan 7:9].'"[71]

What is to be made of this tradition? Recognizing the many difficulties that attend analysis of rabbinica, I would like to make a few cautious suggestions about the contextualization and presentation of this material. First, it should be noted that Aqiba's exegesis has been remembered and presented in a critical light. This is seen clearly in the passage preserved in the Babylonian Talmud. In it Aqiba has been rebuked ("How long will you profane God?"). And in it Aqiba changes his mind, being chided for taking an interest in haggadic exegesis, instead of halakic exegesis, for which this rabbi was justly famous. In the *Tanhuma* passage, Aqiba's earlier interpretation is not mentioned at all, unless it is part of what "our rabbis" said: "And whose are these thrones? [They belong to] the house of David and to the elders of Israel." The midrash goes on to suggest that this is the meaning of Dan 7:9 ("Thrones were set up and the Ancient of Days sat down"). God, along with the elders of Israel, will sit in judgment upon the nations. There is, however, no explicit mention of Messiah.

Secondly, the context of the discussion in *b. Sanh.* 38b is particularly important. The preceding paragraphs address various heresies. The paragraph that immediately precedes the one in which Aqiba's exegesis appears discusses the *minim* who find in passages where God is spoken of in the plural evidence for the plurality of the Godhead (cited, among others, are Gen 1:26 and 11:27). Our paragraph, with its discussion of the significance of the plurality of the "thrones" in Dan 7:9, is part of this discussion. It is indeed significant that Aqiba's interpretation was placed in such a pejorative context. The implication is that Aqiba's suggestion that "David" (i.e. the Messiah) would take his seat next to God himself implied some sort of sharing of divine authority and status. Not only did Aqiba's contemporary, Yose the Galilean, object, but it is quite evident that the later editors of the Babylonian gemara saw this as dangerously similar to the various heresies (such as Christianity and Gnosticism) in which it was believed that there were two or more "Powers" in heaven.

Thirdly, the denigration of Aqiba's exegesis and his subsequent

---

[71]   My translation. Bracketed material comes from other editions of *Tanhuma*.

change of mind probably constitute a fictive scene. It is not likely that
Aqiba expounded upon the meaning of the "thrones" of Dan 7:9, was
challenged on the spot, and then immediately abandoned his
interpretation. I suspect that what we have here is a simplification,
partly authentic and partly fiction. Aqiba probably did interpret
Daniel the way the tradition remembers, and he may very well have
eventually changed his mind, possibly after ben Kosiba's defeat. But it
is possible that Aqiba's interpretation paralleled too closely Christian
interpretation in which Jesus was conceptualized as the enthroned and
deified Son of man of Daniel 7. It could have been for this reason that
the rabbinic tradition presents the tradition the way it does. Aqiba is
promptly challenged and just as promptly drops his interpretation. The
motivation probably had as much to do with preserving Aqiba's
reputation, as it had to do with countering a heretical exegesis and, if
part of his evaluation of Simon ben Kosiba, a dangerous and failed
exegesis.

Fourthly, did Aqiba's exegesis have antecedents? It evidently did, as
is seen in *1 Enoch*, where at many points Daniel 7 is alluded to and
interpreted: "pain shall seize [rulers] when they see that Son of Man
sitting on the throne of his glory" (62:5; for more parallels see above).
Daniel 7 does not explicitly state that the "Son of Man" of v. 13 will sit
on a throne. Verse 26 does say, however, that "the court will sit in
judgment" (cf. v. 10), but it is not clear if the Son of Man is part of this
court. Aqiba understood the plural "thrones" of v. 9 as implying that
the Messiah would sit next to God. *1 Enoch*'s statement that the Son of
Man will sit on a throne is probably the exegetical bridge between
Daniel and Aqiba. This seems to be the idea in Matt 25:31: "When the
Son of Man comes in his glory, and all the angels with him, then he will
sit on his glorious throne" (cf. Mark 13:26).

Although Aqiba is supposedly rebuked for his earlier interpretation
of Dan 7:9, other rabbis also applied parts of Daniel 7 (esp. vv. 13-14)
to the Messiah (see *b. Sanh.* 96b-97a, 98a; *Num. Rab.* 13.14 [on 7:13];
Midr. Ps. 21.5 [on 21:7]; 93.1 [on 93:1]) and to his "elect" (*Midr.
Tanḥ.* B, *Qedošim* §1). There is especially interest in the cloud
imagery. In *b. Sanh.* 96b-97a Messiah is called "Bar Naphle," an
expression behind which lies a pun referring to the "fallen" tent of
David (from the Hebrew נֹפֶל–cf. Amos 9:11) and to the one who comes

with the "clouds" (from the Greek νεφέλη–cf. LXX Dan 7:13).[72] Elsewhere are expressed alternative expectations, depending upon Israel's moral condition: "If they [the Israelites] are meritorious, [Messiah will come] on 'the clouds of heaven' [alluding to Dan 7:13]; if not, [Messiah will come] 'lowly and riding upon an ass' [alluding to Zech 9:9]" (b. Sanh. 98a). Finally, the cloud imagery appears in two of the Targums in which Moses and David are compared: "Moses shall go forth from the wilderness and the King Messiah from the height.[73] The one shall lead the way on top of a cloud and the other shall lead the way on top of a cloud" (Frag. Tg. Exod 12:42; cf. Tg. Neof. Exod 12:42).

A few other traditions attributed to Aqiba are worth brief notice. The first concerns the duration of the messianic reign: "How long will the days of the Messiah last? Rabbi Aqiba said, 'Forty years—as long as the Israelites were in the wilderness.' . . . Rabbi Judah the Prince said, 'Four hundred years—as long as the Israelites were in Egypt. Rabbi Eliezer said, 'A thousand years'" (Midr. Tanh., 'Eqeb §7). Rabbi Aqiba's expectation seems to be limited to one generation, or to the length of adult life expectancy (in contrast to Eliezer and Judah), such as would have been the case had Simon ben Kosiba succeeded in gaining independence for Israel.

Of related interest is tradition in which Aqiba speculates about what will signal Messiah's approach: "How can one tell when the King Messiah is coming? Rabbi Aqiba [some MSS. read Eliezer] said: 'Near the days of the Messiah ten territories will be swallowed up, ten territories will be overturned, ten territories will have their inhabitants put to death" (Pesiq. R. 1.7).[74] In the same passage Aqiba is said to have speculated at one time that Messiah would appear forty years after the destruction of the Temple. There is also a tradition in which Aqiba predicts the regathering of the ten northern tribes ('Abot R. Nat. [A] 36.4; cf. m. Sanh. 10:3, where Aqiba is said to hold the opposite opinion), a hope to which the Targum (cf. Tg. Isa 53:8: "He [i.e., Messiah] will bring back our exiles"; Tg. Hos 2:2; Tg. Song 1:8) and other rabbinic passages (cf. b. Qidd. 70b; Midr. Ps. 122.4 [on

---

72 See Freedman, "Sanhedrin," 654, n. 2.

73 The word רומא can be read either רוּמָא ("height") or רוֹמָא ("Rome"). The former makes the best sense, given the subsequent reference to cloud.

74 Trans. based on W. G. Braude, Pesikta Rabbati (2 vols., YJS 18; New Haven and London: Yale University, 1968) 1.48.

122:4]; *Amida* §10) give expression. According to another tradition
(*b. Sanh.* 97b) Aqiba is criticized, along with others, for having
attempted to predict the coming of the Messiah.

The general impression one receives from these traditions, all of
which admit to uncertainties of date and provenance, is that Aqiba was
known to have entertained messianic speculations. Evidently he made
predictions of when the Messiah would appear, what signs would
attend his approach, and how long his rule would perdure. The latter
point is interesting, for if this tradition is authentic—that Aqiba
thought the reign of Messiah would be for forty years—then he and
others may very well have entertained the advent of a Messiah who
was, in the words of Mildenberg, "a man like themselves." The only
truly apocalyptic feature of the messianology that is attributed to
Aqiba is his interpretation of Dan 7:9, which may have relevance for
Jesus research.

AQIBA'S MESSIANOLOGY AND THE CHRISTOLOGY OF JESUS

Aqiba's exegesis of Dan 7:9, which understands the plural "thrones"
to imply one throne for God and one throne for his Messiah, could
have important relevance for our study of early christology, perhaps
even for Jesus' self-understanding. Several statements in the Gospels,
not all from Jesus, reflect Daniel 7. The request of James and John to
sit on Jesus' right and left (Mark 10:37-40) is likely based on this
passage. Jesus' promise to his disciples that when he sits on his throne
they "will also sit on twelve thrones, judging the twelve tribes of
Israel" (Matt 19:28 = Luke 22:28-30) likely reflects Daniel 7 (along
with Psalm 122). Just as the rabbinic tradition suggests that it was in
response to impressive deeds on Simon's part that Aqiba recognized
Simon as Messiah, so in Mark's Gospel Simon Peter recognizes Jesus as
Messiah (Mark 8:29), probably in response to his miracles. One thinks
also of Mark 14:61-62 where Jesus affirms that he is the Messiah, the
Son of God, and that he will be seen seated at the right hand of God,
coming with the clouds of heaven.[75] If we apply Aqiba's exegesis to
this statement, then Jesus is claiming that he will sit on a throne in the
presence of God. The High Priest's cry of "Blasphemy!" roughly
parallels Rabbi Yose's exclamation, "Aqiba, how long will you treat

---

[75]   For a defense of the historicity of this passage, see chap. 11 below.

the Divine Presence as profane!"[76] Daniel 7, moreover, solves the difficulty in understanding how Jesus could both be "seated" (stationary) and yet be "coming" (moving): The throne belonging to the Ancient of Days is the throne chariot ("its wheels were burning fire"). Although such a claim at first blush might seem too extreme, too apocalyptic, to have been uttered by the pre-Easter Jesus (hence the critical assumption that it represents a post-Easter confession of the early Church), the fact that Aqiba speculated, on the basis of Daniel 7, that the Messiah, whom he identified as Simon ben Kosiba, would sit next to God should put the tradition of Jesus' similar claim in a new light. Remember, too, that it was not necessary for Simon to be viewed in supernatural terms (or as resurrected) for Aqiba to think of him in messianic terms, and as possibly sitting next to God himself (though whether in "this world" or in the "world-to-come" is not clear). Likewise, it should no longer be supposed that only belief that Jesus had been resurrected and carried up to heaven can account for messianic recognition ("You are the Messiah") or even for a claim to sit next to God. In other words, the recognition of Simon ben Kosiba as Israel's Messiah suggests that the christology reflected in Mark 14:61-64 is Jewish, Palestinian, and not necessarily generated by Easter faith and Hellenistic ideas of an exalted human being.

There are other pertinent texts and questions that will have to be taken into consideration. A fuller comparison of the messianology of Aqiba with that of Jesus will be undertaken in chap. 11 below.

---

[76]   See D. R. Catchpole, *The Trial of Jesus* (SPB 18; Leiden: Brill, 1971) 140-41.

CHAPTER FIVE

JESUS AND JEWISH MIRACLE STORIES

One of the important positive steps taken by most scholars of the Third Quest is a willingness to view the miracle stories of Jesus in the context of the *Sitz im Leben Jesu*, rather than limiting them to the *Sitz im Leben der Gemeinde*. This chapter argues for the authenticity of the miracle tradition in general and offers a comparative survey of the miracle stories attributed to certain rabbis, or "holy men."[1]

THE HISTORICITY OF THE MIRACLES OF JESUS

It was stated in chap. 1 above that criteria have been worked out for establishing the probability of the authenticity of the miracle tradition in general and the authenticity of particular miracle stories. The valid criteria, in my opinion, are as follows:

1. Multiple Attestation. Tradition that is found in two or more independent sources (such as Mark and Q) enjoys a stronger claim to authenticity than does tradition found in only one source.[2] Multiple attestation, of course, is no guarantee that a given story is authentic, no more than single attestation proves that a given story is inauthentic. The miracle tradition is attested in Mark, Q, and the fourth Gospel (as

---

[1] For general bibliography, see P. Fiebig, *Jüdische Wundergeschichten des neutestamentlichen Zeitalters* (Tübingen: Mohr [Siebeck], 1911); A. Guttmann, "The Significance of Miracles for Talmudic Judaism," *HUCA* 20 (1947) 363-406; S. Safrai, "The Teaching of the Pietists in Mishnaic Literature," *JJS* 16 (1965) 15-33; H. van der Loos, *The Miracles of Jesus* (NovTSup 9; Leiden: Brill, 1965) 139-50; J. Neusner, *A Life of Yohanan ben Zakkai* (2nd ed., SPB 6; Leiden: Brill, 1970); G. Vermes, *Jesus the Jew: A Historian's Reading of the Gospels* (London: Collins, 1973) 58-82; idem, "Hanina ben Dosa," in Vermes, *Post-Biblical Jewish Studies* (SJLA 8; Leiden: Brill, 1975) 178-214; J. Nadich, *Jewish Legends of the Second Commonwealth* (Philadelphia: Jewish Publication Society of America, 1983) 194-200, 255-59, 296 n. 93, 396 n. 149; C. Brown, "Synoptic Miracle Stories: A Jewish Religious and Social Setting," *Forum* 2.4 (1986) 55-76.

[2] See C. A. Evans, "Authenticity Criteria in Life of Jesus Research," *CSR* 19 (1989) 3-31, esp. 8-10; J. P. Meier, *A Marginal Jew: Rethinking the Historical Jesus* (ABRL; New York: Doubleday, 1991) 174-75.

well as in material found only in Luke ["L"] and, possibly, in Matthew
["M"]). The attestation of the miracle tradition in Q is significant, for it
(the miracle tradition) apparently does not have the programmatic
theological and christological function in this putative source that it
does in Mark. Not only does Q narrate a miracle story (Matt 8:5-13 =
Luke 7:1-10; cf. John 4:46-54),³ it contains sayings, judged by many to
be authentic, that presuppose Jesus' miracles (Matt 11:2-6 = Luke
7:18-23; Matt 10:8 = Luke 10:9; Matt 11:21-23 = Luke 10:13-15; Matt
13:16-17 = Luke 10:23-24; Matt 12:43-45 = Luke 11:24-26). Some of
these sayings appear in Mark as well (e.g. Matt 12:27 = Luke 11:19; cf.
Mark 3:23) and so represent true examples of tradition multiply
attested. Moreover, Paul's reference to the "signs of a true apostle" (2
Cor 12:12), which he believes were wrought through him by Christ
(Rom 15:19), certainly implies that an early miracle tradition,
understood to be rooted in Jesus's ministry and continued in the
ministries of his disciples, was known to him. Lastly, hostile
interpretations of Jesus' miracles, particularly with respect to the
exorcisms, both in early traditions (e.g. Matt 9:34; 12:24 = Luke
11:18; Mark 3:22) and later (e.g. Celsus, in Origen, *Contra Celsum*
1.6, 38, 68; *b. Sanh.* 43a), offer a measure of support to the
authenticity of the miracles; for the miracles are not denied, only
criticized. For these reasons and for others, several scholars argue for
the essential historicity of the miracle tradition.⁴

---

3   R. Bultmann (*The History of the Synoptic Tradition* [Oxford: Blackwell,
1972] 64, 328) regards Matt 8:5-13 = Luke 7:1-10 as a later Hellenistic intrusion
(perhaps as a variant of Mark 7:24-31) into the earlier, Palestinian material that for
the most part makes up Q. Bultmann's analysis, however, seems controlled by his
questionable assumption that the miracle tradition originated in Hellenistic, non-
Palestinian circles of the early Church.

4   A. George, "Les miracles de Jésus dans les évangiles synoptiques,"
LumVie 33 (1957) 7-24; R. Latourelle, *The Miracles of Jesus and the Theology of
Miracles* (New York: Paulist, 1988) 56-58. Because of its wide and early attestation
R. H. Fuller (*Interpreting the Miracles* [Philadelphia: Westminster, 1963] 24-29)
finds the evidence in favor of the general tradition of exorcisms "little short of
overwhelming" and the healing miracles "very strong." More recently G. H.
Twelftree ("EI ΔΕ . . . ΕΓΩ ΕΚΒΑΛΛΩ ΤΑ ΔΑΙΜΟΝΙΑ . . .," in D. Wenham and
C. Blomberg [eds.], *The Miracles of Jesus* [Gospel Perspectives 6; Sheffield:
JSOT, 1986] 361-400) has concluded that there is "more than sufficient evidence to
affirm that Jesus was an extremely successful exorcist" and that "in many ways
Jesus seems to have been a man of his time in that he used readily recognizable

2. Dissimilarity. Tradition that cannot easily be explained as having originated in the early Church or having been taken over from Jewish traditions is said to be dissimilar (or distinctive) and therefore has a reasonable claim to authenticity.[5] Are the miracles of Jesus distinctive from the legends and traditions of the Mediterranean world? Despite efforts to interpret Jesus as a Jewish holy man (e.g. Vermes[6]), on the one hand, or as a magician or Hellenistic wonderworker (e.g. Smith[7]), on the other, most scholars have recognized that the miracles of Jesus resist such simple categorization. Unlike Ḥoni or Ḥanina ben Dosa, rarely does Jesus *pray* for healing or for other miracles. One thinks of Ḥoni standing in his circle beseeching God to give his people a "rain of goodwill, blessing, and graciousness" (*m. Ta'an.* 3:8; cf. Josephus, *Ant.* 14.2.2 §25-28) or Ḥanina who prayed with his head between his knees, knowing that his prayer has been heard when it comes fluently (*y. Ber.* 5.5; *b. Ber.* 34b). Jesus' style is very different. He speaks the word and the cure is effected. Moreover, he speaks and acts in his own name. He says, "I will it" (Mark 1:41; 2:11), not "God wills it."[8] More importantly, neither Ḥoni nor Ḥanina was remembered as the leader of a renewal movement. Most scholars, therefore, hesitate to follow Geza Vermes fully.[9] So it is in the case of comparisons made with magic. There are superficial parallels, to be sure, but there are so many important features missing that few have followed Morton Smith.[10]

---

techniques" (p. 393).

5   See Evans, "Authenticity Criteria," 15-16; Meier, *A Marginal Jew*, 171-74.

6   Vermes, *Jesus the Jew*, 58-82.

7   M. Smith, *Jesus the Magician* (San Francisco: Harper & Row, 1978) 140-52.

8   Latourelle, *Miracles of Jesus*, 58-60.

9   For criticisms, see E. P. Sanders, *Jesus and Judaism* (London: SCM; Philadelphia: Fortress, 1985) 170-72; H. C. Kee, *Medicine, Miracle and Magic in New Testament Times* (SNTSMS 55; Cambridge: Cambridge University, 1986) 82; B. Witherington, *The Christology of Jesus* (Minneapolis: Fortress, 1990) 157-60.

10   For criticisms, see W. Wink, "Jesus as Magician," *USQR* 30 (1974) 3-14; B. F. Meyer, *The Aims of Jesus* (London: SCM, 1979) 158; Sanders, *Jesus and Judaism*, 165-69; Kee, *Medicine, Miracle and Magic*, 115-17; E. M. Yamauchi, "Magic or Miracle? Disease, Demons and Exorcisms," in Wenham and Blomberg (eds.), *The Miracles of Jesus*, 89-183, esp. 94-97. J. M. Hull (*Hellenistic Magic and the Synoptic Tradition* [Naperville: Allenson, 1974] 144-45) concludes: "Jesus did not think of himself as a magician." Sanders (*Jesus and Judaism*, 169) agrees,

Scholars have accordingly concluded that Jesus' ministry of miracles was in important ways distinctive.[11]

But the criterion of dissimilarity functions in another way as well. Not only are the miracles of Jesus culturally distinctive in important ways, they appear to be only incidental to early Christian preaching. In other words, the miracles and the lessons that they often teach do not regularly advance uniquely Christian ideas. A few do, of course. The Johannine miracles of the water turning into wine (John 2:1-11) and the raising of Lazarus (John 11:38-44) advance important Christian doctrines (viz., the soteriological significance of Jesus' death, or "hour of glorification"). But these (relatively late) exceptions prove the basic point.[12] Most of the miracle tradition, especially that found in the earliest sources, does not function in this manner. Jesus casts out demons, cures lepers, raises up the lame. To be sure, some moral lessons are drawn from the miracles (e.g. Gal 3:5), but they are at the fringes of the Christian kerygma, not its heart.[13] For Paul, the gospel centers on the death and resurrection of Jesus, not his exorcisms or healings. The apologetic found on the lips of the Lucan Peter (Acts 2:22: "a man attested to you by God with mighty works and wonders and signs which he did in your midst") is meant primarily to demonstrate the innocence of Jesus (Acts 2:23: "this Jesus . . . you crucified and killed"), not his messianic credentials. It is his resurrection, not the miracles (or teaching, for that matter), that stands at the heart of the kerygma (Acts 2:32-36: "This Jesus God raised up . . . Let all the house of Israel therefore know assuredly that God has made him

---

saying that Jesus' miracles were such that they were open to differing interpretations, and that critics could view them as acts of magic, if they wished. For more on this point, see M. J. Geller, "Jesus' Theurgic Powers: Parallels in the Talmud and Incantation Bowls," *JJS* 28 (1977) 141-55.

[11]   A. Vögtle, "Jesu Wundertaten vor dem Hintergrund ihrer Zeit," in H. J. Schultz (ed.), *Die Zeit Jesu* (Stuttgart: Kreuz, 1966) 83-90; ET: "The Miracles of Jesus against Their Contemporary Background," in Schultz (ed.), *Jesus in His Time* (Philadelphia: Fortress, 1971) 96-105; idem, "Wunder," *LTK* 10.1257-58.

[12]   The miracle tradition has been thoroughly reworked in the fourth Gospel. The miracles have been theologized as "signs," probably, in my view, as part of the Johannine community's polemic with the synagogue (cf. 1 Cor 1:22: "the Jews require a sign"; Mark 8:12: "Why does this generation seek after a sign?").

[13]   It is worth noting that in the one New Testament writing that offers instruction concerning healing (Jas 5:14-15), anointing with oil is prescribed, something that Jesus, so far as our sources tell us, never did.

both Lord and Christ"; Rom 1:1-4: "the gospel concerning his Son, who was . . . designated Son of God in power by his resurrection from the dead"). Even the aforementioned apostolic deeds of power were not understood as an apologetic for the kerygma, but as an apologetic for one's claim to apostolic office.

3. Embarrassment. Edward Schillebeeckx and John Meier refer to the criterion of "embarrassment," which calls attention to sayings or actions that were potentially embarrassing to the early Church and/or the evangelists.[14] The assumption here is that such material would not likely be invented or, if it was, be preserved. The preservation of such material, therefore, strongly argues for its authenticity. The baptism of Jesus by John is a prime example of tradition highlighted by this criterion. Mark, the earliest Gospel, records the event with little commentary and apparently with little embarrassment (Mark 1:9). Matthew has the Baptist initially protest, clearly acknowledging Jesus' superiority (Matt 3:13-15). Luke reports John's imprisonment and then narrates Jesus' baptism, perhaps to avoid telling the reader that Jesus was baptized by John (Luke 3:18-21). The Fourth Gospel says that the Baptist hailed Jesus as the promised Coming One (John 1:29-34) but says nothing of Jesus' baptism. It appears that as we move from the earliest to the last Gospel this tradition is increasingly filtered, probably in response to a growing discomfort with the original form of the tradition.

A similar filtering process can be detected in several places in the miracle tradition. According to Mark 3:20-22 Jesus' family "went out to seize him [Jesus], for people were saying, 'He is mad.'" Assuming that the unity of 3:20-22 is original,[15] people evidently were saying

---

14   E. Schillebeeckx, *Jesus: An Experiment in Christology* (London: Collins; New York: Crossroad, 1979) 93; Meier, *A Marginal Jew*, 168-71. Closely related to this criterion is the criterion of "tradition contrary to the evangelists' editorial tendency"; see C. F. D. Moule, *The Phenomenon of the New Testament* (London: SCM, 1967) 56-76; R. N. Longenecker, "Literary Criteria in Life of Jesus Research: An Evaluation and Proposal," in G. F. Hawthorne (ed.), *Current Issues in Biblical and Patristic Interpretation* (M. C. Tenney Festschrift; Grand Rapids: Eerdmans, 1975) 217-29.

15   See the paragraphing in R. W. Funk (ed.), *New Gospel Parallels* (2 vols., Philadelphia: Fortress, 1985) 1.192, and the discussion in R. Pesch, *Das Markusevangelium* (2 vols., HTKNT 2.1; Freiburg: Herder, 1977) 1.209-10. Many separate 3:20-21 from 3:22-35. According to Bultmann (*History of the Synoptic Tradition*, 13) and others Mark 3:20-21, 31-35 may have been connected,

this about Jesus because of his exorcisms: "He is possessed by
Beelzebul, and by the prince of demons he casts out the demons" (v.
22). Although Matthew and Luke retain this accusation, they omit the
part about Jesus' family trying to seize him (cf. Matt 12:24; Luke
11:15). It is highly probable that Mark's tradition is authentic, but for
obvious reasons the later evangelists wished to sanitize it.[16] Later Mark
tells of the unimpressive results of Jesus' ministry in "his own country"
(evidently Nazareth and vicinity; cf. Luke 4:16), where again, Jesus'
family is mentioned (Mark 6:1-6). We are told that Jesus "could do no
mighty work there" (v. 5) and that he was amazed at the people's lack
of faith (in him). It is difficult to believe that this tradition was
invented either by pre-Marcan tradents or by the evangelist himself,
his secrecy motif notwithstanding.[17] Matthew mitigates the potential
embarrassment of the passage by explaining that Jesus "did not do
many mighty works there, because of their unbelief" (Matt 13:58).
This version implies that Jesus did do a *few* "mighty works" and that

---

with the evangelist inserting 3:22-30. Even if Bultmann is correct, it is likely that
the saying that Jesus was mad had something to do with his exorcisms. See Smith,
Jesus the Magician, 32-33; Pesch, *Markusevangelium*, 1.212.

16   This tradition receives further support by virtue of its coherence with
another story that hints at the tension between Jesus and his family. According to
Mark 3:31-35 members of Jesus' family, standing outside of the house in which
Jesus is teaching, summon him. Jesus' response borders on disrespect and could
imply that there was ill feeling between him and his family: "'Who are my mother
and my brothers?' And looking around on those who sat about him, he said, 'Here
are my mother and my brothers!'" Whereas Matthew takes over the story with
minor editing (Matt 12:46-50), Luke omits the potentially offensive rhetorical
question, "Who are my mother and my brothers?" (cf. Luke 8:19-21). Pace
Bultmann (*History of the Synoptic Tradition*, 29-30, 56), the tradition in Mark
3:20-22, 31-35 did not likely originate in the early Church as a saying on the ideal
disciple. Why would the early Church invent such a potentially embarrassing
vignette in order to have Jesus say something about discipleship?

17   Bultmann (*History of the Synoptic Tradition*, 31) and D.-A. Koch (*Die
Bedeutung der Wundererzählungen für die Christologie des Markusevangeliums*
[BZNW 42; Berlin: de Gruyter, 1975] 149) think that the saying in 6:4 is authentic
but that the story itself is an "imaginary situation" built upon it, perhaps mirroring
the "missionary experience of the Church." This is, of course, possible. Judging by
Matthean and Lucan redaction, however, it is not at all clear that this story
represents the experience of the Church. If it did, why do Matthew and Luke alter it
the way they do? On the unity of the saying and the story see Pesch,
Markusevangelium, 1.316, 321.

the reason he did not do *many* was because of the people's unbelief (whereas in Mark, Jesus "marveled" because of their unbelief). The Lucan evangelist recasts the story completely, suggesting that the people took offense at Jesus when he implied that he would extend messianic miracles and mercies to Gentiles (Luke 4:16-30). Two other Marcan miracles are simply omitted by the later evangelists. In the first Jesus treats a deaf man by putting his fingers in his ears and by spitting and touching his tongue (Mark 7:31-37). In the second Jesus must make two attempts to restore the sight of a blind man (Mark 8:22-26; cf. vv. 23-24: "'Do you see anything?' And he looked up and said, 'I see men; but they look like trees, walking'"). The first story may have been omitted because of its oddness, and perhaps because of its magical connotations,[18] while the second is omitted because it portrays Jesus as struggling to heal.[19] The healing of the Syrophoenician woman's daughter offers a final example (Mark 7:24-30). After initially refusing the woman's request ("Let the children [of Israel] first be fed, for it is not right to take the children's bread and throw it to the dogs"), Jesus acquiesces in response to the woman's intelligent rejoinder ("Yes, Lord; yet even the dogs under the table eat the children's crumbs"). The story does not appear in Luke (which is probably not remarkable, since it falls within the large block of Marcan material that the Lucan evangelist omits), while in Matthew (15:21-28) it is touched up (e.g. the woman respectfully addresses Jesus, the disciples urge Jesus to send her away, Jesus approves of her great faith, etc.). Two factors argue strongly for the authenticity of the Marcan version. First, the story's anti-Gentile orientation tells against a late (and Hellenistic) origin. Secondly, Jesus being bested in an

---

[18]   M. Dibelius, *From Tradition to Gospel* (New York: Scribner's, 1934) 85-86. Because of its supposed magical and thaumaturgical elements K. Kertelge (*Die Wunder Jesu im Markusevangelium: Eine redaktionsgeschichtliche Untersuchung* [SANT 23; Munich: Kösel, 1970] 158) believes that the story derives from the Hellenistic Church. However, touching the disfunctional part of the body and making use of spittle was common enough in Jewish circles (John 9:6; *b. Ber.* 5b; *b. B. Bat.* 126b; *b. Šabb.* 108b; cf. *t. Sanh.* 12.10 where spitting *and uttering an incantation* are condemned). J. M. Hull (*Hellenistic Magic and the Synoptic Tradition* [London: SCM; Naperville: Allenson, 1974] 116-19) notes that Matthew consistently edits out material that connotes magic.

[19]   V. Taylor, *The Gospel According to St. Mark* (London: Macmillan, 1952) 369; Latourelle, *Miracles of Jesus*, 62.

argument (and by a Gentile woman at that!), something unparalleled elsewhere in the Gospels, surely argues for authenticity.[20] It is hard to imagine why the early Church would invent such a potentially embarrassing story.

4. Context and Expectation. It is not clear that healing miracles occupied an important place in first-century Palestinian Messianic expectation. Messianic expectation, as diverse as it was, apparently did not anticipate miracles of the sort and concentration found in the Gospels.[21] Davidic messianology primarily called for a king who would rule Israel and the nations with justice (Isa 11:1-10; 16:5; Jer 23:5; 33:15; Zech 6:12-14), a king who would obey the Law, drive sinners out of Jerusalem (*Pss. Sol.* 17:21-42), and destroy Israel's enemies (4 Ezra 12:31-33). The Spirit, perhaps even a spirit of prophecy (*Tg.* Isa 11:1-2; *Tg.* Ps 72:1), it was thought, would rest upon the Messiah (Isa 11:1-2; 61:1-2). The Messiah was expected to gather and shepherd the people of Israel (Ezek 34:23-24; 37:24) and redistribute them on the land according to their tribes (*Pss. Sol.* 17:26-28). Qumran speaks of an "anointed [or Messiah] of Israel" (CD 12:23; 19:10-11; 20:1; 1QS 9:11; 1QSa 2:11-12, 14, 20-21), who may even be "hailed as the Son of God" (4QpsDan ar[a] 1:9; 2:1-2; cf. Luke 1:32-33).[22] But nothing is said of miracles. Even 4Q521, which does speak of healing—even resurrection—does not say that it is the Messiah who does these things. The context seems to indicate that these are the things that God will do during the messianic era. Mosaic messianology, rooted in the promise of Deut 18:15-19 (parts of which are quoted and applied to Jesus; cf. Acts 3:23; 7:37), hoped for a Priest who would serve with righteousness and justice (*T. Sim.* 7:2; *T. Judah* 21:2; *T. Benj.* 9:2; 4QTest 5-8; cf. 1QS 9:10-11). But again there is no expectation of miracles.

However, this is not to say that miracles would have occasioned surprise. To the extent that Elijah and Elisha provided models for first-century messianic expectation (cf. Luke 4:25-27) there could

---

20 See the discussion in B. D. Chilton, *A Galilean Rabbi and His Bible: Jesus' Use of the Interpreted Scripture of His Time* (Wilmington: Glazier, 1984) 64-66.

21 See Sanders, *Jesus and Judaism*, 163: "[S]ubsequent Jewish literature does not indicate that Jews habitually looked for miracles as a sign of the coming end."

22 Although there is no mention of "Messiah" in the fragmentary 4QpsDan ar[a], it is probable that this is the figure in view. Who else could it be? For more on this text, see chap. 3 above.

have been some expectation of miracles.[23] Moreover, it seems that some "sign from heaven" was expected (Mark 8:11-12; cf. John 2:18; 4:48; 6:30; 1 Cor 1:22). Not only was Jesus himself pressed for such a sign, but several of the various prophetic and/or messianic claimants from the time of Herod until the time of Ben Kosiba promised validating signs of one sort or another, often modeled after the Exodus and the Conquest (cf. Mark 13:22).[24] During the administration of Fadus (44–46 CE), according to Josephus, "a certain impostor named Theudas persuaded the majority of the populace to take up their possessions and follow him to the Jordan River. He stated that he was a prophet and that at his command the river would be parted and would provide easy passage" (*Ant.* 20.5.1 §97-98; cf. Acts 5:36). A decade later an anonymous Jew from Egypt rallied to himself a large following by claiming that at his command the walls of Jerusalem would collapse, allowing them to possess the city (*J.W.* 2.13.5 §261-263; cf. Acts 21:38). These and others promised their people "signs" of freedom and salvation (*J.W.* 2.13.4 §259; 7.11.1 §437-438). Simon ben Kosiba also may have promised and possibly even performed signs. Something apparently convinced Rabbi Aqiba that Simon was Israel's Messiah and fulfilment of the star prophecy (Num 24:17; cf. *y. Ta'an.* 4.5), which in the Targums is explicitly messianic. This possibility is indicated elsewhere. According to Eusebius, "Bar Chochebas . . . claimed to be a luminary who had come down to them from heaven" (*Hist. Eccl.* 4.6.2). According to Jerome, Simon deceived the people with fraudulent miracles (*Against Rufinus* 3.31). Rabbinic legends tell of Simon's remarkable, if not miraculous, feats in battle (*Lam. Rab.* 2:2 §4). In the fifth century one Moses of Crete claimed that at his command the Mediterranean Sea would part and allow Jews to leave Crete and walk to Palestine. The sign did not occur, with the

---

[23]   What role, if any, Elijah played in connection with first-century messianic expectation is not clear. As J. A. Fitzmyer (*The Gospel According to Luke I-IX* [AB 28; Garden City: Doubleday, 1981] 327) has commented: "[N]either in the OT nor in any other pre-Christian Jewish literature is Elijah ever depicted as the precursor of the Messiah." In what sense Elijah was a role model for the awaited Messiah is not much clearer.

[24]   See R. A. Horsley and J. S. Hanson, *Bandits, Prophets, and Messiahs: Popular Movements in the Time of Jesus* (San Francisco: Harper & Row, 1985) 88-189. Horsley and Hanson rightly regard many of these kingly aspirants as in reality messianic claimants.

result that many drowned in the sea (Socrates Scholasticus, *Hist. Eccl.* 7.38; 12.33).

In view of these ideas and experiences it seems highly unlikely that a *Wunder-Jesu* tradition grew up in order to fill out messianic beliefs about Jesus. Messianic beliefs simply did not require a prospective messiah to heal and exorcize demons.[25] One should hardly expect, therefore, early Christians to find it necessary to create such a large number of miracle stories. It is interesting to observe that when Jesus is given the opportunity to offer a sign, the one thing that apparently was expected of agents of salvation, he refuses. This refusal flies in the face of the critical assumption that the miracle stories originated in the Hellenistic Church. If the *Wunder-Jesu* tradition originated in the Hellenistic Church, then why not have Jesus perform a sign that dazzles his opponents? Jesus' refusal, which contemporary skeptics and critics would probably have viewed as *inability*—i.e. when put to the test Jesus failed (here we may invoke the criterion of embarrassment)— strongly tells against such a critical assumption.

5. Effect. According to all four Gospels, crowds listened to and followed Jesus (Mark 2:13; 3:9, 20; 4:1; 5:31; 8:1; 9:14; and parallels). This could be an exaggeration, of course, but in view of the action taken against Jesus it probably is not. Many of the other messiahs and prophets who met violent deaths at the hands of the Romans had also drawn large followings. Smith reasons: "[U]nless Jesus had a large following he would not have been crucified."[26] Most scholars, therefore, seldom question the veracity of the Gospels on this point. The *effect* of Jesus' public ministry was the attraction of multitudes. What was the *cause* of this effect? Why did large crowds follow Jesus? An explanation is required.[27] Smith and Sanders believe, and I think

---

25   A. E. Harvey (*Jesus and the Constraints of History* [London: Duckworth, 1982] 111) thinks that Jesus' ministry of miracles was motivated and guided by the cures described in Isa 35:5-6. This could be, but there are two problems: (1) there is no evidence that in the time of Jesus Isa 35:5-6 was understood this way; (2) Jesus' miracles do not correspond exactly with the list. Exorcism, the most conspicuous of Jesus' miracles, is not one of the cures mentioned in Isaiah. I must agree with Sanders (*Jesus and Judaism*, 163) that it is more likely that Jesus performed those healings "which came to hand."

26   Smith, *Jesus the Magician*, 24.

27   Latourelle (*Miracles of Jesus*, 67) calls this the "Criterion of Necessary Explanation [critère de l'explication nécessaire]."

rightly, that it was Jesus' miracles that attracted the crowds (and not his teaching, at least not initially).[28] As Sanders puts it: "But if it is true that large crowds surrounded him in Galilee, it was probably more because of his ability to heal and exorcize than anything else."[29] I think Smith and Sanders are correct. They reason that it is more likely that miracles, rather than teaching, would have generated large and enthusiastic crowds, crowds that would have alarmed Jewish and Roman authorities. This is corroborated to some extent by the misadventures of persons like Theudas and the Egyptian Jew who would later draw large crowds by promising to perform signs (or miracles).

6. *Coherence.* The miracle tradition also enjoys the support of the criterion of coherence, since several sayings, widely regarded as authentic, discuss or allude to the miracles. Accordingly, the authenticity of the sayings implies the authenticity of the miracle stories. Among these sayings five stand out as having the strongest claim to authenticity. First is Jesus' reply to the charge that he casts out demons by the power of Beelzebul: "If I cast out demons by the power of Beelzebul, by whose power do your sons cast them out? Therefore they shall be your judges. But if by the finger [or Spirit] of God I drive out demons, then the kingdom of God has come upon you" (Matt 12:27-28; Luke 11:19-20). Bultmann believes that this saying can "claim the highest degree of authenticity which we can make for any saying of Jesus."[30] As Meyer has pointed out, the "sheer offensiveness of the charge of sorcery" and the "risk of relativizing the exorcisms of Jesus by reference to those of others" are weighty factors that tell in favor of authenticity.[31] The second passage is the one in which Jesus likens Satan casting out Satan to a kingdom or house divided against itself (Mark 3:24-26). Again, Bultmann classifies this statement among the more certain authentic sayings.[32] Third is the passage in which Jesus likens his battle against Satan as binding a strong man (Mark 3:27). Bultmann thinks that this saying can be ascribed to Jesus with a

---

[28]   Smith, *Jesus the Magician*, 9, 11, 23-24; Sanders, *Jesus and Judaism*, 164-65.

[29]   Sanders, *Jesus and Judaism*, 164.

[30]   Bultmann, *History of the Synoptic Tradition*, 162.

[31]   Meyer, *Aims of Jesus*, 155.

[32]   Bultmann, *History of the Synoptic Tradition*, 105. See also Meyer, *Aims of Jesus*, 156.

measure of confidence.[33] The remarkable implication that Satan has already been defeated likely comes from Jesus, not the early Church. The lack of context and explanation of the saying (such as *when* Jesus defeated Satan) suggests that what we have here is an independent and somewhat isolated bit of authentic tradition.[34] Fourth is the passage in which Jesus replies to the Baptist's question: "Go and tell John what you see and hear: the blind receive their sight and the lame walk, lepers are cleansed and the deaf hear . . ." (Matt 11:5; Luke 7:22-23). Bultmann thinks that the saying may be traced to Jesus, though with some hesitation.[35] In my judgment the authenticity of this saying is very nearly certain, since it is highly unlikely that the early Church would invent an answer to a question in which Jesus' role is called into question ("Are you he who is to come, or shall we look for another?"). The fifth passage is found only in the Lucan Gospel: "Behold, I drive out demons and perform cures today and tomorrow, and on the third day I complete my course" (Luke 13:32). Despite its single attestation, form critics tend to regard it as authentic.[36] In reference to several of the passages just reviewed Taylor rightly comments that "the incidental way in which they tell of 'mighty works' is the best evidence that Jesus wrought them."[37]

7. *Principles of Embellishment.* The observation of features and in some cases patterns of embellishment in later sources provides a measure of corroborating support for the authenticity of some of the miracles already supported by other criteria. A diachronic comparative study of the miracles of Jesus and his approximate contemporaries illustrates this criterion. For example, the earliest and

---

33   Bultmann, *History of the Synoptic Tradition*, 105. See also Meyer, *Aims of Jesus*, 156.

34   C. E. B. Cranfield (*The Gospel according to St Mark* [Cambridge: Cambridge University Press, 1977] 135) regards Mark 3:22-30 as clearly "based on reliable tradition."

35   Bultmann, *History of the Synoptic Tradition*, 128. See also Meyer, *Aims of Jesus*, 157.

36   Dibelius, *From Tradition to Gospel*, 162 (though he doubts that the saying was originally directed against Herod Antipas); Bultmann, *History of the Synoptic Tradition*, 35; V. Taylor, *The Formation of the Gospel Tradition* (London: Macmillan, 1935) 75, 153. See also Meyer, *Aims of Jesus*, 154-55.

37   Taylor, *Formation of the Gospel Tradition*, 120. See also idem, *Mark*, 237, in reference to Mark 3:22-26: "The historical value of the narrative stands high."

best attested miracles of Jewish holy men[38] approximate several of the earliest and best attested miracles of Jesus. But in the passing of time these traditions are noticeably embellished. The later, embellished versions of the miracles of the Jewish holy men in a few instances approximate the later, embellished versions of the miracles of Jesus.[39] Most of these embellishments appear to be motivated out of theological interests. Rabbinic embellishments usually heighten the piety and scrupulousness of observance of the Oral Law, while Christian embellishments quite often are designed to heighten the divinity of Jesus. The value of these late embellishments lies principally in the contrast that the provide with the earlier stories which have a much stronger claim to authenticity.[40]

One interesting example documents how a given teaching, which may or may not have reflected an actual miracle, came to be embellished with illustrative miracles and sayings. According to the Mishnah, one was not to interrupt his recitation of the Shema' "even if a snake was twisted around his heel" (*m. Ber.* 5:1).[41] The Tosefta provides an example of this halakah: "They related about Rabbi Ḥanina ben Dosa that once while he was reciting the Prayer, a poisonous lizard bit him, but he did not interrupt [his recitation]. His students went and found it [the lizard] dead at the entrance to its hole. They said, 'Woe to the man who is bitten by a lizard. Woe to the lizard that bit Ben Dosa'"

---

[38] Such as exorcisms (Eleazar: cf. Josephus, *Ant.* 8.2.5 §46-48), healing (Ḥanina: cf. *y. Ber.* 5.5; *b. Ber.* 34b; *b. B. Qam.* 50a), and even prayers that affect the weather (Ḥoni: cf. Josephus, *Ant.* 14.2.1 §22-24; *m. Ta'an.* 3:8; Gamaliel: *b. B. Meṣia* 59b; Ḥanina: cf. *b. Yoma* 53b). The Mishnah refers to Ḥanina ben Dosa as one of the "men of deeds [מַעֲשֶׂה יְאַנְשֵׁי]" (*m. Soṭa* 9:15). In a portion of the Testimonium Flavianum that is probably authentic Jesus is called a "doer of amazing deeds [παραδόξων ἔργων ποιητής]" (*Ant.* 18.3.3 §63); cf. E. Bammel, "Zum Testimonium Flavianum (Jos. Ant. 18,63-64)," in O. Betz, et al. (eds.), *Josephus-Studien* (Göttingen: Vandenhoeck & Ruprecht, 1974) 9-22.
[39] Such as stretching beams (Ḥanina: cf. *b. Ta'an.* 25a; Jesus: cf. *InfanThom* 11:1-2 [Latin]; *InfanThom* 13:1-2 [Greek A]; *InfanThom* 11:1-3 [Greek B]) or finding an unusual supply of food for wife or mother (Ḥanina: cf. *b. Ta'an.* 24b-25a; Jesus: cf. *Gospel of Ps.-Matthew* 20:1-2; see E. Hennecke and W. Schneemelcher (eds.), *New Testament Apocrypha* [2 vols., London: Lutterworth; Philadelphia: Westminster, 1963] 1.411-12).
[40] See Latourelle, *Miracles of Jesus*, 63.
[41] Trans. from H. Danby, *The Mishnah* (Oxford: Clarendon, 1933) 5.

(*t. Ber.* 3.20).[42] It is possible that the tradition in Tosefta is genuine and perhaps explains what gave rise to the mishnaic halakah in the first place. Then again, Tosefta may preserve nothing more than a pious legend about a famous "man of deeds." In the gemara all sorts of imaginative details are added to this story. Ḥanina is questioned by his pupils ("Master, didn't you feel anything?"); it is noted that a spring of water gushed up from the floor where Ḥanina had been standing and that by drinking from it while praying he had been spared from the effects of the lizard's venom; by way of illustration Ḥanina places his foot over a lizard's hole to be bitten, with the result that Ḥanina is unharmed and the lizard is killed; and Ḥanina is able to draw the moral lesson that "it is not the lizard that kills, it is sin that kills!" (*y. Ber.* 5.1; *b. Ber.* 33a).

A roughly parallel trajectory can be observed in the Jesus tradition. In the Gospels we have a saying about authority over evil: "Behold, I have given you authority to tread upon serpents and scorpions, and over all the power of the enemy; and nothing shall hurt you" (Luke 10:19).[43] The spurious ending to Mark's Gospel may very well reflect this saying: "in my name they will cast out demons . . . they will pick up serpents, and if they drink any deadly thing, it shall not hurt them" (Mark 16:17b-18a). Paul's experience with the serpent may also be an illustration (Acts 28:3-6). Finally, a story that probably originated in the fourth or fifth century may represent yet further development of this tradition: "Now Joseph sent James to gather straw, and Jesus followed after him. And as James gathered straw, a viper bit him and fell to the earth as dead from the venom. But when Jesus saw that, he breathed upon his wound and from that moment James was made whole, and the viper died" (*InfanThom* 14:1 [Latin]).[44]

---

42   Trans. from T. Zahavy, "Berakhot," in J. Neusner (ed.), *The Tosefta* (6 vols., New York and Hoboken: Ktav, 1977-86) 1.18.

43   The authenticity of this saying is much disputed. Bultmann (*History of the Synoptic Tradition*, 158) thought that it was a response to an exaggeration of the importance of miracles. This line of reasoning, however, is questionable. J. A. Fitzmyer (*The Gospel According to Luke X-XXIV* [AB 28A; Garden City: Doubleday, 1985] 859) sees no compelling reason why it cannot be authentic. Jesus' saying may reflect the type of tradition found in *T. Levi* 18:12: "And Beliar shall be bound by him [the coming priest], and he shall give power to his children to tread upon the evil spirits."

44   Trans. from M. R. James, *The Apocryphal New Testament* (Oxford:

Not only do we have late and obvious fictions, but in the transmission of the texts of the Gospels themselves we are able to observe the infiltration of pious legend and embellishment. One thinks of the sweat drops of blood and the appearance of an angel (Luke 22:43-45 [omitted by 𝔓⁷⁵ אᵃ A B T W]), the angel that stirs the pool (John 5:4 [omitted by 𝔓⁶⁶,⁷⁵ א B C* D]), and the aforementioned appearance of the risen Christ who promises his disciples that they can pick up serpents and drink poison (Mark 16:9-20 [omitted by א B 2386]). Another likely candidate, though admittedly there are no extant variants, is the story of the open tombs and the resurrection of saints in Jerusalem (Matt 27:52-53), a tradition, probably based on Ezek 37:12-13 and Dan 12:2, that has been inserted awkwardly into its present context. In the so-called apocryphal gospels which parallel the New Testament Gospels more closely there is evidence of embellishment. The man with the withered hand (cf. Mark 3:1-6 par) says to Jesus: "I was a mason and earned [my] livelihood with [my] hands; I beseech thee, Jesus, to restore to me my health that I may not with ignominy have to beg for my bread" (*GNaz* §10; cited by Jerome, *Comm. Matt.* 12:13).[45] According to Pseudo-Clement (*Hom.* 2:19; 3:73) the Syro-Phoenician woman (cf. Mark 7:24-30) was named Justa and her daughter was named Bernice.

RABBINIC MIRACLE STORIES

There were several Jewish holy men in the time of Jesus, who were well known for mighty acts and remarkable answers to prayer. The lives and activities of five of them compare in various ways to the life and ministry of Jesus. These five are Ḥoni ha-Meʻaggel (first century B.C.E.), Abba Ḥilqiah, grandson of Ḥoni (late first century B.C.E., early first century C.E.), Ḥanin ha-Neḥba, grandson of Ḥoni (late first century B.C.E., early first century C.E.), Ḥanina ben Dosa (first century C.E.), and Eleazar the Exorcist (first century C.E.). The

---

Clarendon, 1953) 65. The Latin *Infancy Gospel of Thomas* is preserved in one MS that dates from the fifth or sixth century. The same story is found in the Greek version A of the infancy gospel (16:1-2; see James, 53-5). For discussion of the dates of the Greek, Syriac, and Latin MSS see Hennecke and Schneemelcher (eds.), *New Testament Apocrypha*, 1.388-92.

[45] Trans. from Hennecke and Schneemelcher (eds.), *New Tesament Apocrypha*, 1.148.

principal features of what is known of them will be briefly reviewed
and where appropriate a few comparisons with Jesus have been drawn.

Ḥoni ha-Me'aggel

In the rabbinic literature Ḥoni is called ha-Me'aggel ("the circle
drawer"). Josephus refers to him as "Onias, a righteous man beloved
by God." He was remembered for praying for rain during a time of
severe drought. When his prayer initially went unheeded, he drew a
circle on the ground and told God that he would not leave it until rain
came (perhaps following the example of Habakkuk; Hab 2:1). Soon it
did rain. The story is found in the Mishnah (m. Ta'an. 3:8; cf. b. Ta'an.
23a) and is alluded to by Josephus (Ant. 14.2.1 §22-24).

The earliest account is provided by Josephus, who is primarily
interested in the Jewish civil war, not Ḥoni's answered prayer. His
allusion to the holy man and to the belief that through his prayer God
sent rain attests to the antiquity of the tradition and offers an important
measure of support for its authenticity. According to Josephus:

> 22'Ονίας δέ τις ὄνομα, δίκαιος ἀνὴρ καὶ θεοφιλής, ὃς ἀνομβρίας ποτὲ
> οὔσης ηὔξατο τῷ λῦσαι τὸν αὐχμὸν καὶ γενόμενος ἐπήκοος ὁ θεὸς ὗσεν,
> ἔκρυψεν ἑαυτὸν διὰ τὸ τὴν στάσιν ὁρᾶν ἰσχυρὰν ἐπιμένουσαν, ἀναχθέντα δ'
> εἰς τὸ στρατόπεδον τῶν Ἰουδαίων ἠξίουν ὡς ἔπαυσεν τὴν ἀνομβρίαν
> εὐξάμενος, ἵν' οὕτως ἀρὰς θῇ κατὰ 'Αριστοβούλου καὶ τῶν συστασιαστῶν
> αὐτοῦ. 23ἐπεὶ δὲ ἀντιλέγων καὶ παραιτούμενος ἐβιάσθη ὑπὸ τοῦ πλήθους,
> στὰς μέσος αὐτῶν εἶπεν· 24ὦ θεὲ βασιλεῦ τῶν ὅλων, ἐπεὶ οἱ μετ' ἐμοῦ νῦν
> ἑστῶτες σὸς δῆμός ἐστι καὶ οἱ πολιορκούμενοι δὲ ἱερεῖς σοί, δέομαι μήτε
> κατὰ τούτων ἐκείνοις ἐπακοῦσαι μήτε κατ' ἐκείνων ἃ οὗτοι παρακαλοῦσιν
> εἰς τέλος ἀγαγεῖν. καὶ τὸν μὲν ταῦτα εὐξάμενον περιστάντες οἱ πονηροὶ
> τῶν Ἰουδαίων κατέλευσαν.

"22Now there was a certain man named Onias, who was righteous
and beloved of God, who at one time during a rainless period
prayed to end the drought; and hearing, God sent rain. This man
hid himself because he saw that the civil war continued unabated,
but taken up to the camp of the Judeans he was asked, just as he
ended the drought through prayer, similarly to place a curse on
Aristobulus and his partisans. 23But though refusing and trying to
beg off, he was compelled by the mob. Standing in their midst, he
said: 24'O God, King of the universe, since those who are now
standing with me are Your people and those who are besieged are
Your priests, I beseech You neither to hearken to those men against

these nor (to hearken to) what these men are asking (You) to perform against those.' And the wicked among the Judeans who stood by stoned him for praying these things."

The Mishnaic account shows no interest in the political issues; its interest is much more theological. According to the Mishna:

1. מעשה שאמרו לו לחוני המעגל התפלל שירדו גשמים:
2. אמר להם צאו והכניסו תנורי פסחים בשביל שלא ימוקו:
3. התפלל ולא ירדו גשמים: מה עשה: עג עוגה ועמד בתוכה ואמר
4. רבונו של עולם בניך שמו פניהם עלי שאני כבן בית לפניך:
5. נשבע אני בשמך הגדול שאיני זז מכאן עד שתרחם על בניך:
6. התחילו גשמים מנטפין: אמר לא כך שאלתי אלא גשמי בורות שיחין ומערות:
7. התחילו לירד בזעף: אמר לא כך שאלתי אלא גשמי רצון ברכה ונדבה:
8. ירדו כתקנן עד שיצאו ישראל מירושלים להר הבית מפני הגשמים:

"[1]Once they said to Honi the Circle-Drawer, 'Pray that rain may fall.' [2]He said to them, 'Go out and bring in the Passover ovens that they may not be softened.' [3]He prayed, but rain did not come down. What did he do? He drew a circle and stood within it and said, [4]'Lord of the universe, Your sons have turned their faces to me, for I am as a son of the house before You. [5]I swear by Your great name that I will not move from here until You have mercy on Your sons.' [6]Rain began dripping. He said, 'Not for this have I prayed, but for rain (that fills) cisterns, pits, and caverns.' [7]It began to come down violently. He said, 'Not for this have I prayed, but for rain of goodwill, blessing, and plenty.' [8]It came down in moderation until Israel went up from Jerusalem to the Mount of the House because of the rain."

What is of concern to the Mishnaic tradition is Honi's apparent familiarity with Heaven. We are told that a certain Simeon ben Shetah expressed disapprobation: "Had you not been Honi, I would have pronounced a ban against you! For were these years like those concerning which Elijah said no rain should fall—for the keys to rainfall were in his hands—would not the result of your action have been the desecration of God's name? But what can I do with you, since you importune God and he performs your will, like a son that importunes his father and he performs his will." Simeon's complaint implies comparison between Elijah and Honi. In a later and textually uncertain tradition the comparison is explicit: "No man has existed comparable to Elijah and Ḥoni the Circle-Drawer, causing mankind to serve God" (*Gen. Rab.* 13.7 [on 2:5]; however, some MSS. omit either Elijah or Ḥoni).

Ḥoni's life and activities present a few points of comparison with the life and ministry of Jesus. Ḥoni's persistence in praying for rain parallels Jesus' similar teaching, as seen in the parables of the Persistent Friend (Luke 11:5-8) and the Importunate Widow (Luke 18:1-8). Ḥoni's filial relationship with God is also interesting. Jesus taught his disciples to pray to God as "Father" (Matt 6:9; Mark 14:36). Moreover, Jesus was regarded as God's Son (Mark 1:11; more on this below). Since there are other examples of the weather being affected through the prayers of the Jewish holy men, this aspect will be discussed below.

Abba Ḥilqiah, grandson of Ḥoni

Abba Ḥilqiah, grandson of Ḥoni (son of Ḥoni's son), a very pious and poor man (worked for hire, wore a borrowed coat, insufficient food for guests), was requested by the rabbis to pray for rain. He and his wife went upstairs and, from opposite corners, prayed. Soon clouds began to form (*b. Taʿan.* 23a–23b). Part of the story reads:

1. אמר לה לדביתהו ידענא דרבנן משום מיטרא:
2. קא אתו ניסק לאיגרא וניבעי רחמי אפשר דמרצי הקדוש ברוך הוא
3. וייתי מיטרא ולא נחזיק טיבותא לנפשין:
4. סקו לאיגרא: קם איהו בחדא זויתא ואיהי בחדא זויתא:
5. קדים סלוק עני מהך זויתא דדביתהו . . . .
6. אמרו ליה ידעינן דמיטרא מחמת . . . .

"¹He said to his wife, 'I know that the rabbis have come on account of rain. ²Let us go up to the roof and pray. Perhaps the Holy One, blessed be He, will have mercy ³and rain will come down, without credit given to us.' ⁴They went up to the roof. He stood in one corner; she (stood) in another corner. ⁵At first the clouds appeared over the corner where his wife (stood) . . . . ⁶They said to him, 'We know that the rain (has come) on your account . . . .'"

Poverty is a feature common to most of the traditions of the holy men. Jesus' lifestyle was also one of poverty: "Foxes have holes, and birds of the air have nests; but the Son of man has nowhere to lay his head" (Matt 8:20; Luke 9:58).

Ḥanan ha-Neḥba

Ḥanan ha-Neḥba (i.e. Ḥanan "the hidden"), grandson of Ḥoni (son of Ḥoni's daugher), was a modest man who used to hide from public view. Like his famous grandfather, Ḥanan gained a reputation for bring down rain through his prayers (*b. Ta'an.* 23b).

‎1. הנחבא בר ברתיה דחוני המגל הוה:
‎2. כי מצטריך עלמא למיטרא הוו משדרי רבנן ינוקי דבי רב
‎3. לגביה ונקטי ליה בשיפולי גלימיה ואמרו ליה
‎4. אבא אבא הב לן מיטרא:
‎5. אמר לפני הקדוש ברוך הוא רבונו של עולם עשה בשביל אלו
‎6. שאין מכירין בין אבא דיהיב מיטרא לאבא דלא יהיב מיטרא:

"¹Ḥanan ha-Neḥba was the son of the daughter of Ḥoni the Circle-Drawer. ²When the world needed rain the rabbis would send school children ³to him and they would seize the hem of his cloak and say to him, ⁴"Father, Father, give us rain!" ⁵Then he would petition the Holy One, blessed be He, "Master of the universe, give rain for the sake of these children ⁶who do not even know enough to distinguish between a Father who gives rain and a father who does not.""

The little children coming to Ḥanan ha-Neḥba, seizing the hem of his cloak, and making a request parallels Synoptic tradition: "They sought him out that they might touch the fringe of his garment; and as many touched it were made well" (Mark 6:56).

Ḥanina ben Dosa

Ḥanina, probably the most famous of the holy men, lived in the town of Arab, a small Galilean village about ten miles north of Nazareth. In *m. Soṭa* 9:15 he is remembered as one of the "men of deeds":

‎משמת רבי חנינא בן דוסא בטלו אנשי מעשה

"When Rabbi Ḥanina ben Dosa died, the men of (great) deeds ceased."

The description, "men of deeds [אַנְשֵׁי מַעֲשֶׂה]," refers to the miracles that were effected through his prayers. Ḥanina was especially famous for his prayers that resulted in healing (*m. Ber.* 5:5):

‎1. אמרו עליו על רבי חנינא בן דוסא
‎2. שהיה מתפלל על החולים ואומר זה חי וזה מת:

3. אמרו לו מנין אתה יודע:

4. אמר להם אם שגורה תפלתי בפי יודע אני שהוא מקבל

5. ואם לאו יודע אני שהוא מטרף:

"[1]They say about Rabbi Ḥanina ben Dosa [2]that he used to pray over the sick and say, 'This one will live,' or 'That one will die.' [3]They said to him, 'How do you know?' [4]He said to them, 'If my prayer is fluent in my mouth, I know that he is accepted; [5]and if it is not, I know that he is rejected.'"

The Babylonia gemara adds further examples. On one occasion he prayed for the son of Gamaliel II (or possibly Gamaliel the Elder). Because the words of his prayer in this instance came fluently, he knew he had been answered. Gamaliel's disciples noted the time and returned to their master to discover that the boy had indeed recovered at the very hour Ḥanina had spoken (b. Ber. 34b; cf. y. Ber. 5.5):

1. תנו רבנן מעשה שחלה בנו של רבן גמליאל:

2. שגר שני תלמידי חכמים אצל רבי חנינא בן דוסא לבקש עליו רחמים:

3. כיון שראה אותם עלה לעלייה ובקש עליו רחמים:

4. בירידתו אמר להם לכו שחלצתו חמה:

5. אמרו לו וכי נביא אתה: אמר להן לא נביא אנכי ולא בן נביא אנכי:

6. אלא כך מקובלני אם שגורה תפלתי בפי יודע אני

7. שהוא מקובל ואם לאו יודע אני שהוא מטרף:

8. ישבו וכתבו וכוונו אותה שעה: וכשבאו אצל רבן גמליאל:

9. אמר להן העבודה לא חסרתם ולא הותרתם אלא כך היה:

10. מעשה באותה שעה חלצתו חמה ושאל לנו מים לשתות:

"[1]The Rabbis taught: Once the son of Rabban Gamaliel became ill. [2]He sent two scholars to Rabbi Ḥanina ben Dosa to ask him to pray for him. [3]As soon as he saw them, he went up to an upper room and prayed for him. [4]When he came down, he said to them, 'Go, the fever has left him.' [5]They said to him, 'Are you a prophet?' He said to them, 'I am neither a prophet nor the son of a prophet. [6]But this I have accepted: If my prayer is fluent in my mouth, I know [7]that he is accepted; and if not, I know that he is rejected.' [8]They sat down and wrote down the exact time. And when they came to Rabban Gamaliel, [9]he said to them, '(By) the (temple) service! You are neither short nor long, but so it was. [10]At that exact time the fever left him and he asked us for water to drink.'"

On another occasion he prayed for the son of Yoḥanan ben Zakkai, Ḥanina's teacher (*b. Ber.* 34b):

1. ושוב מעשה ברבי חנינא בן דוסא שהלך ללמוד תורה אצל רבי יוחנן בן זכאי
2. וחלה בנו של רבי יוחנן בן זכאי: אמר לו חנינא בני בקש עליו רחמים ויחיה:
3. הניח ראשו בין ברכיו ובקש עליו רחמים וחיה:
4. אמר רבי יוחנן בן זכאי אלמלי הטיח בן זכאי את ראשו בין ברכיו
5. כל היום כולו לא היו משגיחים עליו: אמרה לו אשתו וכי חנינא גדול ממך:
6. אמר לה לאו אלא הוא דומה כעבד לפני המלך ואני דומה כשר לפני המלך:

"[1]The deed happened again when Rabbi Ḥanina ben Dosa went to study Torah with Rabbi Yoḥanan ben Zakkai, [2]that the son of Rabbi Yoḥanan ben Zakkai became ill. He said to him, 'Ḥanina my son, pray for him that he may live.' [3]He put his head between his knees and prayed for him and he lived. [4]Rabbi Yoḥanan ben Zakkai said, 'If ben Zakkai had stuck his head between his knees [5]for the whole day, no notice would have been taken of him.' His wife said to him, 'Is Ḥanina greater than you?' [6]He said to her, 'No; but he is like a servant before the king, and I am like a nobleman before the king.'"

There are other stories whereby healing or rescue was effected through Ḥanina's intercession, though these are of a legendary character (cf. *b. B. Qam.* 50a). There is another tradition concerning Ḥanina ben Dosa that may be historical. While praying the Amidah he was bitten by a snake, but he did not break off his prayer. The story is cited as an illustration of a halakah found in *m. Ber.* 5:1:

1. אפלו המלך שואל בשלומו לא ישיבנו:
2. ואפלו נחש כרוך על עקבו לא יפסיק:

"[1]Even if the king salutes him, he may not return the greeting; [2]and even if a snake was twisted around his heel, he may not interrupt (his prayer)."

According to the Tosefta this happened one time to Ḥanina ben Dosa. Of course, it is possible that the tradition is nothing more than a pious story meant to illustrate the halakic ruling. But in my judgment it is equally possible that the halakic ruling owes its inspiration to something that actually happened to Ḥanina. That the story becomes embellished in later traditions is quite clear, but the brief vignette we find in *t. Ber.* 3.20 may constitute reliable historical tradition:

1. אמרו עליו על רבי חנינא בן דוסא שהיה עומד ומתפלל נשכו ערוד ולא הפסיק:
2. הלכו תלמידיו ומצאוהו מת על פי חורו: אמרו
3. אוי לו לאדם שנשכו ערוד אוי לו לערוד שנשך לבן דוסא:

"¹They say about Rabbi Ḥanina ben Dosa that once while he was standing and praying, a poisonous lizard bit him, but he did not interrupt (his prayer). ²His disciples went and found it dead at the mouth of its hole. They said, ³'Woe to the man who is bitten by a lizard. Woe to the lizard that bit ben Dosa!'"

This story is enriched in the Palestinian gemara. We are told that Ḥanina survives the lizard's bite because a spring of water gushed up enabling the praying Ḥanina to drink before the lizard could drink (y. Ber. 5.1).⁴⁶ There is also a parallel account which gives a similar, unhistorical impression, in which Ḥanina offers his heel to a poisonous lizard that has been injuring people. The lizard bites Ḥanina's heel and dies. Then Ḥanina pronounces: "See, my sons, it is not the lizard that kills, it is sin that kills!" (b. Ber. 33a).

Ḥanina also is said to have brought on rain through his prayer (b. Ta'an. 24b; b. Yoma 53b). So impressed with this story Rabbi Joseph commented: "How could the prayer of even the high priest be compared to that of Rabbi Ḥanina ben Dosa?" The parallels with the Elijah/Elisha stories (1 Kgs 17:1 [drought]; 18:45 [rain]) should be noted.

There are other stories of a more fabulous stripe. Once Ḥanina was walking alone at night, when he met the "queen of the demons." She claimed that had he not enjoyed Heaven's protection, she would have harmed him. Ḥanina then banned her from passing through inhabited places (cf. b. Pesaḥ. 112b).

Once a neighbor woman was building a house. After erecting the walls she discovered that the beams for the roof were too short. She went to Ḥanina for help. Playing on her name, Ḥanina said, "May your beams reach!" One Polemo, supposedly an eyewitness, said: "I saw that house and its beams projected one cubit on either side, and people told me, 'This is the house which Rabbi Ḥanina ben Dosa covered with beams, through his prayer'" (b. Ta'an. 25a). Other stories are even more fantastic (cf. b. Ta'an. 25a [oven miraculously filled with loaves,

⁴⁶ According to this amusing legend, the first to drink water lives; the other dies.

the golden table leg, the oil lamp, the goats]; *Eccl. Rab.* 1:1 §1 and *Song Rab.* 1:1 §4 [Ḥanina's stone offering).

Another miraculous story involving Ḥanina concerns the voice from heaven. Although this story is also legendary, it indicates the awe in which this man was held. According to Rab: "Each day a heavenly voice came [from Mount Horeb] and said: 'The whole universe is sustained on account of my son, Ḥanina'" (*b. Ta'an.* 24b; *b. Ber.* 17b, 61b; *b. Ḥull.* 86a; cf. *b. B. Bat.* 74b). Elswhere Rab views Ahab (Elijah's contemporary and foe) as representative of evil, while Ḥanina is representative of good (*b. Ber.* 61b). Such an analogy implies a comparison between Ḥanina and Elijah. Indeed, it may even suggest that Ḥanina was thought to have superseded Elijah. A related tradition calls Ḥanina a "man of rank" (cf. Isa 3:3), who enjoyed the favor of Heaven (*b. Ḥag.* 14a).

Ḥanina's life and activities parallel those of Jesus at many points. In the disputed passage in Josephus (*Ant.* 18.3.3 §63), Jesus is called a "wise man [σοφὸς ἀνήρ]" and a "doer of amazing deeds [παραδόξων ἔργων ποιητής]." Even Robert Eisler, who suspected that the passage had been tampered with, accepted the latter phrase as original, but with a different sense ("astonishing tricks").[47] Recall that Ḥanina was called a "man of doing (or deeds) [אַנְשֵׁי מַעֲשֶׂה]."

The healing of Gamaliel's son at the very "hour" that Ḥanina announced to the disciples that he would recover parallels the Jesus tradition: "The father knew that was the hour when Jesus had said to him, 'Your son will live'" (John 4:46-53; cf. Matt 8:5-13; Luke 7:1-10). The statement itself, "Your son will live," parallels Ḥanina's alternating pronouncements, "This one will live," or "That one will die."

Ḥanina's encounter with the queen of demons is somewhat analogous to Jesus' encounter with the Gerasene demoniac, who ran up and declared that he knew who Jesus was (Mark 5:1-20). The demoniac recognized that he was no match for God's "holy one." Even though there is little reason to believe that this particular Ḥanina story is factual, it offers a useful parallel in that it gives some indication of first-century Palestinian beliefs regarding demons. Elsewhere Jesus has encounters with Satan: the temptations (Matt 4:1-11; Luke 4:1-13),

---

[47] R. Eisler, *The Messiah Jesus and John the Baptist* (trans. A. H. Krappe; London: Methuen; New York: Dial, 1931) 62.

the vision of Satan falling from heaven (Luke 10:17-20), and Satan's demand to have Peter to sift like wheat and Jesus' prayer in his behalf (Luke 22:31-32). More will be said on Jesus's exorcisms below.

The stories about Ḥanina's encounters with poisonous snakes and lizards parallel canonical and non-canonical stories about Jesus. In one place Jesus says: "Behold, I have given you authority to tread upon serpents and scorpions . . . and nothing shall hurt you" (Luke 10:19; cf. Mark 16:18; Acts 28:3-6). Ḥanina's dictum, "See, my sons, it is not the lizard that kills, it is sin that kills!" coheres with Jesus' forgiving sin as either a prerequisite or at least as a corollary of healing (e.g. Mark 2:1-11). The *Infancy Gospel of Thomas* offers an amusing parallel (Greek *Thomas* A 16:1-2; Latin *Thomas* 14:1). On one occasion Jesus' younger brother James was bitten by a poisonous viper. Just as he was about to die, Jesus approached and breathed upon the bite. Immediately James recovered and the viper burst.

Because of their miracles and mighty works Ḥoni and Ḥanina were compared to Elijah, the venerated prophet famous for his mighty deeds (Sir 48:1-16). Jesus was also compared to Elijah (Mark 6:15; 8:28) and may himself have compared his ministry to outcasts and the disenfranchised to the similar ministries of Elijah and Elisha (Luke 4:25-27). On the Mount of Transfiguration he was in Elijah's company (Mark 9:4-5).

Just as the heavenly voiced declared Ḥanina to be "my son," so the heavenly voice spoke at the baptism and transfiguration of Jesus: "You are my beloved Son" (Mark 1:11; 9:7; cf. John 12:28).

The *Infancy Gospel of Thomas* also parallels the story of the stretched beams (Greek *Thomas* A 13:1-2; Greek *Thomas* B 11:1-3; Latin *Thomas* 11:1-2). It seems that Joseph, the father of Jesus, failed to cut two beams precisely the same length. Jesus had him take hold of the short beam and then he stretched it to the proper length. This fanciful story illustrates the parallel tendency of the Jesus/Ḥanina miracle traditions to become increasingly embellished.

Eleazar the Exorcist

Josephus tells us of a certain Eleazar who followed the incantations of Solomon and could draw out demons through a person's nostrils, through the use of the Baaras root (further described in *J.W.* 7.6.3 §180-185). Josephus explains that God gave Solomon "knowledge of the art used against demons for the benefit and healing of humans. He also composed incantations by which illnesses are relieved, and left behind forms of exorcisms with which those possessed by demons drive them out, never to return" (*Ant.* 8.2.5 §45). As to Eleazar's successful employment of these incantations Josephus tells us (*Ant.* 8.2.5 §46-49):

ἱστόρησα γάρ τινα Ἐλεάζαρον τῶν ὁμοφύλων Οὐεσπασιανοῦ παρόντος καὶ τῶν υἱῶν αὐτοῦ καὶ χιλιάρχων καὶ ἄλλου στρατιωτικοῦ πλήθους τοὺς ὑπὸ τῶν δαιμονίων λαμβανομένους ἀπολύοντα τούτων. ὁ δὲ τρόπος τῆς θεραπείας τοιοῦτος ἦν· προσφέρων ταῖς ῥισὶ τοῦ δαιμονιζομένου τὸν δακτύλιον ἔχοντα ὑπὸ τῇ σφραγῖδι ῥίζαν ἐξ ὧν ὑπέδειξε Σολομὼν ἔπειτα ἐξεῖλκεν ὀσφρομένῳ διὰ τῶν μυκτήρων τὸ δαιμόνιον, καὶ πεσόντος εὐθὺς τἀνθρώπου μηκέτ' εἰς αὐτὸν ἐπανήξειν ὥρκου Σολομῶνός τε μεμνημένος καὶ τὰς ἐπῳδὰς ἃς συνέθηκεν ἐκεῖνος ἐπιλέγων. βουλόμενος δὲ πεῖσαι καὶ παραστῆσαι τοῖς παρατυγχάνουσιν ὁ Ἐλεάζαρος ὅτι ταύτην ἔχει τὴν ἰσχύν, ἐτίθει μικρὸν ἔμπροσθεν ἤτοι ποτήριον πλῆρες ὕδατος ἢ ποδόνιπτρον καὶ τῷ δαιμονίῳ προσέταττεν ἐξιόντι τἀνθρώπου ταῦτ' ἀνατρέψαι καὶ παρασχεῖν ἐπιγνῶναι τοῖς ὁρῶσιν ὅτι καταλέλοιπε τὸν ἄνθρωπον. γενομένου δὲ τούτου σαφὴς ἡ Σολομῶνος καθίστατο σύνεσις καὶ σοφία δι' ἥν, ἵνα γνῶσιν ἅπαντες αὐτοῦ τὸ μεγαλεῖον τῆς φύσεως καὶ τὸ θεοφιλὲς καὶ λάθῃ μηδένα τῶν ὑπὸ τὸν ἥλιον ἡ τοῦ βασιλέως περὶ πᾶν εἶδος ἀρετῆς ὑπερβολή, περὶ τούτων εἰπεῖν προήχθημεν.

"I have observed a certain Eleazar, of my race, in the presence of Vespasian, his sons, tribunes and a number of other soldiers, release people possessed by demons. Now this was the manner of the cure: Placing to the nostrils of the demon possessed person the ring which had under the seal a root which Solomon had prescribed, he then, as the person smelled it, drew out the demon through the nostrils. When the person fell down, he adjured the demon, speaking Solomon's name and repeating the incantations which he had composed, never to re-enter him. Then, wishing to persuade and to prove to those present that he had this ability, Eleazar would place at a small distance either a cup full of water or a foot basin and command the demon while going out of the human to overturn it and to make known to those watching that he had left him. And when this happened, the understanding and wisdom of Solomon were clearly revealed, on account of which we felt compelled to speak in order that all might know of the greatness of his nature and divine favor, and that the surpassing virtue of the king might not be forgotten by anyone."

The tradition of Solomon as exorcist par excellence was widespread in late antiquity. The tradition begins in the Bible itself where Solomon is described as unsurpassed in knowledge (1 Kgs 4:29-34). His knowledge of proverbs and plants (1 Kgs 4:32-33) contributed to later speculation that he had mastered the secrets of herbs and spells. And with his knowledge of herbs and spells the king had power over spirits. According to the Wisdom of Solomon, God gave the monarch knowledge of "the powers of spirits and the reasonings of men, the varieties of plants and the virtues of roots; [he] learned what is both secret and what is manifest" (Wis 7:17-21). Solomon's power over demonic forces was appealed to for protection, as has been shown by Aramaic and Hebrew incantations dating from the early centuries of the Common Era. It is to this tradition that Josephus refers in mentioning Eleazar. The tradition was well known in Christian circles. Origen refers to those who attempted exorcisms according to the spells written by Solomon (*Comm. Matthew* 33 [on Matt 26:63]). The pseudepigraphal *Testament of Solomon*, probably written by a Greek-speaking Christian in the second or third century, is wholly dedicated to this theme.[48]

A few of the details recounted by Josephus parallel certain features that appear in the stories of Jesus' exorcisms. Like Eleazar, Jesus was well known for his ability to cast out demons (Mark 1:34, δαιμόνια). In the specific Gospel episodes themselves "evil spirit" and "unclean spirit" (τὸ πνεῦμα τὸ ἀκάθαρτον and τὸ πνεῦμα τὸ πονηρόν) are the preferred terms (e.g. Mark 5:8; Luke 7:21). The possessed "falls" down (Mark 3:11, προσπίπτειν; 9:20, πίπτειν). The exorcist "adjures" the demon (Mark 5:7, ὁρκίζειν) warns it not to return or re-enter (Mark 9:25, μηκέτι εἰσέλθῃς εἰς αὐτόν = μηκέτ' εἰς αὐτὸν ἐπανήξειν [or ἐπανελθεῖν]; Matt 12:44-45 = Luke 11:24-26, εἰσελθεῖν). The demon is cast out demons in Jesus' name (Mark 9:38-39). Eleazar commanded the demon to tip over the wash basin, Jesus ordered the demon to be silent (e.g. Mark 3:12).

The Genesis Apocryphon's retelling of Abram's misadventure with Pharaoh (cf. Gen 12:10-20) offers a pertinent parallel. After taking

48   See D. C. Duling, "Testament of Solomon," in J. H. Charlesworth (ed.), *The Old Testament Pseudepigrapha* (2 vols., Garden City: Doubleday, 1981-83) 1.935-59; idem, "Solomon, Exorcism, and the Son of David," *HTR* 68 (1975) 235-52.

Sarai into his harem, Pharaoh Zoan is oppressed by an unclean spirit. He learns that this spirit will depart from him only on condition of returning Sarai to her husband. Pharaoh Zoan entreats Abram (1QapGen 20:28-29):

[28] 1. וכען צלי עלי ועל ביתי ותתגער מנה רוחא דא באישתא:

2. וצלית על [מג]דפא

[29] 3. הו: וסמכת ידי על [ראי]שה:

4. ואתפלי מנה מכתשא ואתגערת [מנה רוחא] באישתא: וחי:

"¹'But now pray for me and for my house that this evil spirit may be ordered from us.' ²And I (Abram) prayed for that [blas]phemer; ³and I laid hands upon his [he]ad. ⁴The plague was removed from him and the evil [spirit] was ordered [from him]; and he lived."

For discussion of this text, as well as proposed restorations, see the critical work by J. A. Fitzmyer.[49] The topic of laying on of hands raises several points of interest.[50] One is reminded of the infirm woman upon whom Jesus lays his hands (Luke 13:11-13).

The Apocryphal Daniel

In 4QprNab (Prayer of Nabonidus) an unnamed Jew, called a "exorcist," heals the ailing King Nabonidus. The text interesting, for it links healing to forgiveness of sins. The following lines are from fragments 1–3:

1. מלי צלתא די צלי נבני מלך א[רעא די ב]בל מלכא [רבא כדי הוא כתיש]

2. בשחנא באישא בפתגם א[להא עלי]א בתימן [בשחנא באישא]

3. כתיש הוית שנין שבע ומן [אנשא] שוי א[נה וצלית לאלהא עליא]

4. וחטאי שבק לה גזר והוא [גבר] יהודי מ[ן בני גלותא ואמר לי]

5. החוי וכתב למעבד יקר ור[בות הד]ר לשם א[להא עליא וכן כתבת]

"¹The words of the prayer which Nabonidus prayed, the king of

⁴⁹ J. A. Fitzmyer, *The Genesis Apocryphon of Qumran Cave I: A Commentary* (BibOr 18A; Rome: Pontifical Biblical Institute, 1971) 138-41.

⁵⁰ See D. Flusser, "Healing Through the Laying-On of Hands in a Dead Sea Scroll," *IEJ* 7 (1957) 107-108; repr. in Flusser, *Judaism and the Origins of Christianty* (Jerusalem: Magnes, 1988) 21-22; A. Dupont-Sommer, "Exorcismes et guérisons dans les écrits de Qumran," in *Congress Volume, Oxford 1959* (VTSup 7; Leiden: Brill, 1960) 246-61.

[the] la[nd of Bab]ylon, the [great] king, [when he was smitten]
²with the evil disease by the decree of the [Most High Go[d] in
Teima ['With the evil disease] ³was I smitten (for) seven
years and unlike [man] was I made; [and I prayed to the Most High
God,] ⁴and an exorcist remitted my sins for Him; he (was) a Jew
fr[om (among) the deportees. He said to me,] ⁵'Make (it) known and
write (it) down, to give glory and gr[eat hono]r to the name of G[od
Most High.' And thus I have written . . .]"⁵¹

The association of healing with the forgiveness of sins immediately
calls to mind the healing of the paralyzed man in Mark 2:1-12: "And
seeing their faith Jesus says to the paralytic, 'Child, your sins are
forgiven'" (v. 5). It is probable that the Jewish exorcist of the Prayer
of Nabonidus is none other than Daniel. In fact, in line 4 of fragment 4
Fitzmyer and Harrington restore his name: כמה דמא אנתה לד[ניאל] ("how
you resemble Da[niel]").⁵² That the healer is also called an "exorcist"
(גזר) is also noteworthy.⁵³ The word appears in Dan 2:27; 4:4; 5:7, 11.

These healing and exorcism traditions may have an important
bearing on Jesus' ministry and self-understanding. "Then a blind and
dumb demoniac was brought to him, and he healed him, so that he saw.
And all the people were amazed, and said, 'Can this be the son of
David?' But when the Pharisees heard it they said, 'It is only by
Beelzebul, the prince of demons, that this man casts out demons.' . . .
[Jesus replied,] 'if Satan casts out Satan, he is divided against himself;
how then will his kingdom stand? And if I cast out demons by
Beelzebul, by whom do your sons cast them out?' . . . Then some of the
scribes and Pharisees said to him, 'Teacher, we wish to see a sign from
you.' But he answered them, 'An evil and adulterous generation seeks
for a sign; but no sign shall be given it except the sign of Jonah . . . The
queen of the South will arise at the judgment with this generation and
condemn it; for she came from the ends of the earth to hear the wisdom

---

⁵¹ For text, restoration, and translation, see J. A. Fitzmyer and D. J. Harrington, *A Manual of Palestinian Aramaic Texts* (BibOr 34; Rome: Biblical Institute
Press, 1978) 2-3. See also B. Jongeling et al., *Aramaic Texts from Qumran* (SSS
4; Leiden: Brill, 1976) 126-29.

⁵² Fitzmyer and Harrington, *A Manual of Palestinian Aramaic Texts*, 4-5.

⁵³ See W. Kirchschläger, "Exorzismus in Qumran?" *Kairos* 18 (1976) 135-
53, esp. 144-48.

of Solomon, and behold, something greater than Solomon is here. When the unclean spirit has gone out of a man, he passes through waterless places seeking rest, but he finds none. Then he says, "I return to my house from which I came." And when he comes he finds it empty, swept, and put in order. Then he goes and brings with him seven other spirits more evil than himself, and they enter and dwell there; and the last state of that man becomes worse than the first. So shall it be also with this evil generation'" (Matt 12:22-45; cf. Luke 11:29-32, 24-26). When Jesus healed a demonized man the crowd thought of him as the son of David, i.e. one like Solomon. This is evidence of the close association of exorcism and Solomon. It may also indicate that a messianic figure should possess the powers of David's famous son. The religious leaders, however, cast doubt on this inference by suggesting that Jesus is in league with Satan himself (Beelzebul). Jesus replies pointing out how this is illogical. His reference to the exorcisms of their "sons" (as opposed to David's "son"?) and the demons that could return may suggest that Jesus did not think that these exorcisms were entirely successful. In other words, they were not up to standards associated with Solomon, the son of David. Nor were they, by implication, up to the standards of Jesus who was one "greater than Solomon."

Jesus, Rabbis, and Holy Men

Perhaps the most notable feature of Geza Vermes' first book on the historical Jesus was his proposal that Jesus be understood as one of the Jewish "holy men," part of what may be termed "charismatic Judaism."[54] Bruce Chilton has criticized Vermes's hard and fast distinction between rabbis and holy men, isolating Ḥoni and Ḥanina ben Dosa from men such as Yoḥanan ben Zakkai and Eliezer.[55] Chilton's criticism appears to be well founded, for miracles are credited to major rabbis, well known for their teaching, while some teaching is credited to the "holy men." The relevant materials may be surveyed briefly.

Miracles are attributed to well known rabbis: "Let Rabbi Simeon

---

54   Vermes, *Jesus the Jew: A Historian's Reading of the Gospels*, 72-82.
55   B. D. Chilton, *The Temple of Jesus: His Sacrificial Program Within a Cultural History of Sacrifice* (University Park: Penn State University Press, 1992) 92 n. 5.

ben Yoḥai go, for he is experienced in miracles [נוסים]" (*b. Meʿil.* 17b).
"Let the miracle [נס] be performed, no matter how. Thereupon he (the
demon) advanced and entered into the Emperor's daughter. When
(Rabbi Simeon) arrived, he called out, 'Ben Temalion, leave (her),
Ben Temalion, leave (her)!' And as he proclaimed this, he left her" (*b.
Meʿil.* 17b). Several rabbis were remembered to have brought rain
through their prayers (cf. *b. Taʿan.* 24a–25b). It is said (anonymously)
that both Eliezer (late first, early second century C.E.) and Aqiba (late
first, early second century C.E.) were successful in praying for rain,
though apparently the latter enjoyed greater success than the former
(*b. Taʿan.* 25b). Judah the Prince and Joshua ben Levi (early third
century C.E.) also apparently had his prayers for rain answered (*b.
Taʿan.* 24a, 25a). Evidently there was a tradition of requesting major
figures and authorities to pray for rain during periods of drought.
According to Rabbi Samuel bar Naḥmani (ca. 300 C.E.): "When Israel
sins and does evil deeds, the rains are withheld. When they bring an
elder, such as Rabbi Yose the Galilean [ca. 130-140 C.E.], to intercede
for them, the rains fall again" (*y. Ber.* 5.2; cf. *Meg. Taʿan.* [on Adar
§7]: "On the 20th [of Adar] the people fasted for rain, and it was
granted to them"). There may have been other traditions of mighty
deeds accomplished through Yose the Galilean. Abba Silver cites a
tenth-century prayer of a sick man: "Rabbi Yose the Galilean, heal
me!"[56] Such a prayer is evidence of belief that healing could be had
through Yose's intercession. Such an idea likely had its origin in some
remarkable deeds in Yose's lifetime, or in some remarkable legends in
the years following his death. The prayer of a certain pious ḥasid
brought on a flood (*t. Taʿan.* 3.1). To some extent this parallels Ḥoni's
prayer for rain. When the rain began as a drizzle, he asked for
abundant rain. Then it began to pour with the danger of flooding.
Ḥoni's continued petitioning resulted in reducing the rain to
moderation.[57]

Hillel the Elder, with whom no miracles are associated, is called a

---

[56]   A. H. Silver, *A History of Messianic Speculation in Israel* (Gloucester:
Peter Smith, 1978) 22-23.

[57]   It is worth remarking that five of the seven Jewish holy men considered
here were remembered to have had their prayers for rain answered. Ḥanina's
request that the rain stop is particularly noteworthy. In no case does Jesus pray for
rain. But on at least one occasion he commands a storm to stop (Mark 4:35-41; cf.
6:47-52; John 6:16-21).

"ḥasid."[58] His piety and humility are emphasized (cf. *b. Beṣa* 20a; *b. Ketub.* 67b; *b. Šabb.* 31a [the Golden Rule]; *b. Soṭa* 48b; *b. Sukk.* 28a). At the funeral of Hillel, we are told that this lament was uttered (*t. Soṭa* 13.3 = *y. Soṭa* 9.13):

הוי עניו חסיד תלמידו של עזרא:

"Woe for the humble, the saint [חסיד], the disciple of Ezra."

Though frequently associated with miracles, Ḥoni and Ḥanina ben Dosa are nevertheless regarded as teachers.[59] Ḥanina studied under Yoḥanan ben Zakkai (*b. Ber.* 34a) and teaching is attributed to him (cf. *b. Ber.* 33a; *Midr. Mishle* on Prov 11:4; *Baraita deRabbi Eliezer* §29, §31), though often it takes the form of wisdom (cf. *'Abot* 3:10-11; *'Abot R. Nat.* A 22.1). Ḥanina is numbered among the "men of truth" (*Mek.* on Exod 18:21 [*Amalek* §4]). Furthermore, Ḥoni's academic skills were well remembered (*b. Ta'an.* 23a).

What becomes clear is that Jesus' ministry of healing and exorcising blends in well against his Jewish environment. We find little reason to appeal to so-called "Hellenistic" traditions (see the excursus on Apollonius of Tyana that follows this chapter). Nor do we find it warranted to identify Jesus with one particular class of Jewish figures to the exclusion of others. In some ways Jesus resembled the prophets of restoration (as seen in chap. 2 above). In some ways Jesus' messianic ideas coincided with Davidic traditions, possibly even paralleling ideas that may have been associated with Simon ben Kosiba (as seen in chap. 4 above). Even the miracles themselves potentially conveyed messianic and/or restorative significance. In chap. 6 below expressions of Jewish teaching and piety will be considered.

---

[58] For an assemblage of the pertinent texts and (a largely uncritical) discussion of them, see A. Büchler, *Types of Jewish-Palestine Piety from 70 B.C.E. to 70 C.E.: The Ancient Pious Men* (London: Jews' College, 1922; repr. New York: Ktav, 1968) 7-67.

[59] See Vermes, "Hanina ben Dosa," 195-214. Vermes reviews Ḥanina's teaching, finding "a few ethical maxims" (p. 195).

JESUS AND APOLLONIUS OF TYANA

In the early third century C.E. Philostratus of Athens wrote a work entitled *The Life of Apollonius of Tyana*. The author's goal was to defend the legendary first-century sage from recent attacks. Some years later one Hierocles wrote a work entitled *Lover of Truth*, in which he made comparison between Jesus and Apollonius. Eusebius wrote a treatise against this work, entitled, *Against the Life of Apollonius of Tyana*.[1]

Apollonius is said to have performed miracles and even to have been resurrected. The point that Hierocles wished to make is that the miracles of Jesus, no more numerous or significant than those performed by Apollonius, hardly justified the Christians' excessive claim that Jesus was God. Against these claims Eusebius tries to impress upon his readers the significant differences between Jesus and Apollonius his contemporary.

The teachings and activities of Apollonius of Tyana have been of interest to scholars concerned with Jesus research. It has often been suggested, in the past especially, that early Christians and later the evangelists embellished the Jesus tradition along the lines of Hellenistic wonderworkers such as Apollonius. Martin Dibelius and Rudolf Bultmann made form-critical comparisons between the miracles of Jesus and those attributed to Apollonius.[2] On the basis of these comparisons Dibelius and Bultmann were convinced that most of the

---

[1] For a convenient collection of the Philostratus' *Life of Apollonius of Tyana*, letters of Apollonius, and Eusebius' reply to Hierocles, see F. C. Conybeare, *Philostratus: The Life of Apollonius of Tyana* (2 vols., LCL 16-17; London: Heinemann; Cambridge: Harvard University Press, 1912).

[2] M. Dibelius, *From Tradition to Gospel* (London: James Clarke, 1971) 70-103; R. Bultmann, *The History of the Synoptic Tradition* (Oxford: Blackwell, 1968) 218-44. For many parallels, on which Bultmann and Dibelius depended, see O. Weinrich, *Antike Heilungswunder: Untersuchungen zum Wunderglauben der Griechen und Römer* (RVV 8.1; Giessen: Töpelmann, 1909). For a more recent statement, with many proposed parallels, see M. Smith, *Jesus the Magician* (New York: Harper & Row, 1979).

miracle stories neither derived from the historical Jesus nor originated in Palestine; rather, they originated in Hellenism. Dibelius averred: "The Tale-tellers have taken over foreign traits or actions and have Christianized them."[3] Bultmann adds: "the *Hellenistic* origin of [most of] the miracle stories is overwhelmingly the more probable" and "in Mark and most of all in his miracle stories Hellenism has made a vital contribution."[4]

Quite apart from the questionable dichotomy between Palestinian and Hellenistic,[5] the value of the parallels between Jesus and Apollonius (d. 98 C.E.) has in my estimation been exaggerated. Better parallels are seen in the rabbinic traditions, which have been reviewed in the previous chapter, as well as in the Old Testament itself and in some of the pseudepigrapha. A review of the miracles attributed to Apollonius should make this evident. The most important miracle stories include the following:

Healing of the Lame Man

"There also arrived a man who was lame. He was already thirty years old and was a keen hunter of lions; but a lion had sprung upon him and dislocated his hip so that he limped with one leg. However when they massaged with their hands his hip, the youth immediately recovered his upright gait" (*Vit. Ap.* 3.39).

Healing of the Blind Man

"And another man had had his eyes put out, and he went away having recovered the sight of both of them" (*Vit. Ap.* 3.39).[6]

Healing of the Paralytic

"Yet another man had his hand paralysed, but left their presence in

---

3   Dibelius, *From Tradition to Gospel*, 102.

4   Bultmann, *History of the Synoptic Tradition*, 240-41. The emphasis is Bultmann's.

5   The problematical nature of this dichotomy has been helpfully clarified by M. Hengel, *Judentum und Hellenismus: Studien zu ihrer Begegnung unter besonderer Berücksichtigung Palästinas bis zur Mitte des 2 Jh.s v.Chr.* (WUNT 10; Tübingen: Mohr [Siebeck], 1973); ET: *Judaism and Hellenism: Studies in Their Encounter in Palestine during the Early Hellenistic Period* (2 vols., London: SCM; Philadelphia: Fortress, 1974). On the widespread practice of healing, exorcizing, prophecy, and visionary experience in Palestine in the time of Jesus, see *Judaism and Hellenism*, 1.236-41.

6   Trans. by Conybeare, *Philostratus*, 1.317.

full possession of the limb" (*Vit. Ap.* 3.39).

Healing of the Woman who had suffered in childbirth

"And a certain woman had suffered in labour already seven times, but was healed in the following way through the intercession of her husband. He bade the man, whenever his wife should be about to bring forth her next child, to enter her chamber carrying in his bosom a live hare; then he was to walk once round her and at the same moment to release the hare; for that the womb would be extruded together with the foetus, unless the hare was at once driven out" (*Vit. Ap.* 3.39).[7]

Exorcising a Demon from a Young Man

". . . the youth burst out into loud and coarse laughter, and quite drowned his (i.e. Apollonius') voice. The Apollonius looked up at him and said: 'It is not yourself that perpetrates this insult, but the demon [ὁ δαίμων], who drives you on without your knowing it.' And in fact the youth was, without knowing it, possessed by a devil; for he would laugh at things that no one else laughed at, and then he would fall to weeping for no reason at all, and he would talk and sing to himself. Now most people thought that it was the boisterous humour of youth which led him into such excesses; but he was really the mouth-piece of a devil, though it only seemed a drunken frolic in which on that occasion he was indulging. Now when Apollonius gazed on him, the ghost in him began to utter cries of fear and rage, such as one hears from people who are being branded or racked; and the ghost swore that he would leave the young man alone and never take possession of any man again. But Apollonius addressed him with anger, as a master might a shifty, rascally, and shameless slave and so on, and he ordered him to quit the young man and show by a visible sign that he had done so. 'I will throw down yonder statue,' said the devil, and pointed to one of the images which were in the king's portico, for there it was that the scene took place. But when the statue began by moving gently, and then fell down, it would defy anyone to describe the hubbub which arose thereat and the way they clapped their hands with wonder. But the young man rubbed his eyes as if he had just woke up, and he looked towards the rays of the sun, and assumed a modest aspect, as all had their attention concentrated on him; for he no longer showed himself licentious, nor did he stare madly about, but he had returned to his own

---

7   Trans. by Conybeare, *Philostratus*, 1.319.

self, as thoroughly as if he had been treated with drugs; and he gave up his dainty dress and summery garments and the rest of sybaritic way of life, and he fell in love with the austerity of philosophers, and donned their cloak, and stripping off his old self modelled his life in future upon that of Apollonius" (*Vit. Ap.* 4.20).[8]

Raising of the Dead Girl

"Here too is a miracle [θαῦμα] which Apollonius worked: A girl had died just in the hour of her marriage, and the bridegroom was following her bier lamenting as was natural his marriage left unfulfilled, and the whole of Rome was mourning with him, for the maiden belonged to a consular family. Apollonius then witnessing their grief, said: 'Put down the bier, for I will stay the tears that you are shedding for this maiden.' And withal he asked what was her name. The crowd accordingly thought that he was about to deliver such an oration as is commonly delivered as much to grace the funeral as to stir up lamentation; but he did nothing of the kind, but merely touching her, at once woke up the maiden from her seeming death; and the girl spoke out loud, and returned to her father's house, just as Alcestis did when she was brought back to life by Hercules. And the relations of the maiden wanted to present him with the sum of 150,000 sesterces, but he said that he would freely present the money to the young lady by way of a dowry. Now whether he detected some spark of life in her, which those who were nursing her had not noticed,—for it is said that although it was raining at the time, a vapour went up from her face— or whether life was really extinct, and he restored it by the warmth of his touch, is a mysterious problem which neither I myself nor those who were present could decide" (*Vit. Ap.* 4.45).[9]

Miraculous transport of Apollonius from Smyrna to Ephesus

"With such harangues as these he knit together the people of Smyrna; but when the plague began to rage in Ephesus, and no remedy sufficed to check it, they sent a deputation to Apollonius, asking him to become physician of their infirmity; and he thought that he ought not to postpone his journey, but said: 'Let us go.' And forthwith he was in Ephesus, performing the same feat, I believe, as Pythagoras, who was in Thurii and Metapontum at one and the same moment" (*Vit. Ap.*

---

8   Trans. by Conybeare, *Philostratus*, 1.391, 393. One is reminded of the story of the Gerasene demoniac (Mark 5:1-20).

9   Trans. by Conybeare, *Philostratus*, 1.457, 459.

4.10).[10]

Miraculous transport of Apollonius from Rome to Dicaearchia

Facing trial and the possibility of a death sentence, Apollonius bids his friends to go to Dicaearchia, assuring them that "' . . . there you shall see me appear to you.' 'Alive,' asked Damis, 'or how?' Apollonius with a smile replied: 'As I myself believe, alive, but as you will believe, risen from the dead' [ἀναβεβιωκότα]. Accordingly he says that he went away with much regret, for although he did not quite despair of his master's life, yet he hardly expected him to escape death. And on the third day he arrived at Dicaearchia . . ." (*Vit. Ap.* 7.41).[11] Acquited, Apollonius miraculously makes the three-day journey in a single day: ". . . before midday he left the court, and at dusk appeared to Demetrius and Damis at Dicaearchia" (*Vit. Ap.* 8.10).[12] Demetrius then asks if Apollonius is indeed alive. "Whereupon Apollonius stretched out his hand and said: 'Take hold of me . . . but if I resist your touch [ἀπτόμενον] . . .'" (*Vit. Ap.* 8.12).[13]

Ascension of Apollonius

"But about midnight he loosened his bonds, and after calling those who had bound him, in order that they might witness the spectacle, he ran to the doors of the temple, which opened wide to receive him; and when he had passed within they closed afresh, as they had been shut, and there was heard a chorus of maidens singing from within the temple, and their song was this: 'Hasten thou from earth, hasten thou to Heaven, hasten'" (*Vit. Ap.* 8.30).[14] We are then told that the spirit of Apollonius spoke to a young man who doubted the former's immortality (*Vit. Ap.* 8.31).

The miracle stories attributed to Apollonius offer a few general parallels to the miracle stories of the Gospels, but they are not impressive. We encounter elements of gimmickry and trickery on the part of Apollonius, such as removing and replacing his foot in leg

---

[10] Trans. by Conybeare, *Philostratus*, 1.363, 365. One is reminded of the Philip's apparent miraculous transport from Gaza to Azotus (Acts 8:39-40) and the transport of the prophet Habakkuk, via an angel clutching his hair (Bel and the Dragon 33–39; cf. *Life of Habakkuk* 12:7).

[11] Trans. by Conybeare, *Philostratus*, 2.263.

[12] Trans. by Conybeare, *Philostratus*, 2.263.

[13] Trans. by Conybeare, *Philostratus*, 2.361.

[14] Trans. by Conybeare, *Philostratus*, 2.401.

irons while in prison (*Vit. Ap.* 7.38). We find other bizarre elements, such as scaring off an evil spirit by writing a threatening letter (*Vit. Ap.* 3.38) or by making tripods walk and performing other telekinetic acts (*Vit. Ap.* 3.17; cf. Eusebius, *Against the Life of Apollonius of Tyana* 18). There are some interesting parallels to be sure, but Apollonius comes across more as a wizard (of which he is frequently accused). Many of his sayings and actions, moreover, are ostentatious. When the circumstances require, Apollonius does not hesitate to imply that he is a god. Some of his statements, including his apology before Emperor Domitian, smack of conceit and self-importance.

There is also serious question about the credibility of the sources utilized by Philostratus. B. F. Harris has concluded that the life of Apollonius is heavily seasoned with imagination and exaggeration.[15] E. L. Bowie agrees and has criticized scholars for too readily giving credence to the stories attributed to Apollonius of Tyana.[16]

The closest parallels to the miracles of Jesus are not found in Greco-Roman stories, but are found in biblical literature (esp. Elijah and Elisha) and in rabbinic traditions. I prescind from further discussion and recommend to the reader the studies by Barry Blackburn and Erkki Koskenniemi.[17] Koskenniemi criticizes at many points the parallels and conclusions drawn by Bultmann and Dibelius, while both Koskenniemi and Blackburn offer trenchant criticism of the divine man hypothesis.[18]

---

[15] B. F. Harris, "Apollonius of Tyana: Fact or Fiction?" *JRH* 5 (1969) 189-99.

[16] E. L. Bowie, "Apollonius of Tyana: Tradition and Reality," *ANRW* 2.16.2 (1978) 1652-1699.

[17] B. Blackburn, "'Miracle Working ΘΕΟΙ ΑΝΔΡΕΣ' in Hellenism (and Hellenistic Judaism)," in D. Wenham and C. L. Blomberg (eds.), *The Miracles of Jesus* (Gospel Perspectives 6; Sheffield: JSOT Press, 1986) 185-218; E. Koskenniemi, *Apollonius von Tyana in der neutestamentlichen Exegese* (WUNT 2.61; Tübingen: Mohr [Siebeck], 1994).

[18] See also B. Blackburn, *'Theios Aner' and the Markan Miracle Traditions: A Critique of the Theios Aner Concept as an Interpretative Background of the Miracle Traditions Used by Mark* (WUNT 2.40; Tübingen: Mohr [Siebeck], 1991).

CHAPTER SIX

JESUS AND RABBINIC PARABLES, PROVERBS,
AND PRAYERS

Throughout this century scholars have compared the parables of
Jesus with those of the Rabbis.[1] This interest seems to be increasing,

---

[1]   P. Fiebig, *Altjüdische Gleichnisse und die Gleichnisse Jesu* (Tübingen:
Mohr [Siebeck], 1904); idem, *Die Gleichnisreden Jesu im Lichte der rabbinischen
Gleichnisse des neutestamentlichen Zeitalters* (Tübingen: Mohr [Siebeck], 1912);
G. Dalman, *Jesus-Jeshua: Studies in the Gospels* (London: SPCK, 1929); W. O.
E. Oesterley, *The Gospel Parables in the Light of Their Jewish Background*
(London: Macmillan, 1936); J. Jeremias, *The Parables of Jesus* (London: SCM;
New York: Scribner's, 1963); D. Flusser, *Die rabbinischen Gleichnisse und der
Gleichniserzähler Jesus* (Bern: Peter Lang, 1981); C. Thoma and M. Wyschogrod
(eds.), *Parable and Story in Judaism and Christianity* (New York: Paulist, 1989);
B. H. Young, *Jesus and His Jewish Parables* (New York: Paulist, 1989); H. K.
McArthur and R. M. Johnston, *They Also Taught in Parables: Rabbinic Parables
from the First Centuries of the Christian Era* (Grand Rapids: Zondervan, 1990).
For studies principally concerned with the rabbinic parables, see I. Ziegler, *Die
Königsgleichnisse des Midrasch beleuchtet durch die römische Kaiserzeit* (Breslau:
Schlesische Verlags-Anstalt, 1903); I. Abrahams, *Studies in Pharisaism and the
Gospels* (London: Cambridge University Press, 1917; repr. New York: Ktav,
1967) 90-107; A. Feldman, *Parables and Similes of the Rabbis: Agricultural and
Pastoral* (Cambridge: Cambridge University, 1927); P. Fiebig, *Rabbinische
Gleichnisse* (Leipzig: Hinrichs, 1929); R. Pautrel, "Les canons du Mashal
rabbinique," *RSR* 26 (1936) 6-45; 28 (1938) 264-81; J. J. Petuchowski, "The
Theological Significance of the Parable in Rabbinic Literature and the New
Testament," *Christian News from Israel* 23 (1972-73) 76-86; R. M. Johnston,
"Appendix: Parables among the Pharisees and Early Rabbis," in J. Neusner, *A
History of the Mishnaic Law of Purities. Part XIII: Miqvaot* (SJLA 6; Leiden: Brill,
1976) 224-26; D. Stern, "Rhetoric and Midrash: The Case of the Mashal,"
Prooftexts 1 (1981) 261-91; C. Thoma, "Prolegomena zu einer Übersetzung und
Kommentierung der rabbinischen Gleichnisse," *TZ* 38 (1982) 514-31; C. Thoma
and S. Lauer, *Die Gleichnisse der Rabbinen. Erster Teil: Pesiqta deRav Kahana
(PesK). Einleitung, Übersetzung, Parallelen, Kommentar, Texte* (Bern: Peter Lang,
1986); D. Stern, *Parables in Midrash: Narrative and Exegesis in Rabbinic Literature*
(Cambridge: Harvard University Press, 1991) [see pp. 188-205 for discussion of
Jesus' parables].

which is probably a result of, and perhaps to some extent a cause of, the increasing awareness of the importance of studying Jesus within the world of Palestinian Judaism.

There are numerous rabbinic parables, perhaps as many as 2,000 (of which as many as 325 may be tannaitic),[2] a fact which invites and at the same time discourages comparison. H. K. McArthur and R. M. Johnston have identified more than two dozen parables of Jesus that closely parallel rabbinic parables (most are tannaitic).[3] With some modification and expansion they are as follows:

1. The Sower [or the Four Soils] (Mark 4:3-8; Matt 13:3-8; Luke 8:5-8)
   The Four Types of Students (*'Abot* 5:15) [anonymous]

2. The Mustard Seed (Mark 4:30-32; Matt 13:31-32; Luke 13:18-19)
   The Seed under Hard Ground (*b. Ta'an.* 4a) [anonymous]

3. The Wicked Vineyard Tenants (Mark 12:1-11; Matt 21:33-44; Luke 20:9-18)
   The Unworthy Tenants (*Spire Deut.* §312 [on Deut 32:9]) [anonymous]

4. Paying a Debt and Settling a Dispute (Matt 5:25-26; Luke 12:57-59)
   Paying a Debt and Settling a Dispute (*Pesiq. R. Kah.* 18.6) [anonymous]

5. Wise Builder and Foolish Builder (Matt 7:24-27; Luke 6:47-49)
   Wise Builder and Foolish Builder (*'Abot R. Nat.* A 24.1-4) [R. Elisha ben Abuyah, ca. 120 C.E.]
   The Builder with or without Tools (*'Abot R. Nat.* A 22.1) [R. Yoḥanan ben Zakkai, ca. 80 C.E.]

6. The Lost Sheep (Matt 18:10-14; Luke 15:3-7)
   On Who Will Seek the Lost Sheep (*Midr. Ps.* 119.3 [on 119:1]; cf. *Exod. Rab.* 2.2 [on Exod 3:1]: "he placed the lamb on his shoulder"; *Gen. Rab.* 86.4 [on Gen 39:2]) [R. Haggai ben Eleazar, ca. 350 C.E.]

7. The Wise and Foolish Maidens (Matt 25:1-13; cf. Matt 22:1-10; Luke 14:15-24)
   The Wise and Foolish Servants (*b. Šabb.* 153a; cf. *Eccl. Rab.* 9:8 §1; *Midr. Prov.* 16:11) [R. Yoḥanan ben Zakkai, ca. 70-80 C.E.]

---

2   As estimated by Pautrel, "Les canons du Mashal rabbinique," 7. In his dissertation, R. M. Johnston (*Parabolic Interpretations Attributed to Tannaim* [West Hartford: Hartford Seminary Foundation, 1978]) assembles, translates, and comments on 325 parables which are explicitly attributed to Tannaim or are from sources that probably derive from the tannaitic period. On this point, see now McArthur and Johnston, *They Also Taught in Parables,* 9-10.

3   McArthur and Johnston, *They Also Taught in Parables,* 181-96.

8. The Faithful and Unfaithful Servants (Matt 24:45-51; Luke 12:42-46)
   The Wise and Foolish Servants (*Eccl. Rab.* 9:8 §1; cf. *b. Šabb.* 153a)
   [anonymous, based on parable by R. Yoḥanan ben Zakkai, ca. 70-80 C.E.]
   The King's Ungrateful Servants (*S. Elij. Rab.* §12 [55]) [anonymous]

9. The Watchful Householder (Matt 24:42-44; Luke 12:39-40)
   The Wise and Foolish Servants (*b. Šabb.* 153a) [R. Yoḥanan ben Zakkai, ca. 70-80 C.E.]

10. The Talents and the Servants' Stewardship (Matt 25:14-30; Luke 19:12-27)
    The Wife's Stewardship (*Song Rab.* 7:14 §1) [anonymous]
    The King's Steward (*'Abot R. Nat.* A 14.6) [R. Eleazar ben Arak, ca. 90 C.E.]
    The Two Administrators (*Mek.* on Exod 20:2 [*Baḥodeš* §5]) [R. Simon ben Eleazar, ca. 170 C.E.]
    The King's Daughters (*Song Rab.* 4:12 §1) [R. Joshua ben Levi, ca. 220-240 C.E.]

11. The Tares in the Wheat (Matt 13:24-30)
    The Trees of Life and the Trees of Death (*Gen. Rab.* 61.6 [on Gen 25:5]; cf. 83.5 [on 36:39]) [anonymous]

12. The Pearl of Great Value (Matt 13:45-56)
    The Precious Pearl (*Midr. Ps.* 28.6 [on 28:7]; cf. Luke 11:5-8; 18:1-8) [R. Simon, ca. 325 C.E.]

13. The Hidden Treasure (Matt 13:44)
    The Cheaply Sold Field (*Mek.* on Exod 14:5 [*Bešallaḥ* §2]) [R. Yose the Galilean, ca. 120 C.E.]
    The Cheaply Sold Estate (*Mek.* on Exod 14:5 [*Bešallaḥ* §2]; cf. *Pesiq. Rab Kah.* 11.7; *Song Rab.* 4:12 §1; *Exod. Rab.* 20.2, 5 [on Exod 13:17]) [R. Simeon ben Yoḥai, ca. 140 C.E.]

14. The Drag Net (Matt 13:47-50)
    Four Types of Fish (*'Abot R. Nat.* A 40.9) [R. Gamaliel the Elder, ca. 40-50 C.E.]

15. The Unmerciful Servant (Matt 18:23-35)
    The Forgetful Debtor (*Exod. Rab.* 31.1 [on Exod 22:25]) [anonymous]

16. The Generous Employer (Matt 20:1-16)
    The Exceptional Laborer (*Sipra Lev.* §262 [on Lev 26:9]; *Pirqe R. El.* §53) [anonymous]
    The Laborer Paid a Full Day's Wage (*Song Rab.* 6:2 §6; *y. Ber.* 2.8) [R. Zeira, ca. 360-370 C.E.]

17. The Two Sons (Matt 21:28-32)
    The Two Workers (*Exod. Rab.* 27.9 [on Exod 18:1]) [anonymous]

The Two Tenants (*Deut. Rab.* 7.4 [on Deut 28:1]) [anonymous]

18. The Guest without a Wedding Garment (Matt 22:11-14)
    The Guests who brought their own chairs (*Eccl. Rab.* 3:9 §1) [R. Pinḥas, ca. 70-80 C.E.]
    The Wise and Foolish Servants (*b. Šabb.* 153a; cf. *Eccl. Rab.* 9:8 §1; *Midr. Prov.* 16:11) [R. Yoḥanan ben Zakkai, ca. 70-80 C.E.]

19. The Friend at Midnight (Luke 11:5-8)
    The Brazen Daughter and the Polite Daughter (*y. Ta'an.* 3.4; cf *Midr. Ps.* 28.6 [on 28:7]) [R. Aqiba, ca. 95 C.E.]

20. The Insistent Widow (Luke 18:1-8)
    The Brazen Daughter and the Polite Daughter (*y. Ta'an.* 3.4; cf. *Midr. Ps.* 28.6 [on Ps 28:7]) [R. Aqiba, ca. 95 C.E.]

21. The Rich Fool (Luke 12:16-21)
    The Rich Hoarder (*Pesiq. Rab Kah.* 10.3; cf. Sir 11:18-19) [anonymous]

22. The Fruitless Fig Tree (Luke 13:6-9)
    The Fruitless Vineyard (*Exod. Rab.* 43.9 [on Exod 32:11]) [R. Simeon ben Yehozadak, ca. 220-230 C.E.]

23. The Closed Door (Luke 13:24-30)
    The Closed Door (*Midr. Ps.* 10.2 [on Ps 10:1]) [R. Ḥanina (ben Ḥama), ca. 220-230 C.E.]

24. Choosing the Right Place at the Table (Luke 14:7-11)
    (*Lev. Rab.* 1.5 [on Lev 1:1], commenting on Prov 25:6-7 and Ps 113:5-6; cf. Sir 3:17-20) [R. Aqiba and R. Simeon ben Azzai, ca. 120 C.E.]

25. Building a Tower (Luke 14:28-30)
    Counting the Cost of *not* being Reconciled to God (*Pesiq. Rab Kah.*, Sup. 7.3) [R. Jonathan, ca. 270 C.E.]

26. The King Going to War (Luke 14:31-33)
    Counting the Cost of *not* being Reconciled to God (*Pesiq. Rab Kah.*, Sup. 7.3) [R. Jonathan, ca. 270 C.E.]

27. The Lost Coin (Luke 15:8-10)
    The Lost Coin (*Song Rab.* 1:1 §9) [R. Phineas ben Yair, ca. 165-175 C.E.]

28. The Prodigal Son (Luke 15:11-32)
    The Errant Son (*Deut. Rab.* 2.24 [on Deut 4:30]) [R. Meir, ca. 150 C.E.]
    The Repatriated Prince (*Sipre Deut.* §345 [on Deut 33:4]) [anonymous]
    The Returning Prince (*Pesiq. R.* 44.9) [anonymous]
    The Favored Son (*Sipre Deut.* §352 [on Deut 33:12]) [anonymous]

29. The Rich Man and Lazarus (Luke 16:19-31)

The Fate of the Two Men (*Ruth Rab.* 3.3 [on Ruth 1:17], commenting on Eccl 1:15; *Eccl. Rab.* 1:15 §1) [anonymous]

The Two Pious Men and the Tax Collector (*y. Sanh.* 6.23; *y. Ḥag.* 2.27) [anonymous]

30. The Servants Who Have Done Their Duty (Luke 17:7-10)
Servants Who Labor for the Fear of Heaven (*'Abot* 1:3) [Antigonus of Soko, ca. 200? B.C.E.]
Work Claims no Merit (*'Abot* 2:8) [R. Yoḥanan ben Zakkai, ca. 80 C.E.]

31. The Log and the Speck (Matt 7:3-5; Luke 6:41-42)
The Log and the Splinter (*b. 'Arak.* 16b) [R. Tarfon, ca. 120 C.E.]

32. The Two Gates (Matt 7:13-14; cf. Luke 13:24)
The Two Ways (*Sipre Deut.* §53 [on Deut 11:26]; *Midr. HaGadol* on Deut 11:26) [anonymous]

Other tannaitic parables that resemble the parables of Jesus (in theme, style, or details) include the following (principally based on McArthur and Johnston):[4]

1. The Throne and the Footstool (*Gen. Rab.* 1.15 [on Gen 1:1]) [Beth Shammai, ca. 40 C.E.]
2. The Palace (*Gen. Rab.* 1.15 [on Gen 1:1]) [Beth Hillel, ca. 40 C.E.]
3. The Ill-Treated Cupbearer (*m. Sukk.* 2:9) [anonymous]
4. The Well-Rooted Tree (*'Abot* 3:18; cf. *'Abot R. Nat.* A 22.2) [R. Eleazar ben Azariah, ca. 90 C.E.]
5. Ink on Paper (*'Abot* 4:20; cf. *'Abot R. Nat.* A 23.3) [Elisha ben Abuyah, ca. 120 C.E.]
6. The Eater of Ripe Grapes (*'Abot* 4:20; cf. *'Abot R. Nat.* A 23.3 [see Mark 2:22]) [R. Yose ben Judah of Kefar ha-Babli, ca. 190 C.E.]
7. The Inept Servant (*t. Ber.* 6.18) [anonymous]
8. The Lamp Removed (*t. Sukk.* 2.6) [anonymous]
9. The Road between Fire and Snow (*t. Ḥag.* 2.5; cf. *'Abot R. Nat.* A 28.10) [anonymous]
10. The Unfortunate Fugitive (*t. Soṭa* 15.7) [anonymous]
11. The Protected Vineyard (*t. Qidd.* 1.11) [R. Gamaliel II, ca. 80 C.E.]
12. The Married Woman (*t. Qidd.* 1.11) [R. Gamaliel II, ca. 80 C.E.]
13. The Fenced Vineyard (*t. Qidd.* 1.11) [R. Gamaliel II, ca. 80 C.E.]
14. The Two Men who Planned a Wedding Feast (*t. B. Qam.* 7.2) [R. Gamaliel II, ca. 80 C.E.]
15. The Wife Sent Back to Her Father (*t. B. Qam.* 7.3) [R. Yoḥanan ben Zakkai, ca. 70 C.E.]
16. The King Engaged to a Woman (*t. B. Qam.* 7.4) [R. Yoḥanan ben Zakkai, ca.

---

4   McArthur and Johnston, *They Also Taught in Parables*, 18-24.

70 C.E.]

17. The Villager Who Smashed Glassware (*Gen. Rab.* 19.6 [on Gen 3:7]) [R. Yoḥanan ben Zakkai, ca. 70-80 C.E., or R. Aqiba, ca. 120 C.E.]

18. The King's Twin Who Was Executed (*t. Sanh.* 9.7) [R. Meir, ca. 140 C.E.]

19. The Man with a Fine Beard (*b. Ber.* 11a) [R. Eleazar ben Azariah, ca. 80 C.E.]

20. The Fox and the Fishes (*b. Ber.* 61b) [R. Aqiba, ca. 135 C.E.]

21. The King Who Did Not Exempt Himself from Taxes (*b. Sukk.* 30a) [R. Simeon ben Yoḥai, ca. 140 C.E.]

22. The King Who Forgave a Debt (*b. Roš Haš.* 17b–18a) [R. Yose the Priest, ca. 90 C.E.]

23. Giving Promptly and Slowly (*b. Ta'an.* 25b) [R. Samuel the Younger, ca. 90 C.E.]

24. The Trees with Overhanging Boughs (*b. Qidd.* 40b) [R. Eleazar ben Zadok, ca. 90 C.E.]

25. The Retracted Betrothal (*'Abot R. Nat.* A 2.3) [R. Yose the Galilean, ca. 130 C.E.]

26. The Inferior Field (*'Abot R. Nat.* A 16.3) [R. Simeon ben Yoḥai, ca. 140 C.E.]

27. Wise and Foolish Guests at the King's Banquet (*Sem.* 8.10) [R. Meir, ca. 140 C.E.]

28. The Proud Father (*Mek.* on Exod 13:2 [*Pisḥa* §16]) [R. Eleazar ben Azariah, ca. 80 C.E.]

29. The King and His Guards (*Mek.* on Exod 15:2 [*Širata* §3]) [R. Eliezer (ben Hyrcanus?), ca. 90 C.E.]

30. The King Going Out to War (*Mek.* on Exod 20:5 [*Baḥodeš* §6]) [Gamaliel II, ca. 80 C.E.]

31. The King's Images (*Mek.* on Exod 20:16 [*Baḥodeš* §8]) [R. Hanina ben Gamaliel, ca. 85 C.E.]

32. The Foolish Centurion (*Sipre Num.* §131 [on Num 25:1-13]) [R. Aqiba, ca. 130 C.E.]

33. The King Who Repented His Intention to Divorce (*Sipre Num.* §131 [on Num 25:1-13]) [R. Aqiba, ca. 130 C.E.]

34. The Unwise Suitor (*Sipre Deut.* §37 [on Deut 11:10]) [R. Simeon ben Yoḥai, ca. 140 C.E.]

35. The King Who Enforced His Will (*Sipre Deut.* §40 [on Deut 11:12]) [R. Simeon ben Yoḥai, ca. 140 C.E.]

36. The King's Bird (*Sipre Deut.* §48 [on Deut 11:22]) [R. Simeon ben Yoḥai, ca. 140 C.E.]

37. The Frugal Brother and the Wasteful Brother (*Sipre Deut.* §48 [on Deut 11:22]) [R. Simeon ben Yoḥai, ca. 140 C.E.]

38. The Two Wrestlers (*Gen. Rab.* 22.9 [on Gen 4:10]) [R. Simeon ben Yoḥai, ca. 140 C.E.]

39. The King Who Found His Lost Pearl (*Gen. Rab.* 39.10 [on Gen 12:1]; cf. *Ruth Rab.* 8.1 [on Ruth 4:20]) [R. Nehemiah, ca. 150 C.E.]

40. The Foolish Shipmate (*Lev. Rab.* 4.6 [on Lev 4:2]) [R. Simeon ben Yoḥai, ca.

140 C.E.]

Jewish Parables from non-Rabbinic sources:

1. The Trees and the Bramble (Judg 9:7-21)
2. The Poor Man's Ewe Lamb (2 Sam 12:1-4)
3. The Two Brothers and the Avengers of Blood (2 Sam 14:1-11)
4. The Escaped Prisoner (1 Kgs 20:35-40)
5. The Thistle and the Cedar (2 Kgs 14:9)
6. The Fruitless Vineyard (Isa 5:1-7)
7. The Eagles and the Vine (Ezek 17:3-10)
8. The Lion Whelps (Ezek 19:2-9)
9. The Vine (Ezek 19:10-14)
10. The Forest Fire (Ezek 21:1-5)
11. The Seething Pot (Ezek 24:3-5)
12. The Sown Seed (2 Esdras 8:41)
13. The Lame Man and the Blind Man (*Apocryphon of Ezekiel* frag. 1, cited by Epiphanius, *Against Heresies* 64.70.5-17).[5]

The following parables provide a sampling sufficient for purposes of comparison. Most of them are either found in tannaitic sources or are credited to authorities of the tannaitic period. All of them offer significant parallels to the parables of Jesus.[6]

1. The Forgiving King (*b. Roš Haš.* 17b) [Rabbi Yose the priest, ca. 90-100 C.E.]

1. אמשול לך משל: למה הדבר דומה: לאדם שנושה בחבירו מנה
2. וקבע לו זמן בפני המלך: ונשבע לו בחיי המלך הגיע זמן
3. ולא פרעו בא לפייס את המלך:
4. ואמר לו עלבוני מחול לך לך ופייס את חבירך:

"¹I will give you a parable. To what does this matter compare? To a man who lent his neighbor a mina ²and fixed a time (for repayment) in the presence of the king. When the time came in the life of the king ³and he did not pay, he went to the king to be forgiven. ⁴He (the king) said to him. 'My wrong is forgiven you,

---

5   T. W. Manson (*The Teaching of Jesus: Studies of Its Form and Content* [2nd ed., Cambridge: Cambridge University Press, 1935] 61-64) classifies the first and fifth examples as "fables," rather than parables.

6   The Parable of the Unworthy Tenants (*Spire Deut.* §312 [on Deut 32:9]) is a very important parable for studying the parables of Jesus. It and the Parable of the Unhappy Tenant (*Midr. Tanh. B Bešallah* §7) are considered in chap. 10 below.

(but) go and obtain forgiveness from your neighbor.'"

2. On Wisdom and Works ('Abot 3:18) [R. Eleazar ben Azariah, ca. 120 C.E.]

1. כל שחכמתו מרבה ממעשיו למה הוא דומה:
2. לאילן שענפיו מרבים ושרשיו מעטים:
3. והרוח באה ועוקרתו והופכתו על פניו:
4. שנאמר והיה כערער בערבה ולא יראה כי־יבוא טוב
5. ושכן חררים במדבר ארץ מלחה ולא תשב:
6. אבל כל שמעשיו מרבים מחכמתו למה הוא דומה:
7. לאילן שענפיו מעטים ושרשיו מרבים שאפילו כל־הרוחות:
8. שבעולם באות ונושבות בו אין מזיזים אותו ממקומו:
9. שנאמר והיה כעץ שתול על־מים ועל־יובל ישלח שרשיו:
10. ולא יראה כי־יבא הם והיה עלהו רענן:
11. ובשנת בצרת לא ידאג ולא ימיש מעשות פרי:

"¹Every one whose wisdom is greater than his deeds—to what may he be compared? ²To a tree whose branches are many and its roots few. ³And the wind comes and uproots it and overturns it upon its face; ⁴as it is said, 'And he shall be as a shrub in the desert, and shall not see any good come. ⁵And he shall dwell in the parched places of the wilderness, in an uninhabited salt land' (Jer 17:6). ⁶However, every one whose deeds are greater than his wisdom—to what may he be compared? ⁷To a tree whose branches are few and its roots many, so that if all the winds of ⁸the world come and blow on it, it cannot be moved from its place; ⁹as it is said, 'And he shall be as a tree planted by the waters, which spreads out its roots by the river. ¹⁰And it will not be afraid when heat comes, but its leaf will be green. ¹¹And in the year of drought it will not be troubled, nor will cease from yielding fruit' (Jer 17:8)."

3. Wise Builder and Foolish Builders ('Abot R. Nat. A 24.1-2) [R. Elisha ben Abuyah, ca. 120 C.E.] Elisha ben Abuyah says:

1. אדם שיש בו מעשים טובים ולמד תורה הרבה למה הוא דומה:
2. לאדם שבונה אבנים מלמטה ואחר כך לבנים אפילו
3. באים מים הרבה ועומדין בצידן אין מחין אותן ממקומן:
4. ואדם שאין בו מעשים טובים ולמד תורה למה הוא דומה:
5. לאדם שבונה לבנים תחילה ואחר כך אבנים אפילו:
6. באים מים קימעא מיד הופכין אותן:

"¹One in whom there are good works, who has studied much
Torah, to what may he be compared? ²To a person who builds first
with stones and afterward with bricks: ³even when much water
comes and collects by their side, it does not dislodge them. ⁴But one
in whom there are no good works, though he studied Torah, to
what may he be compared? ⁵To a person who builds first with
bricks and afterward with stones: ⁶even when a little water gathers,
it overthrows them."⁷

4. The King's Wise and Foolish Servants (*b. Šabb.* 153a; cf. *Eccl. Rab.* 9:8 §1; *Midr. Prov.* 16:11) [R. Yoḥanan ben Zakkai, ca. 70-80 C.E.]

1. משל למלך שזימן את עבדיו לסעודה ולא קבע להם זמן:
2. פיקחין שבהן קישטו את עצמן וישבו על פתח בית המלך:
3. אמרו כלום חסר לבית המלך:
4. טיפשין שבהן הלכו למלאכתן:
5. אמרו כלום יש סעודה בלא טורח:
6. בפתאום ביקש המלך את עבדיו:
7. פיקחין שבהן נכנסו לפניו כשהן מקושטין:
8. והטיפשים נכנסו לפניו כשהן מלוכלכין:
9. שמח המלך לקראת פיקחים וכעס לקראת טיפשים:
10. אמר הללו שקישטו את עצמן לסעודה ישבו ויאכלו וישתו:
11. הללו שלא קישטו עצמן לסעודה יעמדו ויראו:

"¹It compares to a king who summoned his servants to a banquet
but did not set a time for them. ²The wise ones adorned themselves
and sat at the door of the house of the king. ³They said, 'Can there
be anything lacking in the house of the king?' ⁴The fools went about
their errands. ⁵They said, 'Can there be a banquet without labor?'
⁶Suddenly the king desired his servants. ⁷The wise ones entered
before him adorned. ⁸And the fools entered before him soiled. ⁹The
king rejoiced at the wise and was angry at the fools. ¹⁰He said, 'Let
those who adorned themselves for the banquet sit, eat, and drink.
¹¹Let those who did not adorn themselves for the banquet stand and
watch.'"

The version in *Eccl. Rab.* 9:8 §1 adds: "You might suppose that the

---

⁷   Trans. by J. Goldin, *The Fathers according to Rabbi Nathan* (YJS 10; New
Haven and London: Yale University Press, 1955) 103.

latter were simply to depart; but the king continued, 'No, but the former shall recline and eat and drink, while these shall remain standing, be punished, and look on and be grieved.'"

5. The Banquet Guests (*Sem.* 8.10) [R. Meir, ca. 150 C.E.]

1. רבי מאיר מושלו משל למה הדבר דומד:

2. למלך שעשה סעודה וזימן אורחים ולא קבע להם זמן מתי יכנסו:

3. הפקחין שבהן עמדו בתשעה שעות ביום

4. ונכנסו לבתיהם ועלו למטוחידם באורה:

5. האחרים עמדו בשקיעת החמה והניהו חנויות פתוחות ונרות דולקות

6. ונכנסו לבתיהן ועלו למטוחיהן בנרות:

7. האחרים עמדו בשתים ושלשה שעות בלילה הניחו מקצתן חנויות פתוחות

8. ומקצתן נעולות מקצתן נרות דולקות ומקצתן כבו

9. ונכנסו לבתיהן ועלו למטוחיהן באפילה:

10. המשיירים שבסעודה נכנס בהן יין ופצעו זה את זה והרגו זה את זה:

"[1]Rabbi Meir illustrated it with a parable. To what may the matter be compared? [2]To a king who prepared a banquet and invited guests without setting a time when they should go home. [3]The prudent among them got up at the ninth hour [4]and went to their homes and into their beds while it was still light. [5]Others got up at sunset, while the shops were open and the lamps were burning, [6]and went to their homes and into their beds by lamplight. [7]Others got up in the second and third hours of the night, when some shops were open [8]and some closed, some with their lamps burning, some with their lamps extinguished, [9]and went to their homes and into their beds in darkness. [10]Those who remained at the banquet became drunk and wounded and killed each other."

6. The King's Steward (*'Abot R. Nat.* A 14.6) [R. Eleazar ben Arak, ca. 90 C.E.]

1. משל: למה הדבר דומד:

2. לאדם שהפקיד אצלו המלך פקדון:

3. בכל יום ויום היה בוכה וצועק ואומר אוי לי:

4. אי מתי אצא מן הפקדון הזה בשלום:

"[1]A Parable. To what may the matter be compared? [2]To a man to whom the king entrusted an item of value. [3]Every day he was weeping, crying, and saying, 'Woe to me! [4]When will I be released in peace from this trust?'"

7. The Cheaply Sold Field (*Mek.* on Exod 14:5 [*Bešallaḥ* §2]) [R. Simeon ben Yoḥai, ca. 140 C.E.]

1. רבי שמעון בן יוחאי אומר משל: למה הדבר דומה:
2. לאחד שנפלה לו פלטרית במדינת הים בירושה:
3. ומכרה בדבר מועט:
4. והלך הלוקח ומצא בה מטמוניות ואוצרות של כסף
5. ושל זהב ושל אבנים טובות ומרגליות:
6. התחיל המוכר נחנק:

"¹Rabbi Simeon ben Yoḥai used to tell a parable: 'To what may the matter be compared? ²To one to whom has fallen (as) an inheritance a residence in a land across the sea. ³And he sold it for a small amount. ⁴The buyer came and found in it hidden treasures and stores of silver ⁵and gold, and (stores) of precious stones and pearls. ⁶The seller, being choked, was grieved.'"

8. The Two Ways (*Sipre Deut.* §53 [on Deut 11:26]; *Midr. HaGadol* on Deut 11:26) [anonymous]

1. משל לאחד שהיה יושב בפרשת דרכים והיו לפניו שני שבילים:
2. אחד שתחלתו מישור וסופה קוצים:
3. ואחד שתחלתו קוצים וסופו מישור:
4. והיה מודיע את העוברים ואת השבים ואומר להם:
5. אתם רואים שביל זה שתחלתו מישור:
6. בשתים ושלש פסיעות אתה מהלך במישור וסופו לצאת בקוצים:
7. אתם רואים שביל זה שתחלתו קוצים:
8. בשתים ושלש פסיעות אתה מהלך בקוצים וסופו לצאת במישור:

"¹It compares to one who was sitting at a crossroads; and there were two paths before him. ²One started smoothly and ended with thorns. ³One started with thorns and ended smoothly. ⁴And he informed the passersby and the travelers. And he was saying to them: ⁵'Do you see this path which starts smoothly? ⁶For two or three steps you will walk easily, but it ends with thorns. ⁷And do you see this path that starts with thorns? ⁸For two or three steps you will walk through thorns, but it ends smoothly.'"

9. The Repatriated Prince (*Sipre Deut.* §345 [on Deut 33:4]) [anonymous]

1. משל לבן מלך שנשבה כשהוא קטן למדינת הים:
2. אחר ק' שנים אינו בוש לחזור מפני שאומר:
3. לירושתי אני חוזר:

"¹It compares to the son of a king who while small is taken in captivity to a land across the sea. ²After one hundred years, should he desire to return, (he may,) because he can say: ³'I am returning to my inheritance.'"

10. The Two Administrators (*Mek.* on Exod 20:2 [*Baḥodeš* §5]) [R. Simon ben Eleazar, ca. 170 C.E.]

1. משל למלך שמנה לו שני אפיטרופין:
2. אחד ממונה על אוצר של תבן
3. ואחד ממונה על אוצר של כסף ושל זהב:
4. נחשד זה שהיה ממונה על אוצר של תבן:
5. והיה מתרעם על שלא מנו אותו על אוצר של כסף ושל זהב:
6. אמרו לו ריקה אם על אוצר של תבן נחשדת
7. היאך יאמינו אותך על אוצר של כסף ושל זהב:

"¹It compares to a king who appointed to himself two stewards. ²One was appointed over the store of straw ³and the other was appointed over the store of silver and gold. ⁴The one appointed over the store of straw was held in suspicion. ⁵And he griped over the fact that they had not appointed him over the store of silver and gold. ⁶They said to him, 'Good for nothing! If over the store of straw you were held in suspicion, ⁷how could they trust you over the store of silver and gold!'"

The relevance of these parables for comparison with the parables of Jesus should be obvious. The first one resembles Jesus' teaching that reflects popular wisdom. His advice to his disciples to make things right with people before presenting an offering to the Temple (Matt 5:23-24) closely parallels this parable. One must make things right with one's neighbor, as well as making things right with God. One thinks also of the Parable of the Unforgiving Servant, where we find a servant forgiven a great debt by the king but unwilling to forgive a fellow servant's smaller debt (Matt 18:21-35). In this parable the king is understood as God and the servants are understood as human beings.

This is the assumption of the rabbinic parable. Indeed, Rabbi Yose goes on to say that his parable illustrates offenses committed against God and offenses committed against a human being, which is the same premise underlying Jesus' parable. The word "minah" (מָנֶה) is the very word that appears in Luke's version of the Parable of the Minas (Luke 19:12-27, μνᾶ).

The second and third rabbinic parables remind us of Matt 7:24-27 = Luke 6:46-49. The third parable, moreover, recalls certain words and phrases found in Jesus' parables and teachings: "good works" (Matt 5:16); "when much water comes" (Matt 7:25); and the idea of collapse (Matt 7:27; Luke 6:49).

The wise and foolish servants of the fourth parable find their way into several of Jesus' parables. We are reminded of the Parable of the Wicked Servant (Matt 24:45-51), as well as the Parable of the Worthy Servant (Luke 17:7-10). The expanded version of the parable in *Eccl. Rab.* 9:8 §1 parallels Jesus' warning that "the children of the kingdom will be left out" (Matt 8:11-12; Luke 13:28-30). Servants figure prominently in other dominical parables (Matt 18:23-35; 25:14-30; Luke 19:12-27)

The fifth parable's banquet setting parallels some of Jesus' parables in which we hear of invited guests (Matt 22:1-10; Luke 14:15-24). In the rabbinic parable the folly of the guests lay in not knowing when to go home.

The principal figure in the sixth parable is the king's steward who was entrusted with an item of great value. His fear of the king reminds us of the fear of the servant who failed to trade or bank his master's money (Matt 25:14-30 = Luke 19:12-27, v. 21: "I was afraid of you, for you are a severe man").

The seventh parable immediately brings to mind Jesus' Parable of the Treasure Hidden in a field (Matt 13:44). In this instance, the version of the parable as we find it in *GThom* §109 parallels the rabbinic parable more closely: "The kingdom is like a man who had a (hidden) treasure in his field without knowing it. And (after) he died, he left it to his son. The son did not know (about the treasure). He inherited the field and sold (it). And the one who bought it went plowing and found the treasure. He began to lend money at interest to whomever he wished."

The eighth parable's two paths, one that ends with thorns and other that ends smoothly, reminds us of Jesus' wise saying about easy and hard gates: "Enter by the narrow gate; for the gate is wide and the way is easy, that leads to destruction, and those who enter it are many. For the gate is narrow and the way is hard, that leads to life, and those who find it are few" (Matt 7:13-14; cf. Luke 13:24). The two ways image is quite common in early Judaism (cf. Jer 21:8; *Mek.* on Exod 14:28 [*Bešallaḥ* §7]; *b. Ber.* 28b et passim).

The ninth parable tells of a king's son who wishes to return to his home, no matter how long he has been away. We are of course reminded of the Parable of the Prodigal Son and his decision to return home (Luke 15:11-32).

The tenth parable tells of two stewards, one with an important assignment and the other with what appeared to be an unimportant assignment. When the steward with the lowly assignment complained he was told that it was necessary for him to earn the king's trust. We are reminded of the rewards meted out to the faithful servants in the parables of Jesus: "His master said to him, 'Well done, good and faithful servant; you have been faithful over a little, I will set you over much" (Matt 25:21 = Luke 19:17). It may also be noted that the complaining steward is called "Good for nothing," which translates רֵיקָה ("worthless"), which is the word used in Matt 5:22 (ῥακά).

The rabbinic parables also offer formal parallels to the parables of Jesus. Jesus introduces his parables in the manner we have frequently encountered in the rabbinic parables:

> τίνι ὁμοία ἡ βασιλεία τοῦ θεοῦ καὶ τίνι ὁμοιώσω αὐτήν ὁμοία ἐστιν κόκκῳ σινάπεως . . .
> "What is the kingdom of God like and to what shall I compare it? It is like a mustard seed . . ." (Luke 13:18)

> ἄλλην παραβολὴν παρέθηκεν αὐτοῖς λέγων, ὡμοιώθη ἡ βασιλεία τῶν οὐρανῶν ἀνθρώπῳ σπείραντι καλὸν σπέρμα . . .
> He set before them another parable, saying, "The kingdom of Heaven may be likened to a man who sowed good seed . . ." (Matt 13:24)

Jesus' τίνι is the Greek equivalent of the Hebrew לְמָה, which is found in several of the rabbinic parables, while the appearance of ὁμοία o r ὡμοιώθη, or even the simple conjunction ὡς (cf. Mark 4:26, 31), translates the Hebrew דּוֹמָה. Shem-Tob's *Even Bohan* (MS add. no. 26964, British Library, London) presents Matt 13:24 in Hebrew:

וישם לפניהם משל אחר: מלכות שמים דומה לאיש הזורע כשזרעו זרע טוב

And he set before them another parable. "The Kingdom of Heaven compares to a man who sows good seed . . ."[8]

Another formal point of similarity between the parables of Jesus and the rabbis is seen in introducing the application with "thus" or "so": "Thus [οὕτως] it will be at the close of the age . . ." (Matt 12:45); "Thus [οὕτως] also will my heavenly Father do . . ." (Matt 18:35). The Greek οὕτως translates the Hebrew כָּךְ, which frequently appears in the rabbinic parables, applying the parable to the moral lesson that is being made.[9]

It is clear that much can be learned from the rabbinic parables. In them we encounter a pedagogical form that was a favorite of Jesus'. We encounter themes that are similar to those found in dominical parables. The rabbinic parables frequently center on the actions of a king and/or his servants. Almost always this king is to be understood as God. Similarly, most of Jesus' parables focus on the kingdom of God or on God himself. It is sometimes pointed out that herein lies an important difference between Jesus and the rabbis. Whereas the latter spoke often of the king, the former chose to speak of the kingdom. The difference is real, to be sure, but it may not be as great as some have thought. As recent study has shown, for Jesus the kingdom of God seems to have meant the presence and power of God. In other words, the kingdom of God refers to the sphere and activity of God himself. If this is so, and Bruce Chilton's work in this area has lent compelling support to such a concept, then the difference between rabbinic parables which speak of the activity of God the king may not be all that different from the parables of Jesus which speak of the kingdom of God, itself a way of speaking of God.[10]

There is, nevertheless, need for caution in appealing to rabbinic

---

[8]   For text, see G. Howard, *The Gospel of Matthew according to a Primitive Hebrew Text* (Macon: Mercer University Press, 1987) 62.

[9]   For more on the formal and thematic similarities between the parables of Jesus and the parables of the rabbis, see McArthur and Johnston, *They Also Taught in Parables*, 165-80.

[10]   See B. D. Chilton, *God in Strength: Jesus' Announcement of the Kingdom* (SNTU 1; Freistadt: Plöchl, 1979; repr. BibSem 8; Sheffield: JSOT Press, 1987); idem, "Regnum Dei Deus Est," *SJT* 31 (1978) 261-70; idem, "The Kingdom of God in Recent Discussion," in Chilton and Evans (eds.), *Studying the Historical Jesus: Evaluations of the State of Current Research* (NTTS 19; Leiden: Brill, 1994) 255-80.

parables.[11] Not only do these parables come from sources two to four
centuries after the time of Jesus, very few can be traced to the early
tannaitic period. Why this is so is puzzling. But at the same time we
should not suppose that Jesus was the originator of the popular parable,
which was later taken up and developed in rabbinic circles. It is better
to conclude that Jesus' habitual use of parables is itself evidence that
parables were in use in his time but that our sources, outside of Jesus
himself, fail to document this.[12] In all probability Jesus made use of a
known form and of familiar images.[13]

Was there an early rabbinic tradition that was lost? One thinks of the
intriguing opening comment in *m. Soṭa* 9:15: "When Rabbi Meir died,
makers of parables ceased" (משמת רבי מאיר בטלו מושלי משלים). The
statement is hyperbole, to be sure, but at the very least it hints at the
existence of a tradition of parables among the rabbis, for which this
mid-second century Tanna was well known. Yet not that many parables in his name are preserved in the rabbinic writings. At the very
least the saying may attest how incomplete our sources are.

Rabbinic and biblical materials do not provide the only sources that
clarify important features of Jesus' parables. Many of the parables'
details come from the day-to-day activities of life in Palestine. The
Zenon Papyri, for example, in places parallel and at times even clarify
elements presupposed by the parables.

Perhaps the best known are the papyri that deal with the problems
and frustrations of absentee-management of properties and invest-
ments in Galilee, among them a vineyard. We may read the details of
lease agreements; we hear of winepress, fencing, and housing for the
farmers. We hear of trouble with the farmers, in one case the threat of
a strike. We learn of disputes over rent and tax assessments. We even
hear of one incident where Zenon's envoys, sent to collect a debt from
a Jewish man, are "attacked and thrown out of town." The relevance
that these details have for the Parable of the Vineyard Tenants is
obvious (for a much fuller discussion, see chap. 10).

A few other examples may be mentioned briefly. The following

---

[11]   See the caveats expressed by B. B. Scott, *Hear Then the Parable: A Commentary on the Parables of Jesus* (Minneapolis: Fortress, 1989) 13-19.

[12]   McArthur and Johnston, *They Also Taught in Parables*, 165-66.

[13]   Or, as Scott (*Hear Then the Parable*, 18) puts it: "His parables should be
viewed not as carefully composed and written in the modern sense but as composed
out of the elements of a traditional thesaurus."

letter from Somoelis, a guard from Philadelphia, to his employer
Zenon, adds local color to the Parable of the Rich Fool (Luke 12:16-
21):

"And if possible, have another granary made; the present one is not
big enough to hold the year's wheat."[14]

We think of the rich fool in Jesus' parable who ponders what to do
with an unexpectedly large crop: "What shall I do, since I have no
place to gather my fruit? This is what I shall do: I shall tear down my
barns and build bigger ones and there shall gather my wheat and my
goods" (Luke 12:17-18).

From the Fayûm we have a letter to a son from an anxious father
who fears that unless his son comes home soon, the crops will be a
complete loss. Hermocrates writes to his son Chaeras (first century
C.E.):

"Already indeed I have written you regarding the [. . .] and you
neither answered nor came, and now, if you do not come, I run the
risk of losing the lot (of land) which I possess. Our partner has
taken no share in the work, for not only was the well not cleaned
out, but in addition the canal was choked with sand, and the land is
untilled. Not one of the tenants was willing to work it, only I
continue paying the public taxes without getting back anything in
return. There is hardly a single plot that the water will irrigate.
Therefore you must come, otherwise there is a risk that the plants
will perish."[15]

We are reminded of the Parable of the Two Sons (Matt 21:28-31). In
it one of a man's two sons initially refuses to work in his father's
vineyard. Eventually, however, he does his father's bidding. We can
only hope that Chaeras finally obeyed his father and saved the family
farm.

A letter from a prodigal son to his mother provides a delightful real-

---

14   Greek text and trans. from V. A. Tcherikover and A. Fuks, *Corpus Papyrorum Judaicarum* (2 vols., Cambridge: Harvard University Press, 1957-60) 1.138-
39 (no. 12 = PCairZen no. 59.509).

15   For text, see U. Wilcken et al. (eds.), *Aegyptische Urkunden aus den
Königlichen Museen zu Berlin* (4 vols., Berlin: Weidmann, 1895-1912) 2.174; G.
Milligan, *Selections from the Greek Papyri* (Cambridge: Cambridge University
Press, 1912) 60-63 (no. 22).

life parallel (Fayûm, 2nd century C.E.) to the Parable of the Prodigal Son (Luke 15:11-32):

"Antonis Longus to Nilus his mother, many greetings. I pray continually that you are in good health. I make intercession for you daily to the Lord Serapis. I wish you to know that I had no hope that you would go up to the metropolis. For this reason I did not enter the city. But I was ashamed to come to Caranis, because I walk about in rags. I have written to you, because I am naked. I beseech you, mother, be reconciled to me. Furthermore, I know what I have brought upon myself. I have been chastened, even as is necessary. I know that I have sinned [οἶδα, ὅτι ἡμάρτηκα]. I heard from Postumus, who met you in the vicinity of Arsinoë and inopportunely told you everything. Do you not know that I had rather been maimed than know that I still owe a man an obol? . . . come yourself! . . . I have heard that . . . I beseech you . . . I almost . . . I beseech you . . . I wish . . . not . . . to do otherwise. . . . to his mother, from Antonius Longus her son."

Although the last lines are fragmentary, the gist of this unprofessional letter is quite clear. The son of Nilus admits, "I have sinned," just as the prodigal son of Jesus' parable confesses to his father (Luke 15:18, 21: Πάτερ, ἥμαρτον).[16]

Consider also the following letter (256 C.E.) as it relates to the Parable of the Persistent Widow (Luke 18:1-8):

"To Zenon, greetings from Senchons. I petitioned you about my donkey which Nikias took. If you had written to me about her (i.e. the donkey), I would have sent her to you. If it pleases you, command him to return her, in order that we may carry the hives to the pastures, lest they be ruined for you and be of no use to either yourself or the king. And if you examine the matter, you will be

---

16   For Greek text and discussion, see Wilcken et al. (eds.), *Aegyptische Urkunden*, 3.170-71 (no. 846); Milligan, *Selections from the Greek Papyri*, 93-95 (no. 37); A. Deissmann, *Light from the Ancient East* (rev. ed., New York: Harper & Row, 1927) 187-92 + plate; A. S. Hunt and C. C. Edgar, *Select Papyri I* (LCL 266; London: Heinemann; Cambridge: Harvard University Press, 1932-34) 317-19 (no. 120). Impoverished Antonius (or Antonis for short) could not afford a professional scribe, so he wrote the letter himself. His hand is barely legible in places; his grammar is rustic and his spelling is poor.

persuaded that we are useful to you. And I will send the foal of the ass to you. Therefore, I beg and entreat you, that you not put me off. I am a widow woman. Farewell."[17]

JESUS AND JEWISH PROVERBS

Comparison between Jesus' proverbs and those of the rabbis is also of value. Gustaf Dalman identified the following dominical proverbs and maxims, with some modifications and additions, which are also paralleled in Jewish literature:[18]

Jesus	*Jewish Literature*
"Blessed are the poor in spirit, for theirs is the kingdom of heaven" (Matt 5:3).	"Concerning them . . . who are humble of spirit, Scripture declares: 'Thus says the Lord . . . to him who is despised of men . . . Kings shall see and arise, princes shall also bow down' [Isa 49:7]" (*Derek 'Ereṣ Rabba* 2.14).
"Blessed are those who mourn, for they shall be comforted" (Matt 5:4).	"Concerning them who sigh, grieve, and look forward to (national) salvation and mourn for Jerusalem, Scripture declares: 'To grant those who mourn in Zion, giving them a garland instead of ashes' [Isa 61:3]" (*Derek 'Ereṣ Rabba* 2.20),
"Blessed are those who hunger and thirst for righteousness, for they shall be satisfied . . . Blessed are the peacemakers, for they will be called sons of God" (Matt 5:6, 9).	"Concerning them who pursue righteousness, who seek peace for their people, who grieve with the community and stand by them in the hour of their distress, Scripture declares: 'The Lord is good, a stronghold in the day of trouble; and he knows them who take refuge in him' [Nahum 1:7]" (*Derek 'Ereṣ Rabba* 2.24).
"Blessed are the merciful, for they shall obtain mercy" (Matt 5:7).	"So long as you are merciful, He will have mercy on you" (*t. B. Qam.* 9.30 [Gamaliel]; *Sipre Deut.* §96 [on Deut

---

17   For Greek text and discussion, see C. C. Edgar (ed.), *Michigan Papyri.* Vol. 1: *Zenon Papyri* (Ann Arbor: University of Michigan Press, 1931) 90-91 (no. 29); J. L. White, *Light from Ancient Letters* (Foundations and Facets; Philadelphia: Fortress, 1986) 46 (no. 20).

18   Dalman, *Jesus-Jeshua,* 225-32.

13:18]; *b. Sanh.* 51b; cf. *Derek 'Ereṣ Rabba* 2.21). "My people, children of Israel, as our Father is merciful in heaven, so shall you be merciful on earth" (*Tg. Ps.-J.* Lev 22:28).

"Blessed are the pure in heart, for they shall see God" (Matt 5:8).

"Concerning them . . . who are pure of heart, Scripture declares: 'Surely God is good to Israel, even to such as are pure in heart' [Ps 73:1]" (*Derek 'Ereṣ Rabba* 2.19; cf. *Gen. Rab.* 41.1 [on Gen 12:17]; *Midr. Ps.* 24.8 [on Ps 24:4]).

"You are the salt of the earth" (Matt 5:13a; cf. Mark 9:50).

"The Torah has been compared to salt . . . the world cannot exist without salt . . . it is impossible for the world to exist without Scripture" (*Sop.* 15.8). "The salt of money is greed [חסר], but the salt of money is (also) kindness [חסד]" (*'Abot R. Nat.* A 17.4; *b. Ketub.* 66b; cf. *b. Šabb.* 153a).

"But if the salt has lost its flavor, with what is it to be salted?" (Matt 5:13b; cf. Mark 9:50). "If the salt become insipid, with what will it be salted?" (Luke 14:34).

"When salt becomes unsavory with what is it to be salted?" (*b. Bek.* 8b). "The wisdom of the scribes will become insipid" (*m. Soṭa* 9:15).

"You cannot make one hair white or black" (Matt 5:36).

"If all the nations of the world should gather together to make white one wing of a raven they would not be able to accomplish it" (*Lev. Rab.* 19.2 [on Lev 15:25]; cf. *Song Rab.* 5:11 §3).

"Bless those who curse you, pray for those who mistreat you" (Luke 6:28).

"Concerning those who suffer insults but do not insult, who hear themselves reviled and do not answer back, who perform (religious precepts) from love and rejoice in their chastisements, Scripture declares: 'But let those who love him be like the rising of the sun in its might' [Judg 5:31]" (*Derek 'Ereṣ Rabba* 2.13).

"And with what measure you measure, it shall be measured to you again" (Matt 7:2 = Luke 6:38; Mark 4:24).

"With the measure with which one measures, it will be measured to him" (*m. Soṭa* 1:7; *t. Soṭa* 3.1, 2; *Sipre Num.* §106 [on Num 12:1-16]; *b. Soṭa* 8b; *b.*

Sanh. 100b; cf. Wis 11:15-16). "In what measure a man measures, in that measure is it measured to him" (*Frag. Tg.* and *Cairo Tg.* D Gen 38:26). "Moses said to Israel: 'I have measured out to you with the same measure with which you have measured out'" (*Sipre Deut.* §308 [on Deut 32:5]). "All the measures have ceased, yet the rule of measure for measure has not ceased" (*Gen. Rab.* 9.11 [on Gen 1:31]).

"You hypocrite, first remove the beam from your own eye; and then you will see clearly to remove the speck from your brother's eye" (Matt 7:5).

"I wonder whether there is anyone in this generation who accepts reproof, for if one say to him, 'Remove the speck from between your eyes,' he would answer, 'Remove the beam from between your eyes'" (*b. 'Arak.* 16b). "If the judge said to a man, 'Take the splinter from between your teeth, he would retort, 'Take the beam from between your eyes'" (*b. B. Bat.* 15b).

"Ask, and it will be given to you. Seek, and you will find. Knock, and it will be opened to you" (Matt 7:9 = Luke 11:9).

"If someone say to you: 'I have labored and yet I have not found,' do not believe it. 'I have labored and I have found,' believe it" (*b. Meg.* 6b). "(Mordecai) the son of Kish indicates that he knocked at the gates of mercy and they were opened to him" (*b. Meg.* 12b). "A man should always immerse himself in the Mishnayot, for if he knows (them), it will be opened to him" (*Lev. Rab.* 21.5 [on Lev 16:3]).

"So whatever you wish that men would do to you, do so to them; for this is the law and the prophets" (Matt 7:12 = Luke 6:31).

"What is hateful to you, do not do it to your neighbor. This is the whole law and the rest is the interpretation of it" (*b. Šabb.* 31a [attributed to Hillel]). "What you hate for yourself, do not do it to your neighbor" (*'Abot R. Nat.* B §26 [attributed to Aqiba]). "Do what is done to you: accompany [be present at funerals] in order that you may be accompanied. Lament, in order that you may be lamented. Perform the duty of burial, in order that others may perform in on you" (*t. Ketub.* 7:6 [Aqiba]); cf. Tob 4:15; Sir 31:15; *Ep. Arist.* 207; *m. 'Abot* 2:10.

"Do people gather grapes from thorns, or figs from thistles?" (Matt 7:16 = Luke 6:44).

"From the thorn bush comes the rose" (*Song Rab.* 1:1 §6).

"Physician, heal yourself!" (Luke 4:23; cf. Matt 27:42).

"Physician, heal your own lameness!" (*Gen. Rab.* 23.4 [on Gen 4:23-25]).

"Freely you have received, freely give" (Matt 10:8).

"Just as you received it (Torah) without payment, so teach it without payment" (*b. Bek.* 29a; *Derek 'Ereṣ Zuṭa* 2.4).

"Therefore, be wise as serpents, and harmless as doves" (Matt 10:16).

"With Me they are innocent as doves, but with the nations they are wise as serpents" (*Song Rab.* 2:14 §1).

"The disciple is not above his teacher, nor the servant above his master. It is enough for the disciple that he be as his teacher, and the servant as his master" (Matt 10:24; cf. Luke 6:40).

"It is enough for the servant to be like his master" (*Sipra Lev.* §251 [on Lev 25:23]; *b. Ber.* 58b).

"He who finds his life will lose it; and he who loses his life for my sake will find it" (Matt 10:39 = Luke 17:33; Matt 16:25 = Mark 8:34 = Luke 9:24).

"Alexander of Macedon asked the wise men of the South: 'What will a man do that he may live?' And they answered: 'Let him kill himself.' And what should a man do that he may die?' They answered: 'Let him keep himself alive'" (*b. Tamid* 32a). "If it be your will that you should not die, die that you may not die. If it be your will that you should live, live not, so that you may live. It is better for you to die in this world against your will than to die in the world to come" (*'Abot R. Nat.* B §32 [Judah the Prince]).

"We have piped to you, and you have not danced" (Matt 11:17 = Luke 7:32).

"Much as he may sing, it does not enter into the ear of the dancer. Much as he may sing, the son of the fool hears it not" (*Lam. Rab.* Proem §12).

"A woman in the crowd raised her voice and said to him, 'Blessed is the womb that bore you, and the breasts that you

"Blessed are the breasts which you sucked and the womb that bore you" (*Tg. Neof., Ps.-J.* Gen 49:25; cf. *Gen.*

sucked!' But he said, 'Blessed rather are those who hear the word of God and keep it!'" (Luke 11:27-28).

Rab. 98.20 [on Gen 49:25]).

"Whoever has, to him more will be given, and he will have an abundancce; but whoever does not have, from him will be taken away even what he does have" (Matt 13:12 = Mark 4:25 = Luke 8:18; Matt 25:29 = Luke 19:26).

"He who does not increase will decrease" (*'Abot* 1:13 [Hillel]). "A mortal can put something into an empty vessel but not into a full one, but the Holy One, blessed be He, is not so. He puts more into a full vessel but not into an empty one" (*b. Ber.* 40a; *b. Sukk.* 46a) "The Holy One, blessed be He, gave wisdom to the wise . . . and knowledge to them that know understanding" (*Eccl. Rab.* 1:7 §5). "What they desired was not given to them, and what they possessed was taken from them" (*t. Soṭa* 4.17; *Gen. Rab.* 20.5 [on Gen 3:14]).

"He who does not gather with me scatters" (Matt 12:30 = Luke 11:23; cf. Mark 9:40).

"At the time when one gathers—scatter; and at the time when one scatters—gather" (*t. Ber.* 6.24; *y. Ber.* 9.5 [Hillel]; *b. Ber.* 63a; cf. *Pss. Sol.* 4:13; 12:28).

"For out of the abundance of the heart the mouth speaks" (Matt 12:34 = Luke 6:45).

"What was in their hearts was also in their mouths" (*Midr. Ps.* 28.4 [on Ps 28:3]; *Gen. Rab.* 84.9 [on Gen 37:4]). "If the heart has not revealed (the secret) to the mouth, to whom can the mouth reveal it?" (*Eccl. Rab.* 7:2 §1).

"Blessed are your eyes because they see, and your ears because they hear. For truly I say to you that many prophets and righteous persons have longed to see what you see and they did not see them, and to hear what you hear and they did not hear them" (Matt 13:16-17 = Luke 10:23-24).

"Blessed are my eyes that have seen thus" (*b. Ḥag.* 14b). "Blessed are those born in those days (i.e. when the Messiah will appear) to see the good fortune of Israel, which God will bring to pass in the assembly of the tribes" (*Pss. Sol.* 17:44). "Rabbi Eliezer says: 'Whence can you say that a maidservant saw at the sea what Isaiah and Ezekiel and all the prophets never saw? It says about them: "And by the hand of prophets have I given parables" [Hos 12:11(E10)]'" (*Mek.* on Exod 15:2 [Širata' §3]; cf. *Mek.* on Exod 19:11

[*Baḥodeš* §3]).

"When you are invited by any one to a marriage feast, do not sit down in a place of honor, lest a more eminent man than you be invited by him; and he who invited you both will come and say to you, 'Give this place to this man,' and then you will begin with shame to take the lowest place. But when you are invited, go and sit in the lowest place, so that when your host comes he may say to you, 'Friend, go up higher'; then you will be honored in the presence of all who sit at table with you" (Luke 14:8-11).

"Stay two or three seats below your place, and sit there until they say to you, 'Come up!' Do not begin by going up because they may say to you, 'Go down!' It is better that they say to you, 'Go up,' than that they say to you, 'Go down'" (*Lev. Rab.* 1.5 [on Lev 1:1]; cf. Prov 25:6-7).

"For whoever exalts himself will be humbled; and he who humbles himself will be exalted" (Luke 14:11; Matt 23:12).

"God will exalt him who humbles himself, but God will humble him who exalts himself" (*b. 'Erub.* 13b; cf. *b. Sanh.* 17a). "Hillel used to say: 'My humiliation is my exaltation; my self-exaltation is my humiliation'" (*Lev. Rab.* 1.5 [on Lev 1:1]). "Get down to come up and up to come down: Whoever exalts himself above the words of Torah is in the end degraded; and whoever degrades himself for the sake of the words of Torah is in the end exalted" (*'Abot R. Nat.* A 11.2 [Yose]; cf. Ezek 21:26).

"And he was desiring to be filled with the carob-pods that the swine were eating" (Luke 15:16).

"When Israelites are reduced to eating carob-pods, they repent" (*Lev. Rab.* 13.4 [on Lev 11:2]; 35.6 [on Lev 26:3]; *Song Rab.* 1:4 §3; attributed to the Tanna Aha). "The nations of the world say, 'We have no need to eat carob-pods like the Jews'" (*Lam. Rab.* Proem §17; 3:14 §5). "'Why are you eating carob-pods?' He says, 'I do not have honey'" (*Sipre Num.* §89 [on Num 11:7-9]).

"How many servants in my father's house have bread to spare, and I perish with hunger" (Luke 15:17).

"When a son [abroad] goes barefoot [through poverty] he remembers the comfort of his father's house" (*Lam.*

Rab. 1:7 §34 [attributed to "the Palestinian rabbis"]).

"This my son was dead, and is alive again; he was lost, and is found" (Luke 15:24, 32).

"'This son of yours whom you have lost, is he alive or dead?' He answered, 'Alive'" (*Lev. Rab.* 6.6 [on Lev 5:1]).

"Therefore, if your hand or your foot cause you to stumble, cut them off . . ." (Matt 18:8 = Mark 9:43).

"He who says, 'Blind my eye, which is doing me harm,' or 'Chop off my hand, which is doing me harm,' is exempt" (*t. B. Qam.* 9.32; cf. *m. B. Qam.* 8:7).

"It is easier for a camel to go through the eye of a needle than for a rich man to enter into the kingdom of God" (Matt 19:24 = Mark 10:25 = Luke 18:25).

"Know that men are not shown (in a dream) either a golden palm, or an elephant passing through the eye of a needle" (*b. Ber.* 55b; *b. B. Meṣ.* 38b).

"The last will be first, and the first will be last" (Matt 20:16 = Mark 10:31 = Luke 13:30).

"In this world he who is small can become great and he who is great can be made small, but in the world to come he who is small cannot become great nor he who is great small" (*Ruth Rab.* 3.1 [on Ruth 1:17]; cf. *b. B. Bat.* 10b; *b. Pesaḥ.* 50a).

"Peter began to say to him, 'Lo, we have left everything and followed you.' Jesus said, 'Truly I say to you, there is no one who has left house or brothers or sisters or mother or father or children or lands . . . who will not receive a hundred-fold now in this time . . . and in the world to come eternal life'" (Mark 10:28-30 = Matt 19:27-29 = Luke 18:28-30).

"He who accepts the pleasures of this world will be denied the pleasures of the world to come; but he who does not accept the pleasures of this world will be granted the pleasures of the world to come" (*'Abot R. Nat.* A 28.5).

"Many are called, but few are chosen" (Matt 22:14).

"Many have been created, but few will be saved" (4 Ezra 8:3). "There are more who perish than will be saved" (4 Ezra 9:15).

"Out of her poverty she put in all that she had, even her own life" (Mark 12:44 = Luke 21:4).

"Once a woman brought a handful of fine flour, and the priest despised her, saying, 'See what she offers! What is there in this to offer up?' It was shown to him in a dream: 'Do not despise her! It is regarded as if she had sacrificed her own life'" (*Lev. Rab.* 3.5 [on Lev 1:17]).

". . . for I was hungry, and you gave me something to eat; I was thirsty, and you gave me drink; I was a stranger, and you invited me in; naked, and you clothed me; I was sick, and you visited me; I was in prison, and you came to me . . ." (Matt 25:34-46).

"Concerning them who are merciful, who feed the hungry, give drink to the thirsty, clothe the naked, and distribute alms, Scripture declares: 'Say to the righteous that it will go well with them' [Isa 3:10]" (*Derek 'Ereṣ Rabba* 2.21).

"The days are coming when they will say, 'Blessed are the barren, and the wombs that never bore, and the breasts that never gave suck!'" (Luke 23:29).

"Cursed be the breast that gave suck to such a one as this" (*Gen. Rab.* 5.9 [on Gen 1:13]).

"Why do you seek the living among the dead?" (Luke 24:5). "Let the dead bury their own dead" (Matt 8:22 = Luke 9:60).

"Is it the way of the dead to be sought for among the living, or are the living among the dead?" (*Exod. Rab.* 5.14 [on Exod 5:2]; cf. *Lev. Rab.* 6.6 [on Lev 5:1]).

JESUS AND JEWISH PRAYERS

There is no reason to doubt that Jesus and his disciples prayed the traditional Jewish daily prayers. Yet, there are few prayers attributed to Jesus. The few that are attributed to him probably represent either distinctive prayers or prayers uttered on special occasions. The best known prayer, the Lord's Prayer, contains, as we shall see, little that is distinctive. The reason that the prayers are significant for Jesus research lies in the fact that they give us important insights into Jesus' hopes and intentions. To this end, the Lord's Prayer is particularly useful, even if it contains nothing unique or particularly distinctive. In this third and final section of the present chapter the prayers of Jesus and his contemporaries will be compared.[19]

Before examining the prayers attributed to Jesus, it will be helpful to review Jewish prayers whose claim to antiquity is the strongest. Citing *m. Tamid* 5:1 Jacob Neusner remarks that there "is no reason to doubt the existence of a formal liturgy in the Temple. Quite discrete discourse on the disposition of Temple rites after the destruction in 70, moreover, underlines the probability that prior to 70, a formal

---

19   See the outstanding bibliography compiled in J. H. Charlesworth (ed.), with M. Harding and M. Kiley, *The Lord's Prayer and Other Prayer Texts from the Greco-Roman Era* (Valley Forge: Trinity Press International, 1994) 101-257.

liturgy, though in diverse forms, did govern synagogue prayer."[20] The following prayers existed in whole or in part in the tannaitic period, many of them preserving traditions dating to the time of Jesus.[21]

Jewish Prayers

The evidence from early rabbinic literature, Josephus, and Philo makes it clear that Jewish prayers took shape in synagogues or in "prayer-houses" (προσευχαί), as they were often called in antiquity.[22] Jewish prayers originated in the context of Temple worship and were inspired by the commands and examples in Scripture.

1. The Amidah (or Shemone Esra, "Eighteen"), according to the Palestinian Rescension (with suspected later insertions deleted, excepting the late first-century benediction against heretics), reads as follows:

1. ברוך אתה יהוה אלהי אברהם אלהי יצחק ואלהי יעקב:
אל עליון קונה שמים וארץ מגננו ומגן אבותינו:
ברוך אתה יהוה מגן אברהם:

2. אתה גבור חזק חי עולמים מקים מתים מכלכל חיים מחיה המתים:
ברוך אתה יהוה מחיה המתים:

3. קדוש אתה ונורא שמך ואין אלוה מבלעדיך:

---

[20]   J. Neusner, *Judaic Law from Jesus to the Mishnah* (SFSHJ 84; Atlanta: Scholars Press, 1993) 64-72, quotation from p. 66. See also R. Hammer, "What Did They Bless? A Study of Mishnah Tamid 5.1," *JQR* 81 (1991) 305-24.

[21]   For helpful collections of Jewish prayers and critical discussion of them, see J. Heinemann, "Prayers of Beth Midrash Origin," *JSS* 5 (1960) 264-80; idem, *Prayer in the Talmud: Forms and Patterns* (SJ 9; Berlin and New York: de Gruyter, 1977 [orig. Hebrew, 1964]); M. Brocke, J. J. Petuchowski, and W. Strolz (eds.), *Das Vaterunser: Gemeinsames im Beten von Juden und Christen* (Freiburg: Herder, 1974); abridged ET: J. J. Petuchowski and M. Brocke (eds.), *The Lord's Prayer and Jewish Liturgy* (New York: Seabury, 1978); J. J. Petuchowski, *Understanding Jewish Prayer* (New York: Ktav, 1972).

[22]   See M. Hengel, "Proseuche und Synagoge," in G. Jeremias and H. W. Kuhn (eds.), *Tradition und Glaube* (K. G. Kuhn Festschrift; Göttingen: Vandenhoeck & Ruprecht, 1971) 157-84; idem, "Proseuche und Synagoge: Jüdische Gemeinde, Gotteshaus and Gottesdienst in der Diaspora und in Palästina," in J. Gutmann (ed.), *The Synagogue: Studies in Origins, Archaeology and Architecture* (New York: Ktav, 1975) 27-54; S. Talmon, "The Emergence of Institutionalized Prayer in Israel in the Light of the Qumran Literature," in M. Delcor (ed.), *Qumrân: Sa piété, sa théologie et son milieu* (BETL 46; Louvain: Louvain University Press, 1978) 265-84.

ברוך אתה יהוה האל הקדוש:

4. חננו אבינו דעה מאתך ובינה והשכל מתורתך:
ברוך אתה יהוה חונן הדעת:

5. השיבנו יהוה אליך ונשובה חדש ימינו כקדם:
ברוך אתה יהוה הרוצה בתשובה:

6. סלח לנו אבינו כי חטאנו לך: מחה פשעינו מנגד עיניך:
ברוך אתה יהוה המרבה לסלוח:

7. ראה בעניינו וריבה ריבנו וגאלנו למען שמך:
ברוך אתה יהוה גואל ישראל:

8. רפאנו יהוה אלהינו ממכאוב לבנו והעלה רפואה למכותינו:
ברוך אתה יהוה רופא חולי עמו ישראל:

9. ברך עלינו יהוה אלהינו את השנה ושבע עולם מאוצרות טובך:
ברוך אתה יהוה מברך השנים:

10. תקע בשופר גדול לחרותנו ושא נס לקבוץ גליותינו:
ברוך אתה יהוה מקבץ נדחי עמו ישראל:

11. שיבה שופטינו כבראשונה ויועצינו כבתחלה ומלוך עלינו אתה לבדך:
ברוך אתה יהוה אוהב המשפט:

12. למשמדים אל תהי תקוה ומלכות זדון מהרה תעקר:
[בימינו והנצרים והמינים כרגע יאבדו:
ימחו מספר החיים ועם צדיקים אל יכתבו:]
ברוך אתה יהוה מכניע זדים:

13. על גרי הצדק יהמו רחמיך ותן לנו שכר טוב עם עושי רצונך:
ברוך אתה יהוה מבטח לצדיקים:

14. רחם יהוה אלהינו על ירושלם עירך ועל ציון משכן כבודך
ועל מלכות בית דוד משיח צדקך:
ברוך אתה יהוה אלהי דוד בונה ירושלם:

15. שמע יהוה אלהינו בקול תפלתנו כי אל חנון ורחום אתה:
ברוך אתה יהוה שומע תפלה:

16. רצה יהוה אלהינו ושכון בציון ויעבדוך עבדיך בירושלם:
ברוך אתה יהוה שאותך ביראה נעבד:

17. מודים אנחנו לך יהוה אלהינו על כל הטובות החסד שעשיתה עמנו:
ברוך אתה יהוה הטוב לך להודות:

18. שים שלומך על ישראל עמך וברכנו כלנו כאחד:
ברוך אתה יהוה עושה השלום:

1. Blessed are You, O Lord, God of Abraham, God of Isaac, and God of Jacob, God Most High, who are the Creator of heaven and earth, our Shield and the Shield of our fathers. Blessed are You, O Lord, the Shield of Abraham!

2. You are mighty, strong, who live for ever, who raise the dead, who sustain the living, who make alive the dead. Blessed are You, O Lord, who makes alive the dead!

3. Holy are You, and Your Name is to be feared, and there is no God beside You. Blessed are You, O Lord, the holy God!

4. O favor us, our Father, with knowledge from You, and understanding and discernment from Your Torah. Blessed are You, O Lord, who gives knowledge!

5. Cause us to return to You, O Lord, and let us return afresh in our days as in the past. Blessed are You, O Lord, who delights in repentance!

6. Forgive us, our Father, for we have sinned against You. Blot out our transgressions from before Your eyes. Blessed are You, O Lord, who increases forgiveness!

7. Look upon our afflictions and plead our case and redeem us for Your name's sake. Blessed are You, O Lord, Redeemer of Israel!

8. Heal us, O Lord our God, from the pain of our heart, and raise up healing for our wounds. Blessed are You, who heals the sick of His people Israel!

9. Bless for us, O Lord our God, the year and satisfy the world from the store-houses of Your goodness. Blessed are You, O Lord, who blesses the years!

10. Blow the great shofar for our freedom and lift a banner to gather our exiles. Blessed are You, O Lord, who gathers the dispersed of His people Israel!

11. Return our judges as at first and and our counselors as at the beginning, and rule over us You alone. Blessed are You, O Lord, who loves justice!

12. For apostates let there be no hope, and the kingdom of arrogance quickly uproot. [In a moment let the Nazarenes and the heretics be destroyed; let them be blotted from the Book of Life, and with the righteous not be inscribed.] Blessed are You, O Lord, who loves judgment!

13. Toward the proselytes of righteousness may Your mercies be stirred and give to us a good reward together with those who do Your will. Blessed are You, O Lord, who assures the righteous!

14. Have mercy, O Lord our God, on Jerusalem Your city and on Zion the dwelling place of Your glory and on the kingdom of the house of David Your righteous Messiah. Blessed are You, O Lord God of

David, who builds Jerusalem!

15. Hear, O Lord our God, the sound of our prayer, for You are a gracious and merciful God. Blessed are You, O Lord, who hears prayer.

16. Accept (us), O Lord our God, and dwell in Zion and may Your servants serve You in Jerusalem. Blessed are You, O Lord, whom we serve in fearful respect!

17. Thanksgiving we give to You, O Lord our God, for all the good things, the lovingkindness which you have done among us. Blessed are You, O Lord; it is good to give thanks to You!

18. Set Your peace upon Israel Your people and bless us, each and all of us. Blessed are You, O Lord, who makes peace!

2. The Palestinian short form of the Amidah (from *y. Ber.* 4.3) reads:

1. אומר לו הבינו רצה תשובתנו סלח לנו גואלנו רפא חליינו:
2. ברך שנותינו . . . כי מפוזרים אתה מקבץ ותועים עליך לשפוט
3. ועל הרשעים תשית ידך וישמחו כל חוסי בך
4. בבנין עירך ובחדוש בית מקדשך ובצמח דוד עבדך:
5. טרם נקרא אתה תענה שנאמר והיה טרם יקראו ואני אענה
6. עוד הם מדברים ואני אשמע: ברוך אתה יהוה שומע תפלה:

"[1]He said to him, 'Give us discernment, accept our repentance, forgive us, redeem us, heal our sicknesses. [2]Bless our years . . . for You gather the dispersed, and we depend upon You for justice; [3]and against the wicked you raise Your hand; and all who trust in You will rejoice [4]in the rebuilding of Your city and in the restoration of the house of Your sanctuary, and in the sprouting of (the house) of David Your servant. [5]Before we call, You answer, as it says, "Before they call I will answer, [6]while they are yet speaking I will hear" [Isa 65:24]. Blessed are You, O Lord, who hears prayer.'"

3. The Babylonian short form of the Amidah (from *b. Ber.* 29a) reads:

1. רבי יהושע אומר מעין שמנה עשרה: מאי מעין שמנה עשרה:
2. רב אמר מעין כל ברכה וברכה:
3. ושמואל אמר הבינו יהוה אלהינו לדעת דרכיך
4. ומול את לבבנו ליראתך ותסלח לנו להיות גאולים
5. ורחקנו ממכאובינו ודשננו בנאות ארצך ונפוצותינו מארבע תקבץ
6. והתועים על דעתך ישפטו ועל הרשעים תניף ידיך
7. וישמחו צדיקים בבנין עירך ובתקון היכלך

8. ובצמיחת קרן לדוד עבדך ובעריכת נר לבן ישי משיחך:

9. טרם נקרא אתה תענה: ברוך אתה יהוה שומע תפלה:

"¹Rabbi Joshua says: 'An abbreviated Eighteen.' What is an abbreviated Eighteen? ²Rab said: 'An abbreviated form of every blessing.' ³And Samuel said: 'Give us discernment, O Lord our God, to know Your ways; ⁴and circumcise our heart to fear You, and forgive us so that we might be redeemed; ⁵and keep us far from our sufferings, and fatten us in the pastures of Your land, and gather our dispersions from the four corners of the earth; ⁶and let those who wander from Your knowledge be judged, and against the wicked lift up Your hand; ⁷and let the righteous rejoice in the building of Your city and the establishment of Your Temple ⁸and in the exalting of the horn of David Your servant and the preparation of a light to the son of Jesse Your Messiah. ⁹Before we call, may You answer. Blessed are You, O Lord, who hears prayer.'"

On the antiquity of the Amidah, see *Sipre Deut.* §343 (on Deut 33:2), which cites parts of the second and third benedictions ("The great, mighty, and awesome God, You are holy, and Your name is awesome"), part of the eighth ("who heals the sick"), part of the tenth ("who releases the captives"), and part of the seventeenth ("We give thanks to You"). For other parallels with the Amidah, see *m. Yoma* 7:1.[23]

The Hebrew version of Yeshua ben Sira contains apparent allusions to several of the Amidah's petitions. These allusions are found in a psalm added to what according to Greek versification is 51:12. The expanded Hebrew verse reads:[24]

---

[23] For critical discussion, see L. Finkelstein, "The Development of the Amida," *JQR* 16 (1925-26) 1-43, 127-69; idem, "The Origin and Development of the Qedushah," in A. A. Chiel (ed.), *Perspectives on Jews and Judaism* (W. Kelman Festschrift; New York: Rabbinical Assembly, 1978) 61-78; J. Barta, "Das Achtzehngebet—Eine Betrachtung," in Brocke, Petuchowski, and Strolz (eds.), *Das Vaterunser*, 77-89; J. J. Petuchowski, "Das Achtzehngebet," in H. H. Henrix (ed.), *Jüdische Liturgie: Geschichte, Struktur, Wesen* (Freiburg: Herder, 1979) 77-88; R. Kimelman, "The Daily 'Amidah and the Rhetoric of Redemption," *JQR* 79 (1988-89) 165-97; I. Jacobs, "Kingship and Holiness in the Third Benediction of the Amidah and in the Yozer," *JJS* 41 (1990) 62-74.

[24] For text, see I. Lévi, *The Hebrew Text of the Book of Ecclesiasticus* (SSS 3; Leiden: Brill, 1904) 73-74. A. A. Di Lella (*The Hebrew Text of Sirach* [Studies

ויפדני מכל רע	And He rescued me from all evil,
וימלטני ביום צרה	And He delivered me in the day of distress.
על כן הודיתי ואהללה	Therefore, I will thank and praise Him,
ואברכה את שם יהוה	And I will bless the Name of the Lord:
הודו ליהוה כי טוב	[a]Give thanks to the Lord, for He is good,
כי לעולם חסדו	For His lovingkindness lasts forever.
הודו לאל התשבחות	[b]Give thanks to God who is to be praised,
כי לעולם חסדו	For His lovingkindness lasts forever.
הודו לשומר ישראל	[c]Give thanks to the Protector of Israel,
כי לעולם חסדו	For His lovingkindness lasts forever.
הודו ליוצר הכל	[d]Give thanks to the Creator of all things,
כי לעולם חסדו	For His lovingkindness lasts forever.
הודו לגואל ישראל	[e]Give thanks to the Redeemer of Israel,
כי לעולם חסדו	For His lovingkindness lasts forever.
הודו למקבץ נדחי ישראל	[f]Give thanks to the Gatherer of the dispersed of Israel,
כי לעולם חסדו	For His lovingkindness lasts forever.
הודו לבונה עירו ומקדשו	[g]Give thanks to the Builder of His city and sanctuary,
כי לעולם חסדו	For His lovingkindness lasts forever.
הודו למצמיח קרן לבית דוד	[h]Give thanks to Him who makes a horn sprout for the house of David,
כי לעולם חסדו	For His lovingkindness lasts forever.
הודו לבוחר בבני צדוק לכהן	[i]Give thanks to Him who chooses the sons of Zadok to act as priests,
כי לעולם חסדו	For His lovingkindness lasts forever.
הודו למגן אברהם	[j]Give thanks to the Shield of Abraham,
כי לעולם חסדו	For His lovingkindness lasts forever.
הודו לצור יצחק	[k]Give thanks to the Rock of Isaac,
כי לעולם חסדו	For His lovingkindness lasts forever.
הודו לאביר יעקב	[l]Give thanks to the Protector of Jacob,
כי לעולם חסדו	For His lovingkindness lasts forever.
הודו לבוחר בציון	[m]Give thanks to the Chosen One in Zion,
כי לעולם חסדו	For His lovingkindness lasts forever.
הודו למלך מלכי מלכים	[n]Give thanks to the King of the kings of the kings,
כי לעולם חסדו	For His lovingkindness lasts forever.

---

in Classical Literature 1; The Hague: Mouton, 1966] 92) has concluded that this short psalm "dates from pre-Christian times" (see also his discussion on pp. 101-105). Y. Yadin (*The Ben Sira Scroll from Masada* [Jerusalem: Israel Exploration Society and the Shrine of the Book, 1965] 4) dates the Ben Sira scroll from Masada to the late Hasmonean period; but Sir 51:12 is not among the surviving fragments of this scroll.

וירם קרן לעמו	°He has raised up a horn for His people,
תהלה לכל חסידיו	Praise for all His saints,
לבני ישראל עם קרובו	For the sons of Israel—a people near Him.
הללויה	Praise the Lord! (Ps 148:14)

The following parallels are of special interest:

51:12ʲ: מגן אברהם "shield of Abraham" = *Amidah* §1 (cf. both Pal. and Bab.)

51:12ᵉ: גואל ישראל "redeemer of Israel" = *Amidah* §7 (cf. both Pal. and Bab.)

51:12ᶠ: מקבץ נדחי ישראל "gatherer of the dispersed of Israel" = *Amidah* §10 (cf. both Pal. and Bab., which read מקבץ נדחי עמו ישראל)

51:12ᵍ: בונה עירו ומקדשו "builder of his city and his sanctuary" = *Amidah* §14 (cf. both Pal. Bab., which read ירושלם עירך ... בונה ירושלם)

51:12ʰ: מצמיח קרן לבית דוד "who makes a horn to sprout for the house of David" = *Amidah* §15 (cf. Bab., which reads את צמח דוד מהרה תצמיח וקרנו תרום)

On when it is appropriate to pray an abstract of the Amida, see *m. Ber.* 4:3 (to which the gemara of *b. Ber.* 29a applies, which supplies the abstract). This tradition also supports the antiquity of the Amida. On what to insert in the Amida, see *t. Ber.* 3.25. The Amida is discussed at length in *b. Meg.* 17b-18a. Among other things, we are told that the Amidah was edited at Yabneh (יבנה).

On the malediction in the twelfth "benediction": R. Levi said: "The benediction relating to the Minim was instituted in Yabneh" (*b. Ber.* 28b). "Can anyone among you frame a benediction relating to the Minim? Samuel the Lesser arose and composed it. The next year he forgot it [29a] and he tried for two or three hours to recall it, but they did not remove him . . ." (*b. Ber.* 28b–29a).

4. The Qaddish,[25] with which the Lord's Prayer is often compared, reads:

1.   יתגדל ויתקדש שמיה רבא בעלמא דיברא כרעותיה:

---

[25] For discussion of the various forms of the Qaddish, see I. Elbogen, *Der jüdische Gottesdienst in seiner geschichtlichen Entwicklung* (3rd ed., Frankfurt am Main: J. Kauffmann, 1931; repr. Hildesheim: Olms, 1962) 92-98; D. Flusser, "Sanktus und Gloria," in O. Betz, M. Hengel, and P. Schmidt (eds.), *Abraham unser Vater: Juden und Christen im Gespräch über die Bibel* (O. Michel Festschrift; Leiden: Brill, 1963) 129-52; J. Heinemann and J. J. Petuchowski, *Literature of the Synagogue* (New York: Behrman House, 1975) 81-84; B. Graubard, "The Kaddish Prayer," in Petuchowski and Brocke (eds.), *The Lord's Prayer and Jewish Liturgy*, 59-72.

2. ימלוך מלכותיה בחייכון וביומיכון ובחייהון דכל בית ישראל

3. בעגלא ובזמן קריב ואמרו אמן:

4. יהא שמיה רבא מברך לעלם לעלמי עלמיא:

5. יתברך ישתבח ויתפאר ויתרומם ויתעלה ויתהדר ויתהלל ויתנשא

6. שמיה דקדשא בריך הוא

7. לעילא לעילא מכל ברכתא שירתא תשבחתא נחמתא

8. דאמירן בעלמא ואמרו אמן:

9. תתקבל צלותכון ותתעביד בותכון עם בעותהון

10. דכל בית ישראל קדם אבונא דבשמיא ואמרו אמן:

11. יהא שלמא רבא מן שמיא עליכון ועלנא ועל כל קהלהון

12. דכל בית ישראל לחיים ולשלום ואמרו אמן:

[1]May His great name be glorified and sanctified in the world which He created according to His will. [2]May He establish His kingdom in your lifetime and during your days, and during the lifetime of the whole house of Israel, [3]speedily and soon; and say, "Amen."
[Congregational Response:]
[4]May His great name be blessed forever and ever. [5]Blessed and praised, glorified and exalted, extolled and honored, adored and lauded be [6]the name of the Holy One, blessed be He, [7]beyond all the blessings, songs, praises, (and) consolations [8]that are ever spoken; and say, "Amen." [9]May the prayers be accepted and may the supplications be made [10]of all the house of Israel before our Father who is in heaven; and say, "Amen." [11]May there be great peace from heaven upon us and upon all the congregation [12]of the house of Israel for life and peace; and say, "Amen."

5. The Qaddish de-Rabbanan (the "Qaddish of the scholars") reads:[26]

1. יתגדל ויתקדש שמיה רבא דעתיד לחדתא עלמא ולאחיאה מיתיא

2. ולמפרק חייא ולמבני קרתא דירושלם ולשכללא היכלא קדישא ויקירא

3. ולמעקר פלחנא נכראה מן ארעא ולאתבא פלחנא דישמיה לאתריה:

4. בהדריה בזויה וביקריה ימלוך: מלכותיה בחייכון וביומיכון

5. ובחייהון דכל בית ישראל בעגלא ובזמן קריב ואמרו אמן:

6. יהא שמיה רבא וג׳ ואמרו אמן:

7. על ירשאל ועל רבנן ועל תלמידיהון ועל תלמידי תלמידיהון

8. דעסקין באוריתא קדישתא דיבאתרא הדין ודיבכל אתר ואתר:

---

[26]   Some of the elements of this form of the Qaddish appear in the "Burial Qaddish."

9. יהא לכון ולהון ולנא חנא וחסדא ורחמי

10. מן קדם מימרא דישמיא וארעא ואמרו אמן:

11. יהא שלמא רבא מן שמיא וסיועתא ופרקנא ורוחא

12. וחנא וחסדא ורחמי עליכון וג' ואמרו אמן:

[1]May His great name be glorified and sanctified in the future, to renew the world and to revive the dead [2]and to redeem the living and to rebuild the city of Jerusalem and to establish the holy Temple and the glory [3]and to uproot foreign worship from the earth and to restore worship of His name to its place. [4] In His sovereignty and glory He will reign. May He establish His kingdom in your lifetime and during your days [5]and in the lifetime of all the house of Israel, speedily and soon; and say, "Amen." [6]May His great name (be blessed forever and ever); and say, "Amen." [7]For Israel and for our teachers and for their disciples and for the disciples of their disciples [8]who engage in the study of sacred Scripture in this place and in every place [9]may there be to you, to them, and to us grace, lovingkindness, and mercy [10]from before the Memra of heaven; and say, "Amen." [11]May they have great peace from heaven, and assistance and redemption and the Spirit [12]and grace, lovingkindness, and mercy upon you (and upon all the house of Israel); and say, "Amen."

6. A prayer for the blessing for Jerusalem reads:

1. רחם־נא יהוה אלהינו על ישראל עמך ועל ירושלים עירך

2. ועל ציון משכן כבודך ועל מלכות בית דוד משיחך

3. ועל הבית הגדול והקדוש שנקרא שמך עליו:

4. אלהינו אבינו רענו זונו פרנסנו וכלכלנו והרויחנו:

5. והרוח לנו יהוה אלהינו מהרה מכל צרותינו:

6. ונא אל תצריכנו יהוה אלהינו לא לידי מתנת בשר ודם

7. ולא לידי הלואתם כי אם לידך המלאה הפתוחה הקדושה והרחבה:

8. שלא נבוש ולא נכלם לעולם ועד:

9. ברוך אתה יהוה בונה ברחמיו ירושלים: אמן:

[1]Have mercy, O Lord our God, on Your people Israel, and on Jerusalem Your city, [2]and on Zion, the dwelling place of Your glory, and on the kingdom of the house of David Your Messiah, [3]and on the great house, even the Temple that is called by Your Name. [4]Our God, our Father, tend us, feed us, sustain us, maintain

us, and comfort us. [5]Grant us speedy relief, O Lord our God, from all our troubles. [6]And please let us not need, O Lord our God, the assistance of gifts from other people (lit. flesh and blood) [7]nor the assistance of their loans; but only Your hand filled and open, holy and plentiful, [8]that we might not ever be shamed or humiliated. [9]Blessed are You, O Lord, who builds in His mercy Jerusalem. Amen.

The substance of this prayer probably derives from the first century, since the petition in line 3 presupposes the existence of the Temple. The last line of the prayer is a later addition expressing the hope for the rebuilding of Jerusalem.

The Prayers of Jesus

According to the Gospels Jesus prayed (e.g. Mark 1:35; 6:46) and taught his disciples concerning prayer (e.g. Matt 5:44; 6:6, 9; Mark 9:29; 11:24-25). Of Jesus' prayers themselves we have only three (unless we include Johannine material). Two are found in Q. In one (Matt 11:25b-26 = Luke 10:21b) Jesus thanks God for what has been revealed to his followers. The other prayer found in Q is the well known Lord's Prayer (Matt 6:9b-13 = Luke 11:2b-4). The third prayer is found in Mark 14:36 (cf. Matt 26:39, 42; Luke 22:42). In this prayer Jesus anguishes over the approaching "cup" of suffering, but resigns himself to God's will.

It is probable that all three prayers derive from Jesus, though not without some modification, as is especially the case with respect to the Lord's Prayer. All of these prayers reflect Semitic features and themes that cohere with dominical traditions that enjoy the support of various criteria often invoked to establish the authenticity of the tradition. The criterion of "embarrassment" may also apply to two of the prayers. In the prayer of thanksgiving for God's revelation, Jesus implies that his disciples are not among the "wise and understanding." Indeed, they are likened to "infants." It seems unlikely that the early Church would invent a prayer in which the revered original followers of Jesus would be so regarded. A similar argument may be advanced with respect to the prayer in Gethsemane. Here Jesus is portrayed as "falling down" and begging God to take from him the impending cup of suffering. This unflattering picture of a panicky Jesus would have presented some embarrassment to first-generation Christians. If Jesus was the Son of

God and, presumably, knew what he has doing and why he was doing it, why was he seized with such fear? To be sure, the concluding words, "not my will but yours," to a great extent rescues the scene, but the opening words would still prove awkward. Notwithstanding Crossan's recent expressions of doubt, "Few interpreters would deny that the Lord's Prayer in substantial form derives from Jesus of Nazareth."[27]

1. The Prayer of Thanksgiving (Matt 11:25b-26 = Luke 10:21b):

Ἐξομολογοῦμαί σοι, πάτερ, κύριε τοῦ οὐρανοῦ καὶ τῆς γῆς, ὅτι ἔκρυψας ταῦτα ἀπὸ σοφῶν καὶ συνετῶν καὶ ἀπεκάλυψας αὐτὰ νηπίοις. ναὶ ὁ πατήρ, ὅτι οὕτως εὐδοκία ἐγένετο ἔμπροσθέν σου.

"I thank You, Father, Lord of heaven and earth, that You have hidden these things from the wise and understanding and revealed them to infants; yes, Father, for thus was it pleasing before You."

There are several noteworthy parallels:

"I thank You, Father, Lord of heaven and earth"

Amidah §1: אל עליון קונה שמים וארץ מגננו ומגן אבותינו ("God Most High, who are the Creator of heaven and earth, our Shield and the Shield of our fathers"; cf. Gen 14:19, 22). Note the reading in the Even Bohan: בורא שמים והארץ ("Creator of heaven and earth"). Jesus' reference to "the God of Abraham, God of Isaac, and God of Jacob" (Mark 12:26) also parallels the opening words of the first benediction; cf. also 1QapGen 22:16: בריך אברם לאל עליון מרה שמיא וארעא ("Blessed be Abram by God Most High, Lord of heaven and earth"); and lines 20-21: מרים אנה ידי יומא דן לאל עליון מרה שמיא וארעא ("I raise my hand this day to God Most High, Lord of heaven and earth"). Similar language appears in Greek Jewish traditions: ὁ Κύριος τοῦ οὐρανοῦ καὶ τῆς γῆς δώῃ σοι χάριν (Tob 7:17); δέσποτα τῶν οὐρανῶν καὶ τῆς γῆς (Jdt 9:12); δέσποτα . . . τῶν ἐπ' οὐρανοῦ τε καὶ γῆς καὶ θαλάσσης (Josephus, Ant. 4.3.2 §40); Νῦν οὖν, τέκνα μου, καὶ ὑμεῖς ἀγαπήσατε Κύριον τὸν Θεὸν τοῦ οὐρανοῦ καὶ τῆς γῆς (T. Benj. 3:1); εὐλογήσω σε, ὁ Θεὸς τοῦ οὐρανοῦ καὶ τῆς γῆς (4 Bar. 5:32).

---

27   D. Juel, "The Lord's Prayer in the Gospels of Matthew and Luke," PSBSup 2 (1992) 56-70, quotation from p. 57. For the classic interpretation and defense of the authenticity of the Lord's Prayer, see J. Jeremias, Das Vater-Unser im Lichte der neueren Forschung (3rd ed., CH 50; Stuttgart: Calwer, 1965); ET: "The Lord's Prayer in the Light of Recent Research," in Jeremias, The Prayers of Jesus (SBT 6; London: SCM, 1967) 82-107. For his misgivings, see J. D. Crossan, The Historical Jesus (San Francisco: HarperCollins, 1991) 293-94.

"You have hidden these things from the wise and understanding and revealed them to infants"

The substance of this prayer may echo the words of Daniel: . . . διδοὺς σοφίαν τοῖς σοφοῖς, καὶ φρόνησιν τοῖς εἰδόσι σύνεσιν, αὐτὸς ἀποκαλύπτει βαθέα καὶ ἀπόκρυφα . . . Σοι ὁ Θεὸς τῶν πατέρων μου ἐξομολογοῦμαι καὶ αἰνῶ, ὅτι σοφίαν καὶ δύναμιν δέδωκάς μοι, καὶ ἐγνώρισάς μοι ἃ ἠξιώσαμεν παρὰ σοῦ, καὶ τὸ ὅραμα τοῦ βασιλέως ἐγνώρισάς μοι (". . . giving wisdom to the wise, and discernment to those who have understanding, He Himself reveals deep and secret things . . . To You, O God of my fathers, I give thanks and praise, for You have given me wisdom and strength, and have now made know to me what we asked of You, for You have made known to us the king's matter"; Dan 2:21b-23).[28] The language of Wisdom may also be echoed: ὅτι ἡ σοφία ἤνοιξε στόμα κωφῶν, καὶ γλώσσας νηπίων ἔθηκε τρανάς "because wisdom opened the mouth of the dumb, and made the tongues of babes speak clearly" (Wis 10:21). Note also 1QH 7:26-27 ("I praise You, O Lord, for You have enlightened me through Your truth. And Your marvelous mysteries You have made known to me, and Your lovingkindness to a vain man, and Your abundant mercies to him of perverse understanding"), where God is praised for revealing mysteries.

"for thus was it pleasing before You"

The use of the adverb "before" (ἔμπροσθεν) in relation to the Deity recalls usage of the Aramaic adverb קדם, which frequently occurs in contexts of prayer: "Abraham prayed before [קדם] God, and God healed Abimelech" (*Tg. Ps.-J.* Gen 20:17).

2. "Not my will" (Mark 14:36):

Ἀββὰ ὁ πατήρ, πάντα δυνατά σοι· παρένεγκε τὸ ποτήριον τοῦτο ἀπ' ἐμοῦ· ἀλλ' οὐ τί ἐγὼ θέλω ἀλλα τί σύ.

"Abba, Father, all things for You are possible. Take this cup from me; but (I do) not (request) what I want (to happen), but (I request) what You want (to happen)."

This prayer, like the one above, parallels Jewish thought and piety at many points:

"Abba, Father"

Ἀββὰ = אַבָּא. Jeremias had argued that אבא implied intimacy, perhaps even child-

---

28   W. Grimm (*Jesus und das Danielbuch. Band I: Jesu Einspruch gegen das Offenbarungssystem Daniels (Mt 11,25-27; Lk 17,20-21)* [ANTJ 6.1; Frank am Main: Peter Lang, 1984]) has suggested that Jesus' prayer alludes to Daniel's prayer (Dan 2:20-23), but in a very different sense. He thinks that Jesus has intentionally overturned the idea that religious insight, including divine revelation, is reserved for the "wise," that is, for the formally trained and recognized.

like, and that Jesus' practice was unique.[29] Both of these conclusions have been challenged in recent years.[30]

"all things are possible"
The phrase echoes the kind of language that we find in Job 42:2, but not necessarily the passage itself: כל תוכל ולא־יבצר ממך מזמה = πάντα δύνασαι, ἀδυνατεῖ δέ σοι οὐδέν.

"this cup"
"Cup" means fate, i.e. Jesus' impending death. *Frag. Tg.* Gen 40:23 offers a pertinent parallel, where we find "the cup of death" (כסא דמותא). But it is not necessary to appeal to this text, for the metaphorical use of "cup" in the Old Testament conveys a similar meaning (cf. Ps 11:6; Jer 25:15; 49:12; Ezek 23:31-34).[31] See also Mark 10:38 ("Are you able to drink the cup that I drink?").

"But not what I want, but what You want"
see Ps 22:9[21:8] (σωσάτω αὐτόν, ὅτι θέλει αὐτόν = יצילהו כי חפץ בו). Elsewhere the Psalmist affirms his desire to do God's will: לעשות־רצונך אלהי חפצתי (Ps 40:9); τοῦ ποιῆσαι τὸ θέλημά σου ὁ Θεός μου ἠβουλήθην (Ps 39:8). Again, the Psalmist cries out to God: למדני לעשות רצונך כי־אתה אלוהי (Ps 143:10); δίδαξόν με τοῦ ποιεῖν τὸ θέλημά σου, ὅτι Θεός μου εἶ σύ (Ps 142:10). Parallel in rabbinic literature: עשה רצונך בשמים ("Do Your will in heaven"; *t. Ber.* 3.7; *b. Ber.* 29b). Compare also 1 Macc 3:60, which is not a prayer: ὡς δ' ἂν ἦ θέλημα ἐν οὐρανῷ, οὕτω ποιήσει ("But as the will [of God] be in heaven, so he will do [on earth]").

3. The Lord's Prayer comes down to us in two versions, probably both derived from Q, and possibly a third version in the *Didache*:

Matthew 6:9-13	*Luke 11:2-4*
Πάτερ ἡμῶν ὁ ἐν τοῖς οὐρανοῖς,	Πάτερ,
ἁγιασθήτω τὸ ὄνομά σου·	ἁγιασθήτω τὸ ὄνομά σου·
ἐλθέτω ἡ βασιλεία σου·	ἐλθέτω ἡ βασιλεία σου·
γενηθήτω τὸ θέλημά σου,	
ὡς ἐν οὐρανῷ καὶ ἐπὶ γῆς·	

---

29 Jeremias, *The Prayers of Jesus*, 57-65.
30 See G. Vermes, *Jesus the Jew: A Historian's Reading of the Gospels* (London: Collins; Philadelphia: Fortress, 1973) 210-13; R. Quere, "'Naming' God 'Father'," *CTMis* 12 (1985) 5-14; J. Barr, "Abba Isn't Daddy," *JTS* 39 (1988) 28-47; idem, "'Abba, Father' and the Familiarity of Jesus' Speech," *Th* 91 (1988) 173-79; J. H. Charlesworth, "A Caveat on Textual Transmission and the Meaning of *ABBA*: A Study of the Lord's Prayer," in Charlesworth (ed.), *The Lord's Prayer and Other Prayer Texts from the Greco-Roman Era*, 1-14.
31 See M. Black, *An Aramaic Approach to the Gospels and Acts* (3rd ed., Oxford: Clarendon, 1967) 298.

τὸν ἄρτον ἡμῶν τὸν ἐπιούσιον
 δὸς ἡμῖν σήμερον·
καὶ ἄφες ἡμῖν τὰ ὀφειλήματα ἡμῶν,
ὡς καὶ ἡμεῖς ἀφήκαμεν τοῖς
 ὀφειλέταις ἡμῶν·
καὶ μὴ εἰσενέγκῃς ἡμᾶς εἰς πειρασμόν,
ἀλλὰ ῥῦσαι ἡμᾶς ἀπὸ τοῦ πονηροῦ.[32]

τὸν ἄρτον ἡμῶν τὸν ἐπιούσιον
 δίδου ἡμῖν τὸ καθ᾽ ἡμέραν·
καὶ ἄφες ἡμῖν τὰς ἁμαρτίας ἡμῶν,
καὶ γὰρ αὐτοὶ ἀφίομεν παντὶ
 ὀφείλοντι ἡμῖν·
καὶ μὴ εἰσενέγκῃς ἡμᾶς εἰς πειρασμόν.

Our Father, who are in Heaven,	Father,
may Your Name be made holy;	may Your Name be made holy;
may Your kingdom come;	may Your kingdom come.
may Your will be done,	
as it is in Heaven, even on earth.	
Give to us today our daily bread;	Be giving to us today our daily bread;
and forgive us our debts,	and forgive us our sins,
as even we have forgiven our debtors.	for we also forgive everyone who is indebted to us.
And lead us not into temptation,	And lead us not into temptation.
but deliver us from the evil one.	

The Lord's Prayer has often been compared to Jewish liturgical prayers. To illustrate the extent of the Jewishness of the Lord's Prayer Israel Abrahams offered a composite parallel prayer, assembled from lines and phrases of other Jewish prayers (with some modifications):[33]

"Our Father, who art in Heaven.[a] Hallowed be Thine exalted Name in the world Thou didst create according to Thy will. May Thy Kingdom and Thy lordship come speedily, and be acknowledged by all the world, that Thy Name may be praised in all eternity.[b] May Thy will be done in Heaven, and also on earth give tranquility of spirit to those that fear Thee, yet in all things do what seemeth good to Thee.[c] Let us enjoy the bread daily apportioned to us.[d] Forgive

---

32 I am not persuaded that *Did.* 8:2b preserves an independent version of the Lord's Prayer, as has been argued by H. Koester, *Synoptische Überlieferung bei den Apostolischen Vätern* (TU 65; Berlin: Akademie, 1957) 203-209. Of course, if the *Didache* has preserved an independent version, then the prayer's claim to authenticity is strengthened.

33 I. Abrahams, *Studies in Pharisaism and the Gospels* (2 vols., Cambridge: Cambridge University Press, 1917-24; repr. New York: Ktav, 1967) 2.98-99. He says that he borrowed this composite prayer from an anonymous writing, entitled, *Christentum und Judentum, Parallelen*, which he thinks may have been authored by Ismar Elbogen.

us, our Father, for we have sinned;[e] forgive also all who have done us injury;[f] even as we also forgive all.[g] And lead us not into temptation, but keep us far from all evil.[h] For Thine is the greatness and the power and the dominion, the victory and the majesty, yea all in Heaven and on earth. Thine is the Kingdom, and Thou art Lord of all beings[i] for ever. Amen."

Most of the excerpted lines offer close and relevant parallels:

[a] See *Qaddish* §10: אבונא דבשמיא ("our Father in heaven"); *m. Yoma* 8:9: אביכם שבשמים ("your Father who is in heaven"); see especially *m. Sota* 9:15, which is important given its doleful context: על מי לנו להשען: על אבינו שבשמים ("Upon whom may we rely? Upon our Father who is in heaven"). See also *m. 'Abot* 5:20: לעשות רצון אביך שבשמים ("to do the will of Your Father who is in heaven"); *Frag. Tg.* Deut 32:6: הלא הוא אבוכון דבשמיא ("Is he not your Father in heaven?"). The following gives us an example of prayer: "And it came to pass, when Moses had lifted up his hands in prayer to his Father in Heaven [אבוי דבשמיא]" (*Frag. Tg.* Exod 17:11). From Qumran we have 4Q372 1:16, in which we read אבי ואלוהי ("my Father and my God").[34] Compare also Sir 23:1: Κύριε πάτερ καὶ δέσποτα ζωῆς μου. The oldest antecedents may be traced to Isa 63:16: אתה יהוה אבינו גאלנו ("You, O Lord, our Father, our Redeemer"); 64:7[E 8]: עתה יהוה אבינו אתה ("Yet, O Lord, You are our Father"). The brief prayer attributed to Rabbi Aqiba should be noted (*b. Ta'an.* 25b): אבינו מלכנו אין לנו מלך אלא אתה אבינו מלכנו למענך רחם עלינו ("Our Father, our King, we have no king but You. Our Father, our King, for Your sake have mercy upon us").

[b] See *Qaddish* §1: יתגדל ויתקדש שמיה רבא ("May His great name be glorified and sanctified"). The concern for the sanctity of God's name is ancient and scriptural; cf. Lev 22:32: ונקדשתי בתוך בני ישראל ("I will be hallowed [LXX: ἁγιασθήσομαι] among the people of Israel"); Isa 29:23; Ezek 36:23.

[b] See *Qaddish* §2: ימלוך מלכותיה בחייכון ("May He establish His kingdom in your lifetime"). Note also the saying attributed to Rabbi Yoḥanan (*b. Ber.* 40b): כל ברכה שאין בה מלכות אינה ברכה ("Every blessing in which there is no [reference to the] kingdom is not a blessing"). The prediction in *T. Mos.* 10:1 is relevant: *Et tunc parebit regnum illius in omni creatura illius. Et tunc zabulus finem habebit, et tristitiam cum eo adducetur* ("And then his kingdom will appear in his entire creation. And then the devil will come to an end, and sadness will be carried away together with him"). Although preserved in a late Latin text, the *Testament of Moses* probably was written, in Aramaic or Hebrew, some time around 30 C.E. See

---

[34] For text and discussion, see E. M. Schuller, "4Q372 1: A Text about Joseph," *RevQ* 14 (1990) 349-76; idem, "The Psalm of 4Q372 1 Within the Context of Second Temple Prayer," *CBQ* 54 (1992) 67-79.

also *Sib. Or.* 3:46-48 and 3:767, in which predictions are made of the appearance of an eternal kingdom ruled by an immortal king. Note also the *Pss. Sol.* 17:3, which dates to the first century B.C.E.: "But we hope in God our Savior . . . and the kingdom of our God [ἡ βασιλεία τοῦ θεοῦ ἡμῶν] is forever over the nations in judgment." The association of God himself with the kingdom is an important aspect of agreement between Jesus and the Isaiah Targum; cf. *Tg.* Isa 24:23; 31:4; 52:7: אתגליאת מלכותא דאלהיך ("The kingdom of your God is revealed"), which translates the Hebrew מלך אלהיך ("Your God reigns").

c   *t. Ber.* 3.7: עשה רצונך בשמים ממעל ותן נחת רוח ליריאיך בארץ והטוב בעיניך עשה ("Do Your will in Heaven above, and grant ease of spirit to those who fear You on earth, and do what seems good to you"). The statement is repeated in *b. Ber.* 29b with only the slightest variation (מתחת in place of בארץ). There are biblical precedents for this rabbinical language; cf. 1 Sam 3:18: יהוה הוא הטוב בעינו יעשה ("It is the Lord; let him do what is good in His eyes"); 1 Macc 3:60: ὡς δ' ἀν ᾖ θέλημα [τοῦ θεοῦ] ἐν οὐρανῷ, οὕτω ποιήσει [ἐπὶ γῆς] ("But as the will [of God] be in heaven, so he will do [on earth]").

d   See Prov 30:8: הטריפני לחם חקי ("feed me with the bread that is needful for me"); *Mek.* on Exod 16:4 (*Vayassaʿ* §3): מה יאכל היום ("what he eats today"); cf. *b. Beṣa* 16a, where Prov 30:8 is quoted as proof that the New Year's statute (חק) is sustenance for Israel. Jesus' petition for τὸν ἄρτον ἡμῶν τὸν ἐπιούσιον probably alludes to the daily provision of manna in the wilderness (cf. Exodus 16, esp. v. 4: "Behold, I will rain bread from heaven for you; and the people shall go out and gather a day's portion every day").

e   See *Amidah* §6: סלח לנו אבינו כי חטאנו ("Forgive us, our Father, for we have sinned"). In the context of the Lord's Prayer ὀφειλήματα ("debts") means "sins." See 11QtgJob 34:4 (= Job 40:8): ותחיבני על דברת די תזכא ("And would you make me guilty [*or* indebted] so that you would be innocent?"). For the translation of the Hebrew חטא ("sin") with the Aramaic חובא ("debt"), see *Tg.* Isa 1:18; 31:7; 53:12.

f   See *b. Meg.* 28a: כל המעביר על מדותיו מעבירין ממנו כל פשעיו ("He who passes by his measures [i.e. waives his right to retribution] is forgiven all his sins"); in the same passage we read: שרי ליה לכל מאן דצערן ("I forgive all who afflict me"). On "measure" (מדה) as retribution, see Matt 7:2 and *m. Soṭa* 1:7 ("With the measure [במדה] with which one measures, with it will be measured to him"). For more examples, see the proverbial parallels presented above.

g   See *m. Yoma* 8:9: אין יום הכפורים מכפר עד שירצה את חברו ("There is no Day of Atonement which atones, until he has appeased his friend"); and *b. Taʿan.* 16a: אם אין אתה מרחם עלינו אין אנו מרחמים על אלו ("If You will not have mercy on us, we will not have mercy upon these"). See Sir 28:2: ἄφες ἀδίκημα τῷ πλησίον σου, καὶ τότε δεηθέντος σου αἱ ἁμαρτίαι σου λυθήσονται ("Forgive your neighbor the wrong [he has done you], and then your sins will be pardoned when you pray").

h   As in the daily morning prayer; cf. *b. Ber.* 16b: הכי יהי רצון מלפניך יהוה אלהינו

‎ומשטן המשחית ‎... מיצר רע ‎רע ומפגע רע ‎מאדם ... ‎שתצילנו ... ("May it be Your will, O Lord our God . . . to deliver us . . . from an evil man, from an evil occurrence, from the evil impulse . . . and from the Accuser [or Satan] who destroys"); b. Ber. 60b: ‎לידי נסיון ‎עון ולא לידי חטא ולא לידי ‎תביאני ("and do not bring me into sin, or into iniquity, or into temptation"). See also the prayers in b. Qidd. 81b: ‎מיצר הרע ‎יצילנו ‎הרחמן ("O Merciful One, save us from the evil impulse!"); and b. Sukk. 52b. On the antiquity of the idea, see 11QPsa Plea 19:15-16.

i   See 1 Chr 29:11-13: "Thine, O Lord, is the greatness, and the power, and the glory, and the victory, and the majesty; for all that is in the heavens and in the earth is thine; thine is the kingdom, O Lord, and thou art exalted above all" (v. 11, RSV).

One of the points of dispute involving the Lord's Prayer concerns its original language. There are those who have argued that it was originally spoken in Aramaic. At last three points support this position: (1) Aramaic was Jesus' language[35]; (2) The Lord's Prayer can be translated into Aramaic[36]; and (3) the Qaddish, which is the closest parallel to the Lord's Prayer, is in Aramaic. Supporters of the Aramaic original, besides Lohmeyer, would include K. G. Kuhn and G. Schwartz.[37] Nonetheless, some, such as J. Carmignac and J. Starcky, have contended that the original prayer was uttered in Hebrew.[38]

---

35   See J. A. Fitzmyer, "Methodology in the Study of the Aramaic Substratum of Jesus' Sayings in the New Testament," in J. Dupont (ed.), *Jésus aux origines de la christologie* (BETL 40; Gembloux: Duculot, 1975) 73-102; repr. as "The Study of the Aramaic Background of the New Testament," in Fitzmyer, *A Wandering Aramean: Collected Aramaic Essays* (SBLMS 25; Missoula: Scholars Press, 1979) 1-27; idem, "The Languages of Palestine in the First Century A.D.," *CBQ* 32 (1970) 501-31; rev. and repr. in S. E. Porter (ed.), *The Language of the New Testament: Classic Essays* (JSNTSup 60; Sheffield: JSOT Press, 1991) 126-62.

36   E. Lohmeyer, *Das Vater-Unser* (Göttingen: Vandenhoeck & Ruprecht, 1947) 15; cf. J. C. De Moor, "The Reconstruction of the Aramaic Original of the Lord's Prayer," in P. Van der Meer and J. C. De Moor (eds.), *The Structural Analysis of Biblical and Canaanite Poetry* (JSOTSup 74; Sheffield: JSOT Press, 1988) 397-422.

37   K. G. Kuhn, *Achtzehngebet und Vaterunser und der Reim* (WUNT 1; Tübingen: Mohr [Siebeck], 1950) 38-41; G. Schwartz, "Matthäus VI 9–13; Lukas XI 2–4," *NTS* 15 (1968-69) 233-47. The latter's work must be used with caution.

38   J. Carmignac, *Recherches sur le "Notre Père"* (Paris: Letourzey & Ané, 1969) 32-33; idem, "Hebrew Translations of the Lord's Prayer: An Historical Survey," in G. A. Tuttle (ed.), *Biblical and Near Eastern Studies* (W. S. LaSor

The Lord's Prayer appears in Hebrew in the twelfth chapter of Shem
Tob's polemical work *Even Boḥan*:[39]

9.   אבינו יתקדש שמך:

10. ויתברך מלכותך רצונך יהיה עשוי בשמים ובארץ:

11. ותתן לחמנו תמידית:

12. ומחול לנו חטאתינו כאשר אנחנו מוחלים לחוטאים לנו:

13. ואל תביאנו לידי נסיון ושמרינו מכל רע: אמן:

9. Our Father, may Your name be sanctified.
10. And May Your kingdom be blessed; may Your will be done in
    heaven and on earth.
11. And give our bread daily.
12. And forgive us our sins as we forgive those who sin against us.
    [Luke has sin]
13. And do not lead us into the hand of temptation, but keep us from all
    evil. Amen.

Three observations may be made: (1) The opening line parallels
Luke's shorter version (Luke 11:2). (2) *Boḥan*'s חטאת parallels more
literally Luke's ἀμαρτία. (3) The Boḥan does not include the longer
ending found in Matthew's version of the Prayer. This potentially
supports the antiquity of *Boḥan*'s text.

Another item of dispute involves the original form of the Lord's
Prayer. T. W. Manson and Joachim Jeremias long ago contended that
Luke's shorter version was closer to the original length, while the
form of Matthew's wording was closer to the original language.[40]
Today this conclusion is disputed.[41] A new twist has been given to the

---

Festschrift; Grand Rapids: Eerdmans, 1978) 18-79; J. Starcky, "La Quatrième
Demande du Pater," *HTR* 64 (1971) 401-409.

39   For text, see G. Howard, *The Gospel of Matthew according to a Primitive
Hebrew Text* (Macon: Mercer University Press, 1987) 24. One might also compare
the pointed Hebrew translation in F. Delitzsch, הברית החדשה (London: United Bible
Societies, 1960) 9 (for Matt 6:9-13), 127 (for Luke 11:2-4). Shem Tob's full name
was Shem Tob ben Isaac ben Shafrut. Carmignac ("Hebrew Translations," 21-49)
provides fifty Hebrew translations of the Lord's prayer ranging from the ninth to
the eighteenth centuries, as well as many more from the nineteenth and twentieth
centuries.

40   T. W. Manson, "The Lord's Prayer," *BJRL* 38 (1955-56) 99-113;
Jeremias, *Das Vater-Unser*, 15; idem, *The Prayers of Jesus*, 89-94.

41   See J. H. Charlesworth, "A Caveat on Textual Transmission and the

debate by J. C. O'Neill, who thinks that the Matthean and Lucan traditions preserve not a single prayer, but somewhat independent assemblages of Jesus' prayers, which originally were one-sentence utterances appended to the set prayers.[42] Hence he believes that it is better to speak of the "Lord's Prayers" rather than the "Lord's Prayer." The freedom with which prayers could be supplemented, expanded, or contracted (cf. *b. Ber.* 16b–17a) supports O'Neill's hypothesis.

The Prayers and Intentions of Jesus

What do the prayers of Jesus tell us about Jesus and the intentions of his ministry? The perspectives of the two prayers from Q (Matt 11:25b-26 = Luke 10:21b; Matt 6:9b-13 = Luke 11:2b-4) appear to converge on the hope of the appearance of the kingdom. In the first prayer Jesus thanks God for having revealed "these things" to his followers, as opposed to the religious professionals. In the second prayer, the Lord's Prayer (or Prayers), Jesus prays, "Let Your kingdom come!" I suspect that the "these things" (ταῦτα) of the first prayer refer to the signs of the coming kingdom, one of the central requests of the second prayer. I believe this for three reasons. First, no other alternative commends itself. From Jesus' perspective, what could have been hidden from the wise and revealed to the innocent, except the arrival of the kingdom or, at least, the presence of the one who possesses the authority to announce the presence of the kingdom?

Second, the first Q prayer, as indicated in the notes above, may allude to Dan 2:21-23, in which Daniel thanks God for having disclosed the meaning of the king's dream to him. What is significant is that the dream concerns the approach of the kingdom of God, as Daniel explains to Nebuchadnezzar: "And in the days of those kings the God of heaven will set up a kingdom which shall never be destroyed, nor shall its soverignty be left to another people. It shall break in pieces all these kingdoms and bring them to an end, and it shall stand forever" (Dan 2:44). If Jesus' prayer does indeed allude to Daniel's prayer, and the verbal similarities suggest that it does, then it is likely that what Jesus understood to be revealed to him and to his followers was the

---

Meaning of *Abba*: A Study of the Lord's Prayer," in Charlesworth, with Harding and Kiley (eds.), *The Lord's Prayer and Other Prayer Texts*, 1-14.

[42]   J. C. O'Neill, "The Lord's Prayer," *JSNT* 51 (1993) 3-25.

same thing that Daniel had had revealed to him.

Third, the context of Q itself is very suggestive. If, as is widely supposed, Luke has retained the order of Q,[43] then we may have some indication of what "these things" mean and how the first Q prayer relates to the second. This, of course, assumes that the order of this material in Q in some way reflects material related in the *Sitz im Leben Jesu* and not simply later collected by early Christian tradents. As a working hypothesis I shall approach the Q material of Luke 10–11 as though originally related by Jesus and not simply by the Church.

Luke 10:18-20 may have been drawn from Q.[44] If it was, then this may be the beginning point of the material that leads up to and includes the two Q prayers. In Luke 10:18-20 Jesus describes a vision in which he has seen Satan fall from heaven. This probably is meant to signify the collapse of the kingdom of darkness, as it gives way before the advance of the kingdom of God.[45] This then leads to the first prayer, in which Jesus says, "I thank You, Father, Lord of heaven and earth, because you have hidden these things [i.e. indications of the inbreaking of God's kingdom] from the wise and discerning . . ." (Luke 10:21). In the next unit of Q material Jesus explains to his disciples that their eyes are blessed for what they have seen, "for many prophets and kings desired to see what you are seeing and did not see it, and to hear what you are hearing, and did not hear it" (Luke 10:23-24). "What" (ἅ) it is that they are seeing and hearing is surely the inbreaking of the kingdom. Next follows the second Q prayer, the Lord's Prayer (introduced in 11:1 by the Lucan evangelist), in which Jesus petitions God: "May Your name be holy; may Your kingdom [or reign] come" (Luke 11:1). The prayer is followed by an insertion, that may not derive from Q (Luke 11:5-13). Then comes the controversy over casting out demons. Jesus is accused of casting out demons by the

---

43 For a recent discussion of this question, in which it is concluded that Luke preserves the original order of Q, see J. S. Kloppenborg, *The Formation of Q* (SAC; Philadelphia: Fortress, 1987) 64-80.

44 Scholars are about evenly divided on this question; for summary, see J. S. Kloppenborg, *Q Parallels* (Sonoma: Polebridge, 1988) 76.

45 The saying probably alludes to Isa 14:12-20, in which an arrogant king or deity is told, "How you have fallen from heaven . . . You said in your heart, 'I will ascend to heaven; above the stars of God I will set my throne on high . . .' But you are brought down to Sheol . . ." By alluding to this passage, Jesus implies that Satan's kingdom has been defeated.

authority of Beelzebul (Luke 11:14-19). The reference to Beelzebul recalls the earlier vision of his fall from heaven. To this charge Jesus replies: "If it is by the finger of God that I cast out demons, then the kingdom of God has come upon you" (Luke 11:20). Following the discussion of matters pertaining to exorcism, we have a woman cry out from the crowd: "Blessed is the womb that bore you, and the breasts that you sucked!" (Luke 11:27). This beatitude, which was probably proverbial in Jesus' time (cf. *Tg. Neof.* Gen 49:25; *'Abot* 2:8; *2 Bar.* 54:10), probably had an eschatological import, as perhaps is illustrated by a similar beatitude found in some MSS of *Pesiqta de Rab Kahana* 22: "Blessed is the womb from which he (i.e. the Messiah) came forth."

Whether or not this material originally belonged together or was later compiled by Christian tradents, the coherence of it strongly suggests that these units, even if scattered over time and place in Jesus' ministry, do form an ideological unity. The significance of this conclusion lies in seeing the prayers of Jesus as concerned with the kingdom of God.[46] The first prayer thanks God for revealing the presence or inbreaking of the kingdom to the followers of Jesus; the second calls for the coming of the kingdom and petitions God for help in preparing for it. It may be concluded then that Jesus' prayers reflect his concern for the appearance of the kingdom and so are consistent with his parables, which often address issues relating to the kingdom.

---

[46] For a defense of the eschatological import of the Lord's Prayer, see R. E. Brown, "The Pater Noster as an Eschatological Prayer," *TS* 22 (1961) 175-208; repr. in Brown, *New Testament Essays* (Garden City: Doubleday, 1967) 217-53; J. Jeremias, *New Testament Theology* (New York: Scribner's, 1971) 193-203; D. C. Allison and W. D. Davies, *The Gospel According to Saint Matthew* (ICC; 2 vols., Edinburgh: T. & T. Clark, 1988-91) 1.593-94.

PART TWO

JESUS AND HIS OPPONENTS

CHAPTER SEVEN

FROM PUBLIC MINISTRY TO THE PASSION:
CAN A LINK BE FOUND BETWEEN THE (GALILEAN) LIFE AND THE (JUDEAN) DEATH OF JESUS?

The death of Jesus is problematic. How is the historian to account for the crucifixion of an itinerant teacher and miracle worker? To answer this question two important problems must be addressed: (1) how to account for Jesus' execution in Judea at the hands of the Romans and (2) determining what relationship, if any, that execution had to Jesus' earlier Galilean ministry. In his recent and controversial book, *A Myth of Innocence: Mark and Christian Origins*, Burton L. Mack argues that the factors that led to Jesus' execution are unclear[1] and that the Marcan evangelist's linkage of Jesus' public teachings to the story of his death is a narrative fiction.[2] Impressed by Mack's analysis, David Seeley asserts that "Mark concocted the Jewish conspiracy against Jesus for his own, redactional reasons," adding that "the death itself was probably just a mistake."[3]

On the face of it, logic alone suggests the strong probability of a relationship between (a) the execution of a man as "king of the Jews" and (b) well attested traditions that this popular man had been saying things about a kingdom. That Mark's theological interests played an important role in telling the story of Jesus' death cannot, of course, be denied. But have the evangelist's contributions so completely obscured the chain of events that we cannot say with probability what led to Jesus' death? Is the "Jewish conspiracy against Jesus" nothing more than a Marcan concoction? Was the death of Jesus nothing more than a mistake?

---

[1]   B. L. Mack, *A Myth of Innocence: Mark and Christian Origins* (Philadelphia: Fortress, 1988) 88-89.

[2]   Mack, *Myth of Innocence*, 282.

[3]   D. Seeley, "Was Jesus like a Philosopher? The Evidence of Martyrological and Wisdom Motifs in Q, Pre-Pauline Traditions, and Mark," in D. J. Lull (ed.) *Society of Biblical Literature 1989 Seminar Papers* (SBLSP 28; Atlanta: Scholars Press, 1989) 540-49, here p. 548. When Seeley says "mistake," he means that Pilate mistook Jesus' intentions. See comments in chap. 1 above.

Although I suspect that not too many scholars who engage in Jesus research will be unduly troubled by the views of Mack and Seeley, the problem that they have identified is one that has historically proven nettlesome. The diversity of conclusions bears this out. There are those who have argued that the Jews were principally responsible for Jesus' execution,[4] though advocates of this view are scarce these days. There are those who have argued that the Romans were principally responsible.[5] Some have even argued that the Romans alone were responsible.[6] This diversity notwithstanding, something of a consensus has emerged in which most scholars agree that Jesus was executed by the Roman authorities, in collaboration with a few Jewish persons of influence.[7]

One encounters greater diversity of opinion with regard to the question of what charge was brought against Jesus. It has been argued that Jesus and his followers attempted to overthrow the government in Jerusalem and assume command of the Temple Mount. The coup failed and Jesus was executed.[8] Another study concludes that Jesus provoked

---

4   J. Blinzler, *Der Prozess Jesu: Das jüdische und das römische Gerichts-verfahren gegen Jesus Christus auf Grund der ältesten Zeugnisse dargestellt und beurteilt* (Bibelwissenschaftliche Reihe 4; Stuttgart: Katholisches Bibelwerk, 1951; 4th ed., Regensburg: Pustet, 1969); ET: *The Trial of Jesus* (Westminster: Newman, 1959).

5   S. Zeitlin, *Who Crucified Jesus?* (New York: Harper & Row, 1942); J. D. M. Derrett, *An Oriental Lawyer Looks at the Trial of Jesus and the Doctrine of Redemption* (London: School of Oriental and African Studies, 1966); P. Lapide, *Wer war schuld an Jesu Tod?* (Gütersloh: Mohn, 1987).

6   H. Lietzmann, "Der Prozess Jesu," *Sitzungsberichte der Preussischen Akademie der Wissenschaften in Berlin* 14 (1931) 313-22; P. Winter, *On the Trial of Jesus* (Studia Judaica: Forschungen zur Wissenschaft des Judentums 1; Berlin: de Gruyter, 1961; 2nd ed., rev. and ed. by T. A. Burkill and G. Vermes); H. Cohn, *Reflections on the Trial and Death of Jesus* (Jerusalem: Israel Law Review Association, 1967); idem, *The Trial and Death of Jesus* (New York: Harper & Row, 1971).

7   E. Lohse, *Geschichte des Leidens und Sterbens Jesu Christi* (Gütersloh: Mohn, 1964); W. Koch, *Der Prozess Jesu: Versuch eines Tatsachenberichtes* (Berlin and Köln: Kiepenheuer and Witsch, 1969); O. Betz, "Probleme des Prozesses Jesu," *ANRW* 2.25.1 (1982) 565-647; H. Ritt, "'Wer war schuld am Tod Jesu?' Zeitgeschichte, Recht und theologische Deutung," *BZ* 31 (1987) 165-75; R. A. Horsley, *Jesus and the Spiral of Violence: Popular Jewish Resistance in Roman Palestine* (San Francisco: Harper & Row, 1987).

8   S. G. F. Brandon, *Jesus and the Zealots: A Study of the Political Factor in*

deadly opposition because of his charismatic ministry, as Elijah had in his time.[9] Still another contends that Jesus was condemned as a "rebellious elder," for refusing to answer the questions of the ruling priests.[10] One scholar thinks that Jesus was formally charged as a deceiver of the people.[11] Another thinks Jesus' radical views of finding a place for Gentiles in Israel's faith was enough to get him killed.[12] E. P. Sanders has concluded that it was his specific threat to destroy and replace the Temple that provoked the authorities to eliminate Jesus.[13] Faulting this conclusion, Bruce Chilton suspects that Jesus' arrest and execution were the result of a controversial teaching regarding what constituted appropriate sacrifice.[14] I have argued that Jesus was seized for having condemned high-priestly polity and having predicted the destruction of the Temple.[15]

Leaving aside the specific question of what precise charge, if any, Jewish authorities may have brought against Jesus, the present chapter will show that there is considerable evidence of linkage between Jesus' public activities and his crucifixion at the hands of the Romans. This significant evidence, minimized or ignored by Mack and Seeley, primarily consists of two elements: (1) Jesus' proclamation of the Kingdom of God and his subsequent crucifixion as "King of the Jews"; and (2) the appearance of similar, yet independent, linkages in the fourth Gospel and in the Testimonium Flavianum.

Primitive Christianity (Manchester: Manchester University Press; New York: Scribner's, 1967). Similar views had earlier been articulated by Joseph Klausner and Robert Eisler.

9 G. Vermes, *Jesus the Jew* (London: Collins, 1973).

10 J. Bowker, *Jesus and the Pharisees* (New York: Cambridge University Press, 1973).

11 D. Hill, "Jesus before the Sanhedrin—On What Charge?" *IBS* 7 (1985) 174-86.

12 H. Falk, *Jesus the Pharisee: A New Look at the Jewishness of Jesus* (New York: Paulist, 1985).

13 E. P. Sanders, *Jesus and Judaism* (London: SCM; Philadelphia: Fortress, 1985)

14 B. D. Chilton, *The Temple of Jesus: His Sacrificial Program Within a Cultural History of Sacrifice* (University Park: Penn State University Press, 1992).

15 C. A. Evans, "Jesus and the 'Cave of Robbers': Towards a Jewish Context for the Temple Action," *BBR* 3 (1993) 93-110 [revised as chap. 9 below]; idem, "Jesus' Action in the Temple: Cleansing or Portent of Destruction?" *CBQ* 51 (1989) 237-70. See also chap. 11 below.

The evidence suggests that the Marcan narrative, which admittedly has been edited and arranged to promote distinctive features of Marcan theology, provides a plausible link between Jesus' Galilean activities and his subsequent execution in Jerusalem. In short, Jesus made statements about the Kingdom of God and came to be understood as the Anointed King of this Kingdom. When this teaching was promoted in Jerusalem, during the Passover Feast, Jewish and Roman authorities seized Jesus and put him to death. Jesus' death was not simply a misadventure (and so unrelated to his public activities in Galilee), nor did the Marcan evangelist concoct a Jewish conspiracy. The seizure and execution of Jesus constituted, rather, an inevitable result of and reaction to his proclamation and activities.

JESUS' PROCLAMATION OF THE KINGDOM OF GOD

Proclamation

A suggestive indication of linkage between Jesus' Galilean ministry and his Judean death is his proclamation of the Kingdom of God. This proclamation manifests itself in four areas: (1) parables, (2) prayers and promises, (3) miracles, and (4) politics.

1. Parables and the Kingdom. The most promising place to begin is the kingdom theme in the parables. In the parables, the "bedrock" of the dominical tradition,[16] we hear over and over again the opening words of comparison: "The Kingdom of God is like . . ." Several kingdom parables are widely recognized as authentic sayings of Jesus. From Q we have the Parable of the Leaven: "To what shall I compare the kingdom of God? It is like leaven which a woman took and hid in three measures, till it was all leavened" (Luke 13:20-21 = Matt 13:33; cf. *GThom.* §96).[17] Other promising examples include the Parable of

---

16   One recalls J. Jeremias' famous dictum (*The Parables of Jesus* [rev. ed., New York: Scribner's, 1963] 11): "The Parables are a fragment of the original rock of tradition." Recent studies have confirmed this positive assessment; cf. J. D. Crossan, *In Parables: The Challenge of the Historical Jesus* (San Francisco: Harper & Row, 1973); P. B. Payne, "The Authenticity of the Parables of Jesus," in R. T. France and D. Wenham (eds.), *Studies of History and Tradition in the Four Gospels* (Gospel Perspectives 2; Sheffield: JSOT, 1980) 329-44; B. B. Scott, "Essaying the Rock: The Authenticity of the Jesus Parable Tradition," *Forum* 2.3 (1986) 3-53.

17   Crossan, *In Parables*, 38; idem, *The Historical Jesus: The Life of a Mediterranean Jewish Peasant* (San Francisco: HarperSanFrancisco, 1992) 280-81; D. C. Allison and W. D. Davies, *The Gospel According to Saint Matthew* (2 vols.,

the Treasure (Matt 13:44; cf. GThom. §109),[18] the Parable of the Pearl (Matt 13:45-46; cf. GThom. §76),[19] and the Parable of the Mustard Seed (Mark 4:30-32; cf. Luke 13:18-19; GThom. §20).[20] Crossan rightly concludes: "If, therefore, one precise form of the 'Kingdom' phrase goes back to Jesus, it is most likely 'Kingdom of God.'"[21]

ICC; Edinburgh: T. & T. Clark, 1988-91) 2.421. According to the "Red Letter" edition of the parables, the Jesus Seminar gives Matthew's version of the parable a "red" rating and *Thomas'* version a "pink" rating; cf. R. W. Funk et al., *The Parables of Jesus: Red Letter Edition* (Sonoma: Polebridge, 1988) 29; idem and R. W. Hoover (eds.), *The Five Gospels* (New York: Macmillan, 1993) 195, 523.

[18] Crossan, *In Parables*, 34, 54-55, 83; idem, *Historical Jesus*, 281-82; B. B. Scott, *Hear Then the Parable: A Commentary on the Parables of Jesus* (Minneapolis: Fortress, 1989) 395; Allison and Davies, *Matthew*, 2.435. The Jesus Seminar gives "pink" ratings to Matthew and to *Thomas*; cf. Funk et al., *Parables*, 37; idem and Hoover (eds.), *The Five Gospels*, 196, 529.

[19] Crossan, *In Parables*, 34; idem, *Historical Jesus*, 281; Allison and Davies, *Matthew*, 2.437. The Jesus Seminar gives "pink" ratings to Matthew and to *Thomas*; cf. Funk et al., *Parables*, 46; idem and Hoover (eds.), *The Five Gospels*, 196, 515.

[20] Crossan, *In Parables*, 45-51; idem, *Historical Jesus*, 276-79; Scott, *Hear Then the Parable*, 386; R. A. Guelich, *Mark 1-8:26* (WBC 34A; Dallas: Word, 1989) 247. According to the "Red Letter" edition of Mark, the Jesus Seminar gives Mark's version of the parable a "pink" rating and *Thomas'* version a "red" rating; cf. R. W. Funk, *The Gospel of Mark: Red Letter Edition* (with M. H. Smith; Sonoma: Polebridge, 1991) 101; idem and Hoover (eds.), *The Five Gospels*, 59, 484. Most scholars think that the Lucan version of the parable (cf. 13:18-19) is derived from Q, not from Mark; cf. J. S. Kloppenborg, *Q Parallels* (Sonoma: Polebridge, 1988) 148-50; R. H. Gundry, *Mark: A Commentary on His Apology for the Cross* (Grand Rapids: Eerdmans, 1993) 226.

[21] Crossan, *In Parables*, 38; idem, *Historical Jesus*, 284. The phrase, "kingdom of God," is very rare in pre-Christian sources. Outside of the LXX (cf. Wis 10:10 [βασιλεία θεοῦ] and *Pss. Sol.* 17:4 [ἡ βασιλεία τοῦ θεοῦ ἡμῶν]), the phrase does not occur in the Old Testament. No clear example of the phrase has yet been found among the Dead Sea Scrolls, which could be significant, given the frequency of the word "kingdom," especially in the texts found in cave 4. At least two examples have been proposed. 1QSb 3:5 breaks off after מלכות. Some suppose that the line read "kingdom of God (or heaven)," but that is far from certain. R. H. Eisenman and M. Wise (*The Dead Sea Scrolls Uncovered* [Rockport: Element, 1992] 174) restore 4Q525 5:3 to read מלכ[ות אלהים] ("[the kingd]om of God"), but the restoration is risky (see plate 12). Although the expression was not coined by Jesus, its frequent appearance in the dominical tradition suggests that it was a

2. Prayers and Promises of the Kingdom. There is also well attested
tradition in which Jesus prays for and promises to his disciples the
kingdom of God. Q contains several relevant items. There is the
promise that is associated with the Sermon on the Mount and is
presented as part of a beatitude: The marginalized of Jewish society are
told, "Yours is the Kingdom of God" (Luke 6:20 = Matt 5:3; cf.
GThom. §54).[22] Crossan's interpretation of "poor" has implications
for kingdom and politics, which will be considered below. In what is
probably a related saying, Jesus tells his followers to "Seek His
Kingdom" (Luke 12:31 = Matt 6:33) and then expect God to provide
for their needs.[23] In the Lord's Prayer, parts of which probably do
derive from Jesus, Jesus tells his disciples to pray, "Thy Kingdom
come!" (Luke 11:2 = Matt 6:10; cf. *Did.* 8:2).[24] This prayer accurately

---

distinctive feature in his diction; cf. B. F. Meyer, *The Aims of Jesus* (London:
SCM, 1979) 129. B. D. Chilton (*The Glory of Israel: The Theology and Provenience of the Isaiah Targum* [JSOTSup 23; Sheffield: JSOT Press, 1982] 77-81; *A
Galilean Rabbi and His Bible: Jesus' Use of the Interpreted Scripture of His Time*
[GNS 8; Wilmington: Glazier, 1984] 58-63) has argued that Jesus' use of this
expression probably indicates acquaintance with targumic diction, in which this
relatively rare expression (מלכותא דאלהא) also occurs (e.g. *Tg.* Isa 24:23; 31:4;
40:9; 52:7; *Tg.* Obad 21b; *Tg.* Mic 4:7-8; *Tg.* Zech 14:9). Crossan's conclusion,
cited above, is corroborated by Chilton's targumic research: "'The kingdom of
God' was the fundamental element in Jesus' preaching" (Chilton, *The Isaiah
Targum* [ArBib 11; Wilmington: Glazier, 1987] xxvii).

   22   Crossan, *Historical Jesus*, 270-74; Allison and Davies, *Matthew*, 1.436-39.
J. A. Fitzmyer (*The Gospel According to Luke I-IX* [AB 28; Garden City:
Doubleday, 1981] 632) concludes that Matthew's third-person form of the beatitude
is closer to the original. R. H. Gundry (*Matthew: A Commentary on His Literary
and Theological Art* [Grand Rapids: Eerdmans, 1982] 67-68) thinks that Luke's
second-person form is original. The Jesus Seminar agrees, assigning a "red" rating
to Luke 6:20 and a "pink" rating to Matt 5:3; cf. Funk and Hoover (eds.), *The Five
Gospels*, 138, 289.

   23   Cf. Meyer, *The Aims of Jesus*, 167. The authenticity of much of Matt 6:25-
33 is to some extent corroborated by 1 Cor 9:14 ("the Lord commanded that those
who proclaim the gospel should get their living by the gospel"); cf. J. Jeremias,
New Testament Theology: The Proclamation of Jesus (New York: Scribner's,
1971) 236; Sanders, *Jesus and Judaism*, 105; Allison and Davies, *Matthew*, 1.660.
Allison and Davies note that the phrase, "to seek the kingdom," has no precise
Jewish parallel. The Jesus Seminar assigns a "black" rating to this saying; cf. Funk
and Hoover (eds.), *The Five Gospels*, 152, 340.

   24   J. A. Fitzmyer, *The Gospel According to Luke X-XXIV* (AB 28A; Garden
City: Doubleday, 1985) 898-901; Allison and Davies, *Matthew*, 1.592-93, 604.

reflects "Jesus' invocation of the kingdom of God," to quote Crossan in another context, "not as an apocalyptic event in the imminent future but as a mode of life in the immediate present."[25] Again, there are political implications which will have to be taken into account. Finally, Jesus' beatitude that "many prophets and kings desired to see what you see" (Luke 10:23b-24 = Matt 13:16-17) implies the presence of the kingdom.[26]

3. Miracles and the Kingdom. There are indications that Jesus' exorcisms and healing miracles related in various ways to his ideas of the kingdom of God. "But if it is by the finger of God that I cast out demons, then the Kingdom of God has come upon you" (Luke 11:20 = Matt 12:28). If this saying goes back to Jesus, and its oddity counts against its invention by the early church,[27] and if we understand it, Jesus apparently understood his power as an exorcist as evidence of the presence and power of the kingdom. Two paragraphs later, in what probably was material grouped together in Q,[28] Jesus asserts that "Something greater than Solomon is here" (Luke 11:31 = Matt 12:42). If this saying goes back to Jesus,[29] it may have been related to Jesus'

Crossan (*Historical Jesus*, 293-95) does not think that the prayer, in either Matthean or Lucan form, goes back to Jesus, though it does reflect his views. The Jesus Seminar assigns a red rating to the address, "Our Father," and a "pink" rating to the petition itself; cf. Funk and Hoover (eds.), *The Five Gospels*, 148, 325.

[25]   Crossan, *Historical Jesus*, 304.

[26]   As is rightly argued by J. D. G. Dunn, "Matthew 12:28/Luke 11:20—A Word of Jesus?" in W. H. Gloer (ed.), *Eschatology and the New Testament* (Peabody: Hendrickson, 1988) 29-49, esp. 45. Dunn's interpretation is to be preferred over Sanders (*Jesus and Judaism*, 148-49) who argues that the disciples are blessed for having witnessed the appearance of one (i.e. Jesus) who announces the coming of the kingdom. The Seminar assigns a "gray" rating to the saying; cf. Funk and Hoover (eds.), *The Five Gospels*, 192, 322.

[27]   R. Bultmann, *History of the Synoptic Tradition* (Oxford: Blackwell, 1972) 162; N. Perrin, *Rediscovering the Teaching of Jesus* (New York: Harper & Row, 1976) 65: "The saying clearly implies a *Sitz im Leben Jesu*." Allison and Davies (*Matthew*, 2.339) also accept the authenticity of the saying. See also Meyer, *Aims of Jesus*, 154-58; Dunn, "Matthew 12:28/Luke 11:20," 29-49. The Jesus Seminar assigns "pink" ratings to the Matthean and Lucan forms of the saying; cf. Funk and Hoover (eds.), *The Five Gospels*, 185, 329.

[28]   J. S. Kloppenborg, *The Formation of Q: Trajectories in Ancient Wisdom Collections* (SAC; Philadelphia: Fortress, 1987) 121-34.

[29]   Perrin (*Rediscovering the Teaching of Jesus*, 195) and Allison and Davies (Allison and Davies, *Matthew*, 2.357) lean toward authentitiy. The Jesus Seminar,

exorcisms. (The Matthean evangelist clearly believes that there is a connection; cf. Matt 12:22-45.)[30] According to Josephus, it was in the name of Solomon that a certain Eleazar was able to exorcize demons (*Ant.* 8.2.5 §46-49).[31] Accordingly, in healing the demonized, Jesus may have been understood as a Solomon-like figure and, as such, as a "son of David."[32] In one healing miracle, Jesus is actually addressed as "son of David" (Mark 10:47-48).[33] If Jesus were in fact addressed in

---

because the saying is associated with the sign of Jonah, assigned it a "black" rating; cf. Funk and Hoover (eds.), *The Five Gospels*, 188, 332. The saying, "Something greater than Solomon is here," may originally have been independent. In any case, it is an odd christological formulation, if it originated in the early Church. In my judgment it derives from Jesus.

30   The charges and countercharges in Matt 12:22-45 revolve around Jesus' exorcisms. Matthean contextualization of course does not prove that the saying about one "greater than Solomon" originally belonged in a context of controversy over exorcisms, but given the coherence and symmetry of the bitter exchanges (which are examples of "deviance labeling" common to first-century Palestine; cf. B. J. Malina and R. L. Rohrbaugh, *Social-Science Commentary on the Synoptic Gospels* [Minneapolis: Fortress, 1992] 97-99) it does provide a plausible setting.

31   Origen (*Comm. Matt.* 33 [on Matt 26:63]) refers to those who attempted exorcisms according to spells composed by Solomon. The pseudepigraphal *Testament of Solomon*, probably written by a Greek-speaking Christian in the second or third century, is wholly dedicated to this theme. Solomon as master exorcist probably arose as part of the legend of his extensive knowledge of plants and proverbs (1 Kgs 4:29-34; Wis 7:17-21).

32   Note the reading in *T. Sol.* 20:1: "King Solomon, son of David, have mercy on me." On "son of David" as miracle worker, see K. Berger, "Die königlichen Messiastraditionen des Neuen Testaments," *NTS* 20 (1973-74) 1-44, esp. 3-9; E. Lövestam, "Jesus Fils de David chez les Synoptiques," *ST* 28 (1974) 97-109, esp. 100-107; B. D. Chilton, "Jesus *ben David*: Reflections on the *Davidssohnfrage*," *JSNT* 14 (1982) 88-112, esp. 92-96. For criticisms, see Gundry, *Mark*, 600.

33   The Jesus Seminar has given a "black" rating to the conversation between Jesus and blind Bartimaeus; cf. Funk, *Mark*, 169-70. Even if the conversation should be viewed as the creation of the early Church, the episode itself, including the blind man's cry, "Son of David," may well be authentic; cf. Jeremias, *New Testament Theology*, 90. Fitzmyer (*Luke X-XXIV*, 1213) questions the assumption that Mark 10:46-52 is a "community creation." Several scholars have concluded that a core of authentic tradition lies behind the narrative; cf. J. Schmid, *Das Evangelium nach Markus* (RNT 2; Regensburg: Pustet, 1958) 203; C. F. D. Moule, *The Gospel According to Mark* (Cambridge: Cambridge University, 1965) 85; V. Taylor, *The Gospel According to St. Mark* (2nd ed., London: Macmillan,

this manner, messianic connotations are very probable.[34] Jesus'
statement that the "kingdom of God is in your midst" (Luke 17:20-21;
cf. POxy654 §3; *GThom.* §3, §113)[35] could be related to his
exorcisms.

4. Politics and the Kingdom. There are political and social aspects to
Jesus' sayings and actions that relate to his proclamation of the
kingdom. The comparison that Jesus makes between himself and David
in Mark 2:23-26 may be authentic, especially if it is viewed as
originally separate from 2:27-28.[36] Jesus' question ("Have you never
read what David did?") and answer (cf. 1 Sam 21:2-7) probably

---

1966) 446-49; C. E. B. Cranfield, *The Gospel According to Saint Mark* (Cam-
bridge: Cambridge University Press, 1977) 344-45; E. S. Johnson, "Mark 10:46-
52: Blind Bartimaeus," *CBQ* 40 (1978) 191-204; R. Pesch, *Das Markusevangelium*
(HTKNT 2.1-2; Freiburg: Herder, 1989-91) 2.169-71; W. Kirchschläger,
"Bartimäus – Paradigma einer Wundererzählung (Mk 10,46-52 par)," in F. Van
Segbroeck et al. (eds.), *The Four Gospels 1992* (F. Neirynck Festschrift; 3 vols.,
BETL 100; Leuven: Peeters, 1992) 2.1105-23; Gundry, *Mark*, 596-603.

[34]   O. Betz, "Die Frage nach dem messianischen Bewußtsein Jesu," *NovT* 6
(1963) 20-48, esp. 41.

[35]   The Jesus Seminar has given "pink" ratings to Luke 17:20-21 and *GThom.*
§113, but "gray" ratings to the parallels in POxy654 §3 and *GThom.* §3; cf. Funk,
Mark, 200-201; idem and Hoover (eds.), *The Five Gospels*, 364, 472, 531. See
also Crossan, *Historical Jesus*, 282-83.

[36]   Bultmann, *History of the Synoptic Tradition*, 16; J. Gnilka, *Das
Evangelium nach Markus* (EKKNT 2.1-2; Zurich: Benziger, 1978) 119-20; R.
Pesch, *Das Markusevangelium*, 1.179-80; Gundry, *Mark*, 148-49. Though in the
final calculation it rated Mark 2:25-26 "black," the Jesus Seminar was sharply
divided, with six scholars rating the passage "red" and 25 rating it "pink" (as
opposed to the 69 who rated it either "gray" or "black"); cf. Funk, *Mark*, 76-77.
Evidently members of the Seminar felt that the point of the passage focused on
Jesus' disciples and so reflected early community concerns. But is it really probable
that early Christians were challenged by Pharisees for picking grain on the sabbath
and so found it necessary, by way of reply, to create a dominical saying? cf. E.
Haenchen, *Der Weg Jesu* (Berlin: de Gruyter, 1968) 122. It is more likely that the
episode derives from the *Sitz im Leben Jesu*. The allusion to the passage from 1
Samuel, especially the problematic reference to Abiathar (which is locative, not
temporal; cf. Gundry, *Mark*, 141-42), is not typical of Christian usage of the Old
Testament, which normally involves formal quotation. Jesus' challenge, "Have you
never read what David did?" (2:25), seems to be characteristic, even distinctive, of
his use of Scripture; cf. J. A. T. Robinson, "Did Jesus Have a Distinctive Use of
Scripture?" in R. F. Berkey and S. A. Edwards (eds.), *Christological Perspectives*
(H. K. McArthur Festschrift; New York: Pilgrim, 1982) 49-57, esp. 53-57.

implied that he was acting in the role of the awaited Davidide.[37] The Triumphal Entry (Mark 11:1-10), if a core of genuine history does indeed lie behind this narrative, would probably have been understood in a royal sense. One is reminded of Solomon, mounted on a donkey, anointed, and proclaimed king (1 Kgs 1:32-40). Mules were ridden by Mephibosheth (2 Sam 18:9) and Absalom (2 Sam 19:26) in unsuccessful bids to gain the throne. When Jehu was anointed and proclaimed king, garments were placed on the steps before him (2 Kgs 9:12-13). One thinks also of the singing crowds and the waving of palm branches that greeted Simon as he entered Jerusalem (1 Macc 13:51). The kingly dimension becomes overt in the crowd's shout: "Blessed be the kingdom of our father David" (Mark 11:10).[38] The anointing of Jesus (Mark 14:3-9), which in the light of the subsequent Passion came to be related to Jesus' death and burial, originally could very well have been a messianic anointing.[39]

Although precisely what the original point was is debated, the question about scribal messianic ideas ("How do the scribes say that the Messiah is the son of David?" [Mark 12:35-37]), if authentic,[40] may provide additional evidence that Jesus publicly discussed messianic and, by implication, kingly ideas. The fruit of the vine saying ("I shall not drink again of the fruit of the vine until that day when I drink it new in the Kingdom of God" [Mark 14:25])[41] clearly implies that Jesus

---

[37] Betz, "Die Frage nach dem messianischen Bewußtsein Jesu," 41-43.

[38] For arguments in favor of the authenticity of Mark 11:9-10, see Gundry, *Mark*, 631-34. Gundry comments: "The non-quotation of Zech 9:9 in Mark 11:9-10 supports the historicity of the Triumphal Procession, for derivation of the story from Zech 9:9 would probably have left quoted phrases, perhaps quoted statements as well. But we find none" (p. 632).

[39] The word χρίειν (for משׁח) does not appear. In transforming the story into a passion vignette, the deletion of such an overt (and from the Roman point of view treasonable) messianic act should not occasion surprise. That the anointing was originally messianic, see J. K. Elliott, "The Anointing of Jesus," *ExpTim* 85 (1974) 105-107; E. E. Platt, "The Ministry of Mary of Bethany," *TToday* 34 (1977) 29-39. However, Pesch (*Markusevangelium*, 2.332) disagrees.

[40] The Jesus Seminar has given a "black" rating to the saying; cf. Funk, *Mark*, 187-88; idem and Hoover (eds.), *The Five Gospels*, 105. For arguments in favor of the authenticity of Mark 12:35-37, see Gundry, *Mark*, 720-24. Gundry does not think that in this utterance Jesus intended to deny his Davidic descent.

[41] The Jesus Seminar has given a "gray" rating to the saying; cf. Funk, *Mark*, 212; idem and Hoover (eds.), *The Five Gospels*, 117.

expected the appearance of the kingdom. Consistent with this saying is Jesus' promise to his disciples that they "will sit on twelve thrones, judging the twelve tribes of Israel" (Luke 22:30 = Matt 19:28).[42] It is probable that the request of James and John ("Grant us to sit, one at your right hand and one at your left, in your glory" [Mark 10:37]) is closely related to this promise.[43] Jesus' admission that he does not possess the authority to grant such a petition surely argues for authenticity.[44]

Besides the possible identification of Jesus with David, there are indications that Jesus anticipated (and promoted) significant social as well as political changes. Statements such as "Blessed are you poor" (Luke 6:20), "Woe to you who are rich" (Luke 6:24), and "How hard it will be for those who have riches to enter the kingdom of God" (Mark 10:23-27; cf. *Herm. Sim.* 9.20.2b-3; *GNaz.* §16) very probably derive from Jesus and reflect his criticism of a wealthy and oppressive

---

[42]   A saying about the Twelve sitting on thrones would not in all probability be invented by the early Church, given the defection of Judas; cf. Meyer, *Aims of Jesus*, 154; Sanders, *Jesus and Judaism*, 98-106. The Jesus Seminar assigns a black rating to the saying; cf. Funk and Hoover (eds.), *The Five Gospels*, 222-23, 389. The grounds for their rejection of the saying lies in their skepticism toward much of the eschatological tradition, a skepticism which is largely based on a serious misconception of eschatology and how it relates to the Jesus' concept of the kingdom of God; cf. B. D. Chilton, "The Kingdom of God in Recent Discussion," in Chilton and C. A. Evans (eds.) *Studying the Historical Jesus: Evaluations of the State of Current Research* (NTTS 19; Leiden: Brill, 1994) 255-80, esp. 268-70. The nature and extent of the Seminar's confusion are clearly exhibited by the report of J. R. Butts, "Probing the Poll: Jesus Seminar Results on the Kingdom Sayings," *Forum* 3 (1987) 98-128.

[43]   Gundry, *Mark*, 583: "The request of James and John seems to rest on Jesus' promise that the Twelve 'will sit on thrones judging the Twelve tribes of Israel'" (Matt 19:28 = Luke 22:30).

[44]   The Jesus Seminar gives a "black" rating to the whole dialogue; cf. Funk, *Mark*, 167-68; idem and Hoover (eds.), *The Five Gospels*, 94. However, if vv. 38b-39, which might be a Christian insertion, are deleted, what remains could very well derive from the *Sitz im Leben Jesu*: "You do not know what you are asking. To sit at my right hand or at my left is not mine to grant, but it is for those for whom it has been prepared" (vv. 38a + 40). See C. A. Evans, "In What Sense 'Blasphemy'? Jesus before Caiaphas in Mark 14:61-64," in E. H. Lovering (ed.), *Society of Biblical Literature 1991 Seminar Papers* (SBLSP 30; Atlanta: Scholars Press, 1991) 215-34, esp. 227-30 [now revised as chap. 11 below].

establishment of his day.[45] His startling statement that he brings "not peace but a sword" (Matt 10:34-36 = Luke 12:51-53; cf. Luke 12:49) implies that the kingdom that he envisions will divide Jewish society (and not simply families, as might be inferred from the wording of Mic 7:6).[46] Jesus' proverbial statement that "the last will be first, and the first last" (Matt 20:16; cf. POxy654 §4; *GThom.* §4)[47] presupposes such a reordering of society. It is probable, moreover, that the sayings about receiving the kingdom as children (Mark 10:14-15; cf. *GThom.* §22)[48] were originally related to this theme. Probably also related is Jesus' declaration that "among those born of women none is greater than John; yet the least in the Kingdom of God is greater than he" (Luke 7:28 = Matt 11:11; cf. *GThom.* §46).[49] Jesus' saying, "The

---

[45]   Crossan, *Historical Jesus*, 270-76. The Jesus Seminar gives "pink" ratings to vv. 23 and 25; cf. Funk, *Mark*, 162; idem and Hoover (eds.), *The Five Gospels*, 91. On Luke 6:20 and 6:24, see Funk and Hoover (eds.), *The Five Gospels*, 289. The first passage is rated "red," the second is rated "black."

[46]   Meyer (*Aims of Jesus*, 213), Crossan (*Historical Jesus*, 299-300), Allison and Davies (Allison and Davies, *Matthew*, 2.217), and others regard this saying as authentic. On the meaning suggested here, see M. Black, "'Not peace but a sword': Matt 10:34ff; Luke 12:51ff," in E. Bammel and C. F. D. Moule (eds.), *Jesus and the Politics of His Day* (Cambridge: Cambridge University, 1984) 287-94. The Jesus Seminar assigns a "black" rating to the Matthean version of the saying and a "gray" rating to the Lucan; cf. Funk and Hoover (eds.), *The Five Gospels*, 173-74, 342.

[47]   The Jesus Seminar has given Matt 20:16 and the reversed form of the saying in POxy654 §4 "pink" ratings; cf. Funk and Hoover (eds.), *The Five Gospels*, 224. The Marcan (10:31) and Lucan (13:30) forms are rated "gray"; cf. Funk, *Mark*, 164-65; idem and Hoover (eds.), *The Five Gospels*, 93, 347.

[48]   Crossan (*Historical Jesus*, 266-69) and Gundry (*Mark*, 547) argue for authenticity. The Jesus Seminar gives Matt 19:14 = Mark 10:14 = Luke 18:16 a "pink" rating, but gives Mark 10:15 = Luke 18:17 a "gray" rating; cf. Funk, *Mark*, 158; idem and Hoover (eds.), *The Five Gospels*, 89. Crossan's earlier view of Mark 10:13-14 (cf. *In Fragments*, 315-18) is problematic.

[49]   Crossan (*Historical Jesus*, 237-38) argues for the authenticity of both halves of the saying. There is the distinct possibility that the qualification in v. 11b ("yet the least in the kingdom of God is greater than [John]") is not original. The Hebrew Shem-Tob version reads: "Truly I say to you, among all those born of women none has risen greater than John the Baptizer." A similar version is found in Ps.-Clement, *Recognitions* 1.60.1-3. See the discussion in G. Howard, "A Note on Shem-Tob's Hebrew Matthew and the Gospel of John," *JSNT* 47 (1992) 117-26, esp. 124-25. If this reading is original, then the case for its authenticity is strengthened, for it is difficult to imagine the early Church coining such a statement.

Kingdom suffers violence" (Matt 11:12 = Luke 16:16; cf. *GNaz.* §8), is probably a comment on the fate of John.[50] The implication is that Jesus viewed the ruling powers of his day as actively suppressing the kingdom which John had proclaimed and which he (Jesus) had declared was present.

When Jesus tells his disciples that they are not to "lord it over" their followers, as do the Gentiles and rulers of their country (Mark 10:42-44),[51] his egalitarian principles become transparently clear. These principles constituted an important dimension in his under-standing of the kingdom of God and had much to do with his death in Jerusalem.[52] Horsley has concluded that "the [the Synoptic Gospels] indicate rather clearly Jesus had threatened the Temple, that he was understood as an annointed [sic] king, and that he had 'stirred up' the people."[53] Crossan agrees, arguing quitely plausibly that Jesus' criticism of the "non-egalitarian, patronal, and even oppressive" Temple establishment, particularly as publicly demonstrated in the Temple precincts, "could easily have led to arrest and execution."[54] In short, the backdrop to Jesus' arrest and execution was his proclamation and advocacy of a radical change in society; while the specific event that precipitated the arrest itself was the action in the Temple.[55]

If v. 11b is a later gloss, then the original point of the saying may have had more to do with Jesus' unqualified endorsement of John's preaching, which was highly critical of the establishment. For Shem-Tob's Hebrew text of Matt 11:11, see G. Howard, *The Gospel of Matthew according to a Primitive Hebrew Text* (Macon: Mercer University; Leuven: Peeters, 1987) 48. The Jesus Seminar assigns a "gray" rating to Matt 11:11 = Luke 7:28; cf. Funk and Hoover (eds.), *The Five Gospels*, 178, 301.

[50] For arguments favoring authenticity, see Jeremias, *Theology*, 46-47; Allison and Davies, *Matthew*, 2.254. On the interpretation taken here, see Fitzmyer, *Luke X-XXIV*, 1117-18.

[51] The Jesus Seminar has given Mark 10:42-44 a "gray" rating, concluding that these verses "probably vaguely reflect something Jesus might have said"; cf. Funk, *Mark*, 168; idem and Hoover (eds.), *The Five Gospels*, 95. For more confident expressions of authenticity, see Fitzmyer, *Luke X-XXIV*, 1414; Horsley, *Jesus and the Spiral of Violence*, 244-45.

[52] Cf. Horsley, *Jesus and the Spiral of Violence*, 190-208.

[53] Horsley, *Jesus and the Spiral of Violence*, 163; see also idem, "The Death of Jesus," in Chilton and Evans (eds.), *Studying the Historical Jesus*, 395-422.

[54] Crossan, *Historical Jesus*, 360.

[55] Evans, "Jesus' Action in the Temple," 246.

Death

According to the Gospels Jesus, the proclaimer of the Kingdom of God, was crucified in Jerusalem as "the King of the Jews." All four Gospels agree in this, though with some variation:

Matt 27:37:   οὗτός ἐστιν Ἰησοῦς ὁ βασιλεὺς τῶν Ἰουδαίων
Mark 15:26:   ὁ βασιλεὺς τῶν Ἰουδαίων
Luke 23:38:   ὁ βασιλεὺς τῶν Ἰουδαίων οὗτος
John 19:19:   Ἰησοῦς ὁ Ναζωραῖος ὁ βασιλεὺς τῶν Ἰουδαίων[56]

Common to all four are the words ὁ βασιλεὺς τῶν Ἰουδαίων. According to the Gospels these words, which summarized Jesus' crime, were inscribed on a placard or *titulus* placed over his head.[57] There is literary evidence of such posting of an inscription that refers to the crime (Lat. *causa poenae* = αἰτία in Mark 15:26; Matt 27:37) and/or the name of the victim (cf. Suetonius, *Caligula* 32.2 and *Domitian* 10.1; Cassius Dio 73.16.5). In one case the victim carried a placard around the Forum before his crucifixion (Cassius Dio 54.3.6-7). According to Eusebius one of the Christian martyrs was led around an amphitheatre carrying a placard "on which was written in Latin, 'This is Attalus, the Christian'" (*Hist. Eccl.* 5.1.44; cf. John 19:20: "it was written in Hebrew, Latin, and Greek"). Although some scholars have reservations about the historicity of the titulus,[58] most accept it,[59]

---

56   The form of the inscription in the *GPet.* 4.11 (οὗτός ἐστιν ὁ βασιλεὺς τοῦ Ἰσραήλ) is a secondary reformulation based on Matthew that replaces the ethnic designation "of the Jews" to the more theologically acceptable "of Israel." Josephus routinely refers to Herod the Great as "king of the Jews" (*Ant.* 15.10.5 §373; 15.11.4 §409; 16.9.3 §291; 16.10.2 §311). The title as such may have originated with Antony when he gave Herod a kingdom (cf. *J.W.* 1.14.4 §282). The suggestion made by G. M. Lee ("The Inscription on the Cross," *PEQ* 100 [1968] 144) that the variations among the Gospels are due to independent translations of the Latin and Hebrew portions of the inscription (cf. John 19:20) is as implausible as it is unnecessary.
57   Cf. τίτλος (John 19:19-20) and ἐπιγραφή (Mark 15:26; Luke 23:38). The former is a transliteration of the Latin *titulus*, the latter an approximate translation.
58   D. R. Catchpole, "The 'Triumphal' Entry," in Bammel and Moule (eds.), *Jesus and the Politics of His Day*, 319-34, here 328.
59   Winter, *On the Trial of Jesus*, 108; E. Dinkler, *Signum Crucis* (Tübingen: Mohr [Siebeck], 1967) 306; N. A. Dahl, "The Crucified Messiah," in Dahl, *The Crucified Messiah and Other Essays* (Minneapolis: Augsburg, 1974) 1-36; Meyer, *The Aims of Jesus*, 176-78; E. Bammel, "The *titulus*," in Bammel and Moule (eds.), *Jesus and the Politics of His Day*, 353-64.

with some regarding it as "historically unimpeachable."[60] Fitzmyer's reasoning is cogent: "If [the inscription] were invented by Christians, they would have used *Christos*, for early Christians would scarcely have called their Lord 'the king of the Jews.'"[61]

LINKAGE IN INDEPENDENT SOURCES

The Fourth Gospel

According to Mack, "Mark's fabrication of the narrative theme . . . was to provide a narrative theme to link the Jesus traditions with the account of his death."[62] Since this link also appears in the fourth Gospel, Mack believes that the fourth evangelist drew upon Mark. "John's use of just this narrative design apart from knowledge of Mark would constitute a coincidence of fantastic proportions."[63]

It is, of course, possible that the fourth evangelist knew and made use of Mark (and/or the other Synoptic Gospels), and some Johannine scholars argue this position.[64] Others, however, believe that the fourth Gospel is not dependent on Mark or on any of the Synoptic Gospels.[65] If the latter position is correct, then Mack's conclusion that John's "narrative design" is derived from Mark collapses. Nevertheless, even if for the sake of argument we assume that the fourth evangelist was acquainted with one or more of the Synoptic Gospels, it is not at all obvious that the Marcan link between Jesus' miracles and the Jewish

---

[60]   G. Schneider, "The Political Charge against Jesus (Luke 23:2)," in Bammel and Moule (eds.), *Jesus and the Politics of His Day*, 403-14, here 404.

[61]   Fitzmyer, *Luke I-IX*, 773.

[62]   Mack, *A Myth of Innocence*, 282.

[63]   Mack, *A Myth of Innocence*, 225 n. 12.

[64]   Perhaps the ablest proponent of this position is Frans Neirynck; cf. F. Neirynck et al., *Jean et les Synoptiques* (BETL 49; Leuven: Peeters, 1979); idem, "John and the Synoptics: 1975-1990," in A. Denaux (ed.), *John and the Synoptics* (BETL 101; Leuven: Peeters, 1992) 3-61.

[65]   C. H. Dodd, *Historical Tradition in the Fourth Gospel* (Cambridge: Cambridge University Press, 1963) 349; R. Bultmann, *The Gospel of John* (Philadel-phia: Westminster, 1971); J. M. Robinson, "On the *Gattung* of Mark (and John)," in D. G. Buttrick and J. M. Bald (eds.), *Jesus and Man's Hope* (Pittsburgh: Pittsburgh Theological Seminary, 1970) 99-129; D. M. Smith, "John and the Synoptics: Some Dimensions of the Problem," *NTS* 26 (1980) 425-44; P. Borgen, "The Independence of the Gospel of John: Some Observations," in F. Van Segbroeck et al (eds.), *The Four Gospels 1992* (F. Neirynck Festschrift; BETL 100; 3 vols., Leuven: Peeters, 1992) 3.1815-33.

leaders' decision to have Jesus arrested underlies the Johannine plot.

The Testimonium Flavianum

The historicity of Mark's and John's common narrative design, including the linkage between ministry and execution, receives a measure of indirect support from Josephus. A brief account of the ministry and death of Jesus is given in the famous Testimonium Flavianum (*Ant.* 18.3.3 §63-64). Stripped of its obvious Christian interpolations and embellishments, the original form of the text probably read as follows:

> At this time there appeared Jesus, a wise man. For he was a doer of startling deeds, a teacher of people who receive the truth with pleasure. And he gained a following both among many Jews and among man of Greek origin. And when Pilate, because of an accusation made by the leading men among us, condemned him to the cross, those who had loved him previously did not cease to do so. And up until this very day the tribe of Christians (named after him) has not died out.[66]

According to Josephus, Jesus was a παραδόξων ἔργων ποιητής ("doer of startling deeds")[67] and a διδάσκαλος ἀνθρώπων ("teacher of people"), whom Pilate condemned to be crucified, having been accused by τῶν πρώτων ἀνδρῶν ("the leading [Jewish] men"). In this brief passage Josephus does not explain on what grounds Jesus was accused, nor does he explain on what grounds Pilate condemned him to the cross. But he does describe Jesus as a teacher and wonderworker who was crucified at the instigation of the Jewish leaders. Thus, Josephus provides us with an early and independent account which coheres in a significant way with the narrative design common to Mark and John. We need not

---

66   J. P. Meier, *A Marginal Jew: Rethinking the Historical Jesus. Volume One: The Roots of the Problem and the Person* (ABRL; New York: Doubleday, 1991) 61. For competent assessments of the Testimonium Flavianum, see Meier, *A Marginal Jew*, 56-88; idem, "Jesus in Josephus: A Modest Proposal," *CBQ* 52 (1990) 76-103; L. H. Feldman, "The *Testimonium Flavianum*: The State of the Question," in Berkey and Edwards (eds.), *Christological Perspectives*, 179-99.

67   In *m. Soṭa* 9:15 Hanina ben Dosa is described as one of the אַנְשֵׁי מַעֲשֶׂה ("men of deeds"). "Deeds" here probably should be understood as mighty deeds or miracles; cf. M. Jastrow, *A Dictionary of the Targumim, the Talmud Babli and Yerushalmi, and the Midrashic Literature* (2 vols., London: Putnam, 1895-1903; repr. New York: Pardes, 1950) 1.820; G. Vermes, *Jesus the Jew: A Historian's Reading of the the Gospels* (London: Collins, 1973) 79.

conclude that this parallel linkage of teachings/miracles to execution constitutes a fantastic coincidence; rather, it reflects history.[68]

Other Jewish figures from first-century Palestine also provide helpful points of comparison. Josephus, with an obvious critical bias, tells us of the various prophetic claimants who promised their respective contemporaries signs from heaven: "Deceivers and impostors, under the pretence of divine inspiration fostering revolutionary changes . . . led them out into the desert under the belief that God would there give them signs of salvation" (*J.W.* 2.13.4 §259). At least two of these would-be deliverers promised Joshua-like signs. During the administration of Governor Fadus (44–46 C.E.) a man named Theudas declared that at his command the Jordan River would be parted, permitting the prophet and his following to cross (*Ant.* 20.5.1 §97-98; cf. Acts 5:36). Although Josephus does not say, this sign would probably have been understood as the inauguration of a new conquest of the promised land. Evidently the Romans understood it that way, for Fadus sent a squadron of cavalry against them, killing Theudas and many of his followers. Another would-be prophet, a Jew from Egypt (ca. 56 C.E.), led a large number of people to the Mount of Olives in order to demonstrate that at his command the walls of Jerusalem would fall down, enabling him and his followers to gain entry into the city (*Ant.* 20.8.6 §169-170; cf. Acts 21:38). Again Josephus does not say so, but it is quite clear that this Joshua-like sign was meant to overthrow the establishment and inaugurate a new order. And, like Fadus before him, Felix the Roman governor sent troops against the Egyptian and his following.[69]

Although we are told very little about Theudas and the Egyptian Jew, it is quite probable that the Roman attacks against these men were directly in response to their public teachings and activities. The teachings and activities in themselves, of course, would not have aroused such largescale responses. Theudas and the Egyptian Jew had attracted large followings. Herein lies the reason for the respective Roman responses: the combination of proclamations calling for major changes in Israel *and* the ability to inspire large crowds with these proclamations. Would anyone in all seriousness claim that the death of

---

[68]   Josephus' contribution to the study of Jesus' passion is pursued further in chap. 9 below.

[69]   See the fuller discussion of these persons and others in chap. 2 above.

Theudas was "probably just a mistake" and that it resulted from a misunderstanding of his prior activities? So it was in the case of Jesus of Nazareth. He too had proclaimed an imminent change in the social and political order and had succeeded in attracting a large following. Not surprisingly, the powers of his day responded with deadly force.[70]

Conclusion

Evidence and logic strongly suggest that Jesus' death at the hands of the Roman authorities in Judea was the result of his teaching and activities. The inscription, "the king of the Jews," provides a firm link between Jesus' death and his proclamation of the kingdom of God. Furthermore, this inscription provides an important link between Jesus' ministry and the subsequent emergence of New Testament christology, in that while the Romans would have referred to Jesus as "king of the Jews," early Christians would have applied to him the more theologically charged title, "messiah." To be sure, Mark has interpreted many aspects of Jesus' ministry in the light of the passion and the Easter proclamation, but the basic link between Jesus' Galilean life and his Judean death cannot be reduced to nothing more than a narrative strategy.

---

[70]   In his response to the earlier form of this paper at the 1993 SBL meeting in Washington, DC, Richard Horsley rightly emphasized the point that Jesus was an *organizer* and not simply a *proclaimer*. Jesus' promise that his disciples would sit on thrones judging the twelve tribes of Israel (Matt 19:28 = Luke 22:28-30) and the request of James and John to sit on Jesus' right and left (Mark 10:35-40) constitute important evidence of such organization. Professor Horsley's comments and criticisms were greatly appreciated.

CHAPTER EIGHT

JESUS' ACTION IN THE TEMPLE AND EVIDENCE
OF CORRUPTION IN THE FIRST-CENTURY TEMPLE

E. P. Sanders has recently argued that Jesus' action in the Temple
was not a protest against dishonesty or improper religious polity, but a
prophetic demonstration symbolizing the imminent destruction of the
Temple.[1] Jesus' action came to be interpreted by the evangelists, as
seen in Mark 11:15-17 and parallels, as a "cleansing" in order to tone
down its militancy, a militancy which had begun to embarrass the early
Church. In turning over the tables of the money-changers and in
driving out a few of the sacrificial animals, Jesus intended to have his
contemporaries understand that the Temple "made with hands" was
about to be replaced with a Temple "not made with hands." Jesus'
action, therefore, had nothing to do with corruption. In fact, Sanders
goes on to say that he knows of no evidence of corruption in the first-
century Temple.[2] Therefore, the traditional understanding that Jesus
"cleansed" the Temple is unfounded and ought to be dropped.

Sanders's interpretation is certainly fresh and intriguing. But it is
not, however, free from several difficulties. First, there is little
evidence that the early Church, let alone the Marcan evangelist, was
embarrassed over Jesus' critical stance toward the Temple. Second,
there is evidence that there was significant enmity between Jesus and
the Temple establishment. Third, there is no evidence whatsoever that
a messiah or prophet or any other eschatological figure was expected
to destroy the Temple as the necessary prelude to building a new one.
The evidence that the Messiah was expected to build a new Temple is
itself poorly attested (especially for the pre-70 C.E. period), never
mind build a new one when the old one was still standing, indeed, was
undergoing expensive remodeling. Fourth, there is evidence that the
first-century Temple establishment was widely regarded as corrupt
and the Temple in need of purification. Fifth, and finally, there is

---

[1]   E. P. Sanders, *Jesus and Judaism* (Philadelphia: Fortress, 1985) 61-76.
[2]   Sanders, *Jesus and Judaism*, 367 n. 39.

evidence that some Palestinian Jews expected the Temple to be purified in the Eschaton, whether by the agency of the Messiah or by the agency of some other eschatological figure.

I have dealt with several aspects of these five difficulties in a previous publication.[3] In the present study I investigate more thoroughly the evidence that various groups in Jewish society, in Jesus' generation and in the generations that preceded and followed it, regarded the Temple establishment in various ways and to differing degrees as corrupt. This chapter attempts to set forth this evidence and to probe the difficulties of assessing its relevance and meaning.

For centuries interpretation of the Gospels' account of Jesus' action in the Temple has been marred, either by assuming without sufficient supporting evidence that the Temple establishment was thoroughly corrupt, or by the condescending assumption that Jesus and Christianity called for inner, heart-felt religion, as opposed to the external, ritualistic religion of Judaism. It is against the latter aspect that Sanders, in my judgment, has rightly complained. But with regard to the former aspect, Sanders errs in the opposite direction. He assumes without sufficient examination of the data that there is no evidence of corruption, or at least evidence of an assumption of corruption, in the first-century Temple.

EVIDENCE OF CORRUPTION IN THE FIRST-CENTURY TEMPLE

Outside of the New Testament Gospels and other early Christian writings there is significant and, in my estimation, substantial evidence of corruption. This evidence is seen in Josephus, several Pseudepigraphal writings, Targumic traditions, and Rabbinic writings. My procedure is diachronic, moving from late to early materials. I shall examine (1) the relatively abundant post-70 C.E. traditions that reflect upon the first-century Temple, and then (2) the meager materials that specifically relate to the time of Jesus. The purpose here is not simply to catalogue and describe the evidence, but to study it comparatively and in context. My hope is that certain patterns or themes can be

---

3   C. A. Evans, "Jesus' Action in the Temple: Cleansing or Portent of Destruction?" *CBQ* 51 (1989) 237-70. Other problems are raised in M. D. Hooker, "Traditions about the Temple in the Sayings of Jesus," *BJRL* 70 (1988) 7-19; B. D. Chilton, *The Temple of Jesus: His Sacrificial Program With a Cultural History of Sacrifice* (University Park: Penn State Press, 1992) 98-100.

identified that will serve as an aid in identifying more accurately against whom criticisms are leveled, particularly with respect to Jesus' contemporaries.[4]

1. Post-70 C.E. Reflection

Josephus. In addition to an interpretation of the Jewish catastrophe of 70, Josephus provides us with several items of information, some of which parallel other sources, which prove helpful to the present task. Although Josephus provides us with a fairly reliable account of the events of the first century, his biases must be taken into account. He tends to put the priestly aristocracy, as well as the Roman authorities, in a positive light. But he portrays charismatic leaders, prophets, and messianic claimants who called for revolution, as impostors, deceivers, and brigands.[5] Nevertheless, although it is not his intention, Josephus does reveal things about the ruling priests that suggest that there was significant corruption.

In various places Josephus describes the opulence of the Temple and the incredible wealth of its treasury. He tells us that the building and its gates were overlaid with gold, and that over the entrance hung an enormous grape cluster ("as tall as a man") made of gold (*J.W.* 5.5.6 §222-224; 5.5.4 §210-211; *Ant.* 15.11.3 §395). He further reports that "no one need wonder that there was so much wealth in our Temple, for all the Jews throughout the habitable world, and those who worshipped God, even those from Asia and Europe, had been contributing to it for a very long time" (*Ant.* 14.7.2 §110; from §111 to §119 Josephus cites various ancient historians who commented on the wealth of the

---

[4]   For a more detailed assessment of ancient views of the Temple, see J. Ådna, *Jesu Kritik am Tempel: Eine Untersuchung zum Verlauf und Sinn der sogenannten Templereinigung Jesu, Markus 11,15-17 und Parallelen* (dissertation, University of Stavanger, 1993) 123-296. Ådna's scope of investigation is much broader than mine. Although he is primarily concerned with Jesus' action in the Temple (as is my study in the preceding note), he presents almost everything that can be found in the primary literature that is concerned with the renewal of the Temple or with its rebuilding, with or without the assistance of a messianic figure. My purpose in the present chapter is much narrower and much more modest. I would like to express my gratitude to Dr. Ådna for making his dissertation available to me.

[5]   This point has been recently underscored by R. A. Horsley and J. S. Hanson, *Bandits, Prophets, and Messiahs: Popular Movements at the Time of Jesus* (New Voices in Biblical Studies; Minneapolis: Winston, 1985).

Temple).[6] We are also told that "Crassus . . . carried off the money in the Temple, amounting to two thousand talents, which Pompey had left, and was prepared to strip the sanctuary of all its gold, which amounted to eight thousand talents" (*Ant.* 14.7.1 §105; see also 17.10.2 §264-265; *J.W.* 2.14.6 §293).[7] The families of the High Priests also possessed extraordinary wealth. Incredible sums were paid as dowries (*b. Ketub.* 66b) and allowances for perfumes and jewellery (*b. Yoma* 39b; *m. Kelim* 12:7; *m. Šabb.* 6:5). The widows of High Priests were beneficiaries of extremely generous pensions, paid right out of the Temple treasury (*b. Ketub.* 65a, 66b; *Lam. Rab.* 1:16 §51; *b. Giṭ.* 56a). Obviously the mere fact of wealth does not prove the existence of corruption. But it does provide corroborating evidence, should other sources claim corruption.

From Josephus we also learn of the great political power of the Temple establishment. The Temple establishment and the Jewish ruling aristocracy were virtually one and the same, which in Josephus' opinion was ideal: "Could there be a finer or more equitable polity than one which sets God at the head of the universe, which assigns the administration of its highest affairs to the whole body of priests, and entrusts to the supreme High Priest the direction of the other priests? . . . for the appointed duties of the priests included general supervision, the trial of cases of litigation, and the punishment of condemned persons" (*Against Apion* 2.21 §185-187; see 2.22 §188).[8] Later, we are told that the High Priest used to "safeguard the laws, adjudicate in cases of dispute, [and] punish those convicted of crime. Any who disobey[ed] him . . . pay[ed] the penalty as for impiety towards God Himself" (2.23 §194).[9] The power of the ruling priests was by Roman design, for it was the best way to guarantee tranquility and taxation.[10]

---

6   Trans. by R. Marcus, *Josephus VII* (LCL 365; London: Heinemann; Cambridge: Harvard University Press, 1933) 505. See also 2 Macc 3:6: "The treasury in Jerusalem was full of untold sums of money, so that the amount of the funds could not be reckoned." Tacitus, the Roman historian, writes of Jerusalem: "In that place was a Temple of immense wealth" (*Hist.* 5.8.1).

7   Trans. by Marcus, *Josephus*, 503.

8   Trans. by H. St. J. Thackeray, *Josephus I* (LCL 186; London: Heinemann; Cambridge: Harvard University Press, 1926) 367-69.

9   Trans. by Thackeray, *Josephus I*, 371.

10   See R. A. Horsley, "High Priests and the Politics of Roman Palestine," *JSJ* 17 (1986) 23-55, esp. 27-31; ibid, *Jesus and the Spiral of Violence: Popular*

Again, such a political arrangement in itself is not evidence of corruption, but it certainly establishes a context in which political and economic abuses could flourish.

The High Priesthood in the Herodian/Roman period was dominated by four principal families (Boethus, Annas, Phabi, and Kamith). Although there was some rivalry between them, they were for the most part united in common purpose and polity. This unity, moreover, was also promoted through intermarriage (*Ant.* 17.6.4 §164 [Mattaiah, brother-in-law of Joazar]; John 18:13 [Caiaphas, son-in-law of Annas]; *Lam. Rab.* 1:16 §50] [Joshua ben Gamala, married to Martha, granddaughter of Boethus]). Although at the beginning of this period the family of Boethus was dominant, from the time of Annas (6–15 C.E.) on, the family of the latter dominated. In fact, more than half of the 70 year history of the first century high priesthood was in the hands of the family of Annas.

It is also clear from Josephus that the Temple establishment got along fairly well with the Roman government. Richard Horsley has concluded that the four principal priestly families that controlled the Temple establishment of the first century C.E. "maintained a fairly consistent policy and practice of collaboration in the Roman system," especially so prior to the 40's.[11] Again, this is not evidence of corruption, but it does make it easy to understand how bitter resentment toward the ruling priesthood could develop. Indeed, such resentment did develop, manifesting itself in an especially violent manner when at the outset of war with Rome the rebels gained control of Jerusalem. The followers of Menaḥem, one of those who claimed messianic status (*J.W.* 2.17.8 §434), burned the house of Ananias the High Priest (2.17.6 §426). The priest himself was eventually caught and killed (2.17.9 §441). This was one of several acts of violence directed against the Jewish ruling aristocracy.[12] Evidence of economic

---

Jewish Resistance in Roman Palestine (San Francisco: Harper & Row, 1987) 9-15; D. E. Oakman, *Jesus and the Economic Questions of His Day* (SBEC 8; Lewiston and Queenston: Mellen, 1986) 57-72.

[11] Horsley, "High Priests," 31. See Josephus (*Ant.* 18.1.1 §3) where the High Priest Joazar persuades the Jews to cooperate with the Roman census of 6 C.E.

[12] Horsley, "High Priests," 54: "In Jerusalem itself the aristocracy were regularly suspected of planning to surrender the city or to desert to the Romans. Thus they were either confined or executed for treason by the popular forces which

oppression is seen in the burning of the Temple archives, containing the records of debts (*J.W.* 2.17.6 § 426-427).[13]

Bribery and violence at times characterized the Temple establishment's rule, especially in the 50's and 60's. Josephus tells us that former High Priest Ananias enhanced his reputation by supplying people (such as the newly-appointed Roman governor Albinus) with money. We are also told that when Jesus ben Gamaliel (= Joshua ben Gamala) gained the high priesthood (through bribery according to *b. Yebam.* 61a; *b. Yoma* 18a), a feud arose between the latter and his predecessor: "Ananias, however, kept the upper hand by using his wealth to attract those who were willing to receive bribes" (*Ant.* 20.9.4 §213).[14] Josephus himself was victimized by bribes accepted by the High Priest Ananus (*Life* 38-39 §193-196).

Describing the 50's and 60's, Josephus reports that the chief priests sent their servants to take by force the tithes from lower-ranking priests, "beating those who refused to give," with the result that some of the poorer priests starved to death (*Ant.* 20.8.8 §181, 20.9.2 §206-207; cf. rabbinic traditions below). Josephus also tells us that the High Priest Ananus, son of Annas (Luke 3:2), plotted the death of James, the brother of Jesus, and a few others during the interim between Festus and Albinus (*Ant.* 20.9.1 §197-200).

Josephus believes that Jerusalem and her Temple were destroyed because of Israel's gross sin and folly, and that the Temple was burned and leveled as a purification. The murders committed in the very precincts, indeed in one instance at the very altar, of the Temple constituted the most grievous of this sin (*Ant.* 20.8.5 §166; *J.W.* 4.5.2 §323). But Josephus does not regard the priestly establishment itself as corrupt, or as responsible for Jerusalem's destruction. The sinners were not the ruling priests, but the rabble who had called for liberation from Rome, and who had murdered many of the Jewish aristocrats who had opposed them. Others assessed these events differently.

Pseudepigraphal Writings. Several first and second-century C.E. pseudepigraphal writings reflect upon the tragedy of 70. Most of these writings blame Israel as a whole, or at least give no clear indication

---

had taken control of the city." See also Horsley and Hanson, *Bandits*, 223-29.

13   See Horsley, *Jesus and the Spiral of Violence*, 252-53.

14   Trans. by L. H. Feldman, *Josephus IX* (LCL 433; London: Heinemann; Cambridge: Harvard University Press, 1965) 503.

that one group is more culpable than another. According to the *Ladder of Jacob* 5:8-9 (late first-century), the patriarch is told: "And around the property of your forefathers a palace will be built, a temple in the name of your God and of (the God) of your fathers, and in the provocations of your children it will become deserted."[15] After seeing the destruction of the Temple, Abraham asks God why this has happened. He is told (*Apocalypse of Abraham* 27:7): "Listen, Abraham, all that you have seen will happen on account of your seed who will (continually) provoke me because of the body [cf. 25:1,5] which you saw and the murder in what was depicted in the Temple of jealousy, and everything you saw will be so" (late first, early second-century).[16] "Jealousy" could refer either to the competing rebel factions or to the priestly aristocrats vying for office and power. An interpolation in *Life of Adam and Eve* (in several MSS. following 29:3) reads: "and again they will build a house of God, and the latest house of God shall be exalted more highly than before. And once again iniquity will surpass equity" (late first century).[17] Lack of equity implies criticism of the rulers, as opposed to the people in general. According to Pseudo-Philo's *Biblical Antiquities* 19:6-7 (first century) God revealed to Moses that Israel will forget His Law and be deceived, the result of which will be the destruction of their place of worship.[18] Large portions of 4 Ezra (i.e. 2 Esdras 3–14) are given over to a lament for the destruction of Jerusalem and the Temple. Writing *circa* 100 (cf. 3:1), the author wonders why God would allow Rome (see chaps. 11–12) to destroy God's dwelling place (see chap. 10, esp. vv. 7, 20-23, 45, 48). The author concludes that the disaster was the result of

---

15   Trans. by H. G. Lunt, "Ladder of Jacob," in J. H. Charlesworth (ed.), *The Old Testament Pseudepigrapha* (2 vols., Garden City: Doubleday, 1983-85) 2.409.

16   Trans. by R. Rubinkiewicz, "Apocalypse of Abraham," in Charlesworth (ed.), *Old Testament Pseudepigrapha*, 1.702. The description in chap. 27 of the destruction of the Temple is in reference to the Second Temple, and is part of the "early Jewish stratum" (p. 683). See also 25:4-5. See the discussion in Ådna, *Jesu Kritik am Tempel*, 194-95.

17   Trans. by M. D. Johnson, "Life of Adam and Eve," in Charlesworth (ed.), *Old Testament Pseudepigrapha*, 2.270 n. 29b. See the discussion in Ådna, *Jesu Kritik am Tempel*, 170-71.

18   It is possible that the First Temple is in mind, for it is not known if *Biblical Antiquities* was written before or after 70 C.E. See D. J. Harrington, "Pseudo-Philo," in Charlesworth (ed.), *Old Testament Pseudepigrapha*, 2.327 n. i. See the discussion in Ådna, *Jesu Kritik am Tempel*, 193-94.

Israel's sin (6:19; 7:72; 8:26-31; 9:32, 36; 14:31).[19] Finally, according to *Sib. Or.* 4:115-118 (to be dated to just after 80 C.E.): "An evil storm of war will also come upon Jerusalem from Italy, and it will sack the great Temple of God, whenever they put their trust in folly and cast off piety and commit repulsive murders in front of the Temple."[20]

In one writing at least, however, the priesthood itself is directly blamed for the catastrophe. Lamenting the fate of Jerusalem, Baruch says: "You, priests, take the keys of the sanctuary, and cast them to the highest heaven, and give them to the Lord and say, 'Guard your house yourself, because, behold, we have been found to be false stewards'" (*2 Bar* 10:18).[21] Although ostensibly describing the destruction of the First Temple, the author of this early second-century pseudepigraphon is describing the destruction of the Second Temple in 70 C.E. (cf. 1:4; 32:2-4).[22] It is significant that the priests are characterized as "false stewards," a characterization that coheres with some of Jesus' parables (cf. Matt 24:45-51 par; Mark 12:1-9 par; Luke 16:1-8). The same tradition appears in *4 Baruch* (early second century): "But Jeremiah, taking the keys of the Temple, went outside of the city and, facing the sun, he tossed them, saying, 'I say to you, sun, take the keys of the Temple of God and keep them until the day in which the Lord will question you about them. Because we were not found worthy of keeping them, for we were false stewards'" (4:4-5; see rabbinic parallels below).[23] *4 Baruch* is probably dependent on *2 Baruch*,[24] in which case the idea that it was specifically *the priests* (as opposed to the people in general) who were false stewards is original. In reference to

---

[19]   See the discussion in Ådna, *Jesu Kritik am Tempel*, 195, 252-53.

[20]   Trans. by J. J. Collins, "The Sibylline Oracles," in Charlesworth (ed.), *Old Testament Pseudepigrapha*, 1.387. The references to folly, casting off piety, and commiting murders are to the Jews, not to the Romans (pace Collins, p. 387 n. w). See the discussion in Ådna, *Jesu Kritik am Tempel*, 212-13.

[21]   Trans. by A. F. J. Klijn, "2 (Syriac Apocalypse of) Baruch," in Charlesworth (ed.), *Old Testament Pseudepigrapha*, 1.624. There were literal keys of the Temple (cf. Josephus, *Against Apion* 2.8 §108), but they also had taken on a symbolic value (see also Matt 16:19; Rev 3:7). Further references are considered below.

[22]   Klijn, "2 Baruch," 615-18. See the discussion in Ådna, *Jesu Kritik am Tempel*, 196.

[23]   Translation from S. E. Robinson, "4 Baruch," in Charlesworth (ed.), *Old Testament Pseudepigrapha*, 2.418, 419.

[24]   Klijn, "2 Baruch," 620; Robinson, "4 Baruch," 416-17.

Jerusalem, Baruch is warned: "I am going to destroy it for the multitude of the sins of those who inhabit it" (1:1, 8).

Targumic Tradition. The Targums also yield some evidence, principally from Targum Jonathan to the Prophets, that the first-century Temple establishment was remembered as corrupt. This is seen especially in 1 Samuel, Isaiah, and Jeremiah.

1 Samuel. Containing traditions that antedate, as well as post-date, the destruction of the Second Temple,[25] *Tg.* 1 Samuel yields some significant evidence of the belief that the priests of the Second Temple were regarded as corrupt. Chapter 2 contains many editorial insertions and expansions of an apocalyptic nature. Hannah's Song of Praise (vv. 1-10) is transformed, in the Targum, into an apocalypse. She foresees Sennacherib's siege of Jerusalem (v. 2), Nebuchadnezzar (v. 3), the kingdoms of Greece (v. 4), Mordecai and Esther (v. 5a), Rome (v. 5b), eschatological judgment of wicked and righteous (vv. 6-10ab), and the appearance of the Messianic Kingdom (v. 10c). The apocalyptic orientation of the narrative, however, does not end with Hannah's Song. In the verses that follow the sins of the sons of Eli the priest are described. We are told that they "robbed the sacrifices of the Lord" (v. 17; Heb: "treated the sacrifices of the Lord with contempt"). They are later asked: "Why are you robbing my holy sacrificial offering and my offering that I appointed to offer before me in my temple?" (v. 29; Heb: "Why do you kick at my sacrifices and offerings that I commanded?").[26] It is likely that the sons of Eli are to be understood as examples of the priesthood of the Second Temple, if not the priesthood of the first century (as in fact is the case in *b. Pesaḥ.* 57a). The prophecy of the demise of Eli's sons and family gives way, in v. 32, to a prediction of the demise of the Temple establishment: "And you will be seeing the sorrow that will come upon the men of your house because of the sins that you have sinned in my Temple. And afterwards prosperity will come over Israel" (Heb: "Then in distress you will look with envious eye on all the prosperity which shall be bestowed on Israel").[27] It is likely that the meturgeman is here alluding to the first-century priesthood, the priesthood that was destroyed. This is likely

---

[25] See D. J. Harrington and A. J. Saldarini, *Targum Jonathan of the Former Prophets* (ArBib 10; Wilmington: Glazier, 1987) 13.

[26] Harrington and Saldarini, *Former Prophets,* 107.

[27] Harrington and Saldarini, *Former Prophets,* 108.

the case in light of the promise in v. 35 to raise up a faithful priest who will serve the Messiah: "I will raise up before Me a trustworthy priest, who will minister according to my word, my will, and I will establish for him an enduring kingdom and he will serve my Messiah all the days" (Heb: "I will raise up for myself a faithful priest . . . and I will build him a sure house, and he shall go in and out before my anointed for ever").[28] After the corrupt priesthood has been swept away in judgment, a new and faithful priesthood will be established in the Eschaton.

Isaiah. There are at least three major passages in the Isaiah Targum where criticism is directed against the first-century priesthood. The first example is seen in the rewriting of Isaiah's Song of the Vineyard (5:1-7), where the focus has been narrowed from a threat against Judah at large to a threat against the Temple establishment. In place of the Hebrew text's "tower" and "wine press," the Targum reads "sanctuary" and "altar," respectively (v. 2). Because of the moral failing of the ruling priests (v. 7: "oppressors"), God will destroy the "sanctuaries" and the altar (v. 5).[29] This interpretive tradition carries over into the rabbinic literature, where the tower is specifically identified as the Temple, and the wine press the altar (*t. Me'il.* 1.16; *t. Sukk.* 3.15).[30]

The second example is Isa 28:1-13, which has been paraphrased to

---

[28]   Harrington and Saldarini, *Former Prophets*, 108. It is, of course, possible that none other than David and Zadok are in view (as is likely the case in the Hebrew). But judging by Hannah's apocalypse and the redaction of vv. 17, 29 and 32 (including an explicit reference to the Temple), thus making the sins of the priests in Samuel's time conform more closely to those of the first-century priests, it is likely that here also the meturgeman is thinking of some future righteous priest who will faithfully serve the Messiah (compare also *Tg.* Zech 6:13); cf. Chilton, *The Glory of Israel: The Theology and Provenience of the Isaiah Targum* (JSOTSup 23; Sheffield: JSOT, 1983) 23-24; S. H. Levey, *The Messiah: An Aramaic Interpretation* (MHUC 2; Cincinnati: Hebrew Union College-Jewish Institute of Religion, 1974) 36.

[29]   Chilton (*Glory of Israel*, 18) is probably correct when he notes that the plural "sanctuaries" refer to the Temple and the synagogues.

[30]   Chilton, *A Galilean Rabbi and His Bible: Jesus' Use of the Interpreted Scripture of His Time* (Wilmington: Glazier, 1984) 113. The Temple was referred to as a "tower" prior to the first century C.E. (cf. *1 Enoch* 89:56-67). See Mark 12:1-9 where Jesus criticizes the ruling priests, making use of this very passage from Isaiah.

reflect the leadership of the Herodian Temple.[31] Whereas the Hebrew of v. 1 reads, "Woe to . . . the fading flower of its glorious beauty," the Targum reads, "Woe to . . . the foolish master of Israel [who] gives the headgear to the wicked of the sanctuary." The "foolish master" (i.e. the High Priest) will be trampled by the Romans (v. 3).[32] In his place will arise the Lord's Messiah who will make the "house of judgment" (i.e. the Temple and/or the Sanhedrin) pass "true judgment" (vv. 5-6). Similarly in 42:7 it is anticipated that Messiah will "open the eyes of the house of Israel, who have been blind to the Torah" (Heb: "to open blind eyes").[33] The first century priests and scribes have gone astray, not one of them is "innocent of oppression" (28:7-8; cf. *Tg.* Isa 5:7). In vv. 10-13 the meturgeman goes on to criticize the priests for disregarding the Law and for holding the Temple in contempt. This is probably the idea in 53:5, where Messiah "shall build the Temple, which was profaned because of our sins, and which was surrendered because of our iniquities."[34] The reference to "the service of idols" (28:10) is likely hyperbolic ("referring to cooperation with Gentile power"[35]), and is an attempt to criticize the first-century Temple establishment as sharply as possible.

The third example is seen in the oracle concerning the faithful priest Eliakim (Isa 22:20), who becomes in the Isaiah Targum a portrait of Israel's tragedy. Although he is "exalted" (v. 20), and is appointed a "faithful officer ministering in an enduring place" (v. 23; the Hebrew reads, "And I will fasten him like a peg in a sure place"), and into his hand is placed "the key of the sanctuary and the authority of the house of David" (v. 22; the MT reads, "And I will place on his shoulder the key of the house of David"), he nevertheless "will be cut down and fall, and the oracle of the prophecy that was concerning him will be void" (v. 25).[36] It is possible that the positive elements of the Eliakim oracle (vv. 20-24) derive from the period before 70 C.E., while the negative

---

31   Chilton, *Glory of Israel*, 20, 23; ibid, *Isaiah Targum*, 55-57 (and notes).

32   *Tg.* Isa 29:1 probably alludes to the Roman siege and destruction of Jerusalem, while *Tg.* Isa 25:2 seems to reflect the confidence and hope in the period between the two Jewish wars. See Chilton, *Glory of Israel*, 130 n.10; ibid, *The Isaiah Targum* (ArBib 11; Wilmington: Glazier, 1987) 57 (and notes).

33   Levey, *The Messiah*, 60.

34   Levey, *The Messiah*, 64.

35   Chilton, *Glory of Israel*, 23.

36   Trans. by Chilton, *Isaiah Targum*, 44-45.

elements of v. 25 reflect disillusionment following the destruction of the Temple.[37] In fact, it appears that most of the content in chaps. 22–24, according to Bruce Chilton, has been rewritten in view of the Roman defeat, with the criticisms leveled chiefly at the "Temple hierarchy" (see *Tg.* Isa 17:11: "you forsook my service . . . you put off . . . repentance"; 24:5: "annulled the feasts"; 24:6: "deceit" [cf. 5:23]).[38]

Jeremiah. In *Tg.* Jer 7:9 the religious leaders are explicitly called "thieves." In 23:11 the Targum accuses the priests of having "stolen their ways," instead of being "ungodly," as the Hebrew text reads. Frequently the Targum pejoratively refers to "scribe and priest," instead of "prophet and priest," as in the Hebrew text. On other occasions they are called "robbers of money" (8:10; 6:13: "robbers of wealth"). The reference to scribe and priest is noteworthy, for these are the very persons who take exception to Jesus' action in the Temple (see Mark 11:18). Commercialism seems to be the point behind the subtle change in *Tg.* Jer 14:18: "both scribe and priest devote themselves to trade" (MT: "both prophet and priest ply their trade"). In reference to coming judgment, *Tg.* Jer 23:33 says that the scribe and priest will be driven out (instead of being cast off, as it is in the Hebrew). The thrust of the passage seems to be directed primarily at the religious leaders (and not at the people, as it is in the Hebrew).[39] Robert Hayward suspects that these criticisms, which coincide with similar ones found in the writings of Josephus and Qumran, reflect attitudes in Palestine before 70 C.E.[40]

There are other hints in the targumic tradition that are worth noting. In a messianic paraphrase, *Frag. Tg.* Gen 49:12 predicts the appearance of a Messiah who is pure "according to the Halakah, refraining

---

[37]   See Chilton, *Glory of Israel,* 19; ibid, "Shebna, Eliakim, and the Promise to Peter," in J. Neusner, P. Borgen et al. (eds.), *The Social World of Formative Christianity and Judaism* (H. C. Kee Festschrift; Philadelphia: Fortress, 1988) 311-26.

[38]   Chilton, *Isaiah Targum,* 36, 42-48.

[39]   R. Hayward, *The Targum of Jeremiah* (ArBib 12; Wilmington: Glazier, 1987) 37. He observes that the Jeremiah Targum frequently criticizes the priests: they are accused of robbery, being overly concerned about money, failing to enquire of God or showing compassion for the sick, and of having lack of concern for the people.

[40]   Hayward, *Jeremiah,* 37-38, cf. 101 n. 14 (on 18:18), 189 n. 38 (on 51:53).

from partaking of that which is taken by violence or robbery."[41]
According to Deut 16:19, Israel's judges were not to accept bribes.
Frag. Tg. Deut 16:19, however, reads, "you shall not take a monetary
bribe." *Tg.* Ezek 22:26 claims that the priests "misinterpret" the Law
(MT: the priests "have done violence" to the Law). This complaint may
allude to the priests' interpretation of Lev 6:23, whereby they excused
themselves from paying the Temple tax, and to Deut 14:22-23,
whereby the excused themselves from paying tithes (see below). All of
these traditions resemble the criticisms directed at the high priesthood
of the first century. Finally, the eschatological hope for the appearance
of "Elijah the High Priest" (*Tg. Ps.-J.* Exod 40:10; *Tg. Ps.-J.* Deut
30:4; *Tg.* Lam 4:22) may constitute an implied criticism of the
priesthood of the Second Temple.[42]

Tannaitic Traditions. On one occasion R. Simeon ben Gamaliel (ca.
10-80 C.E.) vigorously protested, because the price of a pair of doves
had been raised to one gold denar, a price some twenty-five times the
proper charge (*m. Ker.* 1:7). It should be remembered that the dove
was the poor man's sacrifice (Lev 5:7; 12:8). Such a charge would be
bitterly resented. In this instance, however, Simeon's protest apparently brought about an immediate reduction in the charge.[43] R. Yohanan
ben Zakkai (first century C.E.) condemned the priests' claim that they
were exempt from the half-shekel temple tax: "If a priest did not pay
the shekel he committed sin; but the priests used to expound this
scripture [i.e. Lev 6:23] to their advantage . . ." (*m. Šeq.* 1:4).[44] It was
"in the interests of peace" that no one insisted that the priests pay the
tax. This statement probably alludes to the violence sometimes
suffered by those who opposed the ruling priests. Horsley avers that
the "half-shekel tax was almost certainly a late development in second
Temple times, and its payment was controversial at the time of

---

[41]   Levey, *The Messiah*, 11. Reflecting a similar tradition, *Tg. Ps.-J.* Gen
49:12 says that the Messiah "will not tolerate as food that which is seized by force
or taken by robbery" (Levey, p. 9).

[42]   For a survey of the targumic evidence, see Ådna, *Jesu Kritik am Tempel*,
197-99.

[43]   See B. D. Chilton, *The Temple of Jesus: His Sacrificial Program Within a
Cultural History of Sacrifice* (University Park: Penn State Press, 1992) 102-103.

[44]   Trans. based on H. Danby, *The Mishnah* (Oxford: Clarendon, 1933) 152.

Jesus."[45] Such controversy is likely what lies behind Matt 17:24-27, and perhaps also 4Q159 (which if true, then apparently the Qumran community also took exception to the tax).[46]

There is also Tannaitic tradition claiming that the family of Annas did not tithe their produce, and for this reason their property was destroyed three years before the rest of Israel. Their refusal to tithe was apparently based on an exegesis of Deut 14:22-23, an exegesis for which the rabbis had little sympathy (*Sipre Deut* §105 [on 14:22]). A similar tradition is found in *y. Pe'a* 1.6 and *b. B. Meṣ.* 88a-b. It is possible that the addition in *Tg.* Isa 5:10 ("because of the sin that they did not give the tithes") alludes to this failure to tithe. Apparently the high priestly families profitted in ways that the rabbis considered at best questionable (*m. Šeq.* 4:3-4) and at other times clearly oppressive (*Sipre Deut* §357 [on 34:1, 3]).[47]

The Tannaitic rabbis also preserve tradition, in part corroborated by Josephus (as noted above), that the office of High Priest was often secured through bribery. Commenting on Lev 16:3 ("with this shall Aaron come"), R. Berekiah (second century C.E.) is reported to have said: "But the verse [i.e. Lev 16:3] does not apply to the Second Temple [as it does to the First Temple], because in its time the priests used to outbid one another for the office of High Priest, so that there were eighty High Priests who served (in disorderly succession) in the Temple. Hence the first part of the verse, 'The fear of the Lord prolongs days' (Prov 10:27a), applies to the priests of the First Temple, and the conclusion of the verse, 'the years of the wicked shall

---

45   Horsley, *Jesus and the Spiral of Violence*, 280, and 345 n. 7. See also S. Freyne, *Galilee from Alexander the Great to Hadrian* (Wilmington: Glazier, 1980) 277-81; W. Horbury, "The Temple Tax," in E. Bammel and C. F. D. Moule (eds.), *Jesus and the Politics of His Day* (Cambridge: Cambridge University Press, 1984) 265-86.

46   4Q159 1 ii 6-7: " . . . that a man gives as a ransom for his soul: half a [shekel]. Only once shall he give it during his lifetime." For more on the Temple tax, see Exod 30:13; 2 Chr 24:5; Neh 10:32; Philo, *Spec. Leg.* 1.14 §77-78; *Rer. Div. Her.* 38 §186; Josephus, *J.W.* 6.6.2 §335; 7.6.6 §218; *Ant.* 14.7.2 §110; 16.2.3 §28; 16.6.2-7 §163-173; 18.9.1 §312-313; *m. Šeq.* 1:3; 4:1-2.

47   See R. Hammer, *Sifre: A Tannaitic Commentary on the Book of Deuteronomy* (YJS 24; New Haven and London: Yale University Press, 1986) 378, 380, 512 n. 4. Employing word-play, "Gilead" (Deut 34:1) is understood as a reference to Jerusalem; "Zoar" (34:3) is understood as a reference to the oppressive establishment in Israel (cf. *Mek.* on Exod 17:14-16 [*Amalek* §2]).

be shortened' (Prov 10:27b), applies to the priests of the Second Temple" (*Pesiq. R.* 47.4).[48] The same tradition also appears in *Lev. Rab.* 21.9 (on 16:3), with a slight variation: "In the Second Temple, however, because they used to obtain the office of High Priest for money, or, as some say, because they used to kill each other by means of witchcraft . . . ."[49] It is likely that this tradition particularly has in mind the Herodian/Roman period, for some twenty-eight High Priests (only two of which were from families that had any legitimate claim) held office in little more than one century (from 37 B.C.E. to 70 C.E).

Early Amoraic Traditions. According to early Amoraic traditions, the High Priests of the first century were always wealthier than the other priests. The High Priest was expected "to be greater than his brethren in beauty, strength, wealth, wisdom, and good looks"; for this reason, the other priests on one occasion "filled up [the High Priest's] woodshed with gold denars" (*t. Yoma* 1.6).[50]

The High Priests are accused of defiling the Temple: "'Depart hence, ye children of Eli,' for they defiled the Temple of the Lord" (*b. Pesaḥ.* 57a). "Children of Eli" alludes to the evil sons of Eli, priest of Shiloh, who profited from the sacrifices, engaged in harlotry, and from those who resisted "they took it by force" (1 Sam 2:12-17). It was observed above that *Tg.* 1 Samuel 2 has rewritten the story of these sons, making their sins conform to those of which the first-century priesthood was thought guilty. The sentence, "they took it by force" (1 Sam 2:16), virtually functions as a refrain in the talmudic passage under consideration.

Although they are accused of many cultic violations, the most serious charge, so far as the present study is concerned, is that the High Priests took more than what was lawfully required. This is seen in a discussion of the distribution of the hides of the sacrificed animals. "At first did they bring the hides of Holy Things to the room of *bet*

48   Trans. based on W. G. Braude, *Pesikta Rabbati* (2 vols., YJS 18; New Haven and London: Yale University Press, 1968) 2.808.

49   Trans. based on J. J. Slotki, "Leviticus," in H. Freedman and M. Simon (eds.), *Midrash Rabbah* (10 vols., London and New York: Soncino, 1983) 4.272. In this version R. Aha (third century C.E.) is given credit for the interpretation of Prov 10:27.

50   Trans. based on J. Neusner, *The Tosefta* (6 vols., New York: Ktav, 1977-81) 2.186.

happarvah and divide them in the evening to each [priestly] household which served on that day. But the powerful men of the priesthood would come and take them by force. They ordained that they should divide it on Fridays to each and every watch. But still did violent men of the priesthood come and take it away by force . . . Beams of sycamore were in Jericho. And strong-fisted men would come and take them by force" (*t. Menaḥ.* 13.18-19; cf. *t. Zebaḥ.* 11.16-17; *b. Pesaḥ.* 57a).[51] Apparently the ruling priests (i.e. the "powerful men of the priesthood") were stealing the tithes (hides, in this case) to which the lower-ranking priests were entitled.[52] Because of this practice, it was not long "before the priests covered the face of the entire porch [of the Temple] with golden trays, a hundred by a hundred [handbreadths], with the thickness of a golden denar" (*t. Menaḥ.* 13.18-19; cf. *b. Pesaḥ.* 57a: "they covered the whole Temple with gold plaques a cubit square of the thickness of a gold denar"; *m. Šeq.* 4:4: "What did they do with the surplus of the heave offering? Golden plating for bedecking the Holy of Holies").[53]

In the passages under consideration, four sets of "woes" are recited concerning three of the four principal high-priestly families of the first century: "Concerning these and people like them . . . did Abba Saul ben Bithnith [first century C.E.] and Abba Joseph ben Yoḥanan [first century C.E.?] of Jerusalem say, 'Woe is me because of the house of Boethus. Woe is me because of their staves. Woe is me because of the house of Kathros. Woe is me because of their pen. Woe is me because of the house of Hanin. Woe is me because of their whispering. Woe is me because of the house of Ishmael ben Phabi. For they are High Priests, and their sons [are] treasurers, and their sons-in-law [are] supervisors, and their servants come and beat us with staves" (*t.*

---

51   Trans. by Neusner, *Tosefta*, 5.161.

52   It is probably against this inequity that *t. Yoma* 1.5 speaks: "But in the case of Holy Things . . . the High Priest and the ordinary priest are the same: each receives an equal portion." Trans. based on Neusner, *Tosefta*, 2.186. Although the laws of the Pentateuch did not, with regard to the offerings and tithes, favor the ruling priests over the lower-ranking priests, from the time of Roman control the ruling priests had such privilege (Josephus, *Ant.* 14.10.6 § 202-203 [44 B.C.E.]).

53   Trans. by Neusner, *Tosefta*, 5.161. The talmudic quotation is from H. Freedman, "Pesahim," in I. Epstein (ed.), *The Babylonian Talmud* (17 vols., London: Soncino, 1978) 3.284; the mishnaic quotation is from Danby, *Mishnah*, 156.

Menah. 13.21; cf. *b. Pesah.* 57a; see also *t. Zebah.* 11.16-17; *y. Ma'as. Š.* 5.15).[54] Greed, nepotism,[55] oppression, and violence, according to these rabbinic traditions, characterized the leading aristocratic priestly families. "Boethus" is probably the lower-ranking priest from Alexandria, mentioned by Josephus in *Ant.* 15.9.3 §320, who gave his daughter Mariamme to Herod as wife, and whose son Simon, in return, Herod appointed High Priest (22–5 B.C.E.). The rabbis lament his family's "staves," with which they beat people. This lament, however, is also expressed in regard to the other families, as the concluding line quoted above indicates. (From Josephus, moreover, we learn that the beatings were not perpetrated by the family of Boethus alone [*Ant.* 20.8.8 §181; 20.9.2 §207].) The identity of "Kathros" is less certain. He may be the "Simon Cantheras," son of Boethus, of *Ant.* 19.6.2 §297 and 19.6.4 §313, who served as High Priest (41 C.E.).[56] The rabbis lament his family's pen, "with which they wrote their evil decrees."[57] "Hanin" is none other than Annas of the New Testament (Luke 3:2; John 18:13, 24; Acts 4:6), who served as High Priest (6–15 C.E.) and whose five sons, a grandson, and son-in-law Caiaphas at various times served as High Priest (see *Ant.* 18.2.1 §26; 20.9.1 §198, where he is called Ananus). This family is particularly criticized by the rabbis (*Sipre Deut* §105 [on 14:22]; *y. Pe'a* 2.16; and possibly *m. Ker.* 1:7). In the present text, the rabbis lament his family's "whispering," by which they mean their secret conspiracies to effect "oppressive measures."[58] "Phabi" (or Phiabi) and his son "Ishmael" are mentioned in *Ant.* 18.2.2 §34. The family of Phabi is lamented by the rabbis (according to the parallel passage in *b. Pesah.* 57a) "because of their fists." Phabi's son Ishmael, the successor of Annas, served as High Priest (15–16 C.E.).

---

54   Trans. based on Neusner, *Tosefta*, 5.161-62. The reading is modified slightly in light of the parallel passage in *b. Pesah.* 57a.

55   The Temple treasurer and supervisor (or "captain") were second and third in authority to the High Priest himself. Tosefta's claim that these posts were awarded to relatives is confirmed by Josephus (*Ant.* 20.6.2 §131; 20.9.3 §208; cf. Acts 4:6).

56   The burned out ruins of a mansion and servants' quarters that belonged to "Qatros" (= Cantheras) may have been found in Jerusalem. Within the ruins of the servants' quarters a stone weight was found bearing the inscription: דבר קתרס ("of the son of Qatros").

57   Freedman, "Pesahim," 285 n. 4.

58   Freedman, "Pesahim," 285 n. 2.

Another Ishmael, son of Phabi II, served as High Priest (59–61 C.E.), and is specifically mentioned by Josephus as one of the High Priests whose servants beat the lower-ranking priests (*Ant.* 20.8.8 §179-181; see also 20.9.2 §207).

It is not likely that this rabbinic tradition has in mind only the excesses that took place in the years immediately preceding the war with Rome. The woes are pronounced against three of the principal families that served throughout the first century. The rabbis were also critical of the politics behind the appointment of the High Priests. "When [unacceptable] kings became many, they ordained the practice of regularly appointing priests, and they appointed High Priests every single year" (*t. Yoma* 1.7; cf. *Pesiq. R.* 47.4).[59] The passage goes on to describe the cultic violations and resulting death of one of the High Priests from the family of Boethus (1.8). Moreover, the gold plaques that covered the Temple may be related to the plates of gold that Josephus describes (*J.W.* 5.5.6 §222; cf. *m. Šeq.* 4:4). It is likely that the profiteering and extortion that resulted in the accumulation of so much gold took years, and perhaps had something to do with the refurbishing of the Temple that continued throughout most of the first century.

According to the Tosefta tractate considered above, because of the greed and hatred of the powerful priestly families, the Second Temple was destroyed: "As to Jerusalem's first building, on what account was it destroyed? Because of idolatry and licentiousness and bloodshed which was in it. But [as to] the latter building we know that they devoted themselves to Torah and were meticulous about tithes. On what account did they go into exile? *Because they love money* and hate one another" (*t. Menah.* 13.22, emphasis added).[60] Whereas hating one another could refer to the bloody fighting between the rebel factions during the war, loving money undoubtedly refers to the greed of the high priestly families. Finally, echoing first-century tradition already cited, a rabbinic tradition reads: "This verse [Zech 11:1] refers to the High Priests who were in the Temple, who took their keys in their hands and threw them up to the sky, saying to the Holy One, blessed be

---

59   Trans. by Neusner, *Tosefta*, 2.187. Tosefta's statement is hyperbolic. High Priests were not appointed "every single year" (cf. John 18:13). Some served less than a year, but most served for more than a year.

60   Trans. by Neusner, *Tosefta*, 5.162.

He, "Master of the Universe, here are your keys which you handed over to us, for we have not been trustworthy stewards to do the King's work and to eat of the King's table" (*'Abot R. Nat.* A 4.5; see also B 7 [21-22]).[61]

All of this tradition, of course, is collected, preserved, and edited by the rabbis of a later time, whose criticisms may not always be justified nor accurately represent the facts. Nevertheless, even allowing for bias and exaggeration, there is no justification to regard it as wholesale fabrication, for it comports well with what we find in the Gospels and Josephus, and with many of the apocalyptic traditions considered above.

2. *Tradition Specifically Reflecting the Time of Jesus*

There is little material that can be assigned with any degree of certainty to the specific time of Jesus' adult life (i.e. the 20's and 30's). Our best historical source for the first century is, of course, Josephus, but his writings unfortunately say little about the 20's and 30's that is helpful for the present investigation. Some of the writings of Qumran, of course, may overlap with Jesus' time. Identifying those that do is not easily done. If some writings could be identified, to what extent they actually reflect Jesus' thinking is likewise uncertain. In the commentary on Habakkuk, and elsewhere, the High Priest is customarily referred to as the "Wicked Priest" (1QpHab 1:13; 8:9; 9:9; 11:4), who has robbed the poor (1QpHab 8:12; 9:5; 10:1; 12:10), has amassed wealth (1QpHab 8:8-12; 9:4-5), and has defiled the "Sanctuary of God" (1QpHab 12:8-9). Similarly, 4QpNah 1:11 refers to the "riches that he [the Wicked Priest?] heaped up in the Temple of Jerusalem." All of these complaints certainly cohere closely with the criticisms and complaints that have been examined above. But do these criticisms refer to the first-century priesthood or to the Hasmonean priesthood of the last two centuries B.C.E.? It is likely that the "Wicked Priest" originally did refer to a Hasmonean priest (whether Hyrcanus

---

61   Trans. by on J. Goldin, *The Fathers according to Rabbi Nathan* (YJS 10; New Haven and London: Yale University Press, 1955) 37. This tradition is at times applied to the destruction of the First Temple, cf. *b. Ta'an.* 29a; *Lev. Rab.* 19.6 (on 15:25). It should be noted that comparison between the two Temples, their destructions, and the ensuing exiles, is not rare in the Targums and writings of the rabbis (see *Tg.* Isa 51:19; *Tg.* Ezek 24:6; *Tg. Ps.-J.* Gen 45:15; *t. Menaḥ.* 13.22; *b. Ta'an.* 28b–29a; *Pesiq. R.* 47.4).

or someone else). Of course, because of its eschatological perspective, the first-century C.E. Qumran community may very well have understood the Habakkuk *pesher* to be referring to contemporary High Priests. If it was so understood, how representative was the Qumranian attitude toward Jerusalem's priestly aristocracy? Did Jesus share their attitude?[62]

The same questions can be raised with regard to various pseudepigraphal writings. Although the original references may have been to figures and/or events of an earlier time (cf. *Jub.* 23:21 and *T. Levi* 14:1-6; 17:11, in reference to the second century B.C.E.; *Pss. Sol.* 17–18 and *1 Enoch* 89–90, in reference to the first-century B.C.E.),[63] later generations may have understood (and often probably did understand) their references to be to the "end times," that is, to their own respective times. But these documents are at best of uncertain value because they were composed generations before the time of Jesus. There are, however, at least three sources that directly relate to the time of Jesus.

Josephus and Philo. Other than referring to his appointment (*Ant.* 18.2.2 §35) and his dismissal (*Ant.* 18.4.3 §95), Josephus gives us little direct information about the High Priest Joseph Caiaphas, son-in-law of former High Priest Annas; Philo gives none. From Josephus we learn that Caiaphas was appointed by the Roman governor Valerius Gratus (16–26 C.E.) in either 18 or 19, held office throughout Pontius Pilate's administration (26–36), and was deposed by Vitellius in 36. From Josephus and Philo we learn of three outrages with significant religious implications that Pilate committed during the tenure of Caiaphas. First, Pilate brought into Jerusalem (and possibly into the Temple court) several busts of the emperor Tiberius (*Ant.* 18.3.1 §55-59; *J.W.* 2.9.2-3 §169-174). When the Jewish people discovered this, a "multitude" went to Pilate entreating him to remove the images, for such were contrary to their "laws" (i.e. Exod 20:4). Although at first he refused, the governor finally yielded. What is interesting is that the protest came from the people, not from Caiaphas or from any of the priestly aristocracy. Second, in making use of Temple funds to build

---

62   In my earlier study (Evans, "Jesus' Action in the Temple," 260-62), I suggested that Jesus may very well have held to an opinion approximating that of the Qumran community. See also C. A. Evans, "Opposition to the Temple: Jesus and the Dead Sea Scrolls," in J. H. Charlesworth (ed.), *Jesus and the Dead Sea Scrolls* (ABRL; New York: Doubleday, 1992) 235-53.

63   See the discussion in Ådna, *Jesu Kritik am Tempel*, 181-90.

an aqueduct in Jerusalem (itself probably not an offense, for Temple
funds were often used for civic projects), Pilate apparently dipped into
the "sacred treasury" reserved for the purchase of sacrificial animals
(*Ant.* 18.3.2 §60-62; *J.W.* 2.9.4 §175-177). Again there is popular
protest, but no mention of Caiaphas or, as one would surely expect in a
case involving the treasury, the Temple treasurer. On this occasion
Pilate did not yield, but had his soldiers beat and disperse the crowds.
The third outrage committed by Pilate, according to Philo (*Embassy to
Gaius* 38 §299-305), this time did provoke some of the ruling
aristocracy to protest to Pilate. But their appeal to the governor seems
more concerned with *preventing war*, rather than with the *religious
concerns* to which the populace had given voice. Pilate's administration finally came to an end after he brutally quashed a Samaritan
pilgrimage to Mount Gerizim (*Ant.* 18.4.1 §85-87). Vitellius, Legate
of Syria, ordered Pilate back to Rome (*Ant.* 18.4.2 §88-90), then
visited Jerusalem, where, "guided by [the Jewish] law," he returned the
priestly vestments to the custody of the priests and deposed Caiaphas
(*Ant.* 18.4.3 §90-95; elsewhere Vitellius shows sensitivity to Jewish
feelings, see *Ant.* 18.5.3 §120-123). Mary Smallwood suspects that
Caiaphas was deposed, "because, as an associate of Pilate, he was
unpopular with the Jews."[64] This is likely so, for the Jewish people
expressed appreciation for the actions that Vitellius had taken (*Ant.*
18.5.3 §123: Vitellius "was greeted with special warmth by the Jewish
multitude").[65] I believe that Horsley is correct when he concludes that
these examples suggest "acquiescence in, if not active cooperation
with, Roman rule," on the part of the Jewish priestly aristocracy.[66] It is
probable that the Jewish populace viewed the ruling priests with
mistrust, if not outright contempt.

Another factor that likely would have alienated most Palestinian
Jews from Caiaphas is the fact that he in all likelihood was a member of
the Sadducean party (cf. Acts 5:17). Other High Priests of the

---

[64]   E. M. Smallwood, "High Priests and Politics in Roman Palestine," *JTS* 13
(1962) 14-34, esp. 22; cited with approval by Horsley, "High Priests," 37.

[65]   Trans. by Feldman, *Josephus IX*, 85.

[66]   Horsely, "High Priests," 37. Horsley ("'Like One of the Prophets of Old':
Two Types of Popular Prophets at the Time of Jesus," *CBQ* 47 [1985] 435-63,
esp. 451) notes the significance of the fact that when Jesus son of Ananias
prophesied the doom of Jerusalem and the Temple (*J.W.* 6.5.3 § 300-309) only the
priestly aristocracy tried to silence him.

Herodian/Roman period are identified as Sadducees: Simon, son of Boethus ('*Abot R. Nat.* A 5.2, where Sadducees are called "Boethusians"; so elsewhere in Rabbinic lit.), Ananus, son of Annas (*Ant.* 20.9.1 §199), and Ishmael, son of Phabi II (*b. Yoma* 19b; *t. Para* 3.8; though referred to anonymously). It is likely that many others were adherents.[67] The significance of this observation is seen in comments of Josephus. He tells us that whereas the Pharisees enjoy the favor of the "multitude," the Sadducees ("men of the highest standing"; *Ant.* 18.1.4 §17) have the confidence of the wealthy few and no following from among the general population (*Ant.*13.10.6 §298). Josephus further states that the Sadducees were much more severe in the administration of justice than other groups (*Ant.* 20.9.1 §199). Nevertheless, Sadducean office-holders often grudgingly followed the rules of the Pharisees, "since otherwise the multitudes would not tolerate them" (*Ant.* 18.1.4 §17). Indeed, apparently the Sadducees feared the Pharisees (*b. Yoma* 19b).

Testament of Moses. Although some have argued for a Maccabean date, the allusions to Herod and his successors in chap. 6 have led most scholars to conclude that the *Testament of Moses* was written sometime in the first century.[68] R. H. Charles dated the writing to just prior to 30 C.E., a conclusion with which John Priest and Johannes Tromp agree.[69] Chapter 5 describes the corruption of the Hasmonean priests, chap. 6 describes the oppression of Herod the Great (for 34 years, see v. 6), and chap. 7 apparently describes the priesthood of the first century C.E. The fragmentary chapter reads:[70]

---

[67]   I. Gafni ("The Historical Background," in M. E. Stone (ed.), *Jewish Writings of the Second Temple Period* [CRINT 2.2; Philadelphia: Fortress, 1984] 24) states that "the priestly oligarchy [was] given to Sadducean influence."

[68]   The allusions are obvious: According to 6:2-6 a "rash and perverse" man [Herod] will rule "for thirty-four years." According to 6:7 Herod "will beget heirs [Archelaus, Herod Antipas, Philip] who will reign after him for shorter periods of time." These heirs will be subdued by a "powerful king of the West," i.e. Rome (6:8).

[69]   R. H. Charles, *The Assumption of Moses* (London: Black, 1897) lv-lviii; J. Priest, "Testament of Moses," in Charlesworth (ed.), *Old Testament Pseudepigrapha*, 1.920-21; J. Tromp, *The Assumption of Moses: A Critical Edition with Commentary* (SVTP 10; Leiden: Brill, 1993) 116-17. Even if a Maccabean date is required, then chaps. 6–7 would have to be understood as a later, probably first-century, interpolation.

[70]   Text from Tromp, *Assumption of Moses*, 16; trans. by Priest, "Testament

[1]Ex quo facto finientur tempora momento . . . etur cursus a . . . horae
IIII veniant [2]coguntur secun . . .ae . . . pos . . . initiis tribus ad exitus VIIII
propter initium tres septimae secunda tria in tertia duae . . . [3]Et regnabunt de
his homines pestilentiosi et impii docentes se esse justos, [4]et hi suscitabunt
iram animorum suorum, qui erunt homines dolosi, sibi placentes, ficti in
omnibus suis, et omni hora diei amantes convivia, devoratores, gulae, [5] . . .
[6]. . . bonorum comestores, dicentes se haec facere propter misericordiam . .
. [7]. . . exterminatores, quaerulosi, fallaces, celantes se, ne possent cognosci
impii, in scelere pleni et iniquitate ab oriente usque ad occidentem,
[8]dicentes: 'Habebimus discubitiones et luxuriam, edentes et bibentes. Et
putavimus nos tamquam principes erimus. [9]Et manus eorum et mentes
inmunda tractantes et os eorum loquetur ingentia et super dicent: [10]'Noline
me tange, ne inquines me loco in quo . . .

[1]When this has taken place, the times will quickly come to an end. [. . .]
[3]Then will rule destructive and godless men, who represent themselves as
being righteous, [4]but who will (in fact) arouse their inner wrath, for they
will be deceitful men, pleasing only themselves, false in every way
imaginable, (such as) loving feasts at any hour of the day—devouring,
gluttonous.

[5][Seven-line lacuna] [6]But really they consume the goods of the (poor),
saying their acts are according to justice, (while in fact they are simply)
[7]exterminators, deceitfully seeking to conceal themselves so that they will
not be known as completely godless because of their criminal deeds
(committed) all the day long, [8]saying, "We shall have feasts, even luxurious
winings and dinings. Indeed, we shall behave ourselves as princes." [9]They,
with hand and mind, touch impure things, yet their mouths will speak
enormous things, and they will even say, [10]"Do not touch me, lest you
pollute me in the position I occupy . . ."

The passage is clearly directed against a wealthy, powerful priestly
aristocracy. Since the passage apparently follows the demise of
Herod's sons, the setting of this apocalyptic vision must be the first
century, and probably some time in the 30's. If this is indeed the case,
then what we have here is pre-70 evidence, possibly from the time of
Jesus, of the belief that the priestly aristocracy was corrupt. It is
significant, furthermore, that several of the complaints reflect the very
ones that we observed in the post-70 literature surveyed above. It has
been suggested that the *Testament of Moses* may be of Essene origin,
but it may reflect the concerns of a broader constituency.

---

of Moses," 930. Verses 1-2 and 5-6 are poorly preserved. Priest's translation in
places is speculative. Compare Tromp's translation (p. 17).

CONCLUSION

Taken together, the above evidence clearly demonstrates that various groups, such as some tannaitic and early amoraic rabbis, members of the zealot coalition, Qumran sectarians, and Josephus viewed various priests, High Priests, or priestly families as wealthy, corrupt, often greedy, and sometimes violent.[71]

Of course, just because the Temple establishment was viewed as corrupt, does not mean that it actually was. Nevertheless, our concern is with the public perception, for it is against this public perception that Jesus' action in the Temple would have been interpreted, and perhaps motivated. Had the Temple been generally regarded as free from corruption, and had a messiah, or some other eschatological agent, been expected to tear down and rebuild the Temple, then Jesus' action may very well have been understood as Ed Sanders has suggested. But there simply is no evidence for such a theory. Evidence that the Temple establishment was viewed as corrupt, however, is substantial. This evidence antedates the time of Jesus, is subsequent to the time of Jesus, and can even be traced to the very time of Jesus.

The evidence surveyed above also underscores two important aspects of the social-political and religious situation in pre-70 Palestine. Socially and politically "the fundamental conflict in Jewish Palestine was between the Jewish ruling groups and the Romans on the one side and the Jewish peasantry on the other."[72] With respect to the practice of the cultus itself, a serious "gulf had developed between the legitimating ideals in the Torah and the actions of the actual high priests and their practices in the Temple."[73] The evidence certainly appears to bear out these conclusions of Horsley and Hanson. In my view, Jesus' action in the Temple should be understood as a criticism of

---

[71]   See the summary in Ådna, *Jesu Kritik am Tempel*, 291-95.

[72]   Horsely and Hanson, *Bandits*, 245; Gafni, "Historical Background," 24.

[73]   Horsely, *Jesus and the Spiral of Violence*, 287. During the revolt from Rome, there was an effort to bridge this gulf by replacing the illegitimate Herodian ruling priesthood with survivors of the legitimate line of Zadokite (*J.W.* 4.3.6 §147-149). Horsely and Hanson (*Bandits*, 234) aver: "The parables of Jesus, along with his other sayings, indicate that the Jewish peasantry entertained ideals of a (restored) egalitarian theocracy (the kingdom of God)—inasmuch as it was members of the peasantry who not only heard such sayings, but also preserved and transmitted them [Matt 22:1-14 = Luke 14:15-24; Luke 6:20-26; and Mark 10:23-31 are cited as examples]. The Zealots, however, were now implementing such ideas."

the Temple establishment (whether or not it should be called a "cleansing").[74] It was not, of course, a criticism of the laws and practice of sacrifice.

Several features in the Gospels cohere with these conclusions. The Baptist's scathing prophetic criticism, "You brood of vipers! Who warned you to flee from the wrath to come?" (Matt 3:7b = Luke 3:7b), was likely originally addressed to the priestly aristocracy (and not to the "Pharisees," as in Matthew, nor to the "multitudes," as in Luke), and as such is completely in keeping with the social and religious conditions of Palestine.[75] Jesus' parables concerning poor stewardship also reflect these conditions.[76] The Parable of the Wicked Vineyard Tenants (Mark 12:1-9) threatens the priestly aristocracy with the loss of their position and power. The abuses of power and privilege described in the Parable of the Faithless Servant (Matt 24:45-51 = Luke 12:42-46) probably reflect how the ruling aristocracy was perceived in the minds of Palestinian peasants. Jesus' pronouncement on the half-shekel Temple tax (Matt 17:24-27) may have been a "declaration of independence from the Temple and the attendant political-economic-religious establishment."[77] Jesus' comment regarding the poor widow and the others who were contributing to the Temple's coffers (Mark 12:41-44) was probably a lament—not a word of commendation—and an implicit criticism of the economic oppressiveness and inequity of the Temple establishment. The condemnation of the "scribes" who "devour widows' houses" (Mark 12:38-40) may very well allude to Sadducean scribes and not, as is usually assumed, Pharisaic scribes (see Josephus, *Ant.* 18.1.4 §16).[78] In Jesus' lament for Jerusalem (Matt 23:37-38 = Luke 13:34-35) there are significant parallels to Jeremiah, the prophet who had severely criticized Jerusalem's First Temple (Jer 7:14, 34; 12:7; 22:5; 26:9), whose criticism Jesus may have had in mind when he took action in Jerusalem's Second Temple (Jer 7:11 in Mark 11:17).[79] Various other details during Passion Week cohere with the criticisms of the priestly

---

[74] Jesus' action in the Temple is treated in chap. 9 below.

[75] Horsely and Hanson, *Bandits*, 178-79.

[76] See Oakman, *Jesus and the Economic Questions of His Day*, 95-131.

[77] Horsely, *Jesus and the Spiral of Violence*, 282; Oakman, *Jesus and the Economic Questions of His Day*, 172 n. 30.

[78] See J. Jeremias, *Jerusalem in the Time of Jesus* (London: SCM, 1969) 231.

[79] Horsley and Hanson, *Bandits*, 175.

aristocracy. The priests demand to know by what authority Jesus acted the way he did (Mark 11:27-33). The ruling priests cannot arrest Jesus immediately because of their fear of the multitude (Mark 12:12). Jesus is arrested by "servants of the ruling priests" who are armed with "clubs" (Mark 14:43-50; recall *t. Menaḥ.* 13.21).

In view of the fact that there is no evidence that a messiah was expected to destroy (and then rebuild) the Temple, but was expected to purify Jerusalem,[80] and that the Temple was expected to be purified in the Eschaton, it is highly probable that the unified first-century testimony of the Gospels, to the effect that Jesus "cleansed" the Temple, in all probability represents further evidence that in some Jewish circles the Temple establishment was regarded as corrupt and in need of purging. Therefore, it is questionable to raise objections to the Gospels' interpretation of Jesus' action in the Temple on the grounds that there is no evidence of corruption in the first-century Temple establishment.

---

[80]   Horsley ("Popular Messianic Movements around the Time of Jesus, " *CBQ* 46 [1984] 471-95, esp. 490) suspects that *Pss. Sol.* 17:26, 29, 36 (passages which speak of Messiah purging Jerusalem) may have lain behind Simon bar Giora's "messianic" actions during the siege of Jerusalem. See also Horsley and Hanson, *Bandits*, 125.

CHAPTER NINE

JESUS AND THE "CAVE OF ROBBERS":
TOWARDS A JEWISH CONTEXT FOR THE TEMPLE ACTION

The topic for the 1992 annual IBR meeting in San Francisco was focused on the Jewish matrix of early Christianity. My assignment was to speak on Jesus. Don Hagner's was to speak on Paul.[1] He approached his subject broadly, addressing the larger question of Paul's understanding of God's covenant with Israel and the Gentiles. I approached my subject much more narrowly, focusing on the meaning of Jesus' action in the Temple precincts. I chose this narower topic for three reasons: First, prior to 70 C.E. the religious center of the Jewish people was the Temple. Various groups and individuals may have been critical of the Temple's caretakers, but they were loyal to the institution itself and what it stood for. The large sums of money that poured into its coffers, both from Palestine and from the Diaspora, testify to this deeply felt loyalty. Accordingly, investigation of Jesus' action in the Temple has the potential of taking us to the heart of the larger question of Jesus' relationship to Judaism. Second, Jesus' action in the Temple has drawn considerable scholarly attention in recent life of Jesus research. This is because interpreters have rightly sensed that this action, if understood correctly, potentially clarifies Jesus' mission with respect to Israel and makes intelligible his execution at the hands of the Romans, Israel's overlords. Third, study of Jesus' action in the Temple precincts brings into focus the larger question of what Judaism was and with what features of this faith and practice Jesus either agreed, disagreed, or thought was in need of revision. Therefore, although the focus of this paper is narrow, in that it is limited to a specific Gospel passage, it does hope to make a contribution to the larger topic of Jesus within the first-century Jewish matrix.

In his recent study, *A Myth of Innocence: Mark and Christian*

---

[1]   I. H. Marshall responded to both papers. I greatly appreciated Professor Marshall's comments, as well as those offered by the IBR Fellows. The discussion was stimulating and profitable.

Origins, Burton Mack concludes that Mark's account of Jesus' action in the Temple is a "Markan fabrication."[2] He believes that the incident cannot be historical, because of the "lack of evidence for an anti-temple attitude in Jesus" and because it advances themes that are essential to Mark's agenda.[3] The latter point is not without merit, but the first point begs the question in assuming that in the context of the historical Jesus the action was "anti-temple." Evidently Mack has not taken into consideration the possibility that what Jesus might actually have done was significantly different from the function that the Markan evangelist assigns to it and from what interpreters often say about it.[4] What Jesus was actually doing will be considered in the second part of this study. The first part of the study will rebut Mack's conclusion that the account of the Temple action is nothing more than a literary fiction.[5]

THE AUTHENTICITY OF THE TEMPLE ACTION

The major problem with Mack's conclusion is that it does not adequately explain the appearance of the Temple action found in John 2:13-20. In a footnote he explains his view of the literary relationship between Mark and John, opining that the latter drew upon the former, but not in a slavish, scribal sense. For support, Mack cites the collection of studies edited by Werner Kelber,[6] where a few of the writers suspect that John knew Mark. But what impresses Mack is John's similar narrative design of moving from miracles to passion. This he believes could not possibly be a coincidence, but is evidence of

---

2   B. L. Mack, *A Myth of Innocence: Mark and Christian Origins* (Philadelphia: Fortress, 1988) 292.

3   Mack, *A Myth of Innocence,* 292, cf. pp. 11, 282.

4   In her review A. Y. Collins (*JBL* 108 [1989] 726-29) exposes this fallacy.

5   Mack's book is fraught with problems, not the least of which are his assertions that Mark invented much of the tradition (see esp. chap. 2). His interpretation of Mark and its negative influence in the course of history represents a painful scholarly tour de force. Although at many points sympathetic, even W. Kelber (*CBQ* 52 [1990] 161-63) disagrees with Mack, saying, "Mark cannot be blamed for all the ills of the West stretching from the crusades to the holocaust . . ." (p. 163). The hutzpah on the book's back cover notwithstanding, Mack's imaginative analysis hardly constitutes scholarly progress in the study of Mark and Christian origins.

6   W. H. Kelber (ed.), *The Passion in Mark: Studies on Mark 14–16* (Philadelphia: Fortress, 1976).

Johannine dependence upon Mark.[7] Although nowhere made explicit, presumably the reader is to assume that John's account of the Temple action was taken from Mark.

There are, however, several problems with this line of reasoning. The first, and probably most serious, is its circularity. The studies produced by Kelber and company represent attempts, along standard redaction-critical lines, to unpack Mark's theology. These scholars face the same difficulties that all redaction critics, since the time of Willi Marxsen,[8] have had to face, and that is the problem of trying to distinguish Mark's sources from Mark's additions and revisions. Since we do not possess Mark's sources (as we do those of Matthew and Luke—and here I am assuming Markan priority), an unavoidable element of subjectivity is introduced into our work. The problem becomes acute when we claim that we have detected the presence of Markan redaction, as distinct from his source, only to discover that this putative "redaction" also appears in the fourth Gospel. Such discoveries have led some of the contributors to Kelber's book to make the further claim that John must have been dependent upon Mark.[9] But is it not as likely, if not more likely, that what was tentatively identified as "redaction" in Mark might in reality be "tradition," in view of its appearance in a Gospel thought by many to be independent of the Synoptic tradition?[10] It strikes me as special pleading to prefer a more

7   Mack, *A Myth of Innocence*, 225 n. 12. See also p. 282. At least one scholar has found Mack's reasoning compelling; cf. R. J. Miller, "The (A)Historicity of Jesus' Temple Demonstration: A Test Case in Methodology," in E. H. Lovering (ed.), *Society of Biblical Literature 1991 Seminar Papers* (SBLSP 30; Atlanta: Scholars, 1991) 235-52.

8   W. Marxsen, *Mark the Evangelist: Studies on the Redaction History of the Gospel* (Nashville: Abingdon, 1969).

9   See J. R. Donahue,"Introduction: From Passion Traditions to Passion Narrative," in Kelber (ed.), *The Passion in Mark*, 8-10.

10   With a few exceptions, the persistent trend is to conclude that the Fourth Gospel is independent of the Synoptics. See R. Kysar, *The Fourth Evangelist and His Gospel: An Examination of Contemporary Scholarship* (Minneapolis: Augsburg, 1975); and more recently P. Borgen, "John and the Synoptics," in D. L. Dungan (ed.), *The Interrelations of the Gospels* (BETL 95; Leuven: Leuven University, 1990) 408-37; J. D. G. Dunn, "Let John Be John: A Gospel for Its Time," in P. Stuhlmacher (ed.), *The Gospel and the Gospels* (Grand Rapids: Eerdmans, 1991) 293-322, esp. 299 n. 13. In the recently published *Festschrift* for Franz Neirynck, U. Schnelle ("Johannes und die Synoptiker," in F. Van Segbroeck et al. (eds.), *The Four Gospels 1992* [BETL 100; 3 vols., Leuven: Leuven

subjective source-critical theory, as source critical work in Mark must always be, owing to the fact that its putative sources are no longer extant, to a theory that on all counts should be viewed as less subjective, owing to the fact that the documents in question (i.e. Mark and John) are extant and are therefore available for comparative study.

An example of this problem is seen in Kim Dewey's essay on Peter's denial of Jesus (Mark 14:53-54, 66-72).[11] Dewey believes that the Markan evangelist has intercalated traditions of Peter's denial outside of the High Priest's house and of Jesus' confession inside before the High Priest and the Council. The most compelling evidence of Markan redaction, we are told, is the appearance of an editorial "seam," created by leaving Peter warming himself by the fire (v. 54) and then later, in returning to him (v. 67), using the same language (i.e. "Peter" and "being warmed"). This two-word seam was supposed to have been created when the traditions were spliced together. But what of the similar, indeed, even more pronounced "seam" in the fourth Gospel, where we have not two words in common, but six (cf. John 18:18-25)? Does not its presence call into question these speculative conclusions regarding Markan redaction? Does not the Johannine seam point to a common tradition that antedates both the Synoptic and Johannine traditions? No, we are assured, it does not. The presence of this seam in John, Dewey avers, constitutes evidence that John knew Mark.[12]

There are, however, several problems with Dewey's (and Mack's) conclusion. First, apparently it has gone unobserved that there are examples of such "seams" in Greco-Roman literature which have nothing to do with the splicing together of literary sources.[13] These

University, 1992] 3.1799-1814) and P. Borgen ("The Independence of the Gospel of John: Some Observations," 3.1815-33) plausibly suggest that the Johannine community made use of some of the materials that found their way into the Synoptic Gospels, but that it is highly doubtful that this community made use of one or more of the Synoptic Gospels themselves. Their conclusions are consistent with those of C. H. Dodd a generation ago.

11   K. Dewey,"Peter's Curse and Cursed Peter," in Kelber (ed.), *The Passion in Mark*, 96-114.

12   Dewey,"Peter's Curse and Cursed Peter," in Kelber (ed.), *The Passion in Mark*, 104-105. Dewey is influenced by the earlier work of J. R. Donahue, *Are You the Christ? The Trial Narrative in the Gospel of Mark* (SBLDS 10; Missoula: Scholars, 1973) 58-63, and N. Perrin, *The New Testament: An Introduction* (New York: Harcourt, Brace, Jovanovich, 1974) 229.

13   C. A. Evans, "'Peter Warming Himself': The Problem of an Editorial

seams, which are no more than story-telling devices enabling the narrator to resume a portion of the narrative that for a time had been dropped, are as common to the oral medium as they are to the written.[14] For scholars who attach great importance to the literary aspects of the Gospels and to the literature of the Greco-Roman world, this is a curious oversight. Second, the assertion that John's version of the seam is due to Markan influence is problematic in its own right, when it is observed that outside of the seam itself, remarkably few of the details found in Mark are found in John. The wording of the accusations and the denials is quite different. The accusers in John are not the same as in Mark. Even the physical location of the scene is different in the Johannine version. How and why the fourth evangelist would carefully preserve a Markan seam and then disregard the more significant details of the narrative itself Dewey does not explain. This observation has led Robert Fortna to conclude that the fourth Gospel is literarily independent of the Markan Gospel.[15] Third, the problem is compounded when we observe that neither of the two Gospels that did make use of Mark, namely Matthew and Luke, picked up Mark's seam, though they did carry over most of his details. This observation leads to the plausible supposition that the seam was part of the *oral* tradition, independently preserved in Mark and John, but edited out of the narrative, in the polished *written* traditions of the later Synoptic evangelists.

The problems that arise from the conclusion that the fourth Gospel is dependent upon Mark for its story of Jesus' action in the Temple are similar to those just considered relating to Peter's denial of Jesus. First, the Johannine context, with its setting at the beginning of Jesus' ministry, is completely different from the Markan context. Although the fourth evangelist apparently knows that the Temple action occurred during a feast (either Sukkot or Passover; John 2:23), and so is in

---

'Seam'," *JBL* 101 (1982) 245-49. For two examples in Greco-Roman literature see Achilles Tatius, *Leucippe and Clitophon* 2.1 + 3.1; 11.1 + 12.1.

14 R. H. Gundry (*Mark: A Commentary on His Apology for the Cross* [Grand Rapids: Eerdmans, 1992] 890) cites my study in the preceding note with approval.

15 R. T. Fortna, "Jesus and Peter at the High Priest's House: A Test Case for the Question of the Relation between Mark's and John's Gospels," *NTS* 24 (1978) 371-83. See also P. Borgen, "John and the Synoptics in the Passion Narrative," *NTS* 5 (1958-59) 246-59. Borgen concludes that the common points between John and the Synoptics point to oral tradition.

agreement with the Synoptic tradition at a very important point, evidently he does not associate it with Jesus' final Passover. Second, there are as many differences in the details as there are similarities, with only a meager amount of vocabulary shared by the Markan and Johannine accounts. John introduces oxen and sheep and has Jesus driving them out with a whip. No equivalent of Mark's statement that Jesus did not permit people to carry vessels through the Temple (Mark 11:16) is found in John's version. The quotation of Isa 56:7 and the allusion to Jer 7:11 do not appear in John. Instead, Ps 69:9 is quoted. A related, but very different version of the saying about the destruction of the Temple (Mark 14:58) is found in John's version (John 2:19-21). Of all these differences the last one could plausibly be explained as Johannine redaction, but most of the other differences resist such facile explanation. It is for these reasons and for others that competent Johannine scholars, whose arguments Mack does not take into account, have concluded that the Temple narrative in the fourth Gospel is not derived from the Synoptic tradition.[16]

Mack's rejection of the authenticity of the Temple action is problematic in another area as well. If Jesus did not protest against Temple polity or threaten the Temple establishment, then how are we to account for the involvement of the ruling priests, if not the High Priest himself, in his arrest and subsequent crucifixion? It will not do to delete this tradition as still more Markan fabrication, for it is attested in Josephus, who tells us that the "leading men" accused Jesus before Pilate (*Ant.* 18.3.3 §64). The "leading men" of this statement, which is part of the Josephan account that is today almost universally accepted as authentic,[17] undoubtedly refers to the ruling priests. Jesus' action in

---

    16 C. H. Dodd, *Historical Tradition in the Fourth Gospel* (Cambridge: Cambridge University, 1963); R. E. Brown, *The Gospel According to John I-XII* (AB 29; Garden City: Doubleday, 1966) 118-20. For more recent confirmation of Johannine independence of the Synoptic tradition see B. D. Chilton, "[ὡς] φραγέλλιον ἐκ σχοινίων (John 2:15)," in W. Horbury (ed.), *Templum Amicitiae: Essays on the Second Temple* (E. Bammel Festschrift; JSNTSup 48; Sheffield: JSOT Press, 1991) 330-44, esp. 333-34; M. A. Matson, "The Contribution to the Temple Cleansing by the Fourth Gospel," in E. H. Lovering (ed.), *Society of Biblical Literature 1992 Seminar Papers* (SBLSP 31; Atlanta: Scholars Press, 1992) 489-506, esp. 499.

    17 Cf. L. H. Feldmann, "The *Testimonium Flavium*: The State of the Question," in R. F. Berkey and S. A. Edwards (eds.), *Christological Perspectives* (H. K. McArthur Festschrift; New York: Pilgrim, 1982) 179-99, 288-93; idem,

the Temple, independently attested in Mark and John, remains the best explanation for high priestly opposition to Jesus.

What also leads Mack to suspect that John was familiar with Mark is their common plot. Both depict Jesus as a teacher and miracle worker, whose crucifixion is desired by the Jewish leaders. According to Mack, "John's use of . . . this narrative design apart from knowledge of Mark would constitute a coincidence of fantastic porportions."[18] Here Mack has put his finger on the classic problem that has confronted interpreters since scholarly life of Jesus research got under way: If Jesus was a teacher and miracle worker and no more, then how do we explain his arrest and crucifixion? But if Jesus was a revolutionary, and so got himself executed for acts of sedition, how do we explain the ancient and widespread portrait of him as a teacher and healer? It is the Temple action that provides the vital historical link between Jesus the teacher and miracle worker, on the one hand, and Jesus the crucified criminal, on the other. Jesus' miracles, teaching, and Temple action, as will be shown in the second part of this paper, were all part of a coherent mission and ministry that make sense in and are to a great extent clarified by the Jewish context. His miracles and teaching were not simply acts of kindness and mercy, but were part of an agenda which had the restoration of Israel as its goal. The miracles and teaching anticipated the Temple action, which formed Jesus' final and climactic public teaching. The Temple action was not a random, accidental event, but a deliberate and calculated demonstration.[19]

By denying the historicity of the Temple action, Mack has unwittingly broken the historical and causal link between miracle/teaching and crucifixion. He is then left marveling at the "coincidence" of both Mark and John portraying the wonderworker and teacher as done

---

"Flavius Josephus Revisited: The Man, His Writings, and His Significance," *ANRW* 2.21.2 (1984) 822-35, esp. 822; J. P. Meier, "Jesus in Josephus: A Modest Proposal," *CBQ* 52 (1990) 76-103. M. J. Cook ("Jesus and the Pharisees—The Problem as It Stands Today," *JES* 15 [1978] 441-60) is mistaken when he speaks of a "consensus" among scholars to the effect that the Testimonium Flavium is wholly spurious. The consensus, or at least near consensus, is that Josephus' account has been redacted, but not invented by Christians.

[18]   Mack, *A Myth of Innocence*, 225, n. 12.

[19]   For a recent and compelling defense of the historicity of the Temple action, see J. Ådna, *Jesu Kritik am Tempel: Eine Untersuchung zum Verlauf und Sinn der sogenannten Tempelreinigung Jesu, Markus 11, 15-17 und Parallelen* (dissertation, University of Stavanger, 1993).

away with at the instigation of the religious leaders. Finding such a coincidence "fantastic," he argues that John must have gotten the idea from Mark, who had earlier happened on it as part of his anti-Temple, anti-Judaism theme. But the coincidence of the similar narrative design is adequately and plausibly explained, if the Temple action is accepted as historical.[20]

The historicity of Mark's and John's common narrative design, if not the Temple action itself, receives a measure of indirect support from Josephus, in the passage to which allusion has already been made. According to Josephus, Jesus was a παραδόξων ἔργων ποιητής ("doer of amazing deeds")[21] and a διδάσκαλος ἀνθρώπων ("teacher of men"), whom Pilate condemned to be crucified, having been accused by τῶν πρώτων ἀνδρῶν ("the leading [Jewish] men"). In this brief passage, which comprises all of two sentences, Josephus does not explain on what grounds Jesus was accused, nor does he explain on what grounds Pilate condemned him to the cross. But he does describe Jesus as a teacher and wonderworker who was crucified at the instigation of the Jewish leaders. Thus, Josephus provides us with an early and independent account which coheres in a significant way with the narrative design common to Mark and John. In short, this "narrative design" is not a literary fiction, but a rough approximation of the historical events, independently attested by Mark, John, and Josephus.

THE TEMPLE ACTION IN CONTEXT

In recent years several scholars have rightly emphasized the importance of the Temple action for understanding the factors that led to Jesus' crucifixion and perhaps also for understanding the factors that made up Jesus' mission.[22] Among the most promising of these

---

20 The Temple action explains the overarching narrative design common to Mark and John (i.e. how a religious teacher comes to grief on a Roman cross), even though their respective applications are not limited to the event's original significance. On these applications see below.

21 In *m. Soṭa* 9:15 Hanina ben Dosa is described as one of the אַנְשֵׁי מַעֲשֶׂה ("men of deeds"). "Deeds" here probably should be understood as mighty deeds or miracles; cf. M. Jastrow, *A Dictionary of the Targumim, the Talmud Babli and Yerushalmi, and the Midrashic Literature* (2 vols., London: Putnam, 1895-1903; repr. New York: Pardes, 1950) 1.820; G. Vermes, *Jesus the Jew: A Historian's Reading of the the Gospels* (London: Collins, 1973) 79.

22 S. G. F. Brandon, *Jesus and the Zealots: A Study of the Political Factor in*

studies is that offered by Bruce Chilton, who rightly criticizes the overdrawn inferences of S. G. F. Brandon, who had concluded that Jesus' action in the Temple precincts was nothing less than an attempted (and failed) coup, and the recent novel suggestion of E. P. Sanders, who proposed that Jesus' action was no more than a prophetic gesture announcing the imminent demise and replacement of the old Temple.[23] Chilton interprets Jesus' action against the background of similar actions taken by his approximate contemporaries and against the background of several important and related passages in the New Testament Gospels.

The principal strength of Chilton's approach lies in its comparative analysis. He shows that Jesus' action is quite intelligible when viewed as one of several protests and demonstrations relating to the Jerusalem Temple.[24] Two of the incidents are preserved in the writings of Josephus. The first protest was directed against Alexander Jannaeus during the festival of Tabernacles (*Ant.* 13.13.5 §372-373).[25] The people were incited (probably by Pharisees)[26] to pelt the king with lemons, just as he was about to offer sacrifice. His critics said that "he was descended from captives [cf. *Ant.* 13.10.5 §292] and was unfit to hold office and to sacrifice." What had been the immediate occasion for this demonstration is difficult to say, but concern for sacrificial purity was probably the justification for the action, if not a genuine underlying motivation. Alexander retaliated with his troops, killing some six thousand of the crowd. The second incident occurred in the final months of Herod's life, when two rabbis,[27] through their public

---

Primitive Christianity (Manchester: Manchester University, 1967); idem, *The Trial of Jesus of Nazareth* (New York: Stein and Day, 1968); E. P. Sanders, *Jesus and Judaism* (Philadelphia: Fortress, 1985); B. Chilton, *The Temple of Jesus: His Sacrificial Program Within a Cultural History of Sacrifice* (University Park: Penn State Press, 1992).

23 Chilton, *The Temple of Jesus*, 94-100.

24 Chilton, *The Temple of Jesus*, 73, 100, 183.

25 In his briefer parallel account, Josephus significantly remarks that "it is on these festive occasions that sedition is most apt to break out" (*J.W.* 1.4.3 §88).

26 Earlier, Josephus asserts that "so great is their influence with the masses that even when [the Pharisees] speak against a king or high priest, they immediately gain credence" (*Ant.* 13.10.5 §288). Of course, allowance must be made for Josephus' tendentiousness.

27 Josephus calls these men σοφισταί, which in the singular is probably the equivalent of "rabbi." In *Ant.* 18.3.3 §63 he calls Jesus a σοφὸς ἀνήρ and a

teaching, persuaded several young men to cut down the golden eagle affixed to the gate of the Temple (*J.W.* 1.33.2-4 §648-655; *Ant.* 17.6.2-4 §149-167). Enraged, Herod had the rabbis and the men who had damaged the eagle burned alive, denouncing them as sacrilegious and impious.

Chilton recommends to our attention two other demonstrations in the Temple precincts that do not end in violence, but do reflect popular concerns with Temple polity.[28] Traditions relating to these incidents are preserved in the rabbinic writings. The first episode involves Hillel, who apparently "taught that offerings (as in the case of his own *'olah*) should be brought to the Temple, where the owners would lay hands on them, and give them over to the priests for slaughter."[29] Persuaded by his teaching, a member of the house of Shammai brought three thousand animals to the Temple and gave them to those who were willing to follow Hillel's teaching (*t. Ḥag.* 2.11; *y. Ḥag.* 2.3; *y. Beṣa* 2.4; *b. Beṣa* 20a-b; on the antiquity of the tradition cf. Philo, *Spec. Leg.* 1.37 §198). The second incident involves Simeon ben Gamaliel who in his time protested the exorbitant charge for doves. Simeon countered by teaching the following: "By this Temple! . . . If a woman suffered five miscarriages that were not in doubt or five issues that were not in doubt, she need bring but one offering, and she may then eat of the animal offerings" (*m. Ker.* 1:7). The effect of this teaching, we are told, was to bring about a sharp reduction in the price of doves.

It is in the light of these examples that Chilton interprets the action of Jesus in the Temple precincts. "Jesus can be best understood within the context of a particular dispute in which the Pharisees took part . . . In that the dispute was intimately involved with the issue of how animals were to be procured, it manifests a focus upon purity akin to that attributed to Hillel and Simeon." "Hillel, Simeon, and Jesus are all portrayed as interested in how animals are offered to the extent that they intervene in the court of the Temple in order to influence the ordinary course of worship."[30] Jesus did not attack the sacrificial system or the Temple,[31] nor did he call for a different, more spiritual

---

διδάσκαλος, which might suggest that Josephus regarded Jesus as a rabbi as well.

28   Chilton, *The Temple of Jesus*, 100-103.

29   Chilton, *The Temple of Jesus*, 101.

30   Chilton, *The Temple of Jesus*, 103.

31   Chilton (*The Temple of Jesus*, 100) is certainly correct when he states that Jesus' action had "nothing whatever to do with destroying the fabric of the edifice

religion (as is often asserted in commentaries). Jesus was concerned with the purity of the pragmata of Israel's sacrificial system. Chilton suspects that Jesus' concern, possibly prompted by Caiaphas' apparently recent and novel introduction of animals into the Temple precincts, was similar to that earlier expressed by Hillel.[32] Jesus' action, or "occupation," as Chilton understands it, was "designed to prevent the sacrifice of animals acquired on the site, in trading that involved commerce within the Temple and obscured Pharisaic understanding that those animals were fully the property of [the people] of Israel (as distinct from the priesthood or the Temple)."[33]

The concern that Jesus expressed in the Temple was not, however, an isolated incident, but was a manifestation of important themes that ran throughout his ministry. Chilton identifies several passages in the Gospels which cohere with his interpretation.[34] These include the cleansing of the leper, where Jesus assumes priestly perogatives (Mark

itself." But his statement that Jesus' action was not "immediately directed at . . . the high priests" requires qualification, perhaps more than the adverb "immediately" entails. Since by all accounts the presence and activities of the merchants and money changers within the Temple precincts was by the permission and at the direction of the chief priests, any challenge or criticism leveled at the former implied challenge and criticism of the latter. I think that it is therefore correct to speak of Jesus' criticism of Temple polity.

[32]   Chilton, *The Temple of Jesus*, 107-11; idem, *A Galilean Rabbi and His Bible: Jeus' Use of the Interpreted Scripture of His Time* (GNS 8; Wilmington: Glazier, 1984) 17-18. For an assessment of the relevant rabbinic traditions see V. Eppstein, "The Historicity of the Gospel Account of the Cleansing of the Temple," *ZNW* 55 (1964) 42-58. It is worth noting that Caiaphas' ossuary may have been discovered. On an ornate first-century C.E. ossuary found in Jerusalem's Peace Forest, which is 1.5 km south of the Old City, two inscriptions read: יהוסף בר קיפא (Yehoseph bar Qaipha) and יהוסף בר קפא (Yehoseph bar Qapha). The first inscription runs along the side of the box, the second along the end. This ossuary contained the bones of a sixty year old man (and those of two infants, a toddler, a young boy, and a woman) The bones of the older man may very well be those of Caiaphas the High Priest, to whom Josephus refers as Joseph Caiaphas (cf. *Ant.* 18.2.2 §35 ['Ιώσηπος ὁ Καϊάφας] and 18.4.3 §95 [τὸν ἀρχιερέα 'Ιώσηπον τὸν Καϊάφαν ἐπικαλούμενον]). See Z. Greenhut, "Burial Cave of the Caiaphas Family," *BARev* 18.5 (1992) 28-36, 76; R. Reich, "Caiaphas Name Inscribed on Bone Boxes," *BARev* 18.5 (1992) 38-44, 76.

[33]   Chilton, *The Temple of Jesus*, 111. See also idem, "[ὡς] φραγέλλιον ἐκ σχοινίων," 335-42.

[34]   Chilton, *The Temple of Jesus*, 121-30.

1:40-44), pronouncements regarding the Temple tax (Matt 17:24-26), what is clean and what defiles (Mark 7:1-8, 14-23, though not all of this material derives from Jesus), what his disciples may carry as they travel throughout Israel (Matt 10:9-14; Mark 6:8-10; Luke 9:3-4; 10:4-7), and what constitutes proper giving to the Temple (Mark 7:9-13; 12:41-44). Chilton believes, moreover, that Jesus' remarkable pronouncements relating to forgiveness (Matt 5:23-24; Luke 7:47), "binding and loosing" (Matt 18:18), and the justification of those regarded by the priestly establishment as unclean or outcast (Luke 10:29-37; 18:9-14) are closely linked to his understanding of purity and sacrifice.[35]

The evidence that Chilton has presented appears to sustain the principal elements of his interpretation of Jesus' action in the Temple. But what specific action or teaching precipitated Jesus' arrest and execution? What provoked the High Priest into taking action against Jesus? Chilton believes that it was Jesus' break with the cultus and his teaching that an offering of bread and wine (Mark 14:22-24 par), where the conditions of purity and ownership are met, is to be preferred to the sacrifice of an animal at the Temple. The words of institution in their original sense, Chilton explains, were neither christological nor soteriological. Rather, "body" and "blood" referred to the body and blood of the sacrificial animal, symbolized by bread

---

[35]   Chilton, *The Temple of Jesus*, 130-36; idem, "The Purity of the Kingdom as Conveyed in Jesus' Meals," in Lovering (ed.), *Society of Biblical Literature 1992 Seminar Papers*, 473-88, esp. 484. Matson ("Temple Cleansing," 499-506) argues for a somewhat similar conclusion. See also N. T. Wright, "Jerusalem in the New Testament," in P. W. L. Walker (ed.), *Jerusalem Past and Present in the Purposes of God* (Cambridge: Cambridge University Press, 1992) 53-77, esp. 58. For important criticism of Sanders's *Jesus and Judaism* touching the question of purity in Jesus' teaching see, J. Neusner and B. Chilton, "Uncleanness: A Moral or an Ontological Category in the Early Centuries A.D.?" *BBR* 1 (1991) 63-88, esp. 80-88. P. Richardson ("Why Turn the Tables? Jesus' Protest in the Temple Precincts," in Lovering (ed.), *Society of Biblical Literature 1992 Seminar Papers*, 507-23) argues that Jesus took action in the Temple because of the use of silver Tyrian coins bearing the image of the god Melkart. Such an interpretation does not necessarily compete with that proposed by Chilton. Richardson's interpretation, if valid, supports the hypothesis that purity issues lay behind Jesus' action. Though taking a different tack, Ådna (*Jesu Kritik am Tempel*, 498-520) also finds several lines of continuity between Jesus' action in the Temple and other important aspects of his teaching and activities.

and wine, and not to the body and blood of Jesus.[36] Judas, who was present when Jesus uttered these provocative words, hurried away and reported them to the High Priest. Caiaphas, perceiving the potential economic threat (remember the result of Simeon's teaching) and ideological subversion,[37] made arrangements through Judas to take Jesus quietly and hand him over to the Romans.[38]

Chilton's analysis has much to commend it. His interpretation of Jesus' action in the Temple is compelling, so far as it goes. His contextualization of this action, both in reference to Jesus' contemporaries and in reference to Jesus' related teaching, is persuasive. His work goes a long way in addressing and filling a serious lacuna in life of Jesus research. Nevertheless, nagging questions remain.

First, it is not clear why Caiaphas would take such aggressive action against a teacher who had begun to advocate a view very similar to what apparently was practiced by the Essenes.[39] According to Philo, the Essenes "are men utterly dedicated to the service of God; they do not offer animal sacrifice, judging it more fitting to render their minds truly holy" (*Prob.* 12 §75). Josephus explains that the Essenes had been excluded from the Temple, owing to their distinctive purification rites. Therefore, "they offered their sacrifices among themselves" (*Ant.* 18.1.5 §19). The Dead Sea Scrolls seem to support this claim: "They (the covenanters) shall expiate guilty rebellion and sinful infidelity . . . without the flesh of burnt offering and the fat of sacrifice, but the offering of the lips in accordance with the Law will be an agreeable odor of righteousness, and perfection of way shall be

---

36   Chilton, *The Temple of Jesus*, 152-54; idem, "The Purity of the Kingdom," 487-88. For a recent and enthusiastic endorsement of Chilton's interpretation, see B. Lang, "The Roots of the Eucharist in Jesus' Praxis," in Lovering (ed.), *Society of Biblical Literature 1992 Seminar Papers*, 467-72.

37   As Chilton (*The Temple of Jesus*, 154) puts it: Jesus' "social eating took on a new and scandalous element: the claim that God preferred a pure meal to impure sacrifice in the Temple. Any such claim struck at the conception of the unique efficacy of the cult on Mount Zion. The dispute concerning the pragmatics of purity turned out to strike at an axiom within the ideology of Israel's sacrifice. Eschatological purity had become more important than place, and the authorities of the Temple could never accept any such inversion of their own ideological priorities."

38   Chilton, *The Temple of Jesus*, 151.

39   C. A. Evans, "Opposition to the Temple: Jesus and the Dead Sea Scrolls," in J. H. Charlesworth (ed.), *Jesus and the Dead Sea Scrolls* (ABRL; New York: Doubleday, 1992) 235-53.

as the voluntary gift of a delectable oblation" (1QS 9:3-5).[40] The idea
of spiritual sacrifice probably also explains the temple language that
the community used to describe itself: "The Council of the Community
shall be established in truth as an everlasting planting. It is the House of
holiness for Israel and the Company of infinite holiness for Aaron . . .
appointed to offer expiation for the earth" (1QS 8:5-6).[41] And
elsewhere: "He (God) has commanded a sanctuary of men [מִקְדַּשׁ אָדָם]
to be built for Himself, that there they may send up, like the smoke of
incense, the works of the Law" (4QFlor 1:6-7).[42] Even if Chilton's
novel interpretation of the words of institution be provisionally
accepted, it is far from obvious that Caiaphas would have felt
significantly threatened by a private halakah advocating withdrawal
from the official cultus.[43] Why not ban Jesus from the Temple
precincts, as Caiaphas and/or his high priestly colleagues had banned
certain Essenes?

Second, it is even less clear why the Romans would crucify someone,
in effect, for boycotting the sacrificial system of the Temple. If Jesus'
action constituted a protest and teaching against Temple polity, along
the lines that Chilton has proposed, how are we to account for the
Roman crucifixion? The *titulus* on Jesus' cross ("King of the Jews"
[Mark 15:26; cf. 15:2, 9, 12, 18], that part which is common to all four

40   A. Dupont-Sommer, *The Essene Writings from Qumran* (trans. G. Vermes;
Gloucester: Peter Smith, 1973) 93 and n. 1.

41   Dupont-Sommer, *Essene Writings*, 91.

42   Dupont-Sommer, *Essene Writings*, 311-12; G. Vermes, *The Dead Sea
Scrolls in English* (2nd ed., New York: Penguin, 1975) 246. Dupont-Sommer's
misleading parenthetic insertion, "made by the hands," which appears after "sanctuary," has been omitted. Qumran's stricter and more widely applied rules of purity
are documented in 11QTemple; cf. G. A. Anderson, "The Interpretation of the
Purification Offering (חטאת) in the *Temple Scroll* (11QTemple)," *JBL* 111 (1992)
17-35.

43   To this Chilton (*Temple of Jesus*, 141-46; and personal conversation
following the discussion of my paper) responds by observing that whereas the
Essenes were content to await the final eschatological battle, after which they would
assume control of the Temple, Jesus evidently was calling for the purification of the
Temple in the here and now. Accordingly, Caiaphas could afford to ignore the
Essenes, but he could not ignore Jesus. Perhaps. But the Essenes were boycotting
the Temple activities *in the here and now*. If Caiaphas could afford to ignore them,
why could be not as readily ignore Jesus? Would the High Priest immediately
respond with force after a private teaching? Jesus' advocacy of a boycott would
have been an irritant, but it would have hardly provided grounds for an attack.

Gospels), whose authenticity is very probable,[44] clearly indicates that Jesus was viewed as a messianic royal claimant of some sort. A messianic role would not have been inconsistent with the Temple action, and perhaps would even have required it. One thinks of *Psalms of Solomon* 17–18 in which is described a "Messiah" who will cleanse (καθαρίζειν) Jerusalem and drive out sinners (see esp. 17:30, 36; 18:5). As a messianic claimant, Jesus has challenged Temple polity and in doing so has possibly challenged the ruling authority of the High Priest.[45]

There is an important historical parallel that may clarify the chain of events that begin with Jesus' action in the Temple. According to Josephus (*J.W.* 6.5.3 §300-309):

> Four years before the war . . . there came to the feast, at which is the custom of all Jews to erect tabernacles to God, one Jesus son of Ananias, an untrained peasant, who, standing in the Temple, suddenly began to cry out, "A voice from the east, a voice from the west, a voice from the four winds, a voice against Jerusalem and the sanctuary, a voice against the bridgroom and the bride, a voice against all the people." . . . Some of the leading citizens, angered at this evil speech, arrested the man and whipped him with many blows. But he, not speaking anything in his own behalf or in private to those who struck him, continued his cries as before. Thereupon, the rulers . . . brought him to the Roman governor. There, though flayed to the bone with scourges, he neither begged for mercy or wept . . . When Albinus the governor asked him who and whence he was and why he

---

[44] The authenticity of the *titulus* is accepted by N. A. Dahl, "The Crucified Messiah," in Dahl, *The Crucified Messiah and Other Essays* (Minneapolis: Augsburg, 1974) 1-36; E. Bammel, "The *Titulus*," in Bammel and C. F. D. Moule (eds.), *Jesus and the Politics of His Day* (Cambridge: Cambridge University, 1984) 353-64; and, with caution, M. de Jonge, *Christology in Context: The Earliest Christian Response to Jesus* (Philadelphia: Westminster, 1988) 210. It should be remembered that Antony and the Roman Senate appointed Herod βασιλεὺς Ἰουδαίων (Josephus, *J.W.* 1.14.4 §§282-285), which indicates that the wording of the *titulus* is at least consistent with official Roman terminology. Had Christian Jews invented the *titulus* tradition, we should have expected something like "Jesus, King [*or* Messiah] of Israel," in place of the ethnic/geographical designation "Jews." Note that the chief priests, in marked contrast to the Romans, are said to have mocked Jesus as "the Messiah, the King of Israel" (Mark 15:31). A conflated and secondary form of the *titulus* tradition appears in *GPet.* 4.11: "they wrote upon it: this is the King of Israel." This later tradition has confused the divergent Roman and Jewish forms of the title.

[45] Recall that from the Hasmonean period the High Priest sometimes functioned as Israel's de facto King.

uttered these cries, he gave no answer to these things . . . . Albinus
pronounced him a maniac and released him . . . . He cried out especially at
the feasts. . . . . While shouting from the wall, "Woe once more to the city
and to the people and to the sanctuary . . ." a stone . . . struck and killed
him.

There are several important parallels between the Temple-related
experiences of Jesus of Nazareth and Jesus son of Ananias.[46] Both
entered the precincts of the Temple (τὸ ἱερόν: Mark 11:11, 15, 27;
12:35; 13:1; 14:49; J.W. 6.5.3 §301) at the time of a religious festival
(ἑορτή: Mark 14:2; 15:6; John 2:23; J.W. 6.5.3 §300). Both spoke of
the doom of Jerusalem (Luke 19:41-44; 21:20-24; J.W. 6.5.3 §301),
the Sanctuary (ναός: Mark 13:2; 14:58; J.W. 6.5.3 §301), and the
people (λαός: Mark 13:17; Luke 19:44; 23:28-31; J.W. 6.5.3 §301).
Both apparently alluded to Jeremiah 7, where the prophet condemned
the Temple establishment of his day ("cave of robbers": Jer 7:11 in
Mark 11:17; "the voice against the bridegroom and the bride": Jer 7:34
in J.W. 6.5.3 §301). Both were "arrested" by the authority of
Jewish[47]—not Roman—leaders (συλλαμβάνειν: Mark 14:48; John
18:12; J.W. 6.5.3 §302). Both were beaten by the Jewish authorities
(παίειν: Matt 26:68; Mark 14:65; J.W. 6.5.3 §302). Both were handed

---

46   D. R. Catchpole ("The Problem of the Historicity of the Sanhedrin Trial," in
E. Bammel [ed.], *The Trial of Jesus: Cambridge Studies in Honour of C. F. D.
Moule* [SBT 13; London: SCM, 1970] 47-65, 62 n. 96) summarizes the basic
parallels with Jesus' arrest and trial. He concludes that much historical material can
be gathered from the Gospels' accounts. The parallels that I offer are more detailed.

47   R. A. Horsley ("'Like One of the Prophets of Old': Two Types of Popular
Prophets at the Time of Jesus," *CBQ* 47 [1985] 435-63, esp. 451) rightly draws
our attention to the fact that it was only the priestly aristocracy that tried to silence
Jesus son of Ananias.

This is not to imply, however, that speaking against the Temple was a matter of
little consequence to the Jewish people in general. One thinks of the story of Paul in
the Temple (Acts 21:27-36). When Paul's enemies spotted him, they cried out:
"Men of Israel, help! This is the man who is teaching men everywhere against the
people and the law and this place; moreover he also brought Greeks into the
Temple, and he has defiled this holy place" (Acts 21:28). Paul was then seized,
beaten, and nearly killed. The gravity of such a charge is well documented by the
well known Greek warning inscription: μηθένα ἀλλογενῆ εἰσπορεύεσθαι ἐντὸς
τοῦ περὶ τὸ ἱερὸν τρυφάκτου καὶ περιβόλου, ὃ δ' ἂν ληφθῆ ἑαυτῶι αἴτιος ἔσται
διὰ τὸ ἐξακολουθεῖν θάνατον ("No foreigner is to enter within the balustrade and
embankment around the sanctuary; but whoever should be caught will have himself
to blame for his death which follows"). See Josephus, *Ant.* 15.11.5 §417.

over to the Roman governor (ἤγαγον αὐτὸν ἐπὶ τὸν Πιλᾶτον: Luke 23:1; ἀνάγουσιν . . . ἐπὶ τὸν . . . ἔπαρχον: *J.W.* 6.5.3 §303). Both were interrogated by the Roman governor (ἐρωτᾶν: Mark 15:4; *J.W.* 6.5.3 §305). Both refused to answer the governor (οὐδὲν ἀποκρίνεσθαι: Mark 15:5; *J.W.* 6.5.3 §305). Both were scourged by the governor (μαστιγοῦν/μάστιξ: John 19:1; *J.W.* 6.5.3 §304). Governor Pilate may have offered to release Jesus of Nazareth, but did not; Governor Albinus did release Jesus son of Ananias (ἀπολύειν: Mark 15:9; *J.W.* 6.5.3 §305).[48]

If we focus upon the *reaction* to Jesus' activity in the Temple, then it seems clear that the closest parallel is the experience of Jesus son of Ananias a generation later. The parallels with Hillel and Simeon are helpful in clarifying what may have motivated Jesus of Nazareth, but they are less helpful in clarifying the response of the Jewish and Roman authorities. Jesus son of Ananias evidently did not have any agenda of reform or criticism (as did Hillel and Simeon); nor did he attack the authorities (as did the crowd that pelted Jannaeus or the young men who vandalized the golden eagle). His action consisted of nothing more than a dolorous prediction of the Temple's impending doom.

Jesus of Nazareth, on the other hand, was apparently motivated out of concerns relating to Temple polity. Evidently he took exception to the presence of the animals in the Temple precincts and the attendant commercial activities. What he taught in the Temple on this occasion, of which only fragments are preserved in the Gospels, may very well have paralleled the earlier teaching of Hillel, as Chilton has suggested.

---

48   Both I. H. Marshall and other IBR Fellows raised the possibility, given the numerous verbal parallels, of some sort of literary relationship between *J.W.* 6.5.3 and the passion tradition. Although this possibility was not vigorously pursued during our time of discussion, perhaps a brief reply would be useful. First, the "parallels" comprise no more than nouns of place and context and verbs that mark the various steps in the judicial and penal process. In other words, the parallels are precisely what one would expect in cases where routine actions are being described. Second, aside from the single parallel cluster where we have a common verbal root, preposition, and Roman governor as object, there are no instances of parallel sentences or phrases. Literary relationships are suspected when there is a high concentration of common vocabulary, especially phrases and whole sentences. In short, I think that the common vocabulary adduced above indicates common judicial and penal process, but not literary relationship. There is no indication that the story of one Jesus influenced the telling of the story of the other Jesus.

The comparison is apt. But the reaction of the Temple authorities suggests the presence of a more serious element in Jesus' teaching and action. This element likely consists of some sort of prophetic pronouncement against the Temple, probably related to Jeremiah 7, just as the later oracle of Jesus son of Ananias would also be based on Jeremiah 7.

The evidence for this conclusion is found at four points. First, there is the allusion to the "cave of robbers" of Jer 7:11 (Mark 11:17). This fragment should not be viewed as a Christian embellishment or replacement of something that Jesus had said.[49] Not only is there no indication that Jer 7:11 was employed by the early Church, independently of Mark 11:17 and parallels, to criticize the Jewish Temple, there is evidence in Jewish sources that the Temple establishment of the first century was viewed by some Jews as corrupt and, specifically, guilty of robbery (Josephus, *Ant.* 20.8.8 §181; 20.9.2

---

[49] R. Pesch, *Das Markusevangelium* (HTKNT 2.2; 4th ed., Freiburg: Herder, 1991) 199. However, Sanders and others dismiss Mark 11:17 as inauthentic; cf. Sanders, *Jesus and Judaism*, 66, 363-64 (n. 1), 367 (n. 40). R. Bultmann (*The History of the Synoptic Tradition* [Oxford: Blackwell, 1968] 36) thinks that Mark 11:17 has replaced the older saying about the "house of merchandise" (John 2:16). J. Gnilka (*Das Evanglium nach Markus* [EKKNT 2.2; Zürich: Benziger, 1979] 127) is correct to point out that the introductory clause, "he was teaching and saying to them," is Markan, but that does not mean that the rest of the verse is Markan. Allusion to two or more passages of Scripture is characteristic of Jesus. The presence of "Gentiles" in the quotation of Isa 56:7 has led some to think that this verse was placed on the lips of Jesus to advance or explain the gentile mission. Of course, this may have been the case. But the verse seems to advance gentile proselytization from the perspective of non-Christian Judaism, rather than from that of Christianity. Why would the early Church add a verse that is part of an eschatological vision in which is imagined all the nations of the earth coming to Jersualem and to her Temple to offer sacrifice to God? Would early Christians, with increasing christocentricity and increasing hostility from and toward the Jerusalem religious establishment, have appealed to such a verse? Furthermore, why would Mark invent a saying identifying the Temple as the place of prayer for Gentiles when, by the time of his writing, the Temple no longer existed? Chilton (*The Temple of Jesus*, 119) rightly observes that the Synoptic citation of these verses from Isaiah and Jeremiah "quite clearly indicates an enduring interest in the Temple." In my judgment, the quotation of this verse likely goes back to Jesus, by which he expressed his expectation that Jerusalem's Temple should be worthy of its divine purpose and mission. I think that such an understanding complements very well Chilton's interpretation of Jesus' attempt to occupy and teach in the Temple precincts.

§206-207; 1QpHab 8:12; 9:5; 10:1; 12:10; *T. Mos.* 7:6; *Tg.* 1 Sam 2:17, 29; *Tg.* Jer 8:10; 23:11; *t. Menaḥ.* 13.18-19).[50] Such an utterance on the part of Jesus is, therefore, entirely consistent with the action in the Temple and with what can be known of the pre-70 social and religious setting.[51] Second, the accusation at Jesus' hearing before the Jewish Council that he had threatened to destroy the Temple and raise up a new one (Mark 14:58) coheres with the allusion to Jeremiah 7, a passage that goes on to warn of the (first) Temple's destruction (vv. 12-15). Though admiting that Jesus did predict the Temple's destruction (Mark 13:2), the Markan evangelist is careful to contextualize Jesus's prediction as an introduction to an apocalyptic discourse (Mark 13:5-37), and not as a threat. Indeed, in the apocalyptic context of Mark 13 Jesus' warning against the Temple is transformed into a formal prophecy. It is framing the testimony of the two witnesses as a threat ("He said, 'I will destroy . . .'") that makes the accusation false. In other words, according to Mark, Jesus did not threaten the Temple's destruction ("I will destroy"), but he did warn of it ("not a stone will be left").[52] The third piece of evidence is found in

---

[50] For a survey and assessment of the evidence see my "Jesus' Action in the Temple and Evidence of Corruption in the First-Century Temple," in D. J. Lull (ed.), *Society of Biblical Literature 1989 Seminar Papers* (SBLSP 28; Atlanta: Scholars, 1989) 522-39 [revised and reprinted above as chap. 8]. See also R. A. Horsley, "High Priests and the Politics of Roman Palestine," *JSJ* 17 (1986) 23-55.

[51] Compare also Jesus' statements about the religious establishment's oppression of widows (Mark 12:38-40, 41-44) to Jer 7:6-7 ("if you do not oppress the alien, the fatherless or the widow . . . then I will let you dwell in this place").

M. J. Borg (*Conflict, Holiness and Politics in the Teachings of Jesus* [SBEC 5; New York: Mellen, 1984] 171-75) accepts the saying found in Mark 11:17 as authentic, but thinks that Jesus uttered it in reference to "violent ones" who congregated in the Temple precincts to plot against Rome. Borg thinks that the word λῃσταί carries the sense often given to it by Josephus. However, this interpretation faces several difficulties: (1) It is highly unlikely that the chief priests, who were Roman allies, would have permitted such persons to occupy any part of the Temple precincts. (2) Why would chief priests have challenged Jesus (Mark 11:27-33) for criticizing such persons? (3) If Jesus spoke against such would-be insurrectionists, why then did he overturn the tables and concern himself with the sacrificial animals? It is better to interpret λῃσταί in Mark 11:17 in light of the context of Jeremiah 7, rather than in light of Josephan usage. See further M. D. Hooker, "Traditions about the Temple in the Sayings of Jesus," *BJRL* 70 (1988) 7-19, esp. 17-18.

[52] Sanders (*Jesus and Judaism*, 61-76), who regards Mark 14:58 as authentic,

the scene that follows Jesus' appearance before the High Priest. When pronounced guilty by Caiaphas and the Council, the attendants mock Jesus with calls to "prophesy" (Mark 14:65). Such mockery, which is likely not Christian invention (though there is evidence of Christian attempts to introduce christological implications),[53] coheres with the proposed scenario that the arrest of Jesus of Nazareth, like the later arrest of Jesus son of Ananias, was precipitated by a warning of the Temple's doom, not simply by a new teaching calling for modification of the sacrificial pragmata or, having failed to bring about such modification, for sacrifice outside of the auspices of the Temple priesthood. The fourth and final indication that Jesus warned of the Temple's destruction at the time that he took action in the Temple precincts is seen in the Johannine version (2:13-20), where Jesus says: "Destroy this sanctuary and in three days I will raise it up" (v. 19).[54]

---

argues that Jesus did in fact threaten to destroy the Temple and erect its messianic replacement within three days. This interpretation is problematic at many points. See my "Jesus' Action in the Temple: Cleansing or Portent of Destruction?" *CBQ* 51 (1989) 237-70; Chilton, *The Temple of Jesus*, 98-99.

   Jesus' prediction of the Temple's destruction probably had been no more than a part of his teaching in the Temple precincts, but came to be emphasized in the light of the events of 66–70. Indeed, the allusion to Jeremiah's "cave of robbers" probably had more to do with criticizing Temple polity than with predicting the Temple's destruction; cf. Chilton, *The Temple of Jesus*, 119. Mark apocalypticizes the prediction (Mark 13) and subordinates it to his anti-Temple theme, whereby Jesus and his new community replace the Temple establishment (Mark 12:10-11; 14:58). John subordinates the destruction prophecy quite transparently to his christology, whereby Jesus is presented as the new Sanctuary, destroyed but resurrected on the third day (John 2:19-22).

   53   Matt 26:68 reads: "Prophesy to us, you Christ!" Further christianization is seen in *GPet.* 3.9, which has collapsed the appearances before the Council and the Roman governor and has the people strike and whip Jesus, saying, "With such honor let us honor the Son of God."

   54   B. F. Meyer, *The Aims of Jesus* (London: SCM, 1979) 181; Matson, "Temple Cleansing," 505; J. P. M. Sweet, "A House Not Made with Hands," in Horbury (ed.), *Templum Amicitiae*, 368-90, esp. 371; Wright, "Jerusalem in the New Testament," 58-60. According to Chilton ("[ὡς] φραγέλλιον ἐκ σχοινίων," 341) Jesus (in John 2:19) has accused the Temple establishment of destroying the Sanctuary: "Jesus' act amounts to an attempt to prevent that destruction. Far from being an attempt to prophesy the ruin of the Temple, Jesus' aim was purification, along the lines of stopping illicit trade (cf. Zech. 14.21c)." This may be, but the persistence of the tradition to the effect that Jesus did predict the Temple's destruction (cf. Acts 6:13) does suggest that Jesus spoke of it. In my judgment,

The reference to Jeremiah's "cave of robbers" constitutes an important link between Jesus' action in the Temple and his execution.[55] The allusion to Jeremiah supports Sanders's contention that at the time of his action in the Temple Jesus spoke of the Temple's destruction,[56] though not in the sense that Sanders proposed. And it was this prophetic warning, and not simply a teaching that was contrary to official Temple polity, that prompted Caiaphas actively to seek the destruction of Jesus.[57]

The reaction of Jewish and Roman authorities to Jesus of Nazareth is analogous to their reaction to Jesus son of Ananias. Had Albinus found the son of Ananias sane and dangerous, in all probability he would have had him executed. But in the case of Jesus of Nazareth, who entertained messianic ideas, who had a following, who challenged the polity of the chief priests, and who evidently was found sane and dangerous, execution was deemed expedient.[58]

Jesus condemned Temple polity (perhaps suggesting that it was the polity itself that threatened the Temple with destruction) and warned that if corrections were not forthcoming the fate of the Herodian Temple would follow that of the Solomonic Temple (just as centuries earlier Jeremiah warned his contemporaries that the fate of the Solomonic Temple would follow that of the House of God at Shiloh).

[55] So also Ådna, *Jesu Kritik am Tempel*, 567.

[56] Sanders, *Jesus and Judaism*, 61.

[57] As is rightly emphasized by Ådna, *Jesu Kritik am Tempel*, 451-81, 574.

[58] Remember, too, that Caiaphas and Pilate evidently got along well, so the latter may have been more willing to acquiesce to the demands of the former (a point which serves Chilton's interpretation equally well). On the simultaneous removal of Caiaphas and Pilate from their respective offices, suggesting that they worked well together, see E. Bammel, "Pilatus' und Kaiphas' Absetzung," in Bammel, *Judaica* (WUNT 37; Tübingen: Mohr [Siebeck], 1986) 51-58. It is likely that Albinus did not enjoy a cordial relationship with any of the several High Priests (Joseph Cabi son of Simon [61–62 C.E.], who may have been removed from office prior to the arrival of Albinus, Ananus son Ananus [62 C.E.], who put to death James the brother of Jesus and was removed from office, Jesus son of Damnaeus [62–63 C.E.], and Jesus son of Gamaliel [63–64 C.E.]) who served during his brief term in office (62–64 C.E.). The frequent turnover suggests friction between the governor and the High Priests and, in any event, would not have been conducive to the development of good working relations. According to Josephus, especially in the briefer account in the *Jewish War*, the administration of Albinus was marked by cruelty and corruption (*J.W.* 2.14.1 §§272-276; *Ant.* 20.9.1-5 §§197-215).

JESUS AND PREDICTIONS OF THE DESTRUCTION OF
THE HERODIAN TEMPLE

In a lengthy essay I argue that in all probability Jesus did prophesy the destruction of the Jewish Temple and that he did so in response to his quarrel with the religious authorities.[1] As seen in the preceding chapter, as well as in chap. 11 below, I have concluded that Jesus' criticism of the Temple establishment, including a prophecy of coming judgment upon it, was the principal factor that motivated the High Priest and his colleagues to take action against Jesus. In this brief appendix I would like to outline and summarize the various predictions, premonitions, and prophecies of the destruction of the Herodian Temple. Some of this material is post-70 C.E. and so may very well represent *vaticinia ex eventu*, but some of it comes from earlier periods of time.

Testaments of the Twelve Patriarchs

The *Testaments of the Twelve Patriarchs* contain several predictions of destruction, either of the Temple, or of Jerusalem, or both:

> And you shall act lawlessly in Israel, with the result that Jerusalem cannot bear the presence of your wickedness, but the curtain of the Temple will be torn, so that it will no longer conceal your shame. (*T. Levi* 10:3)

> And now, my children, I know from the writings of Enoch that in the end-time you will act impiously against the Lord, setting your hands to every evil deed; because of you, your brothers will be humiliated and among all the nations you shall become the occasion for scorn . . . the impieties of the chief priests . . . You plunder the Lord's offerings; from his share you steal choice parts, contemptuously eating them with whores. You teach the Lord's commands out of greed for gain . . . With contempt and laughter you will deride the sacred things. Therefore the sanctuary which

---

[1]   C. A. Evans, "Predictions of the Destruction of the Herodian Temple in the Pseudepigrapha, Qumran Scrolls, and Related Texts," *JSP* 10 (1992) 89-147.

the Lord chose shall become desolate through your uncleanness, and you
will be captives in all the nations. And you shall be to them a revolting
thing, and you shall receive scorn and eternal humiliation through the just
judgment of God. All who hate you will rejoice at your destruction. (*T.
Levi* 14:1–15:3)

> Now I have come to know that for seventy weeks you shall wander
> astray and profane the priesthood and defile the sacrificial altars. You shall
> set aside the Law and nullify the words of the prophets by your wicked
> perversity. You persecute just men: and you hate the pious; the word of the
> faithful you regard with revulsion. A man who by the power of the Most
> High renews the Law you name "Deceiver," and finally you shall plot to kill
> him . . . on account of him your holy places shall be razed to the ground.
> You shall have no place that is clean, but you will be as a curse and a
> dispersion among the nations until he will again have regard for you, and
> will take you back in compassion. (*T. Levi* 16:1-5)

> My grief is great, my children, on account of the licentiousness and
> witchcraft and idolatry that you practice . . . and you will become involved
> in revolting gentile affairs. In response to this the Lord will bring you
> famine and plague, death and the sword, punishment by a siege, scattering
> by enemies like dogs, the scorn of friends, destruction . . . slaughter . . .
> plunder . . . consumption of God's sanctuary by fire, a desolate land, and
> yourselves enslaved by the gentiles. And they shall castrate some of you as
> eunuchs for their wives, until you return to the Lord in the integrity of heart
> . . . then the Lord will . . . free you from captivity under your enemies. (*T.
> Judah* 23:1-5)[2]

Probably written in the second century B.C.E., these passages
probably have in mind the Hasmoneans. There are several predictions
of the destruction of the Temple and/or holy places. *T. Levi* 10:3, if
genuine, could be a prediction of the Temple's destruction. H. C. Kee
suspects that a Christian scribe has tampered with the text, changing
"garment" to "curtain."[3] *T. Levi* 14 predicts the desolation of the
Temple, possibly reflecting tradition found in Daniel 9. *T. Levi* 15:3,
however, understands this desolation as "destruction," thus in all
probability implying the destruction of the Temple. *T. Levi* 16,

---

2   Trans. based on H. C. Kee, "Testaments of the Twelve Patriarchs," in J.
H. Charlesworth (ed.), *The Old Testament Pseudepigrapha* (2 vols., Garden City:
Doubleday, 1983-85) 1.793, 794, 801.
3   Kee, "Testaments," 1.792 n. b.

evidently reworked by a Christian,[4] contains an explicit reference to the razing of the "holy places." This prediction is not likely an interpolation (whether Christian or Jewish) based on the destruction of the Temple in 70 C.E. Although many inhabitants of Jerusalem were taken to Rome as prisoners (cf. Josephus, *J.W.* 6.9.3 §420; 7.1.3 §21; 7.2.1 §24; 7.5.5 §138), there was not a general dispersion of the people, such as occurred following the defeat of Bar Kokhba. Rather, the language is traditional, probably echoing the exile following the destruction of Jerusalem and the Temple in 586 B.C.E. *T. Judah* 23, however, parallels the disaster of 70 closely enough that one could suspect the presence of an interpolation. Siege, plunder, destruction of the Temple "by fire," and enslavement are all prominent features in Josephus' account. However, some features, such as witchcraft, idolatry, and what sounds like a general dispersion, do not reflect the events of the first century, but have more of the ring of the first destruction and exile. Therefore, the passage "may be an authentic prediction on the analogy of Dan[iel] 9."[5]

1 Enoch

1 Enoch apparently contains two prophecies of the destruction of the second Temple:

> Then I stood still, looking at that ancient house being transformed: All the pillars and all the columns were pulled out; and the ornaments of that house were packed and taken out together with them and abandoned in a certain place in the South of the land. I went on seeing until the Lord of the sheep brought about a new house, greater and loftier than the first one, and set it up in the first location which had been covered up—all its pillars were new, the columns new; and the ornaments new as well as greater than those of the first, (that is) the old (house) which was gone. All the sheep were within it. (90:28-29)
>
> . . . the roots of oppression shall be cut off. Sinners shall be destroyed; by the sword they shall be cut off (together with) the blasphemers in every place; and those who design oppression and commit blasphemy shall perish by the knife.
> Then after that there shall occur . . . the week of righteousness. A sword

---

4   Kee ("Testaments," 1.794 n. a) rightly says that v. 13 is not an interpolation, but a Christian revision.
5   Kee, "Testaments," 1.800 n. a.

shall be given to it in order that judgment shall be executed in righteousness
on the oppressors, and sinners shall be delivered into the hands of the
righteous. At its completion, they shall acquire great things through their
righteousness. A house shall be built for the Great King in glory for
evermore. (91:11-13)

> . . . a royal Temple of the Great One in his glorious splendor, for all
> generations, forever. (4QEng = 1 Enoch 91:13b)[6]

Elsewhere *1 Enoch* claims to predict the destruction of the
Solomonic Temple and the building of the second Temple (*1 Enoch*
89:72-73). This prediction, of course, is a *vaticinium ex eventu*. But in
the passages cited above, which probably date from the Maccabean,
even pre-Maccabean period,[7] the destruction of the second Temple and
its replacement with a new, eschatological Temple seem to be
envisioned. According to Lloyd Gaston the "ancient house" of 90:28 is
not in reference to the Temple itself, but to Jerusalem (otherwise, how
can "all the sheep" be "within it"?). He rightly points out that the
Temple is normally called a "tower" (cf. 89:50, 54, 56, 73).[8] Since *1
Enoch* describes the second Temple as polluted (89:73), it is probably
correct to understand that it will be removed, along with the old pillars
and ornaments, and that it will be rebuilt, along with the new pillars,
etc.

The second passage speaks of building a house for the "Great King."
Does the building of this "house" (which in the parallel found in
4QEng is "royal Temple"!) imply that the second Temple will first be
destroyed? Perhaps logic alone requires this, but it is also possible that
the reference to the destruction of the "towers" in v. 9 is what drew the
later material found in vv. 12-17 to chap. 91. Accordingly, the scribe

---

6   Trans. based on E. Isaac, "1 (Ethiopic Apocalypse of) Enoch," in
Charlesworth (ed.), *The Old Testament Pseudepigrapha*, 1.71, 73 and n. f2.

7   Isaac, "1 Enoch," 7, following R. H. Charles, "Book of Enoch," in R. H.
Charles (ed.), *The Apocrypha and Pseudepigrapha of the Old Testament* (2 vols.,
Oxford: Clarendon, 1913) 170-71. 90:28-29 is dated 165–161 B.C.E.; 91:11 105-
104 B.C.E.; and 91:12-13 pre-Maccabean.

8   L. Gaston, *No Stone on Another: Studies in the Significance of the Fall of
Jerusalem in the Synoptic Gospels* (NovTSup 23; Leiden: Brill, 1970) 114; cf. P.
Volz, *Die Eschatologie der jüdischen Gemeinde im neutestamentlichen Zeitalter
nach den Quellen der rabbinischen, apokalyptischen und apokryphen Literatur
dargestellt* (2nd ed., Tübingen: Mohr [Siebeck], 1934) 217.

who added vv. 12-17 and its prediction of the building of a house for God may have thought that the destruction of the "towers" in v. 9 implied that the second Temple, as one of the "towers," will be destroyed and thus will be in need of rebuilding.

Sibylline Oracles

The *Sibylline Oracles* appear to contain, if not a prediction of the Temple's destruction, at least a prediction of an attempt to destroy the Temple:

> But again the kings of the peoples will launch an attack together against this land, bringing doom upon themselves, for they will want to destroy the Temple of the Great God and most excellent men when they enter the land. The abominable kings, each one with his throne and faithless people, will set them up around the city. (3:665)[9]

It is highly unlikely that this oracle is based on the events of 70, or even was colored by them (as is the one found in 5:398-402), for there were no "kings" who assaulted the Temple during that conflict (cf. Jer 34:1). J. J. Collins believes that it is a part of a much larger section written in the period 163-145 B.C.E.[10] The oracle probably alludes to various Ptolemaic and Seleucid monarchs, among them Antiochus IV. It is, of course, possible that the oracle continued to be interpreted, well past the Greek period, as prophetic and, therefore, as yet to be fulfilled.

Qumran

A few of the writings of Qumran predict the destruction of the High Priest, and probably his supporters, but it is unclear if the Temple itself was expected to be destroyed:

> And as for that which he said, "Because you have plundered many nations, all the remnant of the peoples will plunder you" [Hab 2:8], the explanation of this concerns the last priests of Jerusalem who heap up riches and gain by plundering the peoples. But at the end of days, their riches, together with the fruit of their plundering, will be delivered into the hands of the army of the Kittim [i.e. the Romans]; for it is they who are "the remnant

---

9   Trans. based on J. J. Collins, "Sibylline Oracles," in Charlesworth (ed.), *Old Testament Pseudepigrapha*, 1.377.

10   Collins, "Sibylline Oracles," 1.354-55.

of the peoples." (1QpHab 9:2-7)

> The explanation of this word [i.e. Hab 2:17] concerns the Wicked Priest inasmuch as he will be paid his reward for what he has done to the Poor . . . For God will condemn him to destruction even as he himself planned to destroy the Poor. (1QpHab 12:3-5)

> "For a lion went to enter in, a lion cub" [Nahum 2:12]. [The explanation of this concerns Deme]trius king of Yawan who sought to enter Jerusalem on the counsel of those who seek smooth things [in 88 B.C.E; cf. Josephus, *Ant.* 13.14.2 §379-383; *J.W.* 1.4.5 §93-95]. [But he did not enter, for] from Antiochus until the rising of the commanders of the Kittim [God did not deliver it] into the hand of the kings of Yawan [i.e. the Ptolemies and Seleucids]. But afterwards it will be trampled under foot [by the Kittim]. (4QpNah 1:1-3)[11]

> And I shall sanctify my [sanc]tuary with my glory for I shall cause my glory to dwell upon it until (?) the day of blessing (?) on which I shall create (anew) my san[ctuary (?)] to prepare it for myself for all [t]ime according to the covenant which I made with Jacob at Bethel. (11QTemple 29:8-10)

> . . . I shall sanctify . . . and ma[ke] . . . house which you shall build . . . (11QTemple 30:1-4)[12]

It is not obvious if the plundering and destruction of the Wicked Priest entails destruction of the Temple as well. (In 1QpHab 9:9-11 he is "delivered into the hands of his enemies to humble him with a destroying blow.") It might be, especially if 11QTemple's hope for a new sanctuary, a "house which [the righteous] will build," was understood to imply that the old building was to be destroyed. J. Maier, however, thinks that 11QTemple is speaking only of the Temple that Israel was to build in the promised land;[13] but others think that it is eschatological.[14] E. P. Sanders finds in "until [עַד] the day of

---

11 Trans. based on A. Dupont-Sommer, *The Essene Writings from Qumran* (Gloucester: Peter Smith, 1973) 264, 267, 268.

12 Trans. based on J. Maier, *The Temple Scroll: An Introduction, Translation & Commentary* (JSOTSup 34; Sheffield: JSOT Press, 1985) 32.

13 Maier, *The Temple Scroll*, 86.

14 B. Thiering, *"Mebaqqer* and *Episkopos* in the Light of the Temple Scroll," *JBL* 100 (1981) 59-75, esp. 60-61; B. Z. Wacholder, *The Dawn of Qumran: The Sectarian Torah and the Teacher of Righteousness* (Cincinnati: Hebrew Union College, 1983) 21-23.

blessing" a hint that the Temple will come to an end.[15] But there is also the possibility that this new building approximates the "sanctuary of men," or spiritual Temple, mentioned in 4QFlor 1:6,[16] in which case the text probably implies nothing of the fate of the Temple. The pesher on Nahum may be referring to Pompey's conquest of Jerusalem in 63 B.C.E., which is what André Dupont-Sommer thinks.[17] This may be correct, but it is also possible that this exegesis came to be regarded as a yet-to-be-fulfilled prophecy of a Roman trampling of Jerusalem.

Jesus of Nazareth

Jesus of Nazareth predicted the destruction of Jerusalem and its Temple:

> O Jerusalem, Jerusalem, killing the prophets and those who are sent to you! How often would I have gathered your children together as a hen gathers her brood under her wings, and you would not! Behold, your house is forsaken. (Luke 13:34-35a par)

> And when he drew near and saw the city he wept over it, saying, "Would that even today you knew the things that make for peace! But now they are hid from your eyes. For the days shall come upon you, when your enemies will cast up a bank about you and surround you, and hem you in on every side, and dash you to the ground, you and your children within you, and they will not leave one stone upon another in you; because you did not know the time of your visitation." (Luke 19:41-44)

> And as he came out of the Temple, one of his disciples said to him, "Look, Teacher, what wonderful stones and what wonderful buildings!" And Jesus said to him, "Do you see these great buildings? There will not be left here one stone upon another, that will not be thrown down." (Mark 13:1-2 par)

---

15   E. P. Sanders, *Jesus and Judaism* (Philadelphia: Fortress, 1985) 85. On עד as the correct reading, see Sanders, 370 n. 18. The eschatological orientation of the text becomes probable if we follow Florentino García Martínez's restoration of בריה ("creation") instead of ברכה ("blessing") in 11QTemple 29:9-10: "until the day of creation, when I shall create My Temple and establish it for ever"; cf. F. García Martínez, *Qumran and Apocalyptic: Studies on the Aramaic Texts from Qumran* (STDJ 9; Leiden: Brill, 1992) 205.

16   For a discussion of this question see Gaston, *No Stone on Another*, 127-28, 164; and Sanders, *Jesus and Judaism*, 84-85.

17   Dupont-Sommer, *The Essene Writings*, 268 n. 3.

But when you see Jerusalem surrounded by armies, then know that its desolation has come near. Then let those who are in Judea flee to the mountains, and let those who are inside the city depart, and let not those who are out in the country enter it; for these are days of vengeance, to fulfill all that is written. Alas for those who are with child and for those who give suck in those days! For great distress shall come upon the earth and wrath upon this people; and they will fall by the edge of the sword, and be led captive among all nations; and Jerusalem will be trodden down by the Gentiles, until the times of the Gentiles are fulfilled. (Luke 21:20-24 par)

We have heard him say, "I shall destroy this handmade sanctuary and after three days I raise up another not handmade." (Mark 14:58 par; cf. John 2:19: "Destroy this sanctuary and in three days I shall raise it up.")

And there followed him a great multitude of the people, and of women who bewailed and lamented him. But Jesus turning to them said, "Daughters of Jerusalem, do not weep for me, but weep for yourselves and for your children. For behold, the days are coming when they will say, 'Blessed are the barren, and the wombs that never bore, and the breasts that never gave suck!' Then they will begin to say to the mountains, 'Fall on us'; and to the hills, 'Cover us.' For if they do this when the wood is green, what will happen when it is dry?" (Luke 23:27-31)

An increasing number of scholars has come to the conclusion that Jesus did predict the Temple's destruction. Usually most are willing to accept the version found in Mark 13:2, "There will not be left here one stone upon another, that will not be thrown down," but many suspect that much of the remaining material has been heavily redacted by early Christians, either shortly before the Temple's destruction, or shortly after. The accusation of the "false" witnesses (Mark 14:57-58) presents special problems. In what sense is it false? Did Jesus actually threaten to destroy the Temple? Sanders thinks that he did.[18] I think that it is more likely, however, that Jesus predicted that the Temple would be destroyed and that he and/or his community would replace it. More will be said about this below.

Lives of the Prophets

The *Lives of Prophets*, probably pre-70,[19] contains two prophecies

---

[18]   Sanders, *Jesus and Judaism*, 71-76.
[19]   On the date of the *Lives of the Prophets* C. C. Torrey (*The Lives of the Prophets* [SBLMS 1; Philadelphia: SBL, 1946] 11) concluded that "the probability

of the destruction of the first-century Temple:

> And he [Jonah] gave a portent concerning Jerusalem and the whole land, that whenever they should see a stone crying out piteously the end was at hand. And whenever they should see all the gentiles in Jerusalem, the entire city would be razed to the ground. ([*Life of Jonah*] 10:10-11)[20]

> And concerning the end [συντέλεια] of the Temple he [Habakkuk] predicted, "By a western nation it will happen." "At that time," he said, "the curtain [ἄπλωμα] of the Dabeir [i.e. the Holy of Holies] will be torn into small pieces, and the capitals of the two pillars will be taken away, and no one will know where they are; and they will be carried away by angels into the wilderness, where the Tent of Witness was set up in the beginning." ([*Life of Habakkuk*] 12:11)[21]

Douglas R. A. Hare believes that these prophecies are not based upon the events of 70 C.E. In reference to the prophecy credited to Jonah, he thinks that rather than the Romans, the prophecy seems "to reflect uneasiness regarding the increasing number of gentile visitors and/or residents, which threatened to change the character of Israel's holy city."[22] He adds that the "prophecy of 10:11 is best taken as reflecting an earlier situation, not the bitter experience" of 70 C.E.[23] In reference to Habakkuk's prophecy of the Temple's destruction at the hands of a "western nation," Hare similarly concludes that the "prediction of [*Lives*] 12:11 that the Temple will be destroyed by a Western nation was probably understood as referring to the Romans, but nothing requires that it be taken as a prophecy after the fact; the accompanying statements have the ring of unfulfilled predictions."[24]

I think that Hare is correct. But what about the tearing of the curtain? Could this be a *vaticinium ex eventu*? Probably not, for Josephus says nothing of the Temple veil(s) being torn to pieces. Rather, the veils (καταπετάσματα), vestments of the priests, and

---

is very strong . . . that the work was composed and given out before the year 80." D. R. A. Hare ("The Lives of the Prophets," in Charlesworth [ed.], *The Old Testament Pseudepigrapha*, 2.381 n. 11) dates much of the material before 70.

20   Trans. based on Hare, "Lives of the Prophets," 2.393.
21   Trans. based on Hare, "Lives of the Prophets," 2.393-94.
22   Hare, "Lives of the Prophets," 2.393 n. i.
23   Hare, "Lives of the Prophets," 2.381 n. 11.
24   Hare, "Lives of the Prophets," 2.381 n. 11.

several items belonging to the Temple were surrendered intact to the Romans (*J.W.* 6.8.3 §389-391) and were probably among the items carefully put on display in the newly constructed "Temple of Peace" (*J.W.* 7.5.7 §158-162). Even Mark 15:38, which says that "the veil [καταπέτασμα] of the Temple was torn in two from top to bottom," does not likely reflect either Josephus or *Lives*. Nor does it seem likely that *Lives* is dependent here on Mark.

Josephus

Josephus himself, who evidently prophesied Vespasian's elevation to Roman emperorship (*J.W.* 3.8.9 §400-402; cf. Tacitus, *Hist.* 1.10; 2:1; 5.13; Cassius Dio, *Hist. Rom.* 66.1.2-4; Suetonius, *Div. Vesp.* 4.5; Appian, *Hist. Rom.* 22, according to Zonaras, *Epitome Hist.* 11.16), also claims to have predicted the destruction of the Temple and the defeat of the Jewish rebels:

> But as . . . Josephus overheard the threats of the hostile crowd, suddenly there came back into his mind those nightly dreams, in which God had foretold to him the impending fate of the Jews and the destinies of the Roman sovereigns . . . he was not ignorant of the prophecies in the sacred books. (*J.W.* 3.8.3 §351-352)

This prophecy clarifies Josephus' occasional fatalistic statements: "That building, however, God, indeed long since, had sentenced to the flames" (*J.W.* 6.4.5 §250). But what "prophecies in the sacred books" did Josephus have in mind? He relates two of them, albeit in very cryptic terms:

> Who does not know the records of the ancient prophets and that oracle [χρησμός] which threatens this poor city and is even now coming true? For they foretold that it would then be taken whenever one should begin to slaughter his own countrymen. (*J.W.* 6.2.1 §109)

> Thus the Jews, after the demolition of Antonia, reduced the Temple to a square, although they had it recorded in their oracles that the city and the sanctuary would be taken when the Temple should become foursquare (τετράγωνος). (*J.W.* 6.5.4 §311)[25]

There is some speculation that the first passage, the one alluding

---

[25]   Trans. based on H. St. J. Thackeray, *Josephus II* and *III* (LCL 203, 210; Cambridge: Harvard University, 1927-28) 2.675, 3.407, 447, 467.

to an "oracle" that speaks of fratricide, may have been dependent on *Sib. Or.* 4:115-118: "An evil storm of war will also come upon Jerusalem from Italy, and it will sack the great Temple of, whenever they put their trust in folly and cast off piety and commit repulsive murders in front of the Temple."[26] But this prophecy is clearly a *vaticinium ex eventu*, for the lines that follow (lines 119-127) unmistakably describe Nero, the bloody imperial succession, the arrival of Titus, the burning of the Jerusalem Temple, and the slaughter of the Jewish people. The allusion to the eruption of Vesuvius in 79 C.E. (lines 128-129) only confirms that these lines were written sometime after 80.[27] But is this the oracle that Josephus had in mind? It probably is not, for chronological reasons, if for no other. *The Jewish War* was written between 75, when the Temple of Peace was completed, and 79, the year that Vespasian died. Near the end of his account Josephus mentions the Flavian Temple (*J.W.* 7.5.7 §158), whose completion Cassius Dio (*Hist. Rom.* 66.15) dates to 75. We thus know that *War* itself was later than 75, but we also know that Vespasian was presented with a copy before his death.[28] It is not likely, therefore, that Josephus had seen the prophecy now preserved in the *Sibylline Oracles*. It is more likely that Josephus had in mind an oracle based on the Jewish scriptures (see below).

Perhaps the most remarkable oracle is that attributed to one Jesus, son of Ananias, who for seven and a half years proclaimed the doom of Jerusalem and her Temple. According to Josephus:

> Four years before the war . . . one Jesus, son of Ananias ['Ιησοῦς . . . τις υἱὸς 'Ανανίου] . . . who, standing in the Temple [ἱερόν], suddenly began to cry out:
> "A voice from the east,
> "A voice from the west,
> "A voice from the four winds,
> "A voice against Jerusalem and the Sanctuary [ναός],
> "A voice against the bridegroom and the bride,
> "A voice against all people" (*J.W.* 6.5.3 §301)

---

26   Thackeray, *Josephus*, 3.406-7 n. b. Translation based on Collins, "Sibylline Oracles," 1.387.
27   See Collins, "Sibylline Oracles," 1.382.
28   Thackeray, *Josephus*, 2.xii.

"Woe to Jerusalem!" (*J.W.* 6.5.3 §306)

"Woe once more to the city and to the people and to the Sanctuary [ναός]
. . . and woe to me also" (*J.W.* 6.5.3 §309)[29]

Josephus tells us that this Jesus, a "rude peasant," was arrested by
leading citizens and was severely chastised. When he continued to cry
out as before, he was taken before the Roman governor, who had him
"flayed to the bone with scourges" (*J.W.* 6.5.3 §302-304). Albinus
decided that he was a maniac, and so he released him (§305). Jesus
continued to proclaim his foreboding oracle, until he was killed by a
siege stone catapulted over the city wall (§309).

Yoḥanan ben Zakkai and Zadok

Apparently two Tannaim predicted the destruction of the first-
century Temple:

> Forty years before the destruction of the Temple the western light went
> out, the crimson thread remained crimson, and the lot for the Lord always
> came up in the left hand. They would close the gates of the Temple by night
> and get up in the morning and find them wide open. Said Rabban Yoḥanan
> ben Zakkai [1st cent.] to the Temple, "O Temple, why do you frighten us?
> We know that you will end up destroyed. For it has been said, 'Open you
> doors, O Lebanon,[30] that the fire may devour your cedars' [Zech 11:1]."[31]
> (*y. Soṭa* 6.3)

> During the last forty years before the destruction of the Temple the lot
> [for the Lord] did not come up in the right hand; nor did the crimson-
> colored strap become white; nor did the western-most light shine; and the

---

29   Trans. based on Thackeray, *Josephus*, 3.463-67.
30   "Lebanon" is understood to refer to the Temple: "'And Lebanon,' meaning
the Temple, as in the passage: 'Open your doors, O Lebanon' [Zech 11:1]" (*Mek.*
on Exod 17:14 [*Amalek* §2]). This equation is based on a word-play between לבנון
("Lebanon") and לבן ("white"); see *Tg.* Hab 2:17 where "Lebanon" = the Temple.
Cedars from Lebanon were used, of course, in the construction of the Temple (1
Kgs 5:6). Elswhere Lebanon was closely associated with the Temple (cf. Isa
60:13). For further discussion, see G. Vermes, *Scripture and Tradition in Judaism*
(SPB 4; 2nd ed., Leiden: Brill, 1983) 26-39; M. N. A. Bockmuehl, "Why Did
Jesus Predict the Destruction of the Temple?" *Crux* 25.3 (1989) 11-18, esp. 13-14.
31   Trans. from J. Neusner, *Messiah in Context: Israel's History and Destiny*
in Formative Judaism (Philadelphia: Fortress, 1984) 112.

doors of the Temple would open by themselves, until Rabbi Yoḥanan ben
Zakkai rebuked them, saying: "Temple, Temple, why will you be the alarm
yourself? I know that you will be destroyed, for Zechariah ben Ido has
already prophesied concerning you: 'Open your doors, O Lebanon, that the
fire may devour your cedars" [Zech 11:1]."[32] (*b. Yoma* 39b)

[When Vespasian objected to Yoḥanan ben Zakkai's greeting, "Vive
domine Imperator," Yoḥanan explained:] "If you are not the king, you will
be eventually, because the Temple will only be destroyed by a king's hand;
as it is said, 'And Lebanon shall fall by a mighty one' [Isa 10:34]."[33] (*Lam.
Rab.* 1:5 §31)

Rabbi Zadok [1st cent.] observed fasts for forty years in order that
Jerusalem might not be destroyed, [and he became so thin that] when he ate
anything the food could be seen [as it passed down his throat].[34] (*b. Giṭ.*
56a)

It says, "Open your doors, O Lebanon, that the fire may devour your
cedars" [Zech 11:1]. This refers to the high priests who were in the Temple,
who took their keys in their hands and threw them up to the sky, saying to
the Holy One, blessed be He, "Master of the Universe, here are Your keys
which You handed over to us, for we have not been trustworthy custodians
to do the King's work and to eat of the King's table."[35] (*'Abot R. Nat.* [A]
4.5)

Yoḥanan ben Zakkai and other rabbis apparently tried to persuade
the rebels to surrender to the Romans. Nearly murdered for his failure
to support the rebellion, Yoḥanan finally escaped the city, being
carried out in a coffin (*Lam. Rab.* 1:5 §31; *b. Giṭ.* 56a-b; *Abot R. Nat.*
[A] 4.5). According to the tradition in *Lamentations Rabbah* Zadok's
life was spared at Yoḥanan's request.

Examination of these traditions and oracles that speak of the coming destruction of the Herodian Temple reveals that they are almost

---

[32] Trans. based on L. Jung, "Yoma," in I. Epstein (ed.), *The Babylonian
Talmud* (18 vols., London: Soncino, 1978) 4.186.
[33] Trans. based on J. Neusner, *A Life of Rabban Yohanan ben Zakkai* (SPB
6; Leiden: Brill, 1962) 40.
[34] Trans. based on M. Simon, "Gittin," in Epstein (ed.), *The Babylonian
Talmud*, 9.257.
[35] Trans. based on J. Goldin, *The Fathers according to Rabbi Nathan* (YJS
10; New Haven and London: Yale University, 1955) 37.

always based upon the language and oracles of the classic prophets of the Old Testament. This observation also applies to the predictions of Jesus. Virtually every phrase reflects the language and imagery of the prophets who spoke of the destruction of the Solomonic Temple.

My study of these predictions and the factors that may have occasioned them has led me to the following four conclusions:

1. As did many others, Jesus predicted the destruction of the Herodian Temple. This tradition is well attested and is corroborated in a variety of ways.

2. As did many others, Jesus employed the language of the classical prophets, particularly Jeremiah and Ezekiel, whose oracles were concerned with the Babylonian destruction of the Solomonic Temple, in predicting the Herodian Temple's destruction. Moreover, Jesus even alluded to some of the same complaints (e.g. Jer 7:11).

3. There is substantial evidence of corruption in the Herodian Temple establishment. Furthermore, there is evidence of sectarian and peasant resentment toward the ruling establishment (i.e. ruling priests, Roman authorities). Jesus' action in the Temple (the so-called "cleansing") was in all probability related, indeed, possibly the occasion for a prophetic word against the Temple.

4. The fact that the first-century Temple was built by Herod may have been a factor in anticipating its destruction. Built by Herod and administered by corrupt non-Zadokite ruling priestly families, the Temple faced certain destruction. However, whether or not this was a factor in Jesus' actions or in his prediction of the Temple's destruction is not certain. It must remain no more than a speculation. That he was critical of the Herodian dynasty and that Herod Antipas took an malevolent interest in Jesus seem likely.[36]

---

36   Evidence and arguments for points 2–4 will be found in Evans, "Predictions of the Destruction of the Herodian Temple."

CHAPTER TEN

GOD'S VINEYARD AND ITS CARETAKERS[1]

Martin Hengel's study of the Parable of the Vineyard Tenants (Mark 12:1-12) clarified the historical realism of the details that make up the parable.[2] His work has effectively answered critics who have from time to time claimed that the parable is unrealistic and so in all probability arose in the early Church as an allegory based on the life and death of Jesus.[3] Both of Hengel's principal conclusions, viz. that the parable is authentic dominical tradition and that the parable is a judgment parable, are fully justified.[4] It is the purpose of this chapter

---

[1]   Part of this chapter is a revision of my brief study, "On the Vineyard Parables of Isaiah 5 and Mark 12," *BZ* 28 (1984) 82-86.

[2]   M. Hengel, "Das Gleichnis von den Weingärtnern Mc 12:1-12 im Lichte der Zenonpapyri und der rabbinischen Gleichnisse," *ZNW* 59 (1968) 1-39.

[3]   For a summary of the objections that have been and can be raised against the realism and authenticity of the parable, see W. G. Kümmel, "Das Gleichnis von den bösen Weingärtnern (Mk 12, 1–9)," in O. Cullmann and P. H. Menaud (eds.) *Aux Sources de la Tradition Chrétienne, Mélanges offerts à Maurice Goguel* (Bibliothèque Théologique; Neuchâtel and Paris: Delachaux et Niestle, 1950) 120-31; repr. in Kümmel, *Heilsgeschehen und Geschichte* (ed. E. Grässer et al., MTS 3; Marburg: N. G. Elwert, 1965) 207-17; idem, *Promise and Fulfillment: The Eschatological Message of Jesus* (SBT 23; Naperville: Allenson, 1957) 82-83; C. E. Carlston, *The Parables of the Triple Tradition* (Philadelphia: Fortress, 1975) 178-90. Because of the lack of realism Carlston concludes that it is "highly unlikely that this parable is to be ascribed to Jesus" (p. 187). Objections based on the unrealistic aspects of the parable have been answered, however, by E. Linnemann, *Gleichnisse Jesu: Einführung und Auslegung* (Göttingen: Vandenhoeck & Ruprecht, 1961) 36-37; ET: *Parables of Jesus: Introduction and Exposition* (London: SPCK, 1966) 28-29, which Hengel ("Das Gleichnis von den Weingärtnern," 9-11) cites with approval and to which he adds further pertinent observations; and esp. K. R. Snodgrass, *The Parable of the Wicked Tenants* (WUNT 27; Tübingen: Mohr [Siebeck], 1983) 31-40.

[4]   This appears to be the scholarly consensus today, though with much disagreement over how much of the parable belongs to the original form, which Gospel source preserves the original form, and just exactly what it meant in the *Sitz im Leben Jesu*. See B. B. Scott, *Hear Then the Parable: A Commentary on the Parables of Jesus* (Minneapolis: Fortress, 1989) 237-53; R. W. Funk et al. (eds.), *The Parables of Jesus* (Sonoma: Polebridge, 1988) 50-51; R. W. Funk and R. W.

to offer additional support and to answer critics who in more recent years accept the authenticity of Mark 12:1-9, but not that of the concluding quotation of Ps 118:22-23, and who reject the autobiographical interpretation of the parable. Mark 12:1-12 reads:

1. Καὶ ἤρξατο αὐτοῖς ἐν παραβολαῖς λαλεῖν, Ἀμπελῶνα ἄνθρωπος ἐφύτευσεν καὶ περιέθηκεν φραγμὸν καὶ ὤρυξεν ὑπολήνιον καὶ ᾠκοδόμησεν πύργον καὶ ἐξέδετο αὐτὸν γεωργοῖς καὶ ἀπεδήμησεν. 2. καὶ ἀπέστειλεν πρὸς τοὺς γεωργοὺς τῷ καιρῷ δοῦλον ἵνα παρὰ τῶν γεωργῶν λάβῃ ἀπὸ τῶν καρπῶν τοῦ ἀμπελῶνος· 3. καὶ λαβόντες αὐτὸν ἔδειραν καὶ ἀπέστειλαν κενόν. 4. καὶ πάλιν ἀπέστειλεν πρὸς αὐτοὺς ἄλλον δοῦλον· κἀκεῖνον ἐκεφαλίωσαν καὶ ἠτίμασαν. 5. καὶ ἄλλον ἀπέστειλεν· κἀκεῖνον ἀπέκτειναν, καὶ πολλοὺς ἄλλους, οὓς μὲν δέροντες, οὓς δὲ ἀποκτέννοντες. 6. ἔτι ἕνα εἶχεν υἱὸν ἀγαπητόν· ἀπέστειλεν αὐτὸν ἔσχατον πρὸς αὐτοὺς λέγων ὅτι Ἐντραπήσονται τὸν υἱόν μου. 7. ἐκεῖνοι δὲ οἱ γεωργοὶ πρὸς ἑαυτοὺς εἶπαν ὅτι Οὗτός ἐστιν ὁ κληρονόμος· δεῦτε ἀποκτείνωμεν αὐτόν, καὶ ἡμῶν ἔσται ἡ κληρονομία. 8. καὶ λαβόντες ἀπέκτειναν αὐτόν καὶ ἐξέβαλον αὐτὸν ἔξω τοῦ ἀμπελῶνος. 9. τί [οὖν] ποιήσει ὁ κύριος τοῦ ἀμπελῶνος; ἐλεύσεται καὶ ἀπολέσει τοὺς γεωργούς καὶ δώσει τὸν ἀμπελῶνα ἄλλοις. 10. οὐδὲ τὴν γραφὴν ταύτην ἀνέγνωτε,

Λίθον ὃν ἀπεδοκίμασαν οἱ οἰκοδομοῦντες,
οὗτος ἐγενήθη εἰς κεφαλὴν γωνίας·

11. παρὰ κυρίου ἐγένετο αὕτη
καὶ ἔστιν θαυμαστὴ ἐν ὀφθαλμοῖς ἡμῶν;

12. Καὶ ἐζήτουν αὐτὸν κρατῆσαι, καὶ ἐφοβήθησαν τὸν ὄχλον, ἔγνωσαν γὰρ ὅτι πρὸς αὐτοὺς τὴν παραβολὴν εἶπεν. καὶ ἀφέντες αὐτὸν ἀπῆλθον.

HISTORICAL REALISM

Hengel brought to our attention the relevance of Zenon's third century B.C.E. archive of letters for a better understanding the background of the Parable of the Vineyard Tenants (or Farmers). The difficulties of administering commercial farms and vineyards, almost always from a distance, are amply and colorfully illustrated in this correspondence. The paragraphs that follow draw upon the sources

---

Hoover (eds.), *The Five Gospels* (New York: Macmillan, 1993) 510-11. The latter works, both produced by the Jesus Seminar, accept the authenticity of the Vineyard Parable as it is preserved in the *Gospel of Thomas* (§65). European scholars also incline to accepting the authenticity of the parable; cf. M. D. Hooker, *The Gospel according to Saint Mark* (BNTC; London: Black, 1991) 273-75; M. Hubaut, "La parabole des vignerons homicides: son authenticité, sa visée première," *RTL* 6 (1975) 51-61; H.-J. Klauck, *Allegorie und Allegorese in synoptischen Gleichnistexten* (Münster: Aschendorff, 1978) 308-309; J. Nolland, *Luke 18:35–24:53* (WBC 35C; Dallas: Word, 1993) 949-50.

below, which have been abbreviated acccordingly:

BGU	*Aegyptische Urkunden aus den staatlichen Museen zu Berlin: Griechische Urkunden* (4 vols., Berlin: Weidmann, 1895-1912)
CPJ	V. A. Tcherikover and A. Fuks (eds.), *Corpus Papyrorum Judaicarum* (2 vols., Jerusalem: Magnes Press; Cambridge: Harvard University Press, 1957-60)
PCairZen	C. C. Edgar, *Catalogue général des antiquités égyptiennes du Musée du Caire: Zenon Papyri* (4 vols., Cairo: Service des antiquites de l'Egypt, 1925-31; repr. Hildesheim and New York: Olms, 1971)
PCol	W. L. Westermann and E. S. Hasenoehrl (eds.), *Zenon Papyri: Business Papers of the Third Century B.C. Dealing with Palestine and Egypt* (Columbia Papyri: Greek Series 3; New York: Columbia University Press, 1934)
Pestman	P. W. Pestman (ed.), *Greek and Demotic Texts from the Zenon Archive* (Papyrologica Lugduno-Batava 20A; Leiden: Brill, 1980)
PLond	F. G. Kenyon and H. I. Bell (eds.), *Greek Papyri in the British Museum* (5 vols., London: Oxford University Press, 1893-1917)
PRyl	C. H. Roberts and G. E. Turner (eds.), *Catalogue of the Greek and Latin Papyri in the John Rylands Library Manchester* (vol. 4, Manchester: Manchester University Press, 1952)
PMich	C. C. Edgar, *Zenon Papyri in the University of Michigan Collection* (Michigan Papyri 1; Ann Arbor: University of Michigan Press, 1931)
PPetrie	J. P. Mahaffy and J. G. Smyly (eds.), *The Flinders Petrie Papyri with Transcriptions, Commentaries and Index* (3 vols., Proceedings of the Royal Irish Academy 8, 9, and 11; Dublin: Academy House, 1891-1905)
PSAAthen	Papyri of the Societas Archaeologica Atheniensis
PSI	G. Vitelli et al. (eds.), *Publicazioni della Società italiana per la Ricerca dei Papiri greci e latini in Egitto: Papiri greci e latini* (15 vols., Florence: E. Ariani, 1912-79)
SPap	A. S. Hunt and C. C. Edgar, *Select Papyri* (2 vols., LCL 266, 282; London: Heinemann; Cambridge: Harvard University Press, 1932-34)
White	J. L. White, *Light from Ancient Letters* (Foundations and Facets; Philadelphia: Fortress, 1986)

Zenon son of Agreophon, the Caunian (cf. PCairZen 59.257), was in the employ of one Apollonius, a διοικητής ("minister [of finance]"), in the service of Ptolemy II Philadelphus, king of the Ptolemaic empire (282–246 B.C.E.), which at that time included Egypt and Palestine. Zenon worked for Apollonius in an official capacity, overseeing much of the latter's imperial busineṣ activities. Zenon also served as manager of Apollonius' estate in Philadelphia. In the 27th year of the

reign of Philadelphus (259 B.C.E.) Zenon traveled extensively through
the length and breadth of Palestine tending to the business of
Apollonius.[5] Among other things, Zenon oversaw the development
and management of various orchards and vineyards, including one in
Beth Anath of Galilee. Many of the details and problems with which he
had to deal provide an illuminating backdrop against which Jesus'
Parable of the Vineyard Tenants should be understood. A few other
related papyri that are not part of the Zenon archive will also be cited
and discussed.

Lease Agreements. PCairZen no. 59.257 (252 B.C.E.) describes a
sharecropping agreement: "Let Zenon deduct for him in respect of the
rent due for the 35th year corn at whatever price it may be being sold
at the threshing-floor . . . ."[6] The lease agreements concerning a
vineyard in PRyl no. 583 (170 B.C.E.) and a farm in PRyl no. 582 (42
B.C.E.) are instructive. The latter guarantees shares of the harvest and
outlines the consequences should anyone renege. The former reports
that "Nicomachus, son of Ph[. . . .]ades of Halicarnassus, successor to
his father's holding, has leased to Apollonius son of Apollonius,
Persian of the Epigone, the somewhat sandy vineyard [ἀμπελών]
situated near the same Philadelphia." It is quite possible that
Apollonius the father in this lease is either Apollonius, Zenon's
superior, or his son of the same name. We cannot be sure, given the
popularity of this name. The lease goes on to spell out the following
provisions: "for the first year for a rent of two-thirds of all the fruits
[καρποί] and produce that grow in this vineyard [ἀμπελών]; viz., when
all fruits [καρποί] have been turned into wine and deductions made for
the apomoira due to the Treasury, wages for the treaders, hire of
winepress [ληνός] and a contribution (in the month of the vintage?) of a
half kados to the agricultural guild, the must remaining shall be
divided into three portions, of which Nicomachus shall take two and
Apollonius one. Each shall provide jars for himself and as required for
the apomoira according to the proportions of his lease, and each shall

---

5   See the discussion in M. Rostovtzeff, *A Large Estate in the Third Century
B.C.* (University of Wisconsin Studies in the Social Sciences and History 6;
Madison: University of Wisconsin Press, 1922); C. C. Edgar, *Zenon Papyri in the
University of Michigan Collection* (Michigan Papyri 1; Ann Arbor: University of
Michigan Press, 1931) 1-60; *CPJ* 115-30; Hengel, "Das Gleichnis von den
Weingärtnern," 11-16; idem, *Judaism and Hellenism* (2 vols., London: SCM;
Philadelphia: Fortress, 1974) 1.32-57.
6   Pestman 102-103.

carry down the jars for himself to the winepress [λήνος] . . ."

Two other lease agreements are noteworthy for their provisions dealing with failure and disobedience. In the first lease (*SPap* no. 203; 259 B.C.E.) strong incentives are put in place to see to it that the land is properly sown and harvested. Apollonius directs that the manager of the farm shall "himself exact payment from the disobedient cultivators" (αὐτὸς δὲ πρασσέτω παρὰ τῶν γεωργῶν τῶν ἠπειθηκότων). The second (*SPap* no. 39 = PCol no. 270; 256 B.C.E.) is a lease of a portion of Apollonius' estate, through the finance minister's trusted agent Zenon, to three men "of the Macedonian Epigone." This lease is quite similar to PRyl no. 583. With respect to payment the lessees are to "measure out the corn for rent at the granary in Philadelphia in accordance with the ordinance concerning corn-collecting." However, "if they fail to do as they have agreed, Zenon shall be at liberty to lease the land to others."

Development. Although poorly preserved, it is clear that PCairZen no. 59.162 contains instructions relating to the development of vineyards and orchards: "We have sent to Philadelphia [ten thousand] vine cuttings [φυτὰ ἀμπέλινα], one thousand five hundred [young plants], and five [hundred] pomegranate . . . of the servants. Therefore diligently . . . plant [φυτεύειν] . . . ."[7] In PSAAthen no. 4 Isocrates, the "winemaker" (οἰνοποιός), instructs one Bion to fence in (περιφραχθῆι) the vineyard, to protect its shoots from being eaten by animals.[8] In *PSI* no. 624 Zenon, possibly writing in his own hand, gives instructions relating to the care of the vineyard (ἀμπελών) and the securing of its fruit (καρποί).[9] In *PPetrie* no. 13 Zenon instructs Kleon to open the sluicegates because the water level in the canal is too low to irrigate the land adequately.[10] In *PSI* no. 1013 Nicon reports to Zenon that the gardeners have been paid and he now thinks it is necessary to dig a trench around the vineyard (ἀμπελών).[11] See also the instructions to Panakestor, one of Zenon's associates, given in PCairZen no. 59.816 (257 C.E.): καὶ μὴ ἀργήσηι μέρος μηθὲν τῆς γῆς ("no portion of the land should remain uncultivated").[12] PRyl no. 583 requires Apollonius "to prune the vine moderately and exactly, to attend properly to the

---

7   Pestman 121.
8   Pestman 199-200.
9   Pestman 228-30.
10   Pestman 266-67.
11   Pestman 155-56.
12   White 43-44.

dressing of the young vines, to keep the ground of the property clear of weedy growth . . . and is to maintain the cross-trenches dug [διωρυγμένας] and clean and the property fenced [περιφραγμένον]; he is to clear out the drains and fence the conduit facing the [. . .] and lead it through for watering; and when the lease has expired, he is to deliver the ground of the property in clean condition and the cross-trenches clean, as is presently stated."

Inspection. PLond no. 1948 (257 B.C.E) reads: παραγενόμενος δὲ καὶ εἰς Βαιτανῶτα καὶ παραλαβὼν Μέλανα ἐπῆλθον τὰ φυτὰ καὶ τἆλλα πάντα. ἱκανῶς οὖ<μ>μοι δοκεῖ κατειργάσθαι, ἔφη δὲ εἶναι τὴν ἄμπελον μυριάδας ὀκτώ. κατασκευάκει δὲ καὶ φρῆρ καὶ οἴκησιν ἱκανήν. ἔγευσεν δὲ καὶ τοῦ οἴνου, ὃν οὐ διέγνων πότερον Χῖός ἐστιν ἢ ἐπιχώριος ("As soon as I had come to Beth-Anath and had consulted Melas, I inspected the plants and everything else. It seems then to me to be properly done, and he said that there were 80,000 vines. He had also built a well and sufficient housing; and he tasted the wine, which I did not know whether it was from Chios or from the country").[13]

Disputed Tax Assessments and Rents. SPap no. 265 (= PCairZen 59.236; 254 or 253 B.C.E.) is a petition to the διοικητής Diotimus: "My father is being wronged by Theocles the former steward of the Aphroditopolite nome and Petosiris the royal scribe. For in calculating the tax to be paid on the vineyards they used to take the produce of the last three years and make the third part of this the basis of the tax, but in the case of my father they have calculated the tax on the average of the last two years, saying that his vineyard was recently planted."

PRyl no. 578 (ca. 58 C.E.) is a petition from a Jewish man named Judas, who farms (γεωργῶν) near Philadelphia. He claims that he has worked hard and has paid his annual rent satisfactorily. But Marres the village scribe has, "contrary to what is right," changed the agreement and now charges too much.

Theft and Neglect. CPJ no. 14 (= PSI no. 393; 241 B.C.E) describes theft from a vineyard leased to tenant farmers and the declaration made by the "vinedressers, the tenants of the vinyard belonging to Zenon and Sostratos" (ἀμπελουργῶν τῶν ἐξειληφότων τὸν Ζήνωνος καὶ Σωστράτου ἀμπελῶνα). It is interesting to note that one of the vinedressers was named Σαμοῆλις, which is very probably a Semitic

---

13 See Hengel, "Das Gleichnis von den Weingärtnern," 12 and n. 46. On the restoration of οὖμ (= οὖν), see Hengel, 13 n. 46a.

name (perhaps a variant of שְׁמוּאֵל, Samuel).[14] Of the risks of managing
a vineyard the desperate letter of a father to his son is illustrative:
"Already indeed I have written you regarding the [. . .] and you
neither answered nor came, and now, if you do not come, I run the risk
of losing the lot (of land) which I possess. Our partner has taken no
share in the work, for not only was the well not cleaned out, but in
addition the canal was choked with sand, and the land is untilled. Not
one of the tenants [γεωργῶν] was willing to work it, only I continue
paying the public taxes without getting back anything in return. There
is hardly a single plot that the water will irrigate. Therefore you must
come, otherwise there is a risk that the plants will perish" (*BGU* 2.174;
1st cent. C.E.).[15]

   Labor Problems. PSI no. 502 (257 B.C.E.) is a letter from
Panakestor to Zenon in which the former expresses dismay that there
has been no report about τῆς συντιμήσεως καὶ τῆς συναγωγῆς τοῦ
σπόρου ("the value of the harvest"). The letter goes on to describe the
tenant farmers' (γεωργοί) dissatisfaction with the terms of evaluation
and their going on strike by taking up residence in a temple: οἱ δ᾽ ἐπὶ
μὲν τοῦ παρόντος ἔφασαν βουλευσάμενοι ἀποφανεῖσθαι ἡμῖν, μετὰ δ᾽
ἡμέρας δ̄ καθίσαντες εἰς τὸ ἱερὸν οὐκ ἔφασαν . . . συντιμήσεσθαι "They
said that after having deliberated for a while they would give us their
answer and, after four days, having taken up residence in the temple,
they said that they did not want to agree to any evaluation . . . ."[16]

   CPJ no. 15 (= PCairZen no. 59.367; 240 B.C.E.) is a letter from
Zeno to partner Sostratos concerning neighbors of their leased
vineyard (referred to in *CPJ* no. 14 above) who are creating problems
for the workers: "Samoelis and Alexander have been prevented by the
[. . .] from travelling through the vineyards, and [. . .] the reeds(s)
[. . .] by us in the area of the second dike by the canal, they protested
that they [. . .] the vineyard, but were resigning it since they could not
get to it from one side, and it was impossible to travel all the way
through the vineyards. They add that for some time those in charge of
this part were reasonable, but now they too keep them out. So take

---

   14   Σαμοῆλος occurs in Jewish inscriptions; cf. W. Horbury and D. Noy,
Jewish Inscriptions of Graeco-Roman Egypt (Cambridge: Cambridge University
Press, 1992) 51 (= *CIJ* no. 1451), 127 (= *CIJ* no. 1469). Horbury and Noy (p.
54) think the name is one of several Greek forms for the Hebrew name Samuel.
   15   See G. Milligan, *Selections from the Greek Papyri* (Cambridge: Cambridge
University Press, 1912) 60-63.
   16   White 41-43.

thought and consider [. . .] how to prevent them from abandoning the vineyard, so that so great a sum of money should not be lost." The same papyrus concludes with a note addressed to Samoelis and Alexander: "I understand that, though you have leased the 60-arourai vineyard with a plentiful supply of reeds you are intending to default in your agreement with me. I am writing so that you may undestand [. . .] the vineyard [. . .] (to break) the law [. . .] for neither [. . .]." Although the papyrus is fragmentary, the gist of the problem faced by Zeno and his lessees is obvious.

PSI no. 554 (258 B.C.E.), which is poorly preserved and may have come from Beth Anath,[17] describes difficulties dealing with rebellious tenant farmers, who are exhorted: καὶ αὐτακτεῖν, καὶ ὅτι ἐὰν ταῦτα ποιῶσιν τεύξονται παρὰ σοῦ πάντων τῶν φιλανθρώπων. καὶ ταῦτα παρακαλέσαντες ἀπεστείλαμεν αὐτούς ("also to observe order [*or* pay fully and punctually]; and should they do these things, they will gain from you (Apollonius) all every human kindness. With these exhortations we sent them."[18] The writer of this letter has resorted to pleading with his subordinates that they keep in line.

Rejected Emissaries. Another good example is seen in Zenon's attempt to collect a debt from a Jewish man in Judaea named Jeddous[19] (*CPJ* no. 6 = PCairZen no. 59.018; 258 B.C.E.). Zenon's agent, a man named Alexandros, sent a servant with Straton to the debtor. Alexandros writes to a colleague explaining his lack of success: ἐκομισάμην τὸ παρὰ σοῦ ἐπιστόλιον, ἐν ὧι ὑπέγραψάς μοι τήν τε παρὰ Ζήνωνος πρὸς Ἰεδδοῦν γεγραμμένην, ὅπως ἄν, ἐὰμ μὴ ἀποδιδῶι τἀργύριον Στράτωνι τῶι παρὰ Ζήνωνος παραγενομένωι, ἐνέχυρα αὐτοῦ παραδείξωμεν αὐτῶι. ἐγὼ μὲν οὖν ἄρρωστος ἐτύγχανον ἐκ φαρμακείας ὤν, συναπέστειλα δὲ Στράτωνι παρ᾽ ἡμῶν νεανίσκον καὶ ἐπιστολὴν ἔγραψα πρὸς Ἰεδδοῦν. παραγενόμενοι οὖν εἶπόν μοι μηθένα λόγον πεποιῆσθαι τῶι ἐπιστολίωι μου, αὐτοῖς δὲ χεῖρας προσενεγκεῖν καὶ ἐγβαλεῖν ἐκ τῆς κώμης. γέγραφα οὖν σοι ("I have received your letter, to which you added a copy of the letter written by Zenon to Jeddous saying that unless he gave the money to Straton, Zenon's man, we were to hand over his pledge to him (Straton). I happened to be unwell as a

---

17   So V. Tcherikover, "Palestine under the Ptolemies: (A Contribution to the Study of the Zenon Papyri)," *Mizraim* 4-5 (1937) 9-90, esp. 45. Tcherikover is certain that the letter refers to labor difficulties in Beth Anath.

18   See Hengel, "Das Gleichnis von den Weingärtnern," 14-15.

19   Ἰεδδοῦς is the Greek form of ידוע (see LXX Neh 12:12 where the Greek form is Ἰδούα; and Josephus, *Ant.* 11.7.2 §302 where it is Ἰαδδοῦς).

result of taking some medicine, so I sent a young man, a servant of mine, to Straton, and wrote a letter to Jeddous. When they returned they said that he had taken no notice of my letter, but had attacked them and thrown them out of the village. So I am writing to you"). This cavalier treatment is significant and will be discussed shortly.

Another letter from the Zenon archive is illustrative of this kind of problem. An exasperated corn-measurer swore out the following affidavit: "Seeing that in spite of Zenon's order that I should be employed in the granary Kleitarchos and Maron and Anosis have expelled my assistants from the granary [τοὺς ὑπηρέτας μου ἐγβεβλήκασιν ἐκ τοῦ θησαυροῦ] and employ the measurers of Stotoëtis, I have withdrawn from the granary with my assistants until Zenon arrives" (PMich no. 52; 250 B.C.E.).

Seeking Redress. PCol no. 54 (250 B.C.E.), a διάλογος πρὸς Θεόπομπον ("a reckoning against Theopompos"), provides an example of the legal steps that must be taken in order to prepare for action against lessees in violation of the lease agreement (see also PCairZen no. 59.666). Another fragmentary letter (*CPJ* no. 16 = PCairZen no. 59.618 + pl. XI), clearly a petition to the king, apparently from Zenon himself or on his behalf, complains of a failure of payment: οὐ[κ ἀποδί-δωσιν. δέομαι οὖν σου . . .] συντάξαι Ζήνωνι τ[. . . ἐπιδ]εί ξ[ωμεν τ]ὰ διὰ τῆς [ἐντεύξεως . . . ἐπὶ σὲ καταφυ]γὼν τὸν κοινὸν πάν[των σωτῆρα]. εὐ-[τύχει. ἀπόστ]ειλον πρὸς ἡμᾶς ὅπως περὶ τῶν ἐγ[καλουμένων] ("he refuses to pay. Therefore I beg you [. . .] to order Zenon [. . .] let us hand over the property mentioned in the (petition) [. . .] or the value [. . .] appealing to you, impartial saviour of all men. Farewell. Send him to me that (I may examine him) about the accusations"). The request to hand over the property may have to do with a provision in the lease that would grant the lessor the "liberty to lease the land to others," as in PRyl no. 583 above.

SPap no. 279 (= PRyl no. 119) is petition in which a debtor complains to Claudius Cronius, the magistrate of Alexandria (54–67 C.E.), that his creditor, a man named Musaeus, had wrongly foreclosed on a portion of the debtor's land and had seized some of the revenues. Apparently the creditor did not want the debt paid off, so that he could take permanent possession of the debtor's property: "He (i.e. the creditor) refused (a plan of repaying the debt), having grown covetous of it owing to the amount of its yearly produce." The petition goes to say: "We have therefore been robbed on every side by this man, against whom we made petitions and presented reports many in number, which he scorned in virtue of his superior local power, and we served a summons upon him and his sons Hermophilus and Castor to go down to the court, but making light of it his sons did not appear."

The verbal and conceptual parallels between the papyri and the Parable of the Vineyard Tenants are numerous and impressive. The most important include the following: "planting" (φυτεύειν; PCairZen no. 59.162; Mark 12:1); developing "vineyards," collecting "fruit," and operating a wine "press" (ἀμπελών, καρποί, and λήνος; PSI no. 624; PRyl no. 583; Mark 12:1 [ὑπολήνιον]); building ("tower" in Mark 12:1; "housing" in PLond no. 1948); fencing in the vineyards (PSAAthen no. 4: περιφραχθῆι; PRyl no. 583: περιφραγμένον; Mark 12:1: περιέθηκεν φραγμόν); "digging" and "hewing" (PRyl no. 583: διωρυγμένας; Mark 12:1: ὤρυξεν); leasing the vineyard to tenant "farmers" (PSI no. 502; SPap no. 203: γεωργοί; Mark 12:1: γεωργοί); "sending" servants (CPJ no. 6: συναπέστειλα; Mark 12:2, 4-5: ἀπέστειλεν), who were "cast out" (CPJ no. 6: ἐγβαλεῖν ἐκ τῆς κώμης; PMich no. 52: τοὺς ὑπηρέτας μου ἐγβεβλήκασιν ἐκ τοῦ θησαυροῦ; Mark 12:8: ἐξέβαλον αὐτὸν ἔξω τοῦ ἀμπελῶνος). Both the papyri and the parable expect redress of the wrongs suffered (CPJ no. 16; Mark 12:9).

An important point that must not be overlooked is that these "tenants" were not always poor farmers. Indeed, the lessee was often a fairly well to do individual. Like the Jewish man Jeddous or the dishonest creditor Musaeus, such an individual might not always be cooperative or respectful of the servants of a foreign creditor (or a local debtor). If the tenants are understood as local people of means and influence, then understanding the tenants of Jesus' parable as the religious authorities makes good sense. Jesus' followers, many of whom were probably Galilean peasants, would have recognized that the tenants of the parable were not the field workers but the lessees who will manage and profit from the vineyard.

FORM-CRITICAL CONSIDERATIONS

The Parable of the Vineyard Tenants immediately calls to mind several rabbinical parables. To cite the opening part of a parable attributed to Rabbi Simeon ben Halafta: "To what may this be compared? To one man living in Galilee and owning a vineyard in Judea, and another man living in Judea and owning a vineyard in Galilee" (Midr. Tanḥ. B Qedošin §6). One also thinks of the parable applied to Egypt, which had once enslaved Israel: "They were like robbers who had broken into the king's vineyard and destroyed the vines. When the king discovered that his vineyards had been destroyed, he was filled with wrath, and descending upon the robbers, without help from anything or anyone, he cut them down and uprooted them as they had done to his vineyard" (*Exod. Rab.* 30.17 [on Exod 21:18).[20] Another parable, attributed to Rabbi Simeon ben Yoḥai (ca. 140 C.E.), equates Israel to a vineyard, and appeals to Isa 5:7:

> Rabbi Simeon ben Yoḥai said: "Why was Israel likened to a vineyard? In the case of a vineyard, in the beginning one must hoe it, then weed it, and then erect supports when he sees the clusters [forming]. Then he must return to pluck the grapes and press them in order to extract the wine from them. So also Israel—each and every shepherd who oversees them must tend them [as he would tend a vineyard]. Where [in Scripture] is Israel called a vineyard? In the verse, 'For the vineyard of the Lord of Hosts is the House of Israel, and the seedling he lovingly tended are the men of Judah' [Isa 5:7]" (*Midr. Prov* 19:21).[21]

Another parable that has nothing to do with a vineyard or farming nevertheless well illustrates betrayal of a trust and the exaggerated naivete of the protagonist:

> The parable, as told by Rabbi Yose the Galilean, concerned a mortal king who had set out for a city far across the sea. As he was about to entrust his son to the care of a wicked guardian, his friends and servants said to him: My lord king, do not entrust your son to this wicked guardian. Nevertheless the king, ignoring the counsel of his friends and servants, entrusted his son to the wicked guardian. What did the guardian do? He proceeded to destroy the king's city, have his house consumed by fire, and slay his son with the sword. After a while the king returned. When he saw his city destroyed and desolate, his house consumed by fire, his son slain with the sword, he pulled out the hair of his head and his beard and broke out into wild weeping, saying: Woe is me! How <foolish> I have been, how senselessly I acted in this kingdom of mine in entrusting my son to a wicked guardian! (*Sed. Elij. Rab.* §28 [150]).[22]

These parables parallel at many points the principal elements that

---

[20] Trans. by S. M. Lehrman, "Exodus," in H. Freedman and M. Simon (eds.), *Midrash Rabbah* (10 vols., London and New York: Soncino, 1983) 3.367.

[21] Trans. by B. L. Visotzky, *The Midrash on Proverbs* (YJS 27; New Haven and London: Yale University Press, 1992) 89. I have modified the text slightly.

[22] Trans. by W. G. Braude and I. Kapstein, *Tanna Děḇe Eliyyahu: The Lore of the School of Elijah* (Philadelphia: Jewish Publication Society, 1981) 369. The translation has been slightly modified.

make up Jesus' Parable of the Vineyard Tenants. Rabbi Simeon's parable speaks of absentee vineyard owners. The next parable talks of an angry king who takes vengeance on men who had violated his vineyard. The third parable is based on Isaiah 5, as is Jesus' Parable of the Vineyard Tenants. Note too how Simeon ben Yoḥai mixes his metaphors by introducing "shepherds." Jesus likewise mixes metaphors by appending a proof text about "builders." The fourth parable, attributed to Yose the Galilean (2nd cent. C.E.), describes a remarkably foolish and incautious king who entrusts his son to a villain. Several details of this parable have significance for Jesus' parable, especially in view of the questions raised about its authenticity. In Yose's parable we have a man who appears utterly to lack common sense. Against the advice of friends and counselors he entrusts his son to a man known to be a "wicked guardian." But the actions of the guardian are just as difficult to comprehend. We are not told that he stole anything or profitted in any way by his actions. He destroys the king's city, burns down his house, and murders his son. What could he possibly have hoped to gain? Did he imagine that he could get away with these crimes? Would not every hearer of this parable suppose that the king would send troops after the guardian and have him executed? These are the same kinds of questions critics have raised against the authenticity of the Parable of the Vineyard Tenants. How could the owner of the vineyard be so foolish and so reckless with the lives of his servants and especially with the life of his son? What could the tenants realistically have hoped to gain? Did they not know that the owner had the power to come and destroy them? Did they really imagine that they could inherit the vineyard?

Questions such as these do not constitute valid objections against the authenticity of parables. The incomprehensible folly of the king in Yose's parable should not cast doubt on the question of its authenticity (note too that Yose applies the parable to God's trusting Nebuchadnezzar!). Nor should the folly of the vineyard owner and the vineyard tenants cast doubt on the authenticity of Jesus' parable. These parables do indeed provoke these kinds of questions—for ancient hearers as well as modern. But the shocking details and the questions they raise are supposed to lead the hearers to grasp and apply the intended lesson.

The following parables offer the most important rabbinic parallels to the Parable of the Vineyard Tenants. Both are anonymous and from the Tannaic period.

1. The Unworthy Tenants (*Spire Deut.* §312 [on Deut 32:9]):

1. ‏משל למלך שהיה לו שדה ונתנה לאריסים:
2. ‏התחילו האריסים נוטלים וגונבים אותה:
3. ‏נטלה מהם ונתנה לבניהם
4. ‏התחילו להיות רעים יותר מן הראשונים:
5. ‏נולד לו בן אמר להם צאו מתוך שלי:
6. ‏אי אפשר שתהיו בתוכה תנו לי חלקי:

"¹It compares to a king who owned a field and who gave it over to tenants. ²The tenants took it (but) robbed him. ³(Then) he took it away from them and gave it to their sons, ⁴(but) they turned out to be even worse than the first ones. ⁵(Then) a son was born to him; he said to them: 'Get off my property. ⁶You can no longer remain there; give back to me my property.'"

This parable is used to illustrate why it was God favored Isaac and his descendants over Ishmael and his descendants. The former were worthy (it is asserted), the latter were not.

2. The Unhappy Tenant (*Midr. Tanh.* B *Bešallaḥ* §7):

1. ‏למה הדבר דומה למלך שהיה לו בן קטן והיה לו אוסיא:
2. ‏והיה מבקש לצאת למדינת הים:
3. ‏אמר לאריס אחד שיהא משמרה
4. ‏ושיהא אוכל מפירותיה עד שיעמוד בנו על פרקו:
5. ‏ואחר כך נותנה לו כשגדיל בנו של מלך בקש האוסיא:
6. ‏מיד התחיל האריס קורא ווי:

"¹To what may the matter be compared? (It is) like a king who had a small son and owned an estate. ²And it happened that he (the king) wished to move to a foreign land. ³He spoke to a tenant, that he should guard (the estate) ⁴and enjoy its produce until his son should wish it to be delivered to him. ⁵When the son of the king was grown, he claimed the estate. ⁶Immediately the tenant began to cry woe."

It is then explained that the parable illustrates the Canaanites, who were premitted to inhabit the land of Israel, as tenants, until such time God would bring Israel out of Egypt to its possession. When God brought the Israelites into the promised land and evicted the tenants, the Canaanites cried woe.

Troublesome tenants drive both of these parables. The first one reveals a degree of patience and trust that is hard to imagine. Why did the king think that the sons of the wicked tenants would be any more trustworthy than their fathers? Why does he wait until the birth of his son before evicting them? The answers to these questions lie in the parable's application. The parable is made to fit biblical history, not human pyschology or the norms of common sense. According to the biblical story, God favored Isaac and his descendants, not Ishmael and his descendants. The parable attempts to illustrate and clarify this story. The parable is not an attempt to portray the actions of reasonable, prudent people.

From this we can see how the elements of exaggeration, even implausibility, work in the Jewish parables. They make the point, or points, of the parable in the strongest and most memorable terms,[23] yet they reflect stories or traditions that form common, familiar ground. Many of Jesus' parables reflect these features. The Parable of the Vineyard Tenants, complete with its quotation of Ps 118:22-23, would be at home in the rabbinic corpus and I doubt that had it been found there it would have caused any one to wonder about its unity or authenticity.[24]

Nevertheless, as interesting and as revealing as the parallels with rabbinic parables are, comparison of Jesus' parables with those of the Old Testament may prove to be more fruitful. In the case of the Parable of the Vineyard Tenants we do not have to look far for a relevant parallel. Because the parable's scenario derives from Isa 5:1-7, which is itself a parable, we would do well to begin with it. The text reads (according to the MT, as translated by the RSV):

1. Let me sing for my beloved a love song concerning his vineyard:
   My beloved had a vineyard on a very fertile hill.
2. He digged it and cleared it of stones, and planted it with choice vines;
   he built a watchtower in the midst of it, and hewed out a wine vat in it;
   and he looked for it to yield grapes, but it yielded wild grapes.
3. And now, O inhabitants of Jerusalem and men of Judah,
   judge, I pray you, between me and my vineyard.
4. What more was there to do for my vineyard, that I have not done in it?
   When I looked for it to yield grapes, why did it yield wild grapes?

---

23   As has been rightly noted by others; cf. B. B. Scott, *Hear Then the Parable: A Commentary on the Parables of Jesus* (Minneapolis: Fortress, 1989) 35-42.

24   On the problem of using rabbinic parables as models and background of Jesus' parables, see Scott, *Hear Then the Parable*, 13-19; and the discussion in chap. 6 above.

5. And now I will tell you what I will do to my vineyard.
   I will remove its hedge, and it shall be devoured;
   I will break down its wall, and it shall be trampled down.
6. I will make it a waste;
   it shall not be pruned or hoed, and briers and thorns shall grow up;
   I will also command the clouds that they rain no rain on it.
7. For the vineyard of the Lord of hosts is the house of Israel,
   and the men of Judah are his pleasant planting;
   and he looked for justice, but behold, bloodshed;
   for righteousness, but behold, a cry!

Recently several studies have appeared attempting to clarify the form and function of the so-called "Song of the Vineyard" of Isa 5:1-7. After surveying a number of proposals John Willis concluded that Isa 5:1-7 must be understood as a parable,[25] since the pericope possesses the elements which are deemed essential to the parable genre: (1) a simple lesson is intended; (2) correspondence between parabolic figures and real characters is present; (3) legal elements often found in other parables are present (e.g. 2 Sam 12:1-7; 14:1-24; 1 Kgs 20:35-42); and (4) a *specific* situation is depicted rather than a *typical* condition.[26] Gale Yee has agreed with Willis that of all the genres which have been proposed only that of parable is satisfactory.[27] Yee has moved beyond Willis, however, in arguing that Isa 5:1-7 constitutes a specific type of parable, namely, that of the juridical parable, which in Isa 5:1-7 has been introduced as a song: "Within the overall framework of a song the parabolic element operates covertly to bring about the hearers' own judgment against themselves."[28] Herein lies the essential ingredient of the juridical parable: the effect of bringing the hearers to self-condemnation. However, Yee concedes that not all of the elements of the typical juridical parable are to be found in the son of Isa 5:1-7. In a brief study subsequent to that of Yee's Gerald Sheppard has tried to show that Isa 5:1-7 is indeed an instance of the juridical parable.[29] He has concluded that the parable is not incomplete when it is understood that Isa 3:13-15 "contains the

---

25   J. T. Willis, "The Genre of Isaiah 5:1-7," *JBL* 96 (1977) 337-62.

26   Willis, "Genre," 360-62.

27   G. A. Yee, "The Form-Critical Study of Isaiah 5:1-7 as a Song and a Juridical Parable," *CBQ* 43 (1981) 30-40.

28   Yee, "Form-Critical Study," 40.

29   G. T. Sheppard, "More on Isaiah 5:1-7 as a Juridical Parable," *CBQ* 44 (1982) 45-47.

missing parts of an original, juridical parable preserved mostly in Isa 5:1-7."[30] Thus, it would appear that a consensus has emerged in which Isaiah's Song of the Vineyard is understood as an instance of the genre juridical parable.

The juridical parable is represented in the synoptic tradition as well (e.g. Mark 12:1-11; Matt 18:23-35; 21:28-35; Luke 7:36-50; 10:29-37). Like Isa 5:1-7 these parables lead the listeners to self-judgment.[31] It is of special interest to note that the juridical parable found in Mark 12:1-11 is itself based upon Isaiah's Song of the Vineyard. Although the Marcan parable has a different thrust (having altered the roles of the parabolic figures), its function is quite similar and, in its present form, particularly appropriate to Marcan theology. A comparative study of the respective vineyard parables proves instructive with respect to first-century exegetical traditions and Jesus' use of them.

In the Isaianic parable the prophet likens the "house of Israel and the men of Judah" (v. 7a) to a vineyard which the Lord has planted and to which he has given ample and loving care (vv. 1b-2b). Despite the Lord's provision, however, the vineyard yields "wild grapes" rather than the expected "good grapes" (vv. 2c, 4b). Instead of justice and righteousness the Lord finds murder and oppression (v. 7b) and so forewarns of devastating destruction (vv. 5-6). In the Marcan parable Isaiah 5 provides the point of departure on which the new parable may be constructed. The following words are drawn from Isa 5:1-2: ἀμπελῶνα ... ἐφύτευσεν, καὶ περιέθηκεν φραγμὸν καὶ ὤρυξεν ὑπολήνιον καὶ ᾠκοδόμησεν πύργον (Mark 12:1). In Jesus' version of the parable there is concern with the vineyard tenants rather than with the quality of the fruit. The wicked tenants refuse to hand over the fruit of the vineyard to its owner, committing a series of murderous offenses against his servants and son, the result of which is their own judgment and destruction. That this parable does function as a juridical parable is suggested by the question of v. 9a: "What will the owner of the vineyard do?" Although Mark supplies Jesus' answer (v. 9b), the answer is obvious and would be acknowledged by his audience. The juridical nature of the parable becomes unmistakably clear with the

---

30   Sheppard, "More on Isaiah 5:1-7," 46.

31   M. Boucher (*The Mysterious Parable: A Literary Study* [CBQMS 6; Washington: Catholic Biblical Association, 1977] 84) finds this idea to be basic to most of the Synoptic parable tradition and states: "It would be best, perhaps, to say that the parables are the means both by which God judges the hearers, and by which the hearers bring judgment upon themselves."

Marcan conclusion: "And they tried to arrest him . . . for they perceived that he had told the parable against them . . ." (v. 12).

TRADITION-CRITICAL CONSIDERATIONS

The meaning of Jesus' parable cannot be appreciated apart from the Jewish interpretation of Isaiah's Son of the Vineyard. At some point subsequent to the Babylonian exile and during the emergence of the targumic traditions Isa 5:1-7 came to be understood as a prediction of the Temple's destruction. This fact is evident by the paraphrase of *Tg. Isa* 5:1-7:

1. אמר נבייא אשבחיה כען לישראל דמתיל בכרמא זרעיה דאברהם
רחמי תושבחת רחמי לכרמיה עמי חביבי ישראל יהבית להון אחסנא
בטור רם בארע שמינא:

2. וקדישתנון ויקרתינון וקיימתינון כמיצב גפן בחירא ובבית מקדשי ביניהון
ואף מדבחי יהבית לכפרא על חטאיהון אמרית דיעבדון עובדין טבין
ואינון אבאישו עובדיהון:

3. נבייא אימר להון הא בית ישראל מרדו מן אוריתא ולא צבן למתב
וכען יתבי ירושלם ואנש יהודה דינו כען דינא קדמי מן עמי:

4. מא טבא אמרית למעבד עוד לעמי ולא עבדית להון מא דין אמרית
דיעבדון עובדין טבין ואינון אבאישו עובדיהון:

5. וכען אחוי כען לכון ית דאנא עתיד למעבד לעמי אסליק שכינתי
מנהון ויהון למיבז איתרע בית מקדשיהון ויהון לדיש:

6. ואשוינון רטישין לא יסתעדון ולא יסתמכון ויהון מטלטלין
ושביקין ועל נבייא אפקיד דלא יתנבון עליהון נבואה:

7. ארי עמיה דיהוה צבאות בית ישראל ואנש יהודה נצבא דחדותיה אמרית
דיעבדון דינא והא אנוסין דיעבדון זכו והא אינון מסגן חובין:

Bruce Chilton's translation is as follows, with the Targum's departures from the Hebrew emphasized:

"*1The prophet said*, I will sing now for *Israel—which is like a vineyard, the seed of Abraham, my friend—my friend's* song for his vineyard: *My people*, my beloved *Israel, I gave them a heritage* on a *high* hill *in* fertile *land. 2And I sanctified them* and *I glorified them* and *I established them as the plant of a* choice vine; and *I* built *my sanctuary* in *their* midst, and I even *gave my altar to atone for their sins; I thought that they would do good deeds, but they made their deeds evil. 3Prophet, say to them, Behold, the house of Israel have rebelled against the law, and they are not willing to repent.* And now, O inhabitants of Jerusalem and men of Judah, judge now *my case against my people.* ⁴What more *good did I promise* to do for my *people* that I have not done *for them*? When *I thought they would do good deeds*, why *did they make their deeds evil*? ⁵And now I will tell you what I *am about to do* to my *people*. I will *take up my Shekhinah from them*, and *they* shall be for *plundering*; I will break down *the place of their sanctuaries*, and *they will be* for trampling. ⁶And I will make them [*to be*] *banished; they* will not be *helped* and *they* will not be *supported*, and *they will be cast out* and *forsaken*; and I will command the *prophets* that *they prophesy* no prophecy concerning them. ⁷For the *people* of the LORD of hosts is the house of Israel, and the men of Judah his pleasant plant; *I thought that they would perform* judgment, but behold, *oppressors; that they would act innocently*, but behold, *they multiply sins.*"³²

The Aramaic version adds to the passage three very important elements:³³ (1) Isaiah's Song of the Vineyard is introduced in explicitly parabolic terms: "I will will now sing to Israel, which is likened [מתיל] to a vineyard." The Aramaic מתל is the equivalent of the Hebrew משל, "to compare" or to "recite a parable." Such an explicit identification coheres with Jesus' own parabolic employment of words and imagery from the Isaianic passage. (2) In place of the various words that speak of building and digging, we have references to a "high" hill (i.e. the Temple Mount), to a "sanctuary," and to an "altar" for making atonement. The passage has taken on a distinctly cultic frame of reference. Indeed, the specific identification of the "tower" and "wine vat" with the Temple and altar, respectively, is emphasized in Tosefta (cf. *Me'il.* 1.16; *Sukk.* 3.15) in the context of a discussion of the Temple. According to the latter passage:

ויבן מגדל בתוכו זה היכל

יקב חצב בו זה מזבח

וגם יקב חצבו זה השית

---

³²   Trans. by B. D. Chilton, *The Isaiah Targum* (ArBib 11; Wilmington: Glazier, 1987) 10-11. For text and translation, see also J. F. Stenning, *The Targum of Isaiah* (Oxford: Clarendon, 1949) 16-17.

³³   Although I have developed my own ideas concerning what contribution that the Isaiah Targum may make in the interpretation of the Parable of the Vineyard Tenants, I acknowledge my debt to Bruce Chilton's researches in this topic. For a convenient presentation, see his *A Galilean Rabbi and His Bible: Jesus' Use of the Interpreted Scripture of His Time* (GNS 8; Wilmington: Glazier, 1984) 111-14.

"'And he built a watchtower in the midst of it'—this is the sanctuary. 'He hewed out a wine vat in it'—this is the altar. 'And he hewed out a wine vat in it'—this is the (water) channel."

That such tower symbolism was current in the first century is supported by passages in *1 Enoch* which refer to the Temple as the "tower." With reference to the Babylonian destruction we read: "I saw how he left that house of theirs and that tower of theirs and cast all of them into the hands of the lions—(even) into the hands of all the wild beasts—so that they may tear them into pieces and eat them. . . . Then they burned that tower and plowed that house. And I became exceedingly sorrowful on account of that tower, for that house of the sheep was being plowed; thereafter I was unable to see whether those sheep could enter that house" (89:56, 66b-67).[34] That "tower" here in *1 Enoch* refers to the Temple is made clear enough by the description of the rebuilding under Persian rule: "They again began to build as before; and they raised up that tower which is called the high tower. But they started to place a table before the tower, with all the food which is upon it being polluted and impure" (89:73).[35] This same Enochic tradition is alluded to in the *Epistle of Barnabas* in the context of polemic against Judaism:

> Finally, I will also speak to you about the temple, and how those wretched men went astray and set their hope on the building, as though it were God's house, and not on their God who created them. For they, almost like the heathen, consecrated him by means of the temple. . . . For because they went to war, it was torn down by their enemies, and now the very servants of their enemies will rebuild it. Again, it was revealed that the city and the temple and the people of Israel were destined to be handed over. For the Scripture says: "And it will happen in the last days that the Lord will hand over the sheep of the pasture and the sheepfold and their watchtower to destruction." And it happened just as the Lord said (16:1-2a, 4b-5).[36]

---

34   The translation is from E. Isaac, "1 (Ethiopic Apocalypse of) Enoch," in J. H. Charlesworth (ed.), *The Old Testament Pseudepigrapha* (2 vols., Garden City: Doubleday, 1983-85) 1.67-68.

35   Isaac, "1 Enoch," 69.

36   Trans. from J. B. Lightfoot and J. R. Harmer, *The Apostolic Fathers* (2nd ed., rev. and ed. by M. W. Holmes; Grand Rapids: Baker, 1989) 183. In n. 135 the source for the quotation is described as "uncertain," but reference is made to *1 Enoch* 89:56-66. K. Lake (*Apostolic Fathers I* [LCL 24; London: Heinemann; Cambridge: Harvard University, 1912] 396) cites *1 Enoch* 89:55, 66, 67 in the margin.

It is likely that *1 Enoch* 83–90 was written before the emergence of Christianity and if this section was originally composed in Aramaic, as R. H. Charles suspected,[37] then the suggestion that the tower symbolism had already found its way into the emerging targumic tradition prior to the Synoptic tradition becomes plausible. (Indeed, it is probable that *1 Enoch* reflects the Aramaic tradition itself.) The recent publication of 4Q500 lends additional support to this interpretation. This fragmentary text appears to be part of a midrashic interpretation that views the vineyard of Isa 5:1-7 as a metaphor of Jerusalem and her Temple. Lines 2–7 read as follows:[38]

.2   בכ]איכה ינצו ו[
.3   ]יקב תירושכה [ב]ני באבני[
.4   [לשער מרום הקודש]
.5   [מטעכה ופלגי כבודכה ב]
.6   [כפות שעשועיכה]
.7   [וכר]מכה

2 . . . your baca trees will blossom and . . .
3 . . . a wine vat built among stones . . .
4 . . . before the gate of the holy height . . .
5 . . . your planting and the streams of your glory . . .
6 . . . the branches (which make) your delights . . .
7 . . . your vine[yard . . .]

The reference in line 3 to the "wine vat built among stones" is an unmistakable allusion to Isa 5:2. This reference helps restore "your vineyard" in line 7, thereby giving us an allusion to Isa 5:1. The "gate of the holy height" refers to the Temple. "Height" (מרום) agrees with the Targum's "high" (רם) hill. The reference in line 5 to the "streams" of God's glory agrees with Tosefta's second interpretive assignment given the phrase in *t. Sukk.* 3.15. As seen above, the Tosefta not only understands "he dug a wine vat" as a reference to the altar (which agrees with the Targum), it repeats the phrase, "*and* he dug a wine vat," interpreting it as a reference to the water channel, which streams

---

37   Charles, *APOT* 2.164.

38   See M. Baillet, *Qumrân Grotte 4 III (4Q482–4Q520)* (DJD 7; Oxford: Clarendon, 1982) 78-79 + pl. 27; J. M. Baumgarten, "4Q500 and the Ancient Conception of the Lord's Vineyard," *JJS* 40 (1989) 1-6; J. Marcus, *The Way of the Lord: Christological Exegesis of the Old Testament in the Gospel of Mark* (Louisville: Westminster/John Knox, 1992) 120.

forth from the altar (cf. *m. Yoma* 5:6; *m. Mid.* 3:3).[39] These additional points of coherence strongly suggest that the cultic interpretation preserved in the Targum predates the New Testament.

(3) The Aramaic tradition also introduces into the passage the language of "heritage" or "inheritance": "I gave them an inheritance [אחסנא] on a high hill."[40] We have here another important element of thematic and dictional coherence with Jesus' parable's reference to the hope of acquiring possession of the κληρονομία (Mark 12:7).

The significance of the Aramaic's introduction of Temple imagery lies in the fact that divine judgment is now specifically directed against the religious establishment. According to the Targum God will take up his Shekinah from his people and will break down their sanctuaries (*Tg.* Isa 5:5). Taking up his Shekinah is to be understood as the destruction of the Temple itself, while breaking down the sanctuaries may refer either to the other buildings within the precincts or to synagogues.[41] The relevance of the Aramaic tradition for a proper appreciation of the interpretive function that Isa 5:1-7 has for the Parable of the should now be obvious.[42]

---

39   This observation has been made by Baumgarten, "4Q500," 2.

40   Note that the meturgeman translates the Hebrew נחלה ("inheritance") with אחסנא every time the word appears in Isaiah (19:25; 47:6; 63:17). In all three passages the LXX translates κληρονομία.

41   The latter possibility has been suggested by B. Chilton, *The Glory of Israel: The Theology and Provenience of the Isaiah Targum* (JSOTSup 23; Sheffield: JSOT Press, 1982) 18; idem, *The Isaiah Targum*, 11 (notes on "5:1–5:15").

42   In all probability the wording of the LXX has influenced the parable as we now have it in Mark, but it is going too far to claim that the parable is a creation of the Greek-speaking Church; cf. E. Schweizer, *The Good News according to Mark* (Atlanta: John Knox, 1970) 239. There are some Semitic features which should be taken into account: (1) Mark retains the verbs in the third person and not the first person as in the LXX. (2) Mark has ὑπολήνιον rather than the LXX's προλήνιον. It is true that יקב may mean either "wine press" (προλήνιον) or "wine vat" (ὑπολήνιον), but Mark's variation suggests independence of the LXX. (3) Mark's parable describes murder, which may reflect the reference to "bloodshed" (or "murder") in Isa 5:5. The LXX instead reads "injustice." (4) Mark 12:9 predicts the destruction of the tenants, an aspect which may very well reflect the Hebrew tradition in which it is stated that the vineyard will be dismantled and made a "desolation." The LXX, however, does not provide an equivalent. On the Semitisms of the parable, see Hengel, "Das Gleichnis von den Weingärtnern," 7-8 n. 31; M. Y.-H. Lee, *Jesus und die jüdische Autorität* (FB 56; Würzburg: Echter, 1986) 80.

The "vineyard" refers to Israel, or the people of God,[43] the "tenants" refer to Israel's religious leaders, and the various servants no doubt are meant to be understood as the prophets of old. But does the "son" refer to Jesus? Here many interpreters who accept the authenticity of Mark 12:1-9 express doubts about the identification of the son as Jesus. Closely connected to this doubt is the quotation of Ps 118:22-23 at the conclusion of the parable. Appeal to the Aramaic version of this Psalm may help clear up some of the questions involved in this issue. The entire passage is worth quoting:[44]

19. פתחו לי מעלני קרתא דצידקא אעול בהון אשבח יה:
20. דין מעלנא דבית מקדשא דיהוה צדיקיא ייעלון ביה:
21. אהודי קדמך ארום קבלתא צלותי והוית לי לפריק:
22. טליא שביקו ארדיכליא הות ביני בניא דישי וזכה לאתמנאה למליך ושולטן:
23. מן קדם: יהוה הות דא אמרו ארדיכליא היא פרישא קדמנא אמרו בני דישי:
24. דין יומא עבד יהוה אמרו ארדיכליא נדוין ובחדי ביה אמרו בני דישי:
25. בבעו מינך יהוה ‹פרוק› כדון אמרו ארדיכליא
　　　בבעו מינך יהוה אצלח כדון אמרו ישי ואנתתיה:
26. בריך דאתי בשום מימרא דיהוה אמרו ארדיכלי יברכון
　　　יתכון מן בית מקדשא דיהוה אמר דוד:
27. אלהא יהוה אנהר לנא אמרו שבטיא דבית יהודה
　　　כפיתו טליא לניכסת חגא בשושלוון עד די תקרבוניה
　　　ותדון אדמיה בקרנת מדבחא אמר שמואל נבייא:

19. Open to me the gates of the city of righteousness; I will enter by them and praise the Lord.
20. This is the gate of the house of the sanctuary of the Lord; the righteous enter by it.

43　　This symbolism occurs elsewhere in the Old Testament (cf. Isa 27:2-6; Jer 2:21; 12:10; Hos 10:1; Ezek 15:6; 19:10; Ps 80:8-18) and continues in rabbinic literature as well (cf. St-B 2.563-64). John 15:1-5 echoes this tradition, though the evangelist owes his language to Jer 2:21 rather than to Isa 5:1-7, for the LXX version of the former reads ἄμπελος … ἀληθινή ("true vine"), whereas the Hebrew reads זֶרַע אֱמֶת ("true seed"). While in the fourth Gospel it is Jesus who is described as God's vine (some Syrian versions read "vineyard"), there is patristic evidence that the Church came to regard itself as the "beloved vineyard" of Isa 5:1-7; cf. *Apostolic Constitutions* 1.1.1.

44　　The Aramaic text is from P. de Lagarde, *Hagiographa Chaldaice* (Leipzig: Teubner, 1873) 70. See also L. Díez Merino, *Targum de Salmos* (Bibliotheca Hispana Biblica 6; Madrid: Consejo Superior de Investigaciones Científicas, 1982) 91. I would like to express my thanks to Prof. Edward M. Cook for reviewing my translation of the text.

21. I will give thanks before You, for You have received my prayer and You have become for me a Savior.

22. The boy which the builders abandoned was among the sons of Jesse and he is worthy to be appointed king and ruler.

23. "From before the Lord this came about," said the builders. "It is marvelous before us," said the sons of Jesse.

24. "This is the day the Lord has made," said the builders. "Let us rejoice and be glad in it," said the sons of Jesse.

25. "If it please You, O Lord, <save us> now," said the builders. "If it please You, O Lord, prosper (us) now," said Jesse and his wife.

26. "Blessed is one who comes in the name of word of the Lord," said the builders. "They will bless you from the house of the sanctuary of the Lord," said David.

27. "The Lord God has enlightened us," said the tribes of the house of Judah. "Bind the lamb for the festival sacrifice with chains until you sacrifice it, and sprinkle its blood on the horns of the altar," said Samuel the prophet.

The Aramaic version of Ps 118:19-27 also points to important points of thematic and exegetical coherence with the Parable of the Vineyard Tenants. The most dramatic interpretation in the Targum concerns v. 22, which is part of the Psalm 118 quotation that concludes the parable. The Targum reads: "The boy which the builders abandoned was among the sons of Jesse and he is worthy to be appointed king and ruler." The Aramaic טליא ("boy") probably derives from a word play involving הָאֶבֶן ("the stone") and הַבֵּן ("the son"). Such a word play in Hebrew, reflected in the targumic tradition, but not preserved in the LXX, suggests that the quotation derives from Jesus and not from the Greek-speaking Church (as many interpreters suppose). The linkage between the quotation and the parable, which tells of a rejected son, becomes much closer.[45] It has also been suggested that the Aramaic paraphrase is evidence that the Psalm was understood in a messianic sense prior to the rise of Christianity.[46] This is possible, given the reference to being "worthy to be appointed king and ruler." The son of Jesse referred to here is David, of course, who is mentioned by name in v. 26.

---

[45] See Snodgrass, *The Parable of the Wicked Tenants*, 95-106, 113-18.

[46] See B. Gärtner, "טליא als Messiasbezeichnung," *SEÅ* 18-19 (1953-54) 98-108. There is no evidence in the early rabbinic literature that Ps 118:22 was understood in a messianic sense. For a late, possibly messianic interpretation, see *Esth. Rab.* 7.10 (on Esth 3:6). For arguments that Ps 118:25-26 was understood in a messianic sense at the time of Jesus, see J. Jeremias, *The Eucharistic Words of Jesus* (London: SCM, 1990) 256-62.

The picture of the "builders" in the Targum is somewhat ambiguous. They are the ones who "abandoned" the boy. Yet, as the Psalm progresses it seems that they come to recognize his worth, as the exchange in v. 26 may imply. As in the Targum, religious authorities were sometimes called "builders." We see this in rabbinic literature,[47] but more importantly we find it in Qumran where it is quite negative.[48] Of special importance is the appearance of Psa 118:22 in Acts 4:11 where the builders are specifically identified as members of the Sanhedrin.

In my judgment the Aramaic tradition, with its witness to the stone-son word play, argues for the originality of the quotation of Ps 118:22-23 as the conclusion of the Parable of the Vineyard Tenants. This observation undermines the claim that the quotation is nothing more than the product of the Greek-speaking Church, which made christological use of Psalm 118 (cf. Acts 4:11; Eph 2:20; 1 Pet 2:7; *Barn.* 6:4). The quotation is assimilated to the LXX in the translation and transmission of the dominical tradition in Greek-speaking circles. But the origin of the quotation is best explained against the *Sitz im Leben Jesu*. I would rather suggest that the early Church's interest in Psalm 118 arose because of Jesus' prior use of it in this very parable.[49]

Because Isa 5:1-2 was only alluded to, and not quoted, its presence in

---

47 "R. Yohana said: 'These are scholars, who are engaged all their days in the upbuilding of the world'" (*b. Šabb.* 114a); "[When quoting Isa 54:13], do not read *banayik* ['your children'] but *bonayik* ['your builders']" (*b. Ber.* 64a); Rabbi Zeira called Rabbi Hila a "builder of scholarship [בניה דאורייתא]" (*y. Yoma* 3.5); cf. 1 Cor 3:10: "as a wise master-builder I laid a foundation"; LXX Isa 3:3: "(The Lord will remove from Judah) master-builder and wise lecturer"; Philo, *Som.* 2.2 §8: "(Allegory is the) wise master-builder." In both passages the Greek expression is σοφὸς ἀρχιτέκτων.

48 "Such men are builders of a rickety wall" (CD 4:19, alluding to Ezek 13:10); ". . . those who build the wall and cover it with whitewash" (CD 8:12); "[God hates the] builders of the wall" (CD 8:18).

49 The point of the quotation is not so much the vindication of the stone/son, as it is a threat against the Temple establishment. That is, the stone which the builders have rejected will in fact became the principal stone. The builders (i.e. Temple establishment) may think that in rejecting the son the matter is concluded; but it is not. The rejected son will in fact become the principal player in the emergence of a new establishment. The rejected son is worthy, as the Aramaic version puts it, to be appointed king and ruler. In the parable proper Jesus is not necessarily predicting his death, as much as he is describing the utter futility of the tenants' opposition to the owner's wishes. They can kill his servants, even his son, but they cannot keep the vineyard. The son that they have rejected will nevertheless assume the leadership.

the developing Greek tradition faded from the parable, to the point of disappearance. This is seen in Luke's version of the parable, which retains scarcely a trace of the passage, and in *GThom* §65, whose form in all probability derives secondarily from the New Testament Gospels, especially from Luke.[50]

Before concluding this part of the discussion one more point needs to be considered. The tenants' statement, "Come let us kill him" (δεῦτε ἀποκτείνωσεν αὐτόν), repeats the very words uttered by the brothers of Joseph (cf. Gen 37:20).[51] This allusion to the well known story of fraternal treachery contributes to the theme of inheritance and of the rivalry that often plays a part.[52] The allusion may also account for the description of the son of the parable as the owner's "beloved son" (Mark 12:6: υἱὸν ἀγαπητόν), for in Gen 37:3 we are told that Jacob "loved [ἠγάπησεν] him (Joseph) more than all his brothers" (cf. Gen 44:20). If this is so, then the parable may be hinting that the treachery of the tenants is also fraternal in the sense of Israelites killing Israelites. We should remember that the brothers of Joseph were jealous, not only because their father favored his younger son, but because the dreams of Joseph foretold his future exaltation over his older brothers.

Concluding Comments

There are many factors that argue strongly for the authenticity of the Parable of the Vineyard Tenants, including the quotation of Ps 118:22-23. First, the evidence from the papyri, particularly that of the Zenon archive, shows that the fictional scenario of the parable is neither unimaginable nor alien to Palestinian culture. Secondly, the related rabbinical parables make it clear that it is not unusual for the characters in parables to act in illogical and unreasonable ways. To complain of the vineyard owner's rash decision to send his son or of the murderous folly of the tenants does not tell against the authenticity

---

[50] For criticisms of arguments for the antiquity, independence, and superiority of the readings in the *Gospel of Thomas*, see J. H. Charlesworth and C. A. Evans, "Jesus in the Agrapha and Apocryphal Gospels," in B. Chilton and C. A. Evans (eds.), *Studying the Historical Jesus: Evaluations of the Current State of Research* (NTTS 19; Leiden: Brill, 1994) 479-533, esp. 496-503.

[51] Hengel, "Das Gleichnis von den Weingärtnern," 18 and n. 60. The words agree with the LXX exactly, but the Greek is a literal translation of the Hebrew. The Pentateuch Targums also translate the Hebrew literally.

[52] As noted by Scott, *Hear Then the Parable*, 252.

of the parable. Thirdly, to observe that the parable is a partial allegory roughly reflecting Israel's traditions of the rejected prophets, or even the rejected Joseph, also does not tell against the authenticity of the parable. As was observed in the case of the rabbis, parables often presupposed various elements of the biblical story, such as how God relates to Israel and to the Gentiles. Fourthly, several important points of targumic coherence with the parable argue for the antiquity, if not authenticity, and unity of the parable. Fifthly, Jesus' anticipation of violent opposition, as we must conclude if we accept the whole of Mark 12:1-11, also does not provide legitimate grounds for rejecting the authenticity of the parable. Jesus' criticism of the Temple establishment, which is well established and makes sense in his time (see chaps. 7 and 9 above), and the Temple establishment's reaction to him (see chaps. 11 and 12 below) provide a coherent context against which the Parable of the Vineyard Tenants, in its entirety, may be properly understood. I think that it is a questionable procedure to remove the parable from its extant context (which dates to a generation of the life of Jesus), to declare that parts of it do not fit, and then to assert that we can never recover the original point of the parable.[53] The point of the parable was clear to Jesus' original hearers, friends and foes alike, though by the time it was committed to writing some of the interpretive assumptions that underlay, even generated, it were either forgotten or not completely understood by Greek-speaking Christians.

The parable offers a sharp prophetic criticism of the Temple establishment and a warning that its days of administration were nearing an end. It is to the theme of its opposition to Jesus that we shall now turn.

---

[53] Deleting the quotation of Psalm 118:22-23 from the conclusion of the parable has contributed to much of the confusion over the meaning of the parable in the *Sitz im Leben Jesu*. This confusion is well illustrated by the several shifts in J. D. Crossan's attempts to interpret the parable as it is found in *Thomas*; cf. J. D. Crossan, "The Parable of the Wicked Husbandmen," *JBL* 90 (1971) 451-65; idem, *In Parables: The Challenge of the Historical Jesus* (New York: Harper & Row, 1973) 86-96; idem, "The Servant Parables of Jesus," *Semeia* 1 (1974) 17-62, esp. 17-55; idem, "Structuralist Analysis and the Parables of Jesus," *Semeia* 1 (1974) 192-221, esp. 208-209; idem, "Parable, Allegory, and Paradox," in D. Patte (ed.), *Semiology and the Parables* (Pittsburgh: Pickwick, 1976) 247-81, esp. 264-73. B. J. Malina and R. L. Rohrbaugh (*Social-Science Commentary on the Synoptic Gospels* [Minneapolis: Fortress, 1992] 255) also abandon the context that the Gospels give the parable and so can say no more than that the parable "may well have been a warning to landowners expropriating and exporting the produce of the land." This banal interpretation hardly does justice to the thrust of the parable.

CHAPTER ELEVEN

IN WHAT SENSE "BLASPHEMY"?
JESUS BEFORE CAIAPHAS IN MARK 14:61-64

Jesus' response to the question of Caiaphas, in which he affirms that
he is "the Christ the Son of the Blessed," whom Caiaphas and company
"will see" as "Son of Man seated at the right hand of Power and coming
with the clouds of heaven" (Mark 14:61-62), provokes the cry of
"blasphemy!" (Mark 14:64). Many scholars have wondered why, and
for good reason. Claiming to be Israel's Messiah was not considered
blasphemous.[1] Although disparaging them as impostors and opportunists, Josephus never accused any of the many would-be kings and
deliverers of first-century Israel as blasphemers. Perhaps a more
telling example comes from rabbinic tradition. Rabbi Aqiba's proclamation of Simon ben Kosiba as Messiah was met with skepticism, but
not with cries of blasphemy (cf. *y. Ta'an.* 4.5; *b. Sanh.* 93b.) Even

---

[1]   W. L. Lane (*The Gospel of Mark* [NIC; Grand Rapids: Eerdmans, 1974]
536) argues that "anyone who [was in prison and deserted by his followers, but
nevertheless still] proclaimed himself to be the Messiah could not fail to be a
blasphemer who dared to make a mockery of the promises given by God to his
people." This is no more than an assumption. There is no evidence that a claim to
be Messiah, under any circumstances, was considered blasphemous (pace J. C.
O'Neill, "The Silence of Jesus," *NTS* 15 [1969] 153-67; idem, "The Charge of
Blasphemy at Jesus' Trial before the Sanhedrin," in E. Bammel [ed.], *The Trial of
Jesus: Cambridge Studies in Honour of C. F. D. Moule* [SBT 13; London: SCM,
1970] 72-77). According to O'Neill, "it was an understood maxim of the law that
the man who claimed to be Messiah in so many words was guilty of blasphemy and
worthy of death" ("The Charge of Blasphemy," 77). Where is the evidence for this?
The statement in Matt 11:27 could be relevant: "No one knows the son, except the
Father." See also *Pss. Sol.* 17:22: "Behold, Lord, and raise up for them their king,
the son of David, in the time that you know, God, to rule over Israel your servant."
That is, no one knows who the Son of God (i.e. the Messiah) is, except God who
will, in his own good time, make him known. Jesus' affirmation, in response to the
question of Caiaphas (Mark 14:61-62), could have been perceived as presumptuous
for affirming what only God was to disclose. But would such a confession have
been considered blasphemous?

claiming to be *son of God* was not necessarily blasphemous, for there is biblical precedent for such an expression (Pss 2:7; 82:6; 2 Sam 7:14).[2] Admittedly, later rabbinic and targumic traditions tend to shy away from this title, possibly as a reaction to Christianity (see 2 Sam 7:14 and 1 Chr 17:13 in the Targum; and *Exod. Rab.* 29.5 [on Exod 20:2], where God says, "I have no son"; cf. *y. Ta'an.* 2.1). But these traditions do not necessarily reflect first-century thinking.

Recently Joel Marcus has suggested that Jesus' claim of divine sonship "would have fallen on Jewish ears as a claim to commensurability with God."[3] Marcus could be correct, for the charge of blasphemy in John 10 was occasioned by claims of sonship and unity with God: "Do you say, 'You blaspheme,' because I said, 'I am the son of God'?" (John 10:36). Otto Betz has argued similarly: "Jesus blasphemed God because, despite his powerlessness, he would be equal to him."[4] But the Johannine version may very well reflect late first-century Christian polemic with the synagogue. If it does, then it may have been the *post-Easter Christian understanding* of the messiaship and sonship of Jesus that provoked from Jewish circles charges of blasphemy. If this is the case, then one could argue that the charge of blasphemy in Mark likewise reflects later Jewish-Christian controversy and that therefore the cry of blasphemy attributed to Caiaphas is not authentic. This is in fact the conclusion reached by E. P. Sanders in a recent study, in which he repeats and refines points made in an earlier work.[5] If Caiaphas' cry

---

2   An Aramaic fragment found at Qumran (Cave 4) reads: "[He] shall be great upon the earth, [O King!] . . . he shall be called [son of] the [g]reat [God], and by his name shall he be named. He shall be hailed (as) the Son of God, and they shall call him Son of the Most High (J. A. Fitzmyer, *The Gospel According to Luke I-IX* [AB 28; Garden City: Doubleday, 1981] 347). To whom reference here is being made is not clear, but there is no hint that calling this person [Messiah?] "son of God" is inappropriate. See further discussion of this text in chap. 3 above.

3   Joel Marcus, "Mark 14:61: 'Are You the Messiah-Son-of-God?'," *NovT* 31 (1989) 125-41, quote from p. 141.

4   O. Betz, "Probleme des Prozesses Jesu," *ANRW* 2.25.1 (1982) 565-647, quote from p. 636. Betz also argues that "such a false messianic claim, of course, also endangers the Temple and the Holy City."

5   E. P. Sanders, *Jesus and Judaism* (London: SCM; Philadelphia: Fortress, 1985) 309-18 (with notes on pp. 409-11); idem, *Jewish Law from Jesus to the Mishnah* (London: SCM; Philadelphia: Trinity Press International, 1990) 57-67 (with notes on pp. 338-39). In the latter study, Sanders (p. 61 and p. 338, n. 14) cites M. Hengel (*Studies in the Gospel of Mark* [Philadelphia: Fortress, 1985] 37-38) as supporting his view that the two passages in Mark (Mark 2:5-7; 14:61-64),

of blasphemy is to be accepted as historical, then a better explanation of Jesus' assertion and the High Priest's reaction is needed.

The present study will approach this problem in three sections. The first section will examine the narrower issue that asks in what sense Jesus' response could have been construed as blasphemy. It will be shown that although Jesus may have pronounced the Divine Name (as the rules of *m. Sanh.* 7:5 require in cases of capital blasphemy), the grounds for the charge of blasphemy remain obscure. The second section will propose a solution. The third section will examine the christology of Rabbi Aqiba, a christology that prompted a colleague to accuse the famous rabbi of profaning God. In this section the christologies of Jesus and Aqiba will be compared. Arguments in support of the essential historicity of Mark 14:61-64 will be offered.

WHEREIN LIES JESUS' BLASPHEMY?

If claiming to be Messiah, even "Messiah son of God," was not in itself a blasphemy, then what was? There are two components to this problem. The first has to do with the biblical and early Jewish understanding of what constituted "blasphemy," particularly from a legal point of view (i.e. blasphemy as a crime that warranted a death sentence). The second has to do with what specific part of Jesus' assertion in Mark 14:62 would have been regarded as blasphemy.

Blasphemy in the Bible and Early Judaism

The relevant materials are adequately surveyed in the studies by Sanders and H. W. Beyer.[6] It will only be necessary to summarize the data briefly. According to Exod 22:27(E28) Israelites were commanded not to curse [לֹא תְקַלֵּל] God. On one occasion this commandment was broken (Lev 24:10-16). The blasphemer "pronounced the Name and cursed [וַיְקַלֵּל]" and so was stoned. Although the LXX does not translate

---

in which Jesus is accused of blasphemy, represent "the work of the author" (i.e. the evangelist Mark). It is not clear, however, that this is actually Hengel's position. According to the context of his discussion (*Mark*, 37-38 and 142 n. 26), Mark has *selected and arranged* his material, not created it. Note too the skepticism expressed by M. de Jonge, *Christology in Context: The Earliest Response to Jesus* (Philadelphia: Westminster, 1988) 210: "Mark's account of the trial before the Sanhedrin in 14:55-65 too clearly serves Mark's own Christological purpose to be a useful historical source."

6   H. W. Beyer, "Βλασφημέω, κ.τ.λ.," *TDNT* 1 (1964) 621-25; Sanders, *Jewish Law*, 57-60.

these passages using the word βλασφημεῖν, Josephus does: "Let him who blasphemed [βλασφημήσας] God be stoned, then hung for a day, and buried dishonorably and in obscurity" (*Ant.* 4.8.6 §202). Elsewhere the Greek tradition does employ βλασφημεῖν (and cognates βλασφημία and βλάσφημος) in translating גָּדַף (2 Kgs 19:6, 22; cf. Isa 37:6, 23; Ezek 20:27; Ps 44:16), נָאַץ/נֶאָצָה (Isa 52:5 [cited in Rom 2:24]; Ezek 35:12; cf. 2 Sam 12:14; 2 Kgs 19:3; Isa 37:3; Ps 74:10, 18), יָכַח (2 Kgs 19:4), שָׁלָה (Dan [θ] 3:29 [96]), and the euphemism בֵּרֵךְ (Isa 66:3; cf. 1 Kgs 21:10, 13; Job 1:5; 2:9). Βλασφημεῖν and cognates occur in those books of the Greek tradition where there either was no Hebrew original or the Hebrew original is no longer extant (Tob [א] 1:18; Wis 1:6; Sir 3:16; Bel [θ] 8 [9]; 2 Macc 8:4; 9:28; 10:4, 34, 35, 36; 12:14; 15:24).

Both Josephus and Philo were influenced by the language of the LXX. The former believed it wrong even to blaspheme pagan gods "out of respect for the very word 'God'" (*Against Apion* 2.32 §237; *Ant.* 4.8.10 §207; cf. Acts 19:37: "these are not men who blaspheme our goddess"). The same idea is found in the latter (*Vit. Mos.* 2.26 §205; *Spec. Leg.* 1.7 §53).[7] In essence blasphemy constituted words or actions contemning what was regarded as sacred, particularly God himself (cf. *Against Apion* 1.11 §59; 1.25 §223; 1.31 §279; 2.13 §143).

The same broad usage is found in the writings of the New Testament. Jesus is accused of blaspheming for pronouncing the forgiveness of a man's sins, presumably an encroachment of God's perogative (Mark 2:5-7 = Matt 9:2-3 = Luke 5:20-21), and later he himself warns of blasphemy against the Holy Spirit (Mark 3:28-30 = Matt 12:31-32 = Luke 12:10). In the dispute over purity, Jesus cites blasphemy as one of the many defilements that proceed from the human heart (Mark 7:21-22 = Matt 15:18-19). One evangelist describes the mockery of Jesus as blasphemy (Luke 22:65). Stephen is accused of "speaking blasphemous words against Moses and God" (Acts 6:11) and "speaking words against this holy place [i.e. the Temple] and against the Law" (6:13). Evidently, part of this blasphemy had to do with "saying that Jesus the Nazarene will destroy this place" (6:14). After his defense, Stephen is stoned (Acts 7:58). Already mentioned is the threat of stoning Jesus for having claimed equality with God (John 10:31-36). Following Jewish

---

7   This idea is based on the LXX's translation of אֱלֹהִים as θεοί in Exod 22:28[27].

precedent, Christians regarded speaking against Jesus and Christian teaching as blasphemy (Acts 13:45; 18:6; 26:11; 1 Tim 1:20; 6:1; Titus 2:5; James 2:7; Rev 2:9; 13:1, 5, 6; 16:9, 11, 21; 17:3).

Based on Lev 24:16, Philo believed that the death penalty is called for if one utters the name of God in an inappropriate context (*Vit. Mos.* 2.37-38 §203-206). His interpretation is consistent with the view later expressed in the Mishnah. According to the Mishnah blasphemy is among the various offenses that warrant stoning (*m. Sanh.* 7:4). But what kind of blasphemy warrants a death sentence? "'The blasphemer [הַמְגַדֵּף]' is without guilt until he pronounces the Name" (*m. Sanh.* 7:5; cf. 6:4: "Why is this person hanged? Because he cursed the Name"). This opinion is based on Lev 24:11 ("he pronounced the Name and he cursed"). To be convicted, however, there must be two or three witnesses (cf. 7:5), an opinion based on Deut 19:15 ("only on the evidence of two witnesses, or of three witnesses . . . shall a charge be sustained"). In other words, if a person clearly pronounced the Divine Name, and was overheard by two or more credible witnesses, then that person was liable to capital punishment. It is not clear if other forms of blasphemy warranted a death sentence.

"Blasphemy" in Jesus' Answer

When Jesus is asked, "Are you the Christ the son of the Blessed?," he answered, "I am, and you will see the son of man seated at the right hand of Power and coming with the clouds of heaven" (Mark 14:61b-62). We are told that Caiaphas responded demonstratively. Several features of his response seem to cohere with Mishnaic law: (1) the tearing of his robes (Mark 14:63a; cf. *m. Sanh.* 7:5, 8, 10; for biblical precedent see 2 Kgs 18:37; 19:1); (2) the rhetorical question, "What further need do we have of witnesses?" (Mark 14:63b; cf. *m. Sanh.* 7:5); (3) the claim of blasphemy (Mark 14:64a; cf. *m. Sanh.* 7:5); and (4) the condemning of Jesus as deserving of death (Mark 14:64b; cf. *m. Sanh.* 6:4; 7:5). One might conclude that this exchange between Jesus and Caiaphas is a textbook example of the case outlined in the Mishnah. It is not, however, for one important element is apparently missing: the pronunciation of the Divine Name. It is not missing, of course, if one understands Jesus' first two words, "I am" (ἐγώ εἰμι), as a deliberate allusion to Yahweh ("He is"),[8] instead of simply an affirmation to

---

8   Cf. Exod 3:14: "God said to Moses, 'I am [ἐγώ εἰμι] who I am.'"

the question posed (i.e. "Yes, I am [the son of the Blessed]").[9] But this interpretation is very doubtful; and Sanders rightly rejects it.[10]

The rules for sentencing a blasphemer, which are laid out in *m. Sanh.* 7:5, could have relevance, but some express doubts because Jesus does not actually utter the Tetragrammaton.[11] Robert Gundry has recently suggested that Jesus actually said "at the right hand of Yahweh."[12] He appeals to *Sanhedrin*'s requirement that public reports of the blasphemy use a substitute for the Divine Name. The passage reads:

1. המגדף אינו חיב עד שיפרש את השם: אמר רבי יהושע בן קרחה
2. בכל יום דנין את העדים בכנוי יכה יוסי את יוסי:
3. נגמר הדין לא הורגים בכנוי אלא מוציאים את כל האדם לחוץ
4. ושואלים את הגדול שבהן ואומרים לו אמור מה ששמעת בפרוש
5. והוא אומר והדינים עומדין על רגליהן וקורעין ולא מאחין:
6. והשני אומר אף אני כמוהו והשלישי אומר אף אני כמוהו:

[1]"The blasphemer" [Lev 24:16] is without guilt until he pronounces the Name. Says Rabbi Yehoshua ben Qarḥa: [2]"On every day (of the trial) they examined the witnesses with a substituted name, (such as) 'May Yose strike Yose.' [3]When they completed the proceedings, they did not execute (him) with the substituted name (only), but they sent all the people outside [4]and asked the chief (witness) among them and said to him, 'Say what you heard exactly.' [5]And he says (it); and the judges stand up on their feet and tear (their garments), and they may not mend (them again). [6]And the second witness says, 'I also (heard) the same,' and the third says, 'I

---

9   E. Stauffer, *Jesus and His Story* (London: SCM; New York: Knopf, 1960) 102, 142-159; cited by Sanders, *Jewish Law*, 339 n. 19. It should be noted that some MSS. read συ εἶπας ὅτι ἐγώ εἰμι (Θ *fam*[13] arm); cf. Matt 26:64. For a defense of the shorter reading see R. Kempthorne, "The Marcan Text of Jesus' Answer to the High Priest," *NovT* 19 (1977) 198-208.

10   Sanders, *Jewish Law*, 65. Betz ("Prozess Jesu," 634) also rejects this interpretation.

11   E. Schweizer (*The Good News according to Mark* [Atlanta: John Knox, 1970] 331) has said: "Since only those cases were regarded as blasphemy where the most holy Name was uttered, the sentencing of Jesus to death for this statement can hardly be thought to be justified." Sanders (*Jewish Law*, 67) suspects that blasphemy probably had nothing to do with Jesus' trial and execution.

12   R. H. Gundry, *Mark: A Commentary on His Apology for the Cross* (Grand Rapids: Eerdmans, 1993) 915-18.

also (heard) the same.'"

Gundry argues that Jesus actually did utter the Tetragrammaton in his reply to the question of Caiaphas: "I am (the Messiah, the son of the Blessed); and you will see the son of man seated at the right hand of Yahweh, coming with the clouds of heaven." It is in the public report of what Jesus said, that the circumlocution "Power" makes its appearance. I think Gundry is correct.[13] But I do not think that his explanation of the actual basis of the accusation of blasphemy has been fully established. He makes the interesting and plausible suggestion that the charge of the false witnesses, viz. that Jesus had boasted that he would destroy the handmade Temple and replace it with one not handmade (Mark 14:58), may have implied that Jesus had assumed divine perogatives with respect to the destruction and replacement of the building.[14] But the testimony of the witnesses does not agree and Jesus remains silent, neither denying nor affirming the truthfulness of the charge. In any event, this charge provides neither the basis for Jesus' condemnation nor occasions the charge of blasphemy.

We return to the guiding question at the beginning of this study: wherein lies Jesus' blasphemy? He has affirmed that he is the Messiah son of God, which in itself is not blasphemous. He has provided solid grounds for his execution, so far as the Romans would be concerned. In claiming to be at some time "seated at the right hand of Yahweh," he was only alluded to a Davidic tradition that may have been understood in a messianic sense at that time. Again, this in itself does not necessarily constitute blasphemy. Uttering the Divine Name, especially in the context of quoting Scripture and if with all proper reverence, is not blasphemous.

TOWARDS A SOLUTION

I think that Jesus' reply to Caiaphas was regarded as blasphemous

---

13   In the earlier version of this chapter, which appeared in the *Society of Biblical Literature 1991 Seminar Papers*, I noted Gundry's proposal, which I had heard him present at the 1990 SBL meeting in New Orleans. At the time I considered it a possibility. Having perused the arguments in his recently published commentary on Mark I am now fully persuaded that this position is sound.

14   See Gundry, *Mark*, 900-901. J. Ådna (*Jesu Kritik am Tempel: Eine Untersuchung zum Verlauf und Sinn der sogenannten Tempelreinigung Jesu, Markus 11, 15-17 und Parallelen* [dissertation, University of Stavanger, 1993] 576) has reached a similar conclusion.

not because he acknowledged that he was the Messiah, or even the "son-of-God-Messiah," as Marcus has argued. It even may not have been blasphemy in saying that he would sit at God's right hand. I think what made his reply a scandalous blasphemy lay in the combination of the phrases from Psalm 110 and Daniel 7. The text (i.e. Mark 14:62), broken down into its three principal components, with bracketed Old Testament allusions, reads as follows:

ἐγώ εἰμι

1. ὄψεσθε τὸν υἱὸν τοῦ ἀνθρώπου [cf. LXX Dan 7:13: ὁ υἱὸς ἀνθρώπου]

2. ἐκ δεξιῶν καθήμενον τῆς δυνάμεως [cf. LXX Ps 109:1: κάθου ἐκ δεξιῶν μου; and possibly 109:2: ῥάβδον δυνάμεώς σου]

3. καὶ ἐρχόμενον μετὰ τῶν νεφελῶν τοῦ οὐρανοῦ [cf. Θ Dan 7:13: μετὰ τῶν νεφελῶν τοῦ οὐρανοῦ . . . ἐρχόμενος]

As I see it, there are two principal problems with this tradition: (1) the problematic and controversial self-designation "son of man"; and (2) the odd juxtaposition of being *seated*, which implies being stationary, and *coming*, which obviously implies movement. This awkwardness has led Donald Juel to conclude that "two separate scenes" have been combined.[15] Some also see (3) a problem with Mark's circumlocutions "Blessed," and "Power," suspecting that these are Marcan and possibly not genuine Jewish expressions. Before the question of blasphemy can be resolved, these three problems must be addressed.

Son of Man

Recently, convincing arguments have been put forward in support of the authenticity of the self-designation "son of man."[16] Ben

---

15 D. H. Juel, *Messiah and Temple: The Trial of Jesus in the Gospel of Mark* (SBLDS 31; Missoula: Scholars, 1977) 95.

16 E. Stauffer, "Messias oder Menschensohn," *NovT* 1 (1956) 81-102; E. Schweizer, "The Son of Man," *JBL* 79 (1960) 119-29; I. H. Marshall, "The Synoptic Son of Man Sayings in Recent Discussion," *NTS* 12 (1966) 327-51; R. T. France, "The Servant of the Lord in the Teaching of Jesus," *TynBul* 19 (1968) 26-52; R. N. Longenecker, "'Son of Man' as a Self-Designation of Jesus," *JETS* 12 (1969) 151-58; S. Kim, *The "Son of Man" as the Son of God* (WUNT 30; Tübingen: Mohr [Siebeck], 1983); R. Bauckham, "The Son of Man: 'A Man in My Position' or 'Someone'," *JSNT* 23 (1985) 23-33; M. Casey, "General, Generic and Indefinite: The Use of the Term 'Son of Man' in Aramaic Sources and in the Teaching of Jesus," *JSNT* 29 (1987) 21-56. See the excursus in J. Nolland, *Luke*

Witherington's competent survey concludes that the ideas underlying the *Similitudes of Enoch* (i.e. *1 Enoch* 37–71) did not derive from Christian ideas based on the Gospels, as J. T. Milik had argued,[17] but from Jewish, Palestinian, non-Christian ideas likely in circulation during the time of Jesus.[18] This conclusion, which today enjoys widespread scholarly support, is important for research into the meaning of the Synoptic son of man sayings, for in the *Similitudes* the "Son of Man" is depicted as a judge, as he is in the Gospels, particularly as seen in Mark 14:62.[19]

The usage of the epithet, "Son of Man," in the *Similitudes* raises, however, an important question. Whereas there it seems to have a "semi-titular" function, does it have this function in the Gospels? How this question is answered usually plays a part in the question of the authenticity of the Synoptic "son of man" sayings. It is sometimes pointed out that the authentic son of man sayings are self-referential (i.e. "son of man" = "I")[20] or generic (i.e. "son of man" = "a human being" or "a man")[21] and that sayings that understand "son of man" in a technical or titular sense are either inauthentic[22] or in reference to someone other than Jesus himself.[23] Recent studies by Marinus de Jonge and Bruce Chilton rightly argue for the generic sense of the

---

9:21–18:34 (WBC 35B; Dallas: Word, 1993) 468-74.

[17]   J. T. Milik, *The Books of Enoch* (Oxford: Clarendon, 1976) 91-92.

[18]   B. Witherington, III, *The Christology of Jesus* (Minneapolis: Fortress, 1990) 235.

[19]   Witherington, *Christology of Jesus*, 235. For a much more thorough examination of the Son of Man sayings in the Gospels, see pp. 233-62.

[20]   As in G. Vermes, "The Use of בר נש/בר נשא in Jewish Aramaic," in M. Black, *An Aramaic Approach to the Synoptic Gospels and Acts* (3rd ed., Oxford: Clarendon, 1967) 310-28; idem, *Jesus the Jew* (London: Collins, 1973) 160-91; idem, "The Son of Man Debate," *JSNT* 1 (1978) 19-32.

[21]   J. A. Fitzmyer, *A Wandering Aramean: Collected Aramaic Essays* (SBLMS 25; Missoula: Scholars Press, 1979) 143-60; idem, "Another View of the 'Son of Man' Debate," *JSNT* 4 (1979) 58-68.

[22]   E. Käsemann, "Sentences of Holy Law in the New Testament," in Käsemann, *New Testament Questions of Today* (Philadelphia: Fortress, 1969) 66-81, esp. 77-78; P. Vielhauer, "Jesus und der Menschensohn," *ZTK* 60 (1963) 133-77.

[23]   R. Bultmann, *Jesus and the Word* (New York: Scribner's, 1934) 30-31, 49; G. Haufe, "Das Menschensohn-Problem in der gegenwärtigen wissenschaftlichen Diskussion," *EvT* 26 (1966) 130-41.

idiom and try to account for its arthrous usage.[24] They plausibly
suggest that the definite article in ὁ υἱὸς τοῦ ἀνθρώπου be understood in
terms of specificity (and not in a titular sense). The specific "son of
man" (or human) to which the definite article refers is the one
described by Daniel. In favor of their suggestion is the occasional
association in the dominical tradition of the "son of man" with Daniel 7
and with no other Old Testament passage.

What images the "son of man" of Daniel 7 may have conjured up in
first-century Jewish thinking may be clarified in important ways by
the description of the "Son of Man" in *1 Enoch* 62. There are several
passages that are particularly instructive. The "Lord of the Spirits"
will sit "down on the throne of his glory" (v. 2). With him will sit the
"Son of Man," also on a "throne of glory" (v. 5; cf. 69:27, 29). The
"elect" will stand before him (v. 8). Sinners, including kings,
governors, and high officials, will be judged (vv. 9-12). Indeed, these
earthly lords will "fall down before him on their faces, worship and
raise their hopes in that Son Man" (v. 9). The righteous and the elect
will never again see the face of sinners, but will abide in the presence
of the Son of Man forever (vv. 13-16). If such an exegesis as this were
commonly associated with Daniel 7, which speaks of the setting up of
thrones (v. 9), sitting in judgment (vv. 10, 26), the subjugation of
nations, kings, and kingdoms (vv. 14, 17, 25, 27), and everlasting rule
(vv. 14, 18, 27), then a background that is more than adequate for the
Synoptic son of man sayings is at hand.

---

24   M. de Jonge, *Christology in Context: The Earliest Response to Jesus*
(Philadelphia: Westminster, 1988) 169-71, 207; B. D. Chilton, "The Son of Man:
Human and Heavenly," in F. Van Segbroeck et al. (eds.), *The Four Gospels 1992*
(F. Neirynck Festschrift; BETL 100; Leuven: Peeters, 1992) 1.203-18. Chilton cites
C. F. D. Moule (*The Origin of Christology* [Cambridge: Cambridge University
Press, 1977] 14; idem, "Neglected Features in the Problem of the Son of Man," in
Moule, *Essays in New Testament Interpretation* [Cambridge: Cambridge University
Press, 1982] 75-90, esp. 82-85) for having drawn attention to the importance of the
article. Moule rightly concluded that the article specified the "son of man" of Daniel.
See now I. H. Marshall, "The Synoptic 'Son of Man' Sayings in the Light of Linguistic Study," in T. E. Schmidt and M. Silva (eds.), *To Tell the Mystery: Essays
on New Testament Eschatology* (R. H. Gundry Festschrift; JSNTSup 100; Sheffield: JSOT Press, 1994) 72-94. Marshall concludes that "Jesus could and did use
the phrase (א)אנשׁ בר to refer to himself as the Danielic Son of man but in such a
way that the phrase could also function as a form of self-reference that would not
necessarily carry this full connotation every time he used it and to all his hearers"
(p. 94).

But it needs to be emphasized that, with the apparent exception of *1 Enoch*, "son of man" is not a messianic title; it is a generic reference to the human class. But the "son of man" of Daniel 7 is in all probability a messianic figure. He is a messianic figure not because he is called "son of man"; he is a messianic figure because God gives him the kingdom and, along with the saints, he overcomes Israel's enemies. This does not mean that every reference to "son of man" would have elicited messianic thoughts, but some references to *the* "son of man," that is, the one who comes with the clouds, would elicit such thinking.

Seated and Coming

The alleged discrepancy of being "seated at the right hand" and yet "coming with the clouds of heaven" disappears when the following three points are taken into consideration: (1) the similarity of the respective contexts of Daniel 7 and Psalm 110, (2) the combination of the two passages in Jewish exegesis, and (3) a commonly overlooked aspect of the Danielic description of the Divine throne. Because these three points have not been adequately taken into consideration, Jesus' answer has not in my judgment been fully understood. The Old Testament texts are as follows:

Daniel 7: 9-10, 13-14

‎9. חָזֵה הֲוֵית
‎עַד דִּי כָרְסָוָן רְמִיו וְעַתִּיק יוֹמִין יְתִב
‎לְבוּשֵׁהּ ׀ כִּתְלַג חִוָּר וּשְׂעַר רֵאשֵׁהּ כַּעֲמַר נְקֵא
‎כָּרְסְיֵהּ שְׁבִיבִין דִּי־נוּר גַּלְגִּלּוֹהִי נוּר דָּלִק:

‎10. נְהַר דִּי־נוּר נָגֵד וְנָפֵק מִן־קֳדָמוֹהִי
‎אֶלֶף אַלְפַיִם [אַלְפִין] יְשַׁמְּשׁוּנֵּהּ
‎וְרִבּוֹ רַבְוָן [רִבְבָן] קֳדָמוֹהִי יְקוּמוּן
‎דִּינָא יְתִב וְסִפְרִין פְּתִיחוּ:

‎13. חָזֵה הֲוֵית בְּחֶזְוֵי לֵילְיָא
‎וַאֲרוּ עִם־עֲנָנֵי שְׁמַיָּא כְּבַר אֱנָשׁ אָתֵה הֲוָה
‎וְעַד־עַתִּיק יוֹמַיָּא מְטָה וּקְדָמוֹהִי הַקְרְבוּהִי:

‎14. וְלֵהּ יְהִיב שָׁלְטָן וִיקָר וּמַלְכוּ
‎וְכֹל עַמְמַיָּא אֻמַיָּא וְלִשָּׁנַיָּא לֵהּ יִפְלְחוּן
‎שָׁלְטָנֵהּ שָׁלְטָן עָלַם דִּי־לָא יֶעְדֵּה
‎וּמַלְכוּתֵהּ דִּי־לָא תִתְחַבַּל:

9. ἐθεώρουν ἕως ὅτου θρόνοι ἐτέθησαν, καὶ παλαιὸς ἡμερῶν ἐκάθητο, καὶ τὸ ἔνδυμα αὐτοῦ ὡσεὶ χιὼν λευκόν, καὶ ἡ θρὶξ τῆς κεφαλῆς αὐτοῦ ὡσεὶ ἔριον καθαρόν, ὁ θρόνος αὐτοῦ φλὸξ πυρός, οἱ τροχοὶ αὐτοῦ πῦρ

φλέγον·

10. ποταμὸς πυρὸς εἶλκεν ἔμπροσθεν αὐτοῦ, χίλιαι χιλιάδες ἐλειτούργουν αὐτῷ, καὶ μύριαι μυριάδες παρειστήκεισαν αὐτῷ· κριτήριον ἐκάθισεν, καὶ βίβλοι ἠνεῴχθησαν.

13. ἐθεώρουν ἐν ὁράματι τῆς νυκτὸς καὶ ἰδοὺ μετὰ τῶν νεφελῶν τοῦ οὐρανοῦ ὡς υἱὸς ἀνθρώπου ἐρχόμενος ἦν καὶ ἕως τοῦ παλαιοῦ τῶν ἡμερῶν ἔφθασεν καὶ ἐνώπιον αὐτοῦ προσηνέχθη.

14. καὶ αὐτῷ ἐδόθη ἡ ἀρχὴ καὶ ἡ τιμὴ καὶ ἡ βασιλεία, καὶ πάντες οἱ λαοί, φυλαί, γλῶσαι αὐτῷ δουλεύσουσιν· ἡ ἐξουσία αὐτοῦ ἐξουσία αἰώνιος, ἥτις οὐ παρελεύσεται, καὶ ἡ βασιλεία αὐτοῦ οὐ διαφθαρήσεται.

Psalm 110:1-6

1. לְדָוִד מִזְמוֹר
נְאֻם יְהוָה ׀ לַאדֹנִי שֵׁב לִימִינִי
עַד־אָשִׁית אֹיְבֶיךָ הֲדֹם לְרַגְלֶיךָ׃

2. מַטֵּה־עֻזְּךָ יִשְׁלַח יְהוָה מִצִּיּוֹן
רְדֵה בְּקֶרֶב אֹיְבֶיךָ׃

3. עַמְּךָ נְדָבֹת בְּיוֹם חֵילֶךָ
בְּהַדְרֵי־קֹדֶשׁ מֵרֶחֶם מִשְׁחָר
לְךָ טַל יַלְדֻתֶיךָ׃

4. נִשְׁבַּע יְהוָה ׀ וְלֹא יִנָּחֵם
אַתָּה־כֹהֵן לְעוֹלָם עַל־דִּבְרָתִי מַלְכִּי־צֶדֶק׃

5. אֲדֹנָי עַל־יְמִינְךָ
מָחַץ בְּיוֹם־אַפּוֹ מְלָכִים׃

6. יָדִין בַּגּוֹיִם מָלֵא גְוִיּוֹת
מָחַץ רֹאשׁ עַל־אֶרֶץ רַבָּה׃

1. Τῷ Δαυίδ ψαλμός.

Εἶπεν ὁ κύριος τῷ κυρίῳ μου Κάθου ἐκ δεξιῶν μου, ἕως ἂν θῶ τοὺς ἐχθρούς σου ὑποπόδιον τῶν ποδῶν σου.

2. ῥάβδον δυνάμεώς σου ἐξαποστελεῖ κύριος ἐκ Σιών, καὶ κατακυρίευε ἐν μέσῳ τῶν ἐχθρῶν σου.

3. μετὰ σοῦ ἡ ἀρχὴ ἐν ἡμέρᾳ τῆς δυνάμεώς σου ἐν ταῖς λαμπρότησιν τῶν ἁγίων· ἐκ γαστρὸς πρὸ ἑωσφόρου ἐξεγέννησά σε.

4. ὤμοσεν κύριος καὶ οὐ μεταμεληθήσεται Σὺ εἶ ἱερεὺς εἰς τὸν αἰῶνα κατὰ τὴν τάξιν Μελχισέδεκ.

5. κύριος ἐκ δεξιῶν σου συνέθλασεν ἐν ἡμέρᾳ ὀργῆς αὐτοῦ βασιλεῖς·

6. κρινεῖ ἐν τοῖς ἔθνεσιν, πληρώσει πτώματα, συνθλάσει κεφαλὰς ἐπὶ γῆς πολλῶν.

First, the respective contexts of Daniel 7 and Psalm 110 are quite similar. Both speak of the subjugation of Israel's enemies, including kings (Dan 7:14, 26; Ps 110:1, 5, 6), both speak of rule over God's people (Dan 7:14 ; Ps 110:3), and both speak of judgment (Dan 7:10, 22, 26; Ps 110:6). The juxtaposition in Mark 14:62 of phrases from these passages may be evidence of a wider comparison of these two texts, such as what may in fact be the case with respect to the *Similitudes* (see below). The similar themes would certainly facilitate a wider comparison.

Second, Daniel 7 and Psalm 110 are combined in later Jewish exegesis: "And in one place in the Writings it is written, 'The Lord said to my lord, "Sit at my right hand" [Ps 110:1],' and it is also written: 'Behold, one came with the clouds of heaven, as a son of man' [Dan 7:13]" (*Midr. Ps.* 2.9 [on 2:7]; cf. 18.29 [on 18:36]).[25] There is no indication that this exegesis either reflects or seeks to contradict Christian exegesis. Although preserved in writings that clearly post-date the New Testament, this tradition likely represents an independent exegesis. The combination of Daniel 7 and Psalm 110 in Jesus, if not in the *Similitudes* themselves,[26] suggests that this exegesis, in one form or another, existed at least as early as the first few decades of the first century.[27] The juxtaposition of these texts, therefore, does not constitute an argument against the authenticity of Mark 14:62.

Third, the juxtaposition of being seated and coming is not odd when one realizes that what is being spoken of is God's chariot throne.[28] Jane

---

[25]   Trans. based on W. G. Braude, *The Midrash on the Psalms* (2 vols., YJS 13; London and New Haven: Yale University, 1959) 1.40-41.

[26]   As texts that speak of the Son of Man sitting with, or next to, God would seem to imply (cf. *1 Enoch* 45:3; 55:4; 62:5). See Witherington, *Christology of Jesus*, 260-61.

[27]   The "son" (בֵּן) and "son of man" (בֶּן־אָדָם) of Ps 80:16(E15) and Ps 80:18 (E17) have in the Targum been taken in a messianic sense. This may be pertinent for the present concerns, not simply because we have an instance of messianic interpretation of the phrase, "son of man," but we have one in the context of a reference to God's "right hand." The Targum reads: "And the stock which Your right hand has planted and upon the King Messiah [מלכא משיחא] whom You have made strong for Yourself" (*Tg. Ps* 80:16). In v. 18 the "son of man" is translated literally as בר נש, but the context requires that he be understood as parallel to the "King Messiah" of v. 16. In LXX Ps 79:15 "son" is expanded to υἱὸς ἀνθρώπου. Also of possible relevance is the messianic paraphrase found in *Tg. 1 Chr* 3:24, where we are told that the name of King Messiah is "Anani" (ענני). "Anani" comes from Dan 7:13, which speaks of the coming of a son of man "with the clouds [ענני] of heaven."

[28]   Gundry (*Mark*, 887) suggests that Caiaphas and company will see the son

Schaberg has argued that Mark 14:62 reflects merkabah tradition in which Jesus (or the early Church, as she thinks) sees himself as a "co-occupant of the divine throne."[29] She concludes that this explanation accounts for the anomaly of the Son of man sitting and yet coming with the clouds: He is sitting on the throne, which is itself part of God's chariot. This interpretation is supported by Dan 7:9: "thrones were placed and one that was ancient of days took his seat . . . his throne was fiery flames, its wheels were burning fire" (cf. Ezekiel 1, 10).[30] The throne that was set up was none other than God's chariot throne, as is made clear by the reference to the burning wheels. This could be the idea in *1 Enoch* 51:3: "In those days the Elect One shall sit on my throne." That this is what Jesus may have had in mind is supported by Rev 3:21: "He who conquers, I will grant him to sit with me on my throne, as I myself conquered and *sat down with my Father on his throne*" (emphasis added). A similar idea is also found in Philo, who says that the Logos sits in God's chariot next to God himself (cf. *Fug.* 19 §101).[31] Indeed, the concept is well known in the Greco-Roman world, as illustrated by a coin minted in Rome in 55 C.E., which depicts "divine" Claudius seated at the right hand of Augustus atop a chariot drawn by four elephants.[32]

---

of man first seated and then coming. This is possible, but I should think that before resorting to a sequential understanding of the two present-tense participles, one should first try to explain them in terms of concurrence.

[29]   J. Schaberg, "Mark 14.62: Early Christian Merkabah Imagery?" in J. Marcus and M. L. Soards (eds.), *Apocalyptic and the New Testament* (J. L. Martyn Festschrift; JSNTSup 24; Sheffield: JSOT, 1989) 69-94, quote from p. 85.

[30]   Daniel's indebtedness to Ezekiel was noted long ago by J. W. Bowman, "The Background of the Term 'Son of Man'," *ExpTim* 59 (1947-48) 283-88, esp. 285.

[31]   This conclusion was first presented at the 1991 SBL meeting in Kansas City, Missouri; cf. C. A. Evans, "In What Sense 'Blasphemy'? Jesus before Caiaphas in Mark 14:61-64," in D. J. Lull (ed.), *Society of Biblical Literature 1991 Seminar Papers* (SBLSP 30; Atlanta: Scholars Press, 1991) 215-34. It was gratifying to see the appearance of M. Hengel, "'Setze dich zu meiner Rechten!' Die Inthronisation Christi zur Rechten Gottes und Psalm 110,1," in M. Philonenko (ed.), *Le Trône de Dieu* (WUNT 69; Tübingen: Mohr [Siebeck], 1993) 108-94. Working independently, Hengel has come to the same conclusion. He provides a much fuller investigation of the Old Testament background of enthronement. Other aspects of his study will receive attention below.

[32]   For photograph and description of this coin, which is an aureus, see H. Mattingly, *Coins of the Roman Empire in the British Museum. Volume I: Augustus*

What we have here may not be an independent Christian apocalyptic tradition, but a tradition ultimately dependent upon what lies behind Mark 14:62.[33] In other words, Jesus' words in Mark 14:62 were understood as implying that Jesus anticipated sharing God's chariot throne. Such a claim would surely have been scandalous, for the idea of a mortal sitting on God's throne was unthinkable.[34] A later Jewish exegesis illustrates the unthinkableness of the concept: "'Solomon sat on the throne of the Lord' [1 Chr 29:23]. Is it possible that flesh and blood could sit on the throne of the Lord? Is it not written, 'His throne was fiery flames, and its wheels burning fire' [Dan 7:9]? What then do the words, 'Solomon sat on the throne of the Lord,' mean? They mean that like his Maker, Solomon was able to render judgments without witnesses and without warning" (*Midr. Ps.* 72.2 [on 72:1]).[35]

Blessed and Power as References to God

Some question the authenticity of Mark 14:61-62 because "Blessed" (εὐλογητός) and "Power" (δύναμις) were not common circumlocutions for the Divine Name. Years ago Gustaf Dalman suggested that הַמְבוֹרָךְ in *m. Ber.* 7:3 (cf. *y. Ber.* 7.3; *b. Ber.* 50a; *1 Enoch* 77:2), which he translated "the Blessed One," is a Hebrew equivalent.[36] Juel disagrees regarding "Blessed" as a "pseudo-Jewish expression" that cannot be viewed as something that Caiaphas could have said.[37] He argues that the examples in *Berakot* probably should not be understood as substantive, but adjectival: "who is blessed." It is, of course, possible that this is exactly the way it should be understood in Mark 14:61: "the

---

to Vitellius (London: British Museum, 1965) 201 + pl. 38. I wish to thank my colleague James M. Scott for calling this coin to my attention. For additional material on Paul's use of these traditions, see J. M. Scott, "The Triumph of God in 2 Corinthians 2:14: Another Case of Merkabah Mysticism in Paul," *NTS*, forthcoming.

[33] So also Hengel, "'Setze dich zu meiner Rechten!'," 151, 163, 177, 188.

[34] So also Hengel, "'Setze dich zu meiner Rechten!'," 174, 177. Hengel thinks that such a concept would have been viewed as an *Ungeheuerlichkeit*. Hengel suggests that "dieser unsagbar kühne und zugleich anstößige Schritt" in the formation of New Testament christology is owing to Jesus himself. See also D. R. Catchpole, *The Trial of Jesus: A Study in the Gospels and Jewish Historiography from 1770 to the Present Day* (SPB 18; Leiden: Brill, 1971) 140-41.

[35] Translation based on Braude, *Midrash on the Psalms*, 1.558.

[36] G. Dalman, *The Words of Jesus* (Edinburgh: T. & T. Clark, 1909) 200. See also Betz, "Prozess Jesu," 633.

[37] Juel, *Messiah and Temple*, 77-79. See also J. Klausner, *Jesus of Nazareth: His Life, Times, and Teaching* (London: Allen & Unwin, 1925) 342.

son of the One who is blessed" (cf. Rom 1:25; 9:5).[38] In either case, I do not think that calling Mark's phrase a "pseudo-Jewish expression" is justified. Moreover, Marcus thinks it unwise, in light of the "fragmentary nature of our sources for first-century Judaism," to dismiss the authenticity of the expression.[39] Its rarity within the extant sources does suggest that it was not a common way of referring to God. Perhaps it was for this reason that the Matthean evangelist altered Mark's "son of the Blessed" to "son of God" (Matt 26:63). In my opinion, Mark's "the Blessed" is not an *abbreviation* of the ubiquitous rabbinic circumlocution, "the Holy One blessed be He" (הקדוש ברוך הוא), but is a *forerunner* of the later, expanded rabbinic expression.[40]

The expression "Power" as a substitute for God is better attested, being found in a saying attributed to Rabbi Ishmael: "It was said by the mouth of the Power [הַגְּבוּרָה]" (*Sipre Num.* §112 [on 15:31]; cf. *b. 'Erub.* 54b; *b. Yebam.* 105b; *Tg.* Job 5:8: "from the Power [תקיפא]"; 14:18 [var.]; 18:4 [var.]). There are references to "the Power that is above [כח של מעלה]" (*Sipre Deut.* §319 [on 32:18]) and "in the eyes of the Power [הַגְּבוּרָה]" (*'Abot R. Nat.* [A] 37.12).[41] Note also *1 Enoch* 62:7: "For the Son of Man was concealed from the beginning, and the Most High One preserved him in the presence of his power." It is also possible that the word "Power" was suggested by Ps 110(109):2 ("the Lord will send forth from Zion the rod of your power [עז/δύναμις]").

Summary

Thus far I think that the following things can be said. First, it is not likely that Jesus was accused of blasphemy for affirming Caiaphas' question about his messianic identity, although there is a remote possibility that accepting the title "Messiah son of God" might have provoked such a response, especially if Jesus had actually pronounced the Divine Name. Second, the juxtaposition of sitting and coming proves to be meaningful and coherent. Third, it is in this odd juxtaposition that we probably have found our solution, for surely Jesus' claim to share God's throne and to come in judgment upon Caiaphas and the Temple establishment would have prompted the High Priest to

---

38   One is reminded of the call to prayer in the synagogue: בָּרְכוּ אֶת יהוה הַמְבֹרָךְ ("Bless the Lord the Blessed" or "Bless the Lord who is blessed").

39   Marcus, "Mark 14:61," 127 n. 6.

40   So Gundry, *Mark*, 909-10.

41   See E. E. Urbach, *The Sages: Their Concepts and Beliefs* (Cambridge: Harvard University Press, 1975) 80-96.

accuse Jesus of blasphemy, whether or not the Divine Name was pronounced. Though if the Divine Name was pronounced, as Gundry has argued, the grounds for a capital charge of blasphemy would be secure. Even if the Divine Name was not pronounced, such a claim would have qualified as blasphemy according to the usage of the word in the writings of Philo and Josephus. Jesus' claim would have been understood as denigrating God and as threatening the High Priest, Israel's ruler. This will be made clearer shortly. Fourth, Jesus' acceptance of the title "Messiah" would obviously have carried with it political, as well as religious implications. That alone would have warranted the handing over of Jesus to Pilate. But the claim to be seated on God's throne, coming in judgment, would have carried with it not only only political implications, but potentially blasphemous theological implications as well. If Jesus' dangerous political claims could be construed as blasphemy, it would have been much easier for Caiaphas, at a time when many Passover pilgrims were present in Jerusalem, to hand over to the Romans a popular Galilean teacher and healer.

THE CHRISTOLOGIES OF JESUS AND RABBI AQIBA
A POSSIBLE PARALLEL

Because of his interpretation of Daniel 7 and because of his endorsement of the messianic candidacy of Simon ben Kosiba (see chap. 4 above), the messianic ideas, or "christology," of Rabbi Aqiba (ca. 50–135 C.E.) could have some important bearing on the question of the meaning and authenticity of Mark 14:61-64. But how useful are post-New Testament rabbinic traditions for research in the life of Jesus? Since the tendency in the rabbinic materials was either to suppress or ignore ideas, exegeses, and traditions that supported or complemented Christian doctrines, particularly those which contrasted sharply with Jewish beliefs (e.g. the messiahship and divinity of Jesus, the Trinity), the preservation of such materials (e.g. Aqiba's theologically and politically dangerous christology) may indicate that such materials were early and widespread and therefore not easily suppressed. This is similar to the Gospel authenticity criterion of tradition contrary to editorial tendency and dissimilar to the theological interests of the community. The christology of Aqiba seems to meet these criteria. Although there are important parallels, nowhere in this rabbi's christology do I detect dependence upon or polemic against distinctive Christian ideas.

Rabbi Aqiba evidently held to a christology that entertained ideas of
a mortal Messiah, such as someone like Simon ben Kosiba, who,
enthroned next to God himself, would reign for forty years and would
regather the lost tribes of Israel. It is, of course, possible that the forty
year reign was thought to be earthly, while the enthronement was
heavenly. In any case, it is significant that Aqiba understood such a
potentially blasphemous interpretation of Daniel 7 to have been fulfilled in a mortal like Simon. Evidently Aqiba viewed the Messiah as
mortal, so far as life on earth was concerned, for he expected him to
reign but one generation. And yet Aqiba expected the Messiah to sit on
a throne next to God himself. It is the combination of these ideas—
Messiah will sit next to God/Simon ben Kosiba is Messiah—that is
potentially so meaningful for our understanding of Jesus and Daniel
7.[42]

Comparison of the respective christologies of Jesus and Aqiba is
instructive, for they are mutually clarifying.[43] Reasoning principally
from coherence, arguments for the authenticity of Mark 14:61-64 will
now be offered.

Mark 14:61-64 and Related Authentic Tradition

The strongest claim to the authenticity of Mark 14:61-64 is seen in
its coherence with Jesus' promise to his disciples that they will someday sit with him on thrones in the Kingdom of God. This tradition is
clearly based upon Daniel 7.[44] Jesus apparently understood himself in
terms of Daniel's "son of man," to whom the kingdom would be given
(cf. Dan 7:14; *1 Enoch* 69:29; *Pss. Sol.* 17:44), and his disciples as the
"saints" to whom judgment would some day be given (cf. Dan 7:22).

---

[42]   Hengel ("'Setze dich zu meiner Rechten!'," 174) has also observed the
importance of Aqiba's exegesis. Hengel (p. 169) also rightly draws our attention to
4Q491, yet another instance where our thinking overlaps. The hymn found in
4Q491 11 i 11-18, epecially if Morton Smith's interpretation is correct (see Smith,
"Ascent to the Heavens and Deification in 4QM^a," in L. H. Schiffman [ed.],
*Archaeology and History in the Dead Sea Scrolls: The New York University
Conference in Memory of Yigael Yadin* [JSPSup 2; Sheffield: JSOT Press, 1990]
181-88), may offer documentation that ideas of human beings entering heaven and
sitting next to God were entertained by some Jewish mystics. See my discussion of
this scroll in chap. 3 above.

[43]   For Aqiba's christology, one should refer to chap. 4 above.

[44]   Juel (*Messiah and Temple*, 158-59) regards Matt 19:28 = Luke 22:28-30
and Mark 14:62 as "seemingly indisputable allusions" to Daniel 7.

This is likely what lies behind the tradition found in Mark and Q:

From Mark:

And [James and John] said to him, "Grant us to sit, one at your right hand and one at your left, in your glory." But Jesus said to them, "You do not know what you are asking . . . to sit at my right hand or at my left is not mine to grant, but it is for those for whom it has been prepared." (10:37-40)

From Q:

Truly, I say to you, in the new world, when the son of man shall sit on his glorious throne, you who have followed me will also sit on twelve thrones, judging the twelve tribes of Israel. (Matt 19:28)

You are those who have continued with me in my trials; and I assign to you, as my Father assigned to me, a kingdom, that you may eat and drink at my table in my kingdom, and sit on thrones judging the twelve tribes of Israel. (Luke 22:28-30)[45]

According to Rudolf Bultmann, "it is unquestionably the risen Lord who speaks [in Matt 19:28 = Luke 22:28-30] . . . We are dealing with a formulation deriving from the early Church, for it was there that the Twelve were first held to be judges of Israel in the time of the end."[46] More recently F. W. Beare has opined that "it is not conceivable that Jesus could ever have spoken these words. They come from a Palestinian Christianity dominated by vivid apocalyptic expectations couched in traditional Jewish imagery . . . [It does] not come from earliest times. The kind of exaltation of the apostles, the notion of them as a collegiate body governing the church, belongs to the second generation (or later)."[47]

---

[45] Scholars are divided over the origin of this tradition. Some believe the Matthean and Lucan forms derive from Q or from different recensions of Q. Others believe that they derive from M and L. See J. S. Kloppenborg, *Q Parallels* (Sonoma: Polebridge, 1988) 202. Virtually all regard these as divergent forms of the same saying.

[46] R. Bultmann, *The History of the Synoptic Tradition* (Oxford: Blackwell, 1968) 158-59. Elsewhere Bultmann says that this tradition "is related to the inner life of the early Church" (p. 163).

[47] F. W. Beare, *The Gospel according to Matthew* (San Francisco: Harper & Row, 1981) 400. The form of the tradition as it appears in Rev 3:21 ("He who conquers, I will grant him to sit with me on my throne, as I myself conquered and sat down with my Father on his throne") is a later "universalizing of a saying which applied originally only to the Twelve"; cf. Bultmann, *Synoptic Tradition*, 159, n. 4. Relevant also is 1 Cor 6:2: "Do you not know that the saints will judge [κρινοῦσιν]

Nevertheless, in recent years scholars have come to regard this tradition as authentic. Sanders argues convincingly that it would have been highly unlikely for the early Church to have created a saying about the Twelve sitting on twelve thrones, when the early Church knew that one of the Twelve (Judas) had betrayed Jesus.[48] This is no doubt the reason why Luke omitted "twelve," and simply spoke of the disciples sitting on "thrones judging the twelve tribes."[49] Ben Meyer argues, moreover, that surely Jesus anticipated vindication for himself and for his disciples.[50] The saying as it is preserved in Matt 19:28 = Luke 22:28-30 is an expression of such anticipation.[51]

The same arguments may be offered for the authenticity of Mark 10:37-40. Indeed, additional reasons support the authenticity of this passage. First, it paints a discreditable picture of the disciples James and John.[52] It is highly unlikely that the early Church would have invented such a tradition, though it might have been retained for edifying purposes. Secondly, the limitation placed on Jesus ("to sit at my right hand or at my left is not mine to grant") surely does not derive from the early Church, nor does it reflect the Jewish principle that the Master has the authority to assign seats on his right and left (cf. b. 'Erub. 54b). But the saying does cohere with Ps 110:1. In other words, Jesus knows that *only God* has the authority to assign seats; he does not.[53]

---

the world?"

[48]   Sanders, *Jesus and Judaism*, 98-99. Cf. I. H. Marshall, *Commentary on Luke* (NIGTC; Grand Rapids: Eerdmans, 1978) 815.

[49]   So J. A. Fitzmyer, *The Gospel According to Luke X-XXIV* (AB 28A; Garden City: Doubleday, 1985) 1419.

[50]   B. F. Meyer, *The Aims of Jesus* (London: SCM, 1979) 209.

[51]   See also W. G. Kümmel, *Promise and Fulfillment* (SBT 23; London: SCM, 1957) 47.

[52]   V. Taylor, *The Gospel according to St. Mark* (London: Macmillan, 1952) 439; C. E. B. Cranfield, *The Gospel according to St Mark* (Cambridge: Cambridge University Press, 1959) 336.

[53]   I suspect that these related traditions from Mark and Q were originally part of a unified saying, perhaps something like this: "The sons of Zebedee said to him, 'Grant us to sit, one at your right hand and one at your left, in your glory.' But Jesus said to them, 'You do not know what you are asking. To sit at my right hand or at my left is not mine to grant, but it is for those for whom it has been prepared. Truly I say to you, when I sit on my glorious throne, you who have followed [or continued with] me will also sit on twelve thrones, judging the twelve tribes of Israel.'"

The authenticity of this tradition gains further support when its meaning is properly assessed. Daniel 7 is not the only Old Testament passage that lies behind these traditions of sitting on Jesus' right and left and judging the twelve tribes of Israel. It is likely that Ps 122:3-5 ("Jerusalem . . . to which the tribes go up . . . There thrones for judgment were set, the thrones of the house of David") has also contributed to this eschatological saying.[54] This is indeed likely, for both passages, Daniel 7 and Psalm 122, are cited side by side in a rabbinic exegesis that anticipates the day when God and Israel's elders will sit in judgment upon the peoples of the world (cf. *Midr. Tanḥ.*, B *Qedošim* §1, discussed above in chap. 4; cf. *Midr. Ps.* 122.6 [on 122:5]). By means of the exegetical principle of *gezera šawa*, the rabbis have linked the two texts by the words "thrones" and "judgment." Linkage was also facilitated because of Daniel 7's messianic overtones and because of Psalm 122's explicit reference to "the house of David." It is this combination and, to a large extent, this kind of exegesis that in all probability lie behind Jesus' sayings.

Jesus saw himself as the "son of man" who will sit on one of the "thrones" of Dan 7:9 (in agreement with Aqiba's [early] understanding of this verse) and, along with his disciples, who displace the "elders of Israel,"[55] will judge the tribes (as suggested by Ps 122:3-5). The meaning of "judging [κρίνοντες] the twelve tribes" should probably be understood in the Old Testament sense of "ruling" (see LXX Judg 3:10 where κρίνειν translates שָׁפַט), and very likely had no punitive connotation (as in later Christian and Jewish exegesis).[56] A close

---

54   Not many commentators have seen the allusions to Daniel 7 and Psalm 122; Fitzmyer (*Luke X-XXIV*, 1419) sees Ps 122:4-5 lying behind Luke 22:30; R. H. Gundry (*Matthew: A Commentary on His Literary and Theological Art* [Grand Rapids: Eerdmans, 1982] 393) recognizes the parallels between Daniel 7 and Matt 19:28; Marshall (*Luke*, 818) rightly sees the presence of both Old Testament passages behind the saying.

55   D. Zeller, *Kommentar zur Logienquelle* (SKKNT 21; Stuttgart: Katholisches Bibelwerk, 1986) 88.

56   Christians understood Matt 19:28 as predicting punitive judgment of Israel. After citing the verse, Origen says that "the just will judge the twelve tribes of Israel which have not believed" (*Com. Matt.* 15.24). Chrysostom asks: "What is the meaning of 'judging the twelve tribes of Israel'? It means 'condemning them'" (*Hom. Matt.* 64.2). Perhaps in response to this kind of interpretation, the rabbis think that Ps 122:5 implies the judgment of "the nations of the world" (*Midr. Ps.* 122.6 [on 122:5]). In the targum, the idea of judgment drops out altogether: "For there thrones will be set in Jerusalem, thrones in the Temple for the kings of the

parallel is found in the *Psalms of Solomon*: "[Messiah] will gather a holy people whom he will lead in righteousness; and he will judge [κρινεῖ] the tribes of the people" (17:26; cf. 17:29; Ps 2:10; 1 Macc 9:73). In effect, Jesus has promised his disciples a place in his government.

But part of this task will be the regathering of the twelve tribes in order to reconstitute and renew Israel, something that most of the other messianic claimants, especially ben Kosiba, hoped to accomplish.[57] It is very likely that this is what such sayings as those under consideration imply. This is in part why Richard Horsley, in keeping with the idea in the Book of Judges, translates Matt 19:28 as "sitting on twelve thrones *liberating* the twelve tribes of Israel" (my emphasis).[58] Not only does Jesus' promise cohere with the rabbinic expectation, at least as it has been expressed in *Midrash Tanḥuma*, that the "great ones" of Israel will sit upon the various thrones that will be set up in Jerusalem, but it coheres with Aqiba's expectation that the ten lost tribes of the north will someday be regathered.

The implication of this interpretation is clear. If Jesus, drawing upon the imagery of Daniel 7 and Psalm 122, promised his disciples thrones, then the statement that is attributed to him in Mark 14:62, a statement that reflects the same understanding of Daniel 7, has a reasonable claim to authenticity. Moreover, making this statement to the High Priest is also contextually appropriate, for it implies that his rule will be displaced by Jesus' rule. Indeed, the sayings in Mark 10 and Matt 19:28 = Luke 22:28-30 offer a critique of one aspect of the Jewish interpretation of Daniel 7 in suggesting that the "great ones" of Israel will be those who humble themselves. The thrones for judgment

---

house of David."

[57] The precise cause of the Bar Kokhba revolt is not clear. According to Cassius Dio (*Hist. Rom.* 69.12.1-2) Hadrian provoked the war by erecting a temple dedicated to Zeus on the very spot where once the Jewish Temple stood. Chrysostom (*Oration against the Jews* 5.10) believed that the Jews attempted to rebuild their temple during the war. According to the *Scriptores Historiae Augustae* (*Life of Hadrian* 14.2) the Emperor outlawed cicumcision (*mutilare genitalia*). Appian (*Syrian War* §50) speaks of oppressive measures and Jewish hatred of Hadrian (cf. *Gen. Rab.* 63.7 [on Gen 25:23]). Most of these reasons suggest that Simon was probably motivated for religious reasons. The Bar Kokhba letters make it clear that he was religiously observant. For a fuller discussion, see chap. 4.

[58] R. A. Horsley, *Sociology and the Jesus Movement* (New York: Crossroad, 1989) 119.

will not be given to Israel's current rulers (e.g. the High Priest, ruling priests, members of the Sanhedrin), i.e. those who exalt themselves (cf. *T. Moses* 7); the thrones will be given to Jesus' followers who have humbled themselves, as seen in their willingness to serve, rather than be served.[59]

Mark 14:61-64 and the Historical, Political, and Social Context

Secondary support for the authenticity of Mark 14:61-64 is found in the observation that Rabbi Aqiba interpreted Daniel 7 messianically (as did many Rabbis) and identified (as probably many other rabbis did) a human being, Simon ben Kosiba, as Israel's Messiah. Such an identification by a revered rabbi lends plausibility to Jesus' self-identification as the Messiah who would sit next to God. In other words, it is not necessary to suppose that such "high christology" must have arisen in the early Church, following the Easter proclamation. Lending further support to the tradition's authenticity is the fact that many persons aspired to messianic recognition in the generation before Jesus, and in the two or three generations that followed. Some of these persons aspired to be "king," others claimed to be prophets of renewal, probably in accordance with the prophet-like Moses theme.[60]

Mark 14:61-64 and the Parable of Wicked Vineyard Tenants

There is evidence elsewhere that Jesus viewed himself as God's Son. This is seen especially in the Parable of the Vineyard Tenants (Mark

---

59   O. Betz (*Jesus und das Danielbuch, Band II: Die Menschensohnworte Jesu und die Zukunftserwartung des Paulus (Daniel 7, 13-14)* [ANTJ 6.2; Frankfurt am Main: Peter Lang, 1985] 175-76) sees in this concept a deliberate reversal on the part of Jesus of Daniel's idea that the Son of Man will be served. Betz believes that Jesus thought that he must first serve and suffer before he can be exalted and served. This leads me to think that Jesus' ideas of the son of man who suffers may very well have derived from his understanding of Isaiah 53, as has been argued by P. Stuhlmacher, "Existenzstellvertretung für die Vielen: Mk 10,45 (Mt 20,28)," in R. Albertz et al. (eds.), *Werden und Wirken des Alten Testaments* (C. Westermann Festschrift; Göttingen: Vandenhoeck & Ruprecht, 1980) 412-27; repr. in Stuhlmacher, *Versöhnung, Gesetz und Gerechtigkeit: Aufsätze zur biblischen Theologie* (Göttingen: Vandenhoeck & Ruprecht, 1981) 27-42.

60   G. Theissen ("Die Tempelweissagung Jesu: Prophetie im Spannungsfeld von Stadt und Land," *TZ* 32 [1976] 144-58) suspects that Jesus' utterances against the Temple, which he thinks are likely authentic, may reflect widespread rural opposition to the Temple establishment. For a discussion of these claimants see Horsley and Hanson, *Bandits*, as well as chap. 2 above.

12:1-12), a parable which increasingly scholars are coming to regard as authentic (see chap. 10 above).[61] Against the older assertion that the parable was a creation of the early Church depicting what had happened to Jesus,[62] it has been pointed out that the parable warns of the coming judgment of the wicked tenants and says nothing of the son's vindication. Moreover, murdering the son and then casting him "outside" (v. 8) of the vineyard (which, according to this view, is Jerusalem) does not parallel Jesus' experience. Jesus was first taken outside of Jerusalem and then was put to death.[63] Finally, Klyne Snodgrass has recently made a good case for the authenticity of the concluding citation of Ps 118:22-23.[64] He argues that the rejected stone of the Ps 118:22 (which in the Targum reads: "the boy which the builders abandoned") makes up an essential part of the parable and must not be viewed as a later, secondary addition. (For further arguments in support of this position, see chap. 10 above.)

Assuming that this parable does indeed derive from Jesus, we learn several significant facts about Jesus' self-understanding: (1) Jesus viewed himself as God's "son,"[65] sent to the religious authorities, the caretakers of God's vineyard, Israel; (2) Jesus viewed the religious authorities as corrupt and under the threat of divine judgment (which is likely how the action in the Temple should be understood); and (3)

---

61   C. H. Dodd, *The Parables of Jesus* (2nd ed.; New York: Scribner's, 1961) 96-102; M. Hengel, "Das Gleichnis von den Weingärtnern Mc 12:1-12 im Lichte der Zenonpapyri und der rabbinischen Gleichnisse," *ZNW* 59 (1968) 1-39; J. Jeremias, *The Parables of Jesus* (3rd ed.; London: SCM, 1972) 70-77; Cranfield, *Mark*, 366-68; J. D. Crossan, "The Parable of the Wicked Husbandmen," *JBL* 90 (1971) 451-65; Fitzmyer, *Luke X-XXIV*, 1279-80. J. H. Charlesworth, *Jesus within Judaism* (ABRL; New York: Doubleday, 1988) 139-53.

62   In the past this parable was viewed as inauthentic because of its allegorizing features; cf. Bultmann, *Synoptic Tradition*, 177, 205; Kümmel, *Promise and Fulfillment*, 83. Schweizer (*Mark*, 239) thinks that the parable is a creation of the Greek-speaking Church. Such a view overlooks the Semitic and Jewish exegetical features that run throughout the parable, including the citation of Ps 118:22-23.

63   Charlesworth, *Jewish within Judaism*, 141.

64   K. R. Snodgrass, *The Parable of the Wicked Tenants: An Inquiry into Parable Interpretation* (WUNT 27; Tübingen: Mohr [Siebeck], 1983) 111

65   For surveys of references to "son of God" in early Judaism, see M. Hengel, *The Son of God* (Philadelphia: Fortress, 1976), and Charlesworth, *Jesus within Judaism*, 149-53. In view of the evidence, Charlesworth concludes that "it simply will no longer suffice to attribute all references to 'son' or 'Son of God' to the needs and proclamation of the early Church" (p. 152).

assuming that the quotation of Ps 118:22-23 was an original and authentic part of this parable, Jesus understood himself, the "corner-stone,"[66] as the antithesis, indeed, the very replacement of the religious leaders, the "builders."[67] All of these elements cohere with the trial scene that Mark provides us.

Miscellaneous Considerations

There are other objections raised against the authenticity of Mark 14:61-64 which the above discussion has not taken into account. They may now be considered. First, Sanders thinks that the blasphemy charge may function as a sort of diversion, drawing the readers' attention away from the real charge brought against Jesus: his threat to destroy the Temple. Sanders thinks that Mark attempted to tone down Jesus' harsh criticism and demonstration against the Temple establish-ment. I find this line of interpretation problematic, for Mark's redactional thrust appears to run in precisely the opposite direction. The evangelist has *emphasized* the antagonism between Jesus and the Temple establishment, not toned it down.[68] In view of this it is not at all apparent that the Temple charge is a piece of embarrassing historical tradition that Mark felt compelled to revise and push aside in favor of the charge of blasphemy. In favor of the authenticity of Mark 14:62 is the fact that by 70 C.E., about the time the Gospel of Mark was written, Jesus' prediction made to Caiaphas and company ("you will see the Son of Man . . .") could easily have been construed as having failed. Or, as Witherington puts it: "Mark 14:62 has good claims to authenticity, for the church would not make up what appeared to be an

---

66 There are messianic implications associated with the "corner stone" (פִּנָּה רֹאשׁ): "Out of them shall come forth the corner stone [פִּנָּה], out of them the stake . . ." (Zech 10:4); but in the targum: "Out of him comes his king, out of him comes his Messiah . . ."; recall the exegesis of Deut 33:16 in *Sipre Deut* §353 (on Deut 33:16) above, where רֹאשׁ was interpreted messianically.

67 Some rabbis and religious leaders sometimes referred to themselves as the "builders" of Israel (*b. Šabb.* 114a; *b. Ber.* 64a; cf. 1 Cor 3:10). Qumran offers a few negative references, obviously meant to denigrate the establishment's self-description: "Such men are builders of a rickety wall" (CD 4:19, alluding to Ezek 13:10); ". . . those who build the wall and over it with whitewash" (CD 8:12); "[God hates the] builders of the wall" (CD 8:18).

68 See C. A. Evans, "Jesus' Action in the Temple: Cleansing or Portent of Destruction?" *CBQ* 51 (1989) 237-70, esp. pp. 238-43.

unfulfilled prophecy."[69]

Second, some redaction critics think that they find several tell-tale signs of the evangelist's editorial activity in Mark 14:61-64 and so conclude that the pericope is wholly or mostly inauthentic. In my judgment these redaction critical claims have overestimated the extent of the Marcan evangelist's creative activity. For example, John Donahue gets himself into trouble in trying to make his case that the Marcan trial scene is largely the creation of the evangelist.[70] His attempt to show that the intercalation of Peter outside by the fire and Jesus inside before the religious authorities runs shipwreck on the fact that the same "intercalation" occurs in John 18. Donahue is therefore forced to claim that John derived this intercalated presentation from Mark, something that is highly unlikely and highly problematic.[71] It is much more likely that the trial material, though in some measure edited and arranged by the evangelist, is traditional.

Third, Norman Perrin's conclusion that Mark 14:62 is inauthentic, owing its origin to a Christian pesher on Dan 7:13 and Ps 110:1,[72] runs into serious trouble when it is observed that, possibly apart from Rev 3:21, there is little evidence in the New Testament that the early church understood Jesus' saying, much less created it. When Stephen is martyred he says: "Behold, I see the heavens opened and the son of man standing at the right hand of God" (Acts 7:56). The allusion to Mark 14:62, and its components from Daniel 7 and Psalm 110, is obvious. But Jesus is described as *standing*, not *sitting*. It may be that the Lucan evangelist, or in this case the tradition before him, did not fully understand the dominical saying. Elsewhere Luke seems to understand the tradition in terms of Messiah Jesus sitting on the throne of his father David (Luke 1:32; Acts 2:30). In Paul, Jesus sits not on God's throne, but on the βῆμα—the judgment seat (2 Cor 5:10; cf. Rom 14:10). The idea is somewhat parallel, for Jesus will judge, or govern, his people (cf. Matt 19:28; Luke 22:28-30). In Hebrews, Jesus, the

---

69   Witherington, *Christology of Jesus*, 258.

70   J. Donahue, *Are You the Christ? The Trial Narrative in the Gospel of Mark* (SBLDS 10; Missoula: Scholars, 1973).

71   See R. T. Fortna, "Jesus and Peter at the High Priest's House: A Test Case for the Question of the Relation between Mark's and John's Gospels," *NTS* 24 (1977-78) 371-83; C. A. Evans, "'Peter Warming Himself': The Problem of an Editorial 'Seam,'" *JBL* 101 (1982) 245-49.

72   N. Perrin, "Mark 14:62: The End Product of a Christian Pesher Tradition?" *NTS* 13 (1966) 150-55.

High Priest, is "seated at the right hand of the throne of Majesty in heaven" (8:1; cf. 12:2). Jesus is not seated on the throne, nor do these texts have anything to do with judgment. Only in the Apocalypse does it appear that the idea has been preserved (Rev 3:21; cf. 22:1, 3).[73] Moreover, Betz's argument that the nocturnal hearing before Caiaphas, as well as other aspects of Jesus' ministry and teaching, is clarified by Nathan's oracle (2 Samuel 7) should be taken seriously.[74] There is little evidence, apart perhaps from Heb 1:5 where 2 Sam 7:14 is quoted, that early Christians elaborated upon or even recognized the significance of this passage. That it nevertheless clarifies Jesus' ministry, especially the hearing before Caiaphas, the trial before Pilate, and the subsequent crucifixion, complete with the *titulus* that proclaims Jesus "King of the Jews," is support for the essential history of the Marcan trial narrative. In other words, it does not appear to be a Christian exegesis or apologetic of some sort, but a reasonably accurate, though truncated and not always understood, report of what happened.

Concluding Remarks

On historical and exegetical grounds it seems that Jesus was one among many who offered restoration and renewal to oppressed and beleaguered Israel of the early first century C.E. His "christology," evidently similar to that of Rabbi Aqiba at several important points, was in direct conflict with the interests of the Jerusalem ruling establishment. The Marcan trial scene, obviously an edited, truncated, and incomplete version, is probably accurate in reporting that Jesus

---

[73] In his response to the earlier form of this paper (see n. 31 above), John Dominic Crossan defended Perrin's pesher interpretation, arguing that the presence of ὄψεσθε echoes Zech 12:10, which had become an important text for early christology (cf. John 19:37; Rev 1:7). But such an echo is unlikely (Zech 12:10 reads ἐπιβλέψονται); cf. F. H. Borsch, "Mark xiv.62 and I Enoch lxii.5," *NTS* 14 (1967-68) 565-67. Crossan's principal objection to the authenticity of the exchange between Jesus and Caiaphas rested upon the assumption that the disciples, not being present at the hearing before the Sanhedrin, could never have learned what had transpired. Not only does such an assumption fly in the face of probabilities (surely word would have gotten around), but it fails to take into account the custom of publishing a capital decision.

[74] Betz, "Prozess Jesu," 625-28; cf. idem, "Die Frage nach dem messianischen Bewußtsein Jesu," *NovT* 6 (1963) 20-48, esp. 34-37; idem, *Was wissen wir von Jesus?* (Stuttgart and Berlin: Kreuz, 1965) 59-62.

actually met Caiaphas and offended him (which coheres with the Temple action and the subsequent arrest, involving servants of the High Priest). The Marcan scene is probably also accurate in reporting that Jesus acknowledged his divine sonship and described that sonship in terms of Daniel 7 and 2 Samuel 7. In my judgment, scholars should no longer set this tradition aside as inauthentic. To do so is to exclude an important aspect of Jesus' self-understanding.[75]

---

[75] I would like to thank Professors John Dominic Crossan and James H. Charlesworth, who responded to an earlier form of this chapter at the 1991 SBL meeting in Kansas City, MO. Their comments and criticisms were very helpful.

SYNTHESIS

FROM ANOINTED PROPHET TO ANOINTED KING: PROBING ASPECTS OF JESUS' SELF-UNDERSTANDING

The most problematical aspect of the historical Jesus has to do with his self-understanding. The interpreter is faced with several difficult questions. Did Jesus think of himself as Israel's Messiah? And, if so, in what sense? Did he think of himself as the Son of God? And, again, if he did, in what sense? Quite apart from the question of the authenticity or inauthenticity of the relevant materials, scholars are faced with the diversity of and apparent discrepancies within the tradition itself. Among the best attested facts concerning Jesus' identity is his recognition as a prophet (e.g. Mark 6:4)[1] and his crucifixion as the "king of the Jews" (Mark 15:26 par).[2] If Jesus acted and understood himself as a prophet, how and why was he executed as "king of the Jews"? If Jesus understood himself as a royal messianic figure, how do we explain the well-attested tradition that he spoke of himself as a prophet?

This chapter will attempt to make a modest contribution to the latter questions. To the degree that it is successful some light should be thrown on the former questions concerning Jesus' self-understanding.

DEFEATED KINGS AND PERSECUTED PROPHETS

Since Jesus was crucified as "king of the Jews," it is only natural to compare him to other would-be Jewish kings in his time. But such comparison yields many differences, not similarities.[3] According to

---

[1]   The Jesus Seminar assigns a "pink" rating to Mark 6:4; John 4:44; *GThom* §31; cf. R. W. Funk and R. W. Hoover (eds.), *The Five Gospels* (New York: Macmillan, 1993) 63, 412, 490. For support of the authenticity of the saying, see R. H. Gundry, *Mark: A Commentary on His Apology for the Cross* (Grand Rapids: Eerdmans, 1993) 296-300.

[2]   N. A. Dahl, "The Crucified Messiah," in Dahl, *The Crucified Messiah and Other Essays* (Minneapolis: Augsburg, 1974) 1-36; E. Bammel, "The *titulus*," in Bammel and C. F. D. Moule (eds.), *Jesus and the Politics of His Day* (Cambridge: Cambridge University Press, 1984) 353-64; Gundry, *Mark*, 958-59.

[3]   The well known exception to this conclusion is S. G. F. Brandon, *Jesus*

Josephus, these men were little more than brigands who hoped to seize power and royal honor. Allowing for his bias, it is clear that those who attempted to install themselves as kings of a liberated Israel were quasi-military figures at the head of large followings, which in some cases approximated well armed armies.[4]

There were at least three such men in the time following the death of Herod the Great (4 B.C.E.).[5] Judas son of Hezekiah the "brigand chief" plundered the royal arsenals and attacked other kingly aspirants (*J.W.* 2.4.1 §56; *Ant.* 17.10.5 §271-272). Simon of Perea, a former royal servant, "was bold enough to place the diadem on his head" and to proclaim himself βασιλεύς (*J.W.* 2.4.2 §57-59; *Ant.* 17.10.6 §273-276). Simon is mentioned by the Roman historian Tacitus: "After Herod's death, a certain Simon assumed the name king [*regium nomen*] without waiting for Caesar's decision" (*Hist.* 5.9.2). The most significant kingly claimant, at least so far as duration is concerned, was Athronges the shepherd of Judea, who evidently exercised control over parts of Judea from 4 to 2 B.C.E. According to Josephus, this man "dared to gain a kingdom," "put on the diadem," and was called βασιλεύς (*J.W.* 2.4.3 §60-65; *Ant.* 17.10.7 §278-284). All three of

---

and the Zealots: A Study of the Political Factor in Primitive Christianity (Manchester: Manchester University Press; New York: Scribner's, 1967); idem, *The Trial of Jesus of Nazareth* (New York: Stein and Day, 1968). The other well known military interpretation had been offered earilier by R. Eisler, *ΙΗΣΟΥΣ ΒΑΣΙΛΕΥΣ ΟΥ ΒΑΣΙΛΕΥΣΑΣ: Die messianische Unabhängigkeitsbewegung vom Auftreten Johannes des Täufers bis zum Untergang Jakobs des Gerecten* (2 vols., Heidelberg: Winter, 1929-30); ET: *The Messiah Jesus and John the Baptist* (London: Methuen; New York: Dial, 1931).

This approach has been criticized and abandoned. See M. Hengel's review of Brandon, *Jesus and the Zealots*, in *JSS* 14 (1969) 231-40, as well as his *War Jesus Revolutionär?* (CH 110; Stuttgart: Calwer, 1970); ET: *Was Jesus a Revolutionist?* (Philadelphia: Fortress, 1971). For other negative assessments of Brandon's conclusions, see E. Bammel, "The Revolution Theory from Reimarus to Brandon," in Bammel and Moule (eds.), *Jesus and the Politics of His Day*, 11-68, esp. 37-43; E. P. Sanders, *Jesus and Judaism* (London: SCM; Philadelphia: Fortress, 1985) 68; B. Chilton, *The Temple of Jesus: His Sacrificial Program Within a Cultural History of Sacrifice* (University Park: Penn State Press, 1992) 92-100.

4   Although it is somewhat dated, M. Hengel's *The Zealots* (Edinburgh: T. & T. Clark, 1989) still remains an invaluable study of the Jewish freedom movement of the first century.

5   What follows briefly treats the more significant figures that are covered more fully in chap. 2 above.

these men and their followings were attacked and defeated by Roman troops.

During the first great war with Rome (66–70 C.E.) several men vyed for power; at least three of them appear to have attempted to gain recognition as Israel's king.

The first of these kingly aspirants was one Menaḥem, either son or grandson of Judas the Galilean. Josephus tells us that Menaḥem (ca. 66 C.E.) plundered Herod's armory at Masada, arming his followers as well as other "brigands," and then "returned like a king [βασιλεύς] to Jerusalem, became the leader of the revolution, and directed the siege of the palace." His followers occupied the Roman barracks and eventually caught and killed Ananias the high priest. As a result of his accomplishments, Josephus tells us, Menaḥem, believing himself unrivalled, became an "insufferable tyrant [τύραννος]." Finally, insurgents loyal to Eleazar son of Ananias the high priest rose up against him. Menaḥem, "arrayed in royal [ἐσθῆτι βασιλικῇ] apparel," was attacked while in the Temple. Although he initially managed to escape and hide, he was eventually caught, dragged out into the open, tortured, and put to death (*J.W.* 2.17.8-9 §433-448).

There can be little doubt as to Menaḥem's ambitions. He hoped to become king of a newly liberated Israel.[6] Like the kings of Israel's golden age, he worshiped at the Temple. Josephus's description (*J.W.* 2.17.9 §444) suggests that Menaḥem's worship had an official air about it. But Menaḥem's brutality, low birth, and failure to win over an influential priestly figure who would serve at his side, led to his sudden and violent demise.

The second would-be ruler was John of Gischala. Initially he was commander of the rebel forces in Gischala (*J.W.* 2.20.6 §575). He later became part of the zealot coalition (*J.W.* 4.1.1-5 §121-146; 5.3.1 §104-105; 5.6.1 §250-251) which, having been forced to retreat into Jerusalem, gained control of most of the city and installed a high priest of its own choosing (*J.W.* 4.3.6 §147-150; 4.3.8 §155-161). It is true that this installation reflects popular desire to reform the ruling priesthood, but the installation itself could be an indication of John's assumption of kingly authority (though it must be admitted that John's direct involvement is not made explicit).

Although Josephus describes him as little more than a power-hungry

---

6   See the helpful discussion in Hengel, *The Zealots*, 293-97.

brigand (*J.W.* 2.21.1 §585-589), apparently John did have kingly aspirations. Josephus tells us that he aspired to "tyrannical power [τυραννιῶντι]," "issued despotic [δεσποτικώτερον] orders," and began "laying claim to absolute sovereignty [μοναρχίας]" (*J.W.* 4.7.1 §389-393). Fearing the possibility that John might achieve "monarchical rule [μοναρχίας]," many of the zealots opposed him (*J.W.* 4.7.1 §393-394; see also 4.9.11 §566, where the Idumeans turn against the "tyrant"). When the city was finally overrun, John surrendered and was imprisoned for life (*J.W.* 6.9.4 §433). Later in his account of the Jewish war Josephus evaluates John much in the same terms as he does Simon bar Giora (*J.W.* 7.8.1 §263-266; in 4.9.10 §564-565 they are compared as the tyrants "within" and "without" Jerusalem; in 6.9.4 §433-434 Josephus also compares their respective surrenders).[7]

The third and best known royal aspirant of the great war with Rome was Simon bar Giora, a man from Gerasa (or Jerash).[8] Simon distinguished himself with military prowess and cunning (*J.W.* 2.19.2 §521; 4.6.1 §353; 4.9.4 §510; 4.9.5 §514-520). He drew a large following by "proclaiming liberty for slaves and rewards for the free" (*J.W.* 4.9.3 §508; 4.9.7 §534 ["forty thousand followers"]). His army was "subservient to his command as to a king [βασιλέα]" (*J.W.* 4.9.4 §510). Josephus avers that early on in his career Simon had shown signs of being tyrannical (*J.W.* 2.22.2 §652 [τυραννεῖν]; 4.9.3 §508 [ὁ τυραννιῶν]; 5.1.3 §11; 7.2.2 §32 [ἐτυράννησεν]; 7.8.1 §265 [τύραννον]). Simon subjugated the whole of Idumea (*J.W.* 4.9.6 §521-528). The ruling priests, in consultation with the Idumeans and many of the inhabitants of the city, decided to invite Simon into Jerusalem to protect the city from John of Gischala (*J.W.* 4.9.11 §570-576). Simon entered the city and took command in the spring of 69 C.E. (*J.W.* 4.9.12 §577). Among the leaders of the rebellion "Simon in particular was regarded with reverence and awe . . . each was quite prepared to take his very own life had he given the order" (*J.W.* 5.7.3 §309). After the city was overrun, Simon, dressed in white tunics and a purple mantle, made a dramatic appearance before the Romans on the very spot where the Temple had stood (*J.W.* 7.2.2 §29). He was sent to Italy (*J.W.* 7.5.3 §118), put on display as part of the victory celebration in

---

7   Hengel (*The Zealots*, 298) rightly notes that the Romans evidently did not regard John of Gischala as on the same level as Simon bar Giora.

8   See Hengel, *The Zealots*, 297-98.

Rome (*J.W.* 7.5.6 §154),[9] and was finally executed (*J.W.* 7.5.6 §155).

The early second century saw the rise of yet two more would-be deliverers of Israel. During the reign of Trajan the Jewish inhabitants of Judea, Egypt, and Cyrene revolted (114 or 115 C.E.). According to Eusebius they rallied to one Lukuas, "their king" (*Hist. Eccl.* 4.2.1-4). Cassius Dio mentions this revolt, but calls the Jewish leader Andreas (*Hist. Rom.* 68.32; 69.12-13). Eusebius says that General Marcius Turbo "waged war vigorously against [the Jews] in many battles for a considerable time and killed many thousands" (*Hist. Eccl.* 4.2.4). Although Dio's claim that hundreds of thousands perished is probably an exaggeration, the papyri and archaeological evidence confirm that the revolt was widespread and very destructive.[10]

The most famous of Israel's defeated liberators was Simon ben Kosiba (132–135 C.E.). Although rabbinic legends pass on many critical (and untrustworthy) things about Simon, the evidence would suggest that initially he was popular and successful. Only with the greatest difficulty was Emperor Hadrian able to subdue Simon's forces. Again reliable data are scarce but sufficient to indicate that this second great war was very destructive and costly for both sides.[11] Although it is disputed, the evidence appears also to be sufficient to conclude that Simon came to be regarded as Israel's king, probably in some sort of messianic sense.[12]

The various would-be messiahs in the time of Jesus are not particularly close parallels. But the deadly opposition that they faced is quite understandable. Being a prophet and being executed for it in themselves present to modern interpreters no special difficulty. From the period of Jesus we have several examples of prophets who drew crowds and in many instances led movements. A review of the better known figures will be helpful.

---

9   There is no better reminder of this grim occasion than the relief found on the inside of the Arch of Titus (in Rome).

10   See E. Schürer, *The History of the Jewish People in the Age of Jesus Christ* (3 vols., rev. and ed. by G. Vermes, F. Millar, and M. Black; Edinburgh: T. & T. Clark, 1973-87) 1.530-34; E. M. Smallwood, *The Jews under Roman Rule: From Pompey to Diocletian* (SJLA 20; Leiden: Brill, 1981) 389-427; and the details provided in chap. 2 above.

11   See Schürer, *History of the Jewish People*, 1.534-57; Smallwood, *The Jews under Roman Rule*, 428-66.

12   See chap. 4 above for the evidence and arguments in support of this view.

Richard Horsley divides these prophets into two groups. He calls one group "popular prophets." These prophets had followings, in some cases large ones. These prophets, modeling themselves after Israel's charismatic leaders of the past, called for change and evidently anticipated heavenly assistance. The second group is made up of "oracular prophets." These figures made predictions, announced the need for change, and modeled themselves after Israel's classical oracular prophets. Prophets from both of these groups frequently encountered deadly opposition.[13] The popular prophets will be considered first.

Theudas. During the administration of Governor Fadus (44–46 C.E.) a certain Theudas appeared, claiming to be a prophet and urging the Jewish people to join him at the Jordan where the river would be parted (Josephus, *Ant.* 20.5.1 §97-98; cf. Acts 5:36). In all probability Theudas understood himself as some sort of successor to Moses, who, like Joshua of old, would lead the people back into the promised land. Perceiving the revolutionary potential of these activities Fadus dispatched the cavalry, routing the prophet's following and killing the prophet himself.

Anonymous Egyptian Jew. Some years later, during the administration of Governor Felix (ca. 56 C.E.), a Jewish man from Egypt came to Jerusalem also claiming to be a prophet. He gathered around himself a following on the Mount of Olives, promising that at his command the walls of the city would collapse, enabling their entrance into the city. Once again the Roman governor perceived a threat and so dispatched troops. The prophet's following suffered many casualties and was dispersed, but the prophet himself managed to escape (Josephus, *Ant.* 20.8.6 §169-172; cf. Acts 21:38, where a Roman tribune asks Paul if he were this Egyptian fugitive).

Anonymous "Impostor." Josephus describes the activities of yet another prophet who promised Jews "salvation and rest" if they followed him into the "wilderness." As had his predecessors, Governor Fadus (ca. 61 C.E.) dispatched troops who killed the "impostor" and his following (Josephus, *Ant.* 20.8.10 §188).

Jonathan the refugee. Following the Roman victory over Israel, one Jonathan, a weaver, fled to Cyrene. There he gathered in the desert a

---

13   See R. A. Horsley and J. S. Hanson, *Bandits, Prophets, and Messiahs: Popular Movements at the Time of Jesus* (Minneapolis: Winston, 1985; repr. San Francisco: Harper & Row, 1988) 135-89. For a fuller treatment of the prophetic figures, see chap. 2 above.

following of poorer Jews promising to show them "signs and apparitions." The Roman governor Catullus (ca. 71 C.E.) dispatched troops who routed Jonathan's following and captured the prophet himself.[14] He would later be executed by Vespasian (Josephus, *J. W.* 7.11.1 §437-442; *Life* 76 §424-425).

The danger to the establishment that these popular prophets posed is obvious. Roman action in every case was calculated to pre-empt what was probably correctly perceived as the initiation of social and political upheaval. The action that Pilate took against the Samaritan prophet and his following should also be seen in this light (Josephus, *Ant.* 18.4.1 §85-87). The Samaritan's quest for the lost vessels of the Samaritan temple in all probability was part of the Samaritan hope of the appearance of the "Restorer" or Taheb in fulfillment of the promise of Deut 18:15-19. The Taheb would find the lost vessels and "announce all things" (cf. John 4:25). Although Josephus does not call the Samaritan a "prophet," the man's actions clearly cohere with this expectation of the "prophet like Moses." Pilate's brutal action becomes understandable, for he assumed that the gathering at Mount Gerizim was nothing less than a prelude to insurrection.

Common to all of these "popular prophets" was large followings. Roman violence should not occasion surprise. But even "oracular prophets," such as John the Baptist and Jesus ben Ananias, ran the risk of execution, if their oracles were sufficiently disturbing to those who wielded political power.

John the Baptist. In the New Testament Gospels (but not in Josephus) John the Baptist is explicitly identified as a prophet, both in Mark and parallels (cf. Mark 11:32 = Matt 21:26 = Luke 20:6) and in Q (cf. Matt 11:7-9 = Luke 7:24-26). Consistent with this explicit identification is the appearance of John's name in the company of prophets, again both in Mark and parallels (cf. Mark 8:28 = Matt 16:14 = Luke 9:19; Mark 6:14-15 = Luke 9:7-8) and in Q (cf. Matt 11:12-13 = Luke 16:16). This early and widespread tradition in all probability derives from the *Sitz im Leben Jesu*.[15] That Josephus does not himself refer to John as a

---

[14] Josephus calls Jonathan a member of the Sicarii, not a prophet (§437). But Jonathan's promise to show "signs" to his following "in the wilderness" fits the description of the other would-be prophetic deliverers. Note too the suggestive reference to his "exodus" [τὴν ἔξοδον αὐτοῦ]" (§439).

[15] It is significant that in the Fourth Gospel, reflecting a later period when rivalry between the followers of Jesus and the followers of John had intensified,

prophet is not surprising, given his largely negative portrayal of the "prophets" (often called "impostors" or "false prophets") who were his contemporaries. The absence of such identification in Josephus, therefore, should not in itself cast doubt on the reliability of the prophetic identification of John in the Gospels.[16]

Josephus refers to John ("called the Baptist") as a "good man" (ἀγαθὸς ἀνήρ), who:

> commanded the Jewish people to lead righteous lives, to practise justice towards their fellows and piety towards God, and so doing to join in baptism. In his view this was a necessary preliminary if baptism was to be acceptable to God. They must not employ it to gain pardon for whatever sins they committed, but as a consecration of the body implying that the soul was already thoroughly cleansed by right behaviour. [*Ant.* 18.5.2 §117]

According to Josephus, Herod's only reason for disposing of John was because of his popularity and a general fear of an uprising. The real reason likely had to do with Herod's divorce and remarriage (which is emphasized in Mark 6:17-29 and to which Josephus later alludes in 18.5.4 §136), which created for the Galilean tetrarch serious political problems. John's criticisms came at a time when Herod could ill afford erosion of public support.

According to the Gospels John preached "a baptism of repentance for the forgiveness of sins [ἁμαρτίαι]" (Mark 1:4-5; Luke 3:3; and, with some variation, Matt 3:1-2, 5-6). Josephus also refers to "sins" (ἁμαρτάδες), but not to "repentance." However, repentance of some sort is probably in view in the explanation that John required

---

John the Baptist explicitly and emphatically denies a prophetic identification (cf. John 1:19-28). John's duty primarily consists of bearing witness to Jesus (cf. John 1:15, 19, 23, 32, 34; 3:26-30). Even when it comes to baptizing, Jesus outperforms John (cf. John 3:22; 4:1-2).

16   For studies that place John in the context of "oracular prophets," as opposed to "action prophets" who led movements, see D. E. Aune, *Prophecy in Early Christianity and the Ancient Mediterranean World* (Grand Rapids: Eerdmans, 1983) 129-32; R. A. Horsely, "Popular Messianic Movements around the Time of Jesus," *CBQ* 46 (1984) 471-95; idem, "'Like One of the Prophets of Old': Two Types of Popular Prophets at the Time of Jesus," *CBQ* 47 (1985) 435-63; idem and J. S. Hanson, *Bandits, Prophets, and Messiahs: Popular Movements at the Time of Jesus* (Minneapolis: Winston, 1985) 175-81. John's Elijah-like trappings, which cannot all be credited to early Christian interpretation and embellishment, further support the Baptist's prophetic identification. See M. Hengel, *The Charismatic Leader and His Followers* (Edinburgh: T. & T. Clark, 1981) 36 n. 71.

"righteous lives" and "consecration of the body implying that the soul was already thoroughly cleansed by right behaviour."

Once again one can understand why a prophet such as John would have made the establishment nervous. His widespread popularity and his calls for reform could have easily generated a popular movement, such as those led by Theudas or the Jew from Egypt. This would especially be the case if John actually did speak of judgment and the "kingdom of God."[17]

Jesus ben Ananias. The activities and experience of a later oracular prophet named Jesus ben Ananias (62–69 C.E.) are quite instructive.[18] According to Josephus (*J.W.* 6.5.3 §300-305):

> Four years before the war . . . there came to the feast, at which is the custom of all Jews to erect tabernacles to God, one Jesus son of Ananias, an untrained peasant, who, standing in the Temple, suddenly began to cry out, "A voice from the east, a voice from the west, a voice from the four winds, a voice against Jerusalem and the sanctuary, a voice against the bridgroom and the bride, a voice against all the people." . . . Some of the leading citizens, angered at this evil speech, arrested the man and whipped him with many blows. But he, not speaking anything in his own behalf or in private to those who struck him, continued his cries as before. Thereupon, the rulers . . . brought him to the Roman governor. There, though flayed to the bone with scourges, he neither begged for mercy nor wept . . . When Albinus the governor asked him who and whence he was and why he uttered these cries, he gave no answer to these things . . . . Albinus pronounced him a maniac and released him.

Unlike John the Baptist there is no indication that Jesus ben Ananias had a following of any sort or enjoyed any popularity. Unlike John who preached and baptized in the wilderness, Jesus uttered his dolorous oracle within Jerusalem itself. Although he evidently did not call for change, nor challenged his contemporaries to repent, the mere fact that he pronounced woes upon the city, its people, and its Temple was enough to prompt the "leading citizens" (lit. "first men," i.e. ruling priests; cf. *Ant.* 11.5.3 §140-141; 18.5.3 §121) to seek his death.

But John the Baptist and Jesus ben Ananias did have something in common: Their movements did not result in military clashes. No

---

[17]   According to Q (Matt 3:7-10 = Luke 3:7-9; Matt 3:11 = Luke 3:16-17) John spoke of judgment, but it is only in Matthean redaction that John speaks of the approach of "the kingdom of God" (Matt 3:2). This utterance appears to have been drawn from Mark 1:15, where it is credited to Jesus.

[18]   See the more detailed discussion above in chap. 9.

battles had to be fought to take them into custody. They offered no resistance, but were taken easily. So far as we know, not one of their hearers was attacked or arrested. In the case of the former, because he was deemed to pose a real threat to the political well-being of the tetrarch Herod Antipas, he has put to death. In the case of the latter, because he was deemed to pose no threat to Roman administration of Judea, he was scourged and released. The absence of military action constitutes a major point of distinction between the oracular prophets and the popular prophets who led various movements.

The case of Jesus ben Ananias, however, is of special interest. Although he assumed the role of an oracular prophet, had no army of followers, and threatened no action against the ruling establishment, the Jewish ruling establishment nonetheless wanted the man put to death. The pronouncement of doom upon the city and its people apparently was sufficiently offensive and threatening. Why was this the case? Although certainty cannot be obtained, we may suppose that the threat itself implied some sort of deficiency on the part of the religious leaders. If they were leading Israel's worship and cultic practices properly, God's blessings should be expected. The threat of divine judgment, however, implied the opposite. Jesus ben Ananias' allusion to Jeremiah 7 may have recalled the sharp prophetic criticism leveled against the ruling priests of late seventh century B.C.E. This would have only further implied that the ruling priests of the first century C.E. were corrupt and possibly the principal cause of divine judgment. Pronouncements of doom upon the city and its Temple, especially ones echoing the language of a passage such as Jeremiah 7, would surely have been understood as implicit criticism of the Temple establishment. Such criticism would have been both offensive and threatening. Consequently we should not be surprised that the authorities presented the prophet to Governor Albinus, requesting the man's death.

There are certain features of the prophets, both the "popular" ones and the "oracular" ones, that parallel aspects of Jesus' activities. Like the popular prophets, Jesus spoke of social change. He proclaimed the appearance of the kingdom of God and, like John the Baptist, summoned Israel to repentance. His message and activities attracted a large following. His opponents demanded "signs," which often were offered by people like Theudas. Like the oracular prophets, Jesus prophesied certain things. Of special interest is his criticism of the

ruling priesthood and his apparent prediction of the destruction of the
city and its Temple. Like Jesus ben Ananias, Jesus of Nazareth also
appealed to Jeremiah 7. By doing this he evidently implied that the fate
that overtook the Solomonic Temple might overtake the Herodian
Temple.

If prophet remains the best analogue for Jesus, how did that eventually translate into "king of the Jews"?

MESSIANIC PROPHETIC TRADITIONS

There are some traditions where prophetic and Davidic ideas
converge. In both the Hebrew and Greek versions of 1 Sam 16:13 we
are told that following the anointing, the "Spirit of the Lord came
mightily upon David from that day forward." Although the biblical
text says nothing about prophecy, Josephus' retelling of the story does:
"Then, in the sight of David, he (Samuel) took oil and anointed him
and spoke softly into his ear, explaining that God had chosen him to be
king . . . and the Deity abandoned Saul and passed over to David, who,
when the divine spirit [τὸ θεῖον πνεῦμα] had removed to him, began to
prophesy [προφητεύειν]" (Josephus, *Ant.* 6.8.1 §165–6.8.2 §166).

Josephus' paraphrase appears to presuppose an interpretive tradition. The final line in 11QPsª 27:11 is instructive:

כול אלה דבר בנבואה אשר נתן לו מלפני העליון

All these he (David) spoke through prophecy which was given him from before
the Most High.[19]

In rabbinic traditions David is numbered among the prophets.
According to the gemara on *m. Soṭa* 9:12 ("When the first prophets
died"): "Who are the first prophets? Rabbi Huna said: 'They are David,
Samuel, and Solomon'" (*b. Soṭa* 48b).

There are several important passages in the Targums that ascribe
prophecy to David and his son Solomon. This observation could be
significant in view of the fact that both served to one degree or another
as models for messianic traditions.

The Hebrew reading, "And David spoke to the Lord" (2 Sam 22:1),
in the Targum becomes: "And David *gave praise in prophecy before*

---

19   For text, see J. A. Sanders, *The Psalms Scroll of Qumrân Cave 11* (DJD 4;
Oxford: Clarendon, 1965) 92.

the Lord [ושבח דויד בנבואה קדם יוי]."[20]

The Targum also paraphrases David's oracle in 2 Sam 23:1-4. The Hebrew reads: "Now these are the last words of David: The oracle of David, the son of Jesse, the oracle of the man who was raised on high, the anointed of the God of Jacob, the sweet psalmist of Israel: 'The Spirit of the Lord speaks by me, his word is upon my tongue. The God of Israel has spoken, the Rock of Israel has said to me: When one rules justly over people, ruling in the fear of God, He dawns on them like the morning light . . .'" In the Targum this passage becomes prophetic and messianic: "And these are *the words of the prophecy of David that he prophesied* [פתגמי נבואת דויד דאתנבי] *for the end of the world, for the days of consolation that are to come . . . David said: 'By a spirit of prophecy* [ברוח נבואה] *before the Lord I am speaking these things . . . appoint for me the king, that is the Messiah to come who will arise and rule . . .'"[21]

Even the listing of David's "mighty men" in 2 Sam 23:8 is enhanced in the Targum in suggestive ways: "These are the names of the mighty men who were *with David: a mighty man, head of the armies, sitting on the thrones of judgment, and all the prophets and elders surrounding him, anointed with the anointing of holiness . . .*"[22] This Aramaic paraphrase should be compared to Jesus' statement to his disciples: "You who have followed me will also sit on twelve thrones, judging the twelve tribes of Israel" (Matt 19:28; cf. Luke 22:29-30).

Solomon, the son of David, is also presented as a prophet in the targumic tradition. Whereas in the Hebrew 1 Kgs 5:13 (E 4:33) tells us that Solomon "spoke of trees, from the Cedar that is in Lebanon to the hyssop that grows out of the wall," the Targum paraphrases: *"And he prophesied* [ואתנבי] *about the kings of the house of David who would rule in this world in the world of the Messiah; and he prophesied* [ואתנבי] about the beast and about the bird . . ."[23] The reference to

20 Trans. by D. J. Harrington and A. J. Saldarini, *Targum Jonathan of the Former Prophets* (ArBib 10; Wilmington: Glazier, 1987) 200 (with emphasis showing departures from the Hebrew).
21 Trans. by Harrington and Saldarini, *Targum Jonathan of the Former Prophets*, 203 (with emphasis showing departures from the Hebrew).
22 Trans. by Harrington and Saldarini, *Targum Jonathan of the Former Prophets*, 204 (with emphasis showing departures from the Hebrew).
23 Trans. by Harrington and Saldarini, *Targum Jonathan of the Former Prophets*, 220 (with emphasis showing departures from the Hebrew).

"trees" suggested kingly figures (cf. Ezek 17:22-24; Dan 4:10-26).

According to *Tg.* 1 Kgs 6:11 Solomon received a word of prophecy: "And there was *a word of prophecy* [נבואה] *from before the Lord with* Solomon, saying: 'This house that you are building . . . '"[24] And finally, Ps 72:1 is paraphrased: "*By the hand* of Solomon, *spoken through prophecy* [נבואה]. O God, give the King *Messiah* the laws of Your *justice*, and Your righteousness to the son of King *David.*"[25]

As important as these passages are, there are two others, in which Messianic expectation in the Targums is associated with prophecy, that are of greater significance.

The first is Isa 11:1-2, which in the Hebrew reads: "There shall come forth a shoot from the stump of Jesse, and a branch shall grow out of his roots. And the Spirit of the Lord shall rest upon him, the spirit of wisdom and understanding, the spirit of counsel and might, the spirit of knowledge and the fear of the Lord." In the Targum it is paraphrased: "And a *king* shall come forth from the *sons* of Jesse, and *the Messiah* shall *be exalted* from *the sons of* his *sons*. And upon him shall rest *the* spirit *of prophecy*,[26] a spirit of wisdom and under-standing, a spirit of counsel and might, a spirit of knowledge and the fear of the Lord."[27] The reading רוח נבואה ("the spirit of prophecy") is found in the First and Second Rabbinic Bibles, the Antwerp Polyglot, and Codex Reuchlinianus. Although Bruce Chilton's comment that the reading is a secondary insertion may be correct, the data he cites are open to other interpretations. He states that "prophecy in the Tg is quite specifically connected with the holy spirit."[28] He then cites *Tg.* Isa 40:13; 42:1; 44:3. Of these the first is a good example ("Who has established the holy spirit in the mouth of all the prophets?"). But while the second and third examples refer to the "holy spirit," they make no explicit reference to prophets or prophecy. In *Tg.* Ps 45:3 and

---

24   Trans. by Harrington and Saldarini, *Targum Jonathan of the Former Prophets*, 222 (with emphasis showing departures from the Hebrew).

25   Trans. based on S. H. Levey, *The Messiah: An Aramaic Interpretation* (MHUC 2; Cincinnati: Hebrew Union College, 1974) 115 (with emphasis showing departures from the Hebrew).

26   Lagarde, Stenning, Sperber, and Chilton read "a spirit from before the Lord" (ותשרי עלוהי רוח [נבואה] מן קדם יהוה).

27   Trans. based on B. D. Chilton, *The Isaiah Targum* (ArBib 11; Wilmington: Glazier, 1987) 28.

28   Chilton, *The Isaiah Targum*, 28.

Tg. 2 Sam 23:2 we have examples of "spirit of prophecy," without the presence of the adjective "holy." *Tg.* Isa 11:2 could very well be a third example.

The second important passage is *Tg.* Ps 45:3(E2). The Hebrew reads: "You are the fairest of the sons of men; grace is poured upon your lips; therefore God has blessed you forever." The Targum paraphrases the passage: "*Your beauty, O King Messiah,* surpasses that of the sons of men. *The spirit of prophecy* [רוח נבואה] *has been bestowed* upon your lips; therefore, *the Lord* has blessed you forever."[29] It is interesting to observe that the Hebrew's "grace" (חן) in the Aramaic becomes "the spirit of prophecy." We immediately think of Luke 4:16-30, where Jesus reads Isa 61:1-2 ("The Spirit [πνεῦμα] of the Lord is upon me . . . He has anointed [ἔχρισεν] me") and the congregation is impressed by "the words of grace [τῆς χάριτος] that proceeded from his mouth" (Luke 4:22). When Jesus adds the comment, "No prophet [προφήτης] is acceptable in his home country" (Luke 4:24), we have all four elements observed in the Hebrew and the Aramaic paraphrase of this verse: spirit, prophecy, anointed, and grace. It is probable that these elements constitute a constellation of messianic and prophetic ideas, a constellation that is associated with Ps 45:3 and Isa 61:1-2.

The association of anointing with prophecy is made explicit in the Old Testament. One thinks of Ps 105:15 = 1 Chr 16:22: "Touch not my anointed ones [משיחי], do my prophets no harm!" The parallelism here clearly implies that the "anointed ones" are the "prophets." We also think of God's command to Elijah that he anoint (משח) Elisha to be prophet in his place (1 Kgs 19:16). Although in the Old Testament it is never said of the law-giver and prophet Moses (Deut 34:10) that he is anointed, in 4Q377 2 ii 5 we read of "Moses His anointed."

In a series of studies Chilton has argued convincingly that the content of Jesus' preaching and teaching, as well as his style, was to a significant extent influenced by the targumic tradition, especially as it is found in the Isaiah Targum.[30] It may be in the targumic tradition that we find an important part of the answer to the question with which

---

29   For Psalms Targum, see Paul de Lagarde, *Hagiographa Chaldaice* (Leipzig: Teubner, 1873); P. Churgin, *Targum Ketubim* (New York: Horeb, 1945) [Hebrew]. Trans. based on Levey, *The Messiah*, 109 (with emphasis showing departures from the Hebrew).

30   B. D. Chilton, *A Galilean Rabbi and His Bible: Jesus' Use of the Interpreted Scripture of his Time* (GNS 8; Wilmington: Glazier, 1984).

this chapter began. In the targumic tradition we find prophecy and royal messianic ideas associated. We find the same association in the Gospels with reference to Jesus. The prophetic dimension of his public activities is plainly evident, the kingly aspect of his execution is quite probable, and the Davidic flavor of public reactions are also probable, even if particular episodes are disputed.

In conclusion we may return to the question of the linkage between Jesus' death in Jerusalem and his Galilean teaching, a question addressed above in chap. 7. Not only is it very probable that Jesus' crucifixion at the hands of the Roman governor is in some sense the result of his proclamation of the kingdom of God, it is also probable that Jesus' reputation as a prophet and his criminal conviction as "king of the Jews" are not evidence of a shift in Jesus' self-understanding or a shift in how the public perceived him. These two identifications do not stand in tension but are two facets of a unified tradition, especially as seen in the targumic tradition, a tradition with which Jesus was familiar and by which he had been influenced. Jesus is the anointed son of David, whose anointing is prophetic and which not only authorizes Jesus to proclaim the presence of the kingdom but to demonstrate its presence through acts of healing, especially exorcisms. This latter point is quite significant in view of the association of Solomon, the son of David, with exorcisms.[31]

JESUS AND DAVIDIC TRADITIONS

There are indications of other Davidic or messianic activities on the part of Jesus. These will be treated in summary fashion only. Jesus' action in the Temple (Mark 11:15-18 par) may have been a "cleansing"[32] on the order of what *Pss. Sol.* 17:30 seems to have anticipated: "And he (i.e. the son of David, the Lord Messiah, cf. vv. 21, 32) will

---

[31]   One thinks of Matt 12:22-28, where following an exorcism the crowd wonders if Jesus is the "son of David." Jesus then declares that his exorcisms demonstrate that the kingdom of God has indeed come. In short, Jesus may very well have thought of himself as a davidic Messiah, but it was a messiah of his own interpretation. The *Davidssohnfrage* posed in Mark 12:35-37 was probably a challenge directed against popular interpretation, not a denial of Davidic messiahship.

[32]   E. P. Sanders (*Jesus and Judaism* [London: SCM; Philadelphia: Fortress, 1985] 61-76) argues that Jesus' action in the Temple was not a cleansing. His argument is problematic at many points. See C. A. Evans, "Jesus' Action in the Temple: Cleansing or Portent of Destruction?" *CBQ* 51 (1989) 237-70.

glorify the Lord in a distinguished place over all the earth. And he will cleanse [καθαριεῖ] Jerusalem in holiness, as it was even from the beginning." It is possible that a cleansing of the Temple would have been understood to be part of this cleansing of Jerusalem.[33] It is possible that the "distinguished place" (ἐπίσημος) refers to the Temple Mount. If this is so, then the possibility that the cleansing of Jerusalem was meant to include a cleansing of the Temple is significantly increased.

Jesus' favorite self-designation, "son of man," is linked in at least two places with Davidic tradition. After appealing to the example of David and his men (Mark 2:23-27), Jesus says that the "son of man is lord of the Sabbath" (Mark 2:28). The confession before Caiaphas in Mark 14:61-62 links "Christ son of God" (v. 61) with the "son of man at the right hand" (v. 62). Here we have linkage of the son of man of Daniel 7 with the enthroned Davidide of Psalm 110.[34]

Blind Bartimaeus twice calls Jesus "son of David" (Mark 10:47, 48), while the triumphal shouts include the reference to "the coming kingdom of our father David" (Mark 11:10). Apart from the Matthean and Lucan genealogies, little is made in the Gospels or anywhere else in the New Testament of Jesus' Davidic descent; yet it is presupposed (cf. Rom 1:3). I believe that it is probable that Jesus was in fact a descendant of David. Mark 12:35-37 should not be understood as a repudiation either of Davidic descent or of the importance of David for messianic ideas.[35] It also should be noted that Jesus' quotation of Ps 110:1, which in the Hebrew and in the LXX is thought of as Davidic, also draws upon Ps 8:6 (ὑποκάτω τῶν ποδῶν αὐτοῦ) where we find "son

---

[33] So A. Chester, "The Sibyl and the Temple," in W. Horbury (ed.), *Templum Amicitiae* (E. Bammel Festschrift; JSNTSup 48; Sheffield: JSOT Press, 1989) 37-69, here p. 55. For further discussion and pertinent bibliography, see J. Ådna, *Jesu Kritik am Tempel: Eine Untersuchung zum Verlauf und Sinn der sogenannten Tempelreinigung Jesu, Markus 11,15-17 und Parallelen* (dissertation, University of Stavanger, 1993) 270-74, 294. Ådna also thinks that *Pss. Sol.* 17:30 anticipates the cleansing of the Temple by a Davidide.

[34] On the authenticity and meaning of the exchange between Caiaphas and Jesus, see chap. 11 above.

[35] See Gundry, *Mark*, 722-23. Gundry rightly asks how, apart from the authenticity of Mark 12:35-37, can we account for the Church's reluctance to refer to Jesus as "son of David" even though the Church accepts Jesus' Davidic descent? "Jesus' questions [in 12:35, 37] inoculated most of his followers against the term" (p. 722).

of man" (8:4: υἱὸς ἀνθρώπου).[36] If this is correct, we then have three instances where "son of man" is linked with Davidic tradition.

Jesus' prediction of the Temple's destruction (Mark 13:2) and the allegation that he threatend to destroy the Temple and build another "in three days" (Mark 14:58; cf. Acts 6:13) may have had to do with Davidic messianic expectation (as is seen in 2 Samuel 7). The Johannine version of this saying may preserve the original meaning of the statement: "Destroy this Temple [i.e. go on doing things incorrectly and so bring about its destruction] and in a short time I, as the son of David, will raise up a new one."[37] But there is probably more to this complicated tradition.

The qualifiers, "made with hands" and "not made with hands" in all probability derive from Daniel 2 and may have played a part in Jesus' understanding of the role of the Danielic son of man.[38] The vision of Daniel 2 describes the messianic stone that was not made by human hands: "a stone was cut out of the mountain without hands [λίθος ἄνευ χειρῶν], and it beat to pieces" the image that represented the various kingdoms (Dan 2:44-45). This stone is the kingdom of God that shall stand "for ever" (alluding to 2 Sam 7:13-14), the kingdom that shall be given to the son of man and to the saints. Thus, what is "made with/without hands" is not the Temple, but the kingdom. This hope of a divine kingdom has relevance for the son of man material in Daniel 7.

In a recent study Wofgang Bittner has shown how many of the attributes and awards bestowed upon the son of man figure of Daniel 7

---

[36] Gundry (*Mark*, 721) suspects that the appearance of "son of man" in Psalm 8 is what may have led Jesus to allude to it in his quotation of Ps 110:1. The Hebrew reads (v. 5) בֶּן־אָדָם. The Targum reads בר נשא for "man" as well as for "son of man."

[37] See B. F. Meyer, *The Aims of Jesus* (London: SCM, 1979) 181-82. For similar interpretations, see R. E. Brown, *The Gospel According to John I-XII* (AB 29; Garden City: Doubleday, 1966) 122; B. D. Chilton, "[ὡς] φραγέλλιον ἐκ σχοινίων (John 2.15)," in Horbury (ed.), *Templum Amicitiae*, 330-44, esp. 341-42. Qumran may have anticipated the erection of a new Temple, as may be seen in 11QTemple 29:9-10: "until the day of the creation [reading בריה instead of ברכה], when I shall create my Temple and establish it forever"; cf. F. García Martínez, "The 'New Jerusalem' and the Future Temple of the Manuscripts from Qumran," in García Martínez, *Qumran and Apocalyptic: Studies on the Aramaic Texts from Qumran* (STDJ 9; Leiden: Brill, 1992) 180-213, esp. 205.

[38] I disagree with Meyer (*Aims of Jesus*, 301 n. 16) who thinks that these qualifiers come from later Christian interpretation.

correspond in important ways to Davidic traditions.[39] Among the most significant would be the promise of an eternal kingdom and dominion over the Gentiles. The promise echoes similar expressions in the Davidic traditions (cf. 2 Sam 7:12-16; Psalms 2, 110; Isa 9:2-7; 11:1-10; Mic 5:1-5[E2-6]). It is interesting to observe that 4QpIsa[a] 7-10 iii 24, which in commenting on Isa 11:2 says that "God will give him a throne of glory." The "throne of glory" coheres with Daniel 7's thrones (v. 9) and glory that is showered upon the son of man (v. 14) and with the similar language found in the Similitudes of Enoch: "Pain shall seize them when they see that Son of Man sitting on the throne of his glory" (*1 Enoch* 62:5).[40]

I think that Jesus did anticipate setting up a messianic administration that would displace the religious establishment of Jerusalem. We see this in Jesus' reply to James and John (Mark 10:35-40), which clearly anticipates the disciples sitting with Jesus. We see this in Jesus' promise to the twelve that they would someday sit on thrones judging the twelve tribes of Israel (Matt 19:28 = Luke 22:28-30). This saying combines Danielic son of man imagery with Davidic tradition (adding additional support to Bittner's line of argument).[41] Thus, the reference to building a new Temple "without hands" may have originally referred—in a manner approximating that of Qumran (e.g. 4QFlor 1:6: אדם מקדש; "a sanctuary of men")—to this new community, the nucleus of the small but growing kingdom. Because of the close association between Jesus and his followers, the Johannine evangelist understands this new Temple as a reference to the resurrection of Jesus' body (John 2:22). But originally the "made with/without hands" qualifiers were in reference to opposing communities—Jesus' (which is messianic, "made without hands") and the ruling priests' (which is worldly,

---

[39]   W. Bittner, "Gott – Menschensohn – Davidssohn: Eine Untersuchung zur Traditionsgeschichte von Daniel 7, 13f.," *FZPT* 22 (1985) 343-72, esp. 356-64.

[40]   Trans. by E. Isaac, "1 (Ethiopic Apocalypse of) Enoch," in J. H. Charlesworth (ed.), *The Old Testament Pseudepigrapha* (2 vols., Garden City: Doubleday, 1983-85) 1.43. Although containing many useful insights, I hesitate in following Bittner's conclusion ("Gott – Menschensohn – Davidssohn," 371) "that in the figure of the son of man of Daniel 7 God himself . . . is proclaimed as the eschatological Davidic Messiah."

[41]   The Q saying reflects Daniel 7 (son of man sitting on throne of glory) and Ps 122:1-5 (thrones of the house of David set up in Jerusalem, where the tribes will go up). These passages are combined in an interesting exegesis in *Midr. Tanḥ.* B, *Qedošim* §1; see chaps. 4 and 11 above.

"made with hands"). Because Jesus prophesied the Temple's destruction and the demise of the ruling priests along with it, Jesus' "made
with/without hands" qualifiers became associated with the Temple
complex itself. Thus the charge brought against Jesus by the "false"
witnesses (Mark 14:58) was indeed false.

Jesus' crucifixion as the "king of the Jews" (Mark 15:26 par)[42]
provides further evidence of a messianic and probably Davidic orientation on the part of Jesus. In an important collection of essays treating
the theme of the trial of Jesus, Ernst Bammel concludes: "It follows
that the mention of an execution on the cross says less about the authority which called for it than about the kind of crime with which the
victim was charged."[43] Bammel's point is well taken. The crime of
Jesus, in the eyes of Rome, lay in his assumption of royal perogatives.
Hints of these royal perogatives remain in the Gospel traditions.[44] The

---

[42]   J. E. Allen, "Why Pilate?" in E. Bammel (ed.), *The Trial of Jesus* (C. F. D.
Moule Festschrift; SBT 13; London: SCM, 1970) 78-83. It is concluded that the
Sanhedrin found Jesus deserving death, but had to hand him over to Pilate in order
for there to be a death sentence and execution. To justify the execution of Jesus,
Pilate had to write, "The King of the Jews," and the Jews had to accept it (see John
19:21-22). See also E. Bammel, "Die Blutgerichtsbarkeit in der römischen Provinz
Judäa vor dem ersten jüdischen Aufstand," in Bammel, *Judaica* (WUNT 37;
Tübingen: Mohr [Siebeck], 1986) 59-72. Bammel concludes that John 18:31 ("It is
not lawful for us to put anyone to death") is historical.

[43]   E. Bammel, "Crucifixion as a Punishment in Palestine," in Bammel (ed.),
The Trial of Jesus, 162-65, quotation from p. 165. Reprinted in Bammel, *Judaica*,
76-78. See the recent assessment and summary in M. Hengel, *Crucifixion: In the
Ancient World and the Folly of the Message of the Cross* (London: SCM; Philadelphia: Fortress, 1977) esp. 84-85; J. A. Fitzmyer, "Crucifixion in Ancient Palestine,
Qumran Literature, and the New Testament," *CBQ* 40 (1978) 493-513; repr. in
Fitzmyer, *To Advance the Gospel: New Testament Studies* (New York: Crossroad,
1981) 125-46. Fitzmyer's essay is especially valuable for its assessment of the
skeletal remains found at Giv'at ha-Mivtar and for its interpretation of 4QpNah 3-4 i
1-11 (esp. 7-8) and 11QTemple 64:6-13. For more on 4QpNah, see M. Horgan,
Pesharim: Qumran Interpretations of Biblical Books (CBQMS 8; Washington:
Catholic Biblical Association, 1979) 158-91; M. A. Knibb, *The Qumran Community* (Cambridge: Cambridge University Press, 1987) 212-13. For another recent
discussion of crucifixion, see J. Zias and J. H. Charlesworth, "CRUCIFIXION:
Archaeology, Jesus, and the Dead Sea Scrolls," in Charlesworth (ed.), *Jesus and
the Dead Sea Scrolls* (ABRL; New York: Doubleday, 1992) 273-89.

[44]   See esp. M. Hengel, "Jesus, der Messias Israels," in I. Gruenwald et al.
(eds.), *Messiah and Christos: Studies in the Jewish Origins of Christianity* (D.

most obvious example, and one that can hardly be called a "hint," is
Jesus' entrance into Jerusalem mounted on a donkey.

Conclusion

The evidence is such that there is no warrant to conclude, as has
Burton Mack recently, that there is no meaningful connection between
Jesus' public ministry and his crucifixion.[45] Jesus' death in Jerusalem
was the inevitable result of his proclamation of the kingdom of God
and of various actions that not only implied that it was very near, even
beginning to appear, but also implied that Jesus thought of himself as
the "son of man" to whom would be given authority and the kingdom. I
have to concur with the conclusion reached years ago by Gösta
Lindeskog: "Man kann . . . nicht die Leidensgeschichte von dem
Wirken Jesu isolieren."[46] The Galilean prophet proclaimed a Danielic
kingdom that could only be realized after much struggle and suffering.

Flusser Festschrift; TSAJ 32; Tübingen: Mohr [Siebeck], 1992) 155-76.

[45] B. L. Mack, *A Myth of Innocence: Mark and Christian Origins* (Philadelphia: Fortress, 1988) 88-89. See the criticisms offered above in chap. 7.

[46] G. Lindeskog, "Der Prozess Jesu im jüdisch-christlichen Religionsgespräch," in O. Betz, M. Hengel, and P. Schmidt (eds.), *Abraham unser Vater*
(O. Michel Festschrift; AGSU 5; Leiden: Brill, 1963) 325-36, here p. 334.

EPILOGUE

JESUS AND HIS CONTEMPORARIES

In an Epilogue written for a collection of recent studies treating various aspects of Jesus research, Helmut Koester expresses a measure of "misgivings about the entire enterprise."[1] Alluding to a recent publication by his long-time friend and colleague Dieter Georgi, Koester comments on the oft-observed tendency of scholars to impose their personal values and the values and assumptions of western society upon the sources under investigation.[2] It seems inevitable that the "historical" Jesus that emerges holds much in common with the scholar who discovered him. I alluded to this problem in the Preface to this book and I would like now to return to it in this Epilogue. I suppose one Epilogue deserves another.

There is little in Koester's Epilogue with which I disagree. His and Georgi's comments about the tendencies among scholars to be influenced by modern western culture cannot be gainsaid. But I wonder if Koester has fully grasped how most of the participants of the "Third Quest" understand their task. One sentence in the last paragraph of Koester's Epilogue is quite revealing: "Political, social, and environmental problems of our age will not be cured through the ever renewed search for the exemplary personality of Jesus and his wisdom, in order to legitimize the individual's search for perfection and success."[3]

This statement seems to suggest that Koester views Jesus research much in the same way that it was viewed by many of the scholars who participated in the Old and New Quests. If this is indeed how Koester understands the current "situation" of Jesus research, then I believe he

---

[1]   H. Koester, "The Historical Jesus and the Historical Situation of the Quest: An Epilogue," in B. D. Chilton and C. A. Evans (eds.), *Studying the Historical Jesus: Evaluations of the State of Research* (NTTS 19; Leiden: Brill, 1994) 535-45. The quotation is from p. 535.

[2]   Cf. D. Georgi, "The Interest in Life of Jesus Theology as a Paradigm for the Social History of Biblical Criticism," *HTR* 85 (1992) 51-83. Georgi maintains that Christianity's quest for the historical Jesus has been conditioned by social values far more than Albert Schweitzer had realized.

[3]   Koester, "The Historical Jesus and the Historical Situation of the Quest," 544-45.

has primarily in mind German scholarship, which tends to be highly theologically oriented, not American and British. Most of the major figures involved in current research pursue their work without these concerns in mind.[4] Included among these figures are the contributors to the book in which Koester's Epilogue appears.[5]

Not only does Koester's statement pass a gratuitous judgment upon what really is a historical task, I suspect many will strongly disagree with its theological assumptions. I can well imagine many theologians asserting that humanity's numerous ills can in fact be cured through the search and discovery of the "exemplary personality of Jesus and his wisdom." But whether or not this is so, the historian's responsibility is to reconstruct the thought and activity of Jesus of Nazareth and his world, as capably as the available sources will permit. How useful this reconstruction might be for theological purposes, the historian will have to leave to theologians, clerics, and philosophers to decide.

Koester's misgivings notwithstanding, I think Jesus research is valuable for several reasons. First, interest in the historical Jesus has the same claim to legitimacy as does interest in any other historical figure. If the study of history, the quest to understand what happened and where we and our cultures came from, has value, then study of the life and thought of one who so dramatically impacted near eastern and western civilization seems entirely appropriate.

Second, I do not see how the study of Christian and Jewish origins can be served by neglecting the study of the historical Jesus. Should those capable of responsible study surrender the field to the quacks and media sensationalists? Carlston rightly asserts that the "topic is too important to be neglected."[6]

Third, Jesus research, including the flawed Old and New Quests, has yielded numerous positive results. Many of the advances in biblical literature and history in the last two centuries have been prompted by it. It is reasonable to assume that continuing research will lead to

---

4   E. P. Sanders, *Jesus and Judaism* (London: SCM; Philadelphia: Fortress, 1985) 2; J. P. Meier, *A Marginal Jew: Rethinking the Historical Jesus* (ABRL: New York: Doubleday, 1991) 197. Both Sanders and Meier consciously separate the historical task from the question of theology and personal relevance.

5   See especially the sage comments of C. E. Carlston ("Prologue," in Chilton and Evans [eds.], *Studying the Historical Jesus*, 1-8), a colleague and contemporary of Koester's, who was an active participant in the New Quest and in the interpretation of Bultmann and his legacy.

6   Carlston, "Prologue," 8.

further discoveries and insights.

Fourth, I imagine that there are good theological reasons for wishing to know more about the historical Jesus. To me it seems only reasonable for Christians to want to know more about the person who founded the Christian faith. But I shall leave this part of the question to Koester and the heirs of Bultmann and to those who wish to debate with them.

The preceding chapters have touched on several of the issues that attend Jesus research and form the backdrop against which this figure should be studied. Many of these issues have been raised but have been considered only briefly. Others have been explored in more detail. One point that has become clear is that the similarities between Jesus and his Jewish contemporaries are numerous and significant. Very little, perhaps nothing, of Jesus' teachings and activities, when viewed individually, are truly unique.

Jesus prayed and taught in the manner of the popular preachers and teachers of his time. He interpreted Scripture much as the popular preachers and teachers did. In places Jesus' use of the Old Testament reveals familiarity with the Aramaic paraphrases, suggesting that his understanding of Scripture in large measure took shape in the context of the synagogue. Jesus proclaimed the appearance of the kingdom of God, something longed for by many of his contemporaries, though strongly opposed by many who were secure in positions of power and wealth.

Jesus was a successful exorcist and healer. These healings were understood as indications of the presence of God, which was evidence of the inbreaking of the kingdom of God. Jesus demanded repentance and a return to the ethical laws of the Pentateuch and their applications found in the prophets. These demands carried with them serious implications for the ruling elite. Not surprisingly, Jesus was opposed by the ruling elite; his message and authority were rejected.

This opposition and rejection probably led to an intensification of Jesus' criticism of the ruling elite. He condemned it and predicted dire consequences for the city and the Temple establishment. Jesus' words and actions provoked the religious leaders and led them to seek his destruction. Following his arrest, Jesus affirmed, at some point in his interrogation, his messianic identity as he understood it and in so doing provided the grounds for a Roman execution as "king of the Jews."

Some time later, his followers, fully persuaded that Jesus had been resurrected, proclaimed him Israel's Messiah. This proclamation, to be sure, was the result of Easter, but the *messianic identification* itself arose from Jesus' teaching and activities. A non-messianic teacher or prophet would not have been proclaimed "Messiah," even if his followers believed him to have been resurrected. (Had either Aqiba or Yose the Galilean made post-mortem appearances to their disciples, would messianic categories have occurred to any of them?) It was Jesus' promise of kingdom and salvation, the essential elements of the messianic task, that resulted in the emergence of a *christology*, not the Easter discovery alone.

It is hoped that *Jesus and His Contemporaries: Comparative Studies* will make a modest contribution to the ongoing investigation of Jesus and his world. The contribution lies not so much in new conclusions, for there are very few, but in the emphasis on a proper comparative and contextualized approach. In my judgment, the work that properly takes into consideration the Jewish Palestinian backdrop of Jesus and his contemporaries will prove to be the work that makes the lasting contributions. I would like to encourage fellow questers to eschew the trendy, politically correct, but largely ahistorical and noncontextual, presentations of Jesus. The shelf-life of these books, especially those that pander to the media, is short. Legitimate Jesus research should be firmly grounded in history, archaeology, and the primary texts. Much of this material has yet to be fully studied; and new materials continue to come to light. This is a propitious time to be engaged in Jesus research; the opportunities have never been greater.

BIBLIOGRAPHY

Abegg, Jr., M. G. "Messianic Hope and 4Q285: A Reassessment." *JBL* 113 (1994) 81-91.

Aberbach, M. and Grossfeld, B. *Targum Onkelos to Genesis.* New York: Ktav, 1982.

Abrahams, I. *Studies in Pharisaism and the Gospels.* 2 vols. Cambridge and London: Cambridge University Press, 1917-24. Repr. New York: Ktav, 1967.

Achtemeier, P. J. "Gospel Miracle tradition and the Divine Man." *Int* 26 (1972) 174-97.

—. "Miracles and the Historical Jesus: A Study of Mark 9:14-20." *CBQ* 37 (1975) 471-91.

Ådna, J. *Jesu Kritik am Tempel: Eine Untersuchung zum Verlauf und Sinn der sogenannten Tempelreinigung Jesu, Markus 11, 15-17 und Parallelen.* Dissertation. Stavanger: University of Stavanger, 1993.

Aegyptische Urkunden aus den staatlichen Museen zu Berlin: Griechische Urkunden. 4 vols. Berlin: Weidmann, 1895-1912.

Aldwinckle, R. F. "Myth and Symbol in Contemporary Philosophy and Theology: The Limits of Demythologizing." *JR* 34 (1954) 267-79.

Aleksandrov, S. "The Role of 'Aqiba in the Bar-Kokhba Rebellion." *REJ* 132 (1973) 65-77.

Allegro, J. M. "Fragments of a Qumran Scroll of Eschatological Midrashim." *JBL* 77 (1958) 350-54.

—. "Further Messianic References." *JBL* 75 (1956) 174-87.

—. *Qumrân Cave 4 I (4Q158–4Q186).* DJD 5. Oxford: Clarendon, 1968.

Allen, J. E. "Why Pilate?" *The Trial of Jesus: Cambridge Studies in Honour of C. F. D. Moule.* SBT 13. London: SCM, 1970. Pp. 78-83.

Allison, D. C. and Davies, W. D. *The Gospel According to Saint Matthew.* 2 vols. Edinburgh: T. & T. Clark, 1988-91.

Amousine, J. D. "A propos de l'interpretation de 4 Q 161 (fragments 5–6 et 8)." *RevQ* 8 (1974) 381-92.

Anderson, G. A. "The Interpretation of the Purification Offering (חטאת) in the *Temple Scroll* (11QTemple)." *JBL* 111 (1992) 17-35.

Aulén, G. *Jesus i nutida historisk forskning.* 2nd. ed. Stockholm: Verbum, 1974. ET: *Jesus in Contemporary Historical Research.* Philadelphia: Fortress, 1976.

Aune, D. E. "A Note on Jesus' Messianic Consciousness and 11Q Melchizedek." *EvQ* 45 (1973) 161-65.

—. *Prophecy in Early Christianity and the Ancient Mediterranean World.* Grand Rapids: Eerdmans, 1983.

—. "The Use of ΠΡΟΦΗΤΗΣ in Josephus." *JBL* 101 (1982) 419-21.

Aytoun, R. A. "The Servant of the Lord in the Targum." *JTS* 23 (1921-22) 172-80.

Baillet, M. *Qumrân Grotte 4 III (4Q482–4Q520).* DJD 7. Oxford: Clarendon, 1982.

Baillet, M., Milik, J. T., and de Vaux, R. *Les 'Petites Grottes' de Qumrân: Exploration de la falaise, Les grottes 2Q, 3Q, 5Q, 6Q, 7Q à 10Q, Le rouleau de cuivre.* DJD 3. Oxford: Clarendon, 1962.

Bammel, E. "Die Blutgerichtsbarkeit in der römischen Provinz Judäa vor dem ersten jüdischen Aufstand." In Bammel. *Judaica: Kleine Schriften I.* WUNT 37. Tübingen: Mohr (Siebeck), 1986. Pp. 59-72.

—. "Crucifixion as a Punishment in Palestine." In Bammel (ed.). *The Trial of Jesus: Cambridge Studies in Honour of C. F. D. Moule*. SBT 13. London: SCM, 1970. Pp. 162-65. Repr. Bammel. *Judaica. Kleine Schriften I*. WUNT 37. Tübingen: Mohr (Siebeck), 1986. Pp. 76-78.

—. "Jesus as a Political Agent in a Version of the Josippon." In E. Bammel and C. F. D. Moule (eds.). *Jesus and the Politics of His Day*. Cambridge: Cambridge University Press, 1984. Pp. 197-209. Repr. in Bammel. *Judaica: Kleine Schriften I*. WUNT 37. Tübingen: Mohr (Siebeck), 1986. Pp. 289-301.

—. *Judaica. Kleine Schriften I*. WUNT 37. Tübingen: Mohr (Siebeck), 1986.

—. "Pilatus' und Kaiaphas' Absetzung." In Bammel. *Judaica: Kleine Schriften I*. WUNT 37. Tübingen: Mohr (Siebeck), 1986. Pp. 51-58.

—. "The Revolution Theory from Reimarus to Brandon." In E. Bammel and C. F. D. Moule (eds.). *Jesus and the Politics of His Day*. Cambridge: Cambridge University Press, 1984. Pp. 11-68.

—. "The *titulus*." In E. Bammel and C. F. D. Moule (eds.). *Jesus and the Politics of His Day*. Cambridge: Cambridge University Press, 1984. Pp. 353-64.

— (ed.). *The Trial of Jesus: Cambridge Studies in Honour of C. F. D. Moule*. SBT 13. London: SCM, 1970.

—. "Zu 1QS 9, 10f." In Bammel. *Judaica: Kleine Schriften I*. WUNT 37. Tübingen: Mohr (Siebeck), 1986. Pp. 112-14.

—. "Zum Testimonium Flavianum (Jos. Ant. 18,63-64)." In O. Betz et al. (eds.). *Josephus-Studien*. Göttingen: Vandenhoeck & Ruprecht, 1974. Pp. 9-22.

Barnes, T. D. "Legislation against the Christians." *JRS* 58 (1968) 32-50.

Barnett, P. W. "The Jewish Sign Prophets A.D. 40–70—Their Intentions and Origin." *NTS* 27 (1981) 679-97.

Barr, J. "'Abba, Father' and the Familiarity of Jesus' Speech." *Th* 91 (1988) 173-79.

—. "Abba Isn't Daddy." *JTS* 39 (1988) 28-47.

J. Barta, "Das Achtzehngebet—Eine Betrachtung." In M. Brocke, J. J. Petuchowski, and W. Strolz (eds.). *Das Vaterunser: Gemeinsames im Beten von Juden und Christen*. Freiburg: Herder, 1974. Pp. 77-89.

Barthélemy, D. and Milik, J. T. *Qumran Cave I*. DJD 1. Oxford: Clarendon, 1955.

Bauckham, R. "The Son of Man: 'A Man in My Position' or 'Someone'." *JSNT* 23 (1985) 23-33.

Baumgarten, J. M. "4Q500 and the Ancient Conception of the Lord's Vineyard." *JJS* 40 (1989) 1-6.

Beare, F.W. *The Gospel according to Matthew*. San Francisco: Harper & Row, 1981.

—. "Sayings of the Risen Jesus in the Synoptic Tradition." In W. R. Farmer et al. (eds.). *Christian History and Interpretation*. J. Knox Festschrift. London: Cambridge University Press, 1967. Pp. 161-81.

Benoit, P., Milik, J. T., and de Vaux, R. *Les grottes de Murabba'at*. 2 vols. DJD 2. Oxford: Clarendon, 1961.

Berger, K. "Die königlichen Messiastraditionen des Neuen Testaments." *NTS* 20 (1973-74) 1-44.

Betz, H. D. *Lukian von Samosata und das Neue Testament: Religionsgeschichtliche und Paränetische Parallelen*. Berlin: Akademie, 1961.

Betz, O. "Die Bedeutung der Qumranschriften für die Evangelien des Neuen Testaments." *BK* 40 (1985) 54-64. Repr. in Betz. *Jesus: Der Messias Israels. Aufsätze zur biblischen Theologie*. WUNT 42. Tübingen: Mohr (Siebeck), 1987. Pp. 318-32.

—. "Die Frage nach dem messianischen Bewußtsein Jesu." *NovT* 6 (1963) 20-48. Repr. in Betz. *Jesus: Der Messias Israels. Aufsätze zur biblischen Theologie*. WUNT 42. Tübingen: Mohr (Siebeck), 1987. Pp. 140-68.

—. "Jesu Heiliger Krieg." *NovT* 2 (1957) 116-37.

—. *Jesus: Der Messias Israels*. WUNT 42. Tübingen: Mohr (Siebeck), 1987.

—. *Jesus und das Danielbuch, Band II: Die Menschensohnworte Jesu und die Zukunftserwartung des Paulus (Daniel 7, 13-14).* ANTJ 6.2. Frankfurt am Main: Peter Lang, 1985.

—. "Jesus' Gospel of the Kingdom." In P. Stuhlmacher (ed.). *The Gospel and the Gospels.* Grand Rapids: Eerdmans, 1991. Pp. 53-74.

—. "Probleme des Prozesses Jesu." *ANRW* 2.25.1 (1982) 565-647.

—. *Was wissen wir von Jesus?* Stuttgart and Berlin: Kreuz, 1965.

Betz, O. and Grimm, W. *Wesen und Wirklichkeit der Wunder Jesu.* ANTJ 2. Frankfurt am Main and Bern: Lang, 1977.

Betz, O., Haacker, L., and Hengel, M. (eds.). *Josephus Studien.* Göttingen: Vandenhoeck & Ruprecht, 1974.

Betz, O., Hengel, M., and Schmidt, P. (eds.). *Abraham unser Vater: Juden und Christen im Gespräch über die Bibel.* O. Michel Festschrift. AGJU 5. Leiden: Brill, 1963.

Betz, O. and Riesner, R. *Jesus, Qumran und der Vatikan: Klarstellungen.* Giessen: Brunnen; Freiburg: Herder, 1993. ET: *Jesus, Qumran and the Vatican: Clarifications.* New York: Crossroad, 1994.

Beyer, H. W. "Βλασφημέω, κ.τ.λ." *TDNT* 1 (1964) 621-25.

Beyer, K. *Die aramäischen Texte vom Toten Meer.* Göttingen: Vandenhoeck & Ruprecht, 1984.

Bittner, W. "Gott – Menschensohn – Davidssohn: Eine Untersuchung zur Traditionsgeschichte von Daniel 7, 13f." *FZPT* 22 (1985) 343-72.

Black, M. *An Aramaic Approach to the Gospels and Acts.* 3rd ed. Oxford: Clarendon Press, 1967.

—. "Judas of Galilee and Josephus' 'Fourth Philosophy'." In O. Betz et al. (eds.). *Josephus Studien.* Göttingen: Vandenhoeck & Ruprecht, 1974. Pp. 45-54.

—. "Messianic Doctrine in the Qumran Scrolls." In K. Aland and F. L. Cross (eds.). *Studia Patristica 1.* TU 63. 2 vols. Berlin: Akademie, 1957. Vol. 1. Pp. 441-59.

—. "'Not peace but a sword': Matt 10:34ff; Luke 12:51ff." In E. Bammel and C. F. D. Moule (eds.). *Jesus and the Politics of His Day.* Cambridge: Cambridge University Press, 1984. Pp. 287-94.

Blackburn, "'Miracle Working ΘΕΙΟΙ ΑΝΔΡΕΣ' in Hellenism (and Hellenistic Judaism)." In Wenham and Blomberg (eds.). *The Miracles of Jesus.* Gospel Perspectives 6. Sheffield: JSOT Press, 1986. Pp. 185-218.

—. *'Theios Aner' and the Markan Miracle Traditions: A Critique of the Theios Aner Concept as an Interpretative Background of the Miracle Traditions Used by Mark.* WUNT 2.40. Tübingen: Mohr (Siebeck), 1991.

Blinzler, J. *Der Prozess Jesu: Das jüdische und das römische Gerichtsverfahren gegen Jesus Christus auf Grund der ältesten Zeugnisse dargestellt und beurteilt.* Bibelwissenschaftliche Reihe 4. Stuttgart: Katholisches Bibelwerk, 1951. 4th ed. Regensburg: Pustet, 1969. ET: *The Trial of Jesus.* Westminster: Newman, 1959.

Bockmuehl, M. "A 'Slain Messiah' in 4Q Serekh Milḥamah (4Q285)?" *TynBul* 43 (1992) 155-69.

—. "Why Did Jesus Predict the Destruction of the Temple?" *Crux* 25.3 (1989) 11-18.

Boismard, M.-E. "Rapprochements littéraires entre l'évangile de Luc et l'Apocalypse." In J. Schmid and A. Vögtle (eds.). *Synoptische Studien.* A. Wikenhauser Festschrift. Munich: Zink, 1953. Pp. 53-63.

Borg, M. J. *Conflict, Holiness and Politics in the Teachings of Jesus.* SBEC 5. New York and Toronto: Mellen, 1984.

—. *Jesus: A New Vision.* San Francisco: Harper & Row, 1987.

—. "A Temperate Case for a Non-Eschatological Jesus." *Forum* 2 (1986) 81-102.

Borgen, P. "The Independence of the Gospel of John: Some Observations." In F. Van Segbroeck et al (eds.). *The Four Gospels 1992.* F. Neirynck Festschrift. BETL 100. 3 vols. Leuven: Peeters, 1992. Vol. 3. Pp. 1815-33.

—. "John and the Synoptics." In D. L. Dungan (ed.). *The Interrelations of the Gospels.* BETL 95.

Leuven: Leuven University, 1990. Pp. 408-37.

——. "John and the Synoptics in the Passion Narrative." *NTS* 5 (1958-59) 246-59.

Boring, M. E. *The Continuing Voice of Jesus.* Louisville: Westminster/John Knox, 1991.

——. *Sayings of the Risen Jesus: Christian Prophecy in the Synoptic Tradition.* SNTSMS 46. Cambridge: Cambridge University Press, 1982.

Borsch, F. H. "Mark xiv.62 and I Enoch lxii.5." *NTS* 14 (1967-68) 565-67.

Boucher M. *The Mysterious Parable: A Literary Study.* CBQMS 6. Washington: Catholic Biblical Association, 1977.

Bowie, E. L. "Apollonius of Tyana: Tradition and Reality." *ANRW* 2.16.2 (1978) 1652-1699.

Bowker, J. *Jesus and the Pharisees.* New York: Cambridge University Press, 1973.

Bowman, S. "Sefer Yosippon: History and Midrash." In M. Fishbane (ed.). *The Midrashic Imagination: Jewish Exegesis, Thought, and History.* Albany: State University of New York, 1993. Pp. 280-94.

Brandon, S. G. F. *Jesus and the Zealots: A Study of the Political Factor in Primitive Christianity.* Manchester: Manchester University Press; New York: Scribner's, 1967.

——. *The Trial of Jesus of Nazareth.* New York: Stein and Day, 1968.

Braude, W. G. *The Midrash on Psalms.* 2 vols. YJS 13. New Haven: Yale University Press, 1959.

——. *Pesikta Rabbati.* 2 vols. YJS 18. New Haven and London: Yale University Press, 1968.

Braude, W. G. and Kapstein, I. *Tanna Dĕbe Eliyyahu: The Lore of the School of Elijah.* Philadelphia: Jewish Publication Society, 1981.

Braun, H. *Qumran und das Neue Testament.* 2 vols. Tübingen: Mohr (Siebeck), 1966.

——. "The Significance of Qumran for the Problem of the Historical Jesus." In C. E. Braaten and R. A. Harrisville (eds.). *The Historical Jesus and the Kerygmatic Christ: Essays on the New Quest of the Historical Jesus.* Nashville: Abingdon, 1964. Pp. 69-78.

Brocke, M., Petuchowski, J. J., and Strolz, W. (eds.). *Das Vaterunser: Gemeinsames im Beten von Juden und Christen.* Freiburg: Herder, 1974. Abridged ET: J. J. Petuchowski and M. Brocke (eds.). *The Lord's Prayer and Jewish Liturgy.* New York: Seabury, 1978.

Brooke, G. J. "The Amos-Numbers Midrash (CD 7,13b–8,1a) and Messianic Expectation." *ZAW* 92 (1980) 397-404.

——. *Exegesis at Qumran: 4QFlorilegium in Its Jewish Context.* JSOTSup 29. Sheffield: JSOT Press, 1985.

——. "Melchizedek (11QMelch)." *ABD* 4 (1992) 687-88.

Broshi, M. (ed.). *The Damascus Document Reconsidered.* Jerusalem: Israel Exploration Society and the Shrine of the Book, 1992.

Brown, C. *Jesus in European Protestant Thought, 1778–1860.* SHT 1. Durham: Labyrinth, 1985.

——. "Synoptic Miracle Stories: A Jewish Religious and Social Setting." *Forum* 2.4 (1986) 55-76.

Brown, R. E. *The Gospel According to John I-XII.* AB 29. Garden City: Doubleday, 1966.

——. "J. Starcky's Theory of Qumran Messianic Development." *CBQ* 28 (1966) 51-57.

——. "The Messianism of Qumrân." *CBQ* 19 (1957) 53-82.

——. "The Pater Noster as an Eschatological Prayer." *TS* 22 (1961) 175-208. Repr. in Brown. *New Testament Essays.* Garden City: Doubleday, 1967. Pp. 217-53.

——. "The Teacher of Righteousness and the Messiah(s)." In M. Black (ed.). *The Scrolls and Christianity.* SPCK Theological Collections 11. London: SPCK, 1969. Pp. 37-44, 109-12.

Brownlee, W. H. *The Dead Sea Manual of Discipline: Translation and Notes.* BASORSup 10–12. New Haven: American Schools of Oriental Research, 1951.

——. "The Incarnation in the Light of Ancient Scrolls." *The United Presbyterian* 113.5 (1955) 12-13, 15.

——. "Jesus and Qumran." In F. T. Trotter (ed.). *Jesus and the Historian.* E. C. Colwell Festschrift. Philadelphia: Westminster, 1968. Pp. 52-81.

—. "John the Baptist in the New Light of Ancient Scrolls." *Int* 9 (1955) 71-90.

—. *The Meaning of the Qumrân Scrolls for the Bible: With Special Attention to the Book of Isaiah.* Oxford and New York: Oxford University Press, 1964.

—. "Messianic Motifs of Qumran and the New Testament." *NTS* 3 (1956-57) 12-30, 195-210.

—. "The Servant of the Lord in the Qumran Scrolls I." *BASOR* 132 (1953) 8-15.

—. "The Servant of the Lord in the Qumran Scrolls II." *BASOR* 135 (1954) 33-38.

Büchler, A. *Types of Jewish-Palestinian Piety from 70 B.C.E. to 70 C.E. The Ancient Pious Men.* London: Jews' College, 1922. Repr. New York: Ktav, 1968.

Bühner, J.-A. *Der Gesandte und sein Weg im 4. Evangelium: Die kultur- und religionsgeschichtlichen Grundlagen der johanneischen Sendungschristologie sowie ihre traditionsgeschichtliche Entwicklung.* WUNT 2.2. Tübingen: Mohr (Siebeck), 1977.

Bultmann, R. *Die Erforschung der Synoptischen Evangelien.* 2nd ed. Giessen: Töpelmann, 1930. ET: "The Study of the Synoptic Gospels." In Bultmann and K. Kundsin. *Form Criticism.* New York: Harper & Row, 1934. Pp. 11-76.

—. *Existence and Faith.* New York: Harper & Row, 1960.

—. *Die Geschichte der synoptischen Tradition.* 2nd ed. Göttingen: Vandenhoeck & Ruprecht, 1931. ET: *The History of the Synoptic Tradition.* Oxford: Blackwell, 1968.

—. *Jesus.* Berlin: Deutsche Bibliothek, 1926. ET: *Jesus and the Word.* New York: Scribner's, 1934.

—. "Neues Testament und Mythologie." Part II of Bultmann. *Offenbarung und Heilsgeschehen.* BEvT 7. Munich: Kaiser, 1941. Repr. *Neues Testament und Mythologie: Das Problem der Entmythologisierung der neutestamentlichen Verkündigung.* BEvT 96. Ed. E. Jüngel. Munich: Kaiser, 1985. ET: "New Testament and Mythology." In H.-W. Bartsch (ed.). *Kerygma and Myth: A Theological Debate.* London: SPCK, 1957. Pp. 1-44.

—. "The New Approach to the Synoptic Problem." *JR* 6 (1926) 337-62.

—. *Theologie des Neuen Testaments.* 2 vols. Tübingen: Mohr (Siebeck), 1948-53. 5th ed., 1965. ET: *Theology of the New Testament.* 2 vols. New York: Scribner's, 1951-55.

—. *Das Evangelium des Johannes.* KEK 2. Göttingen: Vandenhoeck & Ruprecht, 1964. ET: *The Gospel of John.* Philadelphia: Westminster, 1971.

—. "Zur Frage des Wunder." In R. Bultmann, *Glauben und Verstehen.* 2 vols. Tübingen: Mohr (Siebeck), 1954. 1.214-28. ET: "The Problem of Miracle." *RL* 27 (1958) 63-75.

Burkitt, F. C. *The Gospel History and Its Transmission.* 3rd ed. Edinburgh: T. & T. Clark, 1911.

Burrows, M. *The Dead Sea Scrolls of St. Mark's Monastery.* 2 vols. New Haven: ASOR, 1950.

—. "The Messiahs of Aaron and the New Testament (DSD IX, 11)." *ATR* 34 (1952) 202-206.

Butts, J. R. "Probing the Poll: Jesus Seminar Results on the Kingdom Sayings." *Forum* 3 (1987) 98-128.

Cairns, D. "A Reappraisal of Bultmann's Theology." *RelS* 17 (1981) 469-85.

Calvert, D. G. A. "An Examination of the Criteria for Distinguishing the Authentic Words of Jesus." *NTS* 18 (1972) 209-19.

Cameron, R. *The Other Gospels: Non-Canonical Gospel Texts.* Philadelphia: Westminster, 1982.

Caquot, A. "Le messianisme qumrânien." In M. Delcor (ed.). *Qumrân: Sa piété, sa théologie et son milieu.* BETL 46. Gembloux: Duculot; Louvain: Leuven Univeristy Press, 1978. Pp. 231-47.

Carlston, C. E. *The Parables of the Triple Tradition.* Philadelphia: Fortress, 1975.

—. "A *Positive* Criterion of Authenticity?" *BR* 7 (1962) 33-44.

Carmignac, J. "Le document de Qumran sur Melkisedeq." *RevQ* 7 (1970) 343-78.

—. "Hebrew Translations of the Lord's Prayer: An Historical Survey." In G. A. Tuttle (ed.). *Biblical and Near Eastern Studies.* W. S. LaSor Festschrift. Grand Rapids: Eerdmans, 1978. Pp. 18-79.

—. "Les horoscopes de Qumran." *RevQ* 18 (1965) 199-217.

—. "Notes sur les Peshârîm." *RevQ* 3 (1961-62) 505-38.

—. *Recherches sur le "Notre Père"*. Paris: Letourzey & Ané, 1969. Pp. 32-33.

Cary, E. *Dio's Roman History VIII*. LCL 176. London: Heinemann; Cambridge: Harvard University Press, 1925.

Casey, M. "General, Generic and Indefinite: The Use of the Term 'Son of Man' in Aramaic Sources and in the Teaching of Jesus." *JSNT* 29 (1987) 21-56.

Catchpole, D. R. "The Problem of the Historicity of the Sanhedrin Trial." In E. Bammel (ed.). *The Trial of Jesus: Cambridge Studies in Honour of C. F. D. Moule*. SBT 13. London: SCM, 1970. Pp. 47-65.

—. *The Trial of Jesus: A Study in the Gospels and Jewish Historiography from 1770 to the Present Day*. SPB 18. Leiden: Brill, 1971.

—. "The 'Triumphal' Entry." In E. Bammel and C. F. D. Moule (eds.). *Jesus and the Politics of His Day*. Cambridge: Cambridge University Press, 1984. Pp. 319-34.

Chamberlain, J. V. "Another Thanksgiving Psalm." *JNES* 14 (1955) 32-41.

—. "Functions of God as Messianic Titles in the Complete Qumran Isaiah Scroll." *VT* 5 (1955) 366-72.

—. "Further Elucidation of a Messianic Thanksgiving Psalm from Qumran." *JNES* 14 (1955) 181-82.

Charles, R. H. *The Assumption of Moses*. London: Black, 1897.

—. "Book of Enoch." In R. H. Charles (ed.), *The Apocrypha and Pseudepigrapha of the Old Testament*. 2 vols. Oxford: Clarendon, 1913. Pp. 163-281.

—. *The Greek Versions of the Testaments of the Twelve Patriarchs*. Oxford: Clarendon, 1908. Repr. Hildesheim: Georg Olms, 1960.

—. "The Testaments of the Twelve Patriarchs." In Charles (ed.). *The Apocrypha and Pseudepigrapha of the Old Testament*. 2 vols. Oxford: Clarendon, 1913.

Charlesworth, J. H. "A Caveat on Textual Transmission and the Meaning of *ABBA*: A Study of the Lord's Prayer." In J. H. Charlesworth (ed.), with M. Harding and M. Kiley. *The Lord's Prayer and Other Prayer Texts from the Greco-Roman Era*. Valley Forge: Trinity Press International, 1994. Pp. 1-14.

—. "From Barren Mazes to Gentle Rappings: The Emergence of Jesus Research." *Princeton Seminary Bulletin* 7 (1986) 221-30.

—. *Graphic Concordance to the Dead Sea Scrolls*. Tübingen: Mohr (Siebeck); Louisville: Westminster/John Knox, 1991.

—. *Jesus within Judaism*. ABRL. New York: Doubleday, 1988.

— (ed.). *The Messiah: Developments in Earliest Judaism and Christianity*. Minneapolis: Fortress, 1992.

— (ed.). *The Old Testament Pseudepigrapha*. 2 vols. Garden City: Doubleday, 1983-85.

—. "Research on the Historical Jesus." *Proceedings of the Irish Biblical Association* 9 (1985) 19-37.

Charlesworth, J. H. (ed.), with M. Harding and M. Kiley. *The Lord's Prayer and Other Prayer Texts from the Greco-Roman Era*. Valley Forge: Trinity Press International, 1994.

Charlesworth, J. H. and Evans, C. A. "Jesus in the Agrapha and Apocryphal Gospels." In B. D. Chilton and C. A. Evans (eds.). *Studying the Historical Jesus: Evaluations of the State of Current Research*. NTTS 19. Leiden: Brill, 1994. Pp. 479-533.

Chester, A. "The Sibyl and the Temple." In W. Horbury (ed.). *Templum Amicitiae: Essays on the Second Temple*. E. Bammel Festschrift. JSNTSup 48. Sheffield: JSOT Press, 1989. Pp. 37-69.

Chilton, B. D. "'Amen': An Approach through Syriac Gospels." *ZNW* 69 (1978) 203-11. Repr. in Chilton. *Targumic Approaches to the Gospels: Essays in the Mutual Definition of Judaism and Christianity*. Studies in Judaism. Lanham and London: University Press of America, 1986. Pp. 15-23.

—. "Exorcism and History: Mark 1:21-28." In D. Wenham and C. L. Blomberg (eds.). *The Miracles of Jesus*. Gospel Perspectives 6. Sheffield: JSOT Press, 1986. Pp. 253-71

—. *A Feast of Meanings: Eucharistic Theologies from Jesus through Johannine Circles*. NovTSup 72. Leiden: Brill, 1994.

—. *A Galilean Rabbi and His Bible: Jesus' Own Interpretation of Isaiah*. London: SPCK, 1984. American ed. *A Galilean Rabbi and His Bible: Jesus' Use of the Interpreted Scripture of His Time*. GNS 8. Wilmington: Glazier, 1984.

—. *The Glory of Israel: The Theology and Provenience of the Isaiah Targum*. JSOTSup 23. Sheffield: JSOT Press, 1982.

—. *God in Strength: Jesus' Announcement of the Kingdom*. SNTU 1. Freistadt: Plöchl, 1979. Repr. BibSem 8. Sheffield: JSOT Press, 1987.

—. "The Gospel According to Thomas as a Source of Jesus' Teaching." In D. Wenham (ed.). *The Jesus Tradition Outside the Gospels*. Gospel Perspectives 5. Sheffield: JSOT Press, 1984. Pp. 155-75.

—. *The Isaiah Targum*. ArBib 11. Wilmington: Glazier, 1987.

—. "Jesus and the Repentance of E. P. Sanders." *TynBul* 39 (1988) 1-18.

—. "Jesus *ben David*: Reflections on the *Davidssohnfrage*." *JSNT* 14 (1982) 88-112.

—. "The Kingdom of God in Recent Discussion." In B. Chilton and C. A. Evans (eds.). *Studying the Historical Jesus: Evaluations of the State of Current Research*. NTTS 19. Leiden: Brill, 1994. Pp. 255-80.

—. "The Purity of the Kingdom as Conveyed in Jesus' Meals." In E. H. Lovering (ed.). *Society of Biblical Literature 1992 Seminar Papers*. SBLSP 31. Atlanta: Scholars Press, 1992. Pp. 473-88

—. "Regnum Dei Deus Est." *SJT* 31 (1978) 261-70.

—. "Shebna, Eliakim, and the Promise to Peter." In J. Neusner et al. (eds.). *The Social World of Formative Christianity and Judaism*. H. C. Kee Festschrift. Philadelphia: Fortress, 1988. Pp. 311-26.

—. "The Son of Man: Human and Heavenly." In F. Van Segbroeck et al. (eds.). *The Four Gospels 1992*. F. Neirynck Festschrift. BETL 100. Leuven: Peeters, 1992. Vol. 1. Pp. 203-18.

—. *Targumic Approaches to the Gospels: Essays in the Mutual Definition of Judaism and Christianity*. Studies in Judaism. Lanham and London: University Press of America, 1986.

—. "Targumic Transmission and Dominical Tradition." In R. T. France and D. Wenham (eds.). *Studies of History and Tradition in the Four Gospels*. Gospel Perspectives 2. Sheffield: JSOT Press, 1980. Pp. 21-45.

—. *The Temple of Jesus: His Sacrificial Program Within a Cultural History of Sacrifice*. University Park: Penn State Press, 1992.

—. "[ὡς] φραγέλλιον ἐκ σχοινίων (John 2:15)." In W. Horbury (ed.). *Templum Amicitiae: Essays on the Second Temple*. E. Bammel Festschrift. JSNTSup 48. Sheffield: JSOT Press, 1991. Pp. 330-44.

Chilton, B. D. and Evans, C. A. (eds). *Studying the Historical Jesus: Evaluations of the State of Current Research*. NTTS 19. Leiden: Brill, 1994.

—. "Jesus and Israel's Scriptures." In Chilton and Evans (eds). *Studying the Historical Jesus: Evaluations of the State of Current Research*. NTTS 19. Leiden: Brill, 1994. Pp. 281-335.

Churgin, P. *Targum Ketubim*. New York: Horeb, 1945. [Hebrew]

Clarke, E. G. *Targum Pseudo-Jonathan of the Pentateuch: Text and Concordance*. Hoboken: Ktav, 1984.

Cohn, H. *Reflections on the Trial and Death of Jesus*. Jerusalem: Israel Law Review Association, 1967.

—. *The Trial and Death of Jesus*. New York: Harper & Row, 1971.

Collins, J. J. "The Sibylline Oracles." In J. H. Charlesworth (ed.). *The Old Testament Pseudepigrapha*. 2 vols. Garden City: Doubleday, 1983-85. Vol. 1. Pp. 317-472.

—. "The *Son of God* Text from Qumran." In M. C. De Boer (ed.). *From John to Jesus: Essays on Jesus and New Testament Christology in Honour of Marinus de Jonge.* JSNTSup 84. Sheffield: JSOT Press, 1993. Pp. 65-82.

—. "The Works of the Messiah." *DSD* 1 (1994) 98-112.

Conybeare, F. C. *Philostratus: The Life of Apollonius of Tyana.* 2 vols. LCL 16-17. London: Heinemann; Cambridge: Harvard University Press, 1912.

Cook, M. J. "Jesus and the Pharisees—The Problem as It Stands Today." *JES* 15 (1978) 441-60.

Cranfield, C. E. B. *The Gospel according to St Mark.* Cambridge: Cambridge University Press, 1977.

Cross, F. M. *The Ancient Library of Qumran.* Garden City: Doubleday, 1961.

Crossan, J. D. *The Cross that Spoke: The Origins of the Passion Narrative.* San Francisco: Harper & Row, 1988.

—. *Four Other Gospels: Shadows on the Contours of Canon.* Rev. ed. Sonoma: Polebridge, 1992.

—. *The Historical Jesus: The Life of a Mediterranean Jewish Peasant.* San Francisco: Harper-Collins, 1991.

—. *In Parables: The Challenge of the Historical Jesus.* San Francisco: Harper & Row, 1973.

—. "Materials and Methods in Historical Jesus Research." *Forum* 4.4 (1988) 3-24.

—. "Parable, Allegory, and Paradox." In D. Patte (ed.). *Semiology and the Parables.* Pittsburgh: Pickwick, 1976. Pp. 247-81.

—. "The Parable of the Wicked Husbandmen." *JBL* 90 (1971) 451-65.

—. "The Servant Parables of Jesus." *Semeia* 1 (1974) 17-62.

—. "Structuralist Analysis and the Parables of Jesus." *Semeia* 1 (1974) 192-221.

Cullmann, O. "The Significance of the Qumran Texts for Research into the Beginnings of Christianity." *JBL* 74 (1955) 213-26.

Cureton, W. *Spicilegium Syriacum: Containing Remans of Bardesan, Meliton, Ambrose and Mara bar Serapion.* London: Rivingtons, 1855.

Dahl, N. A. "Der gekreuzigte Messias." In H. Ristow and K. Matthiae (eds.). *Der historische Jesus und der kerygmatische Christus.* Berlin: Evangelische Verlagsanstalt, 1960. Pp. 157-69. ET: "The Crucified Messiah." In Dahl. *The Crucified Messiah and Other Essays.* Minneapolis: Augsburg, 1974. Pp. 1-36.

Dalman, G. *Jesus–Jeschua.* Leipzig: Hinrichs, 1922. ET: *Jesus-Jeshua: Studies in the Gospels.* London: SPCK, 1929. Repr. New York: Ktav, 1971.

—. *Die Worte Jesu: Mit Berücksichtigung des nachkanonischen jüdischen Schrifttums und der aramäistischen Sprache erörtert.* Leipzig: Hinrichs, 1898. Rev. ed., 1930. Repr. Darmstadt: Wissenschaftliche Buchgesellschaft, 1965. ET: *The Words of Jesus.* Edinburgh: T. & T. Clark, 1902.

Danby, H. *The Mishnah.* Oxford: Clarendon, 1933.

Davies, P. R. *The Damascus Covenant: An Interpretation of the "Damascus Document".* JSOTSup 25. Sheffield: JSOT Press, 1982.

de Jonge, M. *Christology in Context: The Earliest Christian Response to Jesus.* Philadelphia: Westminster, 1988.

—. "The Earliest Christian Use of *Christos*: Some Suggestions." *NTS* 32 (1986) 321-43.

—. "Messianic Ideas in Later Judaism." *TDNT* 9 (1974) 509-17.

—. *The Testaments of the Twelve Patriarchs: A Study of Their Text, Composition, and Origin.* Leiden: Brill, 1953.

—. "The Use of ὁ χριστός in the Passion Narratives." In J. Dupont (ed.). *Jésus aux origines de la christologie.* BETL 40. Gembloux: Duculot; Leuven: Leuven University Press, 1975. Pp. 169-92. Repr. in de Jonge. *Jewish Eschatology, Early Christian Christology and the Testaments of the Twelve Patriarchs: Collected Essays.* NovTSup 63. Leiden: Brill, 1991. Pp. 63-86.

—. "The Use of the Word 'Anointed' in the Time of Jesus." *NovT* 18 (1966) 132-48.

de Jonge M. and van der Woude, A. S. "11Q Melchizedek and the New Testament." *NTS* 12 (1966) 301-26.

de Lagarde, P. *Hagiographa Chaldaice.* Leipzig: Teubner, 1873.

——. *Prophetai Chaldaice.* Leipzig: Teubner, 1872.

De Moor, J. C. "The Reconstruction of the Aramaic Original of the Lord's Prayer." In P. Van der Meer and J. C. De Moor (eds.). *The Structural Analysis of Biblical and Canaanite Poetry.* JSOTSup 74. Sheffield: JSOT Press, 1988. Pp. 397-422.

de Nys, M. J. "Myth and Interpretation: Bultmann Revisted." *IJPR* 11 (1980) 27-41.

Deichgräber, R. "Zur Messiaserwartung der Damaskusschrift." *ZAW* 78 (1966) 333-43.

Deissmann, A. *Licht vom Osten: Das Neue Testament und die neuentdeckten Texte der hellenistisch-römischen Welt.* 4th ed. Tübingen: Mohr (Siebeck), 1923. *Light from the Ancient East.* New York: Harper & Row, 1927.

Denker, J. *Die theologiegeschichtliche Stellung des Petrusevangeliums: Ein Beitrag zur Frühgeschichte des Doketismus.* Bern and Frankfurt: Lang, 1975.

Derrett, J. D. M. *An Oriental Lawyer Looks at the Trial of Jesus and the Doctrine of Redemption.* London: School of Oriental and African Studies, 1966.

Dewey, K. "Peter's Curse and Cursed Peter." In W. Kelber (ed.). *The Passion in Mark.* Philadelphia: Fortress, 1976. Pp. 96-114.

Di Lella, A. A. *The Hebrew Text of Sirach.* Studies in Classical Literature 1. The Hague: Mouton, 1966.

Dibelius, M. *Die Formgeschichte des Evangeliums.* Tübingen: Mohr (Siebeck), 1919. ET: *From Tradition to Gospel.* London: James Clarke, 1971.

Díez Macho, A. *Neophyti 1: Targum Palestinense MS de la Biblioteca Vaticana.* 6 vols. Madrid and Barcelona: Consejo Superior de Investigaciones Científicas, 1968-77.

Díez Merino, L. *Targum de Salmos.* Bibliotheca Hispana Biblica 6. Madrid: Consejo Superior de Investigaciones Científicas, 1982.

Dimant, D. "New Light from Qumran on the Jewish Pseudepigrapha — 4Q390." In J. Trebolle Barrera and L. Vegas Montaner (eds.). *Proceedings of the International Congress on the Dead Sea Scrolls—Madrid, 18–21 March, 1991.* 2 vols. STDJ 11. Leiden: Brill, 1992. Vol. 2. Pp. 405-47 + pl. 25.

Dinkler, E. *Signum Crucis.* Tübingen: Mohr (Siebeck), 1967.

Dodd, C. H. *According to the Scriptures.* London: Nisbet, 1952.

——. *Historical Tradition in the Fourth Gospel.* Cambridge: Cambridge University Press, 1963.

——. *History and the Gospel.* New York: Scribner's, 1937.

——. *The Parables of Jesus.* 2nd ed. New York: Scribner's, 1961.

Donahue. J. R. *Are You the Christ? The Trial Narrative in the Gospel of Mark.* SBLDS 10. Missoula: Scholars Press, 1973.

——. "Introduction: From Passion Traditions to Passion Narrative." In W. Kelber (ed.). *The Passion in Mark.* Philadelphia: Fortress, 1976. Pp. 1-20.

Downing, F. G. *Christ and the Cynics: Jesus and Other Radical Preachers in First-Century Tradition.* JSOT Manuals 4. Sheffield: JSOT Press, 1988.

Duling, D. C. "Solomon, Exorcism, and the Son of David." *HTR* 68 (1975) 235-52.

——. "Testament of Solomon." In J. H. Charlesworth (ed.). *The Old Testament Pseudepigrapha.* 2 vols. Garden City: Doubleday, 1981-83. Vol. 1. Pp. 935-59.

Dunn, J. D. G. "Let John Be John: A Gospel for Its Time." In P. Stuhlmacher (ed.). *The Gospel and the Gospels.* Grand Rapids: Eerdmans, 1991. Pp. 293-322.

——. "Matthew 12:28/Luke 11:20—A Word of Jesus?" In W. H. Gloer (ed.). *Eschatology and the New Testament.* G. R. Beasley-Murray Festschrift. Peabody: Hendrickson, 1988. Pp. 29-49.

Dupont-Sommer, A. *The Essene Writings from Qumran.* Gloucester: Peter Smith, 1973.

——. "Exorcismes et guérisons dans les écrits de Qumran." In *Congress Volume, Oxford.* VTSup 7.

Leiden: Brill, 1960. Pp. 246-61.

—. "La Mère du Messie et la mère de l'Aspic dans un hymne de Qoumran." *RHR* 147 (1955) 174-88.

Edgar, C. C. *Catalogue général des antiquités égyptiennes du Musée du Caire.* 4 vols. Cairo: Service des antiquites de l'Egypt, 1925-40.

— (ed.). *Michigan Papyri.* Vol. 1: *Zenon Papyri.* Ann Arbor: University of Michigan Press, 1931.

Ehrlich, E. L. "Ein Beitrag zur Messiaslehre der Qumransekte." *ZAW* 68 (1956) 234-43.

Eisenman, R. H. "A Messianic Vision." *BARev* 17.6 (1991) 65.

—. "The Testament of Kohath." *BARev* 17.6 (1991) 64.

Eisenman, R. H. and Robinson, J. M. *A Facsimile Edition of the Dead Sea Scrolls.* 2 vols. Washington: Biblical Archaeology Society, 1991.

Eisenman, R. H. and Wise, M. *The Dead Sea Scrolls Uncovered.* Shaftesbury: Element, 1992.

Eisler, R. *ΙΗΣΟΥΣ ΒΑΣΙΛΕΥΣ ΟΥ ΒΑΣΙΛΕΥΣΑΣ: Die messianische Unabhängigkeitsbewegung vom Auftreten Johannes des Täufers bis zum Untergang Jakobs des Gerecten.* 2 vols. Heidelberg: Winter, 1929-30. ET: *The Messiah Jesus and John the Baptist.* London: Methuen; New York: Dial, 1931.

Elbogen, I. *Der jüdische Gottesdienst in seiner geschichtlichen Entwicklung.* 3rd ed. Frankfurt am Main: J. Kaufmann, 1931. Repr. Hildesheim: Olms, 1962. ET: *Jewish Liturgy: A Comprehensive History.* Philadelphia: Jewish Publication Society of America, 1993.

Elliott, J. K. "The Anointing of Jesus." *ExpTim* 85 (1974) 105-107.

Ellis, E. E. "Gospels Criticism: A Perspective on the State of the Art." In P. Stuhlmacher (ed.). *The Gospel and the Gospels.* Grand Rapids: Eerdmans, 1991. Pp. 26-52.

Eppstein, V. "The Historicity of the Gospel Account of the Cleansing of the Temple." *ZNW* 55 (1964) 42-58.

Epstein, I. (ed.). *The Babylonian Talmud.* 18 vols. London: Soncino, 1978.

Evans, C. A. "Authenticity Criteria in Life of Jesus Research." *CSR* 19 (1989) 6-31.

—. "'Do This and You Will Live': Targumic Coherence in Luke 10:25-28." In P. V. M. Flesher (ed.). *Targumim and New Testament Interpretation.* Targum Studies. Atlanta: Scholars Press, forthcoming.

—. "In What Sense 'Blasphemy'? Jesus before Caiaphas in Mark 14:61-64." In E. H. Lovering (ed.). *Society of Biblical Literature 1991 Seminar Papers.* SBLSP 30. Atlanta: Scholars Press, 1991. Pp. 215-34.

—. "Jesus and the 'Cave of Robbers': Towards a Jewish Context for the Temple Action." *BBR* 3 (1993) 93-110.

—. "Jesus in Non-Canonical Sources." in B. D. Chilton and C. A. Evans (eds.). *Studying the Historical Jesus: Evaluations of the State of Current Research.* NTTS 19. Leiden: Brill, 1994. Pp. 443-78.

—. "Jesus' Action in the Temple and Evidence of Corruption in the First-Century Temple." In D. J. Lull (ed.). *Society of Biblical Literature 1989 Seminar Papers.* SBLSP 28. Atlanta: Scholars Press, 1989. Pp. 522-39.

—. "Jesus' Action in the Temple: Cleansing or Portent of Destruction?" *CBQ* 51 (1989) 237-70.

—. *Life of Jesus Research: An Annotated Bibliography.* NTTS 13. Leiden: Brill, 1989.

—. "Mishna and Messiah 'in Context': Some Comments on Jacob Neusner's Proposals." *JBL* 112 (1993) 267-89.

—. "Obduracy and the Lord's Servant: Some Observations on the Use of the Old Testament in the Fourth Gospel." In C. A. Evans and W. F. Stinespring (eds.). *Early Jewish and Christian Exegesis: Studies in Memory of William Hugh Brownlee.* Homage 10. Atlanta: Scholars Press, 1987. Pp. 221-36.

—. "On the Vineyard Parables of Isaiah 5 and Mark 12." *BZ* 28 (1984) 82-86.

—. "Opposition to the Temple: Jesus and the Dead Sea Scrolls." In J. H. Charlesworth (ed.). *Jesus and the Dead Sea Scrolls.* ABRL. New York: Doubleday, 1992. Pp. 235-53.

—. "'Peter Warming Himself': The Problem of an Editorial 'Seam'." *JBL* 101 (1982) 245-49.

—. "Predictions of the Destruction of the Herodian Temple in the Pseudepigrapha, Qumran Scrolls, and Related Texts." *JSP* 10 (1992) 89-147.

—. "The Recently Published Dead Sea Scrolls and the Historical Jesus." In B. D. Chilton and C. A. Evans (eds.). *Studying the Historical Jesus: Evaluations of the Current State of Research.* NTTS 19. Leiden: Brill, 1994. Pp. 547-65.

—. *To See and Not Perceive: Isaiah 6.9-10 in Early Jewish and Christian Interpretation.* JSOTSup 64. Sheffield: JSOT Press, 1989.

—. *Word and Glory: On the Exegetical and Theological Background of John's Prologue.* JSNTSup 89. Sheffield: JSOT Press, 1993.

Evans, C. A. and Stegner, W. R. (eds.). *The Gospels and the Scriptures of Israel.* JSNTSup 104. SSEJC 3. Sheffield: JSOT Press, 1994.

Evans, C. A., Webb, R. L., and Wiebe, R. A. *Nag Hammadi Texts and the Bible: A Synopsis and Index.* NTTS 18. Leiden: Brill, 1993.

Falk, H. *Jesus the Pharisee: A New Look at the Jewishness of Jesus.* New York: Paulist, 1985.

Farmer, W. *Jesus and the Gospel: Tradition, Scripture, and Canon.* Philadelphia: Fortress, 1982.

Feldman, A. *Parables and Similes of the Rabbis: Agricultural and Pastoral.* Cambridge: Cambridge University Press, 1927.

Feldman, L. H. "Flavius Josephus Revisited: The Man, His Writings, and His Significance." *ANRW* 2.21.2 (1984) 763-862.

—. "The *Testimonium Flavium*: The State of the Question." In R. F. Berkey and S. A. Edwards (eds.). *Christological Perspectives.* H. K. McArthur Festschrift. New York: Pilgrim, 1982. Pp. 179-99, 288-93.

Ferrar, W. J. *Demonstratio Evangelica.* 2 vols. London: SPCK; New York: Macmillan, 1920.

Fiebig, P. *Altjüdische Gleichnisse und die Gleichnisse Jesu.* Tübingen: Mohr (Siebeck), 1904.

—. *Die Gleichnisreden Jesu im Lichte der rabbinischen Gleichnisse des neutestamentlichen Zeitalters.* Tübingen: Mohr (Siebeck), 1912.

—. *Jüdische Wundergeschichten des neutestamentlichen Zeitalters.* Tübingen: Mohr (Siebeck), 1911.

—. *Rabbinische Gleichnisse.* Leipzig: Hinrichs, 1929.

Finkelstein, L. "The Development of the Amida." *JQR* 16 (1925-26) 1-43, 127-69.

—. "The Origin and Development of the Qedushah." In A. A. Chiel (ed.). *Perspectives on Jews and Judaism.* W. Kelman Festschrift. New York: Rabbinical Assembly, 1978. Pp. 61-78.

—. *The Pharisees: The Sociological Background of Their Faith.* 2 vols. 3rd ed. Philadelphia: Jewish Publication Society of America, 1962.

Fitzmyer, J. A. "'4QTestimonia' and the New Testament." *TS* 18 (1957) 513-37. Repr. in Fitzmyer. *Essays on the Semitic Background of the New Testament.* London: Chapman, 1971. Repr. as SBLSBS 5. Missoula: Scholars Press, 1974. Pp. 59-89.

—. "Another View of the 'Son of Man' Debate." *JSNT* 4 (1979) 58-68.

—. "The Aramaic 'Elect of God' Text from Qumran Cave 4." *CBQ* 27 (1965) 348-72. Repr. in Fitzmyer. *Essays on the Semitic Background of the New Testament.* London: Chapman, 1971. Repr. as SBLSBS 5. Missoula: Scholars Press, 1974. Pp. 127-60.

—. "The Bar Cochba Period." In J. L. McKenzie (ed.). *The Bible in Current Catholic Thought: Gruenthaner Memorial Volume.* New York: Herder and Herder, 1962. Pp. 133-68. Repr. in Fitzmyer. *Essays on the Semitic Background of the New Testament.* London: Chapman, 1971. Repr. as SBLSBS 5. Missoula: Scholars Press, 1974. Pp. 305-54.

—. "The Contribution of Qumran Aramaic to the Study of the New Testament." *NTS* 20 (1973-74) 382-407. Repr. in Fitzmyer. *A Wandering Aramean: Collected Aramaic Essays.* SBLMS 25. Missoula: Scholars Press, 1979. Pp. 85-113.

—. "Crucifixion in Ancient Palestine, Qumran Literature, and the New Testament." *CBQ* 40 (1978) 493-513. Repr. in Fitzmyer. *To Advance the Gospel: New Testament Studies.* New York: Crossroad, 1981. Pp. 125-46.

—. *The Dead Sea Scrolls: Major Publications and Tools for Study.* SBLRBS 20. Atlanta: Scholars Press, 1990.

—. *Essays on the Semitic Background of the New Testament.* London: Chapman, 1971. Repr. as SBLSBS 5. Missoula: Scholars Press, 1974.

—. "Further Light on Melchizedek from Qumran Cave 11." *JBL* 86 (1967) 25-41.

—. *The Genesis Apocryphon of Qumran Cave I: A Commentary.* BibOr 18A. 2nd ed. Rome: Pontifical Biblical Institute, 1971.

—. *The Gospel According to Luke I-IX.* AB 28. Garden City: Doubleday, 1981.

—. *The Gospel According to Luke X-XXIV.* AB 28A. Garden City: Doubleday, 1985.

—. "The Languages of Palestine in the First Century A.D." *CBQ* 32 (1970) 501-31. Rev. and repr. in Fitzmyer. *A Wandering Aramean: Collected Aramaic Essays.* SBLMS 25. Missoula: Scholars Press, 1979. Pp. 29-56. Repr. in S. E. Porter (ed.). *The Language of the New Testament: Classic Essays.* JSNTSup 60. Sheffield: JSOT Press, 1991. Pp. 126-62.

—. "Methodology in the Study of the Aramaic Substratum of Jesus' Sayings in the New Testament." In J. Dupont (ed.). *Jésus aux origines de la christologie.* BETL 40. Gembloux: Duculot, 1975. Pp. 73-102. Rev. and repr. in Fitzmyer. *A Wandering Aramean: Collected Aramaic Essays.* SBLMS 25. Missoula: Scholars Press, 1979. Pp. 1-27.

—. *To Advance the Gospel: New Testament Studies.* New York: Crossroad, 1981.

—. *A Wandering Aramean: Collected Aramaic Essays.* SBLMS 25. Missoula: Scholars Press, 1979.

Fitzmyer, J. A. and Harrington, D. J. *A Manual of Palestinian Aramaic Texts.* BibOr 34. Rome: Pontifical Biblical Institute Press, 1978.

Flusser, D. "Healing Through the Laying-On of Hands in a Dead Sea Scroll." *IEJ* 7 (1957) 107-108. Repr. in Flusser. *Judaism and the Origins of Christianty.* Jerusalem: Magnes, 1988. Pp. 21-22.

—. *Jesus in Selbstzeugnissen und Bilddokumenten* (Rowohlts Monographien 140. Hamburg: Rowohlt, 1968. ET: *Jesus.* New York: Herder & Herder, 1969.

—. *Judaism and the Origins of Christianity.* Jerusalem: Magnes Press, 1988.

—. *Die rabbinischen Gleichnisse und der Gleichniserzähler Jesus.* Bern: Peter Lang, 1981.

—. "Sanktus und Gloria." In O. Betz et al. (eds.). *Abraham unser Vater: Juden und Christen im Gespräch über die Bibel.* O. Michel Festschrift. Leiden: Brill, 1963. Pp. 129-52.

Fortna, R. T. "Jesus and Peter at the High Priest's House: A Test Case for the Question of the Relation between Mark's and John's Gospels." *NTS* 24 (1978) 371-83.

France, R. T. "The Servant of the Lord in the Teaching of Jesus." *TynBul* 19 (1968) 26-52.

Fraser, P. M. "Hadrian and Cyrene." *JRS* 40 (1950) 77-90.

Freedman, H. and Simon, M. (eds.). *Midrash Rabbah.* 10 vols. London and New York: Soncino, 1983.

Freyne, S. *Galilee from Alexander the Great to Hadrian: A Study of Second Temple Judaism.* Wilmington: Glazier; Notre Dame: Notre Dame University Press, 1980.

—. *Galilee, Jesus and the Gospels: Literary Approaches and Historical Investigations.* Philadelphia: Fortress, 1988.

Fuchs, H. "Tacitus über die Christen." *VC* 4 (1950) 65-93.

Fuks, A. "Aspects of the Jewish Revolt in A.D. 115-117." *JRS* 15 (1961) 98-104.

—. "The Jewish Revolt in Egypt (A.D. 115–117) in the Light of the Papyri." *Aegyptus* 33 (1953) 131-58.

Fuller, R. H. *Interpreting the Miracles.* Philadelphia: Westminster, 1963. German ed. *Die Wunder Jesu in Exegese und Verkündigung.* Düsseldorf: Patmos, 1967.

Funk, R. W. (ed.). *The Gospel of Mark: Red Letter Edition.* Sonoma: Polebridge, 1991.

—. (ed.). *New Gospel Parallels.* 2 vols. Philadelphia: Fortress, 1985.

Funk, R. W. et al. (eds.). *The Parables of Jesus: Red Letter Edition.* Sonoma: Polebridge, 1988.

Funk, R. W. and Hoover, R. W. (ed.). *The Five Gospels: The Search for the Authentic Words of Jesus.* New York: Macmillan, 1993.

Gafni, I. "The Historical Background." In M. E. Stone (ed.). *Jewish Writings of the Second Temple Period.* CRINT 2.2. Philadelphia: Fortress, 1984. Pp. 1-31.

Galloway, A. D. "Religious Symbols and Demythologising." *SJT* 10 (1957) 361-69.

García Martínez, F. *Qumran and Apocalyptic: Studies on the Aramaic Texts from Qumran.* STDJ 9. Leiden: Brill, 1992.

Gärtner, B. 'טליא als Messiasbezeichnung." *SEÅ* 18-19 (1953-54) 98-108.

Gaster, M. "The Hebrew Text of one of the Testaments of the XII Patriarchs." *Proceedings of the Society of Biblical Archaeology* 16 (1894) 33-49.

Gaston, L. *No Stone on Another: Studies in the Significance of the Fall of Jerusalem in the Synoptic Gospels.* NovTSup 23. Leiden: Brill, 1970.

Geller, M. J. "Jesus' Theurgic Powers: Parallels in the Talmud and Incantation Bowls." *JJS* 28 (1977) 141-55.

George, A. "Les miracles de Jésus dans les évangiles synoptiques." *LumVie* 33 (1957) 7-24.

Georgi, D. "The Interest in Life of Jesus Theology as a Paradigm for the Social History of Biblical Criticism." *HTR* 85 (1992) 51-83.

Gnilka, J. "Die Erwartung des messianischen Hohenpriesters in den Schriften von Qumran und im Neuen Testament." *RevQ* 2 (1959-60) 395-426.

—. *Das Evangelium nach Markus.* EKKNT 2.1-2. Zurich: Benziger, 1978.

—. *Jesus von Nazaret: Botschaft und Geschichte.* HTKNTSup 3. Freiburg: Herder, 1990.

Goldin, J. *The Fathers according to Rabbi Nathan.* YJS 10. New Haven and London: Yale University Press, 1955.

Goldsmith, D. "Acts 13:33-37: A Pesher on 2 Samuel 7." *JBL* 87 (1968) 321-24.

Gordis, R. "The 'Begotten' Messiah in the Qumran Scrolls." *VT* 7 (1957) 191-94.

Goulder, M. D. "Those Outside (Mk. 4:10-12)." *NovT* 33 (1991) 289-302.

Grabbe, L. L. *Judaism from Cyrus to Hadrian.* 2 vols. Minneapolis: Fortress, 1992.

Graubard, B. "The Kaddish Prayer." In J. J. Petuchowski and M. Brocke (eds.). *The Lord's Prayer and Jewish Liturgy.* New York: Seabury, 1978. Pp. 59-72.

Green, J. B. "The Gospel of Peter: Source for a Pre-Canonical Passion Narrative?" *ZNW* 78 (1987) 293-301.

Greenhut, Z. "Burial Cave of the Caiaphas Family." *BARev* 18.5 (1992) 28-36, 76.

Grelot, P. "Étude critique de Luc 10,19." *RSR* 69 (1981) 87-100.

Grimm, W. *Jesus und das Danielbuch. Band I: Jesu Einspruch gegen das Offenbarungssystem Daniels.* ANTJ 6.1. Frankfurt am Main: Peter Lang, 1984.

Grundmann, W. "Die Frage nach der Gottessohnschaft des Messias im Lichte von Qumran." In S. Wagner (ed.). *Bibel und Qumran: Beiträge zur Erforschung der Beziehungen zwischen Bibel- und Qumranwissenschaft.* H. Bardtke Festschrift. Berlin: Evangelische Haupt-Bibelgesellschaft, 1968. Pp. 86-111.

Guelich, R. A. *Mark 1–8:26.* WBC 34A. Dallas: Word, 1989.

Gundry, R. H. *Mark: A Commentary on His Apology for the Cross.* Grand Rapids: Eerdmans, 1993.

—. *Matthew: A Commentary on His Literary and Theological Art.* Grand Rapids: Eerdmans, 1982.

—. *The Use of the Old Testament in St. Matthew's Gospel.* NovTSup 18. Leiden: Brill, 1967.

Guttmann, A. "The Significance of Miracles for Talmudic Judaism." *HUCA* 20 (1947) 363-406.

Gutwenger, E. "Die Machtweise Jesu in formgeschichtlicher Sicht." *ZKT* 89 (1967) 176-90.

Haenchen, E. *Der Weg Jesu.* Berlin: de Gruyter, 1968.

Hagner, D. A. *The Jewish Reclamation of Jesus: An Analysis and Critique of Modern Jewish Study of Jesus.* Grand Rapids: Zondervan, 1984.

Haines, C. R. *The Correspondence of Marcus Cornelius Fronto II.* LCL. Cambridge: Harvard University Press, 1919-20.

Hammer, R. *Sifre: A Tannaitic Commentary on the Book of Deuteronomy.* YJS 24. New Haven and London: Yale University Press, 1986.

—. "What Did They Bless? A Study of Mishnah Tamid 5.1." *JQR* 81 (1991) 305-24.

Hanson, P. D. "Messiahs and Messianic Figures in Proto-Apocalypticism." In J. H. Charlesworth (ed.). *The Messiah: Developments in Earliest Judaism and Christianity.* Minneapolis: Fortress, 1992. Pp. 67-75.

Hare, D. R. A. "The Lives of the Prophets." In J. H. Charlesworth (ed.). *The Old Testament Pseudepigrapha.* 2 vols. Garden City: Doubleday, 1983-85. Vol. 2. Pp. 379-99.

Harrington, D. J. "The Apocalypse of Hannah: Targum Jonathan of 1 Samuel 2:1-10." In D. M. Golomb (ed.). *"Working With No Data": Semitic and Egyptian Studies Presented to Thomas O. Lambdin.* Winona Lake: Eisenbrauns, 1987. Pp. 147-52.

—. "Pseudo-Philo." In J. H. Charlesworth (ed.). *The Old Testament Pseudepigrapha.* 2 vols. Garden City: Doubleday, 1983-85. Vol. 2. Pp. 297-377.

Harrington, D. J. and Saldarini, A. J. *Targum Jonathan of the Former Prophets.* ArBib 10. Wilmington: Glazier, 1987.

Harrington, D. J. and Strugnell, J. "Qumran Cave 4 Texts: A New Publication." *JBL* 112 (1993) 491-99.

Harris, B. F. "Apollonius of Tyana: Fact or Fiction?" *JRH* 5 (1969) 189-99.

Harvey, A. E. *Jesus and the Constraints of History: The Bampton Lectures, 1980.* London: Duckworth, 1982.

Haufe, G. "Das Menschensohn-Problem in der gegenwärtigen wissenschaftliche Diskussion." *EvT* 26 (1966) 130-41.

Hays, R. B. "The Corrected Jesus." *First Things* (May, 1994) 43-48.

Heinemann, J. *Prayer in the Talmud: Forms and Patterns.* SJ 9. Berlin and New York: de Gruyter, 1977 (orig. Hebrew, 1964).

—. "Prayers of Beth Midrash Origin." *JSS* 5 (1960) 264-80.

Heinemann, J. and Petuchowski, J. J. *Literature of the Synagogue.* New York: Behrman House, 1975.

Henderson, I. "Karl Jaspers and Demythologizing." *ExpTim* 65 (1953-54) 291-93.

—. *Myth in the New Testament.* SBT 7. London: SCM, 1952.

Hendrickx, H. *The Miracle Stories of the Synoptic Gospels.* London: Chapman; San Francisco: Harper & Row, 1987.

Hengel, M. "Aufgaben der neutestamentlichen Wissenschaft." *NTS* 40 (1994) 321-57.

—. "Entstehungszeit und Situation des Markesvangeliums." In H. Cancik (ed.). *Markus-Philologie: Historische, literargeschichtliche und stilistische Untersuchungen zum zweiten Evangelium.* WUNT 33. Tübingen: Mohr (Siebeck), 1984. ET: *Studies in the Gospel of Mark.* Philadelphia: Fortress, 1985. Pp. 1-30, 117-38.

—. *Gewalt und Gewaltlosigkeit: Zur "politischen Theologie" in neutestamentlicher Zeit.* CH 118. Stuttgart: Calwer, 1971. ET: *Victory over Violence.* Philadelphia: Fortress, 1973.

—. "Das Gleichnis von den Weingärtnern Mc 12:1-12 im Lichte der Zenonpapyri und der rabbinischen Gleichnisse." *ZNW* 59 (1968) 1-39.

—. "Hadrians Politik gegenüber Juden und Christen." *JANESCU* 16-17 (1984-85) 153-82.

—. *The "Hellenization" of Judaea in the First Century after Christ.* London: SCM; Philadelphia: Trinity Press International, 1989.

—. "Jesus, der Messias Israels." In I. Gruenwald et al. (eds.). *Messiah and Christos: Studies in the*

Jewish Origins of Christianity. D. Flusser Festschrift. TSAJ 32. Tübingen: Mohr (Siebeck), 1992. Pp. 155-76.

—. *Jews, Greeks and Barbarians.* London: SCM; Philadelphia: Fortress, 1980.

—. *Judentum und Hellenismus: Studien zu ihrer Begegnung unter besonderer Berücksichtigung Palästinas bis zur Mitte des 2 Jh.s v.Chr.* WUNT 10. Tübingen: Mohr (Siebeck), 1973. ET: *Judaism and Hellenism: Studies in Their Encounter in Palestine during the Early Hellenistic Period.* 2 vols. London: SCM; Philadelphia: Fortress, 1974.

—. "Messianische Hoffnung und politischer 'Radikalismus' in der 'jüdisch-hellenistischen Diaspora.' Zur Frage der Voraussetzungen des jüdischen Aufstandes unter Trajan A.D. 115-117." In D. Hellhom (ed.). *Apocalypticism in the Mediterranean World and the Near East. Proceedings of the International Colloquium on Apocalypticism. Uppsala, August 12-17, 1979.* Tübingen: Mohr (Siebeck), 1983. Pp. 655-86.

—. "*Mors turpissima crucis:* Die Kreuzigung in der antiken Welt und die 'Torheit' des 'Wortes vom Kreuz'." In J. Friedrich, W. Pöhlmann, and P. Stuhlmacher (eds.). *Rechtfertigung: Festschrift für Ernst Käsemann zum 70. Geburtstag.* Tübingen: Mohr (Siebeck), 1976. Pp. 125-84. ET: *Crucifixion: In the Ancient World and the Folly of the Message of the Cross.* London: SCM; Philadelphia: Fortress, 1977.

—. *Nachfolge und Charisma: Eine exegetisch-religionsgeschichtliche Studie zu Mt 8,21f und Jesu Ruf in die Nachfolge.* BZNW 34. Berlin: de Gruyter, 1968. ET: *The Charismatic Leader and His Followers.* Edinburgh: T. & T. Clark; New York: Crossroad, 1981.

—. "Probleme des Markusevangeliums." In P. Stuhlmacher (ed.). *Das Evangelium und die Evangelien.* WUNT 28. Tübingen: Mohr (Siebeck), 1983. ET: "Problems in the Gospel of Mark." In P. Stuhlmacher (ed.). *The Gospel and the Gospels.* Grand Rapids: Eerdmans, 1991. Pp. 209-51.

—. "Proseuche und Synagoge." In G. Jeremias and H. W. Kuhn (eds.). *Tradition und Glaube.* K. G. Kuhn Festschrift. Göttingen: Vandenhoeck & Ruprecht, 1971. Pp. 157-84.

—. "Proseuche und Synagoge: Jüdische Gemeinde, Gotteshaus and Gottesdienst in der Diaspora und in Palästina." In J. Gutmann (ed.). *The Synagogue: Studies in Origins, Archaeology and Architecture.* New York: Ktav, 1975. Pp. 27-54.

—. "'Setze dich zu meiner Rechten!' Die Inthronisation Christi zur Rechten Gottes und Psalm 110,1." In M. Philonenko (ed.). *Le Trône de Dieu.* WUNT 69. Tübingen: Mohr (Siebeck), 1993. Pp. 108-94.

—. *Der Sohn Gottes: Die Entstehung der Christologie und die jüdisch-hellenistische Religionsgeschichte.* Tübingen: Mohr (Siebeck), 1975. ET: *The Son of God: The Origin of Christology and the History of Jewish-Hellenistic Religion.* London: SCM; Philadelphia: Fortress, 1976.

—. "Der stellvertretende Sühnetod Jesu: Ein Beitrag zur Entstehung des urchristlichen Kerygmas." *IKZ* 9 (1980) 1-25, 135-47. ET: *The Atonement: The Origins of the Doctrine in the New Testament.* London: SCM; Philadelphia: Fortress, 1981.

—. *Studies in the Gospel of Mark.* Philadelphia: Fortress, 1985.

—. *War Jesus Revolutionär?* CH 110. Stuttgart: Calwer, 1970. ET: *Was Jesus a Revolutionist?* Philadelphia: Fortress, 1971.

—. *Die Zeloten: Untersuchungen zur jüdischen Freiheitsbewegung in der Zeit von Herodes I. bis 70 n. Chr.* AGJU 1. Leiden: Brill, 1961. 2nd ed., 1976. ET: *The Zealots: Investigations into the Jewish Freedom Movement in the Period from Herod I until 70 A.D.* Edinburgh: T. & T. Clark, 1989.

Hennecke, E. and Schneemelcher, W. (eds.). *New Testament Apocrypha.* 2 vols. London: Lutterworth; Philadelphia: Westminster, 1963. Rev. ed. Cambridge: James Clarke; Louisville: Westminster/John Knox, 1991.

Héring, J. "Encore le messianisme dans les écrits de Qoumran." *RHPR* 41 (1961) 160-62.

Higgins, A. J. B. "The Priestly Messiah." *NTS* 13 (1966-67) 211-39.

Hill, D. "Jesus before the Sanhedrin—On What Charge?" *IBS* 7 (1985) 174-86.

—. *New Testament Prophecy*. Atlanta: John Knox, 1979.

Hofius, O. *Jesu Tischgemeinschaft mit den Sündern*. CH 86. Stuttgart: Calwer, 1967.

—. "Unbekannte Jesusworte." In P. Stuhlmacher (ed.). *Das Evangelium und die Evangelien*. WUNT 28. Tübingen: Mohr (Siebeck), 1983. Pp. 355-82. ET: "Unknown Sayings of Jesus." In Stuhlmacher (ed.). *The Gospel and the Gospels*. Grand Rapids: Eerdmans, 1991. Pp. 336-60.

Holladay, C. H. *Theios Aner in Hellenistic Judaism: A Critique of the Use of This Category in New Testament Christology*. SBLDS 40. Missoula: Scholars Press, 1977.

Hooker, M. D. *The Gospel according to Saint Mark*. BNTC. London: Black, 1991.

—. *Jesus and the Servant: The Influence of the Servant Concept of Deutero-Isaiah in the New Testament*. London: SPCK, 1959.

—. "On Using the Wrong Tool." *Th* 75 (1972) 570-81.

—. "Traditions about the Temple in the Sayings of Jesus." *BJRL* 70 (1988) 7-19.

Horbury, W. "The Temple Tax." In E. Bammel and C. F. D. Moule (eds.). *Jesus and the Politics of His Day*. Cambridge: Cambridge University Press, 1984. Pp. 265-86.

Horbury, W. and Noy, D. *Jewish Inscriptions of Graeco-Roman Egypt*. Cambridge: Cambridge University Press, 1992.

Horgan, M. *Pesharim: Qumran Interpretations of Biblical Books*. CBQMS 8. Washington: Catholical Biblical Association, 1979.

—. *Prophecy in Early Christianity and the Ancient Mediterranean World*. Grand Rapids: Eerdmans, 1983.

Horsley, R. A. "Ancient Jewish Banditry and the Revolt against Rome, A.D. 66–70." *CBQ* 43 (1981) 409-32.

—. "The Death of Jesus." In B. D. Chilton and C. A. Evans (eds.). *Studying the Historical Jesus: Evaluations of the State of Current Research*. NTTS 19. Leiden: Brill, 1994. Pp. 395-422.

—. "High Priests and the Politics of Roman Palestine: A Contextual Analysis of the Evidence in Josephus." *JSJ* 17 (1986) 23-55.

—. *Jesus and the Spiral of Violence: Popular Jewish Resistance in Roman Palestine*. San Francisco: Harper & Row, 1987.

—. "Josephus and the Bandits." *JSJ* 10 (1979) 37-63.

—. "'Like One of the Prophets of Old': Two Types of Popular Prophets at the Time of Jesus." *CBQ* 47 (1985) 435-63.

—. "Menahem in Jerusalem: A Brief Messianic Episode among the Sicarii—Not 'Zealot Messianism'." *NovT* 27 (1985) 334-48.

—. "Popular Messianic Movements around the Time of Jesus." *CBQ* 46 (1984) 471-95.

—. "Popular Prophetic Movements at the Time of Jesus: Their Principal Features and Social Origins." *JSNT* 26 (1986) 3-27.

—. "The Sicarii: Ancient Jewish 'Terrorists'." *JR* 59 (1979) 435-58.

—. *Sociology and the Jesus Movement*. New York: Crossroad, 1989.

—. "The Zealots: Their Origin, Relationship and Importance in the Jewish Revolt." *NovT* 28 (1986) 159-92.

Horsley, R. A. and Hanson, J. S. *Bandits, Prophets, and Messiahs: Popular Movements at the Time of Jesus*. Minneapolis: Winston, 1985; San Francisco: Harper & Row, 1988.

Horton, F. L. *The Melchizedek Tradition*. SNTSMS 30. Cambridge: Cambridge University Press, 1976.

Howard, G. *The Gospel of Matthew according to a Primitive Hebrew Text*. Macon: Mercer University Press, 1987.

—. "A Note on Shem-Tob's Hebrew Matthew and the Gospel of John." *JSNT* 47 (1992) 117-26.

Hubaut, M. "La parabole des vignerons homicides: son authenticité, sa visée première." *RTL* 6 (1975) 51-61.

Hull, J. M. *Hellenistic Magic and the Synoptic Tradition.* SBT 28. Naperville: Allenson, 1974.

Hultgård, A. *L'Eschatologie des Testaments des Douze Patriarches.* 2 vols. Stockholm: Almquist & Wiksell, 1977.

Hunt, A. S. and Edgar, C. C. *Select Papyri.* 2 vols. LCL 266, 282. London: Heinemann; Cambridge: Harvard University Press, 1932-34.

Isaac, E. "1 (Ethiopic Apocalypse of) Enoch." In J. H. Charlesworth (ed.). *The Old Testament Pseudepigrapha.* 2 vols. Garden City: Doubleday, 1983-85. Vol. 1. Pp. 5-89.

Jacobs, I. "Kingship and Holiness in the Third Benediction of the Amidah and in the Yozer." *JJS* 41 (1990) 62-74.

Jacobson, A. D. *The First Gospel: An Introduction to Q.* Sonoma: Polebridge, 1992.

James, M. R. *The Apocryphal New Testament.* Oxford: Clarendon, 1953.

Jastrow, M. *A Dictionary of the Targumim, the Talmud Babli and Yerushalmi, and the Midrashic Literature.* 2 vols. London: Putnam, 1895-1903. Repr. New York: Pardes, 1950.

Jeremias, J. *Die Abendmahlsworte Jesu.* 4th ed. Göttingen: Vandenhoeck & Ruprecht, 1967. ET: *The Eucharistic Words of Jesus.* London: SCM, 1990.

——. *Die Gleichnisse Jesu.* 6th ed. Göttingen: Vandenhoeck & Ruprecht, 1962. ET: *The Parables of Jesus.* London: SCM; New York: Scribner's, 1963.

——. *Jerusalem zur Zeit Jesu.* Göttingen: Vandenhoeck & Ruprecht, 1962. ET: *Jerusalem in the Time of Jesus.* London: SCM, 1969.

——. *Neutestamentliche Theologie. Erster Teil: Die Verkündigung Jesu.* Gütersloh: Mohn, 1971. ET: *New Testament Theology: The Proclamation of Jesus.* London: SCM; New York: Scribner's, 1971.

——. *Unbekannte Jesusworte.* Zürich: Zwingli, 1947. 2nd ed. Gütersloh: Bertelsmann, 1951. 3rd ed., 1961. ET: *The Unknown Sayings of Jesus.* London: SPCK, 1957. 2nd ed., 1964.

——. *Das Vater-Unser im Lichte der neueren Forschung.* 3rd ed. CH 50. Stuttgart: Calwer, 1965. ET: "The Lord's Prayer in the Light of Recent Research." In J. Jeremias. *The Prayers of Jesus.* SBT 6. London: SCM, 1967. Pp. 82-107.

Johnson, E. S. "Mark 10:46-52: Blind Bartimaeus." *CBQ* 40 (1978) 191-204.

Johnson, M. D. "Life of Adam and Eve." In J. H. Charlesworth (ed.). *The Old Testament Pseudepigrapha.* 2 vols. Garden City: Doubleday, 1983-85. Vol. 2. Pp. 249-95.

Johnston, R. M. "Appendix: Parables among the Pharisees and Early Rabbis." In J. Neusner. *A History of the Mishnaic Law of Purities. Part XIII: Miqvaot.* SJLA 6. Leiden: Brill, 1976. Pp. 224-26.

——. *Parabolic Interpretations Attributed to Tannaim.* Dissertation. West Hartford: Hartford Seminary Foundation, 1978.

Jongeling, B. et al. *Aramaic Texts from Qumran.* SSS 4. Leiden: Brill, 1976.

Juel, D. "The Lord's Prayer in the Gospels of Matthew and Luke." *PSBSup* 2 (1992) 56-70.

——. *Messiah and Temple: The Trial of Jesus in the Gospel of Mark.* SBLDS 31. Missoula: Scholars Press, 1977.

Kanael, B. "The Historical Background of the Coins 'Year Four . . . of the Redemption of Zion'." *BASOR* 129 (1953) 18-20.

Käsemann, E. *Essays on New Testament Themes.* SBT 41. London: SCM, 1964.

——. "Sentences of Holy Law in the New Testament." In Käsemann. *New Testament Questions of Today.* Philadelphia: Fortress, 1969. Pp. 66-81.

Kee, H. C. "The Bearing of the Dead Sea Scrolls on Understanding Jesus." In R. J. Hoffmann and G. A. Larue (eds.). *Jesus in History and Myth.* Buffalo: Prometheus, 1986. Pp. 54-75.

——. *Medicine, Miracle and Magic in New Testament Times.* SNTSMS 55. Cambridge: Cambridge University Press, 1986.

——. *Miracle in the Early Christian World: A Study in Sociohistorical Method.* New Haven and London: Yale University Press, 1983.

—. "Testaments of the Twelve Patriarchs." In J. H. Charlesworth (ed.). *The Old Testament Pseudepigrapha.* 2 vols. Garden City: Doubleday, 1983-85. Vol. 1. Pp. 775-828.

Kelber, W. H. (ed.). *The Passion in Mark: Studies on Mark 14–16.* Philadelphia: Fortress, 1976.

Keller, E. and Keller, M.-L. *Der Streit um die Wunder.* Gütersloh: Mohn, 1968. ET: *Miracles in Dispute: A Continuing Debate.* London: SCM, 1969. Repr. 1984.

Kempthorne, R. "The Marcan Text of Jesus' Answer to the High Priest." *NovT* 19 (1977) 198-208.

Kenyon, F. G. and Bell, H. I. (eds.). *Greek Papyri in the British Museum.* 5 vols. London: Oxford University Press, 1893-1917.

Kertelge, K. *Die Wunder Jesu im Markusevangelium: Eine redaktionsgeschichtliche Untersuchung.* SANT 23. Munich: Kösel, 1970.

Keylock, L. R. "Bultmann's Law of Increasing Distinctiveness." In G. F. Hawthorne (ed.). *Current Issues in Biblical and Patristic Interpretation.* M. C. Tenney Festschrift. Grand Rapids: Eerdmans, 1975. Pp. 193-210.

Kim, S. *The "Son of Man" as the Son of God.* WUNT 30. Tübingen: Mohr (Siebeck), 1983.

Kimelman, R. "The Daily 'Amidah and the Rhetoric of Redemption." *JQR* 79 (1988-89) 165-97.

Kirchschläger, W. "Bartimäus – Paradigma einer Wundererzählung (Mk 10,46-52 par)." In F. Van Segbroeck et al. (eds.). *The Four Gospels 1992.* F. Neirynck Festschrift. 3 vols. BETL 100. Leuven: Peeters, 1992. Vol. 2. Pp. 1105-23.

—. "Exorzismus in Qumran?" *Kairos* 18 (1976) 135-53.

Klauck, H.-J. *Allegorie und Allegorese in synoptischen Gleichnistexten.* Münster: Aschendorff, 1978.

Klausner, J. *Jesus of Nazareth: His Life, Times, and Teaching.* London: Allen & Unwin, 1925 (orig. Hebrew, 1922).

Klein, M. L. *The Fragment Targums of the Pentateuch According to their Extant Sources.* AnBib 76. 2 vols. Rome: Biblical Institute Press, 1980.

Klijn, A. F. J. "2 (Syriac Apocalypse of) Baruch." In J. H. Charlesworth (ed.). *The Old Testament Pseudepigrapha.* 2 vols. Garden City: Doubleday, 1983-85. Vol. 1. Pp. 615-52.

Kloppenborg, J. A. *The Formation of Q: Trajectories in Ancient Wisdom Collections.* SAC. Philadelphia: Fortress, 1987.

—. *Q Parallels.* Sonoma: Polebridge, 1988.

Knibb, M. A. *The Qumran Community.* Cambridge: Cambridge University Press, 1987.

—. "The Teacher of Righteousness—A Messianic Title?" In P. R. Davies and R. T. White (eds.). *A Tribute to Geza Vermes: Essays on Jewish and Christian Literature and History.* JSOTSup 100. Sheffield: JSOT Press, 1990. Pp. 51-65.

Kobelski, P. J. *Melchizedek and Melchireša'.* CBQMS 10. Washington: Catholic Biblical Association, 1981.

Koch, D.-A. *Die Bedeutung der Wundererzählungen für die Christologie des Markusevangeliums.* BZNW 42. Berlin: de Gruyter, 1975.

Koch, W. *Der Prozess Jesu: Versuch eines Tatsachenberichtes.* Berlin and Köln: Kiepenheuer and Witsch, 1969.

Koester, H. *Ancient Christian Gospels: Their History and Development.* London: SCM; Philadelphia: Trinity Press International, 1990.

—. "Apocryphal and Canonical Gospels." *HTR* 73 (1980) 105-30.

—. "The Historical Jesus and the Historical Situation of the Quest: An Epilogue." In B. D. Chilton and C. A. Evans (eds.). *Studying the Historical Jesus: Evaluations of the State of Research.* NTTS 19. Leiden: Brill, 1994. Pp. 535-45.

—. "History and Development of Mark's Gospel: From Mark to Secret Mark and 'Canonical' Mark." In B. C. Corley (ed.). *Colloquy on New Testament Studies: A Time for Reappraisal and Fresh Approaches.* Macon: Mercer University Press, 1983. Pp. 35-58.

—. *Synoptische Überlieferung bei den apostolischen Vätern*. TU 65. Berlin: Akademie, 1957.

—. "Überlieferung und Geschichte der frühchristlichen Evangelienliteratur." *ANRW* 2.25.2 (1984) 1463-1542.

Koskenniemi, E. *Apollonius von Tyana in der neutestamentlichen Exegese*. WUNT 2.61. Tübingen: Mohr (Siebeck), 1994.

Krupp, M. "The Palestinian Talmud." In S. Safrai (ed.). *The Literature of the Sages. First Part: Oral Tora, Halakha, Mishna, Tosefta, Talmud, External Tractates*. CRINT 2.3. Assen: Van Gorcum; Philadelphia: Fortress, 1984. Pp. 303-22.

Kuhn, K. G. *Achtzehngebet und Vaterunser und der Reim*. WUNT 1. Tübingen: Mohr (Siebeck), 1950.

—. "Die beiden Messias in den Qumrantexten und die Messiasvorstellung in der rabbinischen Literatur." *ZAW* 70 (1958) 200-208.

—. "Die beiden Messias Aarons und Israels." *NTS* 1 (1954-55) 168-79. ET: "The Two Messiahs of Aaron and Israel." In K. Stendahl (ed.). *The Scrolls and the New Testament*. New York: Harper & Row, 1957. Pp. 54-64.

Kümmel, W. G. "Das Gleichnis von den bösen Weingärtnern (Mk 12, 1–9)." In O. Cullmann and P. H. Menaud (eds.). *Aux Sources de la Tradition Chrétienne, Mélanges offerts à Maurice Goguel*. Bibliothèque Théologique. Neuchâtel and Paris: Delachaux et Niestle, 1950. Pp. 120-31. Repr. in W. G. Kümmel. *Heilsgeschehen und Geschichte*. Ed. by E. Grässer et al. MTS 3. Marburg: N. G. Elwert, 1965. Pp. 207-17.

—. *Verheissung und Erfüllung: Untersuchung zur eschatologischen Verkündigung Jesu*. Basel: Majer, 1945. 2nd ed. Zürich: Zwingli, 1953. ET: *Promise and Fulfillment: The Eschatological Preaching of Jesus*. SBT 23. London: SCM; Naperville: Allenson, 1957.

Kurfess, A. "Tacitus über die Christen." *VC* 5 (1951) 148-49.

Kysar, R. *The Fourth Evangelist and His Gospel: An Examination of Contemporary Scholarship*. Minneapolis: Augsburg, 1975.

Lake, K. *Apostolic Fathers I*. LCL 24. London: Heinemann; Cambridge: Harvard University Press, 1912.

Lake, K. and Oulton, J. E. L. *Eusebius: Ecclesiastical History*. 2 vols. LCL 153, 265. London: Heinemann; Cambridge: Harvard University Press, 1926-32.

Lane, W. L. *The Gospel of Mark*. NIC. Grand Rapids: Eerdmans, 1974.

Laperrousaz, E. M. "Le mère du Messie et la mère de l'Aspic dans les Hymnes de Qumrân: Quelques remarques sur la structure de 1QH III, 1–18." In P. Lévy and E. Wolff (eds.). *Mélanges d'histoire des religions offerts à H. C. Puech*. Paris: Presses universitaires de France, 1974. Pp. 173-85.

Lapide, P. *Der Rabbi von Nazaret: Wandlungen des jüdischen Jesusbildes*. Trier: Spee, 1974.

—. *Wer war schuld an Jesu Tod?* Gütersloh: Mohn, 1987.

LaSor, W. S. "The Messiahs of Aaron and Israel." *VT* 6 (1956) 425-29.

—. "The Messianic Idea in Qumran." In M. Ben-Horin et al. (eds.). *Studies and Essays in Honor of Abraham A. Neuman*. Leiden: Brill, 1962. Pp. 343-64.

Latourelle, R. "Authenticité historique des miracles de Jésus: Essai de critériologie." *Greg* 54 (1973) 225-62.

—. "Critères d'authenticité des Évangiles." *Greg* 55 (1974) 609-38.

—. *Miracles de Jésus et théologie du miracle*. Paris: Cerf; Montreal: Bellarmin, 1986. ET: *The Miracles of Jesus and the Theology of Miracles*. New York: Paulist, 1988.

Laurin, R. B. "The Problem of Two Messiahs in the Qumran Scrolls." *RevQ* 4 (1963-64) 39-52.

Lawler, E. G. *David Friedrich Strauss and His Critics: The Life of Jesus Debate in Early Nineteenth-Century German Journals*. New York: Lang, 1986.

Le Déaut, R. *The Message of the New Testament and the Aramaic Bible*. SubBib 5. Rome: Biblical Institute, 1982.

—. "Targumic Literature and New Testament Interpretation." *BTB* 4 (1974) 243-89.

Lee, G. M. "The Inscription on the Cross." *PEQ* 100 (1968) 144.

Lee, M. Y.-H. *Jesus und die jüdische Autorität.* FB 56. Würzburg: Echter, 1986.

Leivestad, R. "Enthalten die Segenssprüche 1QSb eine Segnung des Hohenpriesters der messianischen Zeit?" *ST* 31 (1977) 137-45.

Lentzen-Deis, F. "Kriterien für die historische Beurteilung der Jesusüberlieferung in den Evangelien." In K. Kertelge (ed.). *Rückfrage nach Jesus: Zur Methodik und Bedeutung der Frage nach dem historischen Jesus.* QD 63. Freiburg: Herder, 1974. Pp. 78-117.

Levey, S. H. *The Messiah: An Aramaic Interpretation.* MHUC 2. Cincinnati: Hebrew Union College–Jewish Institute of Religion, 1974.

Lévi, I. *The Hebrew Text of the Book of Ecclesiasticus.* SSS 3. Leiden: Brill, 1904.

Lewis, N. *The Documents from the Bar Kokhba Period in the Cave of Letters: Greek Papyri.* Jerusalem: Israel Exploration Society, 1989.

Licht, J. "An Ideal Town Plan from Qumran—The Description of the New Jerusalem." *IEJ* 29 (1979) 45-59.

Lietzmann, H. "Der Prozess Jesu." *Sitzungsberichte der Preussischen Akadamie der Wissenschaften in Berlin* 14 (1931) 313-22.

Lifshitz, B. "Papyrus grecs du désert de Juda." *Aegyptus* 42 (1962) 240-56 + pls.

Lightfoot, J. B. and Harmer, J. R. *The Apostolic Fathers.* 2nd ed. Rev. and ed. by M. W. Holmes. Grand Rapids: Baker, 1989.

Lindars, B. "Elijah, Elisha and the Gospel Miracles." In C. F. D. Moule (ed.). *Miracles: Cambridge Studies in their Philosophy and History.* London: Mowbray, 1965. Pp. 61-79.

Lindeskog, G. "Der Prozess Jesu im jüdisch-christlichen Religionsgespräch." In O. Betz et al. (eds.). *Abraham unser Vater: Juden und Christen im Gespräch über die Bibel.* O. Michel Festschrift. AGJU 5. Leiden: Brill, 1963. Pp. 325-36.

Linnemann, E. *Gleichnisse Jesu: Einführung und Auslegung.* Göttingen: Vandenhoeck & Ruprecht, 1961. ET: *Parables of Jesus: Introduction and Exposition.* London: SPCK, 1966.

Liver, J. "The Doctrine of the Two Messiahs in the Sectarian Literature in the Time of the Second Commonwealth." *HTR* 52 (1959) 149-85.

Lohmeyer, E. *Das Vater-Unser.* Göttingen: Vandenhoeck & Ruprecht, 1947.

Lohse, E. *Geschichte des Leidens und Sterbens Jesu Christi.* Gütersloh: Mohn, 1964.

—. "Der König aus Davids Geschlecht: Bemerkungen zur messianischen Erwartung der Synagoge." In O. Betz et al. (eds.). *Abraham unser Vater: Juden und Christen im Gespräch über die Bibel.* O. Michel Festschrift. AGJU 5. Leiden: Brill, 1963. Pp. 337-45.

—. *Die Texte aus Qumran: Hebräisch und Deutsch.* Munich: Kösel; Darmstadt: Wissenschaftliche Buchgesellschaft, 1964. 2nd ed., 1971.

Longenecker, R. N. "Literary Criteria in Life of Jesus Research: An Evaluation and Proposal." In G. F. Hawthorne (ed.). *Current Issues in Biblical and Patristic Interpretation.* M. C. Tenney Festschrift. Grand Rapids: Eerdmans, 1975. Pp. 217-29.

—. "'Son of Man' as a Self-Designation of Jesus." *JETS* 12 (1969) 151-58.

Lövestam, E. "Jesus Fils de David chez les Synoptiques." *ST* 28 (1974) 97-109.

Lübbe, J. "A Reinterpretation of 4QTestimonia." *RevQ* 12 (1985-87) 187-97.

Lunt, H. G. "Ladder of Jacob." In J. H. Charlesworth (ed.). *The Old Testament Pseudepigrapha.* 2 vols. Garden City: Doubleday, 1983-85. Vol. 2. Pp. 401-11.

Luz, U. "Rückkehr des mythologischen Weltbildes: Überlegungen bei einer neuen Lektüre von Bultmann's Programm der Entmythologisierung." *Ref* 33 (1984) 448-53.

Mack, B. L. *The Lost Gospel: The Book of Q & Christian Origins.* San Francisco: HarperCollins, 1993.

—. *A Myth of Innocence: Mark and Christian Origins.* Philadelphia: Fortress, 1988.

Mackey, J. P. *Jesus the Man and the Myth.* New York: Paulist, 1979.

Macquarrie, J. "A Generation of Demythologizing." In J. P. van Noppen (ed.). *Theolinguistics.* Brussels: Vrije Universiteit, 1981. Pp. 143-58.

Mahaffy, J. P. and Smyly, J. G. (eds.). *The Flinders Petrie Papyri with Transcriptions, Commentaries and Index.* 3 vols. Proceedings of the Royal Irish Academy 8, 9, and 11. Dublin: Academy House, 1891-1905.

Maier, G. "Zur neutestamentlichen Wunderexegese im 19. und 20. Jahrhundert." In D. Wenham and C. L. Blomberg (eds.). *The Miracles of Jesus.* Gospel Perspectives 6. Sheffield: JSOT Press, 1986. Pp. 49-87.

Maier, J. *Jesus von Nazareth in der talmudischen Überlieferung.* ErFor 82. Darmstadt: Wissenschaftliche Buchgesellschaft, 1978.

——. *The Temple Scroll: An Introduction, Translation & Commentary.* JSOTSup 34. Sheffield: JSOT Press, 1985.

——. *Die Texte vom Toten Meer.* 2 vols. Munich and Basel: Reinhardt, 1960.

Malina, B. J. and Rohrbaugh, R. L. *Social-Science Commentary on the Synoptic Gospels.* Minneapolis: Fortress, 1992.

Maloney, E. C. *Semitic Interference in Marcan Syntax.* SBLDS 51. Chico: Scholars Press, 1981.

Manson, T. W. "The Lord's Prayer." *BJRL* 38 (1955-56) 99-113.

——. *The Teaching of Jesus: Studies of Its Form and Content.* 2nd ed. Cambridge: Cambridge University Press, 1935.

Marcus, J. "Mark 14:61: 'Are You the Messiah-Son-of-God?'" *NovT* 31 (1989) 125-41.

——. *The Way of the Lord: Christological Exegesis of the Old Testament in the Gospel of Mark.* Louisville: Westminster/John Knox, 1992.

Marshall, I. H. *Commentary on Luke.* NIGTC. Grand Rapids: Eerdmans, 1978.

——. "The Synoptic Son of Man Sayings in Recent Discussion." *NTS* 12 (1966) 327-51.

Martin, E. G. "Eldad and Modad." In J. H. Charlesworth (ed.). *The Old Testament Pseudepigrapha.* 2 vols. Garden City: Doubleday, 1983-85. Vol. 2. Pp. 463-65.

Marxsen, W. *Mark the Evangelist: Studies on the Redaction History of the Gospel.* Nashville: Abingdon, 1969.

Matson, M. A. "The Contribution to the Temple Cleansing by the Fourth Gospel." In E. H. Lovering (ed.). *Society of Biblical Literature 1992 Seminar Papers.* SBLSP 31. Atlanta: Scholars Press, 1992. Pp. 489-506.

McArthur, H. K. "The Burden of Proof in Historical Jesus Research." *ExpTim* 82 (1970-71) 116-19.

McArthur, H. K. and Johnston, R. M. *They Also Taught in Parables: Rabbinic Parables from the First Centuries of the Christian Era.* Grand Rapids: Zondervan, 1990.

McNamara, M. *The New Testament and the Palestinian Targum to the Pentateuch.* AnBib 27A. 2nd ed. Rome: Biblical Institute, 1978.

——. *Targum and Testament: Aramaic Paraphrases of the Hebrew Bible: A Light on the New Testament.* Grand Rapids: Eerdmans, 1972.

Mealand, D. L. "The Dissimilarity Test." *SJT* 31 (1978) 41-50.

Meeks, W. A. *The Prophet-King: Moses Traditions and the Johannine Christology.* NovTSup 14. Leiden: Brill, 1967.

Meier, J. P. "The Historical Jesus: Rethinking Some Concepts." *TS* 51 (1990) 3-24.

——. "Jesus in Josephus: A Modest Proposal." *CBQ* 52 (1990) 76-103.

——. *A Marginal Jew: Rethinking the Historical Jesus. Volume One: The Roots of the Problem and the Person.* ABRL; New York: Doubleday, 1991.

Merkel, H. "Appendix: the 'Secret Gospel' of Mark." In W. Schneemelcher (ed.). *New Testament Apocrypha. Volume One: Gospels and Related Writings.* Rev. ed. Cambridge: Clarke; Louisville: Westminster/John Knox, 1991. Pp. 106-109.

——. "Auf den Spuren des Urmarkus? Ein neuer Fund und seine Beurteilung." *ZTK* 71 (1974) 123-

44.

Merkley. P. "New Quests for Old: One Historian's Observations on a Bad Bargain." *CJT* 16 (1970) 203-18.

Meyer, B. F. *The Aims of Jesus.* London: SCM, 1979.

Meyer, R. *Der Prophet aus Galiläa: Studie zum Jesusbild der drei ersten Evangelien.* Repr. Darmstadt: Wissenschaftliche Buchgesellschaft, 1970 (orig. 1940).

Michel, O. "Die Rettung Israels und die Rolle Roms nach den Reden im 'Bellum Iudaicum': Analysen und Perspektiven." *ANRW* 2.21.2 (1984) 945-76.

—. "Studien zu Josephus: Simon bar Giora." *NTS* 14 (1968) 402-408.

Michel, O. and Betz, O. "Von Gott gezeugt." In W. Eltester (ed.). *Judentum Urchristentum Kirche.* J. Jeremias Festschrift. BZNW 26. Berlin: Töpelmann, 1960. Pp. 2-23.

Michl, J. "Der Weibessame (Gen 3,15) in Spätjudentum und frühchristlicher Auffassung." *Bib* 33 (1952) 371-401.

Mildenberg, L. "Bar Kokhba Coins and Documents." *HSCP* 84 (1980) 311-35.

—. *The Coinage of the Bar Kokhba War.* Typos: Monographien zur antiken Numismatik 6. Frankfurt am Main: Sauerländer, 1984.

Milik, J. T. *The Books of Enoch.* Oxford: Clarendon, 1976.

—. "Milkî-ṣedeq et Milkî-reša' dans les anciens écrits juifs et chrétiens." *JJS* 23 (1972) 95-144.

—. *Ten Years of Discovery in the Wilderness of Judaea.* SBT 26. London: SCM, 1959.

Miller, M. P. "The Function of Isa 61:1-2 in 11Q Melchizedek." *JBL* 88 (1969) 467-69.

Miller, R. J. "The (A)Historicity of Jesus' Temple Demonstration: A Test Case in Methodology." In E. H. Lovering (ed.). *Society of Biblical Literature 1991 Seminar Papers.* SBLSP 30. Atlanta: Scholars Press, 1991. Pp. 235-52.

—. (ed.). *The Complete Gospels.* Sonoma: Polebridge, 1992.

Milligan, G. *Selections from the Greek Papyri.* Cambridge: Cambridge University Press, 1912.

Miner, D. F. "A Suggested Reading for 11Q Melchizedek 17." *JSJ* 2 (1971) 144-48.

Moore, C. H. *Tacitus III.* LCL 249. London: Heinemann; Cambridge: Harvard University Press, 1931.

Moule, C. F. D. *The Gospel According to Mark.* Cambridge: Cambridge University Press, 1965.

—. "Neglected Features in the Problem of the Son of Man." In Moule. *Essays in New Testament Interpretation.* Cambridge: Cambridge University Press, 1982. Pp. 75-90.

—. *The Origin of Christology.* Cambridge: Cambridge University Press, 1977.

—. *The Phenomenon of the New Testament.* London: SCM, 1967.

Murphy-O'Connor, J. "A Literary Analysis of Damascus Document VI, 2–VIII, 3." *RB* 78 (1971) 210-32.

—. "The Original Text of CD 7:9–8:2 = 19:5-14." *HTR* 64 (1971) 379-86.

Mussner, F. *Die Wunder Jesu: Eine Hinführung.* Schriften zur Katechetik 10. Munich: Kösel, 1967. ET: *The Miracles of Jesus: An Introduction.* Notre Dame: University of Notre Dame, 1968.

Nadich, J. *Jewish Legends of the Second Commonwealth.* Philadelphia: Jewish Publication Society of America, 1983.

Neirynck, F. "The Historical Jesus: Reflections on an Inventory." *ETL* 70 (1994) 221-34.

—. "John and the Synoptics: 1975-1990." In A. Denaux (ed.). *John and the Synoptics.* BETL 101. Leuven: Peeters, 1992. Pp. 3-61.

Neirynck, F. et al. *Jean et les Synoptiques.* BETL 49. Leuven: Peeters, 1979.

Neusner, J. *A Life of Rabban Yohanan ben Zakkai.* SPB 6. Leiden: Brill, 1962.

—. *A Life of Yohanan ben Zakkai.* 2nd ed. SPB 6. Leiden: Brill, 1970.

—. *Judaic Law from Jesus to the Mishnah.* SFSHJ 84. Atlanta: Scholars Press, 1993.

—. *Messiah in Context: Israel's History and Destiny in Formative Judaism.* Philadelphia: Fortress, 1984.

—. *The Tosefta.* 6 vols. New York and Hoboken: Ktav, 1977-86.

Neusner, J. and Chilton, B. "Uncleanness: A Moral or an Ontological Category in the Early Centuries A.D.?" *BBR* 1 (1991) 63-88.

Neusner, J. et al. (eds.). *Judaisms and Their Messiahs at the Turn of the Christian Era.* Cambridge: Cambridge University Press, 1987.

Newsom, C. *Songs of the Sabbath Sacrifice: A Critical Edition.* HSS 27. Atlanta: Scholars Press, 1985.

Nolland, J. *Luke 9:21-18:34.* WBC 35B. Dallas: Word, 1993.

—. *Luke 18:35-24:53.* WBC 35C. Dallas: Word, 1993.

Oakman, D. E. *Jesus and the Economic Questions of His Day.* SBEC 8. Lewiston and Queenston: Mellen, 1986.

Oesterley, W. O. E. *The Gospel Parables in the Light of Their Jewish Background.* London: Macmillan, 1936.

Olmstead, A. T. "Could an Aramaic Gospel be Written?" *JNES* 1 (1942) 41-75.

O'Neill, J. C. "The Charge of Blasphemy at Jesus' Trial before the Sanhedrin." In E. Bammel (ed.). *The Trial of Jesus: Cambridge Studies in Honour of C. F. D. Moule.* SBT 13. London: SCM, 1970. Pp. 72-77.

—. "The Lord's Prayer." *JSNT* 51 (1993) 3-25.

—. "The Silence of Jesus." *NTS* 15 (1969) 153-67.

Patterson, S. J. *The Gospel of Thomas and Jesus.* Sonoma: Polebridge, 1993.

Pautrel, R. "Les canons du Mashal rabbinique." *RSR* 26 (1936) 6-45; 28 (1938) 264-81.

Payne, P. B. "The Authenticity of the Parables of Jesus." In R. T. France and D. Wenham (eds.). *Studies of History and Tradition in the Four Gospels.* Gospel Perspectives 2. Sheffield: JSOT Press, 1980. Pp. 329-44

Perowne, S. *Hadrian.* London: Hodder and Stoughton, 1960.

Perrin, N. "Mark 14:62: The End Product of a Christian Pesher Tradition?" *NTS* 13 (1966) 150-55.

—. *The New Testament: An Introduction.* New York: Harcourt, Brace, Jovanovich, 1974.

—. *Rediscovering the Teaching of Jesus.* London: SCM; New York: Harper & Row, 1967. 2nd ed. New York: Harper & Row, 1976.

Pesch, R. *Jesu ureigene Taten? Ein Beitrag zur Wunderfrage.* QD 52. Freiburg: Herder, 1970.

—. *Das Markusevangelium.* 2 vols. HTKNT 2.1-2. Freiburg: Herder, 1976-77. 4th ed., 1991.

—. "Zur theologischen Bedeutung der 'Machttaten' Jesu. Reflexionen eines Exegeten." *TQ* 152 (1972) 203-13.

Pestman, P. W. (ed.). *Greek and Demotic Texts from the Zenon Archive.* Papyrologica Lugduno-Batava 20A. Leiden: Brill, 1980.

Petuchowski, J. J. "Das Achtzehngebet." In H. H. Henrix (ed.). *Jüdische Liturgie: Geschichte, Struktur, Wesen.* Freiburg: Herder, 1979. Pp. 77-88.

—. "The Theological Significance of the Parable in Rabbinic Literature and the New Testament." *Christian News from Israel* 23 (1972-73) 76-86.

—. *Understanding Jewish Prayer.* New York: Ktav, 1972.

Petuchowski, J. J. and Brocke, M. (eds.). *The Lord's Prayer and Jewish Liturgy.* New York: Seabury, 1978 [for original German edition, see M. Brocke above].

Petzke, G. *Die Traditionen über Apollonius von Tyana und das Neue Testament.* SCHNT 1. Leiden: Brill, 1970.

Platt, E. E. "The Ministry of Mary of Bethany." *TToday* 34 (1977) 29-39.

Polkow, "Method and Criteria for Historical Jesus Research." In K. H. Richards (ed.). *Society of*

Biblical Literature 1987 Seminar Papers. SBLSP 26. Atlanta: Scholars Press, 1987. Pp. 336-56.

Porter, S. E. "Can Traditional Exegesis Enlighten Literary Analysis of the Fourth Gospel? An Examination of the Old Testament Fulfillment Motif and the Passover Theme." In C. A. Evans and W. R. Stegner (eds.). *The Gospels and the Scriptures of Israel.* JSNTSup 104. SSEJC 3. Sheffield: JSOT Press, 1994. Pp. 396-428.

—. "Jesus and the Use of Greek in Galilee." In Chilton and Evans (eds.). *Studying the Historical Jesus: Evaluations of the State of Current Research.* NTTS 19. Leiden: Brill, 1994. Pp. 123-54.

Priest, J. F. "Mebaqqer, Paqid, and the Messiah." *JBL* 81 (1962) 55-61.

—. "The Messiah and the Meal in 1QSa." *JBL* 82 (1963) 95-100.

—. "Testament of Moses." In J. H. Charlesworth (ed.). *The Old Testament Pseudepigrapha.* 2 vols. Garden City: Doubleday, 1983-85. Vol. 1. Pp. 917-34.

Puech, É. "4Q525 et les péricopes des béatitudes en Ben Sira et Matthieu." *RB* 98 (1991) 80-106.

—. "Une Apocalypse messianique (4Q521)." *RevQ* 15 (1992) 475-519.

—. "Fragment d'une Apocalypse en Araméen (4Q 246 = pseudo-Dan) et le 'Royaume de Dieu'." *RB* 99 (1992) 98-131.

—. "Fragments du Psaume 122 dans un manuscript hébreu de la grotte iv." *RevQ* 9 (1977-78) 547-54.

—. "Notes sur le manuscrit de XIQMelkîsédeq." *RevQ* 12 (1985-87) 483-513.

—. "Le Testament de Qahat en araméen de la Grotte 4 (4QTQah)." *RevQ* 15 (1991) 23-54.

Quere, R. "'Naming' God 'Father'." *CTMis* 12 (1985) 5-14.

Rabin, C. *The Zadokite Documents.* Oxford: Clarendon, 1958.

Rahmani, L. Y. "The Coins from the Cave of Horror." *IEJ* 12 (1962) 200.

Rappaport, U. "John of Gischala: From Galilee to Jerusalem." *JJS* 33 (1982) 479-93.

Reich, R. "Caiaphas Name Inscribed on Bone Boxes." *BARev* 18.5 (1992) 38-44, 76.

Reicke, B. *Handskrifterna från Qumrân.* Symbolae Biblicae Upsalienses 14. Uppsala: Wretmans, 1952.

Reim, G. "Jesus as God in the Fourth Gospel: The Old Testament Background." *NTS* 30 (1984) 158-60.

—. "Joh. 8.44—Gotteskinder/Teufelskinder: Wie antijudaistisch ist 'Die wohl antijudaistischste Äusserung des NT'?" *NTS* 30 (1984) 619-24.

Reinhartz, A. "Rabbinic Perceptions of Simeon bar Kosiba." *JSJ* 20 (1989) 171-94.

Richardson, H. N. "Some Notes on 1QSa." *JBL* 76 (1957) 108-22.

Richardson, P. "Why Turn the Tables? Jesus' Protest in the Temple Precincts." In E. H. Lovering (ed.). *Society of Biblical Literature 1992 Seminar Papers.* SBLSP 31. Atlanta: Scholars Press, 1992. Pp. 507-23

Riesner, R. *Jesus als Lehrer: Eine Untersuchung zum Ursprung der Evangelien-Überlieferung.* WUNT 2.7; Tübingen: Mohr (Siebeck), 1981. 4th ed., 1994.

—. "Der Ursprung der Jesus-Überlieferung." *TZ* 38 (1982) 493-513.

Ritt, H. "'Wer war schuld am Tod Jesu?' Zeitgeschichte, Recht und theologische Deutung." *BZ* 31 (1987) 165-75.

Roberts, C. H. and Turner, G. E. (eds.). *Catalogue of the Greek and Latin Papyri in the John Rylands Library Manchester.* Vol. 4. Manchester: Manchester University Press, 1952.

Roberts, J. J. M. "The Old Testament's Contribution to Messianic Expectation." In J. H. Charlesworth (ed.). *The Messiah: Developments in Earliest Judaism and Christianity.* Minneapolis: Fortress, 1992. Pp. 39-51.

Robinson, J. A. T. "Did Jesus Have a Distinctive Use of Scripture?" In R. F. Berkey and S. A. Edwards (eds.). *Christological Perspectives.* H. K. McArthur Festschrift. New York: Pilgrim, 1982. Pp. 49-57. Repr. in Robinson. *Twelve More New Testament Studies.* London: SCM,

1984. Pp. 35-43.

Robinson, J. M. *A New Quest of the Historical Jesus.* SBT 25. London: SCM, 1959. German ed. *Kerygma und historischer Jesus.* Zürich and Stuttgart: Zwingli, 1960. 2nd ed., 1967.

———. "On the *Gattung* of Mark (and John)." In D. G. Buttrick and J. M. Bald (eds.). *Jesus and Man's Hope.* Pittsburgh: Pittsburgh Theological Seminary, 1970. Pp. 99-129.

———. *The Problem of History in Mark.* SBT 21. London: SCM, 1957.

Robinson, S. E. "4 Baruch." In J. H. Charlesworth (ed.). *The Old Testament Pseudepigrapha.* 2 vols. Garden City: Doubleday, 1983-85. Vol. 2. Pp. 413-25.

Rolfe, J. C. *Suetonius II.* LCL 38. London: Heinemann; Cambridge: Harvard University Press, 1914.

Rosenthal, J. M. "Biblical Exegesis of 4QpIs." *JQR* 60 (1969-70) 27-36.

Rostovtzeff, M. *A Large Estate in the Third Century B.C.* University of Wisconsin Studies in the Social Sciences and History 6. Madison: University of Wisconsin Press, 1922.

Roth, C. "The Pharisees of the Jewish Revolution of 66–73." *JSS* 7 (1962) 63-80.

Rubinkiewicz, R. "Apocalypse of Abraham." In J. H. Charlesworth (ed.). *The Old Testament Pseudepigrapha.* 2 vols. Garden City: Doubleday, 1983-85. Vol. 1. Pp. 689-705.

Safrai, S. "The Teaching of the Pietists in Mishnaic Literature." *JJS* 16 (1965) 15-33.

Safrai, S. and Stern, M. (eds.). *The Jewish People in the First Century.* CRINT 1.1. Assen: Van Gorcum; Philadelphia: Fortress, 1974.

Sanders, E. P. *Jesus and Judaism.* London: SCM; Philadelphia: Fortress, 1985.

———. *Jewish Law from Jesus to the Mishnah.* London: SCM; Philadelphia: Trinity Press International, 1990.

———. *The Tendencies of the Synoptic Tradition.* SNTSMS 9. Cambridge: Cambridge University Press, 1969.

Sanders, E. P. and Davies, M. *Studying the Synoptic Gospels.* London: SCM; Philadelphia: Trinity Press International, 1989.

Sanders, J. A. "From Isaiah 61 to Luke 4." In J. Neusner (ed.). *Christianity, Judaism and Other Greco-Roman Cults.* M. Smith Festschrift. Part One: New Testament. SJLA 12. Leiden: Brill, 1975. Pp. 75-106. Revised and repr. in C. A. Evans and J. A. Sanders. *Luke and Scripture: The Function of Sacred Tradition in Luke-Acts.* Minneapolis: Fortress, 1993. Pp. 46-69.

———. "Ναζωραῖος in Matthew 2.23." In C. A. Evans and W. R. Stegner (eds.). *The Gospels and the Scriptures of Israel.* JSNTSup 104. SSEJC 3. Sheffield: JSOT Press, 1994. Pp. 116-28.

———. "The Old Testament in 11Q Melchizedek." *JANESCU* 5 (1973) 373-82.

———. *The Psalms Scroll of Qumrân Cave 11.* DJD 4. Oxford: Clarendon, 1965.

Sandmel, S. "Parallelomania." *JBL* 81 (1962) 2-13.

Schaberg, J. "Mark 14.62: Early Christian Merkabah Imagery?" In J. Marcus and M. L. Soards (eds.). *Apocalyptic and the New Testament.* J. L. Martyn Festschrift. JSNTSup 24. Sheffield: JSOT Press, 1989. Pp. 69-94.

Schäfer, P. *Der Bar Kokhba-Aufstand: Studien zum zweiten jüdischen Krieg gegen Rom.* TSAJ 1. Tübingen: Mohr (Siebeck), 1981.

———. "Hadrian's Policy in Judaea and the Bar Kokhba Revolt: A Reassessment." In P. R. Davies and R. T. White (eds.). *A Tribute to Geza Vermes: Essays on Jewish and Christian Literature and History.* JSOTSup 100. Sheffield: JSOT Press, 1990. Pp. 281-303.

———. "R. Aqiva und Bar Kokhba." In P. Schäfer (ed.). *Studien zur Geschichte und Theologie des rabbinischen Judentums.* AGJU 15. Leiden: Brill, 1978. Pp. 65-121.

———. "Rabbi Aqiva and Bar Kokhba." In W. S. Green (ed.). *Approaches to Ancient Judaism: Volume II.* BJS 9. Chico: Scholars Press, 1980. Pp. 113-30.

Schalit, A. "Die Erhebung Vespasians nach Josephus, Talmud und Midrasch: Zur Geschichte einer messianischen Prophetie." *ANRW* 2.2 (1975) 208-327.

Schechter, S. *Fragments of a Zadokite Work.* Cambridge: Cambridge University Press, 1910.

Repr. with Prolegomenon by J. A. Fitzmyer. New York: Ktav, 1970.

Schelkle, K. H. "Entmythologisierung in existentialer Interpretation." *TQ* 165 (1985) 257-66.

Schiffman, L. H. *The Eschatological Community of the Dead Sea Scrolls.* SBLMS 38. Atlanta: Scholars Press, 1989.

—. "Messianic Figures and Ideas in the Qumran Scrolls." In J. H. Charlesworth (ed.). *The Messiah: Developments in Earliest Judaism and Christianity.* Minneapolis: Fortress, 1992. 116-29.

—. (ed.). *Archaeology and History in the Dead Sea Scrolls: The New York University Conference in Memory of Yigael Yadin.* JSPSup 8. JSOT/ASOR Monographs 2. Sheffield: JSOT Press, 1990.

Schille, G. *Die urchristliche Wundertradition: Ein Beitrag zur Frage nach dem irdischen Jesus.* Arbeiten zur Theologie 29. Stuttgart: Calwer, 1967.

Schillebeeckx, E. *Jesus: An Experiment in Christology.* London: Collins; New York: Crossroad, 1979.

Schmid, J. *Das Evangelium nach Markus.* RNT 2. Regensburg: Pustet, 1958. ET: *The Gospel according to Mark.* The Regensburg New Testament. Staten Island: Alba House, 1968.

Schnackenburg, R. *Gottes Herrschaft und Reich: Eine biblisch-theologische Studie.* Freiburg: Herder, 1959. ET: *God's Rule and Kingdom.* New York: Herder & Herder, 1963.

Schneider, G. "The Political Charge against Jesus (Luke 23:2)." In E. Bammel and C. F. D. Moule (eds.). *Jesus and the Politics of His Day.* Cambridge: Cambridge University Press, 1984. Pp. 403-14.

Schnelle, U. "Johannes und die Synoptiker." In F. Van Segbroeck et al. (eds.). *The Four Gospels 1992.* BETL 100. 3 vols. Leuven: Leuven University, 1992. Vol. 3. Pp. 1799-1814.

Schubert, K. "Der alttestamentliche Hintergrund der Vorstellung von den beiden Messiassen im Schriftum von Chirbet Qumran." *Judaica* 12 (1956) 24-28.

—. "Die Messiaslehre in den Texten von Chirbet Qumran." *BZ* 1 (1957) 177-97.

—. "Zwei Messiasse aus dem Regelbuch von Chirbet Qumran." *Judaica* 11 (1955) 216-35.

Schuller, E. M. "4Q372 1: A Text about Joseph." *RevQ* 14 (1990) 349-76.

—. "A Hymn from a Cave Four Hodayot Manuscript: 4Q427 7 i + ii." *JBL* 112 (1993) 605-28.

—. *Non-Canonical Psalms from Qumran: A Pseudepigraphic Collection.* HSS 28. Atlanta: Scholars Press, 1986.

—. "The Psalm of 4Q372 1 Within the Context of Second Temple Prayer." *CBQ* 54 (1992) 67-79.

Schürer, E. *The History of the Jewish People in the Age of Jesus Christ.* 3 vols. Rev. and ed. by G. Vermes, F. Millar, and M. Black. Edinburgh: T. & T. Clark, 1973-87.

Schürmann, H. "Zur aktuellen Situation der Leben-Jesu-Forschung." *Geist und Leben* 46 (1973) 300-310.

Schwartz, G. "Matthäus VI 9–13; Lukas XI 2–4." *NTS* 15 (1968-69) 233-47.

Schweitzer, A. *Von Reimarus zu Wrede: Eine Geschichte des Leben-Jesu-Forschung.* Tübingen: Mohr (Siebeck), 1906. ET: *The Quest of the Historical Jesus: A Critical Study of its Progress from Reimarus to Wrede.* London: Black, 1910. Repr. New York: Macmillan, 1968. Rev. ed. *Die Geschichte der Leben-Jesu-Forschung.* Tübingen: Mohr (Siebeck), 1913. 6th ed., 1951.

Schweizer, E. *Das Evangelium nach Markus.* 2n ed. NTD 1. Göttingen: Vandenhoeck & Ruprecht, 1969. ET: *The Good News according to Mark.* Atlanta: John Knox, 1970.

—. "The Son of Man." *JBL* 79 (1960) 119-29.

Scott, B. B. "Essaying the Rock: The Authenticity of the Jesus Parable Tradition." *Forum* 2.3 (1986) 3-53.

—. *Hear Then the Parable: A Commentary on the Parables of Jesus.* Minneapolis: Fortress, 1989.

Seeley, D. "Was Jesus like a Philosopher? The Evidence of Martyrological and Wisdom Motifs in Q, Pre-Pauline Traditions, and Mark." In D. J. Lull (ed.). *Society of Biblical Literature 1989 Seminar Papers.* SBLSP 28. Atlanta: Scholars Press, 1989. Pp. 540-49.

Sellew, P. *"Secret Mark* and the History of Canonical Mark." In B. A. Pearson (ed.). *The Future of Early Christianity.* H. Koester Festschrift. Minneapolis: Fortress, 1991. Pp. 242-57.

Sheppard, G. T. "More on Isaiah 5:1-7 as a Juridical Parable." *CBQ* 44 (1982) 45-47.

Sigal, P. "Further Reflections on the 'Begotten' Messiah." *Hebrew Annual Review* 7 (1983) 221-33.

Silberman, L. H. "The Two 'Messiahs' of the Manual of Discipline." *VT* 5 (1955) 77-82.

—. "Language and Structure in the Hodayot (1QH3)." *JBL* 75 (1956) 96-106.

Silver, A. H. *A History of Messianic Speculation in Israel.* Gloucester: Peter Smith, 1978.

Skehan, P. W. "The Period of the Biblical Texts from Khirbet Qumrân." *CBQ* 19 (1957) 435-40.

Smallwood, E. M. "High Priests and Politics in Roman Palestine." *JTS* 13 (1962) 14-34.

—. *The Jews under Roman Rule from Pompey to Diocletian: A Study in Political Relations.* SJLA 20. Leiden: Brill, 1976.

Smith, D. M. Smith, "John and the Synoptics: Some Dimensions of the Problem." *NTS* 26 (1980) 425-44.

—. "The Problem of John and the Synoptics in Light of the Relation between Apocryphal and Canonical Gospels." In A. Denaux (ed.). *John and the Synoptics.* BETL 101. Leuven: Peeters, 1992. Pp. 147-62.

Smith, M. "Ascent to the Heavens and Deification in 4QM^a." In L. H. Schiffman (ed.). *Archaeology and History in the Dead Sea Scrolls: The New York University Conference in Memory of Yigael Yadin.* JSPSup 2. Sheffield: JSOT Press, 1990. Pp. 181-88.

—. "'God's Begetting the Messiah' in 1QSa." *NTS* 5 (1958-59) 218-24.

—. *Jesus the Magician.* San Francisco: Harper & Row, 1978.

—. "Two Ascended to Heaven—Jesus and the Author of 4Q491." In J. H. Charlesworth (ed.). *Jesus and the Dead Sea Scrolls.* ABRL. New York: Doubleday, 1992. Pp. 290-301.

—. "What is Implied by the Variety of Messianic Figures?" *JBL* 78 (1959) 66-72.

Snodgrass, K. R. *The Parable of the Wicked Tenants.* WUNT 27. Tübingen: Mohr (Siebeck), 1983.

Sperber, A. *The Bible in Aramaic Based on Old Manuscripts and Printed Texts.* 5 vols. Leiden: Brill, 1959-73.

Stanton, G. N. *The Gospels and Jesus.* Oxford: Oxford University Press, 1989.

Starcky, J. "Jérusalem et les manuscrits de la mer Morte." *Le Monde de la Bible* 1 (1977) 38-40.

—. "Les quatre étapes du messianisme à Qumran." *RB* 70 (1963) 481-505.

—. "La Quatrième Demande du Pater." *HTR* 64 (1971) 401-409.

—. "Un texte messianique araméen de la grotte 4 de Qumran." In *Ecole des langues orientales anciennes de l'Institut Catholique de Paris: Mémorial du cinquantenaire 1914-1964.* Travaux de l'Institut Catholique de Paris 10. Paris: Bloud et Gay, 1964.

Stauffer, E. *Jesus: Gestalt und Geschichte.* Dalp-Taschenbücher 332. Bern: Francke, 1957. ET: *Jesus and His Story.* London: SCM; New York: Knopf, 1960.

—. "Messias oder Menschensohn." *NovT* 1 (1956) 81-102.

Stefaniak, L. "Messianische oder eschatologische Erwartungen in der Qumransekte?" In J. Blinzler et al. (eds.) *Neutestamentliche Aufsätze.* J. Schmid Festschrift. Regensburg: Pustet, 1963. Pp. 294-302.

Stegemann, H. "Weitere Stücke von 4QpPsalm 37, von 4Q Patriarchal Blessings und Hinweis auf eine unedierte Handschrift aus Höhle 4Q mit Exzerpten aus dem Deuteronomium." *RevQ* 6 (1967-69) 211-17.

Stein, R. H. "'Authentic' or 'Authoritative'? What is the Difference?" *JETS* 24 (1981) 127-30.

—. "The 'Criteria' for Authenticity." In R. T. France and D. Wenham (eds.). *Studies of History and Tradition in the Four Gospels.* Gospel Perspectives 2. Sheffield: JSOT Press, 1980. Pp. 225-63.

Stendahl, K. *The School of St. Matthew and Its Use of the Old Testament.* Rev. ed. Philadelphia: Fortress, 1968.

——. "The Scrolls and the New Testament: An Introduction and a Perspective." In Stendahl (ed.). *The Scrolls and the New Testament.* New York: Harper, 1957. Repr. New York: Crossroad, 1992. Pp. 1-17.

Stenning, J. F. *The Targum of Isaiah.* Oxford: Clarendon, 1949.

Stern, D. *Parables in Midrash: Narrative and Exegesis in Rabbinic Literature.* Cambridge: Harvard University Press, 1991.

——. "Rhetoric and Midrash: The Case of the Mashal." *Prooftexts* 1 (1981) 261-91.

Steudel, A. "4QMidrEschat: 'A Midrash on Eschatology' (4Q174 + 4Q177)." In J. Trebolle Barrera and L. Vegas Montaner (eds.). *The Madrid Qumran Congress: Proceedings of the International Congress on the Dead Sea Scrolls Madrid 18-21 March, 1991.* STDJ 11. 2 vols. Leiden: Brill, 1992. Pp. 531-41.

Strickert, F. M. "Damascus Document VII 10-20 and Qumran Messianic Expectation." *RevQ* 12 (1985-87) 327-49.

Stuhlmacher, P. "The Theme: The Gospel and the Gospels." In P. Stuhlmacher (ed.). *The Gospel and the Gospels.* Grand Rapids: Eerdmans, 1991. Pp. 1-25.

—— (ed.). *Das Evangelium und die Evangelien: Vorträge vom Tübingen Symposium 1982.* WUNT 28. Tübingen: Mohr (Siebeck), 1983. ET: *The Gospel and the Gospels.* Grand Rapids: Eerdmans, 1991.

Suhl, A. *Die Wunder Jesu: Ereignis und Überlieferung.* Gütersloh: Mohn, 1968.

J. P. M. Sweet, "A House Not Made with Hands." In W. Horbury (ed.). *Templum Amicitiae: Essays on the Second Temple.* E. Bammel Festschrift. JSNTSup 48. Sheffield: JSOT Press, 1991. Pp. 368-90.

Tabor, J. D. "A Pierced or Piercing Messiah?—The Verdict is Still Out." *BARev* 18.6 (1992) 58-59.

Talmon, S. "The Concepts of *Māšîaḥ* and Messianism in Early Judaism." In J. H. Charlesworth (ed.). *The Messiah: Developments in Earliest Judaism and Christianity.* Minneapolis: Fortress, 1992. Pp. 79-115.

——. "The Emergence of Institutionalized Prayer in Israel in the Light of the Qumran Literature." In M. Delcor (ed.). *Qumrân: Sa piété, sa théologie et son milieu.* BETL 46. Louvain: Louvain University Press, 1978. Pp. 265-84.

——. "Waiting for the Messiah: The Spiritual Universe of the Qumran Covenanters." In J. Neusner et al. (eds.). *Judaisms and their Messiahs at the Turn of the Christian Era.* Cambridge and New York: Cambridge University Press, 1987. Pp. 111-37.

Taylor, V. *The Formation of the Gospel Tradition.* London: Macmillan, 1935.

——. *The Gospel According to St. Mark.* 2nd ed. London: Macmillan; New York: St. Martin's, 1966.

Tcherikover, V. A. "Palestine under the Ptolemies: (A Contribution to the Study of the Zenon Papyri)." *Mizraim* 4-5 (1937) 9-90.

Tcherikover, V. A. and Fuks, A. (eds.). *Corpus Papyrorum Judaicarum.* 2 vols. Cambridge: Harvard University Press, 1957-60.

Teeple, H. M. *The Mosaic Eschatological Prophet.* SBLMS 10. Philadelphia: SBL, 1957.

Telford, W. R. "Major Trends and Interpretive Issues in the Study of Jesus." In B. D. Chilton and C. A. Evans (eds.). *Studying the Historical Jesus: Evaluations of the State of Current Research.* NTTS 19. Leiden: Brill, 1994. Pp. 33-74.

Thackeray, H. St. J. et al. *Josephus.* 10 vols. LCL 186, 203, 210, 242, 281, 326, 365, 410, 433, 456. London: Heinemann; Cambridge: Harvard University Press, 1926-65.

——. *Josephus, the Man and the Historian.* New York: Jewish Institute of Religion, 1929.

Theissen, G. "Die Tempelweissagung Jesu. Prophetie im Spannungsfeld von Stadt und Land." *TZ* 32 (1976) 144-58.

—. *Urchristliche Wundergeschichten: Ein Beitrag zur formgeschichtlichen Erforschung der synoptischen Evangelien.* Gütersloh: Mohn, 1974. ET: *The Miracle Stories of the Early Christian Tradition.* Philadelphia: Fortress, 1983.

Thiering, B. "*Mebaqqer* and *Episkopos* in the Light of the Temple Scroll." *JBL* 100 (1981) 59-75.

Thoma, C. "Prolegomena zu einer Übersetzung und Kommentierung der rabbinischen Gleichnisse." *TZ* 38 (1982) 514-31.

Thoma, C. and Lauer, S. *Die Gleichnisse der Rabbinen. Erster Teil: Pesiqta deRav Kahana (PesK). Einleitung, Übersetzung, Parallelen, Kommentar, Texte.* Bern: Peter Lang, 1986.

Thoma, C. and Wyschogrod, M. (eds.). *Parable and Story in Judaism and Christianity.* New York: Paulist, 1989.

Tiede, D. L. *The Charismatic Figure as Miracle Worker.* SBLDS 1. Missoula: Scholars Press, 1972.

Toombs, L. E. "Barcosiba and Qumrân." *NTS* 4 (1957) 65-71.

Torrey, C. C. *The Lives of the Prophets.* SBLMS 1. Philadelphia: SBL, 1946.

Trebolle Barrer, J. and Vegas Montaner, L. (eds.). *The Madrid Qumran Congress: Proceedings of the International Congress on the Dead Sea Scrolls Madrid 18–21 March, 1991.* 2 vols. STDJ 11. Leiden: Brill, 1992.

Trever, J. C. *Scrolls from Qumrân Cave I.* Jerusalem: Shrine of the Book, 1974.

Tromp, J. *The Assumption of Moses: A Critical Edition with Commentary.* SVTP 10. Leiden: Brill, 1993.

Twelftree, G. H. "ΕΙ ΔΕ . . . ΕΓΩ ΕΚΒΑΛΛΩ ΤΑ ΔΑΙΜΟΝΙΑ . . ." In D. Wenham and C. Blomberg (eds.). *The Miracles of Jesus.* Gospel Perspectives 6. Sheffield: JSOT Press, 1986. Pp. 361-400.

Urbach, E. E. *The Sages: Their Concepts and Beliefs.* Cambridge: Harvard University Press, 1975.

van der Loos, H. *The Miracles of Jesus.* NovTSup 9. Leiden: Brill, 1965.

van der Woude, A. S. "Fünfzehn Jahre Qumranforschung (1974–1988)." *TRu* 57 (1992) 1-57.

—. "Le Maître de Justice et les deux messies de la communauté de Qumrân." In *La secte de Qumrân et les origines chrétiennes.* RechBib 4. Bruges: Desclée de Brouwer, 1959. Pp. 121-34.

—. "Melchisedek als himmlische Erlösergestalt in den neugefundenen eschatologischen Midraschim aus Qumran Höhle XI." *OTS* 14 (1965) 354-73 (+ pls. I-II).

—. *Die messianischen Vorstellungen der Gemeinde von Qumrân.* SSN 3. Assen: van Gorcum; Neukirchen: Neukirchen-Vluyn, 1957.

Vermes, G. *The Dead Sea Scrolls in English.* 3rd ed. Sheffield: JSOT Press, 1987.

—. *The Dead Sea Scrolls: Qumran in Perspective.* Philadelphia: Fortress, 1977.

—. *Jesus and the World of Judaism.* London: SCM; Philadelphia: Fortress, 1983.

—. *Jesus the Jew: A Historian's Reading of the Gospels.* London: Collins; Philadelphia: Fortress, 1973.

—. *Post-Biblical Jewish Studies.* SJLA 8. Leiden: Brill, 1975.

—. *The Religion of Jesus the Jew.* London: SCM; Minneapolis: Fortress, 1993.

—. *Scripture and Tradition in Judaism.* SPB 4. Leiden: Brill, 1973.

—. "The Son of Man Debate." *JSNT* 1 (1978) 19-32.

—. "The Use of בר נש/בר נשא/בר נש in Jewish Aramaic." In M. Black. *An Aramaic Approach to the Synoptic Gospels and Acts.* 3rd ed. Oxford: Clarendon, 1967. Pp. 310-28.

Vermes, G., Lim, T. H., and Gordon, R. P. "The Oxford Forum for Qumran Research Seminar on the Rule of War from Cave 4 (4Q285)." *JJS* 43 (1992) 85-94.

Vielhauer, P. "Jesus und der Menschensohn." *ZTK* 60 (1963) 133-77.

Visotzky, B. L. *The Midrash on Proverbs.* YJS 27. New Haven and London: Yale University Press, 1992.

Vitelli, G. et al. (eds.). *Publicazioni della Società italiana per la Ricerca dei Papiri greci e latini in*

Egitto: Papiri greci e latini. 15 vols. Florence: E. Ariani, 1912-79.

Viviano, B. T. "Beatitudes Found Among the Dead Sea Scrolls." *BARev* 18.6 (1992) 53-55, 66.

Vögtle, A. "Jesu Wundertaten vor dem Hintergrund ihrer Zeit." In H. J. Schultz (ed.). *Die Zeit Jesu.* Stuttgart: Kreuz, 1966. Pp. 83-90. ET: "The Miracles of Jesus against Their Contemporary Background." In Schultz (ed.). *Jesus in His Time.* Philadelphia: Fortress, 1971. Pp. 96-105.

—. "Wunder." *LTK* 10.1257-58.

Volz, P. *Die Eschatologie der jüdischen Gemeinde im neutestamentlichen Zeitalter.* 2nd ed. Tübingen: Mohr (Siebeck), 1934. repr. Hildesheim: Olm, 1966.

Wacholder, B. Z. *The Dawn of Qumran: The Sectarian Torah and the Teacher of Righteousness.* Cincinnati: Hebrew Union College, 1983.

Wacholder, B. Z. and Abegg, Jr., M. G. *A Preliminary Edition of the Unpublished Dead Sea Scrolls: The Hebrew and Aramaic Texts from Cave Four.* 3 fascicles. Washington: Biblical Archaeology Society, 1991-94.

Walters, K. H. "The Reign of Trajan, and its Place in Contemporary Scholarship (1960–72)." *ANRW* 2.2 (1975) 381-431.

Wcela, E. A. "The Messiah(s) of Qumran." *CBQ* 26 (1964) 340-49.

Weinrich, O. *Antike Heilungswunder: Untersuchungen zum Wunderglauben der Griechen und Römer.* RVV 8.1. Giessen: Töpelmann, 1909.

Weiss, J. *Die Predigt Jesu vom Reiche Gottes.* Göttingen: Vandenhoeck & Ruprecht, 1892. 2nd ed., 1900. ET: *Jesus' Proclamation of the Kingdom of God.* Chico: Scholars Press, 1985.

Weiss, K. "Messianismus in Qumran und im Neuen Testament." In H. Bardtke (ed.). *Qumran-Probleme.* Berlin: Akademie, 1963. Pp. 353-68.

Wenham, D. and Blomberg, C. L. (eds.). *The Miracles of Jesus.* Gospel Perspectives 6. Sheffield: JSOT Press, 1986.

White, H. *Appian's Roman History II.* LCL 3. Cambridge: Harvard University Press, 1912-13.

White, J. L. *Light from Ancient Letters.* Foundations and Facets. Philadelphia: Fortress, 1986.

Wilcken U. et al. (eds.). *Aegyptische Urkunden aus den Königlichen Museen zu Berlin.* 4 vols. Berlin: Weidmann, 1895-1912.

Willis, J. T. "The Genre of Isaiah 5:1-7." *JBL* 96 (1977) 337-62.

Wink, W. "Jesus as Magician." *USQR* 30 (1974) 3-14.

Winter, P. *On the Trial of Jesus.* Studia Judaica: Forschungen zur Wissenschaft des Judentums 1. Berlin: de Gruyter, 1961. 2nd ed., rev. and ed. by T. A. Burkill and G. Vermes.

Wise M. O. and Tabor, J. D. "The Messiah at Qumran." *BARev* 18.6 (1992) 60-65.

Witherington, B. *The Christology of Jesus.* Minneapolis: Fortress, 1990.

Wright, N. T. "Jerusalem in the New Testament." In P. W. L. Walker (ed.). *Jerusalem Past and Present in the Purposes of God.* Cambridge: Cambridge University Press, 1992. Pp. 53-77.

Yadin, Y. *The Ben Sira Scroll from Masada.* Jerusalem: Israel Exploration Society and the Shrine of the Book, 1965.

—. "Expedition D." *IEJ* 11 (1961) 36-52; 12 (1962) 227-57.

—. "A Midrash on 2 Sam VII and Ps I-II (4 Q Florilegium)." *IEJ* 9 (1959) 95-98.

—. "A Note on Melchizedek and Qumran." *IEJ* 15 (1965) 152-54.

—. *The Scroll of the War of the Sons of Light against the Sons of Darkness.* Oxford: Oxford University Press, 1962.

Yamauchi, E. "Magic or Miracle? Disease, Demons and Exorcisms." In D. Wenham and C. L. Blomberg (eds.). *The Miracles of Jesus.* Gospel Perspectives 6. Sheffield: JSOT Press, 1986. Pp. 89-183.

Yee, G. A. "The Form-Critical Study of Isaiah 5:1-7 as a Song and a Juridical Parable." *CBQ* 43 (1981) 30-40.

Young, B. H. *Jesus and His Jewish Parables.* New York: Paulist, 1989.

Zahrnt, H. *Die Sache mit Gott: Die protestantische Theologie im 20. Jahrhundert.* Munich: Piper, 1966. ET: *The Question of God: Protestant Theology in the Twentieth Century.* New York: Harcourt, Brace & World, 1969.

Zeitlin, S. *Who Crucified Jesus?* New York: Harper & Row, 1942.

—. *The Zadokite Fragments.* JQRMS 1. Philadelphia: Dropsie College, 1952.

Zeller, D. *Kommentar zur Logienquelle.* SKKNT 21. Stuttgart: Katholisches Bibelwerk, 1986.

—. "Wunder und Bekenntnis: zum Sitz im Leben urchristlicher Wundergeschichten." *BZ* 25 (1981) 204-22.

Zias, J. and Charlesworth, J. H. "CRUCIFIXION: Archaeology, Jesus, and the Dead Sea Scrolls." In J. H. Charlesworth (ed.). *Jesus and the Dead Sea Scrolls.* ABRL. New York: Doubleday, 1992. Pp. 273-89.

Ziegler, I. *Die Königsgleichnisse des Midrasch beleuchtet durch die römische Kaiserzeit.* Breslau: Schlesische Verlags-Anstalt, 1903.

Zimmermann, A. F. *Die urchristlichen Lehrer: Studien zum Tradentenkreis der διδάσκαλοι im frühen Urchristentum.* WUNT 2.12. Tübingen: Mohr (Siebeck), 1984.

INDEX OF ANCIENT WRITINGS

6.6 (on Lev 5:1)	275, 276
9.9 (on Lev 7:11-12)	121 n. 88
13.4 (on Lev 11:2)	274
13.5 (on Lev 11:4-7)	72
19.2 (on Lev 15:25)	270
19.6 (on Lev 15:25)	337 n. 61
21.5 (on Lev 16:3)	271
21.9 (on Lev 16:3)	333
35.6 (on Lev 26:3)	274

Numbers Rabbah

13.5 (on Num 7:12)	65
13.14 (on Num 7:13)	208
18.21 (on Num 16:4)	175

Deuteronomy Rabbah

2.24 (on Deut 4:30)	254
7.4 (on Deut 28:1)	254

Ruth Rabbah

3.1 (on Ruth 1:17)	275
3.3 (on Ruth 1:17)	255
8.1 (on Ruth 4:20)	256

Ecclesiastes Rabbah

1:1 §1	235
1:7 §5	273
1:15 §1	255
3:9 §1	254
7:2 §1	273
9:7 §1	145
9:8 §1	252-54, 259

Lamentations Rabbah

Proem §12	272
Proem §17	274
1:5 §31	379
1:7 §34	274-75
1:16 §45	198
1:16 §50	323
1:16 §51	322
2:2 §4	70, 183, 195, 197, 198, 221
2:3 §6	163
3:14 §5	274

Esther Rabbah

3.7 (on Esth 1:9)	198
7.10 (on Esth 3:6)	403 n. 46

Song Rabbah

1:1 §4	235
1:1 §6	272
1:1 §9	254
1:3 §3	198
1:4 §3	274
2:7 §1	72
2:13 §4	177
2:14 §1	272
2:17 §1	198

4:12 §1	253
5:11 §3	270
6:2 §6	253
7:14 §1	253
8:6 §4	198

Midrash Mishle

on Prov 11:4	243
on Prov 16:11	252, 254, 259
on Prov 19:21	391

Midrash on Psalms

1.2 (on Ps 1:1)	60
2.9 (on Ps 2:7)	97, 419
10.2 (on Ps 10:1)	254
14.6 (on Ps 14:7)	115, 173
16.4 (on Ps 16:4)	198
17.13 (on Ps 17:14)	198
18.29 (on Ps 18:36)	419
21.5 (on Ps 21:7)	208
24.8 (on Ps 24:4)	270
28.4 (on Ps 28:3)	273
28.6 (on Ps 28:7)	253, 254
72.2 (on Ps 72:1)	421
75.5 (on Ps 75:11)	163
93.1 (on Ps 93:1)	208
116.1 (on Ps 116:1)	140
119.3 (on Ps 119:1)	252
122.4 (on Ps 122:4)	209-20
122.6 (on Ps 122:5)	427, 427 n. 56

Midrash on Samuel

§5	163

Midrash Tanḥuma

Deut 11:21 (*'Eqeb* §7)	209

Midrash Tanḥuma B

Exod 13:17 (*Bešallaḥ* §7)	257 n. 6, 393
Lev 19:1-2 (*Qedošin* §1)	152, 204, 205, 208, 427, 454 n. 41
Lev 19:1-2 (*Qedošin* §6)	390

Midrash HaGadol

on Deut 11:26	255, 261

Pesiqta Rabbati

1.7	209
15.10	60, 172
15.14/15	121 n. 88
30.3	197
33.6	60
35.4	121 n. 88
44.9	254
47.4	333, 336, 337 n. 61

Pesiqta de-Rab Kahana

5.8	60, 172
5.9	121 n. 88

INDEX OF MODERN AUTHORS